Finance in America

Finance in America

AN UNFINISHED STORY

Kevin R. Brine and Mary Poovey

The University of Chicago Press CHICAGO & LONDON

The University of Chicago Press, Chicago 60637
The University of Chicago Press, Ltd., London
© 2017 by The University of Chicago
All rights reserved. No part of this book may be used or reproduced in any
manner whatsoever without written permission, except in the case of brief
quotations in critical articles and reviews. For more information, contact the
University of Chicago Press, 1427 East 60th Street, Chicago, IL 60637.
Published 2017
Printed in the United States of America

26 25 24 23 22 21 20 19   2 3 4 5

ISBN-13: 978-0-226-50204-5 (cloth)
ISBN-13: 978-0-226-50218-2 (paper)
ISBN-13: 978-0-226-50221-2 (e-book)
DOI: 10.7208/chicago/9780226502212.001.0001

The University of Chicago Press gratefully acknowledges the generous
support of New York University toward the publication of this book.

Library of Congress Cataloging-in-Publication Data

Names: Brine, Kevin R., author. | Poovey, Mary, author.
Title: Finance in America : an unfinished story / Kevin R. Brine and
Mary Poovey.
Description: Chicago ; London : The University of Chicago Press, 2017.
| Includes bibliographical references and index.
Identifiers: LCCN 2017012666 | ISBN 9780226502045 (cloth : alk. paper)
| ISBN 9780226502182 (pbk. : alk. paper) | ISBN 9780226502212 (e-book)
Subjects: LCSH: Finance—United States—History—20th century. |
Finance—United States—History—21st century. | Economics—United
States—History—20th century.
Classification: LCC HG181 .B8345 2017 | DDC 332.0973—dc23
LC record available at https://lccn.loc.gov/2017012666

CONTENTS

Acknowledgments ix

Introduction   1

   I.1   *The Story*   5
   I.2   *What's in a Name? Our Interpretive Position*   15
   I.3   *The Archive*   22
   I.4   *Our Readers and Why This Matters*   26

1   Early Twentieth-Century Origins of American Finance:
    The Rise of the American Corporation and the
    Creation of the Federal Reserve System   28

   1.1   *Valuing the New US Corporations*   28
   1.2   *The Growth of American Public Accounting*   36
   1.3   *Early Twentieth-Century Banking and the Federal Reserve System*   49
   1.4   *The Principles of American Banking*   54

2   Early Twentieth-Century American Economic and Financial Theory   56

   2.1   *The Institutionalism of Thorstein Veblen*   57
   2.2   *Late Nineteenth-Century American Neoclassical Price Theory*
        and the Real US Economy   61
   2.3   *Early American General Equilibrium Theory*   66
   2.4   *An Early Model of Expectations: The Fisher Effect*   72
   2.5   *The Financial View*   76
   2.6   *The Quantity Theory and the Banking View of Money*   81

| 2.7 | *Frank Knight's Theory of Uncertainty* | 87 |
| 2.8 | *American Public Finance: The Personal Income Tax* | 90 |

3   Statistics in America and the Governance of the Modern State | | 96

3.1	*The Statistical Theory of Demand*	96
3.2	*The Harvard Business School Case Method*	100
3.3	*State Data Collection*	103
3.4	*Index Construction and the Dissemination of Data*	105
3.5	*The Challenges of Early Statistical Compilations*	110
3.6	*The Dispute over Index Numbers*	114
3.7	*The Harvard Barometer Project*	119
3.8	*The Pujo Investigation and the "Money Trust"*	121

4   American Finance in the Interwar Period | | 126

4.1	*Transformations in the Interwar Period*	126
4.2	*"New Era Talk" and the Speculative Mania of the 1920s*	127
4.3	*Investment Trusts and the Crash of 1929*	133
4.4	*The New Deal for the American People: Mortgages for All*	138
4.5	*Public Disclosure and the Modern Corporation*	141
4.6	*Security Research*	147
4.7	*The Dividend Discount Model*	153

5   US Finance: Equity and Fixed Income Market Research, 1920–1940 | | 161

5.1	*Midwest Agronomists and the Fortuitous Conjunction*	161
5.2	*Stock Market Skepticism and Sample Theory*	165
5.3	*Stock Forecasting*	171
5.4	*US Common Stock Indexes and Fixed Income Duration*	175

6   Measuring and Taxing the US Economy in the Interwar Period | | 183

6.1	*The Keynesian Revolution*	183
6.2	*Compiling US Income and Production Aggregates*	184
6.3	*The Brookings Institution and the Expenditure Approach*	194
6.4	*Input-Output Accounting for the US Economy*	196
6.5	*Interwar American Fiscal Policy*	201

7   Models of Economies and Finance, 1930–1940 | | 215

| 7.1 | *"Little Model Worlds" and the Econometric Society* | 215 |
| 7.2 | *John Maynard Keynes, John R. Hicks, and Mathematical Economics* | 219 |

7.3   *The IS-LM Model*   225
7.4   *Modeling the Financial View: Marschak's "Theory of Assets"*   227
7.5   *The Keynes-Tinbergen Debate*   238
7.6   *A Macroeconometric Model of the US Economy*   243

8   Postwar Economics in America, 1944–1970   246

8.1   *Postwar Mathematical Economics and Econometrics*   250
  8.1a   The Mathematical Foundations of American Keynesianism   250
  8.1b   The Econometrics of the Probability Approach   253
  8.1c   Mathematical Probability Theory   255
  8.1d   Game Theory and Bayesian Probability   257
  8.1e   Linear Programming of Activities   259
8.2.   *Measurement, Monetarism, Keynesian Stabilization Policies,*
        and Growth Theory   264
  8.2a   Measuring Financial Flows   264
  8.2b   Financial Intermediaries   268
  8.2c   The First Theoretical Account of Financial Intermediation   271
  8.2d   Monetarism   273
  8.2e   The Fed on Trial   276
  8.2f   The Celler-Kefauver Act   280
  8.2g   From Institutionalism to Keynesianism in US Monetary
          and Fiscal Policy, 1950–1968   281
  8.2h   Neoclassical Growth Theory   290

9   Modern Finance   294

9.1   *Origins of Modern Portfolio Theory*   294
  9.1a   Hedging   295
  9.1b   Correlation Analysis and Diversification   299
  9.1c   Subjective Probability Theory   302
  9.1d   Linear Programming and Finance   304
  9.1e   Competitive Equilibrium Theory   304
9.2   *The Years of High Theory*   307
  9.2a   The Capital Asset Pricing Model   307
  9.2b   The Mathematics of Random Processes   308
  9.2c   The Canonization of Modern Finance   313
9.3   *Options Pricing Theory, Financial Engineering, and*
        Financial Econometrics   314
  9.3a   The Theoretical and Mathematical Pillars of Modern Finance   314
  9.3b   Arbitrage Theory   319

9.3c   The Options Pricing Model   320
9.3d   Options Pricing in Continuous Time   323
9.3e   Three Approaches to Pricing Derivatives   325
9.3f   The Arbitrage Theory of Capital Asset Pricing Model   328
9.3g   A Manual for Financial Engineers   329
9.3h   Financial Econometrics   331
9.3i   Efficient Capital Markets II   332
9.3j   Behavioral Finance   334

10 The Transformation of American Finance   337

10.1   *The Inter-Crisis Period: The Volcker Deflation to*
        the Lehman Bankruptcy, 1982–2008   337
10.2   *Early Signs of the Transformation*   ·   343
10.3   *Macroeconomic Theories during the Inter-Crisis Period* 347
        10.3a   New Classical Macroeconomic Theory, Dynamic Stochastic
                General Equilibrium Models, and Real Business Cycle Theory   347
        10.3b   Developments in Information Technology, New Keynesian
                Macroeconomics, the New Neoclassical Synthesis,
                and Hyman Minsky   354
        10.3c   New Research Initiatives   358
10.4   *The Transition to a Market-Based Financial System*   359
        10.4a   Deregulation and the Growth of Finance in America after 1980   359
        10.4b   Securitization and the Shadow Banking System   362
        10.4c   Structured Investment Vehicles   364
        10.4d   Credit Derivatives   365
10.5   *The Market-Based Financial System in Trouble*   366
10.6   *Final Thoughts*   370

Notes 375
Bibliography 449
Index 483

ACKNOWLEDGMENTS

In our decade-long collaboration, we have incurred many debts. The idea to write this history arose in the context of the Re-Enlightenment Project at New York University, which was cofounded by Kevin and Cliff Siskin, with Mary, Peter de Bolla, Lisa Gitelman, David Marshall, William St. Clair, William Warner, and Robert Young as early members. One or both of us subsequently gave papers based on this work at the Re-Enlightenment Project Conference, held at the New York Public Library, Duke University, Cambridge University, the Harvard University Law School, the University of Zurich, Alberta University, the University of Sussex, Uppsala University, and New York University. Under the sponsorship of a research grant from the Norwegian government (CUFF) and with the kind help of Tord Larsen, we presented research talks in Reykjavik, Iceland, and Trondheim, Norway. On these occasions, we greatly benefited from conversations with Ian Baucolm, Sven Beckert, Tom Bender, Jess Benhabib, Ranjeet Bhatia, Elisabeth Bronfen, Brett Christophers, Stefan Collini, Chris Desan, Rupert Gatti, Simon Goldhill, John Guillory, Phil Harper, Ylva Hasselberg, Matt Hockenberry, Peter Knight, Chris McKenna, Perry Mehrling, Frank E. Merle, Ted Porter, Helen Small, Carl Winnerland, and Caitlin Zaloom. We also want to thank Robert Rosenkranz and Bill Janeway, who read early drafts of part or all of the manuscript, and Carol Mandel, who helped direct us to resources at the Elmer Bobst Library and Study Center at New York University. We received funding for this project from the Abraham and Rebecca Stein Faculty Publication Fund at New York University.

For her forbearance, love, and all-round good sense, Kevin acknowledges Jessica E. Smith; and Mary, as always, thanks her dogs Jake and Jamie for not making too much noise while she was writing. We dedicate the book to Mary's father, William Edgar Poovey, who didn't quite make it to see the book in print, but whose spirit is alive in every page.

INTRODUCTION

Finance in America: An Unfinished Story chronicles the history of finance in the United States from the late nineteenth century to the present, the emergence of finance as an object of cultural fascination and subject of academic financial theory, and the innovative financial products created after 1970. These products played a critical role in the transformation of the financial system and contributed to the crisis of 2008. We place the story of finance in the context of developments within the discipline of economics and alongside discussions of US fiscal and monetary policy because isolating finance from the institutional and social contexts in which it grew would make it impossible to grasp how much finance has contributed to—and been shaped by—the nation's history. *Finance in America* is neither a celebration nor an indictment of modern finance. As a history, it provides a long view that seeks to advance the national conversation already underway about the place finance now occupies in the United States and in the global economy as well. The story is unfinished because the fallout of the transformation signaled by the 2008 financial crisis continues to be felt around the world.

The financial crisis of 2008 differed in important ways from the other crises we examine in *Finance in America*, but it would be impossible to understand how this most recent crisis developed without the longer history we provide. This history reveals that finance, as we know it today, emanated from a disparate range of practices, theories, and agendas and only gradually coalesced after World War II into an identifiable set of activities and institutions.

The elusive nature of finance, understood in historical terms, has made writing its history challenging. The challenge comes partly from the daunting mathematical complexity and arcane vocabulary adopted by the applied discipline. Partly, the challenge comes from the intangible nature of finance: finance is grounded in intangible rights to property, contractual or customary; it is a creature of law and legislation and social mores. Its most important forms—such as the corporation, the banknote, and the money market fund—are historically contingent and can appear or disappear as a result of new legislation, changes in accounting rules, or novel institutional arrangements. Financial markets are also driven by intangibles such as changes in taste, information, expectations, and psychology. Today, no one would doubt the importance of finance in America because financial institutions receive extensive media coverage, the Dow Jones Industrial average crawls across TV and PC monitors, and the government regularly releases figures that give official totals for the nation's financial assets, as a percentage of the gross domestic product (GDP): in 1980, the total value of financial assets was five times the US GDP; by 2007, this ratio had doubled.[1] At the end of the nineteenth century, by contrast, even though the United States had an extensive, albeit noncentralized, system of financial institutions, banks and savings associations typically made the news only when one failed; stock exchanges attracted few investors, partly because price information was not widely distributed; and the system of national income accounts to which the GDP belongs had yet to be created. As a consequence, it is impossible to know what percentage of the nation's GDP was represented by financial assets in the 1890s (even though estimates have been made), and, while we can surmise that financial transactions were routinely conducted across the country, we have little data about them.

One place we find early traces of finance is in courses and textbooks that dealt with financial topics—banking, accounting, spending and saving, and, by the 1920s, investing. Another location for discussions of financial topics—the one to which we give the most attention—is works of economic theory. In these books and articles, some early twentieth-century economists elaborated principles and techniques subsequently amalgamated into the core of modern finance. Such topics include Irving Fisher's formulation of a theory of investor expectation based on the routine calculation of present value, which he derived from the work of brokers and actuaries; the accounting principles invented to help manage America's new corporations based on the bookkeeping of the Renaissance merchant; banking theories that elaborated the role of partial reserve banking in money creation; and the quantity and credit views of money. Also critical to the mature subject of finance—now, in the guise of financial theory and modeling—were the distinction Frank Knight drew between measurable risk and unknowable uncertainty, a distinction forgotten by model builders in the lead up to the 2008 crisis; the statistical methods promoted by Henry Ludwell Moore, agronomists, and members of the National Bureau of Economic Research; and innovative ideas about probability championed by Trygve Haavelmo, Jacob Marschak, and John von Neumann and Oskar Morgenstern. Finance as we know it today—the combination of institutions, regulations, asset categories, theories, models, and infrastructure that manages, creates, and studies money, credit, claims, banking, assets, and liabilities—came into being gradually in the course of the decades we survey here. In one sense—as credit or a hedge against the possibility that a crop may fail—finance seems as old as exchange itself. In another sense—as an algorithm that speeds high-volume trades around the world in a fraction of a second—finance seems like a creature of today. While it has no single origin, finance did make itself known in the documents and episodes we describe: the 1907 Bankers' Panic on Wall Street; the report of the Pujo Committee, which exposed a giant "Money Trust" in 1912–13; passage of the Federal Reserve Act in 1913; the marginalist tax policies adopted by the federal government in the 1920s; the speculative schemes and ticker tape machines and investment trusts that proliferated in that decade; and, of course, the Great Depression, the stagflation of the 1970s, and the 2008 global financial crisis. These three crises affected the lives of nearly every American and, individually and collectively, have made it absolutely clear that finance was and is here to stay.

A primary aim of *Finance in America* is to describe the consolidation of finance as a gradual, uneven process without losing sight of the heterogeneity of its components or the capaciousness of what it has now become. In doing so, we have found it useful to invoke a distinction occasionally made by economic and financial theorists—the distinction between the "real" and "financial" "sides" of the economy. Economies do not have "sides," of course, but the metaphor, which comes from the facing pages of an accounting ledger, helps us visualize the distinction between transactions that involve physical goods and services and those composed of credit, claims, and classes of securities. Most US economists in the first half of the twentieth century focused primarily on the real side of the economy, although some, like Irving Fisher, developed ideas that pertain to the financial side, such as the importance of expectations, and others, like Thorstein Veblen, made readers keenly aware of the inherent contradiction between a financial system geared to create profits and a real economy designed to produce useful goods and services. Some economists viewed money, which belongs to both sides of the economy, as neutral in the long run; others treated money as a commodity like any other (subject to the laws of supply and demand); while others—especially after

1960—realized that money represents a site where the real and financial sides of an economy meet. Most often, economists distinguish between what we call the real and financial sides of the economy for theoretical reasons—to delineate the subject they are addressing or to position their work in a tradition of economic analysis.

The capaciousness of finance means that we have had to set limits to what we discuss in this book. Hence, we discuss monetary economics, modern finance, and the evolution of modern capital markets in the United States, but we do not discuss the parallel history of global capital markets and international trade agreements, the US insurance industry, financial information companies, theories of international finance, or globalization. Nor do we discuss numerous sites where ad hoc financial practices are developed, such as bank managers' offices or trading floors. Finally, we have discussed only a limited number of economic theorists. For instance, we discuss American Keynesianism, but do not treat the different approach to Keynesian economics developed by Joan Robinson and her colleagues; nor do we deal with post-Keynesian macroeconomics, structural or information economics, or the diverse approaches now characterized as "heterodox" economics. By the same token, we address a range of institutions that touch on finance but we leave others aside. The institutions we discuss include the modern corporation, the US government, the Federal Reserve system, parts of the US financial system, including financial intermediaries, and some parts of the global financial system. We do not include international institutions like the International Monetary Fund (IMF), multinational corporations, or international financial agreements, like the Basel Accords, nor do we address critical episodes in global finance such as the fall of the USSR, the rise of China's economy, or the creation of the Eurozone. Finally, we focus primarily, although not exclusively, on the United States, even though we recognize that both the theoretical positions we address and the US economy have been and still are shaped in countless ways by international influences. Some of our story's most consequential economists and financial theorists were born, trained, or spent much of their careers in Europe, Russia, or the United Kingdom; and the events we chronicle in chapter 10 would not have occurred had developments in global capital markets not begun to affect the United States after 1970. We set our history in the United States not because this nation is exceptional but because when the limits of American exceptionalism have become clear, as they did in each of the three crises that anchor our story, the consequences proved so dire.

Finance in America does not propose a program to avert future financial crises. While the US economy has rebounded since 2008, the uptick in securities prices and jobs has not benefited all Americans to the same extent. Nor has the average American's understanding of the economy and finance been markedly enhanced by the crisis and its aftermath. Economists and financial theorists continue to speak in highly technical terminology that is almost impossible for outsiders to understand, and even noteworthy attempts to make the disciplines and their models more accessible—such as Dani Rodrik's *Economics Rules* and Ben Bernanke's account of the role played in the crisis by the Fed—constitute frail bridges across the massive gulf that separates economic and financial theory from the everyday language of most Americans.[2] We believe history has the potential to illuminate disciplines now closed to outsiders, not least because the stories contained in *Finance in America* make it clear that, while the pieces fit together, no single outcome is forecast by what has thus far transpired.

I.1. THE STORY

In our account, the history of finance in America is marked by three great crises: the Great Depression, which was a monetary crisis; the stagflation that dominated the 1970s, which was a crisis that originated in the real side of the economy; and the financial crisis of 2008, which was a credit crisis that led to the near-collapse of the global financial infrastructure. The chapters of our book, however, do not focus exclusively on these crises. Instead, we contextualize them in a more capacious account of institutions, theories, and models. In the first six chapters, we examine the period between 1896 and the end of the interwar period. Many, but not all, the developments of these decades can be linked to the methods and concepts introduced by Irving Fisher, professor of political economy at Yale. Fisher brought to American economics the mathematical methods pioneered in Europe, and he also formulated concepts that would prove central to modern finance. These include a theory of investor expectation; a principle called the Fisher effect, which holds that investor expectations are a critical determinant of the nominal interest rate, which led to a new understanding of the role expectations play in investor behavior and asset prices; and a reformulation of the quantity theory of money, which states that the money supply and the price level vary in direct proportion to one another. Fisher was a neoclassical economist—a term we elaborate below—and he was also involved in advancing statistics and statistical techniques like index numbers and econometrics, a practice that combines economic theory, mathematics, and statistics. Many of the prominent economists we discuss in this book, including Joseph Schumpeter, James Tobin, and Milton

Friedman, considered Fisher one of the greatest, if not the greatest, American economist.[3]

Fisher's contributions brought together practices long established in the world of everyday finance, such as compounding interest and estimating prices and the future demand for products, with many of the theories and methods with which academic economists were reshaping their discipline in the first decades of the twentieth century. While finance in its modern form was not part of the US university curriculum in these decades, some of its components were taught in specialized courses on accounting, agricultural economics, banking, or business statistics. As we will see in chapter 3, the case study method of addressing industry pricing and inventory was pioneered at the Harvard Business School between 1909 and 1912. In the first decades of the twentieth century, even in many of Irving Fisher's own works, finance and economic theory were generally two separate subjects, but Fisher did show how the two could join forces, and many of his writings were taken up by later financial theorists, such as Tobin, economic theorists, such as Friedman, and individuals who tried to fuse the two disciplines, such as the post-Keynesian economist Paul Davidson.[4]

In chapter 1, we survey aspects of the historical and institutional context that informed the work of Fisher and other early twentieth-century economists. Most important was the emergence of America's first industrial corporations, which proliferated in what historians call the first merger movement. Following the example of the railroads, industrial corporations became powerful quickly partly because they invented new accounting methods that made it easier for professional managers to launch and control them. These accounting innovations also helped the corporations raise money from a new source—shareholders. In this chapter we also examine financial innovations that supported the new corporations: the introduction of the Federal Reserve system, and the codification of theoretical and practical principles of banking at the turn of the century. In chapter 2, we examine some of the most important economic theories developed in response to these events. These include not only Fisher's neoclassical and mathematical economics, but also Veblen's institutionalist critique of the corporations, John Bates Clark's adaptation of European marginalism to the US context, and Frank Knight's distinction between risk, as a statistically measurable (and thus insurable) version of the unknown, and uncertainty, which he considered beyond statistical analysis because genuinely unknowable. We conclude chapter 2 with a discussion of the fiscal policy adopted by the US government during the 1920s, for this policy explicitly embodied marginalist principles and helped strengthen the second major institution with implications for finance: the federal government.

Chapter 3 focuses on statistics and data, topics with which finance had a special link at the beginning of the twentieth century. At that time, one of the few sources of comprehensive official data came from the US Comptroller of the Currency, and the United States was unique in having a continuous run of securities prices going back to the 1860s. Apart from financial data, however, the US lacked the official records necessary to understand (or tax) the nation's businesses and commercial activities, and the available statistical tools were relatively rudimentary as well. Many economists were wary of statistical analysis, because it seemed to run counter to the deductive nature of most economic theory. Two aspects of this situation began to change in the years leading up to America's entry into World War I: the federal government, bolstered by increased revenue from taxes, began systematically to collect commercial data to prepare for war; and innovations in statistical techniques, like index numbers and time series, made it easier to process and interpret information. While some economists, like Henry Ludwell Moore, embraced statistics, others remained wary; and debates over how one should treat statistical data divided economists during and after the war. As in chapter 1, we place the theoretical and methodological debates among economists in the context of social, institutional, and political developments: the founding of the National Bureau of Economic Research (NBER), early attempts to conceptualize and document the business cycle, and the congressional investigation into the possibility that America's financial system was ruled by a cartel of powerful bankers and industrial magnates. We conclude the chapter with an analysis of one of the earliest comprehensive depictions of the American financial system, Harold Moulton's *The Financial Organization of Society*.

Chapter 4 focuses on the interwar transformation of the US financial system. We discuss these developments as an example of "financialization," but we use the term to refer to the way these decades made finance *visible*, rather than to the growth in the size of the financial sector, however this is measured.[5] In the boom years of the 1920s, when talk of a "new era" and novel investment products catapulted Wall Street to new prominence, then during the Great Depression, as unemployment and failing banks sapped the nation's confidence, financial institutions became objects of the nation's collective fantasies, then targets of concern and legislative reform. We present the 1920s as a brief period of speculative frenzy bracketed, on the one side, by Harold Moulton's plea for the government to deploy "measuring aids of control"—mathematics, statistics, and accounting—to restrain the nation's increasing reliance on credit and, on the other, by the stock market crash of 1929. The crash was soon followed by Roosevelt's New Deal, which used financial reform to impose even stricter controls than Moulton called for. We show how speculation was encouraged by new financial practices, institutions, and products—installment buying, security affiliates, investment trusts—what the crash did to the nation's economy, and how the federal government used federal agencies to formulate and enforce new regulations, reform the Federal Reserve system, and elaborate the federal tax code. We also show how the federal government extended its reach into the US housing market by creating institutions to underwrite mortgages and offering tax incentives to homeowners. Many of the regulations and tax policies implemented under the New Deal remained in place until the 1980s (some exist today), when waves of deregulation, then tax cuts, began to reverse the federal government's attempt to reign in the nation's financial institutions. In this chapter, we also discuss some of the interwar period's most important publications with implications for finance. These include *The Modern Corporation and Private Property*, by Adolf Berle and Gardiner Means, *Security Analysis* by David Dodd and Benjamin Graham, John Burr Williams's *Theory of Investment Value*, and Irving Fisher's *The Stock Market Crash—and After*.

Chapters 5 and 6 explore the ways data and new applications of accounting were used to create new analytic objects, as well as new ways of conceptualizing finance. Chapter 5 deals with research in equity and fixed income and the data sets and analytic tools generated by this research. In this chapter, we detail the contributions made to economic theory and finance by agricultural economists, many working at midwestern land grant universities, and we show how one of the first attempts to apply probability theory to stock prices led Alfred A. Cowles III to prove that professional stock forecasters could not outperform the market. In chapter 6 we turn to the creation of aggregate data sets. We introduce the theoretical contribution of John Maynard Keynes, but devote the bulk of this chapter to efforts to estimate national income and productivity in the 1930s. Focusing on contributions by Simon Kuznets, Milton Gilbert, a group of Brookings Institution economists that included Harold Moulton, and Wassily Leontief, we show how national estimates were supplanted by national income accounts, then augmented by the expenditure approach promoted by Brookings and the input-output accounts developed by Leontief. We conclude the chapter with a discussion of the fiscal policy implemented by the US government in the interwar period.

In chapter 7 we introduce the topic of modeling. So central has model-ing become to the discipline of economics—and, by extension—finance that in 1997, in a survey of his discipline's last fifty years, the Nobel laure-ate Robert M. Solow identified modeling as *the* definitive methodology of economics.[6] Solow associated the advent of modeling with the publication of Keynes's *General Theory of Employment, Interest, and Money* (1936), but we show that Ragnar Frisch, the Norwegian economist and statistician, in-troduced the concept of "little model worlds" in lectures delivered at Yale in 1930. Along with Irving Fisher, Frisch helped found the Econometric Society, and the society's journal, *Econometrica*, provided a venue for de-veloping the new method. Economists began to convert Keynes's theoreti-cal contribution into mathematical models in the months after the *General Theory* appeared, with John R. Hicks's IS-LM model proving especially influential. (The IS-LM model shows the determinant level of national in-come and the interest rate when investment and savings, on the one hand, and the loan market and the money market, on the other, are in equilibrium.)[7] In the late 1930s, working with the London School of Economics economist Helen Makower, Jacob Marschak adapted Keynes's theoretical framework to create a model of investors' decisions about the choice and allocation of fi-nancial assets. Marschak, one of many European émigrés to profoundly affect American economic theory after the rise of the Nazis, went on to head the re-search division of the Cowles Commission, an organization spun off from the Econometric Society. For much of the decade, economists debated how to understand the relationship between models and empirical data. These de-bates are epitomized by the disagreement between the Dutch economist Jan Tinbergen and Keynes, who was generally regarded as the leading economic theorist in the West. One offshoot of the debates was macroeconometrics, which combined Keynes's aggregate approach to economic issues with the methodology and models championed by the Econometric Society.

Models are simulations, which are designed to approximate and simplify real-world situations so that something resembling experiments can be run. Unlike physical scientists, most social scientists do not perform experiments: an economist cannot replay the Great Depression to see if a different combi-nation of public policies and economic factors would have produced a differ-ent outcome. Modeling is a tool that fulfills some of the aims of experimenta-tion because it offers a way to run an "if . . . then" operation: *if* we control for these variables, *then* this set of relations generates this result.[8] Models do not have to be expressed in mathematical language; in chapter 1 we examine an early model designed by Irving Fisher, which consisted of a water-filled cistern in which floating containers exemplified the effects of the money supply on prices. Beginning in the 1930s, however, most economists began to prefer mathematical models to the "literary" modes of theorizing that dominated the writings of earlier economists (including Keynes), and mathematics is now the lingua franca of economic modeling, just as modeling is the characteristic methodology of economics and modern finance.

As simulations, models inevitably inform what we can see of whatever relationship or event they represent. Indeed, the relationship or event presented in the model does not exist *in its model form* outside the model itself, and one of the purposes of models is to create something that does not exist—because it is simpler, more abstract, and more easily manipulated than its real-world counterpart. Many models, as we will see, are designed as guides to policy, so they may be said to have a performative relation to the real world.[9] This is the case with national income models, which we explore in chapter 6. Others are treated as *accurate enough* for specific modes of analysis; this is true, for example, of *ex ante* (before the event or expected) prices, which appear in some kinds of models, whereas others may use only the more exact *ex post* figures. Still other models belong to a complex of related models and are designed to display only one perspective. This is the case with the *fund view* made available in a balance sheet (which is also a model). In the case of corporations, this intentionally partial view began to be supplemented in the second decade of the twentieth century by the *flow view,* when companies began to adopt the income statement. In the case of national accounts, by contrast, the flow view came first, in the national income estimates of the 1930s, and the fund view was added only in the 1960s, when the US government adopted the flow of funds accounts created by Morris A. Copeland in the 1950s. For models designed as policy directives, performativity constitutes an essential measure of the model's success. Models designed to be partial may become performative if they are widely adopted. As we will see in a moment, in the 1970s and 1980s, some financial models did become performative, in the sense that they began to influence the market prices they used as data.[10]

In chapter 8, we explore the components that went into the building of economic models in the middle decades of the twentieth century. Many, although not all these models, used the Keynesian framework. Essentially, the models combined the elements whose history we have been tracing—mathematics (and mathematical economics in particular), statistics, data, and accounting frameworks—but to these they added probability theory, which was a special research interest of the Cowles Commission until 1948. The mathematical part of the models associated with American Keynesianism was developed in works by Paul A. Samuelson and Donald Patinkin; members of the Cowles Commission (especially Trygve Haavelmo) pressed for adding probability theory to the models; game theory, as developed by John von Neumann and Oskar Morgenstern, then adapted by Jacob Marschak, contributed the theoretical components of rational choice and the rational agent; Leonard "Jimmie" Savage reformulated probability theory to accommodate a subjective element; Richard Bellman introduced a dynamic programming equation that helped solve optimization problems; and George B. Dantzig and Marshall K. Wood added to models a technique known as linear programming. Many of these tools were initially developed during World War II, in connection with operations research, and, in the decades immediately after the war, they were adapted for peacetime applications, including economic and financial models.

The 1950s and 1960s also witnessed the publication of empirical studies that proved indispensable to the models developed by economists and financial theorists. In addition to Morris Copeland's work on social money flows, which laid the groundwork for the flow of funds accounts, Raymond Goldsmith completed an NBER project on financial intermediaries, and Milton Friedman conducted empirical research on the money supply. In *Money in a Theory of Finance*, John G. Gurley and Edward S. Shaw published the first theoretical account of the interrelations of the nation's financial markets and institutions. Using data compiled by Copeland, Goldsmith, and Friedman and Anna Jacobson Schwartz, Gurley and Shaw demonstrated that a theoretical model of the entire economy anchored in empirical work could show how financial intermediation worked and how commercial banking was linked to the money supply. All this data fed into Milton Friedman's monetarism and his *Monetary History of the United States*, which he and Schwartz published in 1963. Friedman was a fierce advocate of free market policies and a critic of the Federal Reserve, whose power had just been extended by the 1951 Fed Accord. Friedman also declared himself an enemy of American Keynesianism, even though he largely worked within—albeit against—the aggregate framework Keynes established.

We place the emergence of modeling and the compilation of empirical data within the context of US monetary and fiscal policy between 1950 and 1968. In the 1950s, as inflation began to seem a recurrent feature of the American economy, Washington legislators adopted policies designed to stabilize prices and maintain maximal employment, as the 1946 Employment Act mandated. Economists loosely associated with the institutionalist wing of the discipline staffed the Council of Economic Advisors (CEA), which was also created by the 1946 Employment Act, and the Federal Reserve Board, which was granted increased power by the Fed Accord. Under the leadership of individuals like Arthur F. Burns, Raymond J. Saulnier, and William McChesney Martin, the government used monetary restraint and fiscal prudence to manage the growing economy. When John Fitzgerald Kennedy was elected president in 1960, he brought Keynesian economists into the CEA and onto the Fed Board, and their policies of deficit spending in pursuit of long-term growth culminated in passage of the 1964 Tax Reduction Act, one of the largest tax reductions in American history. The policies of American Keynesians were informed by IS-LM models such as those created by James Tobin and William C. Brainard, which revealed the effects on the nation's economy of financial intermediation by banks. Tobin's models combined support for government management of the financial system (in this case, through monetary controls) with a refusal to use *only* the Fed's monetary controls, unmoored from other fiscal policies. The shift in emphasis by the Kennedy administration—from the institutionalists' stabilization policies to Keynesian policies designed to increase growth—also drew on models developed by Robert M. Solow in the 1950s. These models, which were variants of the growth models first designed in 1939, were the first signs of the supply-side economic policies that were to dominate the decades between 1970 and 2008.

In chapter 9 we examine the emergence of modern finance. This coincided with the appearance of both finance as an identifiable subfield within the discipline of economics (though often housed in business schools) and financial engineering as a practical application of modeling. We show how the emergent discipline of finance was informed by agricultural economists' work on futures markets and hedging and what happened when Harry Markowitz applied linear programming, one of the techniques associated with operations research, to the problem of asset allocation; the outcome was modern portfolio theory. During the next two decades, the remainder of the platform that supports modern finance was put in place: capital asset pricing theory, the efficient market hypothesis, the random walk of stock prices, and the Modigliani-Miller Theorem.

The years of high theory in modern finance extended from 1952 until 1972, when Fischer Black, Myron Scholes, and Robert C. Merton launched the Black-Scholes-Merton options pricing model. The historical context in which this model was created is once more important, although we defer a comprehensive account of the 1970s until chapter 10, where we show how worldwide events, such as the first oil shock in 1973 and the United States' abrogation of the Bretton Woods agreement, helped expose the inadequacies of the assumptions written into the Capital Asset Pricing Model (CAPM) and other financial models (not to mention the demand management policies of Keynesian economics). During the 1970s, these inadequacies were enumerated, on both empirical and theoretical grounds, by Bernard Mandelbrot, Michael C. Jensen, William H. Meckling, Richard Roll, and others. Eventually, even the theorist who coined the phrase "efficient markets" joined in: in 1990 Eugene Fama proclaimed that "beta [the signature measure of the CAPM model] was dead."

The marginalization of CAPM coincided with another phase of the probabilistic revolution in finance, which, in turn, accelerated development of a new generation of financial models. These models, which drew upon and elaborated the Black-Scholes-Merton options pricing model, include no-arbitrage models (APT) and risk-neutral pricing models (RNP). Some are discrete-time models, which address security prices in two-period intervals; others are continuous-time models, which capture the continuous decision making intrinsic to lifetime investing in a stochastic framework.[11] All these models are anchored in the theory of no-arbitrage, instead of the equilibrium assumption that underwrote neoclassical economics and most earlier financial models. All have been used to create new financial products, like collateralized debt obligations and credit derivatives, designed to profit from the volatility that characterized markets in the first decades of the twenty-first century. We discuss financial econometrics, a practice designed to test theories and models by confronting them with data, and Fama's reconsideration of efficient market theory. Both were introduced in the 1980s, in the context of financial deregulation, the disintermediation of financial markets and the elaboration of a shadow banking system, securitization, rapid advances in computing hardware and software, and unprecedented investment by American corporations in the financial sector and by the financial sector in digital technology. As financial engineers created ever-more-exotic derivatives products and more affordable software packages helped financial econometricians identify potentially profitable market inefficiencies and arbitrage opportunities, a market-based, global financial system became visible—a system that was more interconnected and more vulnerable to systemic risk than ever before. We conclude with a discussion of behavioral finance, a research project designed to accommodate investor behaviors that do not conform to the rationality most theoretical models assume.

Chapter 10 explores the factors that led to the transformation of the US (and global) financial systems, the first signs that this transformation was underway, and developments within economic theory that failed to take account of these structural changes. What we see in the decades between 1970 and 2008—which we call the intercrisis period—is an ever-widening mismatch between models designed to drive economic policies and the growth of the financial sector, in the United States but also abroad. As a combination of deregulation, financial disintermediation, and securitization sparked rapid growth in the financial sector after the 1980s, security broker-dealers began to rival commercial banks in supplying credit, especially to the US housing market. Because broker-dealers, along with the structured investment vehicles spun off by some commercial and investment banks, used short-term leverage to purchase illiquid long-term debt (often in the form of asset-backed securities such as securitized mortgages), the financial system became more interconnected and more vulnerable to changes in the overall credit environment. Once homeowners began defaulting on their loans in numbers not anticipated by existing models, the entire system registered the strain. The bankruptcy of Lehman Brothers in September 2008 marked the end of the intercrisis period and the beginning of the worst recession since the Great Depression of the 1930s.

The financial crisis of 2008 was not the first sign that the emergent market-based financial system was vulnerable. In the period between 1987 and 2006, interest rates remained low, economists relied on models that ignored asset bubbles, financial engineers continued to develop exotic financial tools, and Alan Greenspan, chair of the Federal Reserve, repeatedly used the Fed funds rate to quench financial fires by flooding the system with virtually unlimited liquidity. The potential crises Greenspan quieted include the portfolio-insurance related crash of 1987, the fallout of the collapse of Long-Term Capital Management and the Russian default in 1997–98, the collapse of the dot.com asset bubble in 2000, and the stock market response to the 9/11 terrorist attack. Even as Greenspan managed the US economy, however, the structural changes already transforming the country's financial system went unaddressed. The models economists used did not factor in many of the most basic components of finance, and the models used by financial engineers did not recognize that risk could be unknowable and systemic rather than subject to estimation and statistically manageable. The conditions were thus ripe for the rude awakening that occurred in 2008.

I.2. WHAT'S IN A NAME?
OUR INTERPRETIVE POSITION

A brief examination of four concepts and their associated terms will clarify the interpretive position we take in *Finance in America*. The first does not feature in other histories of economics or finance, although a few economists have used its terms.[12] These terms—the real side of the economy and the financial side—capture the sense that economies are composed of parts, which national income accountants in the 1930s called "sectors." Instead of "sectors," we use "sides" to indicate the affinity of these parts of a nation's economy to the accounting practices that exposed the skeleton of corporations and national economies in the early twentieth century: in double entry bookkeeping, the debit and credit accounts of a company's business (or a nation's income and production) are distinguished by the side of the ledger on which they appear, and real transactions—which involve physical commodities or materials—are typically distinguished from financial transactions—which involve capital outlays or debts. We do not believe that the real and financial "sides" of an economy are actually separate—but they are often treated as if they were. We can see this in early attempts to theorize supply and demand, where the commodities at issue were typically real goods or services, not financial assets. We see it again in early national income estimates, where the production of real goods appeared but the channels of financial intermediation did not. One significant storyline of *Finance in America* concerns attempts to integrate the two sides of the economy into a single theoretical account or model. We see such attempts in Jacob Marschak's 1938 model of investment, Gurley and Shaw's 1960 *Money in a Theory of Finance*, James Tobin's 1960s models, and Hyman Minsky's financial instability hypothesis. As we examine various models in chapters 7 through 10, we consistently ask whether they included finance and, if so, how the models dealt with the relationship between the real and financial sides of the economy. In general terms, until economists began to use stock flow analysis or take the fund (as opposed to the flow) view, their models could not accommodate finance. The fact that many growth models, like the dynamic stochastic general equilibrium (DSGE) models used in the first decades of the twenty-first century, did not employ the fund view helps explain why they did not include finance.

Money occupies an especially complicated place in analyses that distinguish between the financial and real sides of an economy, for money is important on both sides. In the real economy, money functions as a unit of account and a medium of exchange. In the financial economy, money is also a medium of exchange, but, in addition, it is a particular kind of asset (a store of value), and a standard of deferred payment. The different roles money plays in the two sides of the economy have led to complications we have tried to parse. Monetarists like Milton Friedman, for example, considered managing a nation's money supply to be the government's most important role in the economy, but while he focused on the supply and demand for the quantity of money, Friedman did not highlight the endogenous role banks and other financial intermediaries play in augmenting the money supply or the importance of the credit channel. By the same token, as the discipline of finance developed its own models and investment products, the real side of economic transactions tended to fade into the background. Some of the more exotic derivatives developed in the last two decades, for example, such as synthetic credit default swaps, require no underlying real asset to anchor their value, and high frequency trading makes money not from trading physical commodities but from capitalizing on high-volume positions taken on split-second differentials in prices that appear on various digital exchanges. In these cases, real commodities never change hands, yet such trades have helped the financial side of the economy grow in volume and value, as a ratio of the nation's GDP. Such complexities in understanding the relationship between the real and financial sides of the economy help explain why writing a history of finance is so challenging.

A second concept, with its related terms, will be more familiar to economic historians. The term *neoclassical economics* was coined by Thorstein Veblen in 1900. Veblen used the term to distinguish between the work of economists like Alfred Marshall and writings by "historical" or Marxist economists. According to Veblen, the former engaged in "taxonomic" projects, which sought "normalities," while the latter pursued an evolutionary inquiry, which assumed only "a cumulative causal sequence," not the kind of "normal cases" preferred by the neoclassicals.[13] Veblen also wanted to distinguish among the economists pursuing taxonomic projects, for Veblen thought that some, like Marshall, were moving toward the evolutionary thinking Veblen considered the future of the discipline, while others, like John Bates Clark, were "classical" in the sense that they were not oriented toward evolutionary thinking but exclusively devoted to finding "normalities."

The difficulties surrounding "neoclassical" arise from the fact that so many people, economists included, have used the term in different ways, almost none of which respect Veblen's original text. As David Colander explains,

[John R.] Hicks and [George] Stigler extended the meaning of neo-classical to encompass all marginalist writers, including [Carl] Menger, [William Stanley] Jevons, and J. B. Clark. Most writers after John Hicks and George Stigler used the term inclusively. Thus it lost its initial meaning. Instead of describing Marshallian economics, it became associated with the use of calculus, the use of marginal productivity theory, and a focus on relative prices. . . . J. M. Keynes, as was his way, disregarded existing usage and developed his own. He lumped Classicals and neo-classicals together, calling them all Classicals—suggesting that the distinctions in pre-Keynesian work were of minor importance. Keynes's use added yet another dimension to the Classical classification: it was a term that was to be contrasted with Keynesian. In the third edition of his principles textbook, Paul Samuelson built on Keynes's classification and turned it around on Keynes by developing the neoclassical synthesis. In the neoclassical synthesis, Keynes's dispute with Classical economists was resolved.[14]

After Samuelson, in Colander's view, the terminological controversy became even more misleading. Colander judges the "current use of the term by historians of thought [to be] schizophrenic and inconsistent," and he recommends avoiding the word altogether. Colander is especially irritated that "neoclassical" has become a term used by "heterodox economists, by many non-specialists, and by historians of thought at unguarded moments, as a classifier for the approach that the majority of economists take today. . . . The worst uses, and the place one hears the term neoclassical most often, is in the discussion of lay people who object to some portion of modern economic thought. To them bad economics and neoclassical economics are synonymous terms."[15]

We take Colander's point that "modern economic thought" is too diverse to be captured by a single term. Indeed, one of the aims of chapter 10 is to display some of this diversity. We also agree with Colander that neoclassical economics, if this term is meaningful at all, died "somewhere between 1935 and 2000," that its "death was gradual" (133), and that the distinctive feature of modern economics is its methodology—its reliance on mathematical modeling: "*the modeling approach to problems is the central element of modern economics*" (137). But it is also the case, even though modern economic practice is diverse, that some economists today still identify a neoclassical core within modern orthodox economics, and they equate the consolidation of this core with the "bald attack on and excommunication of any last vestige of heterodox economics in top-ranked universities through the world."[16] The term *neoclassical* may not be the best term to describe orthodox economics since 2000, but if the discipline is now characterized by virtual unanimity about method and basic assumptions, it seems important to signal that fact.

David Colander is not alone in wanting to ban the term *neoclassical*. In a series of books and articles, Cambridge University's Tony Lawson has also recommended abandoning the term. Lawson justifies his campaign by appeals not to the diversity of projects that characterize the modern discipline but to the ontological error committed by all orthodox economists. While Lawson agrees with Colander that methodology—mathematical modeling— constitutes the distinctive feature of modern economics, he discounts whatever diversity the discipline accommodates because he considers mathematical modeling a fundamentally misleading mode of analysis.

> Certainly the contemporary discipline is dominated by a mainstream tradition. But whilst the concrete substantive content, focus and policy orientation of the latter are highly heterogeneous and continually changing, the project itself is adequately characterized in terms of its enduring reliance, indeed, unceasing insistence, upon the methods of *mathematical modeling*. In effect, it is a form of *mathematical deductivism* in the context of economics. Deductivism is just the doctrine that all explanation be expressed in terms of "laws" or "uniformities" interpreted as (actual or "hypothetical") correlations of even regularities. . . . The methods of mathematical modeling carry ontological presuppositions.

Among these presuppositions are the claims of "regularities at the level of events" and, by extension, that events are discrete or isolated from each other, rather than being part of a process, which is "essentially a process of cumulative causation."[17] According to Lawson, such regularities are rarely to be found in the world, and the continued reliance of orthodox economists on mathematical modeling helps explain why their work has so often been misleading in profound ways.

In *Finance in America*, we have by and large preferred description to critique, even when we are personally sympathetic to critiques like Lawson's. When the economists we discuss use the word neoclassical, we have used the term, and we have regularly applied it to economic work of a certain kind before 2000. We have not tried to draw up a list of attributes associated with neoclassical economics, as Colander does, nor have we elaborated a definition of "classical" that would provide a reference point for its "neo" descendent.[18] While we acknowledge the importance of classificatory categories in any history, our primary goal has been to trace the emergence of finance as a set of practices and theories whose relation to economists' understandings of their own discipline has always been complex—but rarely hindered by economists' disputes over nomenclature. Some early financial theorists, like Irving Fisher and Harry Markowitz, worked within a theoretical framework that can meaningfully be called neoclassical, but this term makes less sense for financial theorists working in the third phase of modern finance, which opened with the Black-Scholes-Merton options pricing model in 1972.

A brief examination of a third concept—which we have not used—reveals much about the limits we have imposed on ourselves in *Finance in America*. The term related to this concept is *neoliberalism*. By and large, neoliberalism is not a term orthodox economists use to describe their work, for it is a critical term that refers to the free-market ideology that can be said to inform economic practice rather than the method or contents of economics, which most orthodox economists believe to be above ideology because they consider economics to be a science. Non-economists, by contrast, and some heterodox economists as well, challenge economists' claim to be scientific by charging the mainstream discipline with complicity in a raft of present-day woes. According to George Monboit, "neoliberalism sees competition as the defining characterization of human relations. It redefines citizens as consumers, whose democratic choices are best exercised by buying and selling, a process that rewards merit and punishes inefficiency. It maintains that 'the market' delivers benefits that could never be achieved by planning." Neoliberalism, Monboit asserts, "played a major role in a remarkable variety of crises: the financial meltdown of 2007–8; the offshoring of wealth and power, of which the Panama Papers offer us merely a glimpse; the slow collapse of public health and education; resurgent child poverty; the epidemic of loneliness; the collapse of ecosystems; the rise of Donald Trump."[19] While we see in contemporary society many of the ills Monboit identifies, we do not use the term *neoliberalism* to connect them, nor do we attribute these problems to the rise of economic orthodoxy or modern finance. To explain our decision, we turn to someone who does: Notre Dame economist Philip Mirowski.

According to Mirowski, neoliberalism rests on a coherent set of principles introduced by Friedrich Hayek and Ludwig von Mises at the first meeting of the Mont Pelerin Society in 1947. While its explicit agenda was to save classical liberalism from the twin specters of Marxist planning and Keynesianism, the society soon expanded into what Mirowski describes as a decentralized "Neoliberal Thought Collective" (NTC) whose power lay in its ability to prosper inside and outside universities, penetrate political parties and corporate management structures, and influence phenomena as disparate as high school textbooks, local government policies, and international monetary agreements. Mirowski enumerates thirteen core principles of neoliberalism and attributes to their implementation much of the damage George Monboit also identifies, but Mirowski focuses his scathing attack on neoliberalism on the discipline of economics and the practices of modern finance.[20]

According to Mirowski, the Federal Reserve "is an avowedly neoliberal institution, and one that relies on its major symbiotic relationship with the American economics profession to skew its membership in a neoliberal direction."[21] He argues that "the economics profession has become beholden to neoliberal institutions, and . . . that garden-variety disagreement [among economists], which might happen under any other circumstances, gets amplified and phase-shifted to produce its real objective, the paralysis of serious reform of the economy" (244). Mirowski agrees that mathematical modeling is now the defining characteristic of economics and finance, but he charges that economists build models not to explain or manage the economy but simply to rationalize "positions/explanations often arrived at elsewhere and by alternative avenues." "Building neoclassical mathematical models in the twenty-first century is a pursuit attuned to appeal to a narrow coterie of refined tastes; one should never confuse it with providing explanations of economic events" (287). Mirowski's blistering analysis culminates in an indictment of the resulting paralysis—the product of agnotology (the intentional manufacture of doubt and uncertainty)—and a malicious conspiracy organized by the "cosmopolitan rich."

> Whether they realize it or not, the kabuki of [economists'] disputations over irrelevant models is one of the more effective interventions in the public sphere, because it distracts attention from far more threatening prospective explanations. These include: the possibility that the financial sector has evolved to the point of cannibalization of the rest of the economy; or that the economics profession played an enabling role in inventing and justifying the most Rube Goldberg of securitizations and alterations of regulations; that neoliberal agnotology has filtered down to the very statistics everyone consults to make sense of economic events; that there is no such thing as the market, but only an array of different markets of varying capacities; that this ecology of markets bears

inherent tendencies toward niche collapse that undermine system operations; and that "free trade" is the cover story for the policies of the class of the cosmopolitan rich who believe they can evade all local consequences of system breakdown. (300)

Mirowski's take-no-prisoners carpet bombing of the economics profession is shrewd and provocative. But his account lacks nuance, and it focuses too narrowly on the postwar period to provide the more textured picture of a discipline forging a core before Mont Pelerin, or to show how the subdiscipline of finance emerged in part from early attempts to organize commercial relations outside a university context.

We do not use the word *neoliberalism* in *Finance in America*, and we believe that our analysis of the emergence of a market-based financial system in chapter 10 reveals a more fundamental shift than simply the extension of neoliberalism, which is Mirowski's concern. We do not use the term *neoliberalism* or address the concept because the term assimilates the history of economics and finance into the current state of these disciplines. It is more difficult to believe that a conspiracy dominates modern finance when one returns to the first decades of the twentieth century, when Irving Fisher struggled to find data for his rudimentary account of the relationship between expectations and interest rates, or even to Jacob Marschak's efforts in the late 1930s to extend the Keynesian framework to investment theory. Even if neoliberalism is now an agenda shared—perhaps unconsciously—by many Wall Street workers, central bank officials, and the "cosmopolitan rich," the history of the emergence of finance from outside and within economics does not coincide with the history of neoliberalism.

The final concept is the most important—and the most problematic, because there is no single term capable of conveying its effects. Certainly, it would be helpful if a single word could capture the impact finance has had on the US and global economies and on culture more generally. To many, *financialization* has seemed the obvious candidate. While we share the sense that some such term could perform important analytic work, we have generally avoided using *financialization* as a catchall term. We do discuss transformations in US financial institutions that some might call *financialization* in chapter 4, but we avoid using *financialization* to convey quantitative or qualitative measures of change.

We take to heart the cautionary note Brett Christophers sounded about *financialization* in 2015. After noting the increased usage of the term—Google Scholar recorded 170 hits between 1996 and 2000; 1,088 between 2001 and

2005; 5,790 between 2006 and 2010; and 12,101 between 2011 and midway through 2014—Christophers warned that financialization lacks precision as a theoretical concept, accuracy as a quantitative measure, and clarity as an analytic tool.[22] Financialization may serve the strategic function of focusing attention on the forces transforming the global economy and culture, Christopher acknowledged, but, thus far, the nature of these changes—much less their causes—remains unclear, and the term has done little to clarify these matters.

We add to Christophers's concern the worry that most discussions of financialization have little to say about "finance" itself. By this we mean not only the institutions and asset classes associated with financial claims and transactions but also the mathematical models by which financial assets are routinely valued today. Most scholarly accounts of financialization also have little to say about the regulations and legal context in which financial trades occur or the ontological regularities they assume. As a result, finance remains hidden in the conceptual black box that has long made it incomprehensible to most people. Meanwhile, *financialization* hints at some portentous transformation already in process without clarifying its nature or explaining how it is changing the world. Our discussion of the emergent market-based financial system, which is global in nature but still only partially visible, offers one contribution to this crucial analytic project but does not invoke the concept of financialization.

To the goal of understanding this process, *Finance in America* contributes a historical account and descriptions of some of the most important financial models. Our story remains unfinished, however, not only because the effects of this transformation are still making themselves felt but also because the analytic work necessary to grasp this process in detail and as a whole remains incomplete. Many contributors from numerous disciplines must work together to give more texture to this picture.

I.3. THE ARCHIVE

Given the number of topics we address in the following chapters, the archive for *Finance in America* is enormous. Our primary texts include canonical works of economic theory but also little-known working papers on asset pricing, as well as textbooks on accounting and mathematical finance. All our sources, both primary and secondary, are printed and digital in form: much as we value archival research and first-person interviews, we elected to write a synthetic history drawn from available sources. Some scholarly works exemplify the capacious approach we have taken, and these have been invaluable guides. Works by Martin J. Sklar and Alfred D. Chandler Jr., for example, clarified the early American corporations; Philip Mirowski's *Machine Dreams* illuminated the relationship between postwar economics and operations research; and our understanding of modern finance has been informed by Peter L. Bernstein's *Capital Ideas*, Perry Mehrling's studies of American monetary thought and Fischer Black; Colin Read's series on modern finance and articles by Geoffrey Poitras and Franck Jovanovic.[23] We have also relied on a series of graduate textbooks to help us parse modern finance. The most helpful include Robert C. Merton, *Continuous-Time Finance*; N. H. Bingham and Rüdiger Kiesel, *Risk-Neutral Valuation: Pricing and Hedging of Financial Derivatives*; John C. Cochrane, *Asset Pricing*; Mark S. Joshi, *The Concepts and Practice of Modern Finance*; Stephen Blyth, *An Introduction to Quantitative Finance*; David M. Kreps, *Microfoundations I: Choice and Competitive Markets*; and Stanley R. Pliska, *Introduction to Mathematical Finance: Discrete Time Models*.[24] Other scholarly studies focused on various parts of this history have also been helpful: David Hendry and Mary S. Morgan on econometrics; Mary Morgan and Marcel Boumans on economic modeling; E. Roy Weintraub on general equilibrium theory and mathematical economics; Donald MacKenzie on financial markets; Greta Krippner on financialization; and Mark Rubenstein on financial theory.[25]

We want to place *Finance in America* alongside two other books that extend or complement the story we tell. The first, William N. Goetzmann's *Money Changes Everything: How Finance Made Civilization Possible*, is one of the few histories that does not equate "finance" with the mathematical subdiscipline of economics inaugurated by the 1952 publication of Harry Markowitz's "Portfolio Selection." Instead, Goetzmann finds the core components of finance in the ancient Near East, and he argues that "financial thinking" and the "financial perspective of time" can be found in Mesopotamian artifacts and Babylonian contracts dating to the second millennium BCE.[26] Goetzmann's capacious, comparative history links financial thinking and practices to the basic components of civilization: writing, cities, architecture, industrialization, social security, contracts, and laws in the Near East, China, Russia, and Europe. *Money Changes Everything* is far more ambitious than *Finance in America*. Indeed, Goetzmann compresses his discussion of the topics we address into the last three of his twenty-nine chapters. As one might expect, Goetzmann's treatment is more cursory than—although not incompatible with—our analysis, and his level of engagement is less scholarly and more autobiographical. With fewer footnotes and more anecdotes,

Money Changes Everything will appeal to readers who want an eyewitness survey of the long sweep of finance, whereas *Finance in America* will attract readers who want an in-depth, extensively documented close-up of the role finance has played in American history and how the United States has given a particular character to the twentieth- and twenty-first-century versions of finance. The two books define "finance" in compatible ways, but where we treat the core ideas of finance as a composite of practices and theories that originated in other sites, Goetzmann claims both that these ideas were present from the beginning and that they were gradually brought together over time. In other words, Goetzmann addresses finance in traditional historical terms, whereas we take a genealogical approach. Finally, Goetzmann offers almost unqualified optimism about the future of finance, which he associates with sovereign wealth funds. Since he says almost nothing about the global financial crisis of 2008 and does not address the structural changes that created a global market-based financial system, his optimism may be warranted, but our more cautionary treatment of financial innovation is informed by events he chose not to include.

The second book complements *Finance in America* but, like *Money Changes Everything*, offers a significantly different emphasis. Thomas Piketty's *Capital in the Twenty-First Century* provides a historical and comparative account of structural inequality since the eighteenth century and across much of the world. Piketty tackles many of the issues we address in *Finance in America*: monetary policy, interest rates, the Federal Reserve, national income accounts, financial intermediaries, and portfolio management, to name a few. Piketty also shares our conviction that useful economic analysis must contain a historical component and that, in his words, "the profession's undue enthusiasm for simplistic mathematical models based on so-called representative agents" was one factor that prevented most economists from recognizing the structural change already underway after 1980.[27] While Piketty agrees that the models that drove much economic analysis during the intercrisis period made finance difficult to see, he is primarily interested in another issue these models obscured: inequality. In Piketty's argument, inequality—in wages, returns on capital, and purchasing power—"contributed to the nation's [the United States'] financial instability" (297). Financial instability in the United States, in turn, interacted with "the structural increase of the capital/income ratio (especially in Europe), coupled with an enormous increase in aggregate international asset positions" (298). The result was the global financial crisis of 2008.

We agree that inequality and financial instability are related features of the intercrisis period, but we think that our analysis of the latter will help readers form a more nuanced understanding of Piketty's analysis of the former. Piketty's data-rich study makes it clear that a great wealth shift has been occurring in the West since 1980: "The richest 10 percent appropriated three-quarters of the growth [in national income]. The richest 1 percent alone absorbed nearly 60 percent of the total increase of US national income in this period. Hence for the bottom 90 percent, the rate of income growth was less than 0.5 percent per year" (297). Piketty explains this wealth redistribution with a simple mathematical formula, which he calls the "fundamental inequality" model: "$r > g$ (where r stands for the average annual rate of return on capital, including profits, dividends, interest, rents, and other income from capital, expressed as a percentage of its total value, and g stands for the rate of growth of the economy, that is, the annual increase in income or output)" (25). Given unequal wealth (capital) and income distribution, he argues, income inequality will continue to grow as long as the rate of return on "capital" outpaces a nation's growth rate. The only thing that could disrupt this trend is the destruction of capital through taxation, appropriation, or war. Piketty's argument turns on the ability to empirically measure the value of capital and income.

In essence, *Finance in America* tells the story of the framework that organizes Piketty's monumental work, as well as the data he amasses to support his argument. We show how national income accounting developed, why the concept of "national wealth" was constructed as it was, how economists and statisticians solved a series of problems that made the kind of aggregate data Piketty relies on seem authoritative, and how mathematical models—models as simple as his but infinitely more complicated ones as well—became the preferred analytic tools (and rhetorical weapons) of economists. Unless one understands how this framework was constructed and naturalized—made to seem like the obvious way to understand economic issues—it is difficult, if not impossible, to see why the empirical measurement of capital and income is more difficult than Piketty implies.[28] In another sense, *Finance in America* provides the analytic framework necessary to understand and evaluate Piketty's important work. Conflating the physical component of "capital," for instance, with its financial component to obtain the "rate of return" obscures a critical distinction that one cannot see until the real and financial sides are separated: one part of the "rate of return" may come from the productive function of the physical or real component of "capital," but another part comes from the rate of interest, which belongs to the financial side of capital.

If readers interested in finance, financial crises, and inequality read *Money Changes Everything*, *Capital in the Twenty-First Century*, and *Finance in*

America, they will have the analytic tools, historical narrative, and statistical data necessary to make better sense of the complicated world we live in today. What they will not have—the book no one has yet written—is a history of the interconnected *global* market that is as historically capacious as Goetzmann's book, as data-rich as Piketty's, and analytic in the way *Finance in America* is. That crucial book still needs to be written.

I.4. OUR READERS AND WHY THIS MATTERS

Given the scope, eclectic archive, and difficulty of many of the texts we address in the following chapters, it is fair to ask why readers without a long-standing interest in the subject might want to give this book a try—especially now that more anecdotal, more journalistic histories are available. Given the proliferation of books on the financial crisis of 2008, moreover, it seems fair to ask if we need another book on this subject. The best answer we can give to the first question is to say that if you've read this far, you may be one of the "earnest readers" we hope to attract. "Earnest readers" is a phrase used by Robert M. Solow and James Tobin in their historical introduction to the economic reports they authored as members of the Council of Academic Advisors under John F. Kennedy. "The Council sought to set forth its principles and to apply them to the United States of the 1960s, in language accessible not just to economists but to all earnest readers," they wrote.[29] We have also tried to write in a language that economists and readers interested in economics and finance will find accessible, but we take the adjective "earnest" to refer to more than the seriousness of our readers. In this period of sound bites and news aggregators, when attention spans seem to shorten every day, readers of this book need to be "earnest" in their focus and willingness to follow several narratives through a story that spans almost a century and a quarter. While the chapters, and even the sections and subsections, of *Finance in America* are modular, in the sense that they are relatively self-contained and can be consulted according to the reader's interest, "earnest" readers who want a longer history of finance will find their efforts repaid, whether they have formal training in economics or not.

In the wake of the financial crisis of 2008, there cannot be too much discussion of economics, finance, and the effects of the transformation we are experiencing. The most recent financial crisis did not provoke the soul-searching among economists some of us hoped it would, but it did allow a wider range of people interested in economic issues to engage in conversations about economics and finance. In the course of these conversations, finance has become visible to an extent and in ways never available before. Few people inside or outside the academy would dispute that changes have occurred in the world's economies in the last thirty years, but there is no consensus on the role economics and finance have played in these changes; nor is there agreement about whether, on balance, the changes have been beneficial or harmful to society as a whole. In *Finance in America: An Unfinished Story*, we want to expand the conversation to include histories of these disciplines, for the long view provides insights no short view can offer.

Early Twentieth-Century Origins of American Finance: The Rise of the American Corporation and the Creation of the Financial Reserve System

1.1. VALUING THE NEW US CORPORATIONS

A nation's economy is simultaneously omnipresent and impossible to see, for an "economy" is a theoretical abstraction, a metaphor that seeks to present an array of disparate transactions, institutions, and conventions as a single, dynamic whole. By the same token, "finance," or the financial "side" of an economy, is also a metaphorical abstraction. Even though the "economy" and its financial "side" are metaphors, however, both abstractions can be treated historically, for the array to which each term refers undergoes change—in terms of size and complexity, in the institutions it contains, and in the theoretical concepts by which individuals struggle to understand their economic environment. One of the major stories of this book concerns the development of techniques and theories designed to render the economy and its financial side visible, and thus comprehensible and measurable: national income and product accounts, flow and fund depictions of the nation's capital, theoretical treatments of financial institutions and financial intermediation. Before these measuring instruments were formalized—indeed, before regional and state markets could be viewed as a *national economy*—the economy and its financial side attracted attention primarily when another kind of event drew attention to them. When a presidential campaign was waged in the name of "free silver," as was the 1896 campaign of William Jennings Bryan, or when a Wall Street panic exposed outrageous shenanigans on the part of bank trust-

ees, as occurred in 1907, Americans undoubtedly turned their attention to the
economy and its financial side. Even though modern analysts have estimated
that the financial industry represented only about 1.5% of the nation's gross
domestic product (GDP) in the middle of the nineteenth century and 3% by
the century's end, economic and financial issues could—and occasionally
did—become newsworthy matters.[1] It was these episodes, as much as theoretical debates about technical matters such as the "quantity theory" versus the
"banking theory" of money, that initially helped form images of an American
economy and its financial side.

This chapter examines some of the developments that helped make the
US economy and its financial side imaginable *before* theoretical measures like
GDP were available. Some of these developments were unmistakable and
have deservedly attracted historical attention, for, at the end of the nineteenth
century and in the first decades of the twentieth, America was undergoing
sweeping changes: the largely agricultural nation was experiencing a gradual
shift of its population to urban centers; a decentralized and complex banking system was being consolidated; and family-owned businesses were being
absorbed by the massive businesses that contemporaries called "trusts" or
"corporations." Other developments, by contrast, were harder to see—if not
wholly invisible to citizens. Alongside an account of some of the most obvious
developments of these decades, we present a history of one of the most consequential but neglected behind-the-scenes developments: the transformation
of the theory and practice of accounting. While invisible to most contemporaries and often overlooked by historians, developments in accounting made
the rise of the American corporation possible; they underwrote the operations of the Federal Reserve system after 1913; and the corporate accounting
structure that was eventually normalized became the backbone of the national
income and production accounts created in the 1930s and 1940s. These developments in accountancy, in turn, were responses to and eventually provided
an answer to a pressing social question: how should the new corporations be
valued?

The problem of corporate valuation became pressing at the beginning of
the twentieth century for two reasons. First, there was no precedent for placing a dollar value on these new companies' assets, which consisted of not only
familiar physical holdings such as buildings and machinery but also intangible forms of property such as the "goodwill" and "earning potential" the
corporation claimed from the companies it absorbed. Second, glowing adver-
tisements drawn up by company promoters often predicted profits that, in the
absence of any track record, looked too good to be true. Worries about what

contemporaries called stock "watering," as well as debates about "capitalization" and "excess" earnings, began to appear in contemporary publications, as the public wondered how to evaluate and understand the implications of this new company form. These issues were eventually addressed, albeit indirectly, by measures taken in the humble realm of accounting.

The impact on the American economy of what historians call the first merger movement was unprecedented.[2] During a very brief period—between 1888 or 1889 and 1903 or 1904—the ruthless competition that had pitted countless numbers of small businesses against each other since the end of the Civil War was supplanted by a form of "co-operation," conducted by approximately 150 large corporations, many of which were formed through the consolidation of previous rivals. One contemporary opined that the new conglomerates added over three and a half trillion dollars of capital value to the US economy, and a modern historian has estimated that more than 1,800 private companies disappeared through consolidation between 1895 and 1904.[3] In 1903, Edward Sherwood Meade, economist at the University of Pennsylvania's Wharton School, argued that "the trusts control the greater part of the output in the industries in which they are formed, 75, 90, 95 per cent being common figures."[4] The range of industries affected by corporatization was broad: following the precedent set by the late nineteenth-century railway companies, new industrial corporations took over energy providers (Standard Oil), food production (American Sugar Refining Company), the manufacture of incidentals and notions (Diamond Match Company, International Thread Company), and the leisure industry (American Bicycle). While spokesmen for some of the new corporations tried to argue that, like the railways and utilities (e.g., gas and street railway companies), these corporations were "public goods," most defended this new way of doing business with some version of the marginalist economic theories we will examine in a moment. Conglomeration, insisted economists like Jeremiah Jenks, professor of political economy at Cornell, was essential to controlling the "wastes" associated with competition, thus increasing productivity at the "margin."[5] "It would seem that if there is any real economic function of combination of capital, whether it has attained monopolistic power or not, it is this: saving the various wastes of competition, in great part by providing for the direction of industrial energy to the best advantage."[6]

The legal imprimatur for the new corporations was provided by a series of rulings, beginning with the Supreme Court's Santa Clara decision in 1886, which indemnified each corporation as a legal "person" with many of the rights an individual enjoyed.[7] Before New Jersey adopted an "enabling" cor-

porate law in 1896, incorporation in the United States required an act of legislation, but the Supreme Court's broadening of the corporation's constitutional
standing helped transform corporate privileges into a generally available right.
Beyond the legal status conferred by incorporation, what distinguished the
new corporations from the private, often-family-owned businesses they supplanted were novel modes of ownership and management. Unlike the family
concern, whose partners contributed the company's working capital, reaped
its profits, and collectively assumed responsibility for its debts, the new corporations were owned in part-shares by large groups of investors who were
often not acquainted with each other or the day-to-day operations of the firm.
The interests of the promoters, underwriters, shareholders, and managers
who brought a new corporation into being and kept its capital flowing were
protected by the law of limited liability, which limited the personal liability of
each individual to the amount he contributed to the firm. Because ownership
was separated from management in the new corporations, the firms required
new accounting procedures that could keep track of the costs of complex production processes, distinguish the capital that kept the firm afloat from the
income eligible for disbursement as dividends, and gauge the relative effectiveness of managers' financial decisions. Because shareholders could buy or
sell financial interests at any time, corporate accountants also had to provide
periodic summaries and records of cash flows so that individual shareholders
would know what they owned. As we will see in chapter 4, these features were
still matters of intense legal and theoretical interest in the 1930s, by which time
their impact on the American economy was visible to everyone.

During the merger movement itself, many economists, like most Americans, did not know quite what to make of the changes transforming American
businesses.[8] Were corporations good for society or harmful? Were they an
inevitable part of the evolution of American capitalism or an opportunistic
attempt to monopolize the nation's resources? Should new tax policies redistribute the corporations' "excess" profits or should tariffs protect them from
international competition? Of all the concerns that swirled around the new
corporations, most vexing were those concerned with valuation. Should a
corporation be valued by the tangible assets it held, like buildings, machinery,
and money in the bank? Or should it be valued by its "intangibles"—its earning potential, the "goodwill" that carried over when one company merged
with another, and the money pledged to the company but not yet paid for
shares? In a series of cases decided between 1886 and 1900, the US Supreme
Court gradually expanded the definition of "property" to include the right
to a reasonable return on investment in intangible assets. These decisions

constitute the legal framework in which we can best understand finance as *claims*. They also led the Yale economist Irving Fisher to redefine "capital" to encompass these claims, which are based not only on legal provisions but also, in practice, on investors' expectations.[9] They also opened onto, and eventually came into alignment with, the redefinition of "capital" that Irving Fisher set out in 1906 in *The Nature of Capital and Income*, a landmark in financial theory that we examine in chapter 2, section 5.

The Supreme Court's ruling that intangible assets constituted property did not help contemporaries value the bonds and securities the corporations wanted to sell. In 1900, the Chicago lawyer and company promoter John Dos Passos explained that the valuation dilemma turned on different understandings of capitalization. "Capitalization is of two kinds; there is a capitalization based on the actual value of the property and a capitalization based on earning power. . . . You will find two classes of people in this country—one in favor of the former method and one in favor of the latter."[10] Each position was supported by both economists and some state legislatures. The first, which favored including in a firm's capitalization only tangible assets, valued (typically) by their historical cost, was endorsed by William Z. Ripley of Harvard and Jeremiah Jenks of Cornell.[11] It was written into the laws of Massachusetts and Connecticut. The second, which included intangibles like goodwill and earning power, was favored by the Wharton School's Meade, who was the nation's first specialist in corporate finance, and, with some reservations, by the New York lawyer Thomas Conyngton, who wrote about corporations under the pseudonym Francis Cooper.[12] This method combined parts of marginalist economic theory with financial concepts drawn from actuarial science, even though neither Cooper nor Meade offered a theoretically consistent defense of privileging earning power over tangible assets. This mode of valuation was enshrined in the corporate laws of New Jersey, West Virginia, and Delaware.

In today's terminology, "capitalization" most often refers to the total dollar value of a company's issued shares, and one can calculate the size of a company by multiplying its outstanding shares by the current market price of one share. In the early twentieth century, a company's promoter set the "par" price of shares when the firm filed for incorporation or, in anticipation of that filing, when the promoter sought financial backing from an underwriter. Instead of using a theory of valuation agreed upon in the corporate world, promoters seem to have based capitalization on some mixture of the value of the assets the new corporation actually held, the goodwill they assumed the corporation would carry over from the companies it absorbed, and the promoters' own hopes and expectations for future earnings. Given this process, which was invisible to the relatively small number of individuals who might have wanted to purchase shares, no one could understand what the promoter had done or judge the fairness of the figure published as the corporation's capital value.

The complex role that promoters played in company flotation helps explain why such evaluations were so difficult. Most contemporaries considered the promoter essential to the formation of a large corporation, for, given the complexity of the transactions involved, someone had to initiate and superintend the process. Writing in 1896, T. C. Frenyear argued that the promoter's "push" was the critical element in company flotation—and that it should be compensated as such. "The conception, the originating, the organizing of an enterprise is the fundamental element of value in it. . . . The most brilliant and the most workable plan may amount to no more than a dream, without push. . . . He who takes the ideas of a genius, worthless ideas, clothes them with outward form and makes them effective; he who takes the gold of the capitalist and gives to it a productive power; he who takes the strong and willing laborer and directs his work in more healthful and profitable channels, is entitled to no mean share in the benefits brought about through his efforts."[13]

Even if contemporaries acknowledged the promoter's importance, the way promoters were compensated led many to suspect that the promoter's interests were too closely related to the value he assigned the corporation. Promoters were often compensated at least partly in company shares, and because the shares of a prospective company had yet to trade on a public exchange, each share's initial value simply represented a percentage of the company's total capitalization, which the promoter set. Since the laws of some states allowed the promoter to include in the company's capitalization intangibles and earning potential, it seemed to some that promoters were serving their own interest by overstating the corporation's value. After all, the promoter was not compensated until he sold his shares, and he could only drive the price of shares up by making the company seem more valuable than it might actually have been.

The controversy over whether the promoter was "watering" a company's shares originated in this process. In contemporary parlance, "watering" stocks referred to any of a number of practices, all of which were thought to misrepresent the relationship between the corporation's legitimate assets and its total capitalization.[14] As Ripley explained, the "baldest and simplest form" of pumping "water" into a corporation's stated value was "simply to declare a stock or bond dividend without putting any additional capital into the company; this constituted an outright gift to shareholders."[15] Stocks could also be watered in other ways: a corporation could issue bonds to purchase securities declared necessary to expand its operations, and then sell the securities and distribute the income in dividends without retiring the underlying debt.[16] Stock watering was thought to be especially prevalent when companies merged. "The constituent companies may be so gerrymandered that successful ones with surplus earnings may average their rate of return downward by combination with other properties less favorably situated," Ripley pointed out. "A weak corporation, whose stock is quoted say at $50, may be merged in a second corporation whose stock is worth $150 per share. The latter may then issue new stock of its own in exchange for the $50 stock, share for share. Such an operation as this . . . establish[es] fictitious capitalization par in excess of the worth of the investment."[17]

While contemporaries agreed that such practices were fraudulent—Francis Cooper described stock watering as an "unmitigated evil"[18]—some commentators, including Cooper, admitted that inflating the new corporation's value was an essential part of the promoter's job, given that he had to attract capital to what was, by definition, a risky venture. As Cooper explained, "usually in the incorporation of a new enterprise . . . the existing value of the enterprise is used only as a basis upon which to build. Future needs must be provided for, present necessities and requirements must be met, and as a result the capitalization actually fixed upon is far in excess of the immediate value of the enterprise."[19] Still thinking about the company's future and its relation to value, Cooper also argued that, beyond tangible assets, capitalization could include "profit probabilities"—and even "profit possibilities." Here he was not referring to compound interest, but simply to the ideas that any viable company had to expect to make money, shareholders were purchasing that expectation, and the promoter's job was to encourage them to do so.[20] That Cooper did not call wagering on these "probabilities" "overcapitalization"— much less "stock watering"—means that the idea of factoring expectations into the calculation of value had begun to gain traction by 1906. As we will see in chapter 2, in that same year, Irving Fisher published a theoretical defense for basing valuation on expectations. Following the publication of Fisher's *The Nature of Capital and Income*, the idea of basing valuation on expectations about future returns was to become one of the cornerstones of modern financial theory. Now we can see that this idea was an important by-product of the valuation controversy.

Whether Cooper, who was a lawyer, not an economist or company promoter, considered the promoter's future-oriented valuation an essential feature of the corporate form or a peculiarity unique to the early phase of company formation is not clear. At least one contemporary economist was willing to speculate on such matters. Not only did Edward Sherwood Meade, the Wharton School economist, sanction factoring a corporation's expected profits into valuations of its capitalization: he also argued that the way promoters financed corporations—by puffing the profits investors could expect—constituted the distinguishing feature of the corporate form. Meade stepped back from presenting this as a universal law of valuation. In fact, he presented corporate finance as a response to a combination of factors that were new at the end of the nineteenth century: "On the one hand the manufacturer was weary of competition and anxious either to combine or to sell. On the other hand stood the public, deeply impressed with the profits of the trust and anxious to buy the shares of industrial combinations if opportunity were given."[21] In Meade's account, the position of the promoter was created to bring these two interests together; and once the promoter appeared, he simultaneously exposed the ambiguities inherent in the process of valuation and devised a way resolve them.

What the promoter discovered when he set out to launch a corporation, according to Meade, was a miniature version of the problem of valuation more generally. In the account books of the companies that wanted to merge the promoter typically uncovered a bewildering variety of bookkeeping systems, definitions of costs, and methods of asset valuation. "Here is one company which charges the cost of new machinery to capital account, and makes an assessment upon its stockholders to pay for all machinery purchased. Another company deducts the expense of machinery from its net receipts before dividends are declared."[22] The solution successful promoters devised was to impose upon the merging companies a single set of accounting rules: using a uniform accounting framework, the promoter was able to restate the companies' earnings in a common form organized by a single set of categories and procedures; this allowed him to set a price for each company and acquire the rights to purchase their assets. With an accounting framework in place and purchasing rights acquired, the promoter could then raise money from an underwriter, for, based on the books that valued the companies in the same way, he could show that the initial capitalization of the new corporation would offset the underwriter's risk.

Meade explicitly applauded the promoter's role—he considered this figure to be "the means of creating a value which did not before exist"[23]—and, to the extent that he recognized that the value the promoter added was tied to expectations about the future, Meade can be said to have glimpsed the theory of valuation by expectation that Fisher was to theorize. But like Cooper, Meade stepped back from endorsing or theorizing such valuation. Instead, he presented it as a departure from what he seems to have considered the normal, more desirable way of valuing a company. Meade acknowledged that, in order to get a corporation going, the promoter had to act upon expectations about future profits: to attract an underwriter, he had to promise that the financier would be able to sell his shares as soon as incorporation occurred, as the promoter also planned to do. And to make this assurance, the promoter, now with the underwriter's help, had to attract numerous risk-seeking investors by promising that the company would be sufficiently profitable to reward initial risk. But the way Meade sums up this process—in which the promoter leverages his own expectations about the future to attract the underwriter's assets and markets speculative shares as investment-quality assets—suggests that Meade considered the entire scheme somewhat shady. "In short, the underwriter asks the public to buy stocks for investment which he would not buy himself."[24]

Meade did not extend the idea that expectations factor into capital valuation into his suggestions for reforming "trust finance."[25] Nor was the debate about stock watering and valuation settled in favor of arguments about prospective earnings. Instead, Meade finally linked valuation by expectations to the problem of "doubtful securities" and "speculative promotion,"[26] and legislators essentially set the problem of stock watering aside when they eliminated the requirement that companies assign a par value to their shares.[27] If potential investors were not tempted to compare the value a company promoter assigned its initial shares with the market value at which those shares traded once the company was launched, the reasoning behind no-par stock went, then the entire problem of "overcapitalization" and stock "watering" would simply disappear. Even if issuing no-par stock did not answer all the questions raised in the debates about company valuation, Meade's description of what the company promoter actually did as he put a corporation together hinted at what would eventually settle such issues. Like the company promoter Meade conjured into being, the flesh-and-blood managers of most American corporations would soon informally address the problems associated with valuation by adopting some version of a uniform set of accounting principles.

1.2. THE GROWTH OF AMERICAN PUBLIC ACCOUNTING

At the beginning of the twentieth century, accountancy in the United States was not universally recognized as a profession; companies, which were not required to provide information to investors or government officials, used idio-syncratic accounting systems tailored to fit their needs; and most accountants focused on the demands of employers rather than trying to develop a standard set of accounting "postulates."[28] Some attempts at professionalizing account-ing had been made in the last decades of the nineteenth century: the Institute for Accountants and Bookkeepers was founded in 1882, and the American As-sociation of Public Accountants was launched in 1887. New York State passed a certified public accountancy law in 1896, but, even though this was a sign of accountancy's professionalization, it effectively put an end to the national as-sociations because separate state societies soon began to pursue state-specific goals. Societies were founded in New York, Pennsylvania, and Illinois; then, in 1902, at the height of the first merger movement, accountants tried to cre-ate another national organization, the Federation of Societies of Public Ac-counting. Disputes over the mission of this society waylaid organizers' efforts, however, and it was not until 1905 that a workable national organization, the American Association of Public Accountants (AAPA), was launched. The AAPA lacked the authority necessary to establish and enforce standards, however, and, as late as 1916, the profession was still at a crossroads: although most accountants recognized that accountancy needed to adopt some kind of standards to gain respect, they did not want to accept federal oversight; and charges that accountants were trying to form their own monopoly sparked some of the same criticisms leveled at the new corporations.[29]

Efforts to gain recognition through professional organizations were sup-ported by the gradual growth of a literature about accountancy, much of which emerged from the college and university business courses where many accountants trained. The first collegiate course in accountancy was taught at the newly founded Wharton School at the University of Pennsylvania in 1882. In its second year, the course used two textbooks: Seldon Hopkins's *Manual of Exhibit Bookkeeping* and C. C. Marsh's *Theory of Bank Bookkeeping and Joint Stock Accounts*. In 1888, the University of Chicago founded the College of Commerce and Politics (later the College of Commerce and Administra-tion), and in 1890, New York University opened the School of Commerce, Accounts, and Finance. At Chicago, where Henry Rand Hatfield taught, the assigned text was by a German author (J. F. Schär); and at New York Univer-sity, unable to find an adequate textbook, Charles Sprague wrote his own, the *Philosophy of Accounts* (1907).[30] The following years saw the publication of two additional American textbooks: William Morse Cole's *Accounts: Their Con-struction and Interpretation for Business Men and Students of Affairs* (1908) and Hatfield's *Modern Accounting: Its Principles and Some of Its Problems*

(1909). In 1916, William Paton, then at the University of Minnesota, and Russell Alger Stevenson, of the University of Iowa, followed these early works with *Principles of Accounting*, which tried to rectify the confusions about terminology that continued to plague accountancy. Paton and Stevenson endorsed the Interstate Commerce Commission's "standard classifications" as "the most logical system of accounting phraseology," thus underscoring the close relationship between accountancy's quest for respect and accountants' acceptance of the government's role in issuing suggested standards.[31]

While a combination of the variety of systems in use and companies' desire to keep their records secret makes it impossible to know whether a single accounting system prevailed in the first two decades of the twentieth century, these textbooks do allow us to identify the principles inherent in the emergent field of corporate accounting, as well as the practices recommended by leading theorists of accounting. Accountancy principles and practices, in turn, occupy a critical position in the history of finance. In the first place, the financial documents developed for use in the new corporations, including the balance sheet and the income statement, separated a company's financial activities from production and sales figures, which showed its role in the real side of the economy. This allowed managers to see the relationship between the company's financial and real activities as separate but related parts. In the second place, as we will see in chapter 6, some of the statisticians who created national income aggregates in the 1930s and 1940s adopted the corporate accounting system as the framework for national income accounts. This means that some of the most consequential measures of national income and growth—GDP and gross national product (GNP)—derive their principles from the form of accounting developed to help managers control and grow the new corporations.

The basic theory of accountancy formulated in the books by Sprague, Hatfield, and Paton endorsed what Sprague called a "proprietorship" application of double-entry bookkeeping. As the name suggests, proprietary theory described the structure of the accounts from the perspective of the owner and assumed that the firm was an extension of the owner(s). It also assumed that all assets, liabilities, expenses, and revenues were accessories of proprietorship and that the primary function of a business firm was to increase its owners' wealth, as signified by the year-end net worth displayed on the company's balance sheet. To enhance a company's net worth, the primary responsibility of the firm's accountants was to distinguish clearly between assets and liabilities—in part so that profits or dividends could be distributed and in part to allow potential lenders, such as banks, to rapidly assess the creditworthiness of the company.[32] This meant that most proprietary theorists recommended against including what Sprague called "alleged assets"—intangibles like goodwill—because they might be said to "water" the company's assets.[33]

In addition to distinguishing between assets and liabilities, proprietary theory required accountants to distinguish between capital and income, with the latter understood simply as "the increase in the beneficial interest accruing to the proprietor." To determine "the net profits of the concern for the period with special reference to the amount of profits available for dividends," the accountant needed to measure the change in "net wealth" that occurred in the period represented by the reckoning.[34] Given their static view of capital, these goals led proprietary theorists to emphasize the balance sheet over any other documents in the bookkeeping system. Emphasizing the balance sheet enabled the accountant to present both the positive items in the business's operation ("Profit, Gain, Revenue, Income, Earnings"—all understood to contribute to "Increase of Wealth") and the negative items ("Loss, Expense, Charge, Outlay").[35] By using the double-entry bookkeeping system and the simple mathematical operations of addition, subtraction, multiplication, and division, the accountant could generate from these composite categories a single number that represented a final statement of the company's year-end worth, which represented the owners' residual claim on assets. In this kind of accounting, it did not matter what the sources of income or expense were, when money was obtained or spent, or when the actual transactions became entries in the accounting books. What mattered was the overall worth of the company, as figured at the end of the accounting period and represented on the balance sheet. The company's owners could evaluate this figure—they could determine whether the company was increasing its wealth or not—by comparing the figures on one year's balance sheet with their counterparts at the ends of other years.

In general terms, proprietary accounting, like other forms of double-entry bookkeeping, was a form of algebra that combined the real side of business (goods) with the financial side (prices) so as to make it possible to solve for the value of specific variables. The rules of double-entry bookkeeping instructed the accountant to group transactions into categories, sum the values of these transactions into a single monetary term, then enter each transaction twice, once as a debit to one account and once as a credit to another, typically on the facing page. This is the "double-entry" for which the system was named in the Renaissance. The double entries enabled the accountant rapidly to assess whether mistakes had been made in the records, for the rules also required the totals of the transactions grouped in each category to equal the totals on the facing page. Thus, any number that was missing could be calculated by inspecting its counterpart, and the accountant could check the records by sequentially striking though the pairs of corresponding figures. He then recorded any excess or deficit not attributable to a recording error in the lower right-hand side of the right page. This figure was carried over, as a credit or a debt, to the next set of accounts. Note that in this process, the quantities of goods bought or sold have been subsumed into their prices.

Central to the double-entry bookkeeping system was a foundational accounting identity: the balance sheet must balance. In practice, this meant that the company's assets had to equal the sum of its liabilities plus the owner's equity: assets = liabilities + equity. Even though assets and liabilities included nonfinancial resources and obligations, the figures that appear in the double-entry accounts are always expressed in monetary terms; a company's well-being was associated with its periodically measured profits, not—or at least not necessarily—with the "permanent interest of the corporation as a going concern."[36] As the final document in the double-entry system, the annual balance sheet thus constituted a year-end summary of the company's overall condition, expressed in financial terms.

Corporate accountants did not uniformly adopt the postulates promoted by accounting theorists, but most did emphasize the balance sheet over other financial documents. Balance sheets were useful to creditors and potential lenders because they summarized the overall health of the company at year's end, as well as the relative liquidity of various assets; and they were useful to owners because they presented a single figure that conveyed the owner's profits at the moment of reckoning. As the new corporations began to dominate American commerce, however, the limitations inherent in relying exclusively on the balance sheet became increasingly obvious. One shortcoming of the balance sheet was its inability to show where profits came from.[37] Another was its indifference to the relationship between the time a transaction occurred and the moment at which it was "realized," or entered into the books. Then too, the balance sheet did not distinguish between the productive or real activities of a company—its manufacturing operations—and its financial activities—its management of interest charges and debt collection, for example. The balance sheet did not allow a manager to track the efficiency of discrete parts of the production process because balance sheets were not drawn up frequently enough, nor did they link the expenses of particular production processes to their costs and overhead. The balance sheet had no place for an accountant to register the depreciation of materials and plant, which was an inevitable part of production processes extended in time and space.

Finally, the balance sheet was not responsive to the new mode of ownership that made the corporations possible. Because ownership of these companies was distributed in part-shares held by a large number of individuals, and because the companies were "going concerns" rather than businesses formed to carry out specific projects, the part-shares owned by individuals had to be linked to the moment of their purchase or sale, and they had to be separable from the business and its ongoing income. To enable investors to buy and sell their shares in different-sized lots at different times and corporate managers to raise capital by issuing new shares, the accountant had to be able to present the company's business as income, not simply as capital or wealth. As Henry Rand Hatfield pointed out, moreover, seeing the corporation's activity this way—as a flow rather than simply as periodic funds—directly addressed the issue of valuation, which so troubled critics of the corporate form: "The public, while a permanent body, is made up of changing individuals. In so far as the body of consumers changes, injustice may be done to the consumers of one or another period, if an expense which should properly be paid by the consumers of one period, is so treated that the consumers of another period are burdened by it. An expense capitalized wrongfully, burdens later consumers. The position is reversed when what is properly a capital expenditure is treated as a current expense."[38]

Even after many accounting theorists agreed that proprietary theory, with its emphasis on the balance sheet, was inadequate to the needs of the new corporations, they did not universally embrace its alternative, a theory known as "entity" theory, which emphasized the company itself instead of the owner(s).[39] Whatever the dispute among theorists, at the level of practice changes had already begun. While the timing of the shift in accounting conventions is impossible to document, it seems clear that within individual corporations, some early twentieth-century accountants had already begun to adapt a technique long in use within industrial firms. This technique was cost accounting. As it was refined and its principles extended, cost accounting provided the basis for a genuine innovation in the history of accounting, for a new financial document—the income statement—made it possible for accountants not only to track and disclose, in monetary terms, the flows of a corporation's business but also to make predictions about future profits.

Cost accounting, or "costing," had been used by many American and British companies since at least the beginning of the nineteenth century. By the early twentieth century, this technique was being taught in some American universities, using textbooks written expressly for classroom instruction.[40] The primary functions of cost accounting were to help managers track costs and to link costs to particular parts of the manufacturing process. Thus, raw goods were treated as assets and valued, typically, at their historical cost, and whatever portion was consumed in the manufacturing process was treated as an expense (assets consumed); the labor and expenses required to transform the raw goods into finished product were generally treated as adding to the value of the asset. When the finished product was sold, expenses incurred in the manufacturing process could be recognized in the accounts. Upon sale, the accumulated costs of the manufactured product were written off as the cost of goods sold. By following these events, a manager could readily identify inefficiencies in various parts of the manufacturing process and take periodic—or, if costing were performed frequently enough, virtually perpetual—stock of the firm's operations. Real components of the production process—raw goods, intermediate goods, and labor, for example—were still subsumed into monetary figures in this accounting process, but, as we are about to see, the narrowly financial aspects of the corporation were also spatially separated from the real processes of production in the income statement itself.

As it was gradually developed at the turn of the twentieth century, the income statement made this costing process visible. Its advantages were not immediately apparent to contemporaries, however, and it received only uneven acceptance by accountants in the field and begrudging acknowledgment in accountancy theory.[41] Arthur Lowes Dickinson, an accountant for the audit firm Price Waterhouse, introduced one prototype of the income statement in a lecture delivered to the Congress of Accountants in 1904, but it is clear from the way Dickinson discussed what he called the "Profit and Loss Account" that he did not consider this as important as the balance sheet. Calling cost accounting "merely an elaboration of ordinary bookkeeping," Dickinson moved immediately from his discussion of the Profit and Loss Account to the kind of consolidated statement epitomized by the balance sheet. Five years later, when Dickinson published his lecture and the form he had described in 1904 (fig. 1), he claimed that this document was "already in fairly general use," but he elaborated no further on its novelty or benefits.[42]

The income statement Dickinson introduced in 1904 was not the first such document proposed in the United States. Dickinson's Profit and Loss Account followed and possibly imitated another version of this form, this one created by the federal government as part of the Revenue Act of 1894. Internal Revenue Form 366 was designed to help the government collect the flat tax imposed on railways and corporations. Like Dickinson's income statement, this form separated operating and financial information and worked its

```
Gross Earnings (whetner sales of products,
    transportation earnings, professional
    earnings, etc.) .......................          $........

Deduct—Cost of Manufacture or Operation:
    (a) Manufacture (for a manufacturing
            concern):
        Labor ...........................   $........
        Material ........................    ........
        General Manufacturing Expenses ...   ........
    (b) Cost of Operation (for concerns not
            manufacturing)
        (Under suitable headings according
            to the nature of the business) ..  $........   $........
Gross Profits .............................              $........
Other Earnings ............................               ........


Deduct—
    Expenses of sale (manufacturing
        business only) ....................   $........
    Expenses of management (if
        distinct from operation) ...........   ........
                                                         $........

Net Profits from Operation ................              $........


Deduct—
    Interest on Bonds .....................   $........
    Other Fixed Charges ...................    ........
                                             ──────────
                                                         $........

Surplus for year ..........................              $........
Extraordinary Profits (detailed) ..........               ........
Surplus brought forward from
    preceding year ........................               ........
                                                         $........


Deduct—
    Extraordinary charges not applicable
        to the operations of the year .......   $........
    Interest and Dividends on Stocks ......    ........
                                             ──────────
                                                         $........

        Surplus carried forward ...........              $........
```

Figure 4.   Dickinson's income statement format.

FIGURE 1. Arthur Lowes Dickinson's income statement. From Arthur Lowes Dickinson, *The Profits of a Corporation: A Paper Read before the Congress of Accountants, at St. Louis, on September 27, 1904* (New York: Jones, Caesar, Dickinson, Wilmot and Co. and Price Waterhouse and Co., n.d.), 28.

way, by means of successively matching costs to income, to a final "amount of net profits," which was the figure subject to taxation. For tax purposes, the government allowed corporations to deduct from net income the interest paid on debt financing but not dividends paid to shareholders.[43] This form all but vanished when the Supreme Court declared the income tax unconstitutional in 1895, but in 1917, eleven years after Dickinson had described his form, the federal government published another income statement, intended, once more, as a model for corporate managers and accountants. This form appeared in the Federal Reserve Board's *Uniform Accounting*, which was part of the *Federal Reserve Bulletin* issued in April of that year (fig. 2). According to Richard A. Brief, this was the first publication that can be said to contain financial reporting *standards* of any kind.[44]

The first three prototypes of the income statement had only minimal success: the Supreme Court voided Internal Revenue Form 366 along with the income tax itself; Dickinson did not promote his Profit and Loss Account as an important innovation; and even though the Federal Reserve Board declared its 1917 form authoritative, the Fed continued to emphasize the balance sheet because commercial bankers—the main audience for its reports— were more interested in liquidity and profits-on-hand than a company's earning capacity or sources of financing.[45] In 1923, the fourteenth edition of the *Accountants' Handbook* printed both Dickinson's form and the slightly amended form then said to be "recommended" by the Federal Reserve, and, while this handbook acknowledged that variation in terminology continued to characterize published statements by corporations, it presented the income statement as an accepted counterpart to the balance sheet.[46] Meanwhile, in 1916, the accountancy theorist William Paton had acknowledged that many accountants were using some version of an income statement and that this document might serve "even the interest of the public." In his influential 1922 textbook on corporate accounting, however, Paton only mentioned in passing what he alternately called "the income sheet" and the "revenue statement."[47]

Once in use, the income statement always forms part of a system of corporate financial documents, the members of which have been valued differently at different times.[48] Like the balance sheet, the early twentieth-century income statement relied on simple mathematical operations (addition, subtraction), and the information it provided was generally arranged in columns, which facilitated rapid computation and analysis. Unlike the balance sheet, however, which supplemented the vertical presentation of various entries with a horizontal display of paired, balancing accounts, the income statement has always been a single vertical column, which is generally divided into three parts.

UNIFORM ACCOUNTING
Form for Profit and Loss Account

Gross sales	$_____
Less outward freight, allowances, and returns	_____
Net Sales	$=======
Inventory beginning of year	_____
Purchases, net	_____
Less inventory end of year	_____
Cost of sales	=======
Gross profit on sales	=======
Selling expenses (itemized to correspond with ledger accounts kept)	_____
Total selling expense	=======
General expenses (itemized to correspond with ledger accounts kept)	_____
Total general expense	=======
Administrative expenses (itemized to correspond with ledger accounts kept)	_____
Total administrative expense	=======
Total expenses	=======
Net profit on sales	=======
Other income:	
Income from investments	_____
Interest on notes receivable, etc.	_____
Gross income	=======
Deductions from income:	
Interest on bonded debt	_____
Interest on notes payable	_____
Total deductions	_____
Net income—profit and loss	_____
Add special credits to profit and loss	_____
Deduct special charges to profit and loss	_____
Profit and loss for period	_____
Surplus beginning of period	_____
Dividends paid	_____
Surplus ending of period	_____

Source: Federal Reserve Board, *Uniform Accounting* (Washington, D.C.: Government Printing Office, 1917).

FIGURE 2. Model income statement for US corporations issued by the Federal Reserve. From Federal Reserve Board, "Uniform Accounting" (Washington, DC: Government Printing Office, 1917).

Even at the beginning of the twentieth century, this division constituted an implicit narrative about the company, which assumed that production could and should be separated from financial activity and that both were related to income: the first part of the statement chronicled the company's manufacturing operation; the second part displayed its financial dealings; and the third part surveyed the company's "surplus." The arrangement of the items in the first two of these parts also told a story, this one chronological and conceptual, for the entries within each category were (and still are) presented in a reducing balance form. This means that the costs of each kind of activity appeared immediately beneath, and then were deducted from, the revenues to which they were related. The reducing balance form allows a reader to rapidly calculate operating costs, or margins, as a percentage of the total in each category. The Federal Reserve form (fig. 2), for example, begins with an entry for "gross earnings" or "gross sales," then sequentially deducts from this figure such activities as "outward freight" and various manufacturing and labor costs in order to generate a final "net sales" figure. This figure, which is an interim total expressed in monetary terms, is then further augmented and depleted by additional line items, priced resources, and costs, each matched to other entries as related transactions. Among the assets in the Federal Reserve form, we find "inventory beginning of year" and "purchases, net"; among the deductions, we find "inventory at end of year," selling and administrative expenses, and "general expenses." This second interim total then appears as "net profit on sales."

The second section of the early twentieth-century income statement, which isolated the company's financial activities, showed how the company was managing its interest income and financial obligations. The Federal Reserve form calls the proceeds from financial activity "other income," thus relegating financial activities to a secondary role in the early corporation. Increases in this section of the Federal Reserve income statement come from "income on investments" and "interest on notes receivable," and its decreases come from "interest on bonded debt" and "interest on notes payable." As in the operating section of the document, deducting costs from the matched income entry generates an interim monetary balance for "net income," which the Federal Reserve form also calls "profit and loss." Then follows the third section of the income statement, the recording of surplus activities. Surplus can consist of special dividends, stock dividends, the prices of returned stock from shareholders, adjustments due to redemptions of capital stock, and so on. Basically, "surplus" refers to financial activities that cannot be captured in the categories of interest received (from investments) or interest paid (on bonds

or other debt). The additions and subtractions carried through the form finally generate the all-important "profit and loss for period," against which
the accountant was to charge the shareholder dividends. The final figure is
"surplus ending of period," which represented the income the corporation
itself had accrued. For shareholders, the most important entry was the "profit
and loss for period," because this was the sum available for dividends—after
enough money had been added to surplus to maintain the corporation as a
going concern or to fund new opportunities from internal cash flow.

The 1904 and 1917 income statements are very simple documents. Unlike
their modern counterparts, they do not contain footnotes that explain complex accounting issues or describe the accountants' methods. Such notes did
not appear until after the 1929 crash made stockholders demand greater clari-
fication about how to interpret financial statements.[49] Even though the Federal Reserve presented its income statement as a model form, moreover, and
an accountants' professional organization (the AAPA) helped create it, US
corporations did not immediately or universally adopt this form, nor did the
income statement immediately displace the balance sheet as the corporation's
most important accounting document.[50] Then, too, a company's decision to
draw up an income statement did not settle important issues like where interest charges should be entered. If such items were entered in the first section
and charged to operating costs, they were deducted from the assets of the
manufacturing process; if they were entered in the second section, they were
deducted from the shareholders' dividends; and if they were entered in the
third section, they were charged to the business entity as a whole, thus diminishing the owners' profits.[51] Latitude about where to enter such items constituted one of the advantages the income statement offered company managers,
for this allowed them to adjust periodic financial reporting in ways that best
served the company's interest. All in all, the very introduction of the income
statement—no matter how unevenly it was adopted—signaled the beginning
of a general shift away from accountancy's endorsement of a static representation of the corporation, which emphasized the year-end financial condition
of the company, the security of its loans, and the realizable value of its assets,
toward recognition of a series of forms that could capture the corporation as a
"going concern," whose activities occurred in time and whose flows of wealth
conveyed the dynamic, complex nature of its operation.

In the early twentieth century, the income statement, used in conjunction
with the balance sheet, offered corporate managers three distinct advantages
over the balance statement alone. All originated in the degree of flexibility and
managerial discretion the income statement allowed. The first had to do with

the difference made by the *timing* of accounting realization—the moment at which individual transactions were entered into the firm's books. Take, for example, the decision about when to recognize accrued income or an accrued receivable. If these were recognized in advance of receipt, they would affect the net value of receivables at the end of the periodic review. If the accountant valued securities at the moment of purchase, the entry would reflect historical cost, or the market price of the shares at the time of purchase; but if he decided to wait and the market price declined, he could charge the decline in market value against expense. Even though decisions about whether to defer recording income or expenses might not permanently affect a company's annual net income, then, material benefits could follow decisions about when to record events.

Privileging the income statement also affected where the accountant recorded business activities. Many decisions about where to record items had to do with matching, the process by which particular expenditures were linked to specific sources of revenue. If, for example, a manager decided to charge the repairs or maintenance of part of the business to the fixed asset account, this would produce a different result than charging such costs to accumulated depreciation. Similarly, estimates of future expenditures or anticipated depreciation charges could be matched with the part of the company's operation that would actually incur these costs or with more general categories, like "depreciation expense" or "accumulated depreciation."

The flexibility that followed from latitude about *when* an item was entered in the books and *where* it was recorded was complemented by how this information could be used by managers and shareholders alike. Indeed, the income statement eventually began to influence how the public understood valuation in general and the value of individual corporations in particular. This influence was rooted in the changing relationship the income statements fostered between accounting practice, corporate self-representation, and the theory of accountancy itself. As long as companies privileged the year-end balance statement because it stressed the proprietors' net worth, accounting entries were treated as records of past events, and this did not encourage managers to use accountants' information to make decisions about the future. Once companies began to produce income statements periodically, however, it became possible to gauge the efficiency and productivity of parts of the organization. As corporate managers used periodic reviews to make predictions about the future, and as they increased the efficiency of the operation to meet future targets, they provided one basis for defusing public concerns about stock watering. Once corporations shifted attention away from a stock's par value, in other words, as derived from the capitalization stated on the balance sheet, and toward the income of the corporation *treated, by successive income statements, as a going concern,* it became possible for investors to figure out how much a company was earning per issued share. Just as company managers began to view the income statement as a decision-making tool within the corporation, shareholders could treat it as a guide to future earnings because this document represented the *earning power* of the business in quantifiable terms, not its theoretical past capitalization.[52] As we will see in chapter 2, Irving Fisher provided a theoretical rationale for accountancy's valuation by the future in 1906, long before use of the income statement was common. And as we will see in chapter 4, when the nation plunged into economic crisis in the 1930s, questions about the fairness of corporate earnings would surface again, even as theorists and lawmakers debated how much information companies should be required to make public.

1.3. EARLY TWENTIETH-CENTURY BANKING AND THE FEDERAL RESERVE SYSTEM

At the beginning of the twentieth century, banking in the United States was still inadequate to the needs of American farmers and businessmen. America was a geographically expansive nation, and the seasonal needs of agricultural parts of the country were not coordinated with capital resources, which were concentrated in the East. With laws restricting the issue of national banknotes, the currency was considered insufficiently elastic for the growing nation. When the election of McKinley waylaid attempts to expand the currency by freely coining silver, contemporaries turned their attention to reform of the monetary and banking systems.

After the failure of two national banks (the First Bank of the United States, 1791–1811, and the Second Bank of the United States, 1816–36) and the end of the greenback era in 1865, the United States relied for its currency issue on notes issued by a complicated mixture of state banks and national banks, as well as on bonds issued by the Comptroller of the Currency. The first national bank (after the two failed attempts) was the First National Bank of Philadelphia (1863). A 10% tax on currency issued by state banks was designed to encourage these banks to become part of a national banking system, which, by 1909, contained 6,865 banks, with almost five billion dollars in individual deposits.[53] In 1913, these banks numbered 21,478.[54] While there was no single coordinating central bank, the Comptroller of the Currency did keep track of these banks through a system of examiners and mandatory reports. After 1870, the Comptroller issued five reports on banking and the currency every year.

One problem with this inadequately supervised banking system was that the capital market was not aligned with the money and credit market. Another was that the accelerating issue of securities by the new corporations gave the false impression that the nation's capital was fluid, when it was actually being converted into the fixed forms that the shares represented. The lack of alignment between markets was especially problematic. The capital market traded claims, like stocks and bonds, through institutions like stock exchanges, which were governed by their own rules until the 1930s. The money and credit market provided businesses resources for day-to-day operations through instruments like short-term, self-liquidating commercial paper. This market included many kinds of institutions, which were subject to various kinds of oversight, including—in the case of the national banks—regulation by the federal government. The money and credit institutions included commercial national and state banks, savings and loan companies, finance companies, credit unions, land banks, and investment banks. These served different purposes, but, among them, the commercial banks played a special role. They were the only institutions that could create credit, through fractional reserve banking, by loaning money in excess of the currency actually deposited by their customers. And, in the absence of a standardized accounting system and before financial documents like balance sheets were routinely available, commercial bankers had the unique ability to monitor firsthand the creditworthiness of potential borrowers.

In periods of crisis, however, commercial banks were vulnerable to runs by panicked customers—in large part because they kept only a fraction of their depositors' assets on reserve. Given the special role commercial banks played, everyone had an interest in containing bank runs, yet bank panics were common in the late nineteenth century, with particularly serious episodes occurring in 1873 and 1893. Before 1907, the New York Clearing House had been able to check bank runs by issuing clearinghouse loan certificates. These allowed banks to monetize their noncurrency assets: by substituting the certificates for currency in clearings, banks were able to free up their gold reserves to pay depositors demanding cash. While issue of these certificates was, strictly speaking, not legal, it was condoned because the certificates circulated only among banks and because some such short-term measure was necessary to restore the system's liquidity.[55]

In 1907, this mechanism broke down, and the near-failure of the money and capital market exposed the weakness of the entire banking and credit system. That the crisis began in the market for copper, a commodity traded like other real staples, also revealed the indissoluble connections between the financial and real sides of the economy. On October 16, F. Augustus Heinze tried and failed to create a bear squeeze on a copper stock traded on the New York Curb Exchange. In the context of a slowing national economy, falling share prices, and particularly illiquid conditions in the fall money market, the revelations following Heinze's failure spooked depositors and investors alike. Heinze turned out to be a director on boards of numerous banks, brokerage houses, and trusts, and he was also in league with many unsavory characters, some of whom were also members of bank boards. Five days after Heinze's position was exposed, depositors began to demand currency from New York trust banks—first, the Knickerbocker Trust, which ceased operation on October 22 after dispersing $8 million in three hours, then the Trust Company of America, and then the Lincoln Trust Company. Meanwhile, in the capital market, the price of call money soared, rising from 6% to 60% to 100% in a matter of hours. Brokerage houses were threatened with failure, and, when New York City's government was unable to sell an issue of bonds needed to raise funds, catastrophe seemed imminent. One contemporary reported the magnitude of the crisis: "There was heavy demand for gold and for money from the NY banks to be transferred to the interior of the country. . . . In the last ten days of 1907 stock market prices fell sharply, clearings decreased, dividends were passed or reduced in many cases, and failure of large corporations and private firms became frequent. The shrinkage in the market value of stock exchange securities alone was estimated as high as $5,000,000,000."[56] In the recession that followed, over 260 banks suspended operations.

A complete catastrophe was averted by a group of wealthy individuals headed by J. P. Morgan, the banking magnate and founder of US Steel. The Morgan group underwrote a 6% bond issue for New York City, persuaded a group of trust presidents to offer a $25 million loan to the New York trusts, and—not incidentally—exchanged higher-quality US Steel paper for a brokerage call loan collateralized by shares in a rival company, thus allowing Morgan's company to absorb a competitor. Even though the immediate crisis was resolved, it was clear to everyone that the existing unsupervised system was badly in need of repair.

The 1907 Panic began in the weakest link of the system—the trusts—because these institutions were subject to less regulation than national and state banks and because, in New York, they did not belong to the clearinghouse system. Trusts offered collateralized loans to businesses that banks would not fund, as well as underwriting security issues. They were not required to maintain the same level of reserves as national and state banks and had less clearing activity than commercial banks. For all these reasons, the portfolios of trusts tended to be riskier, and, because they represented an increasingly large component of the overall system, failure of one or more trusts was especially dangerous: between 1897 and 1907, trust assets grew 244%, whereas national bank assets in the same period drew only 97%.[57]

The overall system was vulnerable not only because it was comprised of so many links and such various institutions but also because commercial banking was theoretically governed by the real bills doctrine, which dictated that banks make only short-term loans, collect in full when loans came due, and loan money only when the borrower or endorser was personally known. In theory, this protected against bank runs because bankers could match assets on hand with the maturity dates of loans outstanding to known borrowers. In practice, however, and especially because the new corporations demanded continuous credit, most borrowers expected to renew loans when they came due. In the face of increasing demand, banks began to issue loans collateralized by companies' assets rather than anchored in the endorsement of a well-known client, and bankers found it increasingly difficult to match demand deposits to the maturity dates of outstanding loans.

It was largely to address the problems exposed by the 1907 Panic that Congress approved the Federal Reserve Act in December 1913—although eleven months were to pass before it was implemented. The act was primarily designed to improve the elasticity of the money supply by creating a lender of last resort. The Fed, which consisted of a politically appointed Federal Reserve Board in the nation's capital and regional banks in important cities, was able to respond to seasonal demands for money expansion and meet the liquidity requirements of banks through its new discount facilities. The act was also designed to eliminate the pyramiding of bank reserves—a process in which interior banks placed part of the reserve they were required to hold in banker balances related to the call loan portfolios of New York commercial and trust banks. As a new bank of issue with broadened eligibility requirements, the Fed provided for the rediscounting of real bills (commercial paper and bankers' acceptances), which banking theorists presented as self-liquidating short-term paper backed by real assets. The new act also required banks to deposit their gold reserves with the central bank. The new system effectively replaced the banks' prior source of short-term liquidity—the call money market—with a real-bill market, and it more efficiently leveraged the nation's gold stock. Call money—so named because redemption could be demanded at any time—was collateralized by the stock exchange and this tied credit to a speculative asset. The real bills in the new market were eligible for rediscount only if they were self-liquidating commercial paper or bankers' acceptances, which were used in foreign trade. Linking the liquidity of banks to bills rather than to call money also upheld the real-bills doctrine, which, as we will see in the next section, satisfied the monetary theorists who supported the banking theory of money over the quantity theory. The Federal Reserve Act also improved the check clearing system by setting up a central clearinghouse that reduced fees and improved efficiency.[58]

The ability of the new central banking system to respond to perceived danger was demonstrated even before the Federal Reserve banks opened their doors. When hostilities broke out in Europe in August 1914, William G. McAdoo, treasury secretary under Woodrow Wilson, preemptively closed the stock exchanges. American exchanges remained closed for an unprecedented four months to forestall the possibility that European demands for gold or attempts to liquidate stock positions would cause a banking crisis in the United States. Closing the exchanges required the issue of special currency, under the Aldrich-Vreeland Act, but ensured that the Federal Reserve system would begin operations with adequate gold reserves in the fall of 1914. McAdoo's intervention once more targeted the critical link between the credit facilities that supported Wall Street and the market financing America's real economy.

In its original form, the Federal Reserve system did not solve all the problems associated with the nation's network of financial intermediaries. It did not prevent banks from pyramiding reserves in New York banks, nor was it immune from political influence, as its founders had envisioned.[59] As we will see, by 1918 banking theorists like Harold Moulton had begun to criticize both the inadequacies of the new banking system and the failure of economists to understand the vital role money plays in every phase of the real economy's productive process. Despite its undeniable shortcomings, however, and even in its early years, the Federal Reserve system did stand guard over the fragile bridge that links promises to pay with short-term flows of cash—the bridge that ties the present to the future.[60] Its efforts to make the nation's currency more elastic and reduce dependence of the money market on the capital market represented the beginnings of reform. The Federal Reserve system began to be reworked almost as soon as it was created because America's entry into World War I meant that, like the banks, the government also needed a lender of last resort. The creation of the Federal Reserve system did not single-handedly transform the geographically expansive and politically divergent

federation of states into a unified economic nation, but it did represent a watershed event in the rise of the finance in the US economy.

1.4. THE PRINCIPLES OF AMERICAN BANKING

The Federal Reserve Act of 1913 was based on a set of principles and the practical experience of bankers. Unlike the quantity theory of money, to which
we turn in section 2.6, these principles were not articulated as an elaborate
or universal theory; they resembled the postulates that anchored work on
accountancy more closely than the full-fledged theories later economists
were to formulate. Sometimes referred to as the commercial loan theory or
the commercial-bill theory of banking, these principles held that the primary
business of banks was to finance current trade, which was generally understood as the trade of commodities.[61] These principles are related to (and, for
some people, were held to include) the real-bills doctrine. At their heart were
two ideas: the funds that back bank issues consist of deposits by members of
the public; and the loans and notes issued by banks (at discount) to support
the commodity trade do not influence prices or increase the amount of long-
term credit outstanding in the nation. In essence, the Federal Reserve Act extended these principles, which were derived from the operations of individual
banks, to the work of the new central bank.

In the new system, individual Federal Reserve banks issued notes, which
were convertible to gold and backed by the self-liquidating short-term commercial loans, or trade acceptances, that commercial bankers had long considered sound, in part because they were integrally linked to operations in
the real economy. But the act also expanded the collateral eligible for backing
the banks' deposit liabilities to include business and farming loans, and this
extension, while responsive to the special situation of the United States, implicitly moved away from the basic principles of the commercial loan theory
because new issues backed by loans that might not be repaid quickly might be
understood to increase existing long-term credit. To contain the implications
of this extension, the framers of the act emphasized the distinction between
two kinds of credit—speculative and productive; the former was not eligible
for discount at the Fed, and the latter was. As Perry Mehrling has pointed
out, this distinction might have worked in theory but it raised new problems
in practice because the rise of the corporations had exacerbated a situation
unique to the United States: American banks held not only credit that fueled
the real side of the economy but also forms of credit intrinsic to the financial
side. "Unlike their British counterparts, and notwithstanding orthodox bank-

ing theory, American banks had always been more or less deeply involved with financing not only working capital but also fixed capital. As a consequence, most banks had substantial holdings of bonds and stocks, loans on bond and stock collateral, and loans on mortgage or real estate collateral, all assets that orthodox banking theory would relegate to savings banks or other long-term investors."[62] This means that extending the principles that based banking on commercial loans to the new central bank raised questions about how and how much the Federal Reserve should actively manage the relationship between the real and financial sides of an economy understood as both separate and inseparable.

These questions were also linked, but not identical, to a dispute between two understandings of the best way to conceptualize "money" and its role in the nation's economy. While these positions were fully articulated only later and in response to subsequent problems, their roots can be found in two early attitudes toward what banks should do, which were in play when the Federal Reserve was created. One position essentially began with the exogenous control of the money supply by the central bank and advocated that this monetary authority should manage the amount in circulation in order to control the price level. This position was linked to Bryan's campaign for free silver; it was given theoretical articulation in Irving Fisher's quantity theory of money; and its modern form, American monetarism, included advocates such as the University of Chicago's Milton Friedman. The second position began with endogenously created money, supplied under the fractional reserve system by the extension of bank credit, and its proponents advocated laissez-faire policies (assuming the gold standard obtained). This position was held by J. Laurence Laughlin, who was the sole economist appointed to the monetary conference convened in 1897 to reform the banking system; it was given theoretical articulation by Allyn Young between 1903 and the late 1920s; and its modern advocates included John G. Gurley and Edward S. Shaw, who stressed the role financial intermediaries play in monetary policy in *Money in a Theory of Finance* (1960). In later chapters we will see how this dispute between forms of monetarism played out and how they shaped understandings of finance.[63]

CHAPTER 2

Early Twentieth-Century American Economic and Financial Theory

Institutional changes and developments in accountancy may have informed the way most Americans understood the economy in the early twentieth century, but a group of academics—initially called "political economists" but increasingly referred to simply as "economists"—also proposed vocabularies and analytic tools capable of representing these phenomena. In this chapter, we examine some of the most important efforts to develop analytic tools appropriate to America's increasingly complicated economic situation. While the details of economists' arguments may seem arcane to a modern reader, these efforts are important because they influenced how subsequent generations of economists viewed—and naturalized—the central metaphor of the "economy." At the same time, these relatively technical debates dictated how the financial "side" of the economy was viewed—if it was visible at all. We conclude with a discussion of debates about taxes because this is the form in which economists' debates hit home to ordinary citizens. We do not consider every American economist who wrote in the period between the 1890s and the 1920s, and we treat some individuals out of chronological order. Highlighting economists whose work contributed to later theoretical work on finance helps focus attention on the way this emphasis gradually emerged within economics; and grouping these theorists into thematic categories should help readers see how central ideas, such as marginalism, were initially formulated. Economists whose ideas were originally—or became—outliers to what was to be the mainstream emphasis of the profession, such as Thorstein Veblen and Frank Knight, are important to themes that return later in our narrative, but the contributions of these individuals were so distinctive that it is difficult to group them with their contemporaries.

At the beginning of the twentieth century, American economists were still struggling to identify the core mission of their discipline and to distinguish its methods from the applied arts of accounting and finance taught in schools of commerce and in accounting, money, and banking courses. A professional organization—the American Economics Association (AEA)—had been created in 1885, but controversies divided its ranks from the outset. Meanwhile, in US universities, economics courses were often taught by members of law or theology faculties. Numerous scholars have detailed the discipline's early struggles, as economists tried to find a coherent program and achieve the social authority many of its practitioners wanted.[1] In this chapter, we describe some of the theories developed by early twentieth-century economists to address the most pressing problems in the real and financial sides of the American economy.

2.1. THE INSTITUTIONALISM OF THORSTEIN VEBLEN

Most historians of economic thought draw a bright line between theorists who treat the economy as a relatively autonomous object of analysis and those who emphasize the historical and institutional contexts in which economic activities take place.[2] While this distinction—between orthodox and heterodox economists—is critical to the history of the discipline, we add to it a second distinction: between economists who emphasize the differences and interrelations between activities that belong to the real side of economy and those that are properly financial and economists who do not. One of the paradoxes of the history we tell is that, as financial activities came to represent an increasingly large percentage of overall US economic activity, orthodox economists paid less attention to the complex relationship between the real and financial sides of the economy, even as the discipline spun off a new subfield to analyze finance on terms specially developed for it.

At the beginning of the twentieth century, one member of the economics profession presented a vivid picture of two separate but inseparable sides of the economy. Because Thorstein Veblen placed his analysis in the institutionalist framework most of his contemporaries were beginning to reject, however, he was viewed—even by his admirers—as marginal to the discipline, and his work is now rarely taught in economics courses.[3] Veblen was not alone in his institutionalist approach to economic problems, nor were institutionalists ignored by their contemporaries or successors.[4] Another early institutionalist, John R. Commons of the University of Wisconsin, was president of the AEA on the eve of World War I, and today, some heterodox economists call themselves "new institutionalists" to mark their affinity with Veblen and Commons. Nevertheless, when Veblen published *The Theory of Business Enterprise* in 1904, he was already departing radically from the path taken by most of his peers.

Born in Wisconsin to a Norwegian farming family, Veblen took a PhD in philosophy at Yale, spent seven years on the family farm, and only belatedly began graduate study in economics. At Cornell University, Veblen impressed Laurence Laughlin, then chair of the department of political economy. In 1892, when Laughlin moved to the University of Chicago to establish a new political economics department, he took Veblen with him. Veblen spent the next fourteen years at Chicago, before moving to Stanford (1906–9), the University of Minnesota (1911–18), and, finally, the New School of Social Research in New York City.

In *The Theory of Business Enterprise* (*TBE*) Veblen explored a series of paradoxes generated by the two separate but inseparable "enterprises" or "employments" that characterized modern society. While these employments had been evolving for decades, Veblen argued that the tensions between what he called the "business enterprise" and the "machine process" had reached new heights because the corporations formed during the merger movement were undermining the most obvious goal of the machine process. Whereas the machine process was dedicated to producing real goods that could satisfy human wants, the business enterprise was devoted to producing financial profits. In a society dominated by the new corporations, as the United States was beginning to be by 1904, the expansion of the business enterprise had begun to hamper industry; parasitic trades, such as advertising, were threatening to choke off the production of serviceable goods; and the system of financing corporations through the sale of bonds and shares was piling an insupportable superstructure of credit and debt on top of the production process. Finally, the governance structure of the new corporations, in which management was separated from ownership, meant that the individuals who ran the companies did so for their own profit, not for the well-being of the shareholders, much less the public. If this situation were to continue, Veblen argued, the relationship between the business enterprise and the industrial process—between the financial and the real sides of the economy—would inevitably cause the business cycle to turn downward. Even worse, because the two groups whose habits of thought and action were governed by their places in this complex situation were developing incompatible ways of thinking, the tension between the business enterprise and the machine process might fuel the rise of socialism among industrial workers, whose engagement in the production process gave them no sympathy for the profit motive that governed the businessmen. "This socialistic disaffection is widespread among the advanced industrial peoples," Veblen warned. "No other cultural phenomenon is so threatening to the received economic and political structure; none is so unprecedented or so perplexing for practical men of affairs to deal with."[5]

Even though *TBE* was not an empirical study, the sources Veblen used to develop his analysis make the influence of the merger movement clear. In 1898, Congress appointed its Industrial Commission to investigate the new trusts, and Veblen carefully studied the nineteen volumes of testimony by industrial magnates published from 1900 to 1902. Using his definition of institutions, the work can be called "institutionalist" because the two dominant enterprises both embodied and fostered habits of thought, which, in turn, were attitudes toward work and value. Whereas those habituated to business thought in terms of individual rights, private property, and profit (*TBE* 151), those habituated to the production process thought in terms of "mechanical efficiency . . . regularity of sequence and mechanical precision, . . . and measurable cause and effect" (*TBE* 147). This also led to two separate understandings of "capital": "'Capital' in the enlightened modern business usage means 'capitalized presumptive earning-capacity'" (*TBE* 65); to the industrial worker, by contrast, "capital" refers to the material assets that feed the production process, including the workers' labor. This division between the ways the two groups understood "capital" was repeated in the difference between the way Veblen understood this foundational concept and the understanding of orthodox economists, to whom he gave the name "neoclassical." In his university lectures on Veblen, Wesley Clair Mitchell, to whom we return in chapter 3, underscored the importance of this distinction among early twentieth-century economists.

> Theorists [neoclassical economists] are accustomed in their treatises to have capital represented as primarily the aggregate of wealth used for the production of other wealth. That is to say, they usually think of capital standing for machinery, buildings, land, etc. Veblen says that if the theorist wants to understand the phenomenon, to think clearly, he must distinguish sharply between the aggregate of material goods which are used in production on the one hand and capital in the business man's

sense on the other. Capital in the business man's sense is a pecuniary magnitude. It is a sum of dollars and cents. On the one hand, it may represent the monetary equivalent of funds which are actually invested in the business. On the other hand in the typical case it does not represent that. It represents the putative earning capacity of the business enterprise capitalized at the prevailing rate of interest.[6]

In many respects, Veblen's understanding of the business conceptualization of capital resembles the theory of capital advanced by Irving Fisher, a peer whose reputation among economists has greatly surpassed that of Veblen. As we will see in our discussion of Fisher's *Nature of Capital and Income* (1906), however, Veblen cast the business definition of capital as one way of understanding this foundational concept, not as a universal principle from which deductive analysis could proceed.

Veblen disagreed with his fellow economists in other matters as well: instead of beginning with the assumption that individuals are rational and animated primarily by self-interest, Veblen insisted that people are creatures of habit and instinct; instead of viewing the price mechanism as the central problem of economics, he thought economists should focus on the growth of institutions, for these both shaped human habits and were amenable to change. For our purposes, Veblen's most important contribution was his emphasis on the novelty—the newness—of what he called the "credit economy," for it was the emergence of this economy *out of* the old "natural economy," by way of an intermediate "money economy," that generated the paradox we emphasize here: the coexistence of real and financial sides of the economy, which are only intermittently theorized by economists.

> What characterizes the early-modern scheme, the "money economy" and sets it off in contrast with the natural economy (distribution in kind) that went before it in Western-European culture, is the ubiquitous resort to the market as a vent for products and a source of supply of goods. The characteristic feature of this money economy is the goods market. . . . The credit economy—the scheme of economic life of the immediate past and the present—has made an advance over the money economy in the respect which chiefly distinguishes the latter. The goods market, of course, in absolute terms is still as powerful an economic factor as ever but it is no longer the dominant factor in business and industrial traffic, as it once was. The capital market has taken the first place in this respect. The capital market is the modern economic feature which

makes and identifies the higher "credit economy" as such. In this credit economy resort is habitually had to the market as a vent for accumulated money values and a source of supply of capital. (*TBE* 75)

The tendency for economists to neglect the relationship between the real and financial sides of the economy stems not only from orthodox economists' failure to treat economic arrangements as historical phenomena, but also from critical overlaps that obscure the interrelation of the two sides. In the first place, as Veblen notes, both the money economy (the real side of the economy) and the credit economy (the financial side) repeatedly "resort" to the market mechanism; the former uses the market as a "vent for products and a source of supply of goods"; the latter uses markets to "vent . . . accumulated money values and [as] a source of supply for capital." In the second place, the real side of the economy assigns values to both input (labor, raw materials) and output (finished products and services) in the very pecuniary terms central to the financial side of the economy (prices). This means that valuation—even in the real side of the economy—always seems to be about prices, just as accountancy always subsumes quantity into price terms.

Even though Veblen's institutionalist approach to economic problems flourished between the two world wars, and despite its persistence among today's new institutionalists, this approach to his discipline remained a minority position. Only intermittently did economists turn to the relationship between the real and financial sides of the economy as a matter of special concern—although, as we will see in a moment, Irving Fisher did offer a financial *view* of economic transactions that was to profoundly influence the eventual emergence of finance as a subfield within economics.

2.2. LATE NINETEENTH-CENTURY AMERICAN NEOCLASSICAL PRICE THEORY AND THE REAL US ECONOMY

In 1900 Veblen coined the phrase "neo-classical" political economy to distinguish the work of some utilitarian price theorists, such as the British economist Alfred Marshall, from the "classical" economists, who included Adam Smith, David Hume, and John Stuart Mill. Marshall had consolidated and extended the marginal utility theory pioneered by William Stanley Jevons, Carl Menger, and Léon Walras in the 1870s. In "Preoccupations of Economic Science III," Veblen explained that these marginalist utility theorists identified "economic laws" in "fundamental theorems [such as] the law of rent, of profits, of wages, of the increasing or diminishing returns of industry, of competitive prices, of cost of production."[7] Late nineteenth-century marginalist economy theory is the ancestor of modern price theory, which was developed in America after World War II by economists such as Milton Friedman and George Stigler at the University of Chicago. Price theory establishes the mechanism by which price determination in competitive markets efficiently allocates resources in the real economy. Price theory, in other words, is the framework economists use to analyze the *real* economy, using the assumptions of neoclassical economics. In the typical setup, money is treated as a medium of exchange and a unit of account, but for pedagogical convenience, money is not treated as a store of value. For this reason, it is often said that price theory and the related general equilibrium theory "abstract" from the world of money and finance.

Late nineteenth-century marginalist utility theorists formulated the laws of supply and demand in scientific terms by analyzing these forces geometrically with graphs and analytically with calculus. They used the latter to quantify the concept of the margin, which is based on the law of diminishing returns or the law of variable proportions. In this form of quantitative marginal analysis, an "infinitesimal" increment produces the maximal benefit (positive utility) or least cost (negative utility). That value comes from the (conceptually, not temporally) "last" increment explains why this set of theoretical principles is said to focus on "marginal utility." The "utility," or desirability, of the unit at the "margin" determines the value of every entity in the set.[8] This notion of the maximum or minimum increment can be quantified by the application of the derivative from calculus, for this provides a method to quantify infinitesimal change. For this reason, calculus is one of the fundamental mathematical tools for neoclassical price theory.

In the late nineteenth century, the American economist John Bates Clark developed a marginal neoclassical theory without resort to calculus by applying the classical example of the marginal productivity of "good labor" to gradations in the fertility of land.[9] Clark, whose primary academic affiliation was with Columbia University, was one of the first American political economists to undertake advanced study in Germany. In Germany in the 1870s, Clark was exposed not only to the historical school, which emphasized some of the issues that preoccupied Veblen, but also to the work of European marginalists.[10] Clark extended the marginalist theory of value to a theory of production and used the neoclassical law of wages, by which the price of wages is set by the marginal contribution of labor to production. Although the price of wages for a firm, or, in aggregate, the total wage cost for a nation, is at least conceptually quantifiable, price theorists faced theoretical quandaries because the historical cost data that was available did not reflect the value of capital. This value was set by discounting capital's productive capacity to the present based on expectations about its return. To develop his neoclassical theory of income distribution and to justify capitalist economics and wage rates, Clark developed a novel theory of a capital fund.

American economists were slow to embrace the terminology of marginalism—the word *marginalism* was not coined until 1914—and the word did not appear in an English dictionary until 1966.[11] Many American economists were also slow to embrace mathematics; in the first decades of the twentieth century, most economists, like the majority of economists for the next half century, presented their ideas in prose sentences, not the mathematical language, equations, and graphs economists commonly use today. Even Clark, who became known as the "American marginalist," avoided mathematical formulations, although he did use diagrams to demonstrate the relative contribution of wages or capital to output. In one sense, then—in his embrace of the neoclassical principle of marginal utility and the metaphor of equilibrium—Clark was the harbinger of things to come in American economics. In another—in his reliance on literary instead of mathematical language—he harkened back to his nineteenth predecessors in political economy.[12]

Clark's major work focused on wages, productivity, and the distribution of income and resources—problems that belong to the real side of the economy. To quantify "capital," Clark drew a distinction between "capital" and "capital goods." For him, the first term referred to the fund of value invested in commodities and the second referred to the commodities themselves; both terms summoned up the world of real production values, not financial value. "Capital consists of instruments of production, and these are always concrete and material."[13] Capital goods are also concrete and material, and both capital and capital goods can be valued in money terms. The difference between the two lay in the permanence and mobility of the former, as opposed to the perishability and immobility of the latter: according to Clark, the fund of capital abides but can transmigrate, via investment, through various capital goods, the nature of which shifts as particular goods are produced and consumed. Unlike Veblen, then, who presented capital as assuming different guises depending on where one stood in relation to the real and financial sides of the economy, Clark was always looking at the real side, where goods are produced and distributed, and where income is a good like any other.

While Clark was not immediately engaged with issues directly relevant to the rise of American finance in the way Veblen was, he did apply marginalist principles to a question that was becoming urgent in late nineteenth-century America: with the western frontier no longer the site of expansive US growth, urban areas increasingly impinging on their rural surrounds, and tensions between workers and employers running high, how could one tell whether the nation's wealth was equitably distributed? During the last three decades of the nineteenth century, striking workers had repeatedly insisted that income distribution was not equitable: wages were too low and the prices of goods set by producers were too high. Whether or not he was directly responding to the deadly Haymarket bombing in 1886, Clark's application of marginalist principles to the production theory of income distribution implicitly addressed the workers' concerns.[14] In a series of articles published between 1888 and 1891, and in the book that synthesized and elaborated these papers (*The Distribution of Wealth*, 1889), Clark explained the ratio between labor and capital, which, he argued, exemplified a "law" that was "as real as gravitation."[15] Cast as a "scientific" proof, Clark's argument demonstrated that wages had to remain relatively low, for increases in population increased the supply of labor and lowered the returns to new capital.[16] "If population be fixed and pure capital increases, what must the new capital do? *It must take less and less productive forms of outward embodiment.* The last new increment will add something to the returns of the man who employs it; it will shape itself into an instrument that will earn something; but the earnings will be less than were those of the earlier instruments of similar cost."[17] By holding another variable constant— this time capital—Clark worked the ratio the other way: if capital is stationary and the number of workers increases, wages will inevitably decrease (61).

Clark was primarily interested in the income distribution to the so-called factors of production—capital and labor. Indeed, the few graphs Clark included show only one curve, angling downward along the vertical axis of price as it moves forward on the horizontal axis of quantity.[18] Clark focused on income distribution because this was the problem at hand: both labor (and its return as wages) and capital (and its return as interest or profit) belong to the supply side of the neoclassical theory of price and value, and the relevant question in the 1880s and 1890s concerned the proper apportionment of the returns to capital or labor. What the marginalist principles show, Clark argued, was clear: if employers were allowed to hire in a fully competitive market, the returns to labor and to capital would both be fair, for even the "marginal man" (the last worker hired or the worker hired to do the least essential work) would receive "the full amount of his product" ("Distribution," 309). Thus the marginalist law "furnishes the ultimate standard of measurement of market value. It . . . identifies production with distribution, and shows that what a social class gets is, under natural law, what it contributes to the general output of industry" ("Distribution," 312–13).

Whether or not Clark's conclusions were as impartial as he claimed, it is important to note the restrictions under which he worked.[19] In the last two decades of the nineteenth century, data that would have allowed an economist to track wages did not exist, and there was no inductive way to tell what the "latest working hour" yielded in particular industries. But Clark did not lament the lack of data—in part, at least, because he realized that returns to labor were *not* in perfect equilibrium with returns to capital. He also knew that the perfect competition necessary to create an equilibrium between supply and demand did not exist, and he saw that American enterprise might not even be tending toward such a theoretically perfect state.[20] In this situation, he promoted his theories as normative statements, not descriptive accounts of actual circumstances.[21] For Clark, the function of economic theory was to persuade his readers that certain conditions *should* obtain, even if the natural laws exemplified by marginalist theory were yet to be realized in fact.

Clark's method generated a "static" picture of an economy in an "unprogressive state." He held one variable after another constant in order to show how each variable worked in relation to the others. He acknowledged that such simplifications created an artificial, "imaginary" representation, yet he insisted that the resulting picture was "realistic." "We make in this way a study that is completely realistic, since the static forces are dominant in the world of actual business. We isolate them, in order that we may know their nature." "In the end," he promised—"although not in this article"—the theorist would be able to "take account of all essential changes that in reality take place, and attain the dynamic laws of distribution" ("Distribution," 290). This static analysis, which relied on the method of *ceteris paribus,* allowed Clark to isolate and examine specific economic relationships sequentially, with the hope of both achieving theoretical consistency and approximating the overall situation in the actual economy. Static analysis was to prove a critical building block of subsequent attempts to depict—and eventually to model—economic forces.[22] The form of neoclassical marginalist argument that John Bates Clark made would play an important role in American finance, for marginalist theories became a critical tool for developing fiscal policy and supporting the free market ideology of competitive free markets.

2.3. EARLY AMERICAN GENERAL EQUILIBRIUM THEORY

The highly abstract, game-theoretic general equilibrium theory (GET), as this was developed by Kenneth Arrow and Gérard Debreu after World War II, was to become one of the most important frameworks of modern finance and modern economics. Even though Arrow and Debreu's general equilibrium theory harkened back to the work of Léon Walras, as this was refined by the Italian theorist, Vilfredo Pareto, and *not* to Irving Fisher's attempt to model the theory of general equilibrium, Fisher's depiction of GET is important for American finance because Fisher's model contained the germ of his monetary theory. Fisher viewed this work, moreover, as supplying the "missing equation" to the general equilibrium theory he worked out in his dissertation.

The dissertation in which Fisher developed his version of GET gave economics—or political economy, as it was known—the methodological turn absent in the work of Clark. Published in 1892 as *Mathematical Investigations in the Theory of Value and Prices,* Fisher's dissertation was later lauded by Paul A. Samuelson as "perhaps the best of all doctoral dissertations in economics."[23] *Mathematical Investigations (MI)* introduced American economists to the general equilibrium paradigm, the mathematical formulation of ordinal marginal utility developed by Léon Walras. As George J. Stigler noted, Fisher's dissertation was "the first careful examination of the utility function and its relevance to demand theory." According to Stigler, Fisher "solved the measurability problem quite satisfactorily for the case in which the marginal utilities of the quantities are independent of one another."[24]

For our purposes, it is important to note that Fisher's dissertation, which operated at a high level of abstraction, dealt with transactions in the real side of the economy by abstracting finance. Although he did discuss the role money plays, he treated money as a unit of account and medium of exchange, not a store of value. Nor did he focus on financial intermediation or financial assets in this work. As we will see in the next two sections, Fisher was soon to take up financial issues and make important contributions to financial theory, but in *Mathematical Investigations,* his primary aspiration was not to link the real side of the economy to finance but to offer a new way of doing economic analysis. Fisher wanted to dispense with the *ceteris paribus* convention used by Clark and other neoclassical economists to analyze price formation in commodity markets and to depict instead the simultaneous interrelation of the exchanged quantities and determined prices for all commodities in an economy composed of many interrelated markets.

In his influential conception of general equilibrium, Walras emphasized aggregates: aggregate supply equals aggregate demand. In Fisher's formulation, by contrast, general equilibrium is attained when the marginal utilities of individual buyers, sellers, and producers equal each other.[25] Considerable mathematical sophistication was required to analyze these equilibrium conditions, and, even though Fisher did not fully implement these techniques, he did gesture toward matrix algebra and vector analysis—the mathematical tools that would allow later economists to represent an economy with many interrelated markets. The notation for these techniques had been used in the theory of thermodynamics developed by one of Fisher's teachers, Willard J. Gibbs.[26]

In *Mathematical Investigations,* Fisher depicted general equilibrium in several different ways: he offered a purely verbal account, sketches of a mechanical model, geometrical graphs, and mathematical analysis. That he used all these strategies suggests both his recognition that each form of representation could highlight some aspects of the equilibrium process[27] and his realization that his preferred mode of representation—mathematics—would not be welcomed by every reader.[28] Almost four decades were to pass before Fisher considered mathematical language sufficiently acceptable to include equations in the body of the text instead of relegating them to appendices.[29] The primary mathematical tool he used here was the analytical simultaneous equation method, as it was then called, which uses algebra to solve for an equilibrium solution. This method requires that the number of equations equal the number of unknowns, with each equation representing a separate market for the commodities exchanged in the economy. Like the other representational modes in his dissertation, Fisher's mathematical analysis was designed to illustrate a fundamental insight: the dependence of value on marginal utility derives from "desire" and the principle of diminishing returns found in production (*MI* 3). In modern mathematical economics, as formulated by Paul Samuelson in the 1940s, the concept of marginal utility based on diminishing returns was replaced by a theory of revealed preference; matrix and vector methods became the preferred techniques for analyzing equilibrium; and what Fisher called the "paradox of cause and effect"—the difficulty of ascertaining how shifts in equilibrium value are influenced by external factors—came to be known as "the identification problem." This problem, which proved to be one of the most challenging for the simultaneous equation method, was to set the terms of much debate about the direction of causality in the real economy.

In addition to introducing mathematics into economic analysis, Fisher also described a physical model that allowed the economist to measure units of desire, the elusive, but all-important driver of consumer demand. In the language of marginalism, desire was expressed in terms of "utility," but utility was notoriously difficult to measure because no unit existed with which it could be quantified. To solve this problem, Fisher invented a measurement unit, called the "util." The physical model Fisher described consisted of a fluid-filled rectilinear container (see fig. 3), inside of which floated a number of smaller cisterns.[30] These cisterns, which varied in size and shape, were attached to each other by horizontal and vertical rods, which extended from the tops of the cisterns to the sides of the rectilinear container. Two rows of cisterns (on the right and left) represented individual consumers, and two other rows (in the front and the back) represented individual commodities. By means of internal partitions made of wood, each of the cisterns in the front and back rows was divided into two parts: the front part represented the physical units in which commodities are valued (e.g., pounds, yards) and the back part represented value in money (dollars). The rods operated in such a way as to "keep the continuous ratio of marginal utilities, the same for all individuals and equal to the ratio of prices" (*MI* 40). Using a system of valves, tubes, stoppers, and pumps to control the inflow and outgo of water, the operator could use the machine to demonstrate a number of relationships among quantities, between kinds of units, and between quantities and units, including prices.[31] The two general principles exemplified by the mechanism as a whole were that all of the interacting parts tended toward general equilibrium and that increasing the amount of money (water) in the system raised the level of all the cisterns to the same degree. The latter, as we will see in a moment, was one of the central tenets of Fisher's monetary theory: it depicts money as an exogenous factor and independent variable rather than viewing money as a store of value or an endogenous product of the financial system itself. The underlying metaphor of Fisher's models was that the quantity of money, like water, would obey the law of gravity. This was not the only metaphor economists used to describe the behavior of money; Morris Copeland, for example, replaced Fisher's "hydraulic" metaphor with a model that depicted money as electricity, and this led to substantially different conclusions about the role money plays in the economy.[32]

As Fisher described it, his model was "the physical analogue of the ideal economic market" (*MI* 44). By making all the "elements which contribute to the determination of prices . . . open to the scrutiny of the eye," Fisher's model allowed the economist to measure the events that occurred in the mechanical representation, as well as to represent them mathematically. Fisher's

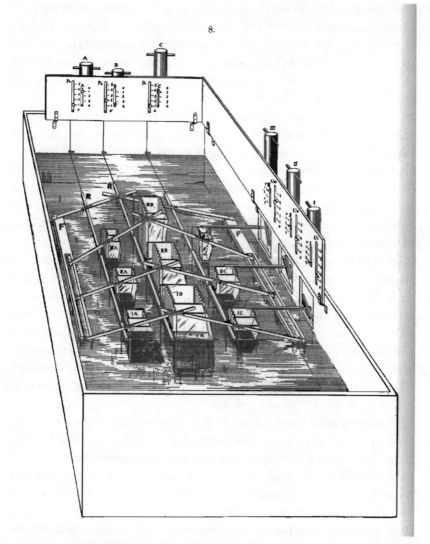

FIGURE 3. Irving Fisher's physical model, which he described as an analogue of an ideal economic market. The fluid-filled rectilinear container holds floating cisterns that rise and fall as the fluid level changes. From Irving Fisher, "Mathematical Investigations in the Theory of Value and Price," *Transactions of the Connecticut Academy* 9 (July 1892): 38.

apparatus thus let him infer and measure what was otherwise simply a theoretical assumption. Fisher was also able to render the units in which the marginal utility for quantities of commodities were measured (gallons, tons, yards) commensurate with the units in which prices were measured (dollars) and thus to calculate the relationship between the movements of the cisterns and changes in price.

In the second part of his dissertation, Fisher extended his quantification of utility; he presented utility as a function not simply of the amount of a single commodity held by an individual but of the available quantities of all commodities. His analysis proceeds in stages, beginning with an economy that contains two commodities consumed by a single individual. Even this small amplification required a shift in the representational medium, for, as Fisher explained, the resulting complexity could not be physically represented unless the size and shape of the cisterns were to change along with each possible relation among the variables. He realized that the new system could be graphed, however, in the form of indifference surfaces in a three-dimensional space. When he extended the analysis to three or more commodities, he had to switch to a mathematical notation that used matrices, for only vector analysis could capture the resulting complexity. In *Mathematical Investigations* as a whole, Fisher's move from one representational mode to another replicated in miniature the strategy Gibbs used in his three most important theoretical works, where he exploited innovative geometric techniques to graph the properties of thermodynamic systems.

In *Mathematical Investigations*, Fisher was not simply drawing an *analogy* between economic concepts and thermodynamics, the discipline in which vector analysis was developed as a way to conceptualize force.[33] Instead, Fisher viewed specific mathematical techniques, including matrices and vector analysis, as peculiarly *fitted* to the theoretical contents of particular economic principles. According to this way of understanding the relationship between mathematical form and theoretical content, a mathematical form can be so appropriate to a theoretical content that, initially at least, the theory cannot be expressed apart from or outside of the mathematical formulation. Over time, the properties of the mathematical instruments used to express the theoretical content become suffused with theoretical meanings that have been developed in economic analysis; and, as the resulting mathematico-economic method of argumentation is naturalized, theory comes to seem indistinguishable from method. This fusion of theory and method would later become central to mathematical modeling, which has become the characteristic method of modern economic analysis.

Fisher did work out a series of analogies between the concepts physicists used to describe force and energy and their economic counterparts. Thus, a particle "corresponds to" an individual; space corresponds to a commodity; force corresponds to marginal utility or disutility; and so on (*MI*, 85). In *Mathematical Investigations,* Fisher even self-consciously meditated on the relationship between economic terminology and the language of what he called mechanics.

> Scarcely a writer on economics omits to make some comparison between economics and mechanics. One speaks of a "rough correspondence" between the play of "economic forces" and mechanical equilibrium. Another compares uniformity of price to the level-seeking of water. Another (Jevons) compares his law of exchange to that of the lever. Another (Edgeworth) figures his economic "system" as that of connected lakes of various levels. Another compares society to a plastic mass such that a "pressure" in one region is dissipated in all "directions." In fact the economist borrows much of his vocabulary from mechanics. (*MI*, 24)

Fisher was invoking both metaphors and mathematical instruments because these representational modes enabled economists to visualize the otherwise elusive economy in ways that otherwise were not possible. The figures Fisher borrowed from physics or mechanics were neither incidental to his theoretical formulations nor a faulty substructure that would collapse as natural scientists reconsidered the kinds of claims they made about the world. Instead, the mathematical figure that was initially borrowed eventually became quite literally indistinguishable from the content it conveyed. As we will see, one result was that economic analysis came to elevate consistency, which is a property of mathematics, over referential validity, which describes the relationship between the model and the world.

Gibbs's matrix and vector analysis permitted Fisher, in theory at least, to extend his depiction of an idealized economy to an infinite number of commodities, and it allowed him to use complex consumer indifference surfaces to show the interplay of the utility and quantity of these commodities over time, based on marginalist principles and sophisticated demand analysis. What Fisher's various approaches could not do was link the dynamics replicated in the machine and captured in the matrix algebra to real-world data or explore the relationship between the real and financial sides of the economy. To do these things, Fisher dropped the method he used in *Mathematical*

Investigations, in which mathematical calculations were used primarily to illustrate an a priori theory, and turned to a method by which buyers and sellers had long calculated the prices of financial assets. Using some of the insights his drawings and mechanism had given him, but relying on this much older method, Fisher discovered that he could address questions about the financial side of the economy, instead of focusing only on supply and demand in the real economy.

2.4. AN EARLY MODEL OF EXPECTATIONS: THE FISHER EFFECT

Mathematical Investigations represents only one part of Irving Fisher's broad and influential engagement with economic issues. In his next major work, *Appreciation and Interest (AI,* 1896), we begin to see the contributions he made to what would become the subfield of finance. This work examines the relationship between commodity prices and the value of money, and it does so not simply in the theoretical terms that defined *Mathematical Investigations,* but also by testing Fisher's theoretical observations empirically, using what was at the time the best data available to suggest the size of the US economy. Empirical testing was important in this project because *Appreciation and Interest* was a response to a practical issue that contemporaries debated in the mid-1890s. The issue was related to the inelastic currency problem addressed by William Jennings Bryan in his campaign for free silver. Because commodity prices had been falling for the last two decades, while the value of gold, on which the US dollar was based, continued to rise, debts incurred at one monetary value had to be repaid in a currency whose value, or purchasing power, had changed.

Many economists had tried to explain the discrepancy between commodity prices and the value of gold, but no one had noticed what Fisher considered central: the "influence of monetary appreciation and depreciation on the rate of interest."[34] Fisher argued that even though the nominal principal repaid by the debtor could be either inflated or depreciated based on changes in the value of currency in relation to gold, if the lender and borrower could anticipate changes in the value of money and build their expectations into an interest rate on which they mutually agreed, no injustice would result. Evidence of this anticipation was later called "the Fisher effect."[35] Because interest is paid in a series of interim payments, the total amount paid over time could compensate for the change that appreciation or depreciation made in the value of money. As Fisher explained, "A farmer who contracts a mortgage in gold is, *if the interest is properly adjusted,* no worse and no better off than if his contract were in a 'wheat' standard or a 'multiple' standard" (*AI* 16; emphasis in original). Fisher's analytical exercise laid the groundwork for the study of the influence of expectations on nominal and real interest rates over the business cycle during inflationary and deflationary periods. This, in turn, encouraged later economists—such as Milton Friedman and Kenneth Rogoff—to address the question of how central banks should respond to such conditions.[36]

To explain how market participants could properly adjust the interest rate, Fisher introduced two kinds of calculations, which, he argued, actual borrowers and lenders routinely performed. The first treated money as a good like any other and involved an algorithm, later called "the Fisher equation," that allowed market participants to relate two sets of values to each other and to move back and forth between the two standards of valuation. Thus, if a debt were contracted in one standard—say, dollars—the farmer had to figure out the value of this debt in wheat, the manufacturer converted it to widgets, and the merchant had to understand it in terms of the commodities he sold. In an economy in which every form of capital commanded its own interest rate, moreover, as Fisher claimed was true in late nineteenth-century America, the dollar standard would be acceptable as long as participants understood how standards behaved in relation to each other. The conventional system of denominating interest rates in the money standard (dollars) could be "just," in other words, even if the value of each standard fluctuated, *if* borrowers and lenders clearly understood the relationship between the interest accruing on one standard (the dollar) and the interest accruing on another (e.g., wheat). A simple formula allowed market participants to calculate such relationships. The formula for calculating "the rate of interest in a (relatively) depreciating standard is equal to the sum of three terms, viz., the rate of interest in the appreciating standard, the rate of appreciation itself and the product of these two elements" (*AI* 9).

The second calculation was derived from and illuminated financial transactions. This calculation figured the "present value" of the future sum that money put out at interest would return by discounting that sum to the present. As Fisher explained, "The ordinary definition of the 'present value' of a given sum due at a future date is 'that sum which put at interest to-day will "amount" to the given sum at that future date'" (*AI* 19). Present-value calculations had routinely been used in insurance, annuity, and fixed-income (bond) transactions since the seventeenth century. Then, as now, they allowed market participants to factor expectations about future changes in the value of money into their business and investment decisions. Instead of requiring complex, on-the-spot calculations, present value is determined by reference to tables that show the geometrical growth over time produced by the compounding of interest. These readily available tables, Fisher pointed out, "are constructed on this principle [compounding] for the practical use of insurance companies in calculating their premiums, and for brokers in determining the comparative methods of various bond instruments" (*AI* 19).[37] Fisher's insight was that the economist could generalize from present-value theory a general claim about the effect of *expectations* on financial matters such as the nominal interest rate.

Fisher argued that farmers and merchants routinely factored into the interest rates they were willing to pay expectations about future changes in the value of money, just as they used informed decisions about the probable yield of their crops or demand for their merchandise to make planting or pricing decisions. To the objection that ordinary farmers and merchants could not make these complicated calculations, Fisher insisted that every participant in the market already routinely followed the trends of relative price changes. As the borrower responded to present changes in the value of money, moreover, he actually affected its future cost, through the market mechanism of supply and demand. The ordinary person's "effort is not to predict the index numbers of Sauerback or Conrad, but to so foresee his own economic future as to make reasonably correct decisions, and in particular to know what he is about when contracting a loan. If gold appreciates in such a way or in such a sense that he expects a shrinking margin of profit, he will be cautious about borrowing unless interest falls; and this very unwillingness to borrow, lessening the demand in the 'money market,' will bring interest down" (*AI* 36).

Fisher's contributions to the debate that had raged since the 1890s, then, consisted of two basic insights. First, because capital must be understood not simply as the *fund* available in the present but also as the *flow* of income from the future, in the form of periodically paid interest, Fisher argued that interest rates could adjust for the changes in standards caused by appreciation and depreciation in the currency used to price debt. The distinction between flow (future interest) and fund (today's price) was also central to the innovations in accounting theory developed to help corporations calculate the value of their assets. Second, because market participants routinely acted on their expectations about the future and their understanding of the principle of compounding when they agreed on interest rates, Fisher elevated the role of expectations—which play a critical role in the financial side of the economy—to new importance in economic analysis. Indeed, his insistence that the behavior of market participants, based on expectations, influences what happens in the market helped shift economists' attention to the process of decision making. As we will see, this became critical to the subfield of finance where, after World War II, price came to be understood as a function of investors' decision-making behavior instead of marginal utility. This change in orientation—from desire to action and choice—was to provide a microeconomic foundation for the macroeconomic models developed in the 1930s.

In Part II of *Appreciation and Interest,* entitled "Facts," Fisher began to test his observations against empirical evidence. Even though this represented a dramatic departure from the approach he promoted in *Mathematical Investigations,* Fisher was adamant that it constituted an advance in economic analysis. "No study of the relation between appreciation and interest would be complete without verification by facts. In imaginary illustrations, such as those used in Part I, it is easy to make calculations agree to the last decimal place; but the figures in which we are really interested must come from actual market quotations" (*AI* 35). Market quotations—the prices actually paid for commodities—regularly appeared in the "multitudes of trade journals and investors' reviews" printed every week (*AI* 37), but as Fisher discovered, corresponding data about the yearly interest rates paid on money was harder to come by. So great a challenge did such data pose that Fisher appended to the text an elaborate compilation of the sources he used to create his figures, which highlights the breaks in the available annual records. The footnotes to the body of Part II also constitute a running commentary on the labor involved in constructing the tables printed in the text. Fisher's statistical test, in other words, while revolutionary in ambition and design, was limited in practice by the same lack of data that John Bates Clark dismissed as irrelevant to economic theory. Unlike Clark, Fisher was clearly frustrated by the inadequacy of the available evidence—both its scarcity and the incommensurate forms it took—and by the relatively rudimentary nature of the tools available to the economist.[38]

Fisher's frustration with the economist's tools is also visible in the caution he issued about index numbers.

> The use of index numbers is itself subject to fatal objection. When unchecked by other statistics they are very misleading. Not only do we reach different results according to the number of commodities and the method of averaging, but the very best methods fail to give a trustworthy measure of ordinary domestic purchasing power, both because they are based on wholesale instead of retail prices, and because they ignore expenditure for house rent and for labor and domestic service, which,

in the family budgets of those who borrow and lend, must form a very large item. (*AI* 81)

Even were the relevant data available, Fisher acknowledged, the economist still would not know "the 'subjective value' or marginal utility of money. The number of dollars at command (*i.e.*, money incomes) must also be considered. And even were our knowledge complete as to the marginal utility of money, as well as its purchasing power, we should be as far as ever from solving the problem of the debtor's loss. The question is not one of appreciation of gold relative to commodities, or to labor, or any other standard. It is, as we have seen, exclusively a question of foresight and of the degree of adaptation of the rate of interest" (*AI* 82). The combination of infuriatingly scarce data and insufficiently sophisticated analytic tools clearly frustrated Fisher, and he also noted—without addressing—the challenging task of modeling expectations (foresight) and behavior (adaptation).[39]

2.5. THE FINANCIAL VIEW

By bringing financial topics like interest rates and financial assets like bonds into his economic analysis, Irving Fisher opened a place for financial theory within the discipline of economics. And by challenging himself and other economists to find the data and statistical tools that would allow theories to be tested, he identified a way to make theory relate to real-world economic transactions. Each of these contributions made an impact on the discipline: not only were financial theory and practice to become important offshoots of economics after 1970, but Fisher's reliance on mathematics and deduction was to reappear in the work of Paul A. Samuelson in the 1940s, and his turn to empirical analysis was to influence the work that Milton Friedman began in the 1930s. In some ways, however, Fisher's greatest contribution to the history of finance was an insight pursued by few subsequent economists. This is what we call the financial view—an all-encompassing understanding of valuation that could include both commodities and financial assets. This understanding of value insists that income should not be equated with money, that money has no intrinsic value, and that the only benefit that accrues from money is consumption, whether this occurs in the present or as an anticipated future event. A more concise way to summarize the primary insight of the financial view is to state its radical theory of value: the value of capital is the future cash flow discounted to the present at the prevailing interest rate.

Fisher developed the financial view in three works published over a quarter of a century. These include *The Nature of Capital and Income* (1906), *The Rate of Interest* (1907), and *The Theory of Interest* (1930). He always considered the first two a pair, but only when he began to revise *The Theory of Interest* (*TI*) did he decide that the three works constituted a single "chain of explanation." "The combined 'impatience and opportunity theory' . . . fits together impatience and opportunity and income. The income concept plays the basic role in the theory of interest."[40] Fisher set out the income concept in *The Nature of Capital and Income* (*CI*), which he presented both as a "philosophy of economic accounting" and "a link long missing between the ideas and usages underlying practical business transactions and the theories of abstract economics."[41] The income concept was one of a series of terms Fisher defined in a new way, which helped reorient economic analysis—not only away from the ethical emphasis we saw in the work of J. B. Clark toward mathematics and philosophy but also away from a focus on the past to an innovative engagement with the future. As we will see, at the heart of this reorientation was the form of property used to great effect by the giant corporations: financial assets, like bonds and equities.

What Fisher did with the foundational terms of the discipline—"income," "property," "capital," "wealth," "interest rate," and "risk"—repelled some of his peers and confused others.[42] By placing *expectations* about future income, as reflected in the actuary's compound-interest table and the bond broker's yield-to-maturity schedule, at the center of value, Fisher turned each of these concepts toward the future.[43] We see this in his definition of "capital-value," which most neoclassical economists viewed as a static sum of past profits. "Were there no expectation of any future income—or, at least, the expectation that there would be an expectation of it—there could be no capital-value. Capital-value, independent of expected income, is impossible" (*CI* 230–31). "Property" also turns to the future in Fisher's account. Instead of viewing property as the contractual right of an owner to material wealth, as classical and neoclassical economists did, Fisher defined property as "the chance of future services of wealth" (335). His elaboration makes clear how far he was departing from tradition: "All wealth is merely existing means towards *future* services, and all property, merely present rights to some of those future services. It is only through the future services that wealth and property are bound together at all. The sequence of ideas is first, present wealth; second, future services; third, present rights to these future services and therefore to the present wealth which yields them. Property is thus always a right to the chance of a future benefit" (*CI* 33–34). The Nobel Laureate Maurice Allais described the importance of Fisher's insight: Fisher "saw with unprecedented clarity that the economic present is no more than the capitalization of the future and that therefore the economic future is only a synthetic projection of the anticipated future."[44] This orientation toward the future was derived from financial assets like equities and bonds, and it now dominates modern finance.

This reorientation also explains why "the income concept plays the basic role in the theory of interest." For if "income" refers to what one anticipates receiving over time, then the decision about whether to spend money in the present or to defer consumption until a later date depends upon one's expectations about the future; and the interest rate, according to Fisher, expresses the relationship between decisions about current versus future consumption. Here we should note that Fisher was not talking about the interest rate that actually obtained in a given borrowing situation, which economists call the nominal interest rate. Instead, he was focused on a purely theoretical concept, the "real interest rate," which is typically defined as the nominal interest rate minus the amount by which the purchasing power of money changes over time. As he developed this idea in *The Theory of Interest,* the real interest rate is a function of two factors. The first, which expresses a relation to the financial side of the economy, involves one's expectations about how future changes in the value of money will affect the ability to consume. The second, which expresses conditions in the real side of the economy, involves the production processes and technological innovations that establish the environment in which consumption and investment take place. The goal of every individual, Fisher assumed, is to maximize the consumption-to-savings ratio, to balance in the best way possible present consumption (also expressed as "the impatience to spend income") with whatever "opportunity" might arise in the future (also expressed as saving). In this scheme, "income" is not simply the money one receives in the present but what one expects to receive *and* the future-oriented series of decisions that follows from this expectation; the real interest rate articulates the relationship among these decisions.

Fisher's reorientation of economic analysis also involved viewing every economic transaction from two perspectives: one emphasizes its static state and the other its temporality, its relation to the future. These perspectives also capture the two views given by the corporate financial documents we have already examined. The first provides the balance-sheet view of a company, which Fisher called the "flash-light picture of capital," and the second gives the income-statement view, which shows "the flow of services from capital through a period of time" (*CI* 66, 333). According to this paradigm, the only way to understand the value of "capital"—to grasp it as "capital-value"—is to invoke its counterpart, income (which is a flow in time). The only way to understand the balance sheet, in other words, is to see it in relation to the income statement.

We don't know for certain whether Fisher had seen the income statement the federal government drew up in 1894 or Dickinson's 1904 form, but *The Nature of Capital and Income* makes it clear that he was familiar with cost accounting, and his references to the document he variously calls the "income account" and the "income-and-outgo account" suggest that he was familiar with the function income statements performed (*CI* 122, 134). What he did in these three works was to combine elements of the double-entry accounting system with the balance-sheet and income-statement views. This allowed Fisher to retain the function of verification inherent in the double-entry system but to add to verification an additional function: calculation or computation, which, for Fisher, could be done using the present-value method he discussed in *Appreciation and Interest*. When one combined the calculations based on actuarial tables with the theory of expectations implicit in his account of interest, the economist had a system of valuation that was expansive, theoretically coherent, and, quite possibly, practical as well. The practical potential of the system came from its roots in the everyday operations of actual accountants, whose guidance, Fisher explained, could have saved economists many mistakes. "A little attention to business bookkeeping would have saved economists from such errors [e.g., overlooking the temporal relation between a stock and a flow]; for the keeping of records in business involves a practical if unconscious recognition of the time principle here propounded. The 'capital account' of a railway, for instance, gives the condition of the railway *at a particular instant of time,* and the 'income account' gives its operation *through a period of time*" (*CI* 59–60).

The practical dimension of Fisher's financial view is reinforced by his discussion of the concrete opportunities that affect decisions about consumption: some, such as "invention and discovery" (*TI* 341), pertain to the real economy, while others, such as the kinds of bonds and loans available at a given time, belong to the financial side of the economy. It is important to remember, however, that Fisher's theory of interest was just that—a *theory* that embraced the assumptions central to neoclassical economics: prices are established by supply and demand, the quantity of money does not affect prices, all contracts will be enforced, and all markets will clear. These assumptions were theoretical rather than realistic, but they allowed Fisher to develop a series of self-consistent pictures of how the two sides of the economy interrelate under increasingly complex conditions. The last of these pictures—each of which anticipates what modern economists would call a model—adds the all-important category of uncertainty to the already complex temporality of the interplay between the impatience to consume and the willingness to defer consumption in favor of anticipated future opportunities. As we will see in section 2.7, the distinction between risk and uncertainty was introduced into economic analysis in the years that separated Fisher's early work from *The Theory of Interest*.

Fisher's turn to the future inevitably introduced uncertainty, for the only thing certain about the future is that we do not know what it will bring. In *The Nature of Capital and Income*, Fisher simply conflated uncertainty and risk, and not until the end of the book did he suggest how his method might accommodate this. In a footnote, Fisher referred the reader to works on "the modern statistical application of probability" (*CI* 410). In 1906, these works included Karl Pearson's *Grammar of Science*, Francis Edgeworth's "Mathematical Theory of Banking," and two attempts to apply probability to the futures and money markets (*CI* 410, n. 1). In this work, Fisher did not elaborate his recommendation that economists replace "guessing about future income conditions" with "the modern statistical application of probability," and nothing in the text suggests that he was thinking in the stochastic terms that economists would soon use to manage risk. Indeed, even in 1930, when he returned to the topic, he did not treat risk in any special way. To him, the mere fact that different interest rates obtained at the same time indicated the presence of uncertainty, and, implicitly, they offered a range of ways to deal with risk. When he named the rates he saw in 1930—"quoted rates on call loans, four months prime commercial paper, prime bankers' acceptances, first mortgages, second mortgages, as well as rates given by savings banks, rates allowed on active checking accounts, pawn shop rates, Morris Plan bank rates, rates realized on government bonds, railroad bonds"—he did not link them to strategies for managing risk (*TI* 207). Fisher had no way to theorize uncertainty or risk, nor did he link various interest rates to probability or risk management. This should not surprise us, for Fisher understood the economic world in the deterministic terms that dominated nineteenth-century political economy, and what he sought were economic "laws," not statistical probabilities.

Even if he did not foresee that his discipline would soon embrace probability instead of searching for laws, the definitions and method Fisher introduced did provide the basic terms by which we now understand finance. As we will see in chapter 9, in the late 1930s Jacob Marschak converted Fisher's insights into a model that could be used to price financial assets. Fisher's mode of valuation is also the basis of capital asset pricing theory, which is one of the cornerstones of modern finance. Jack Hirshleifer, the UCLA economist who helped rehabilitate Irving Fisher's reputation in the 1960s, placed Fisher alongside Adam Smith and John Maynard Keynes in emphasizing the role investment psychology plays in price theory. This conceptual reorientation—the turn to the psychology of expectations about the future, which is the basis of modern finance—has always been implicit in the theory of financial assets, but before the ontology of such assets could be elevated to the level of a concept, it had to be abstracted and theorized. Before the ontology of finance could be modeled, turned into new instruments and products, subjected to meaningful regulation, then freed from regulation again, someone had to understand that the very old practice of buying and selling agricultural futures implied a new way of thinking about value and time. Irving Fisher was among the first to formulate these insights, and, even though he did not think in all the terms used by modern financial theorists, he did forge many of the components of modern finance.

2.6. THE QUANTITY THEORY AND THE BANKING VIEW OF MONEY

Before 1911, most American debates about money focused on three topics: the instability of the price level; the inelasticity of bank notes and credit; and the choice of a metallic standard, which, as we have already seen, pitted gold against a bimetallic standard that would reverse the "outrage" of the 1873 demonetization of silver.[45] Even though economists joined the popular debates · about money, however, they did not develop a general theory of a monetary economy. Since they considered money and pricing to be two different sets of issues, they tended to keep discussions of the two separate. Some economists distinguished between "primary" and "credit" money, and most applied the neoclassical theory of supply and demand to the problem of price, but, as Joseph A. Schumpeter remarked, their "model of the economic process was in all essentials a barter model, the working of which inflations and deflations might disturb but which [was] logically complete and autonomous."[46]

The dominant theoretical position regarding money was the so-called "quantity theory of money" (QTM). Formulated in the sixteenth century in response to the impact of New World gold on European prices, this theory held that the money supply has a direct, proportional relationship to the price level: the more money, the higher the overall price level. In the 1890s, in the American context, this theory was used to support bimetallism, but after the defeat of Bryan and the free silver platform, proponents of the QTM began to separate the theory from bimetallism. Arguing in favor of the gold standard but maintaining that some version of the QTM made sense even when banknotes could not be converted to gold, monetary theorists such as Charles Dunbar, Simon Newcomb, and Edwin Walter Kemmerer attempted to supplement the older version of the theory with a more theoretically and mathematically robust analysis. Most notably, in his 1903 thesis, published in 1907 as *Money and Credit Instruments in Their Relation to General Prices,* Kemmerer added to the QTM equations designed to show the velocity of the turnover of money, the volume of bank deposits subject to checking, and the velocity of the turnover of checks. In Kemmerer's mathematical demonstration, prices are a function of the volume of money in circulation (M), the velocity of money circulation (V), the volume of bank deposits subject to checks (M′), the velocity of check turnover (V′), and the volume of trade (T). This new QTM also allowed for the costs of gold production and changes in business confidence.[47]

Irving Fisher also made important, if complicated, contributions to the quantity theory and the debates about the money supply. He did so primarily in *The Purchasing Power of Money* (1911), where he adopted and slightly altered Kemmerer's formulation. Even though Kemmerer's work preceded his, it is Fisher's formulation of the so-called equation of exchange that has proved influential. In a letter to Kemmerer, Fisher explained that his formulation was inspired by a mathematical consideration: when he counted the equations in the account of commodities markets he had given in *Mathematical Investigations,* he realized that an equation was missing. "It was there [in *Mathematical Investigations*] that I noted that the number of equations necessary for determining individual prices in all cases fell short of the number of unknown quantities to be determined, and, as you know, it is a fundamental principle of algebra and of science that the number of independent determining conditions must be equal to the number of unknown quantities to be determined. This leaves room for the equation of exchange to supply the missing equation, and demonstrates in a beautiful mathematical way the importance of the role this equation plays."[48] Fisher's equation of exchange—$MV + M'V' = PT$—supplied the equation missing from the Walrasian general theory of equilibrium because the equilibrium price of money establishes the purchasing power of money, or its inverse—the price level.

Because Fisher believed that the price level was "normally a passive factor" (the effect, rather than a cause, of the other variables), his interpretation of the equation led to the conclusion, as Milton Friedman later phrased it, that "inflation is always and everywhere a monetary phenomenon." According to

Fisher, this conclusion followed the logic of the model. As in any model, certain assumptions were foundational: money is an independent variable (because it is based on the mechanisms of the gold standard, bank credit formation, and the public's habitual use of hand money); velocity is stable in "normal" times (i.e., times that were not "transitional"); and the level of economic activity is a function of other factors like population growth, technology, institutions, and laws. Assuming these conditions, Fisher then constructed his model: if Money increases (exogenously), Velocity is constant, Trade is independent of monetary conditions (when the economy is in equilibrium), and the Price level is "normally the passive element," then a change in Money will lead to a proportional change in Price. This principle is what Fisher's physical model of floating cisterns was also designed to show: as money (water) was added to the tub, all cisterns (commodity prices) rose.

Several scholars have pointed to complexities that undermine the coherence of Fisher's formulation. Schumpeter, for example, argued that because Fisher's quantity theorem obtained only in equilibrium conditions, not "transitional" periods, the equation of exchange has little purchase. "Since the economic system is practically always in a state of transition or disequilibrium, phenomena that *seem* incompatible with the quantity theorem . . . are almost always in evidence." In acknowledging that the factors that directly influence purchasing power (M, V, and T) are themselves influenced by multiple indirect factors, moreover, Fisher seemed to erode the heart of the quantity theorem. Schumpeter's conclusion is that Fisher adopted "a particularly narrow and inadequate, if not actually misleading, form of his own thought" because his primary goal was to defend his proposed solution to the problem of price fluctuation—the compensated-dollar or "100% reserve" plan. "The theory in the *Purchasing Power of Money* is conceived as a scaffolding for statistical work that in turn was to serve a piece of social engineering."[49]

Whatever the limitations of Fisher's version of the quantity theory, the statistical work to which Schumpeter referred did help illuminate the volume of checking account money (M′) in circulation in the century's first decades. Checks had long been used in Europe and Britain, but the United States was quite late to accept this form of money. Checks only began to rival bills of exchange after passage of the National Banking Acts in the 1860s and the federal issue of silver certificates beginning in the 1880s. Once banks multiplied the number of clearinghouses, which enabled checks to circulate more widely, however, the ratio between checks and all other forms of currency increased dramatically: in 1890, total bank deposits were three times the stock of currency; but by 1914, bank deposits had grown to seven times the stock of currency.[50] Meanwhile, the invention of the telegraph helped lower costs associated with the transfer of funds, just as the development of a national railway system had done in previous decades.

Fisher invoked statistics to show the growing role checks were playing in the monetary landscape of the United States, and, by including in his equation of exchange M′ (demand deposits) as well as M (the quantity of money in circulation), he (like Kemmerer) was making room in "money" for checking deposits. In this regard, Fisher differed from many contemporary economists, who were reluctant to call checking deposits money. While Fisher was aware of the importance of checking deposits, however, and even though he offered a sophisticated account of the role these accounts could play in the business cycle, he stopped short of theorizing the role credit more generally might be said to play in the monetary system.[51] Because of the bank fractional reserve system, which allows individual banks to keep on reserve only a fraction of the credit they extend to customers, the modern check is something like a bridge between the money supply and credit. Indeed, as we are about to see, checks could be said both to extend the purchasing power of gold and to create an elastic source of credit that effectively generated further deposits.[52] When individuals keep money in a checking account, they provide bankers resources for extending more credit to others—just as acceptance of checks by shops and clients also represents credit, at least for the brief period before the check is returned to the bank for payment. If an economist were to begin an account of the monetary system with credit instead of money, he would create a picture that differed in important ways from the quantity theory Fisher endorsed. By 1911, a number of economists had taken this approach and, even though their influence on later monetary theorists was indirect, the position they endorsed provides an important alternative to the quantity theory of money.

As Perry Mehrling has pointed out, "in the history of monetary thought, there have always been two basic approaches to the study of money and banking, whether money or banking is taken as the starting point."[53] The approach that begins with money was associated with the QTM, whether in the populist agitation for free silver or the more abstract theorems formulated by Kemmerer and Fisher. The approach that begins with banking, or credit, was associated in the early twentieth century with the Eastern banking interests that united to defeat Bryan and with the economist who helped launch Thorstein Veblen's career at the University of Chicago, J. Laurence Laughlin. As the allusion to Bryan reminds us, in the period, both positions had political as well as theoretical dimensions. They were, in fact, manifestations of a debate about the role banks should play in American society, as well as two sides in a debate among economists about whether monetary phenomena should be included in theoretical models of the economy.

Fisher and Laughlin directly confronted each other at least twice, at the 1904 and 1911 meetings of the American Economic Association. The second meeting is particularly interesting because, in the roundtable that followed the protagonists' addresses, other economists helped draw out the implications of the position Laughlin had been taking since 1903, when he published *Principles of Money*. As chair of his department and founding editor of the *Journal of Political Economy,* Laughlin had had many opportunities to promote his antiquantity-theory views, but, if anything, his position was losing luster by 1911. At the AEA meeting, Fisher circulated copies of part of his forthcoming book (*The Purchasing Power of Money*), and used his allotted time simply to state the position that seemed to him self-evident: "In my opinion the old quantity theory is in essence correct. . . . The general price level will respond in substantial proportion to the volume of money in circulation."[54] Laughlin, who spoke first, devoted part of his paper to "other things" beyond the demand for gold that had affected prices since 1896. These "other things," which the neoclassical economists were able to ignore because of their reliance on *ceteris paribus,* included, according to Laughlin, the "monopolistic combinations" represented by the new corporations. "The whole *raison d'être* of monopolistic combinations is to control prices, and prevent active competition. As every economist knows, in the conditions in which many industries are today organized, expenses of production have no direct relation to prices. In such conditions, there is a field in which the policy of charging 'what the traffic will bear' prevails; and this includes industries that are not public utilities."[55]

While Laughlin's allusion to the trusts drew some comments from his peers, it was his discussion of credit that proved most provocative. Most controversial was his statement that, through banking, "goods are coined into means of payment." "The effect of credit on prices is to be found mainly in banking facilities by which goods are coined into means of payment, so that, expressed in terms of the standard of gold, they may be exchanged against each other. Thus credit devices relieve the standard to an incredibly great degree from the demand for the use of gold as a medium of exchange" (29). This provoked a begrudging concession from F. W. Taussig, who otherwise supported Irving Fisher's position.

Though I would by no means go to the lengths of Professor Laughlin's reasoning, which seems to imply that every act of exchange supplies automatically its own medium of exchange, it does seem to me that our modern mechanism of deposit banking supplies an elastic source of deposits, which, for considerable periods, enables them to run *pari passu* with the transactions and loans resting on them. In the end, an increase of deposits finds its limit in the volume of cash held by the banks. But there is some elasticity of adjustment, by which loans and deposits increase as fast as transactions or faster; and this accounts in no small degree for the rise in prices during periods of activity. The phenomenon shows itself most strikingly in stock exchange loans, especially in a city like New York. There the business creates for itself quasi-automatically its own medium of exchange.[56]

Taussig's qualified praise was amplified by Ralph H. Hess, who applauded the reference to "goods coined into a means of payment." "It is possible that all legitimate market values, under normal trade conditions, may be liquidized through credit agencies, and the goods in which they are incorporated be thus rendered immediately and conveniently exchangeable. This process may be consummated independently of prices and with slight regard to the actual supply of money. The truth of this assertion is, in fact, demonstrated daily in the marks of trade."[57]

Beyond the intradisciplinary squabbling over theory and method, these exchanges reveal battle lines critical to future debates about how—and whether—economic analysis should deal with new media of exchange, like checks, and with banking and credit more generally. If money is treated as an exogenous factor, as Fisher advocated, then financial intermediation falls beneath the horizon of the economist's gaze and credit looks simply like a loan from one party to another. If money is treated as endogenous, as something that can be created through the banking system, then financial intermediation must become a central part of economic analysis. In the 1920s, these two positions were elaborated in the work of Laughlin and Fisher, on the quantity theory side, and by Allyn Young (following Ralph Hawtrey), on the banking or credit view side. In the 1960s, as we will see in chapter 8, they received yet more attention in the face-off between monetarist Milton Friedman and the Keynesian Edward Stone Shaw. As we will see at the end of this book, the dominance of the first position, to the virtual exclusion of the second, meant that disruptive developments within the financial side of the economy generally slipped below the radar of mainstream macroeconomic theorists until the bottom fell out of the global economy in 2008.

2.7. FRANK KNIGHT'S THEORY OF UNCERTAINTY

Frank H. Knight, who received his doctoral degree from Cornell in 1916, joined the economics department at the University of Chicago in 1927. In the 1930s, Knight was a founding member of the "first Chicago School," and in 1947 he was one of the architects of the Mont Pelerin Society, a group of economists, philosophers, and historians dedicated to promoting free market policies and the principles of an open society in the wake of World War II. For our purposes Knight's most important contribution was the primary distinction he drew in the revised version of his dissertation, published in 1921 as *Risk, Uncertainty, and Profit*. This distinction—between risk and uncertainty—was developed in the context of the changes brought about by the giant corporations; it provided a rationale for the outsized rewards received by company promoters and managers; and it helped justify corporate reliance on credit insurance, a form of casualty insurance relatively new in 1921. Paradoxically, one unintended effect of Knight's distinction was to enhance the confidence later economists were to feel in their ability to model increasingly large segments of the economic world, for, as the domain of calculable risk seemed to grow ever larger, uncertainties that could not be modeled seemed to dwindle in number and importance.

Like Irving Fisher, Knight understood uncertainty to be a critical component of economic analysis, and, like Fisher again, he associated this issue with the future orientation of economic processes. The "forward-looking character of the economic process itself" leads to "the uncertainty problem in economics."[58] Unlike Fisher, however, Knight was not content to treat uncertainty as identical to risk or to see both as essentially matters of subjective belief. Instead, Knight distinguished between two kinds of unknowns, one of which could be "reduced to an objective, quantitatively determinate probability" (231–32) and the other of which could not. The first he designated "risk," and the second "uncertainty." For the kinds of unknowns that constitute risk "the distribution of the outcome of a group of instances is known (either through calculations *a priori* or from statistics of past experience)"; the kind of unknowns that belong to uncertainty, by contrast, defy probability distributions—"the reason being in general that it is impossible to form a group of instances, because the situation dealt with is in a high degree unique" (232).

The distinction Knight drew between risk and uncertainty opened onto possibilities few economists were eager to acknowledge, much less explore.

For, even as economists grew comfortable with statistics and probability—techniques that helped them calculate and manage risk—the possibility that the economic world contained events too rare or idiosyncratic to form part of a homogeneous set threatened to undermine any analysis based in mathematics and logic. In the same year that Knight published *Risk, Uncertainty, and Profit,* John Maynard Keynes raised in passing an even more troubling issue: some future events may be categorically unknowable because data-generating processes may not be stationary.[59] As we will see in chapter 7, section 5, this issue surfaced in Keynes's debate with Jan Tinbergen about the confidence with which economists might extrapolate from data sets; but, for the most part, most economists tended to conflate risk and uncertainty and, increasingly, to ignore the possibilities that human knowledge may have its limits or that once-in-a-lifetime events by definition cannot be known. In chapter 10, we will see how later financial theorists in particular began reluctantly to explore these possibilities, but for almost the entire twentieth century, the discipline of economics acquired its characteristic problems and methods by repeatedly pushing them into the background.[60]

Knight's distinction was a theoretical intervention in economic analysis, but it was also a reflection upon—and, implicitly, a rationale for—the new corporate form, especially the large returns reaped by company promoters and corporate managers. Beginning with the observation that, by the time he was writing, the corporation had become "the typical form of business unit in the modern world" (291), Knight showed how this institution distributed risk and increased efficiency, partly by encouraging specialization. Within the corporation, the most important specialization became "uncertainty-bearing," a task that moved, as the corporation developed, from the company promoter or entrepreneur to the manager (259–60). "With the specialization of function goes also a differentiation of reward" (271), Knight continued. Most employees received wages or "contractual income," which was essentially the "rent" paid for their productive power; but the manager received "profit," which was the return for managing risk. "The only 'risk' which leads to a profit is a unique uncertainty resulting from an exercise of ultimate responsibility which in its very nature cannot be insured nor capitalized nor salaried. Profit arises out of the inherent, absolute unpredictability of things, out of the sheer brute fact that the results of human activity cannot be anticipated and then only in so far as even a probability calculation in regard to them is impossible and meaningless" (310–11). Thus profit is a "pure residual income, unimputable by the mechanism of competition to any agent concerned in its creation" (312). And the corporate manager is entitled to profit because only his judgment can steer the company through these incalculable uncertainties. "The powers and attributes of leadership form the most mysterious as well as the most vital endowment which fits the human species for civilized or organized life. . . . It is the margin of error in this most ultimate faculty of judging faculties whose exercise is the essence of responsible control" (311).

If Knight's elaboration of uncertainty justified paying the corporate manager an outsized proportion of a company's income, his association of risk with actuarial categorization and probability distributions implicitly encouraged companies to purchase insurance for all the eventualities they could insure. The insurance industry was quick to respond to the needs of corporations by developing new forms of casualty insurance. Among these were automobile insurance, which insurance companies presented as a hedge against the loss of a top manager, and credit insurance, which was intended to protect assets when debtors reneged on their obligations. In their promotional book on insurance, industry insiders Robert Riegel and Henry James Loman linked insurance to both uncertainty and credit, and, while they were obviously not using Knight's distinction, their celebration of insurance accords with his account of risk. "If all uncertainty could be removed from business, profits would be sure; insurance removes many uncertainties and to that extent is profitable." Riegel and Loman also made explicit something Knight merely implied—that the more companies could increase the proportion of insurable risk to uninsurable uncertainty, the greater their credit and the larger they could grow. "Credit extension is the most important service in modern business life and is contributed to by practically all forms of insurance."[61]

There are passages in Knight's book that lead one to think he was sympathetic to a theoretical approach responsive to historical change, perhaps even to institutional specificity (cf. 271). This impression, however, is misguided. Knight insisted that "the general laws of choice among competing motives or goods are not institutional" and he stated emphatically that "there are no laws governing the *content* of economic behavior, but there are laws universally valid as to its *form.*"[62] His emphasis on form over content anticipates the affinities between his neoclassical approach and mathematical modeling, which economists began to use in the 1930s and 1940s. As we will see, mathematical modeling depends on the existence of a probability distribution; and Knight's attention to risk, albeit less innovative than his elaboration of uncertainty, was to support subsequent efforts to represent more and more aspects of economic activities in the simplified form consistent with mathematical modeling. Indeed, one might say that despite Knight's effort to theorize uncertainty, and with some notable exceptions (like Keynes), most subsequent economists tended to ignore this distinction and to treat more and more situations simply as risk situations subject to probability and to modeling.

One final sense in which Knight departed from Veblen's institutionalism points to the direction orthodox economic theory was to take after 1920. As we have seen, Veblen provided both a historical account of the move from a barter to a credit economy and a picture of modern society that highlighted lasting tensions between two points of view, one that used production to satisfy basic human wants and one that subordinated this aim to the profit motive. Knight's account emphasized the latter, not as a historically specific outcome of the corporate form but as the expression of a universal economic law; in *Risk, Uncertainty, and Profit,* the need to satisfy human wants, even the desire to consume, is pushed aside by a singular desire to increase wealth. "We can hardly over-emphasize the fact that the dynamic urge back of modern economic life is the desire to increase wealth, rather than a desire to consume goods" (320). This, according to Knight, is the insatiable need gratified by uncertainty, through opportunities created by the modern corporations: "The role of uncertainty in connection with capitalization is to make it possible for an individual through superior judgment or good luck to obtain a large increase in his wealth in a short time" (333). Later economists would develop this observation, just as they capitalized on Knight's comments about risk.

2.8. AMERICAN PUBLIC FINANCE: THE PERSONAL INCOME TAX

The theoretical battles among economists, as well as the consensus around neoclassical principles orthodox economists were beginning to forge, were largely staged within the academic discipline—in university hiring decisions, in the pages of professional journals, or at meetings like the ones where Fisher and Laughlin sparred. Economic theories did have an impact upon American life during these decades, however, and the image of finance that emerged in the first three decades of the century was as informed by the American government's fiscal policies as by these theoretical disputes.

The centerpiece of fiscal policy was a campaign to make taxation more progressive. During the long and contentious debates about taxation, proponents of a progressive income tax explicitly used marginalist arguments—and sometimes marginalist economists—to support their claim that progressive taxation was more socially efficient than tariffs and excise taxes, which disproportionately taxed the less wealthy.[63] Even though several scholars have noted that proponents of federal income tax invoked marginalist principles, few have commented on the way the outcome of this campaign legitimized the future-oriented present-value approach theorized by Fisher in *The Nature of Capital and Income.*[64] The same legislation that made interest and dividends taxable, not incidentally, gave the federal government reliable information about these sources of income—both as components of the taxable income of corporations and individuals and as a proportion of what eventually became visible as the "national income."

The decision to pursue a constitutional amendment legalizing a personal income tax was made several years before the 1913 ratification of the sixteenth amendment. It emanated from an agreement reached around 1908 between Senator Nelson W. Aldrich, the powerful chair of the Senate Finance Committee, and newly elected President William H. Taft. Originally, the two men agreed only to preserve existing tariffs, which were generally considered favorable to large companies, and to tax corporations at a moderate rate *instead* of promoting an income tax. Aldrich reportedly lent his support to the corporation tax bill because he assumed that passage of the corporate tax act would end further discussions of an income tax: "I shall vote for a corporation tax as a means to defeat the income tax," he reportedly told Taft.[65] Taft, by contrast, seized on the idea of a moderate corporate excise tax because he thought this tax—unlike an income tax—would withstand judicial review and, in doing so, lay the groundwork for the income tax. Taft wanted to regulate the new corporations, in other words, but his primary agenda was to pass the constitutional amendment that would make an income tax legal as well.

To make an income tax legal, the Constitution had to be amended because Article 1, section 9 ("Limits on Congress"), links any direct taxation of property to "apportionment"—that is, direct taxes must be proportionately divided among the states according to population. Taft and the legislators who supported taxing income thought a corporate tax would escape the judicial censure that had voided the 1894 income tax because the corporate tax was an indirect tax, not a direct tax. Led by the Democratic first-term member from Tennessee, Cordell Hull, congressional supporters went even further: they argued that exempting intangibles from the property subject to taxation would be unfair. While they successfully argued that interest and dividends should be taxed, both for corporations and individuals, the primary goal of the tax proponents was not to shift the basis of valuation to financial assets, whose value derived from expectations about the future. To today's readers, what the income tax supporters wanted to do seems even more radical than valuing expectations, for their goal was to use taxation to redistribute wealth.[66] In this campaign, the wealth held by the giant corporations seemed like low-hanging fruit, for corporations had been implicitly shielded from federal taxation by Washington's reliance on tariffs, but, as we have seen, their outsized wealth was beginning to arouse popular objections.[67] Passing the Corporation Income Tax Act in 1909 promised to kill two birds with one stone: the legislation targeted the corporations, and it set a precedent for a personal income tax—the measure achieved by the ratification of the Sixteenth Amendment in 1913.

The Corporation Income Tax Act of 1909 may have made corporate assets subject to federal taxation, but the bite it took out of corporate wealth was relatively small: the act established a flat tax rate of 1% on every corporation's "entire net income over and above five thousand dollars." While this rendered "income" a taxable asset under federal law, it also set off a fierce debate about how to define—and account for—this new resource, for the act did not specify how income was to be defined or how net income was to be calculated.[68] For our purposes, the intricacies of the ensuing debates are less important than the mechanism by which a decision (of sorts) was eventually reached. In the end, there were several judicial decisions rather a single, definitive answer, and various courts, including but not limited to the Supreme Court, played a more important role in defining corporate net income than economic theorists, accountancy professors, or politicians. While the Supreme Court decision in the 1920 *Eisner v. Macomber* case is usually cited as establishing "the classic legal definition of income," subsequent court rulings took issue with parts of this decision—and continue to do so. Willard J. Graham, professor of accounting at the University of North Carolina, noted in 1965 that between 1920 and the mid-1960s, state courts regularly disagreed about how to define income. Indeed, Graham argued that using court decisions to define "business income" is futile—even though these decisions *did and still do* establish the parameters within which decisions are made about the corporate income subject to federal taxation: "There is no one legal concept of business income. The courts are concerned with the intent of the various statutes and not with what the measurement of income ought to be."[69]

Debates about how to define income and how (and whether) to break out net income from gross also reverberated throughout discussions of national aggregates in the 1930s, as we will see in chapter 6. For present purposes, it is enough to note that in making corporate income taxable, however it was defined, the Corporate Income Tax Act of 1909 made Fisher's redefinition of this concept relevant, for both this act and the personal income legislation that followed included financial assets—interest, dividends, and rent—in the income to be taxed. When ratification of the Sixteenth Amendment abolished the constitutional mandate that individual taxation be apportioned among states by population, moreover, it set aside one kind of aggregate ("state population"), thus clearing the way for another kind of aggregation, this one associated with *national* income and production "sectors" and "industries." We should also note that, by later standards, the income taxes levied by these two pieces of legislation were minimal. Like corporations, individuals' net incomes over $3000 were subject to a federal tax of only 1%. If an individual's net income reached $500,000, a 6% surcharge was levied. Whatever ideas about wealth redistribution the laws' supporters nourished, the amount of money the new taxes sent to the federal government was relatively small, and, as we are about to see, subsequent measures decreased tax rates even more, as arguments by marginalist economists convinced the taxable public that greater efficiency at the margin meant greater overall returns.

The aftermath of passage of the corporate and individual income tax acts allows us to see the institutional and cultural framework within which economists operated in the 1910s. It also reveals how marginalist theory and the sophisticated mathematics associated with mathematical economics eventually came to be fused to corporate accounting methods; one by-product was a dramatic increase in the number of accountants involved in corporate governance and, as public accountants and national statisticians, in management of the data generated by the new tax laws. As the United States moved toward engagement in World War I, the challenge of defining income and related taxable categories passed from the courts, where previous decisions had been exclusively made, to at least some economists, for the federal government increasingly sought expert advice about what made theoretical, not just legal, sense. Specifically, Washington turned to economists in 1917, when the country decided not to follow Britain's example of using a context-defined "wartime" tax to finance the military campaign. Instead, President Wilson decided to impose a temporary "excess profits" tax to make corporations that seemed to be profiting unduly from the war pay their fair share. Once the United States decided not to adopt the British tax strategy, it faced the problem of identifying which profits were "excess," and this required someone to figure out what "normal" profits were. William G. McAdoo, secretary of the treasury, decided that a university economist was the person to make this decision, and he chose T. S. Adams of Yale. Adams's contribution was important because he brought economists into the political decision-making process. In the end, however, economists did not play the decisive role that McAdoo—and, presumably, many economists—had hoped they would. By the end of 1919, Adams concluded that it was impossible for economists to agree on how to define the "normal" rate of corporate profit so that the government could tax the "excess."[70]

Accountancy theorists played an even more marginal role in defining income in this period, even though their profession ultimately benefited more from the US adoption of income taxes than did the profession of economics. In his 1922 textbook on corporate accounting, William Paton repeatedly refused to provide an unambiguous definition of "gross income" or "net income" (much less "excess profits"). Paton agreed that such issues were critical to the accountant's work—"the development of methods by which the amount of gross earnings may be determined on a rational basis is one of the most serious tasks facing the accountant," he wrote; but he repeatedly backed off the possibility that such a method could be standardized. After devoting chapters to the complications that bedeviled accountants' efforts to establish standard methods and definitions—the preponderance of credit sales, for example, as well as the possibility that stocks on hand could depreciate in value—Paton finally rejected the idea of standards in favor of an appeal to the "full knowledge" that would yield "reasonable results": "all things considered."[71] Despite the absence of an industry-wide standard, accountants as a group benefited from the new tax provisions, for the 1909 Corporate Tax Act made accountants more necessary than ever to corporations, and, as the number of accountants increased, the profession developed increasingly differentiated specialties, like tax accountancy and new variants of public accountancy.

The need to define income for tax purposes also provided the context in which marginalist theories were marketed to government officials and the general public. In some cases, economists directly promoted marginalist assumptions about value, as when T. S. Adams served as a consultant for the Treasury Department, or when J. B. Clark publicly supported progressive taxation in the *New York Times* in 1924; later, Irving Fisher also entered the debate about taxes with his own marginalist views, published as *Constructive Income Taxation* (1942). Indeed, as Mary Murname has argued, the campaign waged in the 1920s to adopt progressive, but *lower,* corporate and individual income tax rates also promoted marginalist ideas, this time substituting for the redistribution argument used in 1909 an argument about *efficiency* taken straight from the pages of the marginalists. The campaign organized to support the Mellon tax plan, and run by new Treasury Secretary Andrew W. Mellon himself, presented marginalist ideas as a commonsense way to think about taxation. If the federal government lowered the top income tax rate for individuals from 77% to 24%, proponents argued, then more people would be willing to pay what they owed and the overall revenue of the government would rise. Constant improvement of efficiency at the margin, Mellon argued, would benefit everyone in the long run. As we see in the repeal of the "excess profits" tax, the triumph of marginalist assumptions even ended the need to define a "normal" rate of profit so that the "excess" could be taxed, for, according to marginalist theorists like Clark, there was no normal rate of profit in a society where competition flourished.[72]

In almost all the debates about defining income after 1909—legal, theoretical, and political—we see the decisive turn to the future introduced by Irving Fisher's financial view. When, for example, the economist E. R. Seligman argued in 1917 that a corporation's "capital" is "the capitalization not only of present income, but of anticipated future income," we hear echoes of Fisher and the logic of financial assets.[73] When the concept of par value was rejected in favor of value that included a discounted stream of future earnings to establish the price of a company's shares, we hear this too. And when we see arguments in favor of the 1920s Mellon tax reform that insisted that high taxes would reduce the value of property by reducing the value of future income, we hear the financial view again. By the end of the First World War, as the federal government began to derive the preponderance of its revenue from income taxes, both corporate and individual, the epistemological shift Fisher inaugurated was well underway. By this time, as we are about to see, the streams of data generated by the new system of taxation had also begun to alter economic theory and practice again, this time through a system of accounting that could measure the wealth of the nation, not just that of its corporations and citizens.

CHAPTER 3

Statistics in America and the Governance of the Modern State

In the first three decades of the twentieth century, government policies intended to address economic issues had something of an *ad hoc* quality. Some, like the Mellon tax plan, drew support from economic theory, but most articulated a hodgepodge of lessons learned from history, ideological conviction, and political expediency. The ability to visualize economic processes and create policies that could respond to or manage them awaited the development of techniques capable of presenting aggregate information in an understandable form. Today, we take for granted the power of "big data," but in the first decades of the century, the scant data that was routinely collected could not be used or augmented until statistical tools, case studies, index numbers, and now-discredited techniques such as economic barometers were refined and made palatable to academics and politicians alike. While the earliest applications of these tools involved prices, they were typically used to illuminate the real, rather than the financial, side of the economy; and when, in 1921, a comprehensive depiction of the financial organization of the United States appeared, its copious information was presented in narrative, not statistical form. As we will see in chapter 4, only with the explosion of securities trading in the mid-1920s were the techniques we describe here used to make finance visible.

3.1. THE STATISTICAL THEORY OF DEMAND

The frustration Irving Fisher expressed about the statistical tools available in 1911 speaks to the balkanization of the disciplines in early twentieth-century

America. Sophisticated statistical work was being done as early as the 1880s, but most of this research was conducted by agronomists, geneticists, and biologists, not by economists, and most people working on the leading edge of statistical analysis were in Britain or Europe.[1] In the United States, a professional organization—the American Statistical Association (ASA)—had existed since 1839, but its influence was negligible: as late as 1909, S. N. D. North, the association's incoming president, complained that the organization "has furnished little direct stimulus to statistical work, has suggested no new methods of procedure, and has not been a rallying point for young men and women who realize the possibilities and the opportunities of this field."[2] Because the data sets statisticians relied on did not exist for earlier periods, North continued, economists trained in the historical school typically did not find statistics useful, and he knew of only one political economist—General Francis A. Walker—who taught statistics in his economics courses.[3]

Indeed, statistics was barely taught at all in American universities, for, apart from Walker, most social scientists did not consider statistics an academic subject.[4] Instead, they associated statistics with the government—with the census, attempts to address labor unrest, and disease maps. Thus, when Henry Ludwell Moore, who had studied economics with J. B. Clark and statistics (briefly) with Karl Pearson in England, set out to elevate the status of statistics, he had to counter skepticism about the discipline's association with the politics of Washington and the shady world of gambling. He also had to locate sources of data sufficiently reliable to make his results seem authoritative.

Moore's primary contribution was to combine neoclassical marginalist theory with a suite of sophisticated statistical tools. His marginalism is apparent from his first major publication, *Laws of Wages: An Essay in Statistical Economics* (1911). Here he engaged the kind of ethical issue Clark had addressed but used statistics to give his analysis the scientific rigor Clark was not always able to achieve. Implicit in Moore's work was the question of whether the government should address workers' complaints about wages by establishing a minimum wage. His explicit analysis, however, focused on workers' strikes: he tested whether strikes exhibit statistical regularities and, if so, whether they could be considered "successful." Based on data drawn from 1881 through 1905, Moore concluded that strikes were "successful" when the workers' stated agenda was to increase their union representation but they were only successful in certain cases when workers were trying to raise wages. And, in confirmation of marginalist theory, he found that strikes were "unsuccessful" when the average wage rate was over the norm and "successful" when the rate was below the norm.[5]

Moore considered himself a "statistical economist," who "proceeds by a progressive synthesis from individual facts to general facts, and from general facts to statistical laws. He expresses the laws in their mathematical form, and, where it is possible, he measures the degrees of association between the related phenomena, expressing them as coefficients of correlation, correlation ratios, or coefficients of contingency, as the case may be" (*Wages* 173). Correlation allowed Moore to measure the relationships among variables; and the simultaneous equation method made it possible to show the inter-relations of multiple factors "in all their complexity" (*Wages* 2). These methods were to become central to the Econometric Society in the 1930s and 1940s.

In *Laws of Wages*, Moore used simple correlation, partial correlation, and regression analysis to link wages to other economic factors. In 1914 he expanded his array of statistical techniques to include multiple correlation, relative changes, and trend ratios. In *Economic Cycles: Their Law and Cause*, Moore produced what Henry Schultz called "the first definitive attack on the problem of deriving the elasticity of demand from statistics." Moore "obtained equations expressing the relations between the quantities demanded and the prices of corn, hay, oats, and potatoes; determined the precision of these equations as formulas for estimating prices; and measured the elasticity of demand for each crop."[6] In *Forecasting the Yield and Price of Cotton* (1917), Moore applied these statistical tools, along with multiple regression and correlation, to cotton prices. This enabled him to create a statistical theory of demand that appealed to both statisticians and economic theorists.

Such tools were not unheard of among agricultural economists of the period, but, as an economist at Columbia University, Moore was in a unique position to promote them to economists in general. He did so by demonstrating that his methods were superior to those currently used by the US government. Moore argued that the US Department of Agriculture's annual crop reports were unreliable because its methods were unscientific: there were no clear definitions of how to measure yield, no one visited the cotton farmers to make sure their reports were accurate, and, most importantly, the government measured only average yields for designated geographical regions and failed to factor change over time into the averages.[7] The result, Moore charged, were imprecise figures and a static picture of prices. This static picture, he continued, repeated the limitation of most economic theory, which was "confined to normalities within an hypothetical, static state" (*Forecasting* 9). For Moore, the reliance on *hypothetical*—i.e., non-data-based—assumptions was as flawed as the *static* picture generated by most economists, and the only way to move forward was to use reliable statistical data and mathematical methods. In one of the few uses of the phrase "mathematical models" we have found in early American economists' writing, Moore made his methodological commitment clear: "The only adequate means of exploiting raw statistics are mathematical models" (*Forecasting* 1).[8]

To improve upon the Department of Agriculture's figures about cotton yields, Moore turned to the Weather Bureau's reports about rainfall and temperatures in the cotton-growing states. The weather bureau reports allowed Moore to provide for the price—or demand[9]—side of the marginalist equation an even greater degree of precision than the government claimed to provide for the supply side (*Forecasting* 10). But Moore's work also targeted the financial implications of the government's misleading data, for he saw that, when the government issued reports, prices on the futures exchanges responded, as speculators bid up or down the price of cotton based on the misleading information printed in the government's *Crop Reporter*. Moore wanted to limit the play of speculation by introducing mathematical methods for more rational trading. "Mathematical methods of probability reduce to system the extraction of truth contained in the official statistics and enable the informed trader to compute, with relative exactitude, the influence upon prices of routine market factors" (*Forecasting* 2).

Forecasting the Yield and Price of Cotton set out in some detail how Moore's statistical mathematics actually worked. First, he assembled the data by presenting it in both tabular and graphical forms. The latter displays the frequency distribution and mean distribution of the data points in scatter graphs, as well as the smooth curves that connect, and thus make sense of, the data points. Second, he translated these geometrical representations into mathematical equations, using both the methodology and symbols of algebra. This involved a series of mathematical theorems, which he assumed in order to guide his mathematical calculations, and mathematical propositions, which he proved. Finally, he worked out the calculations using a range of statistical techniques, which had been developed in connection with the theory of probability popular in the early twentieth century. These included inverse probability techniques, which were designed to estimate the accuracy of the data sample;[10] correlation, by which the relationships either between two or among multiple interdependent factors were represented mathematically; and periodic variation, the correlation of time series that allowed the statistician to determine whether fluctuations, like those in the prices of cotton, were regular (periodic) or not. In addition, Moore used index numbers, to which we return in a moment, to render price and yield data manageable.

These statistical techniques revealed what Moore held to be "empirical laws." These differed from the natural laws Clark and Fisher assumed to be inherent in economic processes; following the principles laid out by Francis Galton and Karl Pearson, Moore presented statistical laws as regularities observable in aggregate phenomena. Because these regularities were empirically observable—given adequate data—they could be used to test the adequacy of the economist's theoretical formulations. Moore emphasized how radical his method was when he contrasted his "statistical theory of multiple correlation" with what he considered to be the most advanced economic method then available: "mathematical economics." We can assume that Moore was alluding to work like Fisher's (even if this seems to oversimplify Fisher's contribution).

> The mathematical method begins with an ultra-hypothetical construction and then, by successive compilations, approaches a theoretical description of the concrete goal. The method of multiple correlation reverses the process: It begins with concrete reality in all of its natural complexity and proceeds to segregate the important factors, to measure their relative strength, and to ascertain the laws according to which they produce their joint effect. [By doing so, the latter method] invests the findings of deductive economics with "the reality and life of fact"; it is the Statistical Complement of Deductive Economics. (*Forecasting* 173)

Not every economist agreed with Moore's contention that statistics could "complement" economic theory. Wesley Clair Mitchell, who also advocated basing economic practice on data, thought that statistical methods were valuable precisely because they challenged theory. Whatever relationship individual economists were to advocate between statistical technique and theory, Moore did help make the "statistical estimation of economic functions an integral part of modern economics," as George Stigler later argued.[11] The correlation techniques he advocated were also to become a cornerstone of the Capital Asset Pricing Model, one of the foundations of modern finance.

3.2. THE HARVARD BUSINESS SCHOOL CASE METHOD

In the early twentieth century, Moore's statistical methods constituted only one approach to the challenge of producing usable aggregates. Another was the case method developed in the Harvard Business School. Even more than Moore's statistical approach, the case method was promoted in the name of "science" and was a deliberate effort to enhance the status of the social sciences.[12] In 1913, Jerome Greene, who had served as secretary to the Harvard Corporation, recommended creating an economic institute that "could do for the social sciences what the Rockefeller Institute had already done for medical science"—that is, put these disciplines on a scientific basis by associating them with reliable, impartial data.[13] Greene approached Edwin F. Gay, dean of the recently founded Harvard Business School (HBS), who had also lobbied for an economic counterpart to the Rockefeller Institute. As dean of a fledgling professional school, Gay was seeking creative ways to run an academic program that lacked adequate financial resources and respect. While the economic institute envisioned by Greene and Gay did not come into being until 1920—and then not as an academic organization—the innovations introduced at HBS did begin to address the problems that insufficient data posed for the social sciences and for business interests alike. When the National Bureau of Economic Research (NBER) was finally created, it employed many of the strategies first developed in the business classrooms at Harvard. Among these was an approach to the data problem that combined the priorities of engineers with a commitment to embedding the results of empirical research in new modes of generalization and aggregation.

Without enough money to hire a full-time faculty, Gay had from the beginning relied on part-time instructors to construct and teach the business curriculum at Harvard. One of these part-timers—Frederick Winslow Taylor—was the gang boss at the Midvale Steel Company's Philadelphia plant. Taylor, who soon became famous for the engineering approach to factory production known as "scientific management," brought to the HBS classroom an emphasis on using careful data collection, standardized manufacturing processes, and a disciplined accounting system to increase a business's productivity. By minimizing waste and maximizing efficiency, Taylor's scientific management was designed to marry information to output and, not incidentally, to make data usable for those who wanted either to sell products or to develop theoretical principles for business instruction.

Taylor's engineering priorities meshed well with Gay's visionary definition of "business" as "the job of *making things (utilities) to sell at a profit— decently.*" This job, according to Gay, required courage, judgment, and "sympathetic tact . . . a kindness of spirit which . . . purifies courage by removing its grossest belligerency and tempers judgment by the understanding heart."[14] The method by which Gay sought to engage the businessman's courage, judgment, and tact was a variant of the case method, which Gay had borrowed from the Harvard Law School. Because no business cases equivalent to judicial cases were available, Gay adopted a "more modest" approach. "Why not ask the businessmen visitors, or the faculty members when they become competent, to present the class with some specific problem and the conditions surrounding it," Gay suggested. "Let the students wrestle with it and submit in writing their suggestions for handling it. Their efforts would form the basis for a critical examination of the whole matter at a subsequent class." To this classroom exercise, which Gay's biographer calls the "problem approach," instructors soon added a "project approach," which required students to visit a factory or company to immerse themselves in its manufacturing and decision-making processes. The project approach was intended to give students firsthand exposure to business and counter the charge that business students were being taught too many abstract theories.[15]

The inductive, data-driven, problem-oriented approach that combined scientific management with hands-on experience was further elaborated when Arch W. Shaw joined the HBS faculty. As the editor of the journal *System*, Shaw had long crusaded to improve business practices. Gay sent Shaw to the Harvard Law School to study the case method, and Shaw soon refined the business-school version of this approach, which he then disseminated in *Approach to Business Problems*, a textbook published in 1916 and adopted by nearly every business school in the country. The book recommended training students with living cases rather than written ones, and it emphasized both the importance of standardized accounting practices and the problem-oriented approach to production and management associated with scientific management and engineering. Shaw also recommended using statistical analysis to make the data collected on-site usable. In June 1909, Shaw lobbied the HBS to create a Bureau of Business Research, whose first project was a statistical response to the request by shoe manufacturers and distributors to study "the spread between factory cost and retail price" of shoes. What the HBS investigators discovered was that they had to create a uniform system of accounting for the shoe industry as a whole before they could collect or analyze data from individual companies. After doing so, the HBS Bureau produced in 1912 "the first standardized cost-analyzing plan in the country." As Gay's biographer notes, this was the last of the marketing projects undertaken by HBS before the war, for lack of funding curtailed further research until 1920.[16]

In the HBS combination of scientific management, a case-method approach to research, a standardized accounting system, and descriptive statistics, we see the germs of the approach taken to data by the government's war commissions and the young NBER. In the initial shoe project, moreover, we see the claim that an inductive method that extracts and statistically analyzes data embedded in individual cases will yield results that are more generally useful: the on-site research that generated information about the cost of manufacturing shoes in particular factories would presumably be useful to the shoe industry as a whole. But the HBS shoe project also alerts us to two issues that continued to haunt this approach. From the point of view of a single industry, like the shoe-making industry, the first issue was legal: if every shoemaker knew how his competitors factored costs into prices, there would be little incentive to innovate because no one could establish a competitive price advantage. In legal terms, as the US Justice Department insisted, the price fixing that might follow would violate the Sherman antitrust law. The second issue emanates from scaling up—in this case from a single shoemaker to the industry as a whole, but, more generally, from a single industry to American industry in general. Once the scale of aggregation increased, how could the analyst create usable aggregates from units that were heterogeneous, partial, and measured differently? Both these issues came to the fore during America's engagement in the European war, and, in some ways, they were resolved by economists' turn to index numbers and estimation techniques.

3.3. STATE DATA COLLECTION

The need to collect more data—and, by extension, to address the kind of problems associated with the case method—was felt as soon as America began preparing to enter the European war. In January 1917, in the wake of the sinking of seven American merchant ships by German submarines, the US government realized it lacked the information about its own maritime and productive capacities needed to begin mobilization. In March of that year, a month before Congress officially declared war, President Wilson addressed the problem of insufficient data by creating the Commercial Economy Board; he charged it with both collecting information about existing productivity and eliminating waste in commercial enterprises. Gay served as a member of the board, but in December he shifted his efforts to the Shipping Board, whose task was to gather more information with an eye to sending American troops to France. In February 1918, the Shipping Board began to work with the War Trade Board, which had been created four months earlier. Gay was asked to create a Division of Planning and Statistics within the Shipping Board to manage the information it gathered about ships and imports. Within the space of only a few months, then, the lack of information necessary to mobilize a war effort had given way to a new challenge: how to use the data now flooding into government agencies.

Edwin Gay was not the only academic drawn into government service by the war. Wesley Clair Mitchell, an economist whose reputation had been established by his first three books—on greenbacks (1903), the relationships among gold, prices, and wages (1908), and business cycles (1913)—served as chair of the Price Division of the War Industries Board (WIB), a commission created in July 1917 to coordinate the purchase and distribution of war supplies, set production quotas, and negotiate price and labor disputes. Mitchell had studied economics at the University of Chicago and joined Columbia University's economics department in 1913. Even before moving to Columbia, Mitchell worried that "one of the great sources of weakness in economics" was theorists' willingness to content themselves with "plausible speculations, attractively presented, instead of insisting on putting their ideas to the final test of correspondence with the facts as they are known."[17] Hoping to correct this weakness, Mitchell devoted his life to collecting data, meditating on the modes by which it could be rendered useful, identifying statisticians trained to apply the latest statistical techniques, and institutionalizing a team approach to solving the data problem.

Mitchell's efforts at WIB were to yield some of the first collections of large-scale price data made public after the war. This price data, once more, was designed to illuminate the real side of the economy, and the release of data also materially affected real production. Advocating at a national level the procedures also promoted by Taylor's scientific management—mass production, standardization, uniform accounting measures, and statistical analysis—the WIB helped increase the level of US production 20% during the war years. In June 1918, the government created a Central Bureau of Planning and Statistics, whose members included Gay, and the Central Bureau soon set up a Statistical Clearing House to organize the responses to its questionnaires. At the end of the war, Gay and Mitchell urged President Wilson to make the Central Bureau a permanent part of government, but, even though the Bureau was charged with one important interwar project (gathering US economic data for the international peace conference), it was not funded after April 1920, and the data-gathering initiative to which Gay and Mitchell contributed had to be taken over by nongovernmental agencies. In 1921, Congress established a Budget Bureau, in the Treasury, whose activities were largely those Gay had envisioned for the Central Bureau. Frustrated by the government's failure to support the Central Bureau, Gay and Mitchell resurrected earlier plans for an independent data-gathering institution and, with the short-term support of the Commonwealth Fund, they founded the National Bureau of Economic Research in 1920.

3.4. INDEX CONSTRUCTION AND
THE DISSEMINATION OF DATA

As important as gathering, aggregating, and managing new data was devising the best way to disseminate it to groups who could put it to good use, especially in the postwar context. The Government Printing Office, which was charged with publishing wartime data, began printing the *Survey of Current Business* in 1921. The *Survey of Current Business*, which is still issued today, was sponsored by the Department of Commerce, under Herbert Hoover's leadership, and "conducted" by the Bureau of the Census, the Bureau of Foreign and Domestic Commerce, and the Bureau of Standards. This report can be taken as representative of the government efforts to collect, arrange, and disseminate what was rapidly becoming an avalanche of wartime data. Instrumental to this effort were index numbers, which use statistical techniques to create a series of aggregate figures that show the behavior of prices, industries, or segments of the economy over time.[18] As we will see in chapter 3, section 6, economists initially disputed the best way to construct index numbers, but even before these disagreements subsided, the texts in which they appeared helped Americans learn to read indexes, and they helped make index numbers seem like the obvious way to make aggregate data usable.

A brief review of index numbers will pay dividends throughout the remainder of this book, for the problems inherent in index-number construction resurface in the next topics we address—sample theory, the statistical concept of the frequency distribution, and Alfred A. Cowles III's analysis of stock market forecasting—and return again in our discussion of the Econometric Society. The naturalization of this construction, moreover—the effacement of the once-contested aspects of index numbers for most of their users—epitomizes the extent to which nearly all economic methods, including those central to modern finance, rest on a kind of cultural amnesia. The index numbers that were generated during World War I were not the first of their kind, nor was the use to which they were put—to represent changes in the relationship between the real and financial sides of the economy—the only function index numbers can serve. But this kind of index number plays such a prominent role in modern economies that we restrict our observation to the price/quantity index numbers, which became the common type after 1900.[19]

Three kinds of data make up every economic transaction: time, price, and quantity. To depict relationships between phenomena in the real side of the economy—such as the total number of bushels of wheat sold—and terms associated with the financial side of the economy—such as the average prices paid for this wheat—the economist constructs an index number, which puts these two factors together in the form of a ratio of the two statistical aggregates. The time component is captured by putting the index numbers into a time series, which shows change over time. The index constructed from these elements—such as the Dow Jones Industrial Index (first published in May 1896)—only shows the price side of the composite *or* the quantity (volume) side: you can have a price index or a quantity index but not both together. As a price index, the Dow has nothing to say about the volume of underlying shares that have been traded.

Because most index numbers combine two kinds of measures—like quantity and price measures—putting the two components together poses a problem: how can one represent in a single number entities measured in different kinds of units? This is the conundrum Ragnar Frisch famously designated "the index-number problem": "The index-number problem arises whenever we want a quantitative expression for a *complex* that is made up of individual measurements for which no common *physical* unit exists. The desire to unite such measurements and the fact that this cannot be done by using physical or technical principles of comparison only, constitutes the essence of the index-number problem and all the difficulties center here."[20]

This problem can be addressed—although not completely solved—by highlighting the ratio between the two parts of the complex rather than the discrepancy between the two measurement units. The ratio between the two parts assumes prominence when the index number—the number that brings the two parts together—is represented as another ratio, this time of whatever point is used as a base in the time series. By constructing a continuous sequence divided into equal segments that represent temporal units (e.g., years or months) and by choosing one point in this sequence to represent the base, the analyst is able to graph the individual index numbers in relation to the base, which is conventionally given the value of 100 so departures from it can be figured as percentages. Changes in the values of the graphed index numbers are thus represented not in physical or price units but simply as a single number: a ratio or percentage of 100. As ratios and when placed in a series showing changes over time, the index numbers collectively reveal the general *tendency* captured by the changes in the values of the numbers. The resulting graph thus allows someone to see this tendency by the rise or fall of a line in relation to the axes of the graph.

Each phase of the index number construction process involves decisions that are simultaneously theoretical and interpretive—and that disappear completely from typical descriptions of the index numbers or time series themselves. Someone must decide how many data points constitute an adequate sample, when the average will be taken, whether the data points captured by the index number will be weighted (and, if so, according to what principle), what intervals constitute the time series, and whether these intervals are homogeneous. Analysts use technical terms to indicate the mathematical and statistical processes by which these decisions are made—for example, averaging, smoothing, trend fitting, regression—but, even though these terms have agreed-upon mathematical and statistical meanings, they also mask the numerous senses in which the resulting numbers, which seem so commonsensical now, are thoroughly imbued with theoretical and interpretive assumptions. When we see a methodologically self-aware commentator like Harvard's Warren Persons state blandly that "each item of each series . . . is a total or average or relative number applying to a definite period of time," we see the process of naturalization at work: the differences between "total," "average," and "relative number" are minimized as he subordinates them to the precision of that "definite" period of time.[21]

During the period we examine here—before the creation of national accounts—index numbers and time series were routinely used to construct general accounts of business conditions—or, one might say, to construct what counted as a picture of overall business for the purpose of the companies, agencies, and individuals who wanted to know about commerce in these terms. These methods underwrote the statistical descriptive approach used in the HBS shoe study, the work of the war commissions, and the NBER work overseen by Mitchell. As we will shortly see, another group of economists would soon add probabilistic elements to these early methods in order to use inferences to make predictions in conditions of uncertainty. As this transition from descriptive to inferential statistics occurred, and as a result of the introduction of new theories about the nature of mathematics and measurement, the epistemological status of empirical data and the theory of empiricism profoundly changed as well. The treatment of data in the modern financial model is based on these momentous changes.

To see how completely and rapidly index numbers were naturalized, it is useful to examine the first issue of the *Survey of Current Business*. This issue consists almost exclusively of tables, each of which displays columns of figures that indicate how various prices have changed over time. No discursive narrative guides the reader through these tables, for, according to the introduction, the way they are constructed enables the reader "to see at a glance the general upward or downward tendency of a movement, which can not so easily be grasped from actual figures." Being able to "see" information in this manner, the authors continue, "will assist in the enlargement of business judgment."[22]

Hoover wanted the information contained in the *Survey of Current Business* to encourage private businesses to help improve the nation's overall economy. Hoover assumed that if business leaders had a better understanding of the nationwide production and sales of various commodities, they would tailor their own activities accordingly. Calibrating the output of individual companies to the demand of the market, in turn, would help ease the short-run but serious price and employment fluctuations that surfaced after the war and, some feared, made the United States vulnerable to labor uprisings and bolshevism.[23] According to Hoover, making information generally available would allow the business sector to govern itself and loosen the stranglehold of big banks and corporations. "To be of value such information must be widely diffused and digested by the business men of the country. It is not enough that the banks and the big business concerns should understand the trends in business; the small manufacturer and the small dealer must have some understanding, too, so that there may be some semblance of unity in action. The Department hopes to reach this audience by offering to them these data" (*Survey* 3).

While most of the data included in the *Survey* concerned the real side of the economy, a few tables did illuminate the financial side. This is the case of a table about bank clearings in New York, which the authors offered as a guide to reading the tables more generally.

Take the figures in the first column of Table 2, which deals with the bank clearings in New York City as reported monthly by Bradstreet. In 1913 the average monthly clearing amounted to $7,886,000,000. This number is allowed to equal 100 on our relative scale. In January, 1920, the total bank clearings were $23,210,000,000, or equivalent to a relative number of 294, when the 1913 average is taken as 100. In June, 1921, bank clearings in New York City were only $16,849,000,000, or on the relative basis only 214. By subtracting 100 from any relative number we obtain at once the per cent increase or decrease above or below the base year. Thus bank clearings in January, 1920, were 194 per cent above the 1913 average, and in June, 1921, they were 114 per cent above the same base. In the number of business failures, as reported in column 3 of Table 2, the relative number for January, 1920, is 43, indicating a decrease for that month of 57 per cent below the 1913 monthly average. (*Survey* 3)

In passing, the authors acknowledged that constructing these figures involved further complexities, but they noted, without elaborating, the decisions their authors made. "In many instances the basic statistics do not go back to the prewar years and, in such cases, averages for the year 1919 have been taken as a base. In a few other cases still other base years have been used for special purposes. . . . Certain commodity movements, such as the production of cottonseed oil, cold-storage holdings, etc., are very seasonal in character. In calculating the index numbers no allowance has been made for this, since it was thought better to let this fact show in the relative figures themselves" (*Survey 3*).

Technically speaking, this passage does not contain index numbers, for its numbers record the sums in dollars that cleared the banks each month, not aggregates of prices and quantities. But the *Survey*'s authors used the index number format (the system of *number relatives*) because it facilitated the comparison they wanted readers to see, and they called their figures "index numbers" because, even by 1921, this term was what readers were looking for. Indeed, the very fact that the *Survey*'s authors could use "index numbers" to refer to a figure that was *not* constructed through the complex process we have described indicates that the process of naturalization was already well underway in 1921 and that discretionary decisions largely passed unnoticed. The *Survey* also contributed to naturalization, of course—paradoxically, even for numbers that resembled, but were not, index numbers in a technical sense.[24]

By presenting only tables of figures, the *Survey* also marginalized the legal and technical issues involved in collecting the data in the first place. The only reference to the contentious campaign Hoover waged to convince trade associations to divulge information is the bland disclaimer that the Department of Commerce "assumes no responsibility" for the "accuracy or correctness" of the numbers (*Survey 3*). We know, however, that Hoover had not only to convince individual businesses to release what they considered proprietary information but also to counter the Justice Department's efforts to restrict this release in the name of free enterprise. Just as President Taft had wanted to use publicity, along with taxation, to control the worst excesses of the corporations, so Hoover believed that making data public would foster healthy competition. To advance this agenda while he was secretary of commerce, Hoover appointed an Advisory Committee on Statistics, with Mitchell, Gay, and other wartime economists as members, and this committee, not surprisingly, urged Hoover to strengthen the government's statistical services. The *Survey* was one response to this recommendation, and, even though the published document articulated Hoover's ambitious goal, it still managed to include only some of the nation's industries. In fact, although one could never tell this from the tables, Hoover's initiative repeatedly encountered resistance, both from the departments of Agriculture and Interior and from members of trade associations. Meanwhile, the Anti-Trust Division of the Justice Department also objected to a project that seemed to violate the Sherman antitrust law. Attorney General Daugherty tried to impose two restrictions on publishing the kind of data Hoover wanted to include in the *Survey*: he insisted that information could only be given to a government agency and that it had to be presented in terms so general that no reader could identify specific firms. Hoover objected strenuously to these restrictions, as well as to the claim that trade association information was, by definition, protected, but efforts to collect and publicize data were repeatedly threatened by attempts to restrict the release of proprietary information in the name of protecting competition. This issue was not even provisionally settled until 1925, when the Supreme Court ruled that exchanges of information among trade groups did not necessarily violate antitrust law.[25]

3.5. THE CHALLENGES OF EARLY STATISTICAL COMPILATIONS

Despite the offstage controversy that surrounded its creation, the *Survey of Current Business* enjoyed immediate success, and from publications like this American business leaders rapidly learned how to use index numbers without pausing over the complexities their construction entailed. Among economists, however, disagreements about index numbers continued, for the decisions required to make them touched on theoretical differences that continued to divide the profession. One position in the decade-long dispute about index numbers is represented by Wesley Mitchell's 1919 reports on the War Industries Board data sets. In *History of Prices during the War*, Mitchell explained that during its unprecedented information-gathering effort, the government agency discovered a veritable "revolution" in prices—fluctuations so sudden and extreme that they tested ordinary forms of measurement. "There has been no other revolution in prices at once so sudden, so violent, and so widespread as the revolution that accompanied the war of 1914–1918," Mitchell asserted.[26] With prices for some commodities increased as much as 5,000% and other commodities having completely vanished, what business leaders needed was not more data about their own industries but some sense of the overall "market trend." The only way to make this visible was to use index numbers and time series. If trends were visible, Mitchell continued, businessmen and government officials could decide whether they should collectively try to control the market. "Is any market trend to be looked for, or will there be miscellaneous shiftings in both directions and prolonged uncertainty? Above all, are future price movements matters which business men and officials should attempt merely to forecast as best they may, or are they matters which men should attempt to control?" (*History of Prices* 3).

To help answer such questions, Mitchell's team at the Price Section constructed indexes for fifty classes of commodities. Even though they set strict limits on their project—they limited their survey to the United States, omitted prices for labor, land, securities, and public utilities, and recorded only wholesale price quotations, not the retail prices actually paid—they still encountered problems. Simply defining "commodity" proved challenging, as did identifying duplicate listings for similar commodities. Then, too, the lack of standardization for many fabricated products was frustrating, as were uneven records of trade statistics, and the need to weight commodities by their relative importance required decisions at every turn. To the challenges posed by categorization, nonstandard commodities, uneven records, and the constant need to exercise discretion, Mitchell added yet one more: how could the analyst decide which factors were causes and which effects? Mitchell refused to address this question, for doing so would have required a level of theoretical generalization with which he was uncomfortable, given the current state of statistical analysis. "No known method of analysis is subtle or powerful enough to disentangle the crossing lines of cause and effect and measure the influence of each factor," he insisted (*History of Prices* 8). Paradoxically, Mitchell's reluctance to engage in speculation also helped naturalize index numbers, for it pushed the interpretive issues implicit in their construction into the background. In the long run, Mitchell's antitheoretical stance also provoked other economists to characterize the NBER's descriptive statistics projects as "measurement without theory," for, in their view, collecting data in the absence of a theoretical framework was a meaningless exercise.[27]

Despite the challenges and judged by almost any criteria, *History of Prices during the War* constituted an enormous advance over previous attempts to generate a national data set. When Mitchell tried to scale up to the international level, however, his staff encountered difficulties even they could not ignore: some countries had collected almost no data or had lost entire industries; commodities were not always the same from country to country; and some currencies had experienced such dramatic fluctuation that comparing prices was impossible. At the conclusion of *International Price Comparisons*, issued by the WIB in 1919, Mitchell admitted that the method used in *History of Prices during the War* would not work for such irregular data. Thus, the report could only present "a series of comparisons between price fluctuations in the United States and in several foreign countries taken one at a time" rather than a picture of a worldwide trend. Unlike the three-stage process of multiplication, addition, and the conversion of aggregates into relatives, which the Price Section statisticians had used for the US data, the index numbers for foreign comparisons were created "by turning actual prices into relatives at the beginning of the computation and then averaging the relatives." The statisticians had to use a different procedure, Mitchell explained, because the foreign figures simply could not be properly weighted.

Under the circumstances, the accomplishment of the Price Section was considerable: it collected at least some price data from thirteen countries, including not only the seven allied nations and two members of the Axis, but also four neutrals (the three Scandinavian countries plus Argentina). Nevertheless, Mitchell knew that his data and methods yielded only limited results. Not only were the data and measurement units incommensurate across nations, but when analysts used different statistical tools, they threatened to make what data existed unusable for anything other than the roughest comparisons. By the end of 1919, Mitchell had come to realize another paradox of index numbers: they were simultaneously essential for depicting large-scale trends and, in conditions of incommensurate or uneven data, virtually useless.

By 1921, when the newly formed NBER published its first report, Mitchell had come to believe that the methodological challenges inherent in index numbers could be minimized if the researchers adopted rigorous methods that promised methodological objectivity. Such methods might not compensate completely for the unevenness of data or offset the need to make discretionary decisions, but they could address the objection that data sets simply reflected the bias of their compilers. This objection had long stalked social scientists and government-sponsored data projects. Indeed, it was largely to counter such suspicions that Jerome Greene and Edwin Gay had initially envisioned creating a social science institute, for one of the most famous early government reports on wage and price data—the 1893 Aldrich Report—had repeatedly been charged with bias.

While the Aldrich Report was often cited as "a great collection of wage statistics,"[28] many critics—including Mitchell—considered its findings deeply flawed on both political and methodological grounds.[29] The study that produced the report was initiated in a period of intense debate about whether businesses, especially the new corporations, were unfairly monopolizing the nation's wealth. When the report concluded, as J. B. Clark had done, that workers' wages were not falling relative to commodity prices, labor unrest erupted anew. Because Aldrich, the powerful chair of the Senate Finance Committee, had used several prominent social scientists to prepare the report, the fledging discipline of economics was tarred with the same brush that blackened the report. When the new NBER decided to take as its first project a study of income in the United States, which was conducted in the immediate wake of the war and in the midst of the brief, but sharp, recession of 1920–21, the organization risked arousing the same hostility that greeted the Aldrich Report. It was in part to neutralize those charges that Mitchell celebrated objectivity in the introduction to *Income in the United States*.

In one sense, Mitchell's introduction to the first NBER report directly engaged the controversy that always surrounds the subject of national income, for he was not afraid to name the volatile issues of distribution and equality. The object of the study, he explained, was to discover "whether the National Income is adequate to provide a decent living for all persons, whether this income is increasing as rapidly as the population, and whether its distribution among individuals is growing more or less unequal."[30] Mitchell thought he could acknowledge these controversial subjects because he used a method that would make the study's findings objective—even if they were not conclusive. After acknowledging that the available data were extremely "miscellaneous" (4) and that the study's conclusions were estimates rather than exact measurements (5), Mitchell explained how his method corrected for bias. He had taken two approaches to national income estimates: one based on income received (taken from income tax returns and reports on wages and salaries), and the other based on income produced (taken from statistics of coal and metals mined, lumber cut, crops grown, and raw materials transported or consumed by manufacture). Two separate teams had worked on the two data sets, and each had prepared an independent estimate. Checking one estimate against the other revealed a maximum discrepancy between the two estimates of only 7%, but, still unsatisfied, Mitchell asked his teams to compare each item in the first data set to its counterpart in the second. No matter what the result, they tried to perfect each figure by going behind the index number to the research that led to its construction. In the end, even though Mitchell admitted that errors varied from item to item and data sources were differentially uneven across various years, he was satisfied that the NBER method checked and double-checked each index number for bias. Even so, Mitchell was careful to state his findings not in definite numbers but in terms of a statistical range: "in the form of ranges within which the National Income will probably fall" (8).

The two approaches the NBER took to national estimates—the income and production approaches—would be adopted in the 1930s in the first official estimates of national income, then supplemented, in the following decade, by a third approach, the expenditure approach. For Mitchell, working before theoretical defenses for these approaches had been articulated—and, in fact, reluctant to allow theory to lead empirical work—the principal advantage of the two-part approach was that it promised to transcend whatever personal convictions a researcher might hold with a degree of objectivity that followed from method. The confidence Mitchell placed in method helps explain why he could simultaneously argue that the NBER's reports must not make explicit policy recommendations (as the Brookings Institution did) and strongly believe that some policies were better than others. For the most part, Mitchell and the NBER were able to walk the line between institutional impartiality and personal partisanship because the organization was not directly funded by any government agency or business interest and because it almost never agreed to undertake a project not originated in-house. The one departure from this last rule—the NBER's involvement in Hoover's attempt to quantify "recent economic changes" in the late 1920s—elicited the very accusations of bias that the bureau had long avoided.[31]

3.6. THE DISPUTE OVER INDEX NUMBERS

For present purposes, *Income in the United States* is primarily important because the limitations Mitchell self-consciously embraced represented a departure from both the explicitly polemical version of political economy practiced by J. B. Clark and the theory-driven deductive method epitomized by Irving Fisher. Like Clark, Mitchell reached the conclusion that income was relatively fairly distributed across the social classes, although he admitted that the war had led to some profiteering. Mitchell based his conclusions not on marginalist principles, however, but on the empirical data his researchers compiled, and setting up separate teams to look at and compare different data sets anchored these conclusions in a methodological rigor that offset at least some of the questions statistical methods could raise. The differences that separated Mitchell from Fisher require more attention, for, during the 1920s, the two economists engaged in an explicit debate about the best method for constructing index numbers. This debate makes it clear that, for economists at least, index numbers had yet to be fully naturalized, even if businessmen and government officials were already using used them to make decisions.

The conflict between Mitchell and Fisher played out in a number of publications, but it can be captured by contrasting Mitchell's *Business Cycles: The Problem and Its Setting* (1927) with Fisher's *The Making of Index Numbers* (1922).[32] Whereas Mitchell insisted that one should construct index numbers to suit the data at hand, Fisher thought it was possible—and preferable—to produce an "ideal" index number, which could be used for every data set. If he could identify a formula for constructing the ideal index number, Fisher believed, he could save economists time, minimize the distortions that followed discretionary choices, and, most importantly, align index numbers with the lawful operations of the economy. While Mitchell and Fisher both wanted to measure something that could not be observed—for Mitchell, this was the business cycle, while Fisher was interested in inflation—and even though both used statistical techniques to represent what they could not see, the two economists differed on whether inductive or deductive methods could best capture unobservable phenomena.

The first point of disagreement concerned equilibrium and the role this concept played in economics. As we saw in chapter 2, Fisher considered equilibrium an inherent law of all economic systems: prices are set when producers and consumers reach agreement, and economies reach—or tend toward—equilibrium because, at the right price, supply is naturally exhausted by demand. Mitchell, by contrast, treated equilibrium as an analogy, and, as a trope borrowed from physics, it seemed to him limiting and flawed. While the analogy could facilitate some kinds of "static" analysis, Mitchell thought it interfered with attempts to understand dynamic phenomena such as business cycles.[33] Mitchell considered equilibrium useful only as an accounting identity: accountants used the idea of equilibrium—or balance—to help master the infinite number of changing factors involved in a business when they implemented the basic income/expenditure relationship in bookkeeping entries. Recording transactions in the double-entry format allowed the manager to see whether income exceeded outlay "by a satisfactory margin of profits" (1927, 187).

> Here is a different conception of equilibrium which may help us—the equilibrium of a balance sheet, or better, of an income and expenditure statement. Such a statement has nothing to do with mechanical forces, and that is a safeguard against false analogies. It deals with pecuniary quantities, and they are genuine elements in our problem. It sums up the results of numerous processes which concern us, through periods

of time which we can divide according to their business characteristics. More than that, the statements for successive periods of the time link into each other, as they should do for our purposes. The statement for one period shows what has happened to certain items included in its predecessor, and shows also certain items the disposition of which will appear in its successor. Finally, the balance which is struck is really a device for finding how much the expenditures and the receipts are out of balance. The difference between these two aggregates of items is put down on the income side as profit and loss, a positive or a negative sum. That feature, too, serves our needs. We have no more warrant for assuming in advance that business processes "tend" to maintain an equilibrium than to assume that they "tend" to get out of balance. What we need when we employ the concept of equilibrium, is a device for showing the relations between the aggregates which stand opposite each other in various processes, as expenditures and receipts stand opposite each other in bookkeeping. Having found equality, or having found one set of items in excess of the other, our problem is to trace the consequences. It is not a foregone conclusion that these consequences will always be of the sort which tend to restore a balance, any more than losses suffered by a business enterprise one year tend to give it profits in the year following. Yet we know that the modern business system does not function smoothly when the aggregates of the opposing items in certain pairs get too much out of balance (1927, 187).

The disagreement over the meaning of equilibrium is linked to another issue that separated Fisher and Mitchell in the 1920s. Fisher's assumptions about immutable laws and his deductive method meant that he was less worried about the fit between whatever empirical observations were aggregated into data sets and the statistical tools applied to them than with the mathematical principles the tools operationalized. Mitchell, by contrast, repeatedly worried that index numbers "would be taken too absolutely as a complete representation of the facts" they aggregated, and, to counteract what he saw as blind, and possibly misleading, faith in indexes, he repeatedly returned to "the actual changes in prices from which they [price indexes] are made, and which they purport to summarize."[34] Fisher did recognize the importance of empirical data, but he wanted to use data to test the adequacy of statistical tools, not evaluate the fit between what Mitchell called "ultimate data" and the index numbers. Even though Fisher insisted that his 1922 book used an "inductive" method, which proceeded "by means of calculations from actual historical data," what he meant by "actual historical data" were the index numbers generated "by Wesley C. Mitchell for the War Industries Board," not the pre-index-number "facts" Mitchell kept invoking. What Fisher wanted to test, in other words, was not the relationship between the index numbers and some kind of raw historical data but the mathematical properties of the formulae and the statistical procedures by which various index numbers were constructed.[35]

In emphasizing the mathematics by which various index numbers were constructed instead of the fit between the index number and the raw data it tried to capture, Fisher took another step toward the formalization of economic analysis, which would culminate in economists' embrace of mathematical modeling. Mitchell, who followed the institutionalist Veblen, called attention to this difference in a footnote: "My understanding is that Professor Fisher draws a sharp line between what is normally true and what is historically true," Mitchell argued. "What is normally true is that which would happen under certain hypothetical conditions which are never fulfilled absolutely. What is historically true is that which actually happens under conditions which combine the factors represented in the theorist's imaginary case with a continually changing host of other factors. Hence relations which hold normally may never be realized historically" (1927, 129 n. 2).

What we see in this sharp disagreement about historical and normal conditions must be understood in the context of developments within the discipline of mathematics and, more narrowly, in the way interwar economists understood the relationship between economics and mathematical and statistical methods. As E. Roy Weintraub has argued, understanding how economics became a mathematical science during the first half of the twentieth century requires us to understand the "changing images of mathematics" during this period; and economics did not become a mathematical science overnight—not simply because a lag separated developments in mathematics and their counterparts in economics but also because different economists embraced these changes to different degrees. Weintraub argues that, at the beginning of the twentieth century, mathematicians' challenges to the foundations of arithmetic and logic began to call into question the physics-based image of mathematics that had obtained in the late nineteenth century. Once physics proved unable to solve problems associated with new discoveries like blackbodies, radiation, and relativity, moreover, mathematics no longer seemed able to provide a secure foundation for physics. "Modeling the concerns of the new physics appeared to require a new mathematics," Weintraub explains, "a mathematics less based on deterministic dynamical systems and more on statistical argumentation and algebra. Consequently mathematical physics was to link up with newer mathematical ideas in algebra (e.g., group theory) and probability theory (e.g., measurement theory), as mathematicians took up the challenge to work on mathematical ideas which could facilitate understanding of the world."[36]

For a neoclassical mathematician-turned-economist like Fisher—who still embraced the physics analogy and the mathematics associated with it—the argument that economic analysis might be liberated from history was exhilarating, for it promised a new way to conceptualize the relationship between mathematical formulations and empirical observations. For an institutionalist economist like Mitchell, by contrast—who was skeptical about both the physics analogy for economics and mathematical methods of any kind—the claim that economic analysis should rest upon mathematical principles seemed at best naïve and at worst dangerous. While Mitchell did embrace a practice he called "mathematical economics," what he meant by this term was quite different than Fisher's practice. Mitchell's version of mathematical economics did not work deductively from logical principles, it did not view mathematical logic as the basis of economic truth claims, and it did not rely on the mathematics used by physicists. Finally, Mitchell's mathematical economics did not assume that a single mathematical formula could—or should—be used to construct index numbers for every empirical situation the economist might encounter. Fisher did assume that such an "ideal" formula existed and, for him, standardizing the method by which index numbers were constructed was essential because doing so would enable the economist to add more dimensions to the problems he was trying to solve.

In Fisher's eyes, "all discussion of 'different formulae appropriate for different purposes' falls to the ground" precisely because the various "legitimate methods of calculating index numbers" all reached "surprising agreement" *when the formulae are "rectified" by a mathematical operation* (1922, 365). "Rectification," which Fisher considered one of the most original contributions of his 1922 book (1922, 366), was designed to align the formulae with each other and thus eliminate "all the sources of distortion or onesidedness" (1922, 364)—that is, to eliminate as much as possible of the bias and "freakishness" that might affect the index numbers.[37] This method involved a number of formal tests, like the "time reversal test" and the "factor reversal test." The former tests whether the formula used to construct an index number gives consistent results if applied going forward and then backward in time. The latter tests whether the formula gives consistent results when applied to prices and to quantities.

In his brief treatment of mathematical notation, Fisher emphasized primarily the flexibility this mode of representation introduced into economic analysis. His formulae "apply if the p's are wholesale prices and the q's are the amount imported into the United States. They apply equally well if the p's are retail prices and the q's are the quantities sold by grocers in New York City. They likewise apply if the p's are rates of wages per hour and the q's the quantities of merchandise transported from New York to Liverpool by all Cunard steamers. They likewise apply if the p's are the prices of industrial stocks and the q's are the number of shares sold by John Smith in January" (1922, "Appendix I," 381). Mathematical notation also made it possible for the first time to address *all* the dimensions Fisher mentions here—prices, quantities, and the time of numerous kinds of transactions conducted by various agents in different intervals and at disparate places. By introducing a mode of representation that could capture the relationships among such factors, all of which are measurable but not by the same units, mathematical notation helped create a new kind of "mathematical economics"—one that opened possibilities for analytic complexity that Mitchell's version did not allow.

3.7. THE HARVARD BAROMETER PROJECT

One further approach to economic statistics and aggregation deserves mention, for this project moved beyond depictions of the real side of the economy to its financial side. Like the case study approach, the Harvard Barometer project originated in Cambridge, Massachusetts. Under the directorship of Warren S. Persons, the Harvard Barometer consisted of a series of related, synthetic statistics that generated the closest approximation to an overall picture of the nation's economy possible before the creation of macroeconomics, national income estimates, and single-figure aggregates like the GDP. With Harvard's endorsement and funding, Persons was able to organize all the industry-specific data sets available in 1918 into a three-part series of indexes that tried to predict turns in the overall business cycle. In so doing, he both drew on and refined existing statistical techniques, used new technical instruments, and shifted the emphasis of statistical analysis from description to inference.[38] His work was explicitly indebted to Moore, he used the trade and inflation indexes created by Irving Fisher, and he positioned his work in the vast area that separated Mitchell's cautious approach from Fisher's more wholehearted embrace of mathematics and theory.[39] In the early 1920s, the Harvard Barometer represented the state-of-the-art statistical tool for representing the nation's economy as a dynamic interaction of real, financial, and monetary factors, but its failure to predict the crash of 1929 largely discredited the project, which was abandoned at the end of the decade.

To create the Harvard Barometer, Persons began with the series of "fundamental statistics" culled from publications such as the *Commercial and Financial Chronicle, Bradstreet's*, the *Iron Age*, and the *New York Journal of Commerce*. The series from which he derived these statistics were long enough to reveal various short-term fluctuations—the monthly series all went back to 1903 and the annual series to 1879—which Persons divided into four kinds: long-term or secular trends; a wave-like or cyclical movement; a seasonal movement within the year; and what he called "residual variations," which were responses to "momentous occurrences" like war.[40] He was primarily interested in the short-term fluctuations, not the trend, seasonal, or residual movements, for these wave-like movements theoretically revealed how interactions among sectors of the economy constituted a deep and consistent rhythm.

To identity the most significant sectors, Persons grouped the series into categories that displayed similar cyclic behaviors. This allowed him to create three synthetic indexes, two of which showed the financial side of the economy, and one of which focused on real production: the speculation index showed average prices of shares; the money market index tracked the short-term credit level, and the business index was composed of the volume of sales and the price level of goods. Using moving averages, regression, and cross-correlation, Persons revealed that these synthetic indexes manifested a regular, lagged relation to each other, which clearly depicted an interplay between real and financial factors. In the cycle's expansionist phase, investors' optimism led to a rise in share prices, reflected in an increase in the speculation index; this led to an increase in the demand for goods and services and to a general rise in prices, which showed up in the business index; and price increases led to an increase in interest rates, which appeared in the money market index. The rise in interest rates marked a turning point, as the decrease in value of fixed income assets led to lowered expectations about the profitability of investments, as reflected in a decrease in the speculation index; decreased investment caused a decrease in demand, then prices, as tracked by the business index; and this led to a decrease in interest rates, which the money market index reflected. Going back to the years with which his indexes began, Persons was able to use commercial data to test his synthetic statistical tool; and from the cyclical movements and interactions the Harvard Barometer displayed, he was able to make predictions about when a new phase of the cycle would begin. Unfortunately, these predictions were not always accurate, as Persons learned when the Barometer failed to anticipate the stock market crash of 1929.

In 1928, a year before the crash discredited the Barometer approach, Oskar Morgenstern, head of the Viennese Institute for the Study of Business Cycles, published a scathing critique of the Harvard Barometer Project. In a review of Morgenstern's article, A. W. Magret summarized Morgenstern's charges. The project of economic forecasting is doomed from the start, Morgenstern argued, because the data is inadequate: it overlooks the nature of economic processes, which do not repeat themselves exactly; and, in an observation that would be echoed by later New Classical economists (see chapter 10, section 3), the forecasts themselves change participants' behavior. "Such forecasts can serve no useful purpose," Magret's summary of Morgenstern's article concluded. "All attempts to develop a formal technique for forecasts are therefore to be discouraged."[41] Even though the Harvard Barometer Project failed, we will see in chapter 5, section 3, another attempt to evaluate forecasting, this time in Alfred A. Cowles's analysis of stock market forecasters. We will also see subsequent attempts to find underlying regularities in financial markets and macroeconomic activities, including business cycles, in modern finance's rational market hypothesis and the related rational expectations hypothesis in macroeconomics.

3.8. THE PUJO INVESTIGATION AND THE "MONEY TRUST"

Henry Moore's studies of cotton prices, the Harvard Business School's case studies, the NBER reports, and government reports published during and immediately after World War I all provided hints about the role played by finance in the first decades of the twentieth century. Index numbers, moreover, which fuse price and quantity ratios, might be said to encapsulate the indissoluble join between the financial and real sides of the economy. Finally, the Harvard Barometer, with its spatial representation of trends in the speculation and money market indexes, on the one hand, and the business index, on the other, was clearly an attempt to make visible the interrelationship of financial and real factors in the US economy. None of these projects, however, attracted the attention of the general public, especially during the tense years of US involvement in World War I and the period of dramatic price rises that followed the conflict. Business leaders no doubt welcomed the government's data, and economists chose sides in the index number controversy, but neither the Commerce Department nor theoretical treatises presented an account of the economy capacious enough or sufficiently compelling to help most Americans see the overall picture to which the data contributed.

Two texts did try to create such a picture, and they seem to have attracted more attention than the more technical works we have examined in this chapter. The first was the publication, in 1913, of the report of a congressional subcommittee charged with investigating the so-called "money trust," a network of 385 overlapping directorships and oversight boards that tied together some of the biggest industries, transportation companies, and financial institutions in America. The subcommittee, which was chaired by Arsene Pujo, a Louisiana Democrat, found an extraordinary set of connections radiating outward from J. P. Morgan, who had saved the New York banks in 1907, to US Steel, the New York Railway Association, and banks like the Continental and Commercial Bank and the First National Trust, to name just a few. In February 1913, the subcommittee presented to Congress an intricate, multicolored chart that linked these concerns to Morgan, as well as a long report spelling out its findings.[42] The report received widespread attention in the nation's newspapers, for it spoke to the common belief that the panic of 1907 had been engineered by a group of financiers who had manipulated the market for personal gain. The report also led J. P. Morgan & Company to draft a defense of financial concentration, excerpts of which also appeared in newspapers. In the company's defense, its director, known as the "Napoleon of Finance," offered a portrait of the US economy that not only drew parallels between its real and financial sides but also insisted that the former could not survive without the latter.

> Just as grain and cotton and manufactures are commodities subject to the unchanging laws of supply and demand, so, in the same way, money and credits are commodities subject to the same unvarying laws, but far more intensely. . . . The steady growth in the size of banks in New York and Chicago and the frequent merger of two or more banks into one institution have erroneously been designated before your Committee as "concentration." This steady growth and these mergers, however, are a development due simply to the demand for larger banking facilities to care for the growth of the country's business. As our cities double and treble in size and importance, as railways extend and industrial plants expand, not only is it natural, but it is necessary, that our banking institutions should grow in order to care for the increased demands put on them.[43]

Whether persuaded by Morgan's depiction of the interpenetration of finance and commerce or by their inability to find evidence of collusion, the subcommittee decided that, even if a money trust did exist, it had not manipulated the markets or caused the panic. There was a legislative response to the investigation, however. In 1914, Congress passed the Clayton Act, which was designed to break up the interlocking system of company directorates.

The second portrait of the interpenetration of the real and financial sides of the US economy appeared in 1921. Written by Harold Glenn Moulton, then an instructor in the School of Commerce and Administration at the University of Chicago, *The Financial Organization of Society* was designed as a textbook for a survey course in financial organization. In his preface, Moulton acknowledged the demand for such a general survey. "Not only are the classes in finance in our colleges, universities, and schools of commerce literally flooded with students; the high schools are also seeking to incorporate the subject in their rapidly developing commercial curricula; Y.M.C.A. and institute study courses in finance are being formed throughout the country; and, more significant still, many business houses, recognizing the dependence of successful business management upon a thorough knowledge of financial principles, are now organizing special courses for their employees and officials" (xi). Even if Moulton's textbook reached only a portion of these venues, it helped shape the way many Americans understood their economy. Its success was also reflected in the increased prominence of its author. In 1927 Moulton became the first president of the Brookings Institution in Washington, DC.

The Financial Organization of Society is an institutionalist account of the range of financial institutions present in the United States, their historical development, and their relationships both with each other and with the real side of the economy. The organizing theme of the narrative is the "dependence of practically all business enterprise upon borrowed funds—that is, upon credit" (xi). According to Moulton, this dependence both fueled the growth of the US economy and almost destroyed it in the wake of the 1907 panic, when it became obvious that no central authority was overseeing credit. It was to remedy this problem that the Federal Reserve system was adopted, he explained: "The Federal Reserve Act . . . undertook to organize the nation's resources and to prevent the recurring collapse of the credit system in times of panic, as well as to minimize the ebb and flow of business activity" (734). In this account, the Federal Reserve system is the link between the financial and real sides of the economy: it controls the first by managing the "credit mechanism" and supports the second by "rendering [credit] subservient to the varying requirements of business" (738).

Following Veblen, Mouton referred to this complex "interdependence of finance and business" (743) as the "credit society" (748), and, like Veblen again, he acknowledged that America's "almost universal expression of modern economic activities and achievements in pecuniary terms has led to an exaltation of the significance of money that has done much to pervert the ideals of society" (744). Nevertheless, his primary goal was not to criticize the resulting organization but simply to explain it—to show how credit flowed from the Federal Reserve through national and state banks, and from these to the businessmen and consumers who made the nation productive. In his account, everyone is—or should be—interested in finance: "Literally almost every individual and every institution is, under modern conditions, vitally interested as an investor in the efficient working of the financial system" (749). His stirring conclusion called readers to see the US economy as a two-sided but singular "organism": "For good or ill the economic system has become predominantly pecuniary; modern life is largely organized about the pecuniary unit of calculation; business processes are everywhere worked out though financial means; and even the larger aspects of economic organization are in no small measure regulated through the intermediation of financial institutions and agencies. There is little exaggeration in saying that the economic society of our times is financially organized and controlled" (773). By making financial intermediation the nexus of the economic system, Moulton elevated finance to a status acknowledged by few of his neoclassical peers, who tended to theorize price formation as a process independent of the institutions in which it occurred.

In addition to creating an influential picture of a two-sided but integrated economy, Moulton also formulated an important account of the relationship between commercial banking and capital formation. Given the tension between short-term credit instruments, to which the real-bills doctrine theoretically limited banks, and the new corporations' need for continuous financing, Moulton argued that unfettered commerce might not solve the credit problem. In the first of a series of articles devoted to "Commercial Banking and Capital Formation," all published in 1918, Moulton called upon economists to focus on the forces transforming American society. "What is needed is a study of the processes by which a percentage of the productive energy of society is diverted from the creation of consumptive goods to the creation of capital goods. It should be a study, moreover, that runs in terms of the institutions through which and by which the capital formation is effected in a complex industrial world. It should be a study, finally, that is not averse to facing the possibility of utilizing social agencies in the control of both the amount and the direction of capital accumulation."[44]

One of these agencies, as we have seen, was the Federal Reserve system, but when America joined the European war effort in 1917, the Fed was saddled with a task that complicated its oversight of capital formation: funding the war effort. It initiated funding by issuing bonds and expanding its open market operations, but no central bank could raise money and manage a nation's credit as long as it was hampered by the real-bills doctrine. This is why Moulton targeted the real-bills doctrine. In his view, long-term claims that traded on securities markets were superior to self-liquidating commercial paper because the former offered greater liquidity. While the latter was supposed to be safe, the fact that commercial paper was not traded meant that this form of credit was not "shiftable," as were long-term securities. The doctrine of "shiftability," which Moulton laid out in subsequent publications, underwrote what became the dominant policy for commercial banks and the Fed. In the 1920s, under the directorship of Benjamin Strong, the Fed began to shift the vast portfolio of US debt as one way to manage the nation's economy and control capital formation. The doctrine that evolved for the central bank, which has been characterized as a doctrine of central bank *responsibility*, thus gradually displaced the not-so-very-old doctrine of *convertibility*. The new doctrine made the Federal Reserve system responsible for overseeing the purchasing power of money, credit, and capital formation, whereas the old scheme merely required the Fed to make sure bank deposits could be converted into lawful currency.[45]

CHAPTER 4

American Finance in the Interwar Period

4.1. TRANSFORMATIONS IN THE INTERWAR PERIOD

The period between 1918 and 1941 witnessed a remarkable transformation of the US financial system. At the beginning of the period, the US dollar was convertible to gold; the Federal Reserve system consisted of twelve relatively independent banks that still responded primarily to regional credit conditions; the nation's thirty-plus stock exchanges were self-regulating institutions, each governed by its own exchange rules and listing requirements; corporations were predominantly regulated through state laws and courts (with the exception of specific Federal Trade Commission and Federal Reserve Board areas of oversight); and securities were largely distributed by investment banks and trusts to relatively small numbers of institutional buyers and wealthy individuals. By the end of the interwar period, as the United States mobilized to enter a second international conflict, all these institutional arrangements had changed: the dollar was devalued by almost 60% against gold; the Federal Reserve was dominated by its Washington branch and had become the lender of last resort for the federal government; stock exchanges and corporations were subjected to new levels of federal oversight; and securities were sold by more institutions to more Americans than ever before.

These dramatic changes were outward signs of the increased importance of the financial side of America's economy, and, along with a handful of key publications, they helped inform ordinary people about how the US financial system that Moulton described in his business school courses worked. Modern analysts estimate that in the middle of the nineteenth century, the financial sector represented approximately 1.5% of the nation's economic activity; in the roaring twenties, this rose above 6%; and, by 1940, it had fallen to 2.4%.[1]

Changes in the financial side reverberated through the real side of the economy as well: during the sharp recession of 1921, the dollar suffered its worst deflation in the nation's history, which translated into an annual decline of 37% in wholesale prices.[2] A seven-year period of economic productivity followed, characterized by innovations such as electrification, improvements in automobiles and roads, new communication technologies, and breakthroughs in the chemical and pharmaceutical industries. During this prosperous period, long bond rates generally declined, the overall value of the stock market rose, the dollar became a global currency, Americans borrowed more money than ever before, and the Federal Reserve system, under Benjamin Strong, tried to stabilize the economy with open market operations. In 1929, all these trends, both monetary and real, began to reverse. During the Great Depression, the value of stocks fell precipitously, industrial production declined by 37%, unemployment rose to 25%, the money supply contracted, and the nation's currency once again deflated sharply. Prices fell 33%. Another reversal began in 1938, once the FDR administration introduced its only Keynesian policy, and the recovery accelerated as Roosevelt responded to the fall of France in June 1940. By November 1941, US unemployment stood at 3.9%.[3]

These unmistakable swings in the real and financial sides of the economy made finance visible to Americans as it had never been before. Even if an individual owned no securities in the 1920s and 1930s, he or she found it impossible to ignore the volatility of the stock market, fluctuations in the purchasing power of the dollar, and the impact of widespread unemployment. As people struggled to understand, measure, and make sense of the "new era" finance of the 1920s, then the financial reforms of the New Deal, new agencies, professions, and specialists emerged to interpret the changing world. By the end of this period, a few American economists began to use a new tool—modeling—to make sense of the interwar developments, including the rise in the financial sector itself.

4.2. "NEW ERA TALK" AND THE SPECULATIVE MANIA OF THE 1920S

In 1920, it was possible to buy or sell securities on at least thirty-three US exchanges, ranging from the New York Stock Exchange housed on Wall Street to the New York Curb Market, located in the winding streets adjacent to the Exchange, to regional markets, like the Chicago and Boston exchanges, to numerous over-the-counter exchanges operating with various degrees of formality. These exchanges used various methods to circulate information to industry insiders, but, by and large, their ability to engage the attention—or attract the money—of the public was relatively limited. Two contemporaries—H. T. Warshow, writing in 1924, and Gardner Means, in 1930—estimated that only about 4.4 million individuals held shares in 1900; by 1920, the number had increased to 12 million.[4] According to another contemporary, Frederick Lewis Allen, in 1920, Americans associated Wall Street with political violence, not financial opportunity. On September 16, a radical group detonated a bomb at the intersection where the headquarters of the J. P. Morgan Bank faced off against the New York Stock Exchange, the Sub-Treasury building, and the US Assay Office. To many, this symbolized the ongoing conflict between the powerful elite and the angry majority. "Government finance, private finance, the passage of private control of industry from capitalist hand to hand: here stood the respective citadels cheek by jowl, as if to symbolize the union into one system of the government and the money power and the direction of business—that system which the radicals so bitterly decried."[5]

Even if Americans were relatively ignorant about Wall Street activities at the beginning of the 1920s, many had already become investors, through the purchase of Liberty and Victory bonds. The first stage of the democratization of the US capital market was a function of wartime necessity, patriotism, and celebrity marketing, not the result of a widespread impression that securities investment could augment individual wealth. The federal government initially promoted the purchase of bonds in its 1917–18 campaign as a way for civilians to support the war effort. Between 1917 and 1919, the government sold $27 billion in Liberty Bonds and Victory Bonds to finance the war against Germany. More than 22 million Americans, from nearly all income groups and occupations, bought war bonds. As Michael E. Parrish notes, this was for many a first taste of the "mysteries of the securities market," and the popularity of the campaign encouraged more individuals to buy stocks and more corporations to issue them: "the spectacular success of the government's wartime bond program encouraged more and more corporations to seek public financing in the next decade."[6]

Although the first issues appeared in large denominations (in 1917, the smallest Liberty Bond was $50), war bonds were rapidly issued in denominations suited to nearly every American. Saving stamp books were given out to school children and a $5 certificate was contemplated for laborers, women, and children.[7] The Liberty Bond campaign brought together individual savers, government officials, and private banks in a network that seamlessly transformed individual savings into interest-bearing investments, which were intended to benefit the individual investor, the government, and the private banks that borrowed from the government in order to lend to the small inves-tor. Not incidentally, for many, this transaction constituted an early example of buying on margin, even as it brought various parts of the financial industry into an even more integrated system. Early in 1917, as James Grant explains,

> it was clear to the Treasury Department that the people's savings would fall short of the needs of the government. To augment the stock of real capital, the government directed the banking system to loan would-be investors the price of their bonds. The Federal Reserve, in turn, would lend to the banks. In effect, the worker-investors would buy on margin—an experience that some of them would repeat in the stock-market boom of the 1920s. [George F.] Baker's bank [the First National Bank of New York] became the very model of the patriotic financial institution. It purchased Liberty bonds for its own account, lent them to facilitate their purchase by others, and took the extra, and at the time novel, step of borrowing from the Federal Reserve Bank of New York to extend its reach.[8]

By 1923, when Calvin Coolidge was sworn in as president, the war was over and the economic and political anxiety of 1920–21 was beginning to fade. Apart from the continuing slide of agricultural prices, the next seven years constituted a period of almost unparalleled economic expansion, aided by the stable dollar, declining interest rates, and strong economic growth. Almost certainly, the increase in the US securities market contributed to this prosper-ity, although exact data are not available.[9] What we do know is that the num-ber of individual investors grew substantially during the 1920s. The 12 million investors Warshow and Means estimated at the beginning of the decade grew in just three years to 14.4 million; and by 1928, the shareholding population had jumped to 18 million. Even more significant were institutional investors, such as national banks and insurance companies, both of which increased holdings of securities in their investment portfolios.[10] Before the stock market crashed in 1929, many Americans believed a "new era" had begun, and tech-nological innovations and the apparently limitless flows of US money seemed to make old truisms obsolete.

Economists at the time, like their counterparts today, did not agree about what caused the stock market boom of the 1920s. Irving Fisher, in the im-mediate aftermath of the crash, justified the "new era" valuation of securities by citing fundamentals related to both the real and the financial sides of the economy. These included enhanced cost savings from the corporate merger movement, a new era of cooperation between labor and capital, scientific innovations applied to business enterprises, the elimination of waste through a better understanding of costs, the plethora of new inventions that promised future payoffs, and financial innovations such as group insurance. Fisher also highlighted the monetary factor so dear to his own heart: the stability of the dollar during the period.[11]

Rather than debate the origins of the boom or the reasons for the 1929 crash, we focus on some of the structural changes that altered the financial sector during the 1920s. These changes affected the infrastructure of finance—both the system of financial institutions Moulton described in 1921 and the extension of intermediation through what two contemporaries called "the machinery for quantity manufacture and distribution" of securities.[12] This machinery, as represented by a new kind of financial institution, the security affiliate, and a modernized version of the old investment trust, not only created, marketed, and helped distribute securities to more investors than ever before. It also helped transform America into the "credit economy" Veblen had foreseen in the first decade of the century.

The security affiliate allowed commercial banks to do what they had previously been forbidden to do: issue and trade securities. The first security affiliate was launched in 1911, as a spin-off of the National City Bank, the predecessor of today's Citibank, which was headquartered in New York. The National City Bank was a commercial bank, which originated in 1812 as the City Bank of New York. For its first one hundred years, it grew at a steady, but unremarkable pace, and its directors operated within the legal constraints imposed on commercial banks, which included the 1864 prohibition on commercial banks' conducting "nonbanking" activities. These included the issue and sale of securities. Under law, securities origination was limited to investment banks, which did not invest their own money or accept deposits but only issued, underwrote, and traded securities for others.

In 1911, the directors of the National City Bank decided to increase the bank's revenue by inventing a new kind of corporation—the National City Company. Because it was not a commercial bank, the National City Company was allowed to provide the investment services denied the bank. In theory, the two companies were distinct, but in practice, the company, as a "security affiliate" of the bank, was simply another part of the commercial bank. As Ferdinand Pecora remarked in the Senate hearings that began in 1932, the bank and its security affiliate were "like one body with two heads."[13] The commercial bank had contributed all the funds ($10 million) necessary to launch the company; National City Bank offered its shareholders discounted shares in the new company; and the commercial bank's shareholders agreed not to exercise voting rights in the company, ceding control instead to three senior officers of the bank. Even the company's nonvoting shares embodied the fusion of the two institutions: the company's shares were printed on the reverse side of the stock certificates of the bank, making it impossible to sell one without selling the other.

When the National City Bank spun off its security affiliate, it chose as president of the new company Charles E. Mitchell, head of a modest investment fund. Mitchell soon transformed what began as a four-person office into a financial juggernaut, with 1,900 employees working in 6 branch offices and selling over $1.5 billion in securities a year. To make their quotas, Mitchell's bond salesmen set up new offices, advertised in national magazines, and hawked their wares by knocking on potential investors' doors. One admiring contemporary remarked that "such methods, pursued with such vigor and on such a scale were revolutionary."[14] In 1921, Mitchell was also made president of the bank; in 1929, he became the bank's chairman as well.[15]

Struck by the success of the National City Company, many state and national banks set up security affiliates of their own; others simply staffed existing bond departments with salesmen and research staffs devoted to security analysis and sales.[16] National banks took the lead in financing securities purchases and lending money on call to speculators and brokers. In the decade from 1921 to 1930, new securities valued at $66,229,000,000 were issued, exclusive of government issues. Much of this was financed by national banks, which enjoyed the trust of their customers and offered both the investment machinery and expert advice necessary to handle this business.[17]

In 1927, passage of the McFadden Act explicitly granted national banks the right to buy and sell bonds; the act also allowed them to open branches. When the act was passed, more than one hundred national banks were already distributing securities through their bond departments. By 1929, the number of national banks, state banks, and affiliates engaged in the securities business had reached 591, up from 277 in 1922.[18] These institutions dealt in nearly every kind of marketable security: US government bonds; the securities of foreign governments; bonds issued by cities and states; and US and foreign corporation bonds and debentures. In the late 1920s, affiliates began to originate and issue common stocks to supply the increasing demand for this riskier kind of security, which was not tied to underlying assets or fixed maturity dates. While the data available for the late twenties allows us only to estimate how many securities were issued by affiliates, one analyst writing in 1941 thought that banks and security affiliates accounted for about half the total volume of securities issued in the last years of the decade.[19]

Security affiliates dramatically increased the numbers of securities on offer in the period but they also posed a legal dilemma. It was virtually impossible to distinguish a security affiliate from the bank that had created it because so many banks followed the example of the National City Bank in giving affiliates a variant of their own names. This made good business sense because it helped the security affiliate capitalize on the bank's goodwill, but the naming overlap could also create confusion when an aggrieved shareholder sought legal recourse. Contributing to the confusion were other practices common to these twinned companies: the two related companies often mixed their profits and expenses; shared parts—but not all—of the same accounting system; and distributed the profits earned by one company to the shareholders of the other. Then, too, directors of related companies often formed chains of affiliates to increase their capital. These complex institutional interrelations were not limited to banks and their security affiliates. When this system of interlocking ownership and affiliation was extended into other kinds of companies, which also issued and financed securities, it became nearly impossible for an investor to have any idea of the actual worth—or meaning—of his holdings. Chains of affiliated companies were especially common—and confusing—in the utilities industry, whose stocks traded with particular volatility at the end of the 1920s. By the summer of 1929, Frederick Allen wrote, the ownership of utilities companies had become so complex that "even the professional analyst of financial properties was sometimes bewildered when he found Company A holding a 20-per-cent interest in Company B, and B an interest in C, while C in turn invested in A, and D held shares in each."[20]

In the 1920s, banks and their security affiliates were not the only financial institutions ready to lend money for investment or purchase securities themselves. Indeed, when the members of the NBER Exploratory Committee on Financial Research, which was convened in 1937, attempted to enumerate the parts of the "system of finance" that had survived the crash and ensuing bank failures, they still found "many thousands of individual institutions characterized by great diversity of size, and by varying degrees of specialization. In it are commercial banks, savings banks, Morris Plan banks, industrial banks, mortgage banks, investment banks, Federal Reserve banks, home loan banks, credit unions, finance companies, insurance companies, investment trusts, security exchanges, brokerage houses, and many others."[21] Not all these institutions issued or underwrote securities, but most were at least indirect participants in the securities market—because they loaned money to institutions that loaned to investors, borrowed from institutions that issued shares, or were part of the elaborate chains of holding companies Allen described.

Even more important than the specifically financial institutions involved in the securities market was the number of corporations loaning their own cash reserves to investors—thus becoming, in effect, financial institutions themselves. It made more sense for a company to raise money by issuing bonds or stocks than borrowing from commercial banks because issuing allowed a company to avoid bank fees, and investors seemed ready to pay virtually any price for company shares. In 1928 and 1929, as opposed to 1926 and 1927, money became expensive, as the Federal Reserve kept the discount rate high in a vain attempt to discourage speculation. The call rate—the rate at which brokers could borrow—moved even higher than the discount rate in early 1929.[22] Despite the cost of money, investors continued to demand shares, and corporations responded by loaning to brokers either the money held in their cash reserves, many of which were at an all-time postwar high, or the assets they raised by floating securities. In their own accounts, corporations usually booked these loans simply as "other loans." The brokers, in turn, loaned the money to consumers who wanted to purchase securities. The result was what Alexander Noyes called "a pretty circle": "What the brokers had thus borrowed they had lent to their own speculating customers; the customers had used it for buying on a margin the outstanding stock of these very corporations."[23] In January 1926, Noyes reported, the outstanding total of these "other loans" was $564,000,000; in early October 1929, the figure stood at $3,941,000,000. During the next seven weeks, as the market crashed, the outstanding amount of "other loans" fell nearly two billion dollars—to $1,982,000,000—and by the end of 1930, the dollar amount was only $363,000,000.[24] Because most of these loans—at every stage of the process—were used to make margin purchases, when corporations or brokers tried to collect outstanding debts, losses cascaded through the entire financial system.

4.3. INVESTMENT TRUSTS AND THE CRASH OF 1929

The risk involved in such unbridled speculation was literally incalculable in 1929: no analytic paradigm existed for factoring risk into securities prices. Some institutions did exist, however, that had the potential to distribute risk, even if this had yet to be theorized. One of these was the investment trust, which originated in Great Britain as a vehicle for pooling investors' money, usually to purchase conservative portfolios, which were managed by professionals. What the bond salesmen Lawrence Chamberlain and William Wren Hay called the "true investment trust" focused on mortgages and bonds, and the only risk such portfolios entailed followed from possible changes in interest rates during the life of the bond.[25] The primary obligation of the investment trust was to repay to its investors the principal they invested; this was underwritten by the fund's equity capital. When the investment trust institution was adapted for the American market, however, it assumed a slightly different form. Instead of simply managing investors' pooled funds, the professional managers who typically founded these trusts also sold shares in the trust itself. Before 1928, the trusts' investments still tended to be relatively conservative, but their structure meant that the risk they took on—and thus the profit they might yield—was greater than for their British counterparts. As Chamberlain and Hay explained, the "funds entrusted are represented by shares in the enterprise and therefore the payment of the principal is not an obligation of the management, irrespective of the earnings of the trust."[26]

Before 1924, according to Chamberlain and Hay, there were relatively few investment trusts in the United States, but in that year, "about as many trusts were formed . . . as in all the preceding years and . . . the capital committed to these ventures in the year 1924 ($75,000,000) was five times as much as in all the years preceding. In 1925, 1926, and 1927 the number of companies grew rapidly and the total capital invested at least doubled each year, so that by the middle of 1928 there were about 200 trusts with an aggregate capital of $1,200,000,000."[27] During the next twelve months, the financial hysteria engulfing the securities market drove up both prices and the volume of shares traded by the investment trusts; and, when the fall began, these shares fell as far and as fast as other holdings in the US market. Because some trusts had been sponsored by investment banks, moreover, with whose extensively leveraged purchases of securities the trusts' interests were intertwined, investors in some US trusts suffered particularly severe losses.

Chamberlain and Hay criticized investment trusts because, after 1928, the shares they traded were primarily common stocks, all of which Chamberlain and Hay considered speculative. The "erroneous belief in 'common stocks as long-term investments,'" they explained, lay at the heart of the suffering the stock market crash inflicted on American investors. They attributed this belief to a book published in 1925, Edgar Lawrence Smith's *Common Stocks as Long-Term Investments*. The bond analysts concluded that Smith's book had distracted investors from more reliable data, such as a company's long-term history of earnings, thus blinding them to the truism that ought to govern investment decisions: "the only certainty of the future price-trend is its uncertainty."[28]

One contemporary who approved of investment trusts was Irving Fisher. To Fisher, in fact, the appearance of investment trusts was one of the few reasons to be optimistic after the crash, for these trusts used protective features unusual among rival financial institutions. First, they plowed their profits back into the fund instead of issuing capital gains as dividends; this plowing-back, Fisher explained, resulted in "an accumulation at compound interest, so to speak." Second, because investment trusts pooled assets, they were able to distribute risk for the individual investor. Finally, trusts used professionals to supply expert assessment and manage stocks; this allowed investors not only to pick the best stocks but also to diversify their portfolios.[29]

Fisher's work explains—and possibly even justifies—one of the profound shifts that has characterized modern investing: the preference, on the part of those who can afford long investment horizons, for stocks over bonds. The question of whether stocks yield greater returns than bonds was a matter of intense debate in the 1920s. By 1930, as we will see in chapter 5, Alfred A. Cowles, founder of the Cowles Commission, had become deeply skeptical about stock forecasters' ability to make accurate predictions about individual stocks. When Cowles developed a more sophisticated analysis of the equities market as a whole, however, he was able to demonstrate empirically that, over time, American stocks as an asset class return a premium over bonds.

As early as 1925, Edgar Lawrence Smith, whose endorsement of common stocks so angered the bond analysts Chamberlain and Hay, had enunciated what has now become one of the most important principles of investment planning: the impact of the holding period on the risk posed by equities.[30] Smith's argument was that the risk of holding stocks declines as the holding period is extended; over longer time periods, and despite the interim volatility of individual stocks, the investor's return will more closely match the long-term positive trend of the overall market. Fisher gave Smith's argument a more precise historical context, as well as a theoretical explanation: at the end of the 1920s, he insisted, investors had a good reason to shift their money out of bonds because bonds, far from being the safe securities investors once believed them to be, had become extremely risky. This risk might have been obscured by "the money illusion"—the common assumption that the purchasing power of a dollar does not change—but it was (and is) very real. When the purchasing power of the dollar falls, as it did between 1901 and 1922, the fixed-dollar-denominated returns and principal repayments of bonds are decimated. Thus, in periods in which the purchasing power of a currency fluctuates, as in the late 1920s, bonds pose a kind of risk that equities do not because fixed income returns (both the income payments and the eventual return of capital) cannot be protected from the debasement of the currency in which the bond is denominated. In such periods, the net advantage in a head-to-head competition between bonds and stocks moves to the latter. Indeed, Fisher concluded, in such periods, "bonds have a speculative character."[31]

Fisher also argued that prudent investors needed to understand the impact of interest rates on both stocks and bonds. Whereas declining rates benefit both stocks and bonds, rising interest rates affect the two asset classes differently. Changes in the interest rate affect the value of all bonds, but some stocks benefit from increasing rates and others perform well for reasons unrelated to changes in rates, such as technological innovations. An investor who owns only bonds thus cannot protect any part of his portfolio as interest rates rise, but a stockholder can neutralize some of the risk posed by changing interest rates through diversification. "If one invests $10,000 in ten different companies, putting $1,000 into each, while he does run a real risk of losing all that he has invested in some one or two of these companies, this risk is mostly offset by the probability that some other company will prosper exceedingly."[32] This explains the advantage that investment trusts offered investors in the 1920s. By pooling the investment dollars of many investors, these trusts took advantage of a probabilistic paradox:

> The more risky the investment would be to a lone individual playing the game, the safer it is, if, by pooling in an investment trust with wide diversification in investment, the individual risk is thereby absorbed. For as the risk grows it can be constantly absorbed by corresponding increases in diversification. Thus the individual member of the trust may gain more on the riskier investments, bought by the trusts at much less than their mathematical value, than if he played the market alone with less risky investments, but bought at much nearer their mathematical value. So the investment trust has proved that speculation can be turned into investment which is much safer than many individual investments in so-called "gilt-edged" securities. And the paradox is that because of the "caution factor" the market value of the riskiest investments has been depressed far below their real mathematical value. The investment trusts, carrying the principle of diversification to wide limits, have managed to get a higher average return from investments which individually would have proved quite risky, while at the same time they have extracted from them largely their elements of risk.[33]

Because investment trusts also offered their clients a "constant inspection or check-up as to the status of companies issuing stocks," they could ensure the "constant turnover" necessary to manage risk through wise diversification. "The sound investor in common stocks must turn them over constantly, selling those that are losing in value and investing in those that are gaining. This function is performed today by skilled investment counsel to a degree that makes investments in common stocks, guarded by their vigilance, safer than the former investment in bonds by individuals."[34]

Fisher's *The Stock Market Crash—and After* was primarily addressed to ordinary readers, including investors who had just suffered catastrophic losses in the 1929 crash. This work has never been embraced by economists, despite the insights it contains. (Only a brief excerpt is included in Fisher's collected works.) Perhaps the prediction of a speedy return to prosperity was too rosy to seem credible in 1930; perhaps the book was simply premature. But, as we are about to see, many of the points Fisher made in this book were soon taken up by other writers, who also wanted to help investors understand the securities market, risk, and how to evaluate companies' shares.

Before turning to these writers, we briefly consider Fisher's next work, *Booms and Depressions: Some General Principles* (1932), for this work was one of the period's few theoretical accounts of the structural relationship between the financial and real sides of the economy. Written before the publication of Keynes's 1936 *General Theory, Booms and Depressions* boldly argued that finance itself—in the form of the structural misalignment between the American currency market and the credit markets—was the proximate cause of the nation's inability to emerge from the Great Depression. Fisher argued that if a nation's currency sharply deflates during an economic downturn in which excess credit is extinguished by bankruptcy, workouts, and debt restructuring, debtors will be left with sizable levels of debt in *real* terms even after a substantial amount of their nominal debt has been extinguished. In such a situation, the perfect storm of unsustainable credit levels and currency deflation creates a downward spiral, which shrinks balance sheets and squeezes the net worth of the nation's businesses, thus impairing their creditworthiness and access to credit. Because many commercial banks, which had supplied credit to the business sector in the 1920s, were also wiped out in the early 1930s, credit flows dried up.[35] To illustrate this thesis, Fisher assembled statistics that showed that between 1929 and 1932, national indebtedness increased by 29% in *real* terms—even though debt had been reduced by a nominal $37 billion. Indebtedness increased, Fisher argued, because of the deflation of the US currency. The lesson Fisher drew from this was unambiguous: the role of the central bank in such a crisis was to do everything possible to "reflate" the currency to prevent further damage. While controversial at the time, Fisher's thesis was later developed by economists like Hyman Minsky and Richard Koos.[36]

4.4. THE NEW DEAL FOR THE AMERICAN PEOPLE: MORTGAGES FOR ALL

After the stock market crash of 1929, the federal government embarked on what President Roosevelt called "a new deal for the American people"—a campaign intended to revive the real side of the nation's economy, in part by reforming its financial side. In a flurry of radical and long-lasting legislative and regulatory measures, the Roosevelt administration sought to provide a social safety net for all Americans by protecting their savings from unstable banks, reforming the laws governing corporate disclosure, and providing resources for unemployment and old age. The regulations associated with the New Deal left no existing financial institution or instrument untouched. New laws also created entirely new institutions, such as the Social Security Administration and the Federal Deposit Insurance Corporation. And, by reworking aspects of both contract and securities law, New Deal legislation recast the terms in which credit, borrowing, investing, and even speculation would be understood for decades.

Emblematic of the way New Deal policies touched both the real and financial sides of the economy was the government's approach to home ownership. The New Deal response to home ownership, in turn, was necessitated by the inadequacy of policies the government had supported in the 1920s. In that decade, home construction was one of the boom industries, and home prices soared, rising by 50% to 75% a year.[37] Herbert Hoover, secretary of commerce, had relentlessly promoted home ownership through a national campaign entitled "Better Homes in America," and with a booklet, *How to Own Your Own Home,* written by John M. Gries and James S. Taylor.[38] In the early 1920s, home ownership had to be so vigorously promoted because few people could afford to buy a home—in part, at least, because borrowing money still carried the taint it had acquired in the late nineteenth century. In order to make borrowing seem virtuous instead of morally dubious—especially in the context of Hoover's much publicized campaign for Thrift—the secretary of commerce mobilized the patriotic overtones of the government's Liberty Bond sales campaign and encouraged Americans to take advantage of installment buying, which was initially developed in the automobile industry.

During the 1920s, Hoover's Thrift Campaign seamlessly knitted together saving-to-spend on war with preserving democracy at home. Promoting home ownership was a critical part of this effort. In the 1924 National Conference on Thrift Education, for example, a spokesperson for the New York State League of Savings and Loan Societies explained that keeping democracy safe required increasing the number of American home owners—something that could be facilitated through the kind of "wise spending" that savings and loan societies encouraged.[39] At the same conference, John Goodell, executive secretary of the National Thrift Committee of the International Committee of the YMCA, underscored the place home ownership occupied in the pantheon of American virtues: "The financial creed [of the YMCA] runs as follows: work and earn; make a budget; record expenditures; have a bank account; carry life insurance; own your own home; make a will; invest in safe securities; pay your bills promptly and share with others. You will notice it completes the circle of personal and family economic education, including earning, spending, saving, investing, and giving" (*Report* 14).

In his *History of the Thrift Movement* (1920), Simon William Strauss repeatedly emphasized that the "wise spending" known as "thrift" was fully compatible with American capitalism. Thrift, Strauss proclaimed, is "the thrift of prudent spending as well as of wise saving."[40] Strauss, who was the first president of the American Society for Thrift, was also an innovative and successful salesman: in 1909, he originated and, for the next two decades, sold real estate mortgage bonds. Marketing the senior bonds as super-safe, Strauss guaranteed purchasers an annual return of 6%. According to an article published in the *New York Evening Post* in 1924, contemporaries equated these bonds with "safe investing."

> Real estate bonds have been sold perhaps more widely than any other type of bond; they have been placed with the small investor so well in cases that many have come to regard them as the personification of safe investing. Real estate mortgage bonds have probably done more to increase the investor class in this country than any other influences since the Government war bonds selling campaigns; they have demonstrated that new buyers of bonds, in large numbers, can be created by intensive merchandising methods (not necessarily undignified methods). In doing this the real estate banker deserves no little appreciation from the bond business in general and from general business and the public at large.[41]

Along with thrift, Hoover's campaign to increase home ownership also rested on the prop of installment buying, which had long been used to help Americans purchase big-ticket items such as farm machinery and sewing machines.[42] In 1919, the General Motors Corporation helped save the automobile industry by creating its own finance company to offer installment plans to consumers. Following the creation of the General Motors Acceptance Corporation (GMAC), other companies followed suit, and, by 1925, the number of finance companies devoted to automobile sales alone had reached sixteen or seventeen hundred, and somewhere in the vicinity of 70% to 75% of all automobile sales were financed through these companies.[43] Installment buying was soon applied to less expensive purchases, such as phonographs, radios, vacuum cleaners, washing machines, refrigerators, and ready-made clothing, but it was also applied to houses, in the form of mortgages, most of which were underwritten not by the US government but by the kind of bonds marketed by Strauss.[44]

For Strauss and purchasers of his bonds, the good times began to end in 1926, when the failure of one of his competitors sparked an inquiry into the real estate mortgage bond industry. With the revelation that many of these ventures were essentially Ponzi schemes, Strauss's bonds lost the popularity they had momentarily enjoyed.[45] By 1929, when the stock market crashed, Americans owed a total of $30 billion in mortgage debt—this, in addition to the $7 billion they owed in other forms of consumer debt.

The government's response was to double down on its campaign for home ownership—not just to support democracy, much less thrift, but because home construction and sales would put Americans back to work. As Marriner Eccles, soon to be FDR's choice to head the Federal Reserve, explained, new housing starts "would affect everyone, from the manufacturer of lace curtains to the manufacturers of lumber, bricks, furniture, cement, and electrical appliances. The mere shipment of these supplies would affect the railroads, which in turn would need the produce of steel mills for rails."[46] To promote home ownership, Roosevelt created the Home Owners' Loan Corporation; beginning in 1933, this agency refinanced more than a million mortgages. Offering for the first time thirty-year fixed-rate mortgages instead of the more typical three- to five-year mortgage that had been the norm, the Home Owners' Loan Corporation helped many Americans stay in their homes. With backing from the Federal Housing Authority (FHA) and the Federal National Mortgage Association (the predecessor of Fannie Mae), these measures made certain that any bank willing to lend would be able to, for the agencies essentially guaranteed that loans not repaid by borrowers would be made good by the government. Fannie Mae was empowered to repurchase loans from banks, thus allowing banks to lend more money than in the past, and the FHA provided insurance for any bank that suffered losses from mortgage loans. By yoking consumer well-being to patriotic values and the financial institutions that underwrote construction and loans, these New Deal policies both put the US government at the center of the housing industry and supported the real and financial sides of the economy at the same time. The financial institutions they created were also the first members of what would eventually become a shadow banking system, which worked alongside the official banking system but outside the purview of regulatory agencies.

4.5. PUBLIC DISCLOSURE AND THE MODERN CORPORATION

Some New Deal reforms were designed to do what existing, but largely ineffectual, state blue-sky laws had tried to do: make modern corporations disclose "exact full information about securities sold."[47] The most important measures in this regard were the Securities and Exchange Acts of 1933 and 1934. These acts, in turn, were formulated as partial responses to a book published in 1932, *The Modern Corporation and Private Property* by Adolf Berle and Gardiner Means, a seminal study that exposes the critical role played by changing conceptions of information as the government tried to make some parts of the US financial system more visible to consumers.

In 1932, Adolf Berle was a Columbia University law professor and member of FDR's "brains trust," and Gardiner Means was an institutional economist who taught at Harvard. Other scholars have focused on important aspects of this book—its anticipation of "agency costs," the analysis of the challenge that the securitization of corporate assets poses to traditional property rights, or its advocacy of the fiduciary or trust paradigm of the duties management owes to shareholders.[48] For our purposes, the heart of *The Modern Corporation* is its engagement with the public securities markets, which the authors describe as "one of the economic enigmas" of the modern financial system.[49] As we saw in chapter 1, one of the distinctive features of the modern corporation is its separation of ownership from control over the company's day-to-day operations. What we have yet to explore are the paradoxical effects of this separation. Among these is a mismatch between the needs of company investors and those of the corporation itself: whereas the former wants to be able to buy and sell securities at will, the latter requires a constant stream of income. The shareholder, who is mortal, needs liquidity; the corporation, which is an immortal "going entity" under the law, needs perpetual flows of capital.

By the early 1930s, the financial needs of the giant corporations were even more voracious than during the initial merger period. At the time Berle and Means collected data for their book, large companies "appear[ed] . . . [to be] growing between two and three times as fast" as all other non-corporate companies (41). The concentration of wealth these corporations represented was equally noteworthy, as was their scale. By 1930, "130 out of the 573 independent American corporations . . . can be classed as huge companies, each reporting assets of over one hundred million dollars. These 130 companies controlled more than 80 per cent of the assets of all the companies represented" (29). The two hundred largest corporations controlled 49.2% of corporate wealth, 38% of business wealth other than banking, and 22% of national wealth (33). The largest nonbanking corporations had assets of over $100 million, and fifteen had assets of over $1 billion (19).

While shareholders as a group had also amassed considerable wealth, the corporate structure deprived them of the ability both to see the company's operations firsthand and to exercise any influence over it. But, as Berle and Means explained, in ceding control to management, shareholders had actually gained something unique to the corporate regime: the ability to cash out part or all their interest at will. This is the second paradox exposed by *The Modern Corporation*: in purchasing equities, shareholders exchange control for liquidity. But liquidity both requires and creates further novelties. The requirement is straightforward: For a liquid form of property to have value, some mechanism must assign it a price. The new product, which is more complex, turns on the reorientation articulated in Irving Fisher's financial view: For the market mechanism to assign the security a price, it must factor in not the value of some underlying asset but the investors' expectations about the future—about whether the company whose shares they hold will distribute part of its profits in dividends and whether their shares will rise in value.[50] And herein lies a third paradox, for the investors' expectations about the company's willingness to pay dividends is, in turn, appraised by the pricing mechanism and factored into the market value of the shares. "Tersely, the shareholder has a piece of paper with an open market value, and as holder of this paper may receive from time to time, at the pleasure of the management, periodic distributions. He is forced to measure his participation, not in assets, but in a market quotation; and this market quotation 'discounts' or appraises the expectation of distributions" (252).

Berle and Means acknowledged that the "corporate security system" is thus based on a peculiar dynamic, the legal status of which primarily matters when it feeds into investors' expectations: "Economically, the various so-called a 'legal rights' or the economic pressures which may lead a management to do well by its stockholders, in and of themselves are merely uncertain expectations in the hands of the individual. Aggregated, interpreted by a public market, and appraised in a security exchange, they do have a concrete and measurable value; and it is to this value that the shareholder must and in fact does address himself. His thinking is colored by it; and in large measure the corporate security system is based on it" (252). Because the mechanism that appraises and prices securities is so central to this system, Berle and Means devoted the last two books of *The Modern Corporation* to the operations of the public security exchanges. By bringing together buyers and sellers, these exchanges rectified the mismatch between the short-term and heterogeneous needs of individual investors and the long-term needs of corporations.

Because they priced shares continuously, the exchanges allowed the shareholders to buy and sell whenever the price was right; because they brought a virtually limitless stream of investors into the market, the exchanges provided the corporations with the flow of capital they craved. In yet another paradox of the corporate system, the exchanges also offered shareholders imaginative rewards even when they did not sell their shares. "A shareholder who possesses common stock in the expectation that it will ultimately pay large dividends, though in fact it is paying none, would, nevertheless, regard his expectations as reasonably satisfied if the price of his stock were to mount steadily so that he could realize his expectation by sale of his security for cash through the machinery of a public market" (247). If the price assigned by the exchange to his securities were to rise, in other words, the shareholder would be satisfied in anticipation of some future sale—whether or not that sale occurred. The exchanges even converted these anticipated rewards into actual lines of credit that otherwise would not exist. This credit could benefit an individual shareholder—by allowing him to borrow against the market value of the shares—and it could benefit the corporation—by allowing the company to borrow against or issue new shares in relation to its capitalized value. This credit could even benefit the nation—by raising the value of its overall productivity—a figure that would soon become visible in the aggregate estimates generated by national income and product accounts.[51]

Berle and Means explained that markets priced securities by processing a flow of information. "Appraisal necessarily turns on information" (259). Some information was elicited by the exchanges, which required "continuous disclosure" from the listed corporations (259); and some appeared in newsletters devoted to the industry (*Poor's, Moody's,* and *Standard Statistics*), as well as newspapers like the *Wall Street Journal* or the *New York Commercial.* Stock tickers also distributed information, this time in a continuous stream, and the buy-and-sell orders that brokers placed generated yet more. "These, and many more besides, constantly pour into the market a running narrative of facts, figures, amounts, opinion, and information of all sorts, which does or is thought to bear upon values of the securities traded in" (259). Even if some of the information was not true, even if the relevant information did not always reach its intended destination, even if an unimpeded flow of perfect information was impossible, "the ideal situation—that of constant running disclosure of all information bearing on value . . . can . . . be approximated; and it certainly is true that the mechanisms of dissemination are so well developed that any facts bearing on values can become common market property almost instantaneously" (259).

The same "constant running disclosure of all information" that allowed exchanges to appraise and price securities should, in theory at least, have given each buyer and seller, no matter how great his resources, the same chance to profit from trade. This "disclosure philosophy," which was embodied in the Securities and Exchange Acts of 1933 and 1934, underwrote Roosevelt's demand that the Wall Street firms "let in the light," and, even if the laws did not require full disclosure, the acts did attempt to use publicity to make the markets police themselves.[52] Before turning to the provisions of the two securities acts, we consider the complexities of the relationship between information and disclosure, for these complexities illuminate both the goals and the limitations of all New Deal efforts to use transparency as an instrument of reform. In their discussion of disclosure, Berle and Means alluded to the present-value theory of stock valuation, and they began to tease out the implications this theory held for corporate liability.

> Granting the economic thesis that a share of stock is primarily a capitalized expectation, valued in an open market appraisal of the situation existing in the corporation and the industry, and granting further that it is reasonably foreseeable (as it certainly is) that appraisals will vary with the information given out, it is not difficult to suppose that the management of a corporation will be liable (a) for willful misstatement of fact designed to induce action on the part of anyone buying or selling in the market; (b) perhaps also on account of a negligent misstatement of fact not designed to induce action in the market but resulting in a material

fluctuation; (c) possibly, for a failure to disclose a material fact leading
to a faulty appraisal. (282)

Looking at the situation as a corporate lawyer, Berle knew it would be difficult
to prove that a corporation was culpable for passing along false or misleading
information, not to mention simply failing to disclose (282).[53] But he and his
co-author also realized that, because of the critical role information played
in pricing, this difficulty could be surmounted by insisting on transparency
at the points at which information originated or was released: the drafting of
the company's charter, its registration with the security exchange, periodic releases of corporate accounts, announcements of extraordinary events, and reports of dividends issued. They argued that the law should not only target the
release of information at special moments when transparency was essential; it
should also restrict some flows of information, primarily insider information,
which, by definition, the public could not see.

Even though *The Modern Corporation and Private Property* focused primarily on the intersection of market transactions and the law, this work did
add the new idea of information to the economic theory that expectation is
a critical component of value. If expectation informs value, as present-value
theory states, and if information informs expectations, as Berle and Means asserted, then the flow of information is a critical component of finance. And if
the financial market is to operate fairly and efficiently, information must be simultaneously released and regulated. Disclosure rules must be superimposed
upon the "open" operations of the security exchanges; corporations must be
compelled to meet specified standards that require publicizing certain "extraordinary facts"; and managers must be forbidden from profiting from information to which they alone are privy (284). Berle and Means reached these
conclusions in *The Modern Corporation and Private Property,* but they also
recognized that such disclosures would be insufficient: "It cannot be said that
disclosures of the kind required furnish all of the information needed for an
accurate appraisal. The formulation of such requirements would probably be
impossible" (280).

Berle and Means were obviously ambivalent about the paradoxes their
investigation exposed. On the one hand, they openly lamented some of the
effects of the corporate transformation of property: the shareholder, owner-
no-more, had become "a risk-taker pure and simple" (297); the "spiritual values" once entwined with property ownership had vanished (64); and shares
of stock, severed from the assets they presumably represented, had been cast
adrift to "glide from hand to hand, irresponsible and impersonal" (250). On

the other hand, Berle and Means also viewed the modern corporation as "a major social institution" (308), whose concentration of economic power enabled big companies to "compete on equal terms with the modern state" (313), and they even imagined that "economic statesmanship" might be the diplomacy of the future (313). The ambivalent tone of the work—elegiac yet celebratory, caustic yet resigned—encapsulates the ambiguities that permeated the entire New Deal, as legislators audaciously tried to remake virtually every financial institution at the same time, while also casting nostalgic glances at the past.

The Securities and Exchange Acts that became law in 1933 and 1934 also conveyed this ambivalence—although it might be more accurate simply to say that they represented compromises between presidential advisers hell-bent on reforming Wall Street and the financiers whose deep pockets kept so many politicians in Washington. The 1933 act assigned regulatory oversight for the financial industry to the Federal Trade Commission (FTC) and included a list of disclosures required of corporations newly listing on Wall Street. It also imposed a twenty-day waiting period between the time a company filed its registration statement and the issue of its shares; this would allow the FTC to examine the company in more detail. The 1933 act did not allow the FTC to evaluate the quality of listed securities, however, nor did it give the FTC authority to enforce existing blue-sky laws. Finally, the act exempted so many kinds of securities—including all those already listed, all bank securities, and all securities issued by both state and federal governments—that few issuing companies were subject to much restraint. Felix Frankfurter, who had lobbied strenuously for a stronger bill, acknowledged the limitations of the act Congress was willing to pass. Calling it "a modest first installment," Frankfurter said that the act was "strong insofar as publicity is potent; it is weak insofar as publicity is not enough."[54] The second Securities and Exchange Act actually weakened regulation of the financial industry. In creating a special agency to oversee Wall Street—the Securities and Exchange Commission (SEC)—the 1934 act freed finance from the more exacting standards of the FTC. The act did give the SEC oversight of stock exchange rules and it required companies that listed on exchanges to file quarterly and annual reports with the SEC. The 1934 act did not specify a mechanism for enforcing anything like the full disclosure of information to shareholders, however, even though it granted the SEC the vague power to issue new rules "in the public interest or for the protection of investors."[55]

As prescient as they were about the role information plays in modern finance, Berle and Means did not theorize their insight, as later economists were to do. Indeed, because modern finance capitalizes expectations in order to appraise the bundle of tangible and intangible property rights represented in securities, the creation of techniques to exploit information rationally and rules to govern its flow would prove critical to future developments in financial theory. Even if they did not develop this theory, and even if the two securities acts they promoted did not immediately realize a new regime of regulatory information, Berle and Means did help investors understand the laws that governed securities transactions, and they also helped administration officials see why unimpeded information flows were critical to the economy.

4.6. SECURITY RESEARCH

A second book, this one published in 1934, also gave contemporaries some insight into how the financial system worked. *Security Analysis,* by Benjamin Graham and David Dodd, has been praised for redefining "the role of academics in relation to the practice of security analysis,"[56] but it also helped raise the credibility of a profession whose reputation suffered in the 1929 crash, gave future Wall Street analysts an invaluable trove of case studies and practical guidelines, and proved that security analysis, while not a science, could be systematized and taught. Like Berle and Means, moreover, Graham and Dodd introduced but did not theorize what were to become critical pieces of modern financial theory: whereas Berle and Means adumbrated but did not develop the role played by information in the market mechanism, Graham and Dodd revealed how asset classes and risk were treated before these concepts were placed on a statistical basis. In the pages of *Security Analysis,* we see concepts emerge that were to be carried over but completely transformed as the information mandated by the new securities laws was collected and as risk was newly theorized.

Benjamin Graham joined Columbia University's evening division of the School of Business Administration in 1928, and he continued teaching at Columbia until 1956, with enrollments in his "Advanced Security Analysis" course sometimes reaching 150 students. David Dodd was Graham's junior colleague at Columbia and went on to a successful career as a financial analyst and adviser. Graham reversed this trajectory, for he came to Columbia from Wall Street. His first job was as an assistant in the bond department of Newburger, Henderson, and Loeb, in 1917, where he created the company's statistical department; he soon became a partner in the firm. Among his technical achievements at Newburger was the development of a method for addressing the problem of stock watering, which had caused so much concern at the beginning of the century. In 1923, Graham left Newburger to become a portfolio manager at Graham Corporation; in 1926, he founded the Benjamin Graham Joint Account, where, through hedging and arbitrage based on the kind of careful analysis now called fundamental research, he and his partners earned impressive returns. When the market crashed in 1929, the fund's earnings followed suit: returns fell 20% in 1929, 50% in 1930, 16% in 1931, and 3% in 1932. Graham thus left Wall Street for Columbia with a track record of extraordinary success and humbling failure. He was later to say that simply keeping his fund alive through the years after the crash was one of his greatest accomplishments.[57]

To understand the fundamental research *Security Analysis* promoted we need to place the 1934 book in the context of the period's securities transactions. These transactions, like their modern counterparts, always had two sides: on the one side, a company's promoter or CFO, often advised by an investment banker, decided how to raise money for the firm—whether, for example, to issue bonds, which had fixed-interest obligations and predetermined expiration dates, or shares, which carried some expectation of periodic dividends, potentially gave the purchaser more interest in the firm, paid market-driven returns, and had no expiration date; on the other side of the transaction, the investor had to decide what to buy to maximize returns and how to insure the safety of his overall investment. It is important to remember that the details of the issuer's side were not visible to the investor—even the new publicity requirements instituted by the 1933 Securities Act did not mandate this level of detail—and that the two sides of the transactions were not temporally aligned. While every purchase involved both an issuer and a buyer, in other words, the corporate decisions that brought the securities to the market in the first place preceded the investor's decision about what securities to buy. After the initial release of a particular issue of securities, moreover, a company could issue additional securities, which could affect the value of the shares already sold.[58]

One way to view the job of a security analyst is to imagine him trying to reconstruct the decisions made on the issuer's side of the transaction in order to judge the value of the securities on offer and determine whether they were overpriced in relation to their "intrinsic value" or priced correctly, in relation to the overall worth of the company and the returns they would yield. For Graham and Dodd, this involved several operations, all of which were made under three crucial assumptions: investment and speculation were antithetical activities; "intrinsic value," while important to the analyst's valuation, often involved approximation; and market price did not always indicate "true value" (22). Graham and Dodd assumed that investment could be distinguished from speculation to justify the profession of security analysis; they assumed that the analyst could approximate intrinsic value because, in the absence of statistical data about asset class returns, they needed some kind of benchmark by which to judge the security's market price; and they assumed that market price and true value could diverge because this divergence yielded the "undervalued securities" they were looking for. Graham and Dodd justified these assumptions by appealing to "facts" and by admitting that definition by negation was sometimes necessary. Thus they acknowledged that it was difficult to draw a bright line between "investment" and "speculation" but insisted that the first depended on the "thorough analysis" of facts.[59] They admitted that "intrinsic value is an elusive concept" (17).[60] And they explained that prices sometimes diverged from intrinsic value because "the market is not a *weighing machine,* on which the value of each issue is recorded by an exact and impersonal mechanism, in accordance with specific qualities. Rather should we say that the market is a *voting machine,* whereon countless individuals register choices which are the product partly of reason and partly of emotion" (23). The image of the market as a voting machine captures Graham and Dodd's perspective on the impeded information flows that so worried Berle and Means: whereas Berle and Means sought legal measures to ensure that information would flow, Graham and Dodd saw in the blocked flows opportunities for shrewd investments. Another way to view the work of the security analyst, in fact, is to say that he exploits blockages in the flows of information; by "shrewd detective work," he can identify bargains where others see only the published prices.

The analysis that Graham and Dodd conducted included, but was not restricted to, the following activities: they reconstructed the processes of corporate accounting and capital budgeting that lay behind the company's issue of a particular security; analyzed the "capitalization structure" of the issuing company and compared the company to others in the same industry (461); analyzed the company's accounts for misrepresentations or omissions; and, most importantly, judged whether at the moment of purchase, a particular security was undervalued by the market. Their focus on the issuing company's "capitalization structure"—what modern analysts call its "capital structure"—is one of the most important contributions of *Security Analysis,* for this focus acknowledges that each issue of securities carries with it designated rights, features, protective provisions, and covenants that affect the investor as much as the issuing firm. (These include the right to vote, the status of the claim in case of bankruptcy, the call on future dividends, and so on.) Looking at the capital structure of a company involved, in essence, using its income statement and balance sheets to see beyond what the documents explicitly revealed—to see how the overall finances of the company were organized. This enabled the analyst to remind an investor that when she purchased a security, she was buying a specific issue, the value of which was partly a function of the entailments with which the security was issued, just as it was partly determined by the company's simultaneous or subsequent securities issues. Because a company had many claims upon it, the investor had to know not simply the price of the security she wanted to buy—much less the single number quoted on an exchange or even on the company's balance sheet; the investor also had to know how the price of this particular issue would be affected by other aspects of the company's capital structure. This is one reason the first noun in Graham and Dodd's book is singular: the security analyst has to examine each security, issue by issue, in relation to the entire suite of liabilities that the company has undertaken.

Within the capital structure of a corporation, the classification of securities into discrete categories is critical, for this both identifies the pertinent features of each group and determines the relationship among groups of securities. One of the secondary aims of *Security Analysis* was to introduce a new system of classification; the book's primary aim was to remind readers that the connotations once carried by terms like "bonds," "preferred stock," and "public utilities" had to be revisited in the wake of the crash. Thus they included extensive anecdotal accounts of bonds, preferred stocks, and common stocks that departed from the norms traditionally associated with each security class. Even though Graham and Dodd were interested in classification, however, they did not use the modern concept of an asset class, nor did they have the statistical data that would allow later analysts to evaluate a particular security in relation to the total return of its asset class. They did repeatedly recommend that an investor increase the safety of her overall holdings by diversification, but they did not have the kind of statistical aggregation that would later anchor asset allocation on a comparable basis. Unlike subsequent theoretical treatments, which would explain the prices of securities through concepts such as randomness, efficiency, information, and market structure, Graham and Dodd's approach to market decisions was pragmatic and commonsensical: they knew that corporations sometimes engaged in "tricky accounting" (390); Wall Street was often willing to accept "sleight-of-hand" in pricing securities (418); and the "topsy-turvy reasoning" of corporate managers might seriously distort the value they assigned an issue (418). To penetrate the smoke-and-mirrors game practiced by corporate accountants and Wall Street brokers, the analyst had to rely not on mathematical calculations or statistical analysis alone but on a combination of quantitative and qualitative analysis (430). Only then did he stand a chance against the limitless repertoire of strategies companies exercised on the other side of the securities transaction. The conviction repeatedly expressed by Graham and Dodd that no formulaic analysis could protect the innocent investor lay behind their skepticism about the effectiveness of the 1933 Securities Act.

> The Securities Act of 1933 aims to safeguard the security buyer by requiring full disclosure of the pertinent facts and by extending the previously existing liability for concealment or misrepresentation. While full disclosure is undoubtedly desirable, it may not be of much practical help except to the skilled and shrewd investor or to the trained analyst. It is to be feared that the typical stock buyer will neither read the long prospectus carefully nor understand the implications of all it contains. Many modern financing methods are not far different from a magician's bag of tricks; they can be executed in full view of the public without it being very much the wiser. (558)

Graham and Dodd realized that the investment environment had changed during the 1920s. At the beginning of the decade, they argued, investors could treat every security as if it were a form of bond because companies were legally required to issue shares of stock at par and to pay dividends out of profits. By the end of the decade, companies were required only to make their balance sheets available to potential investors; no-par stock had long been permissible; and company managers had begun to limit or even curtail dividend issue. In this context, and as bond yields began to fall, investors stopped treating all securities as if they were bonds. They could see that company earnings were exceeding dividend payments; they knew that a company could use its retained earnings to reinvest in its operations; and they began to evaluate securities according to both the undistributed assets of the company and, in anticipation of the yields these assets could generate, according to the returns investors expected shares to generate in the future. By the end of the decade, in the brief but manic phase of the "new era," investors began to demand common stocks over both bonds and preferred stock; and they evaluated the price of common stocks by applying a species of "pseudo-analysis" to whatever facts and figures were available. Unlike Irving Fisher, who had credited equity holders with recognizing the vulnerability of bonds to fluctuating currency values, Graham and Dodd charged that what investors were really doing in the build-up to the crash was simply fleeing the disappointing yields of bonds, assigning undue importance to the value of the intangibles on a company's books, and, essentially, buying any industrial common stock on offer in the irrational belief that the price of every "blue-chip" would continue to rise (4–5, 11, 14).[61]

To restore good judgment to the valuation of common stocks after the crash, Graham and Dodd offered three guidelines, which anticipated modern concepts without placing them on a statistical basis. The first echoed Fisher's endorsement of diversification: investors should think of their investments as a "*group* operation, in which diversification of risk is depended upon to yield a favorable average result" (317). Whereas Fisher had approved of the investment strategy endorsed by Smith's *Common Stocks as Long-Term Investments,* however, Graham and Dodd insisted that investors should focus on the "true P/E [price/earnings] estimate of a company," which stressed "*average earnings,* not *maximum earnings* or *trend of earnings,*" as Smith's P/E ratio did (314). The second maxim extended their earlier comments on the inadequacy of relying exclusively on either quantitative or qualitative tests; select individual securities, they advised, "by means of quantitative and qualitative tests corresponding to those employed in the choice of fixed-value investments" (317). Their third guideline, by contrast, identified the criteria for choosing between bonds and equities; in the case of the latter, "a greater effort is made . . . to determine the future outlook of the issues considered" (317). This anticipation of a "future outlook" should not be confused with valuation based on the expectation of future returns: repeatedly, Graham and Dodd insisted that "analysis is concerned primarily with values which are supported by the facts and not those which depend largely upon expectations. . . . The analyst must take possible future changes into account, but his primary aim is not so much to *profit* from them as to *guard* against them" (38).

This last warning—that the analyst should guard against future changes— opens onto the understanding of risk implicit in *Security Analysis.* Benjamin Graham and David Dodd did not think of risk in relative terms, as later theorists would do; they did not measure risk in relation to an asset class, an investor's portfolio, or the market as a whole. For them, risk had no statistical component; it could not be managed, because, in their account, risk, like loss, was absolute. Risk, in other words, was neither conflated with uncertainty nor opposed to it: Graham and Dodd viewed risk as insurmountable and inevitable. An investor either profited from an individual security or he did not; he either received returns or he did not. Modern portfolio managers and security analysts, engaged in managing large portfolios for institutions with long investment horizons, use statistical measures based on the history of US capital markets to establish a relative risk/reward framework instead of using the absolute risk framework Graham and Dodd assumed. Without a statistical understanding of asset classes or long-term reconstructions of capital market returns, Graham and Dodd could not express confidence that the market will always come back, as their modern contemporaries typically do.

Graham and Dodd did intimate that the evaluation of an individual security should be made in relation to the overall market: the "high" and "low" prices of stocks should always be measured relative to prices on the overall market, they wrote, as well as in relation to the past prices for these shares (321). In passing, they also acknowledged that P/E ratios were relative measures: in criticizing Smith's *Common Stocks as Long-Term Investments,* they noted that the price of a security could rise in relation not only to its own price but in relation to prices of shares on the overall market (314). By and large, however, Graham and Dodd's investment philosophy was anchored in absolute principles: they thought a P/E ratio of 10 was almost always a good investment and that the security analyst could establish a "basis for *conservative* or *investment* valuation," even if this involved some approximation (452). Even if they recommended diversification, they did not work in the theoretical framework that would soon underwrite portfolio analysis; even if they advocated fundamental analysis, they could not foresee how statistical methods would change the way this was used. Benjamin Graham and David Dodd viewed the securities market in fine detail and they exercised exquisite judgment about it, but they finally judged security analysis to be an "art," not part of a science that would make use of mathematics or models. "Investment is by nature not an exact science," they asserted (14). "It must always be remembered that the truth which the analyst uncovers is first of all not the *whole* truth and, second, not the *immutable* truth" (352). "There are no dependable ways of making money easily and quickly," they ruefully concluded, "either in Wall Street or anywhere else" (613).

4.7. THE DIVIDEND DISCOUNT MODEL

In 1938, almost a decade after the stock market crash but with the US economy still enmeshed in the Great Depression, another investor-turned-economist tried to expose the mysteries of the securities market. Unlike Berle and Means, who wrote primarily for policy makers and lawyers, and Graham and Dodd, who wrote for security analysts-in-training, John Burr Williams wanted economists to read his book. Williams considered *The Theory of Investment*

Value a contribution to "Economics as a whole," and he introduced his new technique—"algebraic budgeting"—as a "new tool of great power, whose use promises to lead to notable advances in Investment Analysis."[62] By refusing to apologize for his extensive use of mathematics, as most other economists did, Williams also made the turn only a few economists had made by 1938—a turn to mathematical formalism that was to prove decisive for the discipline. While Williams did not recognize the role risk was to play in modern investment theory, the technique he developed, as well as the mathematical formalism he celebrated, would soon transform the way economic theories were constructed and presented.[63]

Like Benjamin Graham, John Burr Williams gained practical experience working in finance during the 1920s, as a junior investment banker in Boston. His goal, however, was to combine that experience with economic theory. Williams arrived at Harvard along with two of the professors who were to sit on his thesis committee: Wassily Leontief, an economist who had left Kiel in 1931, and the Austrian Joseph Schumpeter, who had previously taught at Bonn. The third member of Williams's dissertation committee, Alvin Hansen, was not to arrive at Harvard until 1937.

As we saw in chapter 3, one of the research programs mounted by the Harvard Economics Department in the 1920s focused on business cycle barometers, a statistical tool for measuring indexes considered essential to the business cycle. Even though the project had been abandoned in 1929, it did leave an influential legacy, for, as a project devoted to compiling and mathematically analyzing time series and large data sets, Warren Persons's work had brought mathematical tools like curve fitting, spectral analysis, and regression and correlation analysis to the attention of Harvard economists. Williams profitably used one technique from the economic statistician's toolkit: the formula for the logistic curve, which was used to fit empirical data to time series trends for phenomena that were rapidly growing, such as expanding populations, profitable new companies, or companies that grew from a one-time stimulation like a merger. The logistic curve had been employed in population studies as early as 1845 because it captured the process of rapid initial growth followed by the slowdown that characterizes a population's maturation. As the statistician Harold Davis explained: "The logistic curve may be regarded as a transition line intermediate between a lower initial level and an upper stable level. In such a transition curve there must necessarily be a point of inflection, where the rate of increase of production begins to decline. . . . The existence of an upper asymptote, the line of complete maturity, is the distinguishing feature of the logistic which makes it superior to a purely exponential law of growth in applications of economic time series."[64]

Williams also adapted a second method long part of the Harvard toolkit—the case study. Williams realized that he could use this method to generate data and test both his economic theories and the predictions made by algebraic budgeting. He devoted Book II of *The Theory of Investment Value* to case studies of General Motors, US Steel, and the Phoenix Insurance Company. Two appendices containing tables of his raw data—showing prices, seasonal bookings, output, and the capitalization structure of the companies—allowed interested readers to evaluate Williams's judgments.

Williams's pivotal contribution was to use the logistic curve to model the prospective pattern of earnings growth of a successful young company, thus predicting the company's future performance. This also established a rational basis for valuation, if the curve's parameters were estimated according to the analyst's research assumptions. This allowed the analyst to break a long time series into smaller units and thus to distinguish between general, seasonal, and whatever local trends he was interested in; Williams identified the point at which the tendency of one segment of the curve shifted into another pattern as the inflection point. Critics of the Harvard Barometer Project had charged that applying this method to the business cycle too often simply confirmed what statisticians expected to find: because identifying and measuring trends and inflection points rested exclusively on the analyst's judgments, statisticians had no external point of reference by which they could evaluate their judgments.[65] Then, too, they were trying to discover *laws* in the data from which they constructed the series and curves, and, once the Depression arrived, they were forced to acknowledge that the trends they thought reflected laws had disappeared. Williams was able to substitute for the notion of an informing law the predicted growth pattern of an individual company by focusing not on aggregate economic processes but on the performance of a single company and by looking toward the future instead of the past. Williams's ultimate goal was to help the investor identify the "true" or "intrinsic" value of a company's equities by predicting the company's future growth pattern. Like Graham and Dodd, in other words, Williams assumed that it was possible to identify the intrinsic value of a stock, but unlike the authors of *Security Analysis,* he provided a mathematical technique for doing so.[66]

Williams's understanding of intrinsic value was modeled on well-known mathematical ideas. The heart of this model—the mathematical machinery that makes it run—is the present-value algorithm, which is the geometric growth rate most familiar to investors as compound interest, or as logarithmic growth. In Williams's view, the valuation of stocks should be patterned on the mathematics that informed the valuation of bonds; the investment value of each kind of security is the sum of its future payments, discounted to the present at the current discount rate. Here is Williams's statement of what he calls "the main thesis of this book":

> Let us define the investment value of a stock as the present worth of all the dividends to be paid upon it. Likewise let us define the investment value of a bond as the present worth of its future coupons and principal. . . . The purchase of a stock or bond, like other transactions which give rise to the phenomenon of interest, represents the exchange of present goods for future goods—dividends, or coupons and principal, in this case being the claim on future goods. To appraise the investment value, then, it is necessary to estimate the future payments. The annuity of payments, adjusted for changes in the value of money itself, may then be discounted at the pure interest rate demanded by the investor. (55)

At this point in his exposition, Williams began to convert these definitions into mathematical equations, but, like other mathematical economists writing in the 1930s, he could not assume that most readers would follow the mathematics. In a footnote addressed to *"the non-technical reader,"* Williams tried to reassure these readers, even though he was clearly encouraging other economists to use mathematics. "It is not necessary to master all of the algebra in the following chapters to understand the rest of this book," Williams explained, "for the text between the equations has been so written as to summarize the argument and make it possible to take the derivation of the formulas for granted" (55, n. 2). Williams clearly stood at a methodological crossroads in the discipline. Soon economists would have two groups of readers: one group would have to take "the derivation of the formulas for granted," if they followed the mathematical argument at all; and the other, which did not dominate the profession until the 1970s, would both reason and express their ideas in mathematical terms.[67]

Williams's work also occupied the crossroads where institutional economics met neoclassical theory. Like institutionalists, he considered the likely effects of "taxation, invention, rearmament, foreign lending, war, and Social Security" (386) as he estimated the long-term interest rate (which informed the final calculation of the discount rate). Williams's reliance on mathematics, by contrast, harkened back to the deductive method associated with neoclassicism. The result of combining these approaches was a formula—we might call it a model—that helped the investor value the price of a stock by predicting its future dividends, then discounting them back to their present value. If the value given by the formula was higher than the price the stock traded for, the investor could assume the stock was undervalued and feel confident in buying it. Today, this is called the dividend discount model, or the Gordon Growth Model.

Williams's valuation technique involved four steps. First, he used the long-term government bond, which is not influenced by the Fed's monetary interventions, to identify what the market thought future real interest rates would be. Second, he made his own judgment about these rates, based on an analysis of the prevailing conditions, and he used this judgment to correct for conditions not built into market expectations. Based on his assessment of the impact that a resumption of inflation was likely to have, for example, which the market had not factored in, and an upward movement in real interest rates, which he thought would accompany recovery from the Depression and the economic stimulus of war preparation, Williams concluded that the 2.78% yield-to-maturity of the long government bond, maturing in 1959, needed to be adjusted upward to 4%. Williams also added a risk premium to the long government bond rate—thus reaching a discount rate for equities of 5¾% (387). Williams cited the common Wall Street practice of including a risk premium for stocks, but, even if it was customary in 1938 to do so, he was the first economist to model and estimate the equity risk premium.[68]

The third step in Williams's method was to forecast the future pattern of earnings for the company. If it was young and growing, Williams used the logistic curve; if it was a monopoly with fixed earnings, like a utilities company, he had to use another distribution because the logistic curve would not fit its growth pattern. Finally, Williams discounted the predicted future earnings back to their present value; this allowed him to arrive at "the pure interest rate demanded by the investor"—the interest rate sufficiently attractive, under these conditions, to make an investor buy. Of the four steps, determining the future pattern of earnings was the most important—but, ultimately, the most challenging. This is where algebraic budgeting entered the process. "The solution . . . consists in making a budget showing the company's growth in assets, debt, earnings, and dividends during the years to come. This budget is not drawn up with debit and credit, however, using a journal and ledger as an accountant would do, but is put into algebraic form in a way that is altogether new to the accountant's art. Then, by manipulation of algebraic symbols, the warp of development is traced through the woof of time with an ease unknown to ordinary accounting" (128). As this passage makes clear, algebraic budgeting combined the abstraction and manipulability of algebra with basic accounting rules and principles, like the accounting identity that requires debits to equal credits. In addition, it relied on a recognized statistical distribution to predict growth. The algebraic equations built on the kind of fundamental analysis promoted by Graham and Dodd, but algebraic budgeting combined this with mathematical equations and statistical probability to model the relationships among various factors out into the future according to both the patterns observed in the past and those the future would probably bring. Williams viewed his innovation as an extension of the tried-and-true mathematics of finance.

> In the science known as the Mathematics of Finance, it has long been the practice to employ algebra in the making of bond tables and the calculation of depreciation; now it would seem to be time greatly to enlarge the scope of that science so as to make it include methods for dealing with *all* kinds of securities, under *all* kinds of conditions. In the past this science could handle only bonds, and even bonds it could not handle if the purchasing power of money or the rate of interest rate was expected to change; now it is desirable to equip it to handle stocks, warrants, and convertible issues, as well as bonds, and to handle bonds also when inflation or deflation impends or when interest rates seem likely to rise or fall. (187)

The conceptual and methodological breakthrough represented by Williams's work depended upon institutional and theoretical factors that converged in the 1930s. On the one side, these factors derived from the general developments in corporate accounting and corporate law we examined in chapter 1: without a stable definition of earnings per share and regular, reliable information about a particular company's book value, return on equity, bond and equity liabilities, and schedule of dividend payments, it would have been impossible even to imagine that such values could be solved by an algebraic equation. While companies were not required to publish any of this information in 1938, the legal consideration that Berle and Means had outlined in 1932—the threat that shareholders would sue if companies did not disclose information—made the release of such information not only imaginable but also, in some cases at least, actual. On the other side, some of these factors were specific to Harvard, where the methodologies of business cycle barometers and case studies had flourished, where the research paradigm of the former had been abandoned yet bequeathed some familiarity with advanced mathematical and statistical techniques, and where a number of theoretically sophisticated economists—among them two notable European émigrés— joined a faculty on the cusp of disciplinary change.

The developments we have surveyed in this chapter, from the "new era" escalation of securities trading, to the stock market crash of 1929, to the government reforms of the 1930s, to the practical and theoretical treatises designed to illuminate the workings of corporate finance and securities exchanges, all raised public awareness about the financial side of the economy, even if awareness took the form of greed or fear. As John Burr Williams's work reminds us, changes in the form and operation of financial institutions occurred alongside innovations in economic theory and method—even if the two were not always directly linked. We must also acknowledge that Williams's work on finance was, strictly speaking, marginal to the discipline; financial topics like asset prices did not receive extended attention until 1952. By the end of the 1930s, as America and the nations of Europe struggled to survive the Great Depression, most economists had turned their attention to more consequential matters. With the publication of John Maynard Keynes's *General Theory* in 1936, work on business cycle analysis was largely supplanted by the new subfield now called macroeconomics, which focuses on the analysis of aggregate processes produced by the interactions of multiple factors, not all of which behave according to the principles economists assign to individual actors. Public finance was placed on a new foundation, which was theorized both in European institutions and in US graduate seminars such as the one Alvin Hansen began teaching at Harvard in 1937; in the 1940s, the policies that grew out of these theories were implemented in Washington, DC, through new budgeting and tax policies. These policies were based on a new understanding of the role that central governments should play in augmenting national income by creating fiscal surpluses and stabilizing the economy's fluctuations through interest-rate management.

The technical foundations of economic work were also changing. Aggregate phenomena like the cyclical components of the business cycle, which were previously represented primarily by graphical indexes of price data, began to be reformulated as algebraic representations, ideally of real data,[69] with the definitions of the aggregates stabilized by the new definitions of national income accounting identities we discuss in chapter 6. After the discipline's short-lived engagement with Keynesianism, which did try to integrate real and financial factors, American economists began to develop models that substituted measures associated with the real side of the economy—like wage units (e.g., hours worked)—for price measures, which come from the financial side. This was intended to abstract from the image of the economy the impact of monetary factors, including inflation, deflation, and all the effects of financial intermediation. As we will see, in the long run, the consequences of depicting the internal mechanisms of the economy in this way were enormous: when the most influential macroeconomic models of the 1980s systematically abstracted financial and monetary factors and assumed that people do not suffer what Irving Fisher called the money illusion, they were unable to keep track of developments that were transforming the financial world of securities trading. Williams's rudimentary model may have stood at several crossroads—where finance met economics, and mathematics met institutionalism—but the divergent paths that soon opened made recognizing any relationship between the trajectories increasingly difficult.

CHAPTER 5

US Finance: Equity and Fixed Income Market Research, 1920–1940

The image of finance generated by developments in the interwar period also had a more technical dimension. In addition to works that presented an overall picture of how financial institutions worked, these decades yielded publications that offered new data about the long-term returns of assets classes, such as equities and bonds. The figures that filled these books may look like straightforward records of stock and bond purchases and sales, but, like index numbers, they were actually the products of complex statistical work, as well as painstaking research and fiercely debated theoretical assumptions. The labor involved in composing this data was largely invisible to contemporaries, and most economic historians have simply neglected it. To interwar investors seeking an advantage in understanding financial markets, however, the data these publications contained was invaluable, as it is now to historians who want to understand the infrastructure of finance in the period.

5.1. MIDWEST AGRONOMISTS AND THE FORTUITOUS CONJUNCTION

At least one of the tributaries that fed the stream of financial data published in the late 1930s originated in an unexpected place: the work done by agricultural economists in the 1920s and the 1930s. These economists, many of whom worked in the land-grant colleges and universities in the American midwest, were among the few to embrace the work of Henry Ludwell Moore when it was initially published. They did so because Moore's methodology provided a way to solve problems encountered every day in the experimental stations and extension programs associated with midwest economics departments—problems involving real-side issues such as quantity and price, supply and demand, and the interaction of multivariate factors. The neo-Walrasian economic theory promoted by neoclassical economists could not accommodate these factors, nor were neoclassical economists typically interested in the practical issues agricultural economists addressed. No one understood the importance of these issues better than Henry A. Wallace, associate editor of his family's newspaper, *Wallace's Practical Farmer*. Wallace was not trained as an economist, nor was he a politician, but he could see from his father's work in Washington, DC, on the Department of Agriculture's Swine Commission, how practical, theoretical, and political issues could combine.

In 1915, before he joined his father in Washington, the younger Wallace wrote to Henry Moore for help. Wallace had read Moore's *Economic Cycles,* and, even though he could not follow the calculations, he could see that Moore's method was relevant to a problem he was trying to solve. "I want to derive the law of demand as you have done for cattle, hogs, and sheep," Wallace wrote, and he asked Moore to recommend a book to teach him statistics and mathematics. Wallace's ultimate goal was not to identify the equilibrium point or marginal utility of farm products, as a neoclassical economist would have done, but to figure out how to intervene in the market to promote greater all-round prosperity. "It is of course right and reasonable that the units of a high acre yield should sell for less per unit than the units of a low acre yield, but is it right and reasonable for the total value of a high acre value to be less than the total value of the low acre yield? In order for truly permanent agriculture to be established would you not regard it as necessary for some price mechanism to be established which would reward farmers the country over for a high acre yield and penalize them for a low acre yield?"[1]

Moore's advice—to read G. Udny Yule's *Introduction to the Theory of Statistics* (1911)—must have been helpful, for by 1920, Wallace had sufficiently mastered the subject to publish the first corn-hog ratios, which divided the price of a bushel of corn by the price of one hundred pounds of pork. By 1923, Wallace was so proficient in the statistical methods of correlation and regression—and in the use of computing machines—that he delivered a series of lectures at Iowa State University. These lectures ultimately led to the publication of a manual entitled *Correlation and Machine Calculation,* which he co-authored with George Snedecor, professor of mathematics at Iowa State.[2]

Iowa State University, the first land-grant college, was thus the needle's eye through which Moore's statistical economics was threaded into agronomics in the 1920s—and, by a fortuitous conjunction, the conduit by which advanced statistical work was incorporated into the compilation of financial data. In that decade, and also at Iowa State, Wallace helped establish the nation's second interwar computing laboratory. The first was at the Bureau of Agricultural Economics in Washington. Initially, Wallace used the tabulators of a Des Moines insurance company, but Snedecor had also leased a card punch machine for his university office, and he performed much of the initial punch work there. By 1925, Snedecor had become the driving force behind the Iowa State computing laboratory, in part because Wallace had begun to devote more time to his hybrid-corn company. Snedecor hired a human computer; then, in 1927, he acquired an electric tabulator, which summarized data and performed the initial calculations that allowed the analyst to fit curves to data. That same year, a corporation called International Business Machines began to lease tabulators to other US universities; the first to acquire them were Cornell, Columbia, the University of Michigan, and the University of Tennessee. The Iowa State laboratory, which Snedecor named the "Mathematical and Statistical Service," was unique, however, in employing both mechanical tabulators and human calculators. The latter were still necessary because punch card machines could only perform the first part of the calculations—reducing data to a series of normal equations. To complete the calculations, human beings had to process the equations, using a mathematical method that Myrrick Doolittle invented in the late nineteenth century.[3]

Iowa State continued to be a center for statistical computing and economic research, especially in the field of agronomics and agricultural research. In 1929, the departments of general, agricultural, and industrial economics were consolidated into a single department; that same year, the university awarded its first PhD in agricultural economics. As the Great Depression intensified the woes of farmers, the research and extension programs at Iowa State expanded, and when Henry A. Wallace, now secretary of agriculture, set up a corn-hog research program, Iowa State was one of the program's most important participants. Under the chairmanship of Theodore W. Schultz, who had been recruited as a young faculty member from the University of Wisconsin, the Economics Department hired important new members: Gerhard Tintner, who joined the faculty in 1937; George J. Stigler, who arrived from the University of Chicago in 1936; and Kenneth Boulding, who was hired in 1943. The mix of interests represented by these individuals shows that the Economics Department at Iowa State University continued to link agricultural economics with new econometric work, which began to appear in 1930: from 1940, Schultz was editor of the *Journal of Farm Economics;* Tintner was book review editor of *Econometrica,* the journal established by the Econometric Society in 1933, and his book entitled *The Variate Difference Method* was jointly published by the Cowles Commission and Iowa State University in 1940. Most importantly, it was through Alfred A. Cowles III, founder of the Cowles Commission, that the statistical work associated with both agricultural economics and econometrics was brought to bear on data derived from the financial side of the economy.

The computing manual published by Wallace and Snedecor in 1925 was also a link between Iowa State University and the methodological innovations soon to be designated econometrics, for this manual helped Harold T. Davis, professor of mathematics at Indiana University, learn the Doolittle method of completing least-squares calculations. With scant funding, Davis set up a small computing laboratory at Indiana University, and he began compiling tables of mathematical functions for researchers who lacked computing facilities. Davis's lasting contribution to the histories of economics, econometrics, and financial data, however, did not emanate from his computing lab but from the contacts he made in the profession and during the summers he spent in Colorado Springs. In the summer of 1931, in Colorado Springs, Charles H. Boissevain, who headed the Colorado Foundation for Research in Tuberculosis, referred to Davis an investment adviser who had come to Boissevain with an unusual question: Was it possible to compute a correlation coefficient in a problem involving twenty-four variables? From the friendship that ensued between Davis and Alfred A. Cowles III came the idea for the Cowles Commission for Research in Economics, the flow of funds from Cowles to the Econometric Society to launch the journal *Econometrica,* and the first application of a statistical method relying on frequency distribution and randomization to financial data. While the story of the link between Cowles, the Econometric Society, and *Econometrica* has been told, the importance of Cowles's use of statistical techniques to investigate financial data has received less attention. The fortuitous conjunction between Davis's interest in mathematics and calculating machines, Cowles's work with stock forecasting, and the work of English biometricians, which we examine in the next section, created an innovative, scientific method for constructing and understanding financial data. This, in turn, provided the cornerstone of what was eventually named the efficient market hypothesis: the idea that stock prices cannot be forecast because their trajectory constitutes a "random walk."[4]

5.2. STOCK MARKET SKEPTICISM AND SAMPLE THEORY

Alfred A. Cowles III came from a prosperous publishing family, with substantial interests in newspapers in Cleveland, Chicago, Washington, Oregon, and Idaho. Cowles began his career at the *Tribune* in Spokane, but, following the path from information to the securities market, he soon moved to an investment company in Chicago, one which specialized in acquiring and restructuring railroads. The company also published a small investment newsletter analyzing the market and offering investment advice.[5] Diagnosed with tuberculosis in the late 1920s, Cowles withdrew from business and moved to Colorado Springs in hopes of improving his health. He continued to supervise his family's investments, but in 1929, when the stock market crashed, he grew skeptical about the entire enterprise of stock forecasting. Since 1928, Cowles had been collecting data about the stock forecasts made by various market newsletters, and in 1931, he wanted to evaluate the predictions made by these and other forecasters. This led to the query Cowles posed to Boissevain, and to Boissevain's suggestion that he contact Davis. Davis, in turn, told Cowles to look into the new computing machine IBM was marketing, the Hollerith Calculator. After visiting a company that used them, Cowles leased a set of computers and, with Davis's help, set up a computing laboratory in Colorado Springs. The two men soon learned that the Hollerith machines could not compute correlations or solve regression equations; Cowles scaled back his research project to a series of calculations the machines could handle; and, with the help of a suite of statistical methods introduced by English biometricians working on real-side problems like crop yields, he developed another method for analyzing stock market forecasts. This method, to which we turn in the next section, involved comparing the forecasts made in the past by the market newsletters, as well as investment decisions made by experienced investors such as insurance companies, both to actual historical prices and to a set of random picks Cowles and his team generated from the available securities. Based on this work, Cowles delivered to the December 1932 joint meeting of the American Statistical Association and the Econometric Society a paper entitled "Can Stock Forecasters Forecast?" The paper, published in *Econometrica* in 1933, introduced some of the most important concepts for what was soon to become the modern discipline of finance.

The problems Cowles confronted in the early 1930s had three components, each of which troubled the collection and use of data, both real-side and financial. First, given that every data set represents only a subset of some

larger, possibly infinite, set of observations, what is the best way to understand the relationship between the finite samples available for analysis and the
larger population to which the sample presumably belongs? Second, given
that what counts as data is shaped by the theoretical assumptions with which
the analyst begins, how can one test the relationship between theoretical hypotheses and the collection and treatment of data? And third, given the in-
evitability of mistakes, how can the analyst determine whether his results are
affected by errors or even by chance?

In a 1927 review of a recently published book, the Columbia statistician
and economist Harold Hotelling suggested that economists might be able to
address these issues by using sample theory, and, more specifically, by reading
the work of Ronald A. Fisher, a British biometrician.[6] If Hotelling was correct, few Americans knew Fisher's work in 1927, even though he had already
published a series of important articles as well as an accessible handbook for
statistical field workers.[7] The British statistician was soon to make a pair of
visits to America, however, and his seminars, lectures, and personal engagements impressed everyone who encountered him. Fisher's first American
visit, in 1932, was occasioned by an invitation from the president of Iowa State
University and George Snedecor, who had co-authored the handbook on correlation and machine calculation with Henry A. Wallace. At the time, Fisher,
who had trained at Cambridge in statistics and genetics, was affiliated with
the Rothamsted Experimental Station, located about twenty-five miles north
of London, where he had been working as a statistician since 1919. Snedecor
was so excited by the contributions Fisher's work could make to agricultural
economics that he vowed to write his own book, which could "lead the beginner" to Fisher's 1925 text.[8] During this visit, in addition to giving lectures
and seminars in Ames, Fisher also visited economists and geneticists in Minneapolis, Chicago, Ithaca, Philadelphia, Boston, and New York. When Fisher
visited the United States a second time, in 1936, he once more served as a visiting professor at Iowa State (where he was awarded an honorary doctorate);
he then traveled to Colorado Springs to lecture to the Cowles Commission, as
well as to Chicago, Ann Arbor, Ithaca, Princeton, Washington, San Francisco,
Berkeley, Palo Alto, and Ottawa. In September of that year, Fisher was one of
sixty-two scholars awarded an honorary doctorate by Harvard University.[9]

For our purposes, Fisher's most important contributions to statistics—and
thus to Cowles's project—consist of a series of techniques that conceptualize
the relationship between the data sample and the larger population to which
it belongs.[10] Fisher did not invent these techniques, but built on work done
in the seventeenth and eighteenth centuries in astronomy, mathematics, and

probability theory as well as on more recent genetic and biometric break-throughs by Galton and Pearson, the last of whom had so impressed Henry Moore. But Fisher brought to these statistical techniques a clarity of thought and precision of method that enabled American economists finally to see why sample theory might matter. Essentially, the techniques enabled the research worker to reason from the sample to the population; measure the strength of the relationship between two (or more) variables; measure the adequacy of the original hypothesis to the existing data; and evaluate the roles that chance and error played in the final results. All these techniques rely on the concept of the frequency distribution, a statistical method of arranging values either found in nature by observation or created through some method of randomization.

Like index numbers, sample theory combines theory with a series of methods developed over time. Sample theory also relies on a number of distributions that mathematicians and theorists have refined over the course of centuries. Among these are the normal distribution, represented by the bell curve, which describes measurements of natural phenomena that include the randomness found in nature; and the binomial distribution, which records phenomena with only two possible variants, like the throws of a coin (heads or tails). Instruction guides taught researchers to recognize the distribution pattern exemplified in a given data set by assembling and organizing the data they collected in the field so they could literally visualize its inherent pattern. This method also allowed them to visualize how a sample related to the hypothetical population to which it belonged and analyze the frequency, within the sample, of the measured attribute. This approach was taken by almost everyone who tried to explain sample theory in the 1930s, including R. A. Fisher and Harold T. Davis, who published one textbook in 1935 applying inferential statistics to economics and another in 1941 on economic time series.

In order to visualize distribution and analyze the correlation among attributes in samples, researchers were advised to organize data in the following manner. Take the information collected in the field and create a table that categorizes the data in some useful ways. (For example, for a study of the relationships between the heights of fathers and the heights of daughters, record each father's height in inches and each daughter's height in the same measurement unit.)[11] Then, take a piece of graph paper and draw two intersecting axes, one horizontal and the other vertical, each corresponding to one of the two relevant variables. (The horizontal, x, axis represents the frequency distribution of the fathers' heights and the vertical, y, axis represents the distribution of the daughters' heights.) Mark off intervals in the field framed by the axes to indicate the units used to quantify each (for example, inches). Next, for each observation, place a dot on the graph that registers the point of intersection of the paired values (for example, the intersection of the data for a specific father x and a specific daughter y). The dot represents the correlation of a given father's height with that of a given daughter. If there is some meaningful relationship between the two variables, a pattern will become visible on the graph paper, formed by the concentration of dots in various parts of the quadrants of the chart. The overall shape of the pattern shows how attributes are correlated with each other, and the density and shape of clustered points can indicate the strength of the covariation of the variables: if diffuse clouds spread evenly across all four quadrants, there may be no correlation between the variables. To render the diagram useful, next fit a straight line or a curve through the cluster of points, following the shape directionally. This is called the regression line. A quantitative analysis of the goodness of fit between the regression line and the cloud cluster of intersecting points allows the researcher to see whether the two variables have a linear relationship. The analyst can then use the frequency distributions of the variables plotted on each axis and the regression line, which shows the nature of their relationship, to generate useful statistics about the variables and their relationship. These statistics include the mean and standard deviation of each distribution, the mean and standard deviation of the regression equation, and the correlation coefficient.[12] These summary statistics constitute the information about the relationship between the variables one can take away from the original data.

In general terms, the elements of this approach to sampling are derived from astronomy, the field in which this kind of analysis was initially worked out: the vertical and horizontal axes might be said to take the place of longitude and latitude measurements, and the dots that compose the scatter diagram resembled the points used to plot the positions of stars in the sky. Beginning with Galton, and using the graphical and algebraic technique of least squares—the mathematical technique by which the regression line was calculated from a scatter diagram—this method was transferred from astronomy to biometrics and then, in the process we are describing, it was transferred again, this time to agronomy, and then on to economics. Each transfer introduced significant changes in the way the relationship between the variables could be constructed and interpreted. Whereas an astronomical observation might be sighted and dated precisely, generate a single measurement of an observable phenomenon, and make sense in relation to the deterministic law that informs it, the correlation of two "variables" in genetics or economics might not indicate any causal connection at all or reveal a natural law. The objects studied by astronomers, biologists, and economists are profoundly different: species are not the same kind of phenomena as planets, and corn prices differ from both. Like an index number, the resulting data point does not represent a discrete measurement of a singular entity made at a particular moment in time. Technically, both the index number and the data point are not measurements at all but ratios or aggregates constructed from elements that are interpretively constructed too, and each of which belongs to another distribution, which belongs, in turn, to an unseen and unmeasured population. Most importantly, the economist faces challenges spared the astronomer and agronomist: unlike the astronomer, the economist is not able to observe the same phenomenon twice, and unlike the agronomist, he cannot perform experiments. Thus, when the techniques of sample theory, including correlation analysis, are transferred to economics, all sorts of issues complicate the relatively unproblematic extrapolations the astronomer, and even the agronomist, make from their observations.

Of all the decisions faced by the researcher, the most critical are the inferences he draws from the plotted, tabular, or mathematically rendered information. Implicitly, these inferences answer a series of questions: What do the statistics generated by the graph, table, and curve reveal about the population to which the data points belong? To what extent do they confirm or qualify the hypothesis that guides the research? To what extent are summary statistics generated by chance or colored by error? How much significance can the researcher claim for his results? For the economist, who cannot test his results by repeating experiments, the burden placed on inference and significance tests is greatest of all.

R. A. Fisher's primary contributions to statistical method consist of three ways to engage these questions—if not precisely to answer them. First, in using the concept of the frequency distribution to move from the sample to the population, Fisher showed how to conceptualize the relationship between part and whole *probabilistically*. In doing so, Fisher was adapting the mathematical theory of probability, which dates to the seventeenth century. Fisher considered probability "the most elementary of statistical concepts," but he wanted to distinguish between mathematical probability and *likelihood,* by which he meant simply "the state of our information with respect to the parameters of hypothetical populations."[13] By conceptualizing the variations that populations inevitably contain probabilistically, Fisher did encourage the researcher to scale up from the sample to the population, but he did not guarantee that a mathematically exact relation would exist between the two. Indeed, Fisher's emphasis on variation de-emphasized the mathematical search for aggregates and averages through techniques like least squares and stressed instead both the patterns of variation and the tools that could measure covariation, or the relationships among variables. (The strength of these relationships is what regression and correlation analyses measure.)

Second, in providing a rationale and a template for experiment design, Fisher showed how techniques like randomization and repetition could address the influence of error and pure chance on experimental outcomes. Meaningful experiments, Fisher explained, should begin with the construction of "a hypothetical infinite population, of which the actual data are regarded as constituting a random sample." To test whether the collected data was truly a random sample of the whole, the researcher should construct additional samples according to a randomizing procedure (like drawing cards from a deck) and test the constructed sample against the collected data. Assuming that each data set belonged to a normal distribution, the investigator could then "evaluate the probability that a worse fit should be obtained from a random sample of the population of the type considered."[14]

Third, by providing techniques that could test the significance of the researcher's concluding statistics, Fisher provided a way to contain the uncertainty inevitably introduced by chance, error, and the possible misalignment of hypothesis and data.[15] Essentially, the tests devised by Fisher were designed to verify the adequacy of the analyst's theoretical hypothesis, his mathematical formulations, and his statistical hypothesis to the available empirical data. This was important because the analyst wanted to know whether the information yielded by his work was significant and, as a logical consequence, how much confidence he could place in it. If the statistical tests verified the adequacy of the hypothesis—as that hypothesis had been adjusted to the empirical data and captured in both mathematical equations and the summary statistics—he could feel sufficiently confident about its usefulness (although not its accuracy) to make claims about how the population would behave in the future.[16] The ability to make predictions explains why this approach is called *inferential* statistics: the inferences the analyst could draw from the sample, according to this method, referred not simply to the present population but also to the future state of that population—to the population extended, probabilistically, through time.

Most obviously, *Statistical Methods for Research Workers* provided a handbook for agricultural scientists and researchers engaged in experiments on real-side factors, such as crop yields, hog prices, and hybrid varieties of grain. Implicitly, however, as Snedecor, Davis, and other members of the Cowles Commission recognized, the book's insights could also shape work with financial data. To see how Fisher's work on real-side problems was used in financial research, we turn to Alfred Cowles's 1933 essay on stock forecasting.

5.3. STOCK FORECASTING

Even after the crash of 1929, Alfred A. Cowles continued to collect market newsletters. By the end of 1931, he had accumulated an almost four-year run of twenty-four of the most widely subscribed newsletters, a collection that allowed him to chart the accuracy of market forecasters from the last gasp of the pre-crash boom to the wheezing bear market of the early 1930s. After meeting Harold Davis at Colorado Springs, acquiring the Hollerith punch card calculator, and gaining some familiarity with the methods of R. A. Fisher and Karl Pearson, Cowles began to see how to apply to the forecasters the kind of statistical tests that biometricians had drawn up.[17] To generate more data, he supplemented the collection of recommendations made by the market newsletters with investment information derived from twenty fire insurance companies and the forecasts offered by sixteen financial publications; he then added the advice given by William Peter Hamilton, one of the proponents of the kind of technical analysis known as the Dow Jones theory. Cowles selected these sources because he considered them representative of their industries; the only exception was the twenty-six-year forecasting record of Hamilton, former editor of the *Wall Street Journal,* which Cowles chose "because of the reputation for successful forecasting which he had established over a long period of years."[18]

The point of the exercise Cowles described in 1933 was to examine whether the stock pickers and market forecasters could forecast—the evidence for which would be whether they outperformed the securities market as a whole.[19] In modern Wall Street terminology, Cowles was testing two kinds of investment processes: securities selection and stock market timing.[20] Cowles's "experiment" was just as practical as R. A. Fisher's agricultural trials—even though Cowles used past performance and not controlled or replicable experiments for his comparisons: just as Fisher was asking which plantings yielded the best crop returns, so Cowles was asking whether stock market advice was worth the money professionals charged. At a theoretical level, however, Cowles was also testing the insight Irving Fisher had introduced in 1906: if, as Fisher argued, value is a function of expectations about the future, then to what extent are individuals' forecasts about the economic future reliable guides to what will happen? Posed in the midst of the greatest depression in United States history and initially delivered in a professional meeting chaired by Irving Fisher himself, this was a radical question indeed. But the answer Cowles delivered on the last day of 1932 was even more shocking. What he discovered—and stated explicitly, if not emphatically, at the conclusion of his paper—was that all the forecasters—the market newsletters, the insurance investors, the financial weeklies, and even the Wall Street expert William Peter Hamilton—"failed to demonstrate that they exhibited skill." The statistical tests Cowles applied to the results of these sources, moreover, indicated that "the most successful records are little, if any, better than what might be expected to result from pure chance" (311).[21]

Given the context in which Cowles delivered his paper—at a joint meeting of the American Statistical Association, the American Economic Association, the American Association for Labor Legislation, the American Farm Economic Association, and the (still relatively young) Econometric Society and in a session entitled "Statistical Forecasting"[22]—it should not surprise us that Cowles, who was not trained as an economist or a statistician, did not take his conclusions to the next, theoretical level. He did not ask, as he was to do four years later, whether the failure of the forecasters to beat a randomly assembled portfolio or to predict the market's activities meant that the market itself was unpredictable (that is, inherently random).[23] Even though he was a wealthy man and a full member of the Cowles Commission, in this gathering of some of the most renowned experts in the world, Cowles was undeniably an amateur. To take the full measure of the implications of Cowles's paper, then, we have to read it carefully.[24] Doing so reveals the influence of the British biometricians and shows how ideas and methods borrowed from Pearson and Fisher began to transform the way the discipline of economics—and what would become the subdiscipline of financial economics—approached the problem of data.

In his paper Cowles did not stress the innovative nature of his ideas. Nevertheless, and especially when read in the context of modern applications, these ideas seem as visionary as Irving Fisher's reorientation of value.[25] Cowles's innovative framework rested on four foundational assumptions, which began with but then adapted R. A. Fisher's statistical method. The first was that the securities market can be considered from the investor's perspective, not simply as an autonomous entity observable from afar. From the investor's point of view, the most important financial data involves the distribution of returns, not a chronological series of prices. This shift from an apparently objective, disinterested perspective to the investor's perspective is the basis of modern capital market theory. In order to emphasize returns, Cowles transformed the available indexes of stock prices into a series of intraperiod changes; these could then be analyzed not only as cumulative returns but also as distributions of returns within a particular period. The decision to focus on such distributions bears traces of R. A. Fisher's method.

Cowles's second assumption was that returns should be evaluated on a total return basis; they should include dividends and other capital changes that accrued to the investor over time. His third assumption was that the appropriate benchmark for analyzing stock market averages was comprised of a broadly representative group of industries, each of whose place in the index was weighted by the market capitalization of the companies that composed the industry—that is, the price of a share for each company multiplied by the number of shares outstanding. Cowles's fourth assumption was that any analysis of the market should be grounded on the most basic, and challenging, feature of stock investing: fluctuations in stock prices. As the English biometricians had demonstrated, in formal, statistical terms, the fluctuations of stock returns could best be measured by variance and standard deviation, which were, in turn, calculated from the distribution of returns over the period in which an investor held the stock.

The four pillars of Cowles's reconceptualization of finance were anchored in the statistical properties of stock indexes and time series, as R. A. Fisher defined them in the context of agricultural research. Cowles demonstrated that the statistical properties of the returns of the market index could be compared to their counterparts in sample stock portfolios and that both could be analyzed statistically. This comparison yielded statistical inferences that allowed an investor to evaluate market returns, both for actual stock portfolios and for portfolios constructed to test the returns of the actual portfolios. In this exercise, the distribution of returns exhibited by an actual or a simulated portfolio corresponded to the biometrician's sample, and the distribution of returns of the market as a whole, over the same period, corresponded to the population. Cowles also borrowed from the biometricians the idea of the summary statistic—as the measure that reduces reams of data to a few meaningful figures, which capture both the variability found in nature between the individual and the population and the correlation of specific attributes to each other. Following Fisher's method, Cowles computed the return and variability of the total return index for the stock market, and he measured its correlation with the total returns and variability of sample portfolios. Based on the comparison of the two, he was able to draw statistical inferences about whether the sample portfolio returns, which the market forecasters produced, were the result of skill or chance. This recasting of financial decision making, so that it highlighted the variance within portfolios as well as their relation to the variability of the market as a whole, is the heart of what is now called portfolio theory.

Cowles used these figures to measure not just cumulative total returns but the variability of returns around the mean. This required him both to find the mean return on individual stocks and portfolios and to evaluate the variability of this return in relation to the standard deviation for the return of the entire market. Given the inevitable volatility of the market as a whole, the risk of individual shares had to be placed in a time frame, calculations about which also had to be figured into the evaluation of asset returns. This juxtaposition created the following volatility metric, which is still used today to measure risk: the greater the time a share is held, the greater its relative volatility. In other words, the deviation of a stock's return from the market's return increases with time. Finally, Cowles realized that evaluating the forecasters' performances, which led to these returns, required him to test these performances probabilistically—that is, against randomly generated portfolios. To construct this test, he used the process of randomization R. A. Fisher recommended as the final check for the significance of any research worker's results.

We can provide a clearer account of Cowles's method by focusing on two of the studies described in 1933. The first deals with the problem of stock selection. In his analysis of the records of the leading financial publications, Cowles found that six of the sixteen services demonstrated success, with the best manager beating the market by 3%; the average of all sample portfolios, however, underperformed by 1.3%. To evaluate whether the best manager's result demonstrated skill or chance, Cowles examined the statistical probability that out of a population of sixteen forecasters, one service would outperform the market by the 3% he had observed. Cowles based his reasoning on the recognition that, in a volatile stock market, prices by definition fluctuate widely; thus, a sample portfolio could be "on the right side of the market" simply by chance. Using the algebra of direct and inverse probability and assuming that stock prices displayed a normal distribution of returns, he showed that there was a 50/50 chance that one portfolio in sixteen would exhibit the degree of outperformance the study found. Specifically, the best forecaster's portfolio outperformed the market in seven out of nine six-month periods with an excess return of 3%. Even though this might look like a demonstration of skill if it were considered in isolation, when it was viewed as one of sixteen attempts to beat the market, the forecaster's success could equally well be the result of chance.

The second study dealt with the issue of market timing. From the recommendations made by the twenty-four financial publications, Cowles created a set of randomly generated portfolios. The study demonstrated that even "where forecasting agencies made gains, even the greatest of these lay within limits equaled by the best of our 24 imaginary records" (319). Admitting that in the case of forecast revisions, it was difficult to create the statistically required number of independent observations, Cowles examined the correlation of each decision about when to invest with a successful prediction. In this case, a comparison of the relevant best and worst forecasters' records demonstrated that the timing decisions for the best manager were weakly correlated with market success, and he found a decided difference between the market timing records of the best and worst forecasters. Using one of the statistical significance tests developed by R. A. Fisher, Cowles identified a "slight" presumption of skill for this forecaster. When he considered all the factors together, however—the technical problems in research design, the similarity of the performance of randomly generated portfolios to the records of actual portfolios, and the weak proof of skill even in the best forecaster—Cowles judged the statistical results of his investigations "inconclusive" (321). The results demonstrated "little, if any, better than what may be expected from pure chance" (324).

In the 1930s, before digital computers, the empirical work and computation necessary to generate these results was prohibitive for most economists. To create his data, the human computers at Cowles had not only to collect lists of historical prices for individual shares, construct historical time series to represent the overall performance of the stocks chosen to represent the securities market, and weight these companies according to their capital values, but also to obtain from financial services companies records of the amounts and timing of the dividends distributed by all the corporations included in the indexes or recommended by a forecaster. As we are about to see, in 1938, the Cowles Commission published the results of the research that informed this study as a record that other researchers could use.

5.4. US COMMON STOCK INDEXES AND FIXED INCOME DURATION

In 1938, the Cowles Commission published the results of Cowles's work—*Common-Stock Indexes, 1871–1937*, with a title page emblazoned with the logo of the Commission: "Science is Measurement." That same year, Frederick

R. Macaulay, who had worked on the NBER's first income study, published *Some Theoretical Problems Suggested by the Movements of Interest Rates, Bond Yields, and Stock Prices in the United States since 1856.* The institutional affiliation of this volume was announced by its preface, written by the NBER's founder, Wesley Clair Mitchell.[26]

These volumes provided contemporaries the technical data absent from works like Berle and Means's *Modern Corporation* and Graham and Dodd's *Security Analysis,* and they continue to be important research tools for today's financial professionals. Cowles provided the intellectual rationale and mathematical methodology for creating capitalization-weighted stock indexes. Cap-weighted indexes, which are ubiquitous today, are used to reconstruct the history of capital markets; measure the performance of investment managers; establish the empirical basis of modern investment theory; and are the basis for constructing index funds, now one of the most common forms of investment. The particular cap-weighted index that Cowles began in 1938 still survives as the Standard and Poor 500.[27] Macaulay developed one of the most important statistics used in modern fixed-income investment, the Macaulay duration. As later refined, this measures the adjusted term to maturity of a bond and is used to gauge and adjust the interest-sensitivity of a bond or portfolio.[28] In keeping with the commitment of the NBER to empirical research, Macaulay also argued strenuously that many economic theories then in circulation, including those set out by Irving Fisher and John Maynard Keynes, were not confirmed by the facts uncovered by his historical research and statistical aggregates. Like Graham and Dodd before him, but now armed with extensive reconstructions of the historical movements of bond yields and trends for various financial instruments and economic aggregates, Macaulay insisted that the facts derived from raw data provided the critical infrastructure of economic analysis—even if these facts were the stylized facts created by statisticians in the offices of the NBER.[29]

The work of Cowles and Macaulay provided a new empirical and statistical foundation for financial analysis, which assumed and built upon the legal and institutional foundation we have already examined. These studies gave finance a "foundation" in the sense that Eugene Fama used that term in 1976.[30] This empirical and statistical foundation became the platform for almost all subsequent financial theorizing: modern financial theory is built upon data sets constructed and described in the way that Cowles and Macaulay recommended. In the long run, this foundation enabled finance to become a relatively autonomous theoretical and applied practice, which was both housed within the academic disciplines of economics and business school programs in finance and practiced outside the university setting, on the physical and virtual exchanges where increasing numbers of shares changed hands as securities trading recovered from the Depression slump.

In some ways, the two researchers approached constructing indexes for securities in different ways—or at least from different perspectives. Cowles approached common-stock indexes from the point of view of the investor, although his investor was a hypothetical construct, who invested continuously during the period from 1871 to 1937, rather than an actual or even an "average" investor.[31] The bulk of the price data with which Cowles worked was supplied by the weekly publications of Standard Statistics; for the period before 1918, the year Standard Statistics began publication, Cowles had to piece together data from various sources—including the indexes Macaulay was constructing for railway stocks. Standard Statistics was the most comprehensive of the available indexes: it covered 351 stocks, whereas the next most comprehensive, Moody's, covered only sixty. Cowles figured that using Standard Statistics indexes allowed him to obtain information for "about 73 per cent of the market value of common stocks listed on all of the exchanges in the United States, and about 77 per cent of those which are sufficiently active to be regularly available for inclusion in an index" (9). Cowles did decide to exclude some available listings—most notably, the listings from the New York Curb Exchange before it moved indoors in 1921—because he considered these to be "unreliable" (6). Cowles's aim was to "portray the average experience of those investing in this class of security [common stocks] in the United States from 1871 to 1937" (2). To capture this "average experience" of a "hypothetical investor" (13), he decided to omit brokerage fees and taxes. He also assumed that the investor reinvested his dividends and redistributed his holdings at the end of every month among all quoted stocks (2). Cowles approached investing on what is now called a total-return basis, and the indexes he constructed also took account of the kind of "pecuniary changes" that could affect an investor's experience. These included the corporation's sale of its own shares for cash, its decision to offer shares below market price to investors, and the payment of dividends in cash (13–14).

Macaulay, by contrast, approached the history of bonds and financial markets as a business-cycle analyst, not someone interested primarily in investor experience. Working with 150 railway bond prices, which spanned the period between 1856 and 1936, Macaulay faced the challenge of creating a continuous time series from data that had not been continuously collected. He also tackled the daunting task of establishing empirical relations between financial aggregates and the real economy. In the largest sense, his aim was to determine "the statistical relations of those rates [interest rates] and [bond] yields to one another, to stock and commodity prices, to the physical and monetary volume of trade, and to credit and banking conditions."[32] As this list suggests, Macaulay's project engaged more sources of data than Cowles's more limited treatment of common stocks, and Macaulay also wanted to distinguish among seasonal, cyclical, and secular trends to make visible the temporal, possibly causal, relationships among movements in the aggregates. Macaulay reasoned that the economist had to make informed assumptions about the source of the volatility in time series—whether it reflected seasonal, cyclical, or secular trends—if he were to measure the correlations among key variables over the course of the business cycle. As we will see, however, Macaulay stopped short of theorizing causal relationships among the movements he documented, and he repeatedly called for economists to confront their theories with the new facts his study established.

The feature that linked the two projects was their shared reliance on a particular index formula to aggregate their data. As we saw in chapter 3, index construction—and the choice of which index formula to use—was essentially a design problem, one that economists and statisticians fiercely debated in the early twenties. Whereas Irving Fisher had insisted that a single, "ideal" index formula could capture all kinds of aggregates, both Cowles and Macaulay took the position that Wesley Mitchell endorsed: one should choose an index formula relevant to the task at hand. In his 1938 volume, Cowles in particular carefully set out the advantages and disadvantages of various index formulae, including Fisher's, but he ultimately selected one that was suited to some of the peculiarities of financial data and that did not involve the extensive computation required by Fisher's ideal index formula. As it turned out, even the formula Cowles chose required considerable computation. In the second edition of *Common-Stock Indexes,* published in 1939, Cowles marveled at the 1,500,000 work-sheet entries the project entailed, as well as the 25,000 computer hours necessary to compile the indexes. Even though he used the IBM Hollerith computer, moreover, most of this computation was performed by human beings: in his preface, Cowles acknowledged the labor performed by five staff members and forty-five Colorado College students, twenty-five of whom were women (vii).

The index formula Cowles and Macaulay chose had several design features: it was weighted by the capitalization of the issuing companies' outstanding securities; returns were chain-linked, interval by interval;[33] the denominator of what Cowles called the "value ratio" (14) contained a divisor that could be adjusted for changes in the capital structure of the company or the composition of securities outstanding in the class; and, as a dividend or interest payment was received, the formula assumed that these were reinvested in the asset class. This total-return calculating procedure allowed the statistician to evaluate any interest- or dividend-generating financial asset on a common basis according to a strictly defined method. Adopting a single formula for constructing index numbers and a common method of calculation, in other words, meant that all financial data sets could speak to each other or be viewed in relation to each other, as Macaulay wanted to do. In short, these two empirical projects, along with others that adopted this design, promised to make US capital markets amenable to comparative statistical analysis—that is, to make them subjects of scientific inquiry.[34] To this end, Cowles and Macaulay chose each element of the index design for a particular reason: Cowles chose to weight the index numbers by capitalization to represent the "average experience" of the "hypothetical investor"; he elected to use a chain-based system instead of Fisher's "ideal" formula both to save on calculations and because chain-linked returns eliminated the impact of the amount of dollars invested in the asset class, period by period; and he chose to assume that dividends and interest payments were reinvested to recognize that, over long investment horizons, the returns from reinvestment represent the preponderance of the investor's cumulative returns.

In his discussion of bond yields and stock prices, Macaulay explained the advantages of using a cap-weighted, chain-linked index formula. In the process, he highlighted the concept of the asset class, which was fundamental to the conceptual work in which he and Cowles were engaged.

> We are concerned with railroad common stocks as a type of security. We are therefore interested in what happened to railroad common stockholders as a class, but not in what would have happened to an individual if he had played the market in this way or that. We are interested in the changing value of the entire railroad system of the country—in so far as market prices can be used to measure changes in that value—rather than in changes in the price of arbitrary and insignificant or fluctuating and misleading units.
>
> And, for such purposes, there is only one index number. Indeed, were it not for changes in the number of shares outstanding and for the occurrence of amalgamations, consolidations and reorganizations with the attendant necessity of substitutions and changes in the lists of stocks used, no question would ever arise. The price per share of each stock would, without discussion, be multiplied by the number of shares

outstanding in order to obtain a figure for the total "equity" value of each corporation—its worth to shareholders. And these totals would then be added together. But, with not only changes in number of shares outstanding but also changes in capital structure that alter or even destroy the significance of the price of "one share," "chain" index numbers become absolutely necessary. (152–53)

Here we see how Macaulay's indexes subjected to statistical measurement some of the issues involving a corporation's capital structure, which Berle and Means described in 1932. As changes occurred in capital structure—when a corporation issued more securities, possibly of a new asset class, or when it issued stock warrants, for example—the value of one share of common stock necessarily changed; and only the chain-linked index numbers could take such alterations into account in the aggregates presented in the time series.

With the publication of these two works, two critical concepts were conceptualized, constructed, and measured: asset class and total return. A third concept central to modern financial theory was later derived from the empirical evidence assembled by Cowles and Macaulay, but these two pioneers did not theorize the concept of risk in the way later theorists were to do: as the standard deviation or variance of the historical total-return data in relation to the asset class. What Macaulay in particular did begin to theorize—although not at great length—was the role played by expectations in the movements of all security prices. Just as Berle and Means had intuited that human expectations about the future constitute critical components of the investing environment, so Macaulay realized, as Mitchell stressed in his introduction to Macaulay's bond book, that "to understand the behavior of bond yields and interest rates it is necessary to take account of futurity" (xii). Taking account of futurity, Macaulay insisted, meant taking into account "human nature," including the hopes and fears that feed expectations. As Macaulay remarked, "It will always be human nature to gamble on whether if one buys at an inflated level he will be able to find a bigger fool than himself to buy from him at a still higher level. The primary reason for the variableness of the economic future to which man must adjust himself lies in man himself" (234).

Alfred Cowles may not have theorized or named the "equity risk premium," but his tables did make visible what Irving Fisher had predicted and John Burr Williams assumed: the greater returns of common stock, on a total-return basis and as an asset class, over bonds and commercial paper. In his description of the "important facts disclosed by the indexes" (40), Cowles confidently spelled out the stylized facts about the relative value of stock and bond investments his tables made clear. "If we add cash dividend payments to changes in the market value of stocks . . . the total return has been 4.8 per cent for the Railroads, 6.1 for the Utilities, 8.3 for the Industrials, and 6.8 for the three groups combined. This is to be compared with an average return of about 4.2 per cent obtainable from high-grade bonds and 4.7 per cent from prime commercial paper for this period" (40–41). Since the period Cowles's tables depicted contained the disastrous fall in securities prices that followed the crash of 1929, he felt justified in endorsing the conclusion Fisher and Williams had reached: over the long run, and despite their volatility, stocks yield higher returns than bonds.

Frederick Macaulay had as much confidence in the methods and concepts that underwrote his tables as did Cowles, but his optimism about how these tables could be used was considerably more qualified. Instead of implying, as Cowles did, that careful attention to long-term empirical research should foster confidence in investment decisions, Macaulay repeatedly expressed his concern that even the most painstaking historical research would never yield forecasting adequate to the complexities of the economic world. So perplexed does he occasionally seem to have been about how—or whether—his empirical data would lead to social improvement that he sometimes called for "control"—measures taken, presumably by legislators, that would render forecasting unnecessary.

> It is, of course, highly desirable to learn how things actually have occurred—and particularly how closely or how distantly they have followed a "rational" pattern; to study the problems of economic prediction even into the fields of "irrational" sequences; to investigate not only the empirical relations between crop sizes and crop prices but also the empirical relations between long and short term interest rates. However, the mere fact that so much effort has already been expended on attempts to improve the quality of empirical forecasting strongly suggests the possibility that no such forecasting will ever be adequate to prevent even such gigantic world-wide economic disturbances as that from which we have but recently emerged.
>
> A more hopeful approach is that of *control.* Instead of attempting to improve the quality of forecasting, we might attempt to make forecasting less necessary. . . . Much can be done by mere legal elimination of conditions that make forecasting particularly important. . . . We must break away from the mysticism of "laissez-faire." Times without number "the invisible hand" has led mankind into the economic ditch. (21)

The heterodoxy of such statements, especially in a historical context haunted by the specter of communism and state planning, was so shocking that twice the director of the NBER, M. C. Rorty, disrupted Macaulay's pessimism with qualifying footnotes.[35]

Despite Macaulay's occasional lament, the bulk of his monumental study was devoted to providing precisely the kind of rigorous statistics that later economists would use to great effect. Indeed, theorizing the causes of the temporal patterns Macaulay so painstakingly brought to light is in large part the central goal of modern monetary economics because his tables enticingly suggest that a determinate relationship ties the financial-side factor of interest rates to the growth or decline of the real economy. Macaulay's carefully constructed stylized facts, created and presented in the true NBER style of resisting premature theory, allowed future economic theorists to ask—and sometimes even to answer—what became the central questions of modern finance. Here, too, Macaulay led the way when he questioned the traditional focus of interest rate theory. "Most interest theories attempt to explain 'pure' interest only. However, the nature of 'pure' interest is invariably left quite obscure. . . . Economists have gradually come to recognize that the interest problem is essentially a numerical problem and should be approached as such. It is fundamentally a problem of *interest rates*. . . . Too little effort has been made to discover all relevant facts about actual rates and their behavior, and from those facts to find out, among other things, how human beings really do function" (6–7). Macaulay's most important contribution to financial *theory* was his insistence that economists focus on a new, empirically observable phenomenon: the system of interest rates, not "the interest rate," the abstraction that had so preoccupied economists like Irving Fisher and the Austrian Eugene Böhm-Bawerk. Macaulay's emphasis on the system of interest rates—that is, the yields, risks, and expected returns on portfolios of financial assets held by households, governments, and corporations—laid the groundwork for modern portfolio theory.

CHAPTER 6

Measuring and Taxing the US Economy in the Interwar Period

6.1. THE KEYNESIAN REVOLUTION

The developments that began to reorient the discipline of economics in the interwar period allowed Americans to see something previously as elusive as finance: the national economy. John Maynard Keynes did not invent macroeconomics, much less the idea of a national economy as a statistical, sectored, calculable entity amenable to governmental budgets and planning.[1] Nevertheless, the conjunction of Keynes's *General Theory of Employment, Interest and Money* (1936), the availability of statistical data about aggregate income and production, the methodology of modeling, and a set of policies that helped some nations throw off the Great Depression has made it nearly impossible not to credit the Keynesian revolution with teaching statisticians the power of national aggregates, governments the benefits of spending, and economists the merits of mathematical modeling. The deep structure of the National Income and Product Accounts was Keynesian; "full" employment in the United Kingdom and the United States was one outcome of increased government spending on defense; and one incentive for economists to adopt mathematical modeling came from efforts to stabilize the meaning of Keynes's treatise.

Keynes's *General Theory*, as its title suggests, also moved some components of finance—interest and money—closer to the center of economic analysis. Because Keynes's analysis was *macro* in scope, however, his work initially elevated the macroeconomic version of finance—the relation between aggregate saving and investment—over the kind of micro decisions about investment we began to explore in chapter 4. As we will see in chapter 9, some economists would soon return to the micro dimension of finance, but the first impact of Keynes's work was to direct attention to concepts that were simultaneously macro in scope and abstract in nature. Despite their names, these concepts— "the consumption function," the "marginal propensity to consume," the "marginal efficiency of capital," and the "liquidity preference"—were not limited to the financial side of the economy. Nor were they immediately ready for data or policy implementation. To render these concepts usable, and to develop Keynes's provocative hints about links between the financial and real sides of the economy, economists had to anchor Keynes's theory in the data national statisticians began to assimilate in the 1930s. If Keynes's work was to "make contact with reality,"[2] economists also had to translate his literary language into mathematical models.

We save our primary discussion of Keynesianism for chapter 8, where we show how his ideas were implemented in the American context. Here we focus on the way national income and production aggregates were created in the 1930s and 1940s, for the outcome of debates about the best way to compile and present aggregate data was instrumental to the form taken by the Keynesian revolution in subsequent decades.

6.2. COMPILING US INCOME AND PRODUCTION AGGREGATES

The twentieth-century efforts to generate estimates of a nation's aggregate income and production were not the first such projects, although the interwar form of these estimates, as well as state sponsorship for national aggregates, were new.[3] The estimates finally published in 1947 as the first official US National Income and Product Accounts (NIPA) were more comprehensive than earlier estimates, and their reliance on sophisticated statistical data was more extensive. These accounts made it possible for the first time to see the nation's economy as a statistical entity, divided into sectors, and reducible to a single number: the gross domestic product (GDP).[4] The estimates could be viewed from three complementary perspectives, which reflected the approaches by which they were created: the income approach, the source of production approach, and the expenditure approach. The invention of national income accounts was arguably the most consequential contribution made by economists to American life in the first half of the twentieth century, for these accounts enabled the federal government to create budgets capable of projecting forward from income and expenses incurred in the past.

In 1932, when the US government sponsored the first official estimates of national income, there was no consensus about the best way to create such estimates. As we saw in chapter 3, in 1920, in an unofficial attempt to generate estimates, the NBER had used income and product approaches. To examine the distribution of income, Mitchell and colleagues' *Income in the United States: Its Amount and Distribution* (1921) highlighted the relationship between national income received (the sum of individual incomes plus corporate surpluses) and income produced (the sum of sources of production, such as the hand trades, manufacturing, and agriculture); to confirm the results, Wesley Mitchell cross-checked the income team's calculations with the findings of the production team. It was this dual view of national income—as income received and income paid out for consumption—that Simon Kuznets presented to the US Senate in his report on *National Income, 1929–1932* (1933). As we show in a moment, in the 1930s, the Brookings Institution created a third approach to national aggregates, the expenditure approach, based on statistics of consumption and investment. Both these approaches—the dual view used by Mitchell and Kuznets and the expenditure approach introduced by the Brookings Institution—combined financial and real-side data, but neither made it possible to see the financial side of the economy clearly.

In the interwar period, national accountants—and legislators—disagreed not only about what data to collect but also about how best to organize and present the results. The eventual outcome—the accounting format used in the 1947 NIPA—was the hard-won outcome of a series of fierce debates about numerous interrelated issues, each of which is simultaneously quite technical and very consequential. Even after this consensus was reached, moreover, two additional views of national aggregates were added to NIPA: the income-output accounts, which we examine below, were added in the 1950s; and flow-of-funds accounts, which we describe in chapter 8, were adopted in the 1960s. It was this last view that finally made visible the flow of financial assets through the nation's economy and the effects of financial intermediation.

We can reduce the issues economists debated in the interwar period to five: scope, valuation, aggregation, netness, and sectoring.[5] *Scope* involves identifying the production activities attributed to the three domestic sectors (households, corporations, and government), and *valuation* involves deciding how, when, and in what terms to assign money values to them. *Aggregation* involves decisions about how to consolidate disparate instances of the same activity into a summary statistic that can reveal growth and development over time. *Netness*, a term introduced by Simon Kuznets, alludes to the question of whether to represent income and production aggregates before or after setting aside deprecation and capital replacement costs. *Sectoring* involves determining the fundamental categories that will organize the system of aggregates. By 1932, it was clear that, even though the government was funded and legitimized by American households, and households also owned corporations as well, government and corporations played such important roles in the nation's economy that they should be artificially treated as statistically and analytically distinct from the household sector. Thus NIPA grouped the nation's economy into four sectors: households, governments, businesses, and "rest of the world." Separating the corporate and government sectors from the household sector made it possible to see the roles played by the burgeoning federal government and the giant American corporations in the nation's economy, and the last category, "rest of the world," made it clear that, even though international ties bound countries together, the United States occupied the center of its own economic universe. While contested to the end, the question of netness was eventually decided in favor of gross figures, and national statisticians accepted common definitions of scope, valuation, aggregation, and sectors as well—just as they eventually agreed that superimposing an accounting framework taken from corporate accounting would make the estimates most usable.

In the interwar period, the dispute about national aggregates had two primary contestants. The first, Simon Kuznets, was a Russian émigré who arrived in the United States in 1922. Kuznets studied with Mitchell at Columbia, worked at the NBER, and, from 1931, taught statistics at the University of Pennsylvania. In 1932, the US Department of Commerce commissioned Kuznets to construct the first official income estimates for the United States, focusing on the years leading up to the Depression.[6] Kuznets presented his first report to the Senate in 1934 and followed this up with more elaborate compilations in 1937 and 1941. The second contestant was Milton Gilbert, who studied with Kuznets at the University of Pennsylvania and worked with him on the first income estimates. As editor of the *Survey of Current Business* since 1939, Gilbert also had considerable experience with commercial aggregates. In 1941, the Department of Commerce approached Gilbert about providing new estimates of income and production so the Roosevelt administration could evaluate whether—and how quickly—the United States could reorient its economy to war production. The work performed by Gilbert and his team continued long past the nation's entry into the war.[7] It culminated in 1947 with *National Income and Product Statistics of the United States, 1929–46,* published as a supplement to the *Survey of Current Business*. These accounts, the NIPA, were the first US estimates organized by the corporate accounting framework.

When Kuznets began work on the national aggregates, he knew economists disagreed about nearly every aspect of this project, including how best to define "national income." Nevertheless, he insisted that a "clear cut, general concept" of this idea existed and should be used: "In current reality, the most clear cut, general concept of national income is income received by individuals; and . . . the uninterrupted flow of commodities and services through the economic system is best arrested for the purpose of analysis and measurement at the point when the stream reaches the living individual, after it leaves the productive units proper and before it has been diverted into the various channels of consumption."[8] This early statement identifies Kuznets's positions on most of the theoretical issues national accountants had to address. "Income received by individuals" identifies his preference for the income approach and the scope of Kuznets's project (individuals carry out the productive activities of the economy), his preferred mode of valuation (factor costs), and his principle of aggregation (scaling up from the individual). In addition, "uninterrupted flow" highlights the flow perspective he endorsed and the model of circulation that underwrote his system; and "measurement at the point when the stream reaches the living individual" indicates his preference for identifying income with final product, not intermediate product (as would be the case if he measured income both when a company bought some commodity, such as pig iron, and then again when that company sold its final product, such as railway track, which was made from the intermediate product). Kuznets emphasized two additional points elsewhere: he wanted net measures, not gross—that is, figured after the deduction of taxes, depreciation, and replacement costs; and he wanted to treat the government as if it were an industry like any other.

Kuznets's position followed from two underlying assumptions: the end goal of economic activity is the consumption of real goods and services; and the purpose of constructing national aggregates is to measure economic welfare, as measured by consumption. Kuznets's ideas were formulated in the context of the 1930s, when the Depression crisis of oversupply failed to abate, and his primary goal was to understand how to tackle the problem of oversupply. Kuznets's preference for net over gross measures reflects his belief that the measures that mattered most were the sums after taxes and depreciation were subtracted. For this reason as well, two of the concepts Kuznets used to organize his system—*national income paid out* and *national income produced*—did not equal each other or form an accounting identity. Instead, national income paid out included the flow of income payments to individuals, while the larger figure, national income produced, added a sum for "business savings" to national income paid out. "Business savings," which was also a net measure deducting business taxes and capital depreciation from companies' undistributed profits, could be either a positive or a negative figure. During the Depression, this aggregate ran red because businesses were not able to accumulate capital.[9] This was one reason businesses were unable to hire and the nation was not able to form new capital for additional investment.

Even though Kuznets considered government one of the nation's principal "industries," he treated government income differently than the incomes of other industries. In the case of government, the two categories that organized Kuznets's system did not equal each other, for Kuznets assumed that, by definition, government could not generate business savings—or, by extension, run the counterpart to business deficits. As a consequence, even though the US government did run substantial deficits during the Depression, Kuznets's system did not treat these deficits as negative "business savings." Because government transactions were not priced in market exchanges, moreover, Kuznets also had to devise a way to value these services that did not involve market prices. To do so, he treated government tax receipts from individuals (income tax) as part of national income paid out and excluded from the aggregate national income all taxes collected from businesses, as well as indirect taxes (e.g., sales and property taxes), since companies subtracted these taxes from their profits in their own accounts. In his system, in other words, Kuznets treated the government as if some of its expenditures benefited individuals while others provided intermediate product to businesses rather than final product to individuals. Examples of the former included government expenditures on education and highways; the latter included income generated by legislation protecting companies from certain kinds of competition or awarding tax breaks.[10]

While Kuznets's aggregates did give the administration a picture of the nation's ability (or failure) to generate capital and produce and circulate real goods and services, neither his definition of national income nor his approach to the problems involved in calculating national aggregates survived the 1930s. This was true not because his system was inherently flawed—good arguments can be made for each of his decisions—but because the situation in which national aggregates were drawn up, and thus the uses for which they were needed, had changed dramatically by the end of the decade. By 1940, it was clear that the United States would soon enter the European conflict and that defense expenditures would have to increase rapidly. When President Roosevelt announced a budget that allotted over half the nation's income to defense spending, it became obvious that national accountants would have to address the question of whether—and how—an economy devoted to supplying national consumption could shift into wartime production. When the Department of Commerce offered Milton Gilbert this challenge in 1941, he also faced a second question Kuznets did not have to address: could the US economy make the transition to war production without succumbing to inflation? Gilbert succinctly described these two issues as follows: "Were the people and their Government together trying to buy more goods than could be produced, and how much more?"[11] From answers to these questions, which Gilbert's aggregates supplied, would come the policies that shaped many Americans' economic experience of the war: heavy taxation, the growth of US debt in the form of Treasury bonds, price controls, and the rationing of some consumer commodities.

To address whether consumer demand was likely to undermine the war effort, Gilbert decided that net national income produced, the aggregate Kuznets preferred, was less useful than gross measures, like gross domestic product and gross national product—aggregates not reduced by subtracting depreciation, costs for upkeep and repairs, and business taxes. This constituted a significant departure from Kuznets's strategy: like Kuznets, Gilbert used both the income and production approaches, but he gave more emphasis to the latter; and Gilbert also incorporated a relatively new approach that estimated national aggregates by expenditure. To make use of the latter, Gilbert valued expenditures at market price; by contrast, he valued national income by factor costs. He figured expenditures at market price because the government's war payouts, the category of most immediate importance, largely consisted of purchases of American industries' goods and services, which were, in practice, valued at market price. He figured income at factor cost because the national income aggregates measured the net value of current output as the sum of net returns to factors of production. Gilbert argued that gross aggregates provided a more appropriate measure for the short-run analysis of war spending because some of what net figures subtracted—like business taxes—were actually available to the government to help fund the war.[12] To generate gross totals, Gilbert had to convert net national income figures, the data set with which he began, into gross aggregates by adding back both the taxes businesses had paid and the depreciation Kuznets had subtracted to produce net aggregates. Following the British statistician Colin Clark, Gilbert called the resulting aggregate "gross national product" or "gross national expenditure at market price."[13] Gilbert decided not to count the interest paid on government debt as part of the nation's income because he argued that government debt, which was undertaken primarily to finance the war, was not analogous to corporate interest payments on outstanding bonds, which should be treated as part of the company's current use of its capital. The former would presumably stop accumulating when the war ended, whereas the latter was an ongoing cost of conducting corporate business.

As Richard Kane has argued, Gilbert's intervention countered other economists' dire predictions about the impact the war was likely to have on the nation's economic well-being. This, in turn, backed Roosevelt's desire to increase the resources devoted to war. By adding to the income and product approaches the new expenditure approach, Gilbert could show what proportions of the national income flowed to consumption and investment. By definition, the residual could be identified as the nation's "savings."[14] Gilbert's decision to highlight GNP also helped policy makers anticipate the inflationary pressures associated with the war, for the "final expenditure" component generated by the expenditure approach allowed the administration to observe changes in the relationship between wages, which tended to increase during the war, and expenditures on consumer goods, which shrank as the production of domestic goods was reduced. Over time, this breakout would also reveal that expenditure on consumer goods tends to be relatively stable as a percentage of the whole, whereas expenditure on investment can fluctuate wildly; this, in turn, would offer a new way to understand the dynamics of business cycles.

The impact of Gilbert's decisions was amplified by his decision to organize the estimates with an accounting framework borrowed from corporate accounting. Morris A. Copeland had suggested doing this in 1932 and, in Britain, a team of national accountants offered a refined version of national accounts in 1941. To many economists, the benefits of an accounting approach seemed obvious: imposing the framework of double-entry accounting on the national aggregates converted the picture of a circular flow, which Kuznets's national income aggregates presented, into a system of inter-related accounts which showed the complex relationships among parts of the economy. The form of the accounts was dictated by the rules of double-entry accounting, which, as we saw in chapter 1, required the income for each sector to equal its outlays and net savings; in addition, by the rule of accounting identities, the total income for the nation had to equal its total expenditure. The result of this representational change was an increase in the level of detail the aggregates provided and, most importantly, a picture that emphasized the national economy's *structure*. Thus, when the ratios among various sectors' incomes or expenditures changed in significant magnitudes and over a long enough period, economists could say that *structural changes* were occurring in the economy, in contrast to other changes that did not alter the relationships assumed to be fundamental.

Placing national aggregates in a double-entry accounting framework not only helped national accountants see the economy in new ways; it also made it easier to estimate some values where data was not available. Unlike corporate accountants, who (ideally) had records of all company transactions, such records were not available to national accountants: some activities considered productive did not occur in a market, and some activities that might have been priced were not. Then, too, the value of long-term or ongoing activities could change as the purchasing power of money changed. To deal with such challenges, national accountants use a technique called imputation. In the absence of actual records, the accountant imputes a value for the service or contribution considered "productive" but not measured through price. The double-entry accounting framework makes imputation easier, for the basic accounting identity—income equals production—means that data that is relatively easy to obtain (the income figures) can be used to impute measures for data more difficult, or impossible, to obtain (the production figures and, in some cases, the expenditure figures). Because this accounting identity, along with the balances it entails, is imposed within each sector, moreover, as well as in the economy as a whole, missing data is effectively generated at every level by the available data.[15]

In 1944, Gilbert explicitly defended imputation by showing how it could calculate the nation's "saving," which is a finance-side category. Gilbert explained that, from a national-income point of view, saving can only be calculated *as a residual*, through imputation, when the accountant subtracts from the total of household incomes the amount individuals spent on consumer goods and services and what they paid in taxes and fees. "The balance of incomes, not spent on consumption or paid in taxes, must constitute saving," Gilbert explained. This breakout, which separated consumption from saving, was critical both because the "saving" figure was the household sector's closest approximation to the "surplus" (or profit) generated and carried over by a business and, as we will see, because the distinction between consumption and saving could be operationalized using Keynesian theory. The imputed "saving" figure also represented the closest approach this accounting system could make to the financial side of the economy.

Using imputation to generate data otherwise unavailable, Gilbert was also able to calculate the size of the government deficit. To do so, he relied once more on the accounting framework. "On the one hand, there are the major categories of Government expenditures—pay of factors of production, purchases of goods and services from private business, and transfer payments. On the other hand, there are Government revenues—personal and business taxes. The missing item needed to balance the expenditure and receipts sides of Government accounts is borrowing, or the Government deficit" (51). By filling in each "missing item needed to balance" two matching accounts and by consolidating and rearranging various entries in his accounts, Gilbert was able to show not only saving and the size of the government deficit, but also that these two figures had a fixed relation to each other—one, he insisted, not affected by inflation. "As statistically measured, savings in excess of private gross capital formation [investment] always equals Government borrowing, whether there is an inflation going on or not." This equation is a product of the double-entry accounting system; the accountant generated it by placing entries in matched accounts so related items could cancel each other out. While Gilbert acknowledged that such figures were products of the accounting system's rules, rather than exact reflections of "a state of balance in the economic system," he considered it adequate to address most readers' fears and doubts.

> This proof may leave the reader uneasy. "What," he may ask, "would happen if sufficient savings are not available and the Government prints money or borrows from the banks to cover the deficit? Will not the deficit exceed savings?" Suppose that in the situation depicted in the summary table the Government prints $10 billion of additional money and spends it on the products of private business. The Government deficit then will have increased by $10 billion. But the same $10 billion also appears as the receipts of private business and, provided there is no change in other items, the undistributed profits of private business will rise by the same amount. Total savings will have increased exactly in the amount of the deficit, and the statistics will not indicate that new money has been created. (50, 55)

By 1944, Gilbert could dismiss concerns like this, for national accounts relying on income, product, and expenditure approaches had provided the administration the tools it needed: "They enabled the Administration to set sights for the war production consistent with the vast productive potential of our economy and they provided the basis for determining the general character of the shift of industries from peace to war production. . . . With the inflation problem too, the income and product statistics have made possible a continuing quantitative appraisal that has been of immeasurable value in mapping the details and timing of the anti-inflation program." What seems to have pleased Gilbert most, however, was that his accounts had also convinced

American businessmen that gross figures would allow them to plan future activities, just as they allowed the government to plan and draw up budgets. "Since the national product statistics provide a historical record of how the output of a particular type of commodity or service fluctuated with output as a whole, [these gross aggregates] are useful to business in determining how a particular industry is likely to change with respect to total output in the future. This is, of course, important in the regular month-to-month appraisal that business men must make of the changes in prospect for their business. . . . It is safe to say that most firms attempting to approach their post-war problems in quantitative terms are making use of gross national product estimates" (57).

After Gilbert's NIPA accounts appeared, Kuznets wrote a harsh critique of the changes in the national estimates; Gilbert and his team responded in an only slightly less caustic article.[16] For our purposes, Kuznets's most important points are his criticisms of Gilbert's use of the double-entry framework, Gilbert's preference for gross over net figures, and his decision to treat government activity as final, not intermediate, product. These objections turned on the degree to which Gilbert's innovations required the national accountant to exercise interpretive discretion. While everyone involved in the debates about national aggregates agreed that the accountant had to make interpretive judgments—and even though Kuznets was the most outspoken proponent of making one's point of view explicit—he nevertheless objected that Gilbert was hiding his own interpretations behind the system of accounting rules. Objecting both to the judgments that led Gilbert to assign some data to one side of the double accounts instead of to the other and to the accounting framework itself, Kuznets opened fire on NIPA.

> If "economic accounting" is used properly to denote a method of approach, the basic concepts of accounting should be applied. . . . But even with more specific definition, there is little in the technique of the system of accounts in and of itself to help us determine the proper scope of national income and the observable flows that represent net yields and those which, from the standpoint of the national economy, represent costs; to decide upon the bases of valuation to be used; and the significant sectors to be distinguished at any level of economic circulation. Indeed, examination of the report fails to convey the impression that the setting up of the accounts assisted in any way in solving these problems of definition and distribution. On the contrary, the impression is that these problems were solved without benefit of the accounts, and that the system of accounts was constructed to fit the solutions. (152–53)

Kuznets's objections clearly followed from his own attempt to grapple with the difficult issues involved in creating national aggregates. "Does a system of accounts help the student deal with the vexing problems of scope, netness, and consistency of valuation that must be resolved when national income is defined as a measure of an economy's *net product?*" he asked (8). But these objections also acknowledge something the Gilbert team did not explicitly address: the sectors into which both teams divided the economy were, in important ways, fundamentally incommensurate. For, unlike households, corporations, and even "rest of the world," governments are not profit-making enterprises; thus, to apply an accounting system devised for the profit-driven corporation to government activity required the accountant to treat national income as corporate revenue, government consumption as tantamount to a company's costs, and the nation's capital formation as profit. Writing in 1958, George Jaszi, one of the members of Gilbert's group, drily acknowledged this lack of fit: "corporate accounting is not indigenous to the soil of the other sectors to which it is transplanted by national accountants."[17]

According to Kuznets, no accounting system could answer the thorny questions the national accountant inevitably faced. And using appeals to accounting rules to efface the decisions the accountant had actually made came perilously close to hiding the degree of discretion the aggregates actually contained. What Kuznets did not say—but a charge implicit in his objection to Gilbert's emphasis on gross measures—is that when Gilbert shifted the representation of the government sector to gross final product, he implicitly equated the growth of government (expenditures and costs) with growth of the nation's economy. This represented a dramatic retreat from the position Kuznets had taken when he argued that the purpose of creating national aggregates was to measure national welfare. When the growth of *government* was equated with the growth of the *nation*, the policy tool the national accountant provided could be used to justify *government growth*—and the national accountant became, de facto, an apologist for—as well as an indispensable member of—the government he measured.

6.3. THE BROOKINGS INSTITUTION AND THE EXPENDITURE APPROACH

The expenditure approach to national estimates, which was incorporated into NIPA along with the income and source of production approaches, has received remarkably little scholarly attention—even though the perspective it affords was critical to showing how financial intermediation affects the economy.[18] The income approach does depict financial activity, of course, in statistics for interest, dividends, and profits, which are proxies for capital as a factor of production. The production approach also includes some financial data in statistics depicting activities of the banking and insurance industries. Only with the expenditure approach, however, did the strategic importance of financial intermediation begin to appear; and even then, the national accounts could not show how flows of capital affected the nation's economy.

The expenditure approach used four additional aggregates—consumers' expenditures on final goods, business expenditures on investments, government expenditures, and net exports—to generate a higher-level, executive view of the economy. This view became influential for policies inspired by Keynes's work because, in his *General Theory,* Keynes argued that the interaction of these four components—consumption, investment, government, and net exports—determines the nation's demand for goods and services. Even though this approach dovetailed with Keynes's policy positions, however, in the United States it originated not exclusively in the work of the Keynesian economists recruited to Washington by the Roosevelt administration, such as Alvin Hansen and Lauchlin Currie, but also in research conducted independently of FDR's initiatives, by economists associated with the Brookings Institution.[19] Like the NBER, Brookings was a not-for-profit, nongovernmental agency that nevertheless had close ties to Washington. It was founded in 1916, as the Institute for Government Research; when merged in 1927 with the Institute of Economics and the Robert Brookings Graduate School, Brookings declared itself the first "fact-based study of national public policy issues," whose aim was to "bring science to the study of government."[20]

The most prominent economists at Brookings in the 1930s were Harold Moulton, Clark Warburton, and Edwin G. Nourse. Taken together, the positions held by these men indicate the enhanced status the discipline of economics was beginning to enjoy in the interwar period: Moulton, the University of Chicago professor we met in chapter 3, became the first head of Brookings; Warburton served as the first president of the Federal Deposit Insurance Corporation; and Nourse later became the first chairman of the Council of Economic Advisors. In the 1930s, they developed an extensive statistical data set that anchored the expenditure approach to national accounting. The results of this research were published in four volumes in 1934 and 1935: *America's Capacity to Consume* (by M. Leven, Moulton, and Warburton, 1934); *America's Capacity to Produce* (Nourse and Associates, 1934); *The Formation of Capital* (Moulton, 1935); and *Income and Economic Progress* (Moulton, 1935). In 1936, at the Wealth and Income Conference sponsored by the NBER, the Brookings' economists reconciled their statistical work with comparable empirical studies conducted by Kuznets on capital formation and by W. H. Lough on consumption.[21] The resulting data provided the statistical foundation for the expenditure approach to national income, as Gilbert incorporated this into the 1947 NIPA.

The theoretical positions held by the Brookings' economists differed in significant ways from Keynes's positions. The former, for example, insisted that the roots of the economic downturn lay in the pattern of income distribution, which favored those with higher incomes, and in the restriction of consumption relative to investment that followed: the wealthy tend to save more of their income. As Harold Moulton explained, the result was "a chronic inability—despite such devices as high pressure salesmanship, installment credits, and loans to facilitate foreign purchases—to find market outlets adequate to absorb our full productive capacity."[22] Moulton also thought that excess savings were primarily funneled into the stock market, where they bid up the price of securities. Despite significant differences, however, most of the components of Keynes's theory were present in the Brookings' economists' work—with the all-important difference that the latter anchored their theoretical positions in extensive statistical work.

6.4. INPUT-OUTPUT ACCOUNTING FOR THE US ECONOMY

NIPA, along with headline figures like the gross domestic product (GDP) and the gross national product (GNP), constitute the most familiar form of information about national aggregates in the United States, but before temporarily leaving the topic of national aggregates, we describe another data set, which was introduced—although not made fully operational—in the 1930s: input-output accounts, also known as the US Industry Accounts. Input-output accounts (IOA) were created during the 1920s and 1930s by Wassily Leontief; they were refined in the 1950s, during the Kennedy administration; and the US Bureau of Economics began regularly preparing input-output tables in 1958 and publishing them in 1964. In 1968, IOA were incorporated into the United Nations' System of National Accounts (SNA). Input-output accounts are based on the mathematical system of vector and matrix algebra, the technique Irving Fisher used in his early work and Paul A. Samuelson embraced in the 1940s. This technique was to prove pivotal in the postwar transformation of economics and in the reworking of mathematical economics more generally.[23]

Wassily Leontief was a German-born émigré who came to America from Russia in 1931. After a year at the National Bureau of Economic Research, Leontief joined the Harvard Economics Department, where he served as one of the directors of John Burr Williams's dissertation. American funding for Leontief's project, which he began before he left Russia, was initially provided by the NBER, but then taken over by the Harvard Committee on Research in the Social Sciences; in 1941, the US Bureau of Labor Statistics assumed responsibility for funding the research.[24] The purpose of IOA was to track flows of resources among sectors so the accountant could visualize the economy as a system of connected and interdependent parts, not simply an overall system of production and consumption, or aggregate savings and investment. To produce this representation, Leontief's IOA sectored the economy by industry, not simply by the large aggregates that organized Gilbert's estimates and the NIPA (household, corporations, and government). Leontief's system resembled NIPA in using an accounting framework, but the IOA framework differed in appearance and objective from the double-entry system intrinsic to NIPA. Arranged in intersecting columns and rows, Leontief's input-output accounts used the concept of linearity, the mathematics of matrices, and vector notation to model the interdependence of various industries and sectors of the economy.

While he published several versions of his accounting system in the 1930s, the best picture of Leontief's input-output accounts appears in *The Structure of American Economy*, the first edition of which was published in 1941 (covering the period from 1919 to 1929); a revised and augmented edition appeared a decade later.[25] In this volume, Leontief explained that input-output economics uses a technology of inferential analysis, which he invented, based on certain highly stylized assumptions about industrial production processes, consumer spending patterns, and savings behavior.[26] These assumptions are stylized because the ideals to which he aspired were not attainable from the available data—or, indeed, from any data: the "production enterprises" could not be classified into homogeneous categories because "the actual process of production and consumption preclude[d] a clean-cut differentiation of industries"; and households could not be "subdivided into separate classes according to the kind of services they provide[d]" because every household provided many kinds of services (20, 21). Leontief's sectors were more granular than their counterparts in Keynesian theory, early income, product, and expenditure estimates, or NIPA, in other words, but the IOA still had to rely on some of the basic theoretical and practical fictions that informed other national aggregates. Like other national accountants, moreover, Leontief also acknowledged a fairly long list of economic activities "completely ignored in our analysis, the most important [of which] are the entire fields of (a) distribution, wholesale and retail, (b) banking and finance, and (c) all non-rail transportation. No less serious is the omission of (d) the budgets of federal, state, and local governments" (21).

The foundations of input-output economics lay in three practices used in disciplines other than neoclassical economics: the *mathematics* of systems of simultaneous linear equations solved by matrix methods; the *statistics* that measured industrial production, household consumption, and revenue expenditure; and the *accounting principles* used to generate the revenue and expenditure entries that appeared on companies' income statements. Leontief described his study as "an attempt to apply the economic theory of general equilibrium—or better, general interdependence—to an empirical study of the interrelations among the different parts of the economy as revealed through the covariations of prices, outputs, investments, and incomes" (3). Thus his goal resembled the aggregative project refined by national accountants in the interwar period, most centrally in finding links between the real and financial sides of the economy; but it differed from both Kuznets's and Gilbert's work in the mathematical method he used and his vision that all interdependent parts of the economy could be connected by superimposing on the data a giant accounting system, whose most relevant document was the income statement. This accounting system provided the basic building block of his model.

The economic activity of the whole country is visualized as if covered by one huge accounting system. Not only all branches of industry, agriculture, and transportation, but also the individual budgets of all private persons, are supposed to be included in the system. Each business enterprise as well as each individual household is treated as a separate accounting unit. A complete bookkeeping system consists of a large number of different types of accounts. For our particular purpose, however, only one is important: the expenditure and revenue account. It registers on its credit side the outflow of goods and services from the enterprise or household (which corresponds to total receipts or sales) and on the debit side the acquisition of goods or services by the particular enterprise or household (corresponding to its total outlays). In other words, such an account describes the flow of commodities and services as it enters the given enterprise (or household) at one end and leaves it at the other. In contrast to a balance sheet, this type of account is related not to a single instant but rather to a period of time, say a year, a month, or a week. (11–12)

The coherence of the IOA system derives from the method of matrix algebra. Matrix algebra was useful because it could handle a large number of simultaneous equations and thus a large number of variables. Not only did it allow Leontief to write the equation system in a compact form, but it also enabled him to test whether a determinate solution existed for the system of equations. To conduct this test, he had to represent each of the elements that populated the model according to certain mathematical properties, including homogeneity, linearity, and the independence of all elements (except the dependent left to close the system). The system also required the number of equations in the overall system to equal the number of unknowns. Leontief arranged these elements in a series of rectangular arrays, each containing numbers, parameters, or variables and each typically enclosed in brackets. The location of each element in a matrix was fixed; each matrix was an ordered set, and, taken together, the number of rows and columns defined its dimension. To use this system, one read across the row, or up and down the column, to identify the row or column vector.

The particular matrix system Leontief used was square; mathematicians call this the Frobenius matrix, after the German mathematician Ferdinand Georg Frobenius. Leontief used the Frobenius matrix because it supported Walrasian general equilibrium theory, which required all economic relations to be represented at the same time. Walrasian general equilibrium theory differed from Marshallian partial equilibrium theory in avoiding the *ceteris paribus* convention, which allowed the economist to set aside some factors or relationships in order to solve for others.[27]

While Leontief did not use *ceteris paribus,* he did finesse certain aspects of the economy to produce his model. He limited production to single technical coefficients that assumed constant returns to scale, for example (37), and he placed restrictions on the substitutability of factors in both production and consumption functions (42). To fit the model protocols, moreover, Leontief also treated the household as an *industry;* this allowed the model to work as a closed system in which all industry factors mutually influenced each other (42).

Households are treated in our theoretical scheme exactly as any other industry. . . . The modern theory of consumers' behavior is, in most aspects of its conceptual development nearly identical with the theory of production. The formal similarity of a system of isoquants and of indifference curves is well established. The analogy can easily be extended by identifying the service output of a household with the production of an enterprise. Certain psychological resistance to this approach—due to memories of ill conceived subsistence cost theories of wages—would disappear as soon as we realize that nothing more is implied by it than the existence of an obvious connection between the expenditures of an individual and the amount of his earnings. (42)

Leontief's decision to treat the household sector "exactly as any other industry" provides one more indication that the influence of the financial sector on the American household was well underway in the interwar period, for household consumption, often using installment buying, was by that time a critical part of the national total.

For our purposes, Leontief's most consequential adjustment concerns his treatment of savings and investment activities. Because his accounting system lacked a fund (or balance-sheet) perspective, he had to estimate coefficients for each sector's investment and savings by inference from flow data. To generate these estimates, he had to make certain modifications:

Introduction of savings and investments obviously requires modification of all the cost equations. . . . The value product of any industry (or household), instead of being simply equal to its aggregate outlays, can now be either larger or smaller. In other words, total cost must now be equated to the total revenue divided by a certain *saving coefficient,* B_i. . . . Whenever B_i is greater than 1, the particular industry shows positive savings; it equals 1 if the total revenue of the enterprise or household exactly covers its outlays; and it becomes smaller than 1 in the case of negative savings, i.e. positive investment. (43)

In Leontief's matrix for 1919, which was partitioned into forty-four industry sectors, a catch-all residual "undistributed sector" was used as a stand-in for the government, banking, and finance sectors. During the three decades after 1919, as we are about to see, government taxes and services grew exponentially, many technological innovations were introduced, and the American household was financialized to a previously unheard-of degree, partly through the expansion of banking and insurance facilities. Leontief's matrices reflected these developments: in the 1939 industry matrix, he added discrete government and aircraft sectors; and he made finance and insurance visible as separate sectors in the 1947 matrix, published in 1951.

Leontief's seminal insight was that the corporate accounting system devised to measure profits (revenue minus costs equals profits) could be used to measure production and value added (output-input) if critical accounting items were imbued with new economic content. He overlaid cost accounting with production accounting by manipulating items on the income statement to reveal measures of production. To do this he generalized the accountant's concept of *cost* so it became the economist's concept of production *input,* and he generalized the accountant's concept of *revenue* to make it production *output.* This adaptation of concepts developed for one discipline (accounting) to the requirements of another (production economics) allowed Leontief to use a double-entry format to systematize and correlate the vast amounts of cost, revenue, and other financial data tabulated and standardized by the Bureau of Labor Statistics, the Census Bureau, the Internal Revenue Service, the Department of Agriculture, and the Federal Reserve—all of which was now available in easily obtainable publications.

6.5. INTERWAR AMERICAN FISCAL POLICY

When the Depression began, American tax policy was relatively simple, at least by contrast to the more complicated tax systems of Great Britain and Germany. In 1930, only 12% of American families were subject to the personal income tax, estate taxes were very low, corporate tax rates stood at 12%, and most individual income tax rates had been dramatically reduced under the progressive tax plans implemented in the late 1920s. The onset of the Depression hit federal revenue hard, however: national income was more than cut in half between 1929 and 1932—it fell from $87.8 billion to $42.5 billion in just three years— and Andrew Mellon, architect of the Mellon Tax Plan and Hoover's Treasury secretary, was forced to ask Congress for a tax increase in 1932. Ogden Mills, Mellon's replacement at the Treasury, was even bolder: recognizing that the base of the American tax system was too narrow, resting as it did primarily on the wealthy and depending on a robust environment for business, Mills recommended restoring tax rates to their 1924 levels, doubling surtax rates, reducing personal exemptions, raising corporate tax rates, and returning estate tax rates to their 1921 level. While the Revenue Act of 1932 did not include all of Mills's suggestions, and while it depended much more heavily on excise taxes than Mill had recommended, it did mark the beginning of the transformation that would turn America's pre-Depression personal income "class tax" into its current "mass tax" system, a transformation that was complete by 1945. The 1932 Revenue Act led to what has been called the largest tax increase in American history because the steep new rates for income tax payers were implemented during a period of a marked decline in nominal GNP.[28]

Taxation is obviously a central plank of public finance, and, for many Americans, it is the most inescapable face of finance. Taxes constitute a major source of government revenue, decisions about how to generate and spend this revenue form the heart of an administration's social policy, and a government's ability to justify its tax policy often determines its success with voters. Decisions about taxation can be made on ethical, political, or economic grounds, and the way these decisions are presented either reinforces or undermines the social fabric of the nation. Thus, taxation is the connective tissue that sutures individuals to their government; tax policies express an administration's values and vision; and the models that began to be applied to tax policy in the late 1930s, along with the budgeting by which taxation was rendered accountable, helped justify the government's demand for money as part of a theoretically coherent contract between those who needed services and protections and the government that provided them.

The debates about the revenue acts passed between 1932 and 1942 expose all these dimensions of taxation, and the application of forward-looking budgeting after 1938 also shows how the modeling Williams developed for corporations in his PhD thesis began to be applied to national fiscal policy. But the history of taxation in this period also reveals a steady, unprecedented rise in the amount of taxation imposed on individuals and corporations. As we survey the debates by which the Roosevelt administration made these tax increases palatable and some of the individuals who helped do so, we should not lose sight of this overall increase, for it constitutes the backbone of the social and fiscal contracts that still anchor America today, as well as the debates that now swirl around taxation. We emphasize this increase—which every contemporary taxpayer will recognize—alongside an aspect of the history of modern tax policy that will surprise most readers, as it would have surprised Americans who lived through the New Deal: the approach to taxation and budgeting implemented after 1938 originated, at least partly, in Germany's short-lived Weimar Republic.

Roosevelt's initial approach to taxation was driven by his strong commitment to tax fairness. His administration's first tax initiatives were attempts to hunt down and prosecute tax evaders. So wide was the net of tax justice that the banker J. P. Morgan and Andrew Mellon, the architect of Hoover's tax reduction plan, were both eventually caught in its snare.[29] The first positive revenue act of the Roosevelt administration was not passed until a year after he took office, and the Revenue Act of 1934 reveals his zeal for identifying tax avoiders and limiting the deductions shareholders could take for stock losses—something that had been permitted by the Revenue Act of 1932. The 1934 Act also continued the policy of tax increases on the wealthy begun by the 1932 act; it levied higher surcharges on higher income tax payers and cut effective rates in the lower tax brackets. In addition, it limited the deductions that partnerships could take for losses in an effort to crack down on the kind of tax avoidance that benefited J. P. Morgan and his partners.[30]

The Revenue Acts of 1935 and 1936 imposed even steeper income tax rates on the wealthy, and they also tackled undistributed profits—the capital reserves built up by corporations and not distributed to shareholders. The debate about taxing undistributed profits had been raging since 1932, but it heated up in 1936, when Harry Morganthau, secretary of the Treasury, began promoting this tax in the name of tax fairness. Others, like Robert H. Jackson, argued that taxing undistributed profits would help prevent the dangerous consolidation of companies—a trend, as we have seen, that also worried Berle and Means. The Revenue Act of 1936 enacted this provision, taxing the undistributed revenues of companies at rates between 7% and 27%, depending on company size and the percentage of profits they retained. This act also raised effective corporate tax rates by approximately 1%.[31] The undistributed-profits tax was extremely unpopular with businesses and shareholders, in part because the tax would have both forced corporate managers to find new sources of capital and reduced returns to investors. The undistributed tax was curtailed by the Revenue Act of 1938, and what was left of it was repealed in 1939. Before this pullback was complete, the Revenue Act of 1937 went after loopholes that allowed some tax payers to reduce their individual tax liabilities. Public debate about loopholes once more raised the issue of tax fairness, especially when some wealthy Americans, including members of the du Pont family, were revealed to have avoided taxes by counting spending on the upkeep of yachts and country estates as deductible business expenses.[32] Tax avoidance, whether on the part of corporations or individual taxpayers, was the clearest target of these revenue acts, and the wealthy bore the burden of both taxation and public outrage.

The tax increases enacted by the mid-1930s legislation were justified not only by appeals to tax fairness but also by the nation's demonstrable fiscal need. Not only had the onset of the Depression radically diminished revenues from personal income and corporations, but, in January 1936, the Supreme Court struck another blow to national solvency when it declared the Agricultural Adjustment Act (AAA) unconstitutional. By voiding this act, the Court deprived the administration of approximately $500 million, generated by the AAA's processing fee. A few weeks later, Congress overrode the president's veto of the soldiers' bonus bill, the cost of which was estimated at an additional $120 million for the current fiscal year. Initially, these losses did not seem likely to be offset by the revenue generated by the Social Security Act of 1935, which, in 1937, was to reach $226 million. (By 1938, this figure was increased by an incremental $515 million; in that year, the GDP was estimated to be slightly more than $80 billion.)[33] In 1936, just over $1.2 million was returned to Social Security beneficiaries, but within a year, the payout had swelled to $10.5 million. In any case, many still blamed the mandatory Social Security tax for catapulting the US economy back into recession in 1937–38.

Between Roosevelt's first year in office and 1938, the president, lawmakers, and popular news sources typically debated revenue bills in ideological terms. Whether cast as a demand to ferret out "tax evaders," to "soak the rich" so as to redistribute corporate profits, to promote "tax fairness," or to use "social taxation" to accelerate the nation's economic recovery, political and popular discussions of taxation in these years tended to be tinged with moralistic overtones, when they were not explicitly phrased in the appeals to fairness and economic justice Roosevelt favored.[34] In 1938, however, a new rhetoric about taxation began to circulate—at least among legislators and in the White House. This rhetoric came from and reflected the administration's new approach to taxation, which was signaled by a reorganization within the US Treasury Department. In 1938, Treasury created a new Division of Tax Research, and, under the leadership of the economist Roy Blough, this division began to bring tax experts into the administration, with an eye to beefing up statistical research, making taxation part of a coherent fiscal policy, and developing budgets that were forward-looking and regularly delivered. Along with experts hired to advise Congress and the president, these specialists helped make taxation a central component of a more focused fiscal policy. After 1938, and as the United States rapidly began to prepare for another war in Europe, taxation came to be treated not as an instrument to ensure social justice or even as a source of federal revenue but as a key part of macroeconomic policy and one cornerstone of national security.

The new approach to taxation symbolized by the 1938 arrival of tax experts in Washington was at least partly a result of discussions held in academic seminars, conferences, and symposia, where economists and political scientists tried to understand the implications of the Roosevelt administration's untheorized responses to the nation's revenue shortfall. Two academic centers were especially important in discussions about fiscal policy. The first was Harvard's Fiscal Policy seminar, which was co-taught by Alvin Hansen and John H. Williams. The seminar first convened in the fall of 1937, and, during its long life, this seminar brought Washington insiders to Cambridge to discuss taxation, budgeting, and fiscal management. Many of the individuals who helped shape the administration's fiscal policies from the late 1930s had some contact with this seminar.[35] In addition to Hansen and John H. Williams, these include four men who became members of the Council of Economic Advisors, four who served as members of the Board of Governors of the Federal Reserve, two who served as undersecretaries of the Treasury, and two who became assistant secretaries for economic affairs.

The Fiscal Policy seminar is best remembered as the point of entry for Keynesian theory into American economics. Two Canadian graduate students who attended Keynes's lectures in England between 1932 and 1935 arrived at Harvard in the fall of 1935 with their seminar notes, and they soon arranged to get an advanced copy of the *General Theory* sent to Harvard as well. Although initially skeptical about the value of Keynes's ideas, Hansen and Williams made Keynes's work the center of the first year's syllabus.[36] While many people now associate New Deal policies, including tax policy, with Keynesian theory, and while these theories were undeniably influential in the 1940s, the policies of the 1930s cannot be directly attributed to Keynes's ideas, no matter how influential Harvard-associated economists such as Lauchlin Currie and Walter Salant became.[37] As Leon Keyserling, chair of the Council of Economic Advisors, remarked, nearly all the New Deal policies were "fully developed before Keynes. . . . From the very beginning of the rising unemployment in 1930, in '30 and '31 and '32, a number of years before the general public really heard of Keynes, public officials—senators like Robert F. Wagner of New York and Edward Costigan of Colorado and Bob La Follette, the younger, of Wisconsin—were introducing bill after bill on public works to take up the unemployment, which was raw Keynesianism but didn't come from Keynes."[38] The economist Paul Sweezy agreed: "The New Deal did not act on Keynesian policies at all," he asserted.[39]

The second academic center where discussions of fiscal policy were held in the 1930s had, in some ways, a more direct impact on the Roosevelt administration's fiscal policies—although not, to be sure, on the bills introduced in Congress in the early 1930s. This was the New School for Social Research, which had been founded in New York in 1920 by, among others, economists

Wesley Clair Mitchell and Alvin Johnson. The New School was initially devoted to adult education, especially in the social sciences. Johnson, who had a special interest in the social sciences, was also the editor of the *Encyclopedia of the Social Sciences,* an ambitious project sponsored by the Carnegie and Rockefeller foundations to put these disciplines on a modern footing. As part of his effort to find authors for the encyclopedia, Johnson kept in touch with European economists. As a result, he was well placed to organize a rescue effort to get some of the most important social scientists out of Germany when that country reinstated its Civil Service Act (the "Law for the Reconstruction of Public Service Appointments") on April 7, 1933. Among the first twelve émigrés Johnson recruited to what he initially called the "University in Exile" was Gerhard Colm, a German trained in sociology who was working at Kiel when the Civil Service Act was reinstated.[40] Colm was one of Germany's foremost analysts of business cycles, and, most relevant to our argument, he was an eloquent spokesperson for viewing taxation and budgeting as central components of a nation's fiscal policy. By focusing on Colm, we show how some of the policies and techniques originally developed in Weimar Germany were brought to the United States, used retrospectively to justify policies that were already in place, and—by implication, at least—made to seem distinctively Keynesian. A discussion of Colm also allows us to show how one version of the modeling that John Burr Williams set out in his PhD thesis was applied to US taxation and budgeting.

Although Gerhard Colm does not seem to have been Jewish, he was one of the first academics dismissed under the Civil Service Act—probably because he had repeatedly and publicly opposed the burgeoning Nazi movement. At the Kiel Institute at the University of Koln, Colm worked alongside other economists who were soon to emigrate voluntarily and go to the United States, like Wassily Leontief, as well as those who were forced to leave by the Nazi crackdown; these included Jacob Marschak, Adolph Lowe, Hans Neisser, and Alfred Kahler.[41] More important for our purposes is Colm's previous position: during the 1920s, he worked for the Reich's Statistical Office, under the leadership of Ernst Wagemann and, more immediately, the statistician Hans Wolfgang Platzer. When Wagemann launched the Institut fur Konjunkturforschung (Institute for Business-Cycle Research, IfK) in 1925, he brought Platzer and Colm into the institute. Under the directorship of Platzer, Colm headed the research team charged with producing an official estimate of the nation's income.

The Statistical Office and the Institut fur Konjunkturforschung belonged to the new national system of economic administration hastily created to deal with the nation's postwar turmoil. While other nations also faced challenges when the First World War ended, Weimar's situation was especially dire. In addition to the demand that Germany pay wartime reparations, the Republic also confronted domestic unrest: a soldiers' strike had paralyzed the military; a separatist movement sprang up on the French border; Bolshevism was a constant threat; and the nation's economy was descending into the hyperinflation that was to climax in 1924. As J. Adam Tooze explains, the Statistical Office and especially the IfK were designed "to combine intensive monitoring of the fluctuations of the economy (Konjunkturbeobachtung) with scientific analysis of the business-cycle (Konjunkturforschung)"[42] in hopes of ending economic instability. Colm's initial work with the IfK centered on evaluating the relatively crude estimates of national income Karl Helffrich had drawn up prior to the war. In 1925, it was critical to construct a reliable estimate of national income because the US-led Dawes Committee, which had provided a temporary judgment on the vexed reparations issue in 1924, had fixed the amount Germany had to pay to a rough index of its national prosperity—that is, to its national income. In 1921, the reparations amount had been set at 269 billion German gold marks. In 1922, in *A Revision of the Treaty*, Keynes argued strenuously that this amount should be reduced, but, like everyone else, Keynes had only Helffrich's questionable figures to work with. The Dawes Committee essentially agreed with Keynes and arrived at the provisional figure of 132 billion, but it too lacked data more reliable than Helffrich's estimates. When the IfK launched its national income project, then, the stakes were high, for the size of the nation's reparations—as well as the amount of money it would have to borrow from the United States to make good on this penalty—depended on these official estimates.

Colm and his team were especially suspicious of Helffrich's figures for prewar tax evasion, which they considered seriously underestimated, but they soon focused on postwar data as well.[43] Colm and colleagues worked within, and presumably shared, the vision Wagemann celebrated: according to Wagemann, a properly constructed system of national accounting could not only make the nation's economy visible but also make it amenable to government planning, if not control. In a perfect marriage of economic expertise and political power, Germany's new national accounting system would not only seek to track the past fluctuations of the economy but also try to master the business cycle in order to manage the future.[44] The accounting system developed and regularly applied by the IfK bears a superficial resemblance to the Harvard business barometers, but whereas that tool presented only an arbitrary collection of symptomatic indicators, the IfK approach highlighted national income as the key descriptive *and* predictive macroeconomic variable. This approach also treated other important variables—the balance of payments, including the balance of interest payments, price data, and unemployment data—as parts of a national economic system. As a result, the IfK team was able to use its measurements of national income to present a new picture of the business cycle. "Extending the data series back to 1890 confirmed [the] initial intuition [that] the economy developed in a wave-like motion. Billions of marks ebbed and flowed through the circuits of production, income and expenditure while, at the same time, an even larger process of production and reproduction developed according to its own rhythm, largely untroubled by the turmoil of the cycle."[45]

Colm took from his work at the IfK both the conviction that statistical research on the business cycle and macroeconomic variables could be fused into a useful picture of a nation's economy and the notion that such research could drive forward-looking government policy. He saw, in other words, that, when treated as components of the flow of a nation's income, taxation, budgeting, and even an administration's announcement of fiscal policy could be used as levers to manage the nation's economy going forward—not simply to monitor or react to economic conditions. In this scheme of things, the expectations of individuals played a crucial role, maximizing information was critical to maximizing income, and effective initiatives could only occur at the aggregate level (in the United States, at the federal level), where what statistical experts could know about the nation's economy as a whole fed directly into the ways policy makers treated economic issues. Taxes, budgets, and fiscal policy were no longer viewed primarily as local or political matters, nor were they incidental necessities subordinate to a political or ethical agenda. From this perspective, they were the essential components of state management and planning, without which no government could hope to succeed.

In 1927, when conditions at the IfK began to deteriorate, Colm left the institute for Kiel, where Leontief, Lowe, Neisser, and Kahler also held professorships.[46] As we have seen, Leontief left Kiel in 1931, initially to join the NBER and then, a year later, the Harvard Economics Department; and Colm, Lowe, Neisser, and Kahler left immediately after the reinstitution of the Civil Service Act, in April 1933. Collectively, these economists are sometimes referred to as the "new classicals" or the "German reform economists" (even though at least three members of the group—Colm, Lowe, and Neisser—did not hold degrees in economics).[47] Among their contributions to economic and financial theory and practice were Lowe's work on the role technical innovation played in the business cycle, Neisser's analysis of the competition between labor and technology in the dynamics of capitalism, Kahler's work on multisector growth models, and Leontief's early development of the input-output model. Here we focus only on Colm's contributions to fiscal policy, for these were to prove most influential in Washington. We also focus initially on the articles Colm published in the interwar period—that is, between the time he arrived in New York in 1933 and 1941, when the United States entered World War II. Even though he had already published extensively in German, only the articles published in English—many of which appeared in *Social Research,* the journal launched by the New School—would have been accessible to most American policy makers.

As Claus-Dieter Krohn has pointed out, in 1933 US work on public finance was "in an archaic state."[48] The American tax system, which, as we have seen, had last been updated with the Mellon Tax Plan of the late 1920s and the Revenue Act of 1932, approached taxes primarily as money withdrawn from productive use in the economy, and a significant number of the relatively small percentage of individuals required to pay income tax regarded tax avoidance as acceptable. Budgeting at the state and federal levels was certainly taken seriously, but budgets tended to be short-term and based on estimates and hopeful projections. The national debt was also not consistently considered central to public finance, much less fiscal policy. Most politicians, including FDR at the beginning of his first term, advocated balancing the national budget, avoiding deficit spending, and reducing taxation as matters of prudent political policy as much as anything else. Even as more reliable economic data became available after 1920, moreover, most economists who might have wanted to construct theories or offer legislators advice about fiscal policy were hampered by uncertainty about how to integrate empirical research and economic theory. As Leontief wryly remarked, in America, empirical research and economic theory "always remained a kind of song with separate piano accompaniment."[49]

One of Colm's first two English-language articles, published in August 1934, was devoted to taxation. Entitled "The Ideal Tax System," the article contrasted America's minimalist approach to taxation with the tax systems of Great Britain and Germany. Colm argued that the Depression was forcing the United States to realize that its present policy of using property taxes, supplemented by scant revenue from income and corporate taxation, to finance government spending could not support the level of government intervention necessary to jump-start the stalled economy. Bringing together his previous work on the business cycle with his sociological interest in the interrelation of fiscal and social issues, Colm argued that, in such a situation, "the development of a cyclical theory of taxation becomes . . . a new task for fiscal science." Economists had to develop a set of "rules of the 'best' tax policy with reference to the business cycle," he argued. If they developed these rules, "taxation could become . . . an instrument of economic planning."[50] Despite his optimistic view that placing taxation at the heart of fiscal policy would open new opportunities for social scientists, Colm was nevertheless pessimistic that the United States could make a coherent tax system play the vital role he envisioned. "In combating cyclical instability, the government must place foremost reliance on instrumentalities other than taxation that affect the economic process more vitally."[51]

Colm developed his most extensive ideas about the theory and practice of fiscal policy in the postwar period, and it is useful to look forward to his more fully articulated ideas. Defining fiscal policy as "government expenditures, revenues, borrowing, and debt management, considered with a view toward their impact on the flow of purchasing power," he placed fiscal policy in a national-income framework, which was, in turn, conceptualized as a "flow" best understood as "purchasing power"—or what Keynes called "effective demand."[52] In an essay written during the administration's debates about what became the 1946 Employment Act, Colm advocated economic projection, using the national budget both for planning and as an incentive to spur business investment; he also emphasized the necessity of generating and using information in fiscal decision making.[53] In "Public Finance in the National Income" (1950), he provided a flow chart that positioned government receipts and expenditures as critical, although special, components of the national income—a topic, as we have just seen, that was both controversial and consequential.[54] And in "National Economic Budgets" (1951), Colm clarified the relationship between national income estimates and the operationalization of these statistics through the budgeting process. Here, as elsewhere, he also tempered his enthusiasm for national planning—a subject that was still controversial in America in the 1950s[55]—with a respectful discussion of the goals of a free-enterprise economy. As always, Colm recommended that the United States pursue a balanced economy rather than a balanced budget and that national economic budgeting, which was "developed as a tool for appraising government fiscal and economic policies" during the extraordinary conditions of depression and war, be used in peacetime to evaluate the government's performance as well as orient its future performance.[56]

For our purposes, Colm's most interesting contribution to interwar finance is an essay published in 1936 in the third volume of *Social Research*. Entitled

"Public Spending and Recovery in the United States," this article attracted the attention of Washington officials, and, soon after it appeared, Colm was invited to join the Bureau of the Budget as a financial expert. Particularly interesting is the resemblance between the method Colm used in this essay and the method John Burr Williams was working out in his thesis. In "Public Spending," Colm did not attempt to model the economy, nor did he use the word *model*—although by 1951, Colm was both using the word and placing models in the context of other forward-looking techniques, including forecasting.[57] In a footnote to the 1936 article added in 1954, Colm also acknowledged that because "the methods for measuring the economic effects of government spending" were relatively unrefined in the mid-1930s, the approach he used would seem "elementary" to readers in 1954. The methodological "refinement" to which he alluded was clearly the translation of literary and graphic representations, which dominate this essay, into "mathematical formulations."[58]

We might call the method Colm developed in 1936 a proto-model. He used it to isolate one aspect of the Roosevelt administration's multifaceted approach to the Depression—hence, to answer a single question: was this spending responsible for inaugurating the economic recovery that seemed to be underway in the United States? (In light of the second economic downturn that began in 1937, Colm's analysis looks premature.) To isolate public spending, the factor he was most interested in, Colm identified, evaluated, and excluded other variables that might also have affected the nation's recovery, such as a drop in the interest rate or the expectation that New Deal measures would increase consumer confidence; and he developed ways to factor in the speed of the transmission of effects, leakage, and multipliers—theoretical concepts he borrowed from J. M. Clark, R. F. Kahn, and John Maynard Keynes, respectively. He also tried to accommodate temporal lags, which would reflect delays in the effects of public spending. He took his data from Simon Kuznets's *Gross Capital Formation, 1919–1933,* an NBER bulletin, and the *Survey of Current Business*—that is, the state-of-the-art statistical sources—as well as some less familiar sources (the Cleveland Trust Company, the National Industrial Conference Board, and the *American Federalist*). He presumably used regression analysis to correlate the relationships between his key variable and other factors, and he generated two charts to illustrate the relationship between his hypothesis—about the amount the nation's income *should* rise if public spending were the decisive factor—and the actual national income. The two charts showed that, with leakages calculated, first, at 50% and then at 33-1/3%, the hypothesis about pump priming was correct: if the leakage was figured at 50%, then 66% of the actual recovery was due to the federal government's deficit spending; if the leakage was figured at 33-1/3%, then 80% of the recovery could be attributed to deficit spending.[59]

Colm's demonstration resembles the models economists would soon embrace because of his use of the "if . . . then" structure: if we include these factors, defined in the following ways, state our foundational assumptions, and derive statistically measurable relationships between our hypothesis about the most significant variable (federal spending) and the available data (about national income), then our outcome graphically confirms (or disproves) the hypothesis with which we began. If we change some of our assumptions (about the percentage of leakage), then the new graph also addresses the hypothesis, this time in relation to the new assumptions. Since Colm could not know precisely what the percentage of leakage was, he concluded that the most plausible answer lay somewhere in between the relationships plotted on the two graphs. Here we see Colm's characteristic modesty: while he presented the relationship the graphs show as reliable, he did not attribute certainty to the results. If anything, his conclusions directed attention to what such proto-models could *not* show, given the limitations of available data and the imprecision of theoretical concepts such as leakage. "Our positive results, especially the figures, must be understood more as illustration than as exact measurements. This study has at least made clear the gaps in our information about facts that ought to be known for a definite answer to our question. The whole problem of leakages, for example, indicates a vast lacuna in our knowledge about fundamental facts in economic development. And yet we think that we can claim at least a certain probability for our assumptions."[60]

Judged in relation to later mathematical models, Colm's method seems relatively rudimentary. Not only was the method for measuring aggregates, such as the effects of government spending or even national income, still something of a patchwork in 1936, but Colm did not use mathematical language, as Williams did, much less sophisticated mathematical techniques, like simultaneous equations or matrix and vector analysis, to figure and represent the *relationships* among various factors. Instead of trying to correlate these relationships, he factored out variables that seemed extraneous, and, while he stated his conclusion in terms that alluded to probability, the "certain probability" he claimed for his conclusion was not a mathematical expression of variance around a mean. While Colm clearly saw the role market agents' expectations play in economic activity, and while he understood that information—or, in this case, the lack thereof—was vital to the actions of both market agents and economists, he did not try to factor expectations or information into his analysis. His proto-model was formulated according to the *ceteris paribus* paradigm familiar to Marshallian economists: all other things being equal, and if these assumptions obtained, then one could draw these conclusions from the available data and theoretical paradigms.

Colm presumably took this approach to Washington in 1938. Working first for the Bureau of the Budget and then as a member of the Council of Economic Advisors, which was advisory to the president of the United States, Colm continued to make substantive contributions to New Deal policy throughout the 1940s. He made important contributions to the Employment Act of 1946; he helped draw up plans for the emergency or extraordinary budget, which was used to finance one-time projects; he staunchly supported future-oriented budgetary planning, which was mandated by the Employment Act; and he published extensively on how to use taxation, national budgets, and budgetary projections to help direct the economy in a free-market society. Colm enjoyed the respect of economic theorists such as Walter S. Salant, who published widely on monetary theory, as well as policy specialists such as Leon Hirsch Keyserling, who served as chair of the Council of Economic Advisors.[61]

The few scholars who discuss Colm treat him either as a particularly successful émigré or as a Keynesian.[62] Certainly, his contemporaries viewed him as "a staunch believer in Keynesianism," and, despite contributing to an issue of *Social Research* that contained critical reviews of Keynes's *General Theory* by Lederer and Neisser, Colm no doubt respected most of Keynes's ideas.[63] Nevertheless, some of the ideas that might have seemed most Keynesian at the time—and that still do so today—actually came from the German reform school of economics. The formulation of these ideas not only preceded Keynes's work but also went much further toward endorsing state planning than Keynes was willing to do. Like many of the New Deal policies in general—especially the reorganization of fiscal policy after 1938—Colm's ideas came to seem Keynesian in retrospect, after Keynes's theories had been recast by Alvin Hansen, after the Harvard Keynesians acquired various administrative positions in Washington, and after Colm tempered some of the more enthusiastic endorsements of state planning that appeared in his early works. Once American economists began to embrace Keynes's theories and Washington drew more Keynesian economists into war work, members of the administration inevitably built on policies already in place, thus making the New Deal initiatives seem more theoretically coherent than they originally were.[64] It was easy to assimilate Gerhard Colm's contributions to the general atmosphere of "Keynesianism" because, like Keynes and his American followers, Colm also wanted the central government to exercise planning and use forward-looking budgets to influence not simply administrative policy but the activities of businesses as well. Like those who supported the early New Deal policies, Gerhard Colm was not, strictly speaking, Keynesian, but it was easy to see him as such because the administrative changes he recommended—which were deeply imbued by the research he had conducted in Weimar Germany—departed so far from the laissez-faire traditions with which most Americans were comfortable.

In 1940, Congress enacted two tax bills, which raised individual and corporate tax rates; an excess profit tax was imposed in 1941, as America prepared to enter World War II, and in 1942, corporate and individual income tax rates were once more raised significantly. All these tax initiatives were formulated in the terms of a systematic, forwarding-looking budgeting process whose theoretical infrastructure we examine in a moment. Most important to the administration's ability to use taxation for such forward-looking budgeting was the creation of the mandatory payroll withholding policy—an accomplishment of the Victory Tax of 1942, which has been called "the greatest tax bill in American history."[65] Withholding taxes from the payrolls of American taxpayers at the point of origin, instead of simply hoping that individuals would voluntarily set aside money for taxes, transformed both Americans' relation to taxation and the income tax itself. Instead of being an estimate, whose collection was unsure, the income tax became a calculable fund that could be used as a basis for future-oriented planning. We can see how powerful a tool this tax had become for managing the nation's economy by contrasting the percentage of American workers who filed individual income tax returns in 1945—90%—to the 12% who filed in 1930.

CHAPTER 7

Models of Economies and Finance, 1930–1940

Since at least the late 1990s, most economists identify modeling as the defining methodology of the discipline.[1] Yet the practice only began to be theorized in the interwar period, and the word *model* was not widely used by economists until the 1940s. Ragnar Frisch introduced the word into the economist's lexicon in 1930, the concept was theorized by Joseph A. Schumpeter in his 1939 book on business cycles, and by 1940, macroeconometricians like Jan Tinbergen routinely used techniques now associated with modeling to represent national economies. The process by which modeling became the preferred method of economists and the way economic modeling came to rely on mathematics provide the critical links between early economic theories and the postwar discipline, and the complex relationship between economic models and finance constitutes an unwritten history of the related but distinct disciplines of economics and finance.

7.1. "LITTLE MODEL WORLDS" AND THE ECONOMETRIC SOCIETY

In 1930, the Norwegian economist Ragnar Frisch visited Yale at the invitation of Irving Fisher. In the first of his Yale lectures, Frisch explained that it was imperative to elevate economics to the level of a "science," and to do so, economists had to combine statistics, the best tool for analyzing data ("The true theorist in economics has to become at the same time a statistician"), with theory ("the attempt at *understanding,* at bringing a rational order into things"). The result, Frisch explained, would not be exact replicas of the real world but simplified simulations, which he called "little model worlds."[2] As Frisch described them, model worlds constitute "an intellectual trick: in our mind we create a little *model world* of our own, a model world which is not too complicated to be overlooked, and which is equipped with points where the mind can get a grip, so that we can find our way through without getting confused. And then we analyse this little model world instead of the real world. This mental trick is the thing which constitutes the rational method, that is, theory" (32).

Frisch acknowledged that a "gap" separated the model world from the observable world—the former was governed by "rational laws," while the latter was subject to "empirical laws"—but he insisted that understanding the model world could illuminate events in the empirical world, even when the model world contained objects the theorist had invented—"transobservational creations." Most of the time, the model world would "consist only in typification, an idealization of some observed empirical law," Frisch explained, but sometimes, by "a kind of heroic guess," the economist could add to the model something he had not observed: "a new kind of object, not resembling anything which is known from actual observations, or it can be a relation between phenomena which are by themselves well known from actual experiences but which have never been observationally related, because nobody has thought of it, or because the phenomena are of such a kind that they cannot be observed together directly with the given technique of observation" (34, 32-33). These "transobservational creations" allowed the theorist, who was "sovereign in the model world, so long as [he did] not break the laws of formal logic," to perform the kind of experiments otherwise unavailable to the economist. This is the "if . . . then" structure of the model we initially saw in John Burr Williams's work on investment. By reducing the variables that make economic transactions so complicated to those considered most relevant, provisionally adopting theoretical assumptions (even when they are unrealistic), and using rigorous mathematical language, the economist's model world allows him to test various hypotheses even when direct observation and experimentation are impossible.

In December of his Yale term, Frisch suggested another way to advance the scientific ambition of economics. This was an international society, whose work would add mathematics to the model's reliance on theory and statistics. At a joint meeting of the American Economic Association and the American Statistical Association, Frisch convened a small group of like-minded scholars, and the Econometric Society was born. Conceived from the beginning as an international institution as well as an interdisciplinary venture, the Econometric Society brought together prominent Europeans, such as Joseph A. Schumpeter, and Americans who had helped shape their respective disciplines in the United States. American charter members included the Iowa State mathematician Harold C. Davis; Columbia professor Harold Hotelling, the statistician who had promoted R. A. Fisher's work; the mathematician Edwin Bidwell Wilson, who was president of the American Statistical Association and author of the most advanced calculus textbook in America; Walter A. Shewhart, an engineer, physicist, and Bell Labs researcher; and Yale economist Irving Fisher, who was elected the society's first president.[3] Alfred A. Cowles III was an early financial supporter of the society.

The draft constitution of the Econometric Society did not stress models per se, but, as Olav Bjerkholt and Duo Qin have pointed out, models constituted the "essential medium"—the only medium—in which the three methods endorsed by the society could be combined.[4] Without modeling, data, in the form of statistics, could not be brought into alignment with economic theory, and both became precise only when expressed in mathematical language. Models became the preferred method of econometrics precisely because the "rational laws" humans create do not—or cannot be known to—correspond to the complicated dynamics of the real and financial sides of actual economies. In 1939, Joseph A. Schumpeter provided a theoretical account of the modeling practice the society used. Schumpeter described models as analytic tools that "fram[e]" the economist's approach to facts. But models are also "framed" by the theories that inform them, and it is this recursive interplay between models and facts that facilitates economic and econometric analysis. The economist must have "tools of analysis," Schumpeter explained, "before we take hold of the material we wish to measure and to understand. A set of such analytic tools, if framed to deal with phenomena which form a distinct process, we call a model or schema of this process."[5]

The Econometric Society almost immediately encountered problems, both theoretical and methodological. The problems stemmed in part from limitations inherent in each of the three practices the society wanted to unite. Statistics were necessary if the econometrician wanted to incorporate data, but statistics, as we began to see in chapter 3, raised theoretical and methodological questions practitioners had yet to resolve; foremost among them were the related issues of sampling (estimation) and inference. The form of mathematics used by most economists in the early 1930s brought a promising degree of precision to the analysis of economic relations but was to prove insufficient to handle the large number of variables intrinsic to econometric analysis. One solution was to limit the number of equations in a given model. As we will see below, this was the path taken by John R. Hicks when he condensed Keynes's *General Theory* into the IS-LM model. Another solution was to use a more sophisticated technique—the simultaneous equation method—to manage more variables. This was the approach of the Cowles Commission, the research branch of the Econometric Society. As we will see, however, the simultaneous equation method had its own limitations, not least of which was the time required to solve the simultaneous equations before technical improvements were made to computing. Finally, economic theory was still a matter of intense dispute in the period, as some practitioners, such as Keynes, continued to use the Marshallian partial equilibrium paradigm and to insist on the priority of theory, while others, such as John Hicks and the economists at the London School of Economics, endorsed Walrasian general equilibrium theory. These problems initially came to the surface in a dispute between Jan Tinbergen, one of the most dedicated of the practical econometricians, and Keynes, who was generally considered the leading economic theorist in the Western world. We return to the debate between Keynes and Tinbergen in section 5, below. The problems reappeared, in a different form, in the debates about probability that occupied members of the Cowles Commission and the Econometric Society in the early 1940s, to which we return in chapter 8. Despite the problems that made econometrics challenging, the modeling approach to economic analysis continued to gain currency in the profession, for it proved remarkably adaptable to almost every theoretical framework and to projects as disparate as creating national aggregates, improving monetary theory, and developing a way to understand the relations between the real and financial sides of the economy.

Before we leave the econometric project, it is worth summarizing its methods and the contributions econometrics made to the discipline of economics. The simultaneous equation method, which was further elaborated at the Cowles Commission in the 1940s under the leadership of Jacob Marschak, is centered on the structural modeling process. It links economic theory stated in a measurable, testable form to statistically aggregated data in a multi-step process intended to bridge the gap between data and theories about how economic relationships work. This approach thus attempts to overcome the limitations of both descriptive statistics and the use of small samples to estimate time series. The process involves three principles: it uses theory to identify relevant variables and relies on the results of statistical estimation to identify additional variables; it uses mainly linear, differential and mixed difference-differential equations to describe the relationships among variables; and it creates a system of interdependent relationships in the model. These principles yield the general form that characterizes today's macroeconometric models: they are "logical systems, in which the behavior of the whole is not always predictable from the nature of the parts which compose the system."[6]

As—or perhaps more—important as this formal procedure were the implications of two decades of development in statistical inference methods. This development began in the 1920s with the integration of probability theory and statistical inference, and its origins can be linked to the work of R. A. Fisher, which we described in chapter 5. In 1932, Jerzy Neyman and Egon Pearson introduced a new paradigm for testing statistical hypotheses, which Abraham Wald developed into a general decision theory from a frequentist point of view, and, in the 1950s Yale University's Leonard Jimmy Savage added to these methods a Bayesian approach to inference.

Meanwhile, in "The Probability Approach in Econometrics" (1944), to which we return in chapter 8, Cowles researcher Trygve Haavelmo challenged the profession to forge a new practice by integrating the inference procedures developed in probability theory, the simultaneous equation method, and general equilibrium theory.[7] Even though the links among these methods were never completed, Haavelmo's challenge signaled that the econometrics project had begun to reshape economics into a discipline whose practitioners could reconceptualize the "error" paradigm of the traditional curve-fitting technique as a probability concept that lives in a stochastic universe and that accommodates not simply errors in measurement, but uncertainty understood as randomness.[8]

7.2. JOHN MAYNARD KEYNES, JOHN R. HICKS, AND MATHEMATICAL ECONOMICS

There is nothing in the nature of modeling that requires the use of mathematics, and, as we saw in Irving Fisher's hydraulic model, models can assume many forms. By the same token, in the 1930s many economists remained skeptical about the value of mathematics, whether they explicitly thought of their work as modeling or not. John Maynard Keynes, for example, whose theoretical work inspired one of the most influential early models, did not think economists needed mathematics to work out their ideas. "Too large a proportion of recent 'mathematical' economics are merely concoctions," Keynes wrote, "as imprecise as the initial assumptions they rest on, which allow the author to lose sight of the complexities and interdependencies of the real world in a maze of pretentious and unhelpful symbols."[9] Despite his reluctance to endorse mathematics, however, and even though he did not develop a sustained account of modeling, Keynes's work is so intimately tied to both methodological innovations that we need briefly to consider the relationship between Keynes and the mathematical form that modeling began to take in the late 1930s.[10] We reserve our most sustained treatment of Keynes's theories for chapter 8.

Mathematical economics is not a field within economics but an approach to economic problems, one that relies on both mathematical equations and the use of mathematical theorems in the reasoning process.[11] As we have already begun to see, the national aggregates created in the 1930s were essentially products of statistical analysis, but mathematical methods such as Leontief's matrix and vector analysis soon made more flexible versions of these aggregates available. As Irving Fisher explained, as soon as economists realized that "the economic world is a world of n dimensions," not the two-dimensional world captured by the supply/demand graph, they could see the value of applying mathematics to economic data.[12] Some economists went further, arguing that economic theory would also benefit from the rigor, clarity, and simplification mathematics brought to the discipline.

One economist who made this argument was John R. Hicks, who taught economics at Cambridge University, where the most influential member of his department was John Maynard Keynes. At the time Keynes published the *General Theory of Employment, Interest, and Money,* Hicks was considered one of the "anti-Keynesians," even though, as we will see in chapter 8, American economists were soon to place Keynes's theories on the foundation Hicks created to forge what has been called the "neoclassical synthesis." Substantial theoretical and methodological differences separate the work of Hicks and Keynes: whereas Hicks endorsed Walrasian general equilibrium theory and wanted to highlight the individual, microfoundational, maximizing behavior of economic agents, Keynes used Marshallian partial equilibrium theory to model the macroeconomic structure generated by abstract interrelating forces such as "propensities" and "preferences," and he believed that "animal spirits," rather than purely rational behavior, motivated individuals.[13] Nevertheless, Hicks was sympathetic to some of Keynes's key departures from classical economic ideas: Hicks agreed that in a period of depression, an economy might reach equilibrium at less than full employment; and that, at critical points in the economic cycle, government fiscal or monetary intervention could stimulate the growth of national income and increase employment without triggering an inflationary response.

As its title suggests, Keynes's *General Theory* aspired to create a "general theory" that would link some parts of the real economy (employment) to features of the financial side of the economy (interest and money). In the context of the argument we are developing here, Keynes's insistence on linking the real and financial sides could have been a watershed moment in the history of economic analysis. As it happens, however, this project did not attract sustained attention, and many of Keynes's contemporaries did not even consider it central to Keynes's project. Joan Robinson, for example, who participated in the Cambridge Circus convened to discuss Keynes's ideas, emphasized Keynes's treatment of the financial side: Keynes's argument demonstrated "that the rate of saving is governed by the rate of investment, that the level of prices is governed by the level of money wages, and that the level of interest rates is governed by the supply and demand of money." By contrast, the Nobel laureate Lawrence Klein highlighted Keynes's contribution to real-side issues: the *General Theory* is "most important as a theory of the determination of the level of aggregate employment and output." And Don Patinkin, who elaborated the microfoundations of Keynes's thesis, also focused on real-side issues: he judged "the essential novelty" of the *General Theory* to be "the argument that an excess aggregate supply exerts a direct depressing effect on the level of output, and that the decline in output itself ultimately eliminates the excess supply and thus brings the economy to a position of unemployment equilibrium."[14] While some economists did see the connection Keynes made between real and financial issues—the American Paul A. Samuelson was among them—many simply emphasized the part of Keynes's theory that intersected with their own research interests.

In many ways, this makes sense, for, as David C. Colander and Harry H. Landreth point out, Keynes failed to develop the "complex core" of his theory. "The Keynesian theoretical revolution was the beginning of a revolution," they argue, "but one which skirted the main issues at debate: the multiplicity of aggregate equilibria and whether dynamic forces were strong enough to return the economy to a unique desirable equilibrium. Instead of focusing on these abstract issues, the Keynesian revolution focused on a different branch of theory—what might be called theoretical policy."[15] Then, too, there was the matter of Keynes's literary style. Paradoxically, the ambiguities generated by Keynes's distinctive style, which is marked by allusions, metaphors, and sharp turns of phrase, contributed not only to his contemporaries' confusion but also to the overall success of the *General Theory*.[16] For, not only did Keynes's vagueness on key issues encourage readers to elaborate a range of theoretical positions, but his stylistic verve virtually begged other economists to recast Keynes's work in mathematical terms that could provide the precision the master withheld.

This is where Hicks stepped in. Hicks saw in Keynes's work not only a theory that linked real and financial parts of the economy but also a bridge between the Walrasian theory of value and monetary theory, which had previously remained two separate wings of economic analysis. The Walrasian theory of value was a theory of marginal utility, which used calculus to quantify demand by means of prices set at the margin; in marginal utility theory, equilibrium is reached when markets for real goods clear at the intersection of supply and demand, and there is no room for finance. Monetary theory, by contrast, did not use marginalist assumptions or calculus but typically relied on the equation of exchange (see chapter 2, section 6). In 1935, when he read a draft of Keynes's work, Hicks began to see that these traditional ways of conceptualizing the theory of value and monetary theory had been superseded by recent work. Economists such as Vilfredo Pareto, for example, had demonstrated that "marginalist utility analysis is nothing else than a general theory of choice, which is applicable whenever the choice is between alternatives that are capable of quantitative expression." Reading Keynes, Hicks realized that the *General Theory* also introduced a theory of choice, this time investment choice. Seeing the similarity between marginalist theory and Keynes's treatment of investment decisions, Hicks saw a way to connect the theory of value with monetary theory. "When Mr. Keynes begins to talk about the price-level of investment goods; when he shows that this price-level depends upon the relative preference of the investor—to hold bank-deposits or to hold securities . . . we have a choice at the margin!"[17] Not only did Hicks see a way to place monetary theory and marginalist theory on the microfoundations of measurable choice; he also created a place within marginal utility theory for a certain understanding of finance—one that viewed finance as a set of interchangeable (but not identical) financial assets, among which the investor repeatedly chooses.

In Hicks's 1935 engagement with Keynes, he emphasized two choices. The first is the point in time at which the individual decides to hold money or purchase a financial asset, and the second involves the kinds of decisions the investor makes. The time-stamped nature of financial decisions helped Hicks see that "the connection between income and the demand for money must always be indirect," and it culminated in theories about intertemporal substitution, choices that investors make in the course of an investment life (4). The second choice involved whether to hold money, which yields no interest, or some material good or financial asset ("capital goods"), which do. "For capital goods will ordinarily yield a positive rate of return, which money does not. What has to be explained is the decision to hold assets in the form of barren money, rather than of interest- or profit-yielding securities" (5). In other words, what Hicks wanted to explain was what Keynes referred to as the "liquidity preference"—the preference some individuals express for hoarding over spending or investing.

Hicks identified several factors that might lead a rational actor to hoard. Among them was the "risk-factor," which could be figured probabilistically, in a way that resembles Frank H. Knight's treatment of risk. "Where risk is present," Hicks explained, "the *particular* expectation of a riskless situation is replaced by a band of possibilities, each of which is considered more or less probable. It is convenient to represent these probabilities to oneself, in statistical fashion, by a mean value, and some appropriate measure of dispersion" (8). Hicks did not consistently emphasize Knight's distinction between statistically calculable risk and uncertainty, however; instead, like many economists, Hicks used the two terms interchangeably, thus effectively reducing uncertainty, which, for Knight, involved unknowns that could not be calculated, to statistically calculable risk. "With uncertainty introduced in the way we have described, the investment now offers a chance of larger gain, but it is offset by an equal chance of equivalent loss" (8). Hicks did explore some of the complexities of risk, however. Like Irving Fisher's discussion of investment banks, Hicks discussed diversification ("When the number of separate investments is very large, the total risk may sometimes be reduced very low indeed" [9]), and he realized that an investor's choices were based on a combination of "objective facts" with a "subjective preference for much or little risk-bearing" (10).

Hicks's 1935 engagement with Keynes also addressed monetary theory. Instead of applying Fisher's equation of exchange, which began with money and essentially disregarded financial intermediation, Hicks invoked the banking-theory or credit view, which began with banking and highlighted the role banks play in creating monetary—or financial—substitutes. "We ought to regard every individual in the community as being, on a small scale, a bank. Monetary theory becomes a sort of generalisation of banking theory" (12). Unlike Walrasian general equilibrium theory, which used an income statement approach to analyze the individual's decisions on the income and expenditure side and the production side of his personal accounts, Hicks explained, this banking-theory approach would focus on the individual's balance sheet. "We shall have to draw up a sort of generalised balance sheet, suitable for all individuals and institutions" (12). As with general equilibrium theory, this revised banking-theory approach to monetary theory would focus on equilibrium—not Walras's price-centered, market-clearing version of equilibrium, however, but the accounting balance between offsetting liabilities and assets, with both sides of the balance sheet constrained by objective investment opportunities and "subjective factors like anticipations" (13). Because this monetary theory had to factor in anticipation, Hicks's version of Fisher's expectations, Hicks admitted that "this purely theoretical study of money can never hope to reach results so tangible and precise as those which value theory in its more limited field can hope to reach" (13).

Hicks valued the "tangible and precise" results that mathematical equations gave economic analysis, and he remained frustrated with Keynes's resistance to mathematical language. We can see the source of Hicks's frustration in Keynes's discussion of the same issue Hicks tackled in 1935. When he examined "the liquidity preference" in chapter 15 of the *General Theory*, Keynes combined a set of generalized abstractions (the "income-motive," the "business-motive," the "precautionary-motive," and the "speculative-motive") with a series of particularized descriptions that qualify the functional relationships that link these abstractions. For example, in his discussion of the relationship between risk and the interest rate, Keynes introduces "moral risk" as a particular kind of risk, and this qualified kind of risk considerably complicates the situation. "Thus the rate of interest which the typical borrower has to pay may decline more slowly than the pure rate of interest, and may be incapable of being brought, by the methods of the existing banking and financial organisation, below a certain minimum figure. This is particularly important if the estimation of moral risk is appreciable. For where the risk is due to doubt in the mind of the lender concerning the honesty of the borrower, there is nothing in the mind of a borrower who does not intend to be dishonest to offset the resultant higher charge."[18]

Keynes's primary aim was to determine how and when intervention by monetary authorities could enhance the economic and financial conditions that determined a nation's level of employment. He was interested in the functional relationship among variables rather than in pursuing a set of universal laws, yet his method was that of a logician rather than a statistician or mathematician, and the combination of abstraction and complicating qualifications in his work confused some readers. Keynes's theories did both draw on and contribute to the national income data we examined in chapter 6, but beyond providing the framework for organizing this data and implementing policies, Keynes's *General Theory* bore only an indirect relation to the national accounts themselves.[19] To render Keynes's *General Theory* really useful, economists wanted to eliminate its ambiguities and give the functional relationships he described a more precise formulation. Once more, John Hicks played a leading role. In 1936, only months after the *General Theory* was published, Hicks offered a mathematical model of the links Keynes drew between the real and financial sides of the economy.

7.3. THE IS-LM MODEL

The first mathematical model of Keynes's *General Theory* was created by Brian Reddaway; this appeared in a review of Keynes's book published in the *Economic Record* in June 1936.[20] Soon other economists weighed in: the first panel of the 1936 meeting of the Econometric Society, which was held in Oxford in September, was devoted to the *General Theory*, and, at the session, Hicks, James Meade, and Roy Harrod all presented mathematical models of Keynes's ideas. The most influential of these—Hicks's IS-LL model (later renamed IS-LM)—was published the next year in *Econometrica*. In the version made famous by Paul Samuelson and Alvin Hansen, this model became both the standard textbook presentation of Keynesian macroeconomics and the model used by policy makers to draft new legislation and justify policies already in place.[21]

Even though Hicks later dismissed the IS-LM model as a "classroom gadget," the graph and the equations that inform it remain both influential and exemplary: they not only contributed to the canonization of a certain understanding of Keynesian theory, which highlights the relationship between the money market and the market for capital goods, but also illustrate the method by which mathematical economists translated literary economics into mathematical models in the period. In this method, the solution of a system of algebraic equations was given economic content, which represented an economy in a state of equilibrium. Hicks's macroeconomic mathematical model was produced at the same time that John Burr Williams was working on his own mathematical model of microeconomic content, which was published in *The Theory of Investment Value* in 1938. As we showed in chapter 4, Williams applied the logistic curve to basic research about corporations to calculate the intrinsic value of a stock. In the article based on his conference paper, "Mr. Keynes and the 'Classics,'" Hicks applied the mathematics of Walrasian equilibrium conditions for the supply and demand of markets to the expenditure perspective on national income to model the relationship between consumption (the real), savings (financial), and investment (financial). In both cases, mathematical modeling proved so persuasive that, even though both models were subsequently criticized for their equilibrium assumptions, each seemed to capture what became a piece of conventional wisdom about the economic world. After Williams's work, investors simply assumed that stocks have intrinsic, or "true," values; after the Keynes-Hicks model, many people came to believe that governments must intervene in economic affairs to stabilize an unruly business cycle. Both these mathematical models—the first based on the corporate accounting framework and the second on the national income accounting framework—are modern constructions that anchor contemporary understandings of how capitalist economies work.

In the *General Theory*, Keynes argued that the abstract drivers of national income—the propensity to consume or save and the inducement to invest— are factors of the marginal efficiency of capital, the liquidity preference, and the consumption function (the ratio of consumption to savings). When Hicks translated these ideas into mathematical language, he altered Keynes's argument in three ways. First, he converted Keynes's accounting framework into a simultaneous equation system. Second, he recast some of the economic relationships Keynes described by adding the effects of changes in the interest rate and income; this allowed him to solve for the equilibrium between the money and capital goods markets simultaneously with the level of national income and interest rates. And third, Hicks reduced the three accounting identities that organized the national income framework to a system of two equations, each representing a market: the market for capital goods (IS) and the money market (LM). This reduction required him to eliminate a common variable (consumption) from the equations. In his conversion of an accounting system into a simultaneous equation system, Hicks presented the accounting identity—investment = savings—as being in equilibrium when (and only when) planned investment and savings are equal (investment minus savings = o).[22]

In the graph by which he illustrated his mathematical model, Hicks depicted the level of national income on the horizontal axis and the interest rate on the vertical axis. The intersections of the curves that represent the capital goods and the money markets depend on the shapes of these curves, which derive from the series of equilibrium points in the real (nonfinancial) side of the economy, when the amount of money individuals elect to save out of the nation's total income equals investment (in the financial side). The money market curve (LM) slopes upward, and the curve that captures the capital goods market (IS) slopes downward. The placement of the two curves shows "the relation between Income and interest which must be maintained in order to make saving equal to investment." The "income and the rate of interest are now determined together at P, the point of intersection of the curves LL [LM] and IS. They are determined together, just as price and output are determined together in the modern theory of demand and supply."[23] By looking at the behavior of the potential placements of the curves and their shapes and slopes, the analyst could see that in the special case of depression economics a change in monetary policy—an increase in the stock of money—would shift both curves to a new point of intersection (the new equilibrium point P) and increase the level of income and employment *without* increasing interest rates, as classical economic theory predicted it would do. At full employment, by contrast, the dynamic predicted by classical theory would obtain.[24]

At the end of his article, Hicks explained how his "little apparatus" improved Keynes's literary exposition, and he mentioned several issues Keynes had failed to address. Keynes did not treat the controversial matter of depreciation, Hicks pointed out; he did not deal with the timing of the economic process, and thus his theory was static, not the kind of dynamic theory interwar economists hoped to generate.[25] Other economists would add to Hicks's list additional omissions in Keynes's *General Theory.*[26] Most important is the point Don Patinkin made a decade later when he began to extend Keynes's work. In order to reconcile Keynes's Marshallian partial equilibrium approach with the Walrasian general equilibrium theory that he, like Hicks, preferred, Patinkin added to the aggregate capital goods and money markets both a micro perspective, which focused on individual decision making, and an additional market: the "bond market." Only by adding this market, Patinkin argued, and only by understanding that all these markets interact with each other, could one understand how prices are set and expectations established, and how uncertainty becomes a calculable factor in the economist's theoretical system. To add the bond market—which was an important component of the financial side of the economy—it was essential to have the *fund* perspective in addition to the flow perspective. And to make this fund/flow perspective operational—useful for work in the actual world—it was essential to have data that showed balance sheets as well as movements of income. It was the fund perspective and the balance sheet values that the NIPA did not provide. For this reason, it was not until the Federal Reserve's flow of funds accounts made balance sheet data available that the omission Patinkin identified in Keynes's *General Theory* could be supplied.[27]

7.4. MODELING THE FINANCIAL VIEW: MARSCHAK'S "THEORY OF ASSETS"

Several of the economists encountered in this and previous chapters were born outside the United States. In addition to Simon Kuznets, Wassily Leontief, Ragnar Frisch, Jan Tinbergen, and Britons like Keynes and Hicks, Joseph A. Schumpeter was European, as were Gerhard Tintner and Adolph Lowe. As many scholars have pointed out, the most vibrant centers of economic research in the early twentieth century were arguably Russia, Austria, and Germany; until the interwar period, the United States was something of a disciplinary backwater—albeit one with great resources—intellectual, institutional, and financial—ready to support promising research.

Of the economists we have examined in detail, only Gerhard Colm immigrated directly to the United States under the pressure of Nazi attacks, which escalated in the early 1930s.[28] Among the other European economists forced to leave Europe by Hitler's regime, another—Jacob Marschak—deserves particular attention because he made discipline-changing contributions to modeling and mathematical economics, and he also helped realize the econometric dream of uniting statistics, theory, and mathematics. Marschak was born in Ukraine in 1898; at the age of nineteen, he served as secretary of labor in the short-lived revolutionary Terek government in the Northern Caucasus; and in 1915–16, he studied with Eugen Slutsky at Kiev, then, in Berlin in 1919, with Ladislaus von Bortkiewicz, the mathematical economist and statistician. Marschak completed a PhD at Heidelberg in 1922, and, from 1928 through 1930, he worked at the Kiel Institute, where Adolph Lowe, Wassily Leontief, and Emil Lederer were also researchers. Marschak was appointed to a position at the University of Heidelberg in 1930, where he taught a popular seminar on Keynes's *Treatise on Money*. When the Nazis dismissed Jewish economists from the universities in April 1933, Marschak had already left Germany—moving through Paris, Vienna, Spain, and the Netherlands to Britain, where he arrived in Oxford in the fall of that year.

At Oxford, Marschak was first appointed to teach economics at All Souls, then he became a reader in statistics; in 1935, he became the founding director of the Oxford Institute of Statistics. It was this organization that sponsored the September 1936 meeting of the Econometric Society where Hicks delivered his paper on Keynes. Marschak was also present at that meeting, and, as we are about to see, he was already working on a model of Keynes's ideas that would complement Hicks's work. For the three years he directed the Oxford Institute, Marschak cultivated economists engaged in empirical research, especially those who, like himself, were émigrés passing through England or seeking a new home. Jan Tinbergen and Ragnar Frisch, who were key players in the development of econometrics, both admired Marschak, and Roy Harrod explained to Keynes in 1938 that "we have a sort of minor Tinbergen here in the form of Marschak."[29] In December of that year, Marschak went to the United States on a one-year fellowship provided by the Rockefeller Foundation, which also helped support the Oxford Institute. In September 1939, Marschak joined the economics department at the New School in New York City. At the New School, Marschak took the position vacated by Gerard Colm, whose travels from Kiel to New York to Washington we have already traced.

To appreciate Marschak's impact on interwar modeling, we need to place his work at the Oxford Institute in the context of the two other British centers of economic research: Cambridge University and the London School of Economics. The Oxford Institute was founded in the context of a fierce debate in England about the best way to study the economy and what the discipline's public role should be. While the London School of Economics (LSE) faculty—even within the economics department—did not endorse a unified position, by the 1930s, this university had become the British center of research on Walrasian general equilibrium theory. Thus John Hicks and other LSE students were encouraged to read not only Alfred Marshall, but also works by Walras, Pareto, Cassel, Barone, von Mises, and the Swedish economist Kurt Wicksell. The Cambridge economics curriculum, by contrast, was dominated by works that emphasized Marshallian partial equilibrium analysis.[30] The two approaches differed in methodology, theory, and attitudes toward the role economists should play in policy debates. In the early 1930s, especially in 1932–33, the rivalry between the two schools was so intense that Hicks found Cambridge, where he had accepted a position, "foreign," and Lionel Robbins described British economics as "red with fraternal strife."[31] In the winter of the year the Oxford Institute was founded, 1935–36, a joint economics seminar, with participants from LSE, Cambridge, and Oxford, helped dissipate the intensity of the rivalry, as most young economists turned their attention to Keynes's work.

Because the London School of Economics had been founded (in 1895) as an alternative to the educational bastions of Cambridge and Oxford, the university prided itself on being more open than the more traditional universities—to older students and to European émigrés, many of whom brought with them a strong commitment to both political engagement and central planning that played less well in the British context. The central figure in the LSE economics department was not an émigré, but he welcomed those who were: it was the Englishman Lionel Robbins, who ascended from the student body to a professorship at LSE in 1929, whose enthusiasm for Ludwig von Mises and the Austrian school opened the door to Friedrich Hayek and others. Robbins invited Hayek to lecture at LSE in 1931, and Hayek joined the faculty later that year. The so-called Robbins Circle in the early 1930s also included Nicholas Kaldor, John Hicks, Abba Lerner, G. L. S. Shackle, Arnold Plant, Ursula Webb, Ronald Coase, Roy Allen, Richard Sayers, and P. Rosenstein-Rodan. Oskar Lange, from Poland, was another influential émigré affiliated with LSE. Lange, who studied there in 1929, returned to England in 1934 and was supported—as so many émigrés were—by a grant from the Rockefeller Foundation.[32]

Even if the rivalry between the Cambridge and LSE brands of economics quieted in 1935, a new dispute erupted the next year, this time primarily among the LSE economists. The LSE general equilibrium theorists, who aspired to bring variables into economic models set aside by Marshallian partial equilibrium work, differed from each other on the question of the political implications of GET. This theory could support *either* the position held by socialists like Evan Durbin and Oskar Lange, which insisted that central planners correct disastrous swings of the business cycle, *or* the free market position held by Hayek, Robbins, and Plant. At stake were understandings of the nature of market adjustment, the consequences of decentralized and incomplete market information, and the motives that drive market participants. The controversy known as the socialist calculation debate was explicitly a debate about whether state governments should intervene in the market, whether, in the absence of market rationality, governments could rationally calculate, set prices, and redistribute resources so as to prevent monopolies and depressions, and whether governments could "encourage" economic agents to adopt identical decision-making processes (or express identical "preference functions") instead of acting in socially counterproductive, self-interested ways.

The controversy did not come to a head until after World War II, when Maurice Allais and other economists angrily rejected Frisch's program to devote econometrics to central planning, but the socialist calculation debate constituted an important part of the matrix in which Marschak made his contributions to microeconomic modeling, in papers that were to help launch modern theories of finance. Marschak's earliest economic publications focused on the socialist calculation controversy, but by the time he turned to the topic of finance in the mid-thirties, he had abandoned the political outspokenness of his youth. Nevertheless, Marschak's engagement with Hicks and Keynes—and with finance in particular—occurred in the context of this debate, and his commitment to general equilibrium theory (and thus to Hicks's project) should be understood as an understated preference for government planning over a strict laissez-faire view of economic decisions. Marschak's preference for planning may seem to resemble Keynes's support for government intervention in a depressed economy, but Marschak's quest to model the rational agent's investment decisions as a series of choices, as well as his reliance on the simultaneous equation method, places the models he created in the framework Hicks endorsed.

Marschak presented an early attempt to create a general equilibrium model that included financial variables expressed in mathematical terms at the fifth European meeting of the Econometric Society, held in Belgium in September 1935. Marschak's paper, entitled "On Investment," set out the methodological preconditions for a model that would measure the "net annual investments in several countries."[33] Clearly already engaged in a version of the capital formation project that occupied Simon Kuznets and Harold Moulton in the United States, Marschak was also in dialogue with Keynes's work on aggregate investment and Hicks's effort to provide a fund perspective on aggregates by adding time stamps to the variables. As he described the genesis of the project, Marschak was working on the problem of capital formation when he realized that economists had to agree on a set of definitions before work could continue. In his "tentative" definitions, Marschak divided assets into two categories: real assets, or "complexes of goods," and financial assets, or "claims." He also clarified the definition of *value* for all assets, both real and financial, as the discount of the asset's future yield on a present-value basis. This framework provided a secure, mathematically derived definition of *investment* over a given time period as the "increment of the value of asset C from point of time n to point of time n + 1."[34] With the methodological clarity provided by a consistent use of present value, Marschak further stabilized the definitions of the real-side variable—"consumption"—and the financial side variable—"investment": "net receipts (or income) of an individual consists of his consumption and investment. The latter may, of course, be negative [and] it should include such assets as good will."[35]

Marschak's reworking of general equilibrium theory has four implications for what would soon become the theoretical infrastructure of modern finance. First, the schema presented the financial side of the economy (claims) as autonomous and independent of the real side (the consumption of commodities or investment goods). Second, Marschak's definition of asset value identified a common measurement standard—present value—for valuation on both sides. Third, the schema defined and justified a new, more inclusive understanding of finance, which placed money on a continuum with shares, bonds, and other financial claims; this schema also accommodated both negative and positive claims and expressly included accounting valuations such as good will. And fourth, Marschak placed the microfoundations of asset valuation, real or financial, in a probabilistic, mean-variance framework based on the investor's expectations, which informed the decisions he made. These insights drew upon and extended points Hicks had made in his 1935 paper, most significantly, the idea that an investor formed expectations about the future yield of an asset not simply as a single payout but as a series of returns, which could be modeled as a frequency distribution of probable returns.[36]

Marschak worked out the implications of the 1935 presentation in two papers written over the next two years and published in 1938. One was written with Helen Makower, a researcher at the Oxford Institute of Statistics, who went on to an illustrious career in economics at LSE.[37] While we do not know whether Marschak or Makower was primarily responsible for the ideas expressed in the papers, comparing the published articles to Makower's LSE doctoral thesis, which the co-authors cite in their first footnote, reveals a progressive degree of generalization and mathematical formalization, which corresponds to Marschak's intellectual preferences.[38] In contrast to Makower's thesis and the jointly authored article, moreover, the paper Marschak published in *Econometrica* translated their shared work into mathematical form— the simultaneous equation method, which was to drive the research program at the Cowles Commission until 1948. Both these facts suggest that, as the collaboration went on, Marschak's ideas prevailed.

These papers were foundational for the theory of assets, one of the cornerstones of modern finance. The ideas they developed were most explicitly spelled out in Makower's thesis, although she relegated the graphs and most of the mathematics to an appendix.[39] As she stated it, Makower's aim was to "extend value analysis . . . to the market for capital goods" within a general equilibrium framework derived from Pareto. To expand the general equilibrium framework, she used the actual prices of capital goods, drew on Irving Fisher's two-period time preference model, highlighted decisions made at the margin, and factored in risk, which she represented as frequency distributions. Her argument was that all these variables were mutually dependent. As a result, she concluded, the "value of assets is . . . determined by the interaction of tastes for quality, time and riskiness of income, with the opportunities to obtain incomes of varying quality, time-distribution and riskiness."[40]

Makower's thesis made two contributions to the theory of assets. First, she carried over and, in some cases, refined the definitions Marschak, elaborating Hicks, introduced in 1935: "assets" give a series of yields over time; "claims" means "all credit instruments, including money"; and "debts" represent negative assets. Second, her treatment of preferences, or "tastes," elaborated the treatment of expectations offered by Hicks and Marschak. Makower interpreted "tastes" as "referring not to definite quantities, but to bundles of more or less probable quantities." This interpretation allowed Makower to quantify preferences; it drew not only on Hicks's 1935 article but also on Lionel Robbins's 1932 *Essay on the Nature and Significance of Economic Science,* which recast economics as "the science of choices."[41] As her reference to "probable quantities" makes clear, this interpretation also led Makower to follow Hicks and Marschak into probability, the mean/variance framework, and frequency distributions.

By adding investment goods to consumption goods, and time preferences and the "taste for risk" to variables more typical of general equilibrium models, Makower hoped to expand the economist's depiction of the economy to include financial assets alongside other consumption goods. In her presentation, a mix of financial assets and consumption goods composes both the individual's initial endowment and the assortment through which he seeks to maximize his preferences; the individual's challenge is to move from the initial endowment to the combination of financial assets and consumption goods that will satisfy his sense of what will serve him best. To understand how the individual allocates resources among various kinds of assets, Makower presented "commodity tastes," "time tastes," and "risk tastes" as a matrix of factors; the individual estimates the value of each of the assets within his mix (and the relative desirability of each, as a ratio of the whole) by calculating the probable yields returned by the commodities and the financial assets over time and by forming expectations about the toll that risk will take—all within the context of his "system of tastes." Makower's work thus reoriented the macroeconomic models Keynes had used toward the individual investor. In so doing, Makower gave the individual's perspective on economic factors that Keynes presented as aggregates (e.g., the "liquidity preference"). In this account, and over time, each part of the investor's portfolio can be "transformed," either because the passage of time changes the value of particular assets or because the investor buys and sells assets with varying return and risk profiles. The goal of these allocation decisions is to maximize the investor's yield, and he or she decides what mix of assets to obtain according to expectations about the future (which are, in turn, shaped by probability distributions), the prevailing market conditions, and the investor's unique "system of tastes." Makower understood that every investor is unique, but, because, in the modern world, "*all* individuals are investors" (as Marschak asserted), she modeled the overall economy as a system in which countless people were simultaneously making similar decisions.[42] Such decisions, all made in the presence of unknowns, determined the prices of both consumption goods and investment goods. It is worth noting here that, even though Makower was taking account of unknown factors, she was silently subsuming Frank Knight's category of "uncertainty" into the statistically calculable category he called risk. The kinds of unknowns she included, in other words, did not defy statistical treatment but used statistical analysis to manage risk.

In "Money and the Theory of Assets," published in *Econometrica* in October 1938, Marschak translated Makower's largely literary account of individual tastes, preferences, decisions, and weighted calculations about future yields into a set of simultaneous equations that modeled the interrelation of these variables. Like Makower, Marschak was directly engaging Keynes's *General Theory*—or, more precisely, he was attempting to replace Keynes's partial equilibrium paradigm with Hicks's general equilibrium approach by adding the all-important variable of financial claims, including money. The challenge faced by anyone attempting to include money in a general equilibrium model, which is anchored in assumptions about the equilibrium between supply and demand, stems from the peculiarities of money. First, unlike commodities, money has no fixed supply: a central bank (like the US Federal Reserve) can increase the money supply by issuing bonds, and the fractional reserve system also allows banks to loan more money than they hold. Second, and again unlike commodities, money has no fixed volume of demand: because it is frictionless, it can have a great impact without being used up. The best way to incorporate financial claims and what Hicks called "barren money" into an equilibrium model was to use not only the flow perspective Keynes used, but also the fund perspective provided by balance sheets, as Hicks intuited. Like Hicks, Marschak realized that value theory and monetary theory could be aligned if one treated both as accounts of decisions. He also saw that doing so would allow the economist to model the complex interrelation between objective conditions (the range of assets available) and subjective factors like expectations and tolerance for risk.

> The unsatisfactory state of Monetary Theory as compared with general Economics is due to the fact that the principle of determinateness so well established by Walras and Pareto for the world of perishable consumption goods and labour services has never been applied with much consistency to durable goods and, still less, to claims (securities, loans, cash). To do this requires, first, an extension of the concept of human *tastes:* by taking into account not only men's aversion for waiting but also their desire for safety, and other traits of behavior not present in the world of perfect certainty as postulated in the classical static econom-

ics. Second, the *production conditions,* assumed here to be objectively given, become, more realistically, mere subjective expectations of the investors—and *all* individuals are investors (in any but a timeless economy) just as all market transactions are investments. The problem is: to explain the objective quantities of goods and claims held at any point of time, and the objective market prices at which they are exchanged, given the subjective tastes and expectations of the individuals at this point of time. (312)

By including financial claims and money, Marschak wanted to provide "a properly generalized Economic theory," by which he meant both a general (not partial) equilibrium perspective and a mathematical (not literary) representation of the interaction of economic variables. Clearing away conventional but distracting terminology (substituting "assets" for the unhelpful term "capital," and "economic determinateness" for the hard-to-define concept of "economic equilibrium"), Marschak managed the kind of ambiguity that emanates from sloppy terminology by applying the simultaneous equation method to Makower's theoretical formulations. This formalization through mathematics further marginalized Knight's version of uncertainty, of course, for mathematical equations cannot even allude to unimaginable states or relationships, even if they do accommodate negative values. The mathematical treatment of the problem enabled Marschak to demonstrate the interrelation of the variables and reserve a place for data that satisfied several relations simultaneously. The resulting series of equations provided a mathematical demonstration that "'in equilibrium,' the price ratio between two sets of assets is equal to their rate of transformation." This formulation established a relationship—the "joint demand and joint supply"—among all kinds of assets: commodity goods, investment goods, and money too.

In his analysis, Marschak did invoke uncertainty ("the actual uncertain world"), but he treated the Knightian version of unknowability as less important than its probabilistic counterpart—in part at least because the former was less amenable to mathematical treatment. Indeed, Marschak introduced the mean/variance framework explicitly in order to calculate the probable results of the investor's decisions.

Since, in the actual uncertain world, the future production situation (technique, weather, etc.) and future prices are not known, the transformation equation $T(a, b, \ldots ; x, y, \ldots) = 0$ is not strictly valid so long as it means that, in the mind of the producer, to each combination of assets there corresponds one and only one n-dimensional set of yield combinations. It is more correct to assume . . . that to each combination of assets there corresponds, in his mind, an n-dimensional joint-frequency distribution of the yields. Thus, instead of assuming an individual who thinks he knows the future events we assume an individual who thinks he knows the probabilities of future events. We may call this situation the situation of a game of chance, and consider it as a better although still incomplete approximation to reality, and to relevant monetary problems, than the usual assumption that people believe themselves to be prophets. (320)

In this passage, Marschak acknowledged that his probability-calculating investor was an assumption, but he was not bothered by the distance between the model investor and its real-life counterpart, for the former was necessary to the mathematical model Marschak was constructing. Without the assumption of an investor who calculates probabilities, the mathematical model would not work because some form of randomness beyond the statistically manageable set could enter the picture. Marschak introduced a second assumption—the analogy between the investment situation and a game of chance—to shore up the first assumption—that the investor calculates probabilities—and he admitted that both merely "approximate" reality. When he established two measurable parameters for each yield—the "mathematical expectation ('lucrativity')" and the coefficient of variation ('risk')"—Marschak downplayed any ambiguity that might follow his reliance on assumptions and analogies, for this embedded his analysis in mathematics, where probability reigns.

By the conclusion of "Money and the Theory of Assets," Marschak had recast Keynes's three macrovariables as variables quantified at the level of the individual investor: Keynes's aggregate "liquidity preference" became how much cash the investor was willing to hold; the "consumption function" became the ratio the individual sought to establish among the assets he holds (including goods and financial claims); and Keynes's "marginal efficiency of capital" became "lucrativity," the individual's mathematical expectation of future yields, understood to operate within conditions of uncertainty. There are signs that Knight's version of uncertainty haunted Marschak's model, however, for Marschak felt the need to remind readers that ordinary statistical distributions might not accommodate extrapolation from observed samples. But even as he raised this possibility, he found a way to minimize its impact by invoking an innovation recently introduced into statistical theory. In the third section of his paper, Marschak suggested using the likelihood principle introduced by Jerzy Neyman instead of the small-sample inference method associated with R. A. Fisher. While it generated distributions less familiar than the Gaussian probability distribution, Neyman's likelihood principle worked better for populations too large or indeterminate to subject to exact measurement than did the small-sample method used for inferring estimations from observable phenomena. By using Neyman's method, Marschak both integrated probability theory into his mathematical framework and helped economists expand the domain of calculable risk, while shrinking the domain of what they had to admit to be genuinely unknowable (Knight's uncertainty).

> In the preceding two sections, the individual was assumed to know the relevant probabilities: the parameters of the transformation function as defined were assumed to be known. But this knowledge of probabilities—a situation approached in the games of chance—is a limiting case only. In reality the man does not regard himself as enabled by his experience to assign definite probabilities to each yield combination. Let the form of the transformation function depend on a set of parameters S. For each set of values, say, S_1 assigned to theses parameters there can be stated a probability $P\ (E/S_1)$ that the actual observed facts E (e.g., the crops and outputs, prices, etc., of the past, or any other information available) would have happened if S_1 was true. We obtain thus a likelihood function $L(S)$ of the variable set S_1, viz., $L(S) = P(E/S)$. . . . Characteristic parameters can be used to measure this: e.g., the steepness of $L(S)$ near its maximum, or some measure analogous to measures of dispersion, or Dr. Neyman's "confidence limits," etc. (323–24)

Marschak's contributions to modern financial theory are considerable: a mean/variance framework for defining risk, the balance-sheet perspective for decision making, a presentation of debts as negative assets, the two-period model of consumption (taken from Irving Fisher), the time-dating perspective (borrowed from J. R. Hicks), and the conviction that every individual is an investor, ceaselessly making decisions by calculating the probabilities of future outcomes, with an eye toward maximizing future yields according to a unique "system of taste." Neither Marschak nor most of his colleagues paused over the relegation of Knightian uncertainty to the margins of economic analysis, for whatever doubts they might have had about whether the economic and financial domains resembled natural phenomena in their statistical regularity seem to have been managed by a new statistical tool, which pushed worrisome kinds of unknowns further away.

7.5. THE KEYNES-TINBERGEN DEBATE

The disagreement among interwar economists known as the Keynes-Tinbergen debate engaged methodological procedures imbued with profound theoretical implications. At the heart of this dispute was a disagreement about whether economy theory could or should be tested by statistical data—and at the core of this question was the issue of whether economic and financial processes are stationary (exhibit statistical regularities). At stake in the debate was not only the methodological project of the Econometric Society but also whether the models created by econometricians could be used to generate policy. To be useful to policy makers, models had to be both relatively simple and reasonably well-fitted to actual economic data. As Jan Tinbergen well knew, meeting these requirements was extremely difficult—a task made even harder by economists who insisted that theory take precedence over statistical evidence.[43]

Jan Tinbergen was a Dutch economist who began his career at the Central Bureau of Statistics in The Hague and who, along with Frisch, was awarded the first Nobel Prize in economics in 1969.[44] In 1936, Tinbergen published in Dutch a twenty-four-equation model of the economy of the Netherlands; and, in 1939, under the sponsorship of the League of Nations, he published a forty-eight-equation model of the US economy for the period 1919–1932.[45] As the title of Tinbergen's English-language study suggests, *Statistical Testing of Business-Cycle Theories* was conceptualized as an extension of the business-cycle research projects conducted at Harvard and the NBER, but the methodology Tinbergen used was an extension of the formal growth and cycle models championed in the 1930s by other members of the Econometric Society.[46] Such models, as Victor Zarnowitz has pointed out, were devoted to "the formulation and interpretation of explicit and complete mathematics of business cycles in highly aggregative form."[47]

One influence on Tinbergen's method was Frisch's "rocking horse" model, which Frisch introduced at the 1933 Leyden meeting of the Econometric Society, devoted to mathematical business-cycle analysis. In a session attended by John Hicks and Henry Shultz among others, Frisch and Michal Kalecki presented models fulfilling the requirements of what they called "dynamic economics." These models were "dynamic" because the time lags were fully specified in the equations; even though these models did not incorporate actual data, they allowed for data to be "time-stamped" in sequential time periods. The models were "determinate" because the causal factors in each equation were fully specified. And they were "complete" because the equation system contained as many equations as unknowns.[48]

In 1936, when Tinbergen published his model of the Dutch economy, he broke with both the descriptive protocols of the NBER business-cycle analyses and the purely mathematical formalism embodied in Frisch's models. Like the 1936 model, his 1939 model of the US economy consisted of a complete system of equations based on statistical evidence, rather than the verbal descriptions and pure mathematics favored by Mitchell and Frisch. Using multiple correlation to fit data to his equations, Tinbergen could test the theories other economists had devised against empirical data. In the first pages of the second volume of the 1939 study, Tinbergen provided a simple example of his method, using only three equations. The first estimated the dependence of the value of investment goods in one period on profits in the prior period, thereby introducing profits as a lagged variable that "explained" future capital formation. The second equation modeled the relationship of consumption outlays to several factors: total wages, the consumption/savings ratio, and the presence of speculative gains; the latter were again a function of prior profits. The third equation defined how profits were calculated. Taken together, the system of three equations was "dynamic" in Frisch's sense of the word.[49] Using the reduced-form method, Tinbergen then eliminated variables to produce a final equation, a difference equation for the time-path of profits, which incorporated the regression coefficients estimated for the structural equations. With this final difference equation, he could measure the time-path of profits, represent it in graphical form, and compare it to the historical time series of actual data. If the simulated path generated by the regression model closely tracked the path of the data, Tinbergen was willing to say that the statistical model "explained" the trend in question. For the purpose of policy analysis or planning, the econometrician could test different hypothetical regression coefficients to judge the sensitivity of the target variable—in the case of this model, profits—to alternative parameters for the wage/consumption, savings, or speculative gains variables.[50]

Tinbergen was fully aware of the challenges confronting the econometrician. Constructing this kind of model for an actual economy, he acknowledged, "is, in many respects, a matter of trial and error. Exactly what variables are to be included and what neglected is not known beforehand; it only becomes apparent as the work progresses."[51] Then, too, the results were bound to be provisional, for correlation, the workhorse of his method, could only show relationships, not causation. For this reason, Tinbergen routinely placed the words *explains* and *explanation* in scare quotes. John Maynard Keynes did not object to Tinbergen's conclusions, which, as we will see at the end of this chapter, generally supported the position Keynes endorsed in the *General Theory*. Instead, Keynes objected to the enterprise itself—to the econometrician's basic claim that statistical data could be used to test, and, by extension, evaluate theories generated through deduction and logic. Behind Keynes's skepticism about method was the deeper worry that economic and financial data might not provide an adequate test for theory because the processes that generated the data might not be stationary.

Keynes expressed his impatience with Tinbergen's work in rhetoric that often verges on bombast: "The worst of him is that he is much more interested in getting on with the job than in spending time in deciding whether the job is worth getting on with."[52] Beneath such rhetorical flourishes, however, lay genuine methodological differences, which highlight some of the limitations of the econometric project. Of the six objections specified by Keynes, three are particularly germane. The first alluded to Tinbergen's acknowledged trial-and-error method: unlike Tinbergen, who wanted to identify the relevant variables through sequences of models, Keynes insisted that the economist had to know in advance, through his *theoretical* analysis, the "significant causes" involved in the economic relationships under investigation. If he did not know all the significant variables before constructing the model, the method of multiple correlation, so central to Tinbergen's work, could not "discover the relative quantitative importance" of the identified factors because unidentified factors might be influencing the ones the economist had specified.[53] In the form of the "identification problem," this issue was to continue to haunt econometricians.

Keynes's second objection targeted Tinbergen's treatment of temporality. Keynes charged that Tinbergen had made up or arbitrarily chosen the time-lags and trends by which his model dealt with time. "To the best of my understanding, Prof. Tinbergen is not presented with his time-lags, as he is with his qualitative analysis, by his economist friends, but invents them for himself. That is to say, he fidgets about until he finds a time-lag which does not fit in too badly with the theory he is testing and with the general presuppositions of his method. . . . The introduction of a trend factor is even more tricky and less discussed. . . . He has persuaded himself, if I follow him correctly, that it does not really make any difference what trend line you take."[54] At stake here was whether economic processes, which Keynes understood to be not stationary but evolutionary, internally uneven, and complexly interwoven with each other—especially over the course of time—could be reduced to a simple model, as Tinbergen was trying to do; and further, whether time was homogeneous—so that the past provided a template for the future—or marked by unpredictable variations.[55] This is one of the central issues still addressed in modern financial econometrics: to what extent can past trends—say, of stock prices—be taken as predictors of future trends?

Keynes's concerns about Tinbergen's treatment of regularity and time lay at the heart of the ontological and epistemological divide that separated the two men. The question concerned "the environment" in which the economist's model placed the economic processes it examined. Designating this "environment"—deciding which factors were internal to it (endogenous) and which external (exogenous), and determining how, if at all, to incorporate randomness into the model—was, and still is, one of the central tasks of the modeler. According to Keynes, the fundamental task confronting the modeler in 1939 was to decide whether the environment was "uniform and homogeneous over a period of time" or, if it was not, to divide up the "period" into segments short enough to find a suitable degree of uniformity.

> Put broadly, the most important condition is that the environment in all relevant respects, other than the fluctuations in those factors of which we take particular account, should be uniform and homogeneous over a period of time. We cannot be sure that such conditions will persist in the future, even if we find them in the past. But if we find them in the past, we have at any rate some basis for an inductive argument. The first step, therefore, is to break up the period under examination into a series of sub-periods, with a view to discovering whether the results of applying our method to the various sub-periods taken separately are reasonably uniform. If they are, then we have some ground for projecting our results into the future.[56]

Keynes judged that Tinbergen's divisions, which simply distinguished between the postwar and prewar periods, were not based on a theoretically sound understanding of the problem of the environment but were simply "a result of the exigencies of the available statistics." Keynes recognized that the problem of the environment was central to the entire project of econometric modeling, for, if economic processes were not organized by stable and homogeneous "structures," then structural functions or equations could not be used to represent them. If change, uncertainty, disequilibrium, and complexity—rather than stability, certainty, equilibrium, and uniformity—characterized the relationships among economic factors, as Keynes believed, then mathematical formalism was simply inadequate, no matter how good the statistical data might be.[57]

While most econometricians closed ranks against Keynes's wholesale critique of their method, the way they did so was to prove critical for the emergence of modern financial theory and practice.[58] For, in turning away from Keynes's understanding of uncertainty (which resembled Knight's but was not identical to it) to a paradigm that quantified randomness and probability, the econometricians provided one element of the matrix from which modern financial theory was born. Of course, this turn away from Keynes's version of Knightian uncertainty, which hinted at unknowns beyond the realm of human knowledge, also helped expand the domain of risk, which could be modeled—and managed—through statistics and probability. Paradoxically, this turn *away* from the understanding of uncertainty common to Knight and Keynes was also a turn *toward* Keynes's *General Theory*, for the project Jacob Marschak launched when he became research director of the Cowles Commission in 1943 was an attempt to model Keynes's ideas. But, in yet another paradox, which emerges only when the histories of econometrics and finance are recounted together, the commission's turn away from one of Keynes's central ideas to his overall project was itself a turn for the organization, this time away from *finance*, which had been the primary interest of the commission's founder, to the kind of macroeconomic view that government policy teams demanded to plan resource allocation in the context of war and its aftermath. As we have seen, in the early work of the commission, Alfred Cowles and Harold Davis used R. A. Fisher's statistical method to investigate investment advisers' track records, in a clear precursor to efficient market theory, and they applied index theory to the construction of a total return series for US stocks, which established the empirical basis for the equity risk premium that drives modern financial valuation models. But this work was simply set aside when the Cowles Commission left Colorado Springs for the University of Chicago in 1938. Marschak, member of the Econometric Society and Cowles Commission and leader of the latter's new research program, briefly returned to the financial interests of Alfred Cowles in his 1938 articles, but even Marschak soon dropped this project and succumbed to the intoxicating allure of modeling the Keynesian system.

7.6. A MACROECONOMETRIC MODEL
OF THE US ECONOMY

Tinbergen's model of supply and demand in US money and capital markets, published in chapter 4 of his League of Nations report, represented a significant milestone in modern macroeconometrics; it was a synthesis of aggregation techniques, regression analysis, and mathematical analysis. As we have just seen, Tinbergen's goal was to test economists' theories about what caused the economic swings of the 1920s and 1930s by applying statistical tools to the available data. Tinbergen took his data from many of the organizations we have already encountered: the NBER; the Brookings Institution; and monetary economists working with Federal Reserve data, such as Roger Angell at Columbia University and Lauchlin Currie at Harvard.[59] The model examined several factors economists considered central to the economic dynamics of the period, including the demand for goods and services and the prices of goods and services. What Tinbergen added set his model apart from other attempts to "explain" the decades in question: "demand and supply in the money and capital markets," the subject of chapter 4. At the beginning of this chapter, Tinbergen acknowledged Makower and Marschak's article, as well as Keynes's *General Theory,* but he did not name two of the factors that clearly informed his treatment of these markets: the microfoundational, decision component Marschak added to Keynes's work and the expenditure approach to national accounting; the latter was instrumental in generating the high level of aggregation that allowed Tinbergen to reveal investment and savings as independent variables—that is, apart from real-side consumption and production activities. Breaking out the markets for money and capital, as Tinbergen did, produced a new statistical view of the relative autonomy and independence—not to mention the importance—of the financial side of the economy as a discrete sector.

Tinbergen's econometric model of the financial sector consisted of a system of forty-eight simultaneous equations, statistically estimated by correlation analysis on historical time series data. The model followed the schema outlined by Marschak: money, which Tinbergen defined as "time + demand deposits of all banks + currency held by the public,"[60] formed a continuum with short claims, bonds, and shares; and the model was sectored by institutional forms of asset ownership (banks, nonfinancial firms, and individuals) (73). "Speculators" act like sectors in Tinbergen's analysis, although, in his original description, he did not designate them a sector—or, to use his term, a *subject.* Each class of subjects makes different kinds of related financial decisions, but all these decisions are based on "maximizing" behavior.

> A parallel may be drawn with the separate maximisation that is often thought to exist for the individual's way of earning and spending income: *first* he trives [*sic*] to get the maximum money income, and *then* he seeks the maximum satisfaction from the given amount of money. Likewise, we may assume that firms decide *first* what is necessary for the course of production (the construction of buildings and machines, the holding of commodity stocks and the amount of debt and shares they are prepared to carry), and *afterwards* how much money they need to keep to these plans. Banks *first* decide how much money they will allow to be in existence, and *then* distribute this amount over short claims and bonds. Speculators *first* determine their holdings, and *then,* if necessary, borrow short credits. (74)

The autonomy and independence Tinbergen's model assumed in the structural equations underscored Marschak's theoretical claim that the mechanisms of the financial sector *cannot* be abstracted from the conditions that obtain in the real economy. This was true for a multitude of reasons: Speculative activity *itself* changes trends in consumption and production in the real side of the economy; above-trend profits provoke responses in multiple channels, by acting upon producer expectations, entrepreneurial spending, and expansion of the wage base; and even modest rates of inflation stimulate investment, consumption, and wage growth. Using correlation fitted to historical data, Tinbergen "explained" household hoarding, the issue of new shares by firms, banks' issuance of new credits, the issue of bonds by the government and firms, and the impact of speculative activity on consumption and savings. His method generated a graphical picture of "the speculative attitude" or "boom psychology" of the 1920s, as well as the hoarding that followed the market crash and ensuing bank failures (106). The conclusions to which the analysis pointed, Tinbergen acknowledged, were that none of the factors most economists emphasized—over-investment, changes in the cost of production, under-consumption, or agricultural factors—played as large a role in the business "cycle" of the period as did monetary factors: speculation played an outsized role in the lead-up to the crash and hoarding helped prolong the depression. The influence of the latter, "which acted through interest rates on share prices, and from them on consumption . . . and investment . . . seems to be the most important from the monetary sphere" (185).

As groundbreaking as Tinbergen's macroeconometric models were, they were not to be the last work in macroeconometrics or in mathematical models. As we see in future chapters, Tinbergen's nonstochastic, deterministic model would be replaced by stochastic modeling; his reliance on correlation analysis would be subjected to a battery of new statistical significance tests; the linearity assumption that was the foundation of both Wassily Leontief's input-output accounts and Tinbergen's models would be exploited by new computational operations; a mathematically deduced definition of risk and diversification would revolutionize portfolio theory; game theory would redefine the prevailing understanding of expectations; and computing and information science would revolutionize the treatment of information and radically transform financial institutions by rendering them interdependent.

CHAPTER 8

Postwar Economics in America, 1944–1970

In general terms, the contributions economists made to the Allied victory in World War II are well known: in addition to holding positions in the Treasury, Commerce, and Agriculture departments of the US government, economists helped develop military applications of resource allocation, solved search problems, developed computational programs to break codes, and addressed estimation problems. As members of the operations research community, economists helped Allied forces locate enemy submarines, weigh low-altitude, high-risk, high-gain bombing raids against their high-altitude, low-risk, low-gain alternatives, and direct resources such as steel to the products considered essential. If resource allocation is one of the fundamental issues addressed by economics as a discipline, then World War II provided economists an unprecedented opportunity to display the practical value of the theories they had painstakingly constructed.[1]

The war also profoundly altered the discipline of economics. As part of the reorganization of science culminating in the National Science Foundation in 1950, funding for economic research began to flow from government-sponsored organizations such as the Office of Naval Research (ONR) and the Air Force's Research and Development Center in Santa Monica (RAND), supplementing more traditional sources such as universities and wealthy patrons. Other changes involved shifts in attitude more difficult to document but no less consequential: as part of the respect accorded mathematics and science after the war, economists basked in the optimism associated with the discipline's more rigorous academic counterparts. The prestige enjoyed by economics—and by some individual economists as well—was one offshoot of the discipline's enhanced reputation, and, as economists as a group gradually embraced the mathematical techniques developed in operations research, linear programming, and game theory, their claim to exercise, rather than just emulate, mathematical rigor began to seem justified.[2]

The postwar discipline of economics also gained credibility because many of its most prominent members pursued research projects developed in relation to a core set of theories and methods, loosely linked to the term "American Keynesian." While some economists vehemently rejected the central tenets of Keynesian economics—Milton Friedman comes to mind—even they tended to formulate their arguments in relation to Keynesian terminology and policies rather than beginning from a new place.[3] Implementing the policies Keynes recommended in *How to Pay for the War* (1940) had helped the United States finance the war and kept inflation under control at war's end— and research projects developed along Keynesian lines made the economists who pursued them seem as farsighted as Keynes.[4] During the quarter century that followed World War II, Keynesian macroeconomic theory was provided with a more robust mathematics, statistical methods capable of incorporating probability and, linking Keynes's ideas to real data, sets of empirical data that brought previously invisible parts of the economic process into relief, and a microfoundation that helped economists ground Keynes's aggregates in the behaviors of individual agents. During the 1960s, American Keynesians joined powerful government agencies in Washington DC such as the Council of Economic Advisors and the Federal Reserve Board of Governors. From these positions, economists were able to implement policies based on the models they had developed in conferences, classrooms, and professional publications. In the 1960s, American fiscal and monetary policy was governed by the US version of Keynesian economics.

Developments within the discipline of economics occurred within the context of a world transformed by the Second World War and new international monetary arrangements. Some aspects of this transformation are critical to understanding postwar developments within US fiscal and monetary policy and the globalization of American finance after the 1960s. From the perspective of the international monetary and financial order, the most enduring agreements that concluded World War II were outlined at the Bretton Woods Conference, held in July 1944. At this conference, representatives of the forty-four Allied nations agreed to a series of measures intended to encourage open markets in real goods and services and capital flows and to manage the Western political-economic order. To promote the stability of exchange rates and regular flows of capital, participants created the International Monetary Fund

(IMF) and pegged exchange rates to the US dollar backed by gold reserves. To assist nations devastated by war, they instituted the International Bank for Reconstruction and Development (IBRD), which oversaw loans intended to rebuild infrastructure and foster economic development. While some of the measures ratified at Bretton Woods failed to take effect—the US Senate refused to accept the International Trade Organization, for example, and the International Clearing Union was also rejected by US representatives—many of these agreements provided a stabilizing context in which most nations, including the United States, could make the transition from wartime to peacetime economic activity.

A second legacy of World War II was less salutary, even for victor nations like the United States. While increased government spending during the war led to a short-run expansion in aggregate demand, as measured by GDP, at the end of the war, the reduction in military expenditure caused a brief economic contraction in the United States. In keeping with the policies Keynes outlined in *How to Pay for the War*, the US government had financed the war with a combination of higher taxes, the liquidity preserved by forced savings in the context of price and wage controls, rationing, reductions in nondefense spending, borrowing from the public (the Liberty and Victory Bonds we examined in chapter 4), and new money issued by the Federal Reserve. The government also instructed private factories to direct production to war materials. During the war, nearly half the nation's GDP was used by the federal government; in 1946, the debt held by the public reached 108.6% of GDP. The postwar contraction was also large, as the nation adjusted to a decrease in government spending from about 40% to about 15% of GDP. This contraction, though large initially, was mild in comparison with the 1919 downturn and ended in 1948.[5]

Even if the postwar economic contraction had no lasting impact on US growth in the 1950s, the transition from war to a peacetime economy did exacerbate anxieties about the twin specters of unemployment and inflation. While the worry that "ongoing inflation" would have an effect on employment only became a concern for US policy makers in the 1940s, and even though employment reached an all-time high during the war, questions about the link between changes in the price level and the level of employment haunted both legislators and economists for much of the next three decades. We have already seen that Milton Gilbert was charged with revising the national accounts to anticipate the inflationary effects of US participation in the war. After the war, policy makers made stabilizing the purchasing power of money a critical policy objective, this time by passing the Employment Act of 1946, which committed the executive branch of the government to ensure both maximal employment and price stability.[6] As we will see, the oscillation between the government's tendency to intervene by setting prices and imposing credit controls and its endorsement of policies that encouraged competitive free-market pricing provoked controversy, and for the next three decades economists debated the best way to understand—or restrict—the role government should play in a competitive market economy.

Additional measures designed to manage the nation's economy included the Fed Accord, an agreement reached between the Treasury and the Federal Reserve in 1951. From its creation in 1913, the main business of the Federal Reserve had been discounting commercial paper: in the context of the gold standard and governed by the real bills doctrine, the Fed financed loans that supported agricultural production and exports. By the mid-1920s, discounting had almost completely disappeared, and the Fed's primary tool for managing short-term interest rates and bank reserves had become open market operations. During the war, the Fed's primary duty was to finance the military and wartime production. To do so, it used historically low interest rates and credit regulations. At war's end, the Employment Act of 1946 increased the Fed's responsibility for economic stabilization, for the act charged the Fed with maintaining economic conditions consistent with full employment. Despite its responsibilities, the Fed was hampered by an ongoing struggle with the Treasury, which was responsible for debt management. Until 1951, debt management was treated as the greatest priority, and the Fed had to consult Treasury before changing interest rates. At the end of the war, Treasury wanted to keep interest rates low—initially because it wanted to float a Victory loan, and then to control the cost of servicing the debt. The conflict between Treasury and the Fed intensified between August and December 1950, and, once the Fed received congressional backing, was finally resolved by the agreement known as the accord. The accord allowed the Federal Reserve to let the rate on long-term government bonds exceed 2.5% and the rate on short-term bonds rise to the discount level. Adopting an "even keel" policy, the Fed agreed to maintain interest rates during periods of Treasury borrowing. This permitted increased growth in the money supply when budget deficits rose, as they did in the 1960s.[7] The Fed Accord effectively transferred the responsibility for monetary policy from executive and congressional oversight to an ambiguously autonomous Fed and set the stage for the growth of the budget of the Board of Governors of the Federal Reserve system. This, in turn, has made the Federal Reserve research staff a major contributor to economic research and data collection, comparable only to the research staff of the International Monetary Fund.

8.1. POSTWAR MATHEMATICAL
ECONOMICS AND ECONOMETRICS

8.1a. The Mathematical Foundations of American Keynesianism

In chapter 6, we described some of the basic principles of John Maynard Keynes's *General Theory*: working at the level of aggregates, Keynes set out a theory intended to address the shortcomings of capitalism that had been exposed by the Great Depression. Keynes wanted to restore stability, efficiency, and the capacity to grow to economies whose productivity remained low and unemployment rates high. In his analysis, the price mechanism, which economists had celebrated since Adam Smith's *Wealth of Nations*, had proved unable to coordinate the general level of output and employment. In periods of instability, he argued, governments should extend their traditional functions in order to regulate aggregate demand and ensure satisfactory aggregate output and employment. Keynes thought that governments should not infringe on individual liberties or initiatives, but he did not devote extensive attention to individuals' behavior—apart from acknowledging the irrational "animal spirits" that sometimes motivate individual actions.

In chapter 7, we examined an early mathematical model of Keynes's ideas, John R. Hicks's IS-LM model, and we showed how Jacob Marschak and Helen Makower drew on Hicks's work to make the Keynesian framework include individuals' self-maximizing decisions about the allocation of money and investments. It was the combination of Keynes's aggregate theories, the method of modeling (often using Hicksian utility calculus), and the microfoundation provided by the assumption of rational self-maximizing agents that constituted the heart of American Keynesianism. A more general reconciliation of the Keynesian macroeconomic framework, Hicks's microfoundations, and Walrasian general equilibrium theory was set out in the 1955 edition of Paul A. Samuelson's *Economics*. Samuelson called this the "neoclassical synthesis."[8] As Peter Howitt has described it, this "synthesis," turned on assuming a difference between short-term and long-term economic phenomena: "Since it was widely believed that wages were less than fully flexible in the short run, it seemed natural to see Keynesian theory as applying to short-run fluctuations and general equilibrium theory as applying to long-run questions in which adjustment problems could be safely ignored."[9]

Within twenty years of the close of World War II, according to Nobel laureate Franco Modigliani, the Hicksian IS-LM paradigm had become almost as familiar to economists as the neoclassical supply-demand paradigm was to an earlier generation.[10] Prominent economists such as R. G. Hawtrey, Jacob Viner, Frank H. Knight, Jacob Marschak, and Alvin Hansen were all engaging with the Keynes-Hicks paradigm in print and in their classrooms.[11] In turn, mathematically inclined doctoral students were encouraged to establish a secure microfoundation for Keynes's macroanalysis. Paul Samuelson and James Tobin were introduced to Keynes's macroanalysis in the Fiscal Policy Seminar, taught by Hansen and John H. Williams at Harvard, and, as a classroom exercise, Samuelson constructed the Hansen-Samuelson multiplier-accelerator model. Samuelson's dissertation was later published as *Foundations of Economic Analysis* (1947). Under the doctoral direction of Marschak at the New School, Franco Modigliani wrote a dissertation on Keynes's liquidity function, published as "Liquidity Preference and the Theory of Interest and Money" (1944). At the University of Chicago, Don Patinkin, a predoctoral fellow at the Cowles Commission for Economic Research and later a doctoral student at Chicago, drew a distinction others were also beginning to make, between microeconomics, which extended the Walrasian general equilibrium system by adding a utility theory of money, and macroeconomics, which modeled the markets for labor services, commodities, money, and bonds to show the effects of an increase in the amount of money or a shift in liquidity preference in a full employment economy and with involuntary unemployment. Patinkin was finally able to unite his work on microeconomics and macroeconomics in *Money, Interest, and Prices* (1956).

Of these works, Samuelson's dissertation was the most methodologically ambitious and influential, in part because it worked out the mathematical framework for American Keynesianism. *Foundations* opens with a demonstration of the unity of neoclassical theories about consumption, production, and exchange based on shared assumptions about maximizing (minimizing) behaviors, which can be expressed in equilibrium equations.[12] Samuelson was not content with earlier economists' equilibrium models, however, and added to their "preliminary spade work" a demonstration showing how diverse families of mathematical systems can be used to characterize diverse kinds of economic phenomena. Whereas the comparative static method proceeds by finding the solution to a system of simultaneous equations, dynamic methods exploit the determinative or stochastic behavior of diverse kinds of linear and dynamic systems over a period of time. With this larger construct, and following Ragnar Frisch's pioneering work on dynamic systems, Samuelson analyzed the "Keynesian System" as a simultaneous equation system containing three functions: a consumption function, the marginal efficiency of capital, and the schedule of liquidity preference (276). The resulting small mathematical model provided one key part of American Keynesianism. Samuelson's mathematical framework is still used to build new models and teach economics in undergraduate and graduate classrooms.

Patinkin's *Money, Interest, and Prices* contributed a second key element to American Keynesianism by integrating monetary theory and value theory.[13] Patinkin's goals were to rescue the quantity theory of money, which we encountered in chapter 2, and to reformulate unemployment as a disequilibrium phenomenon.[14] He was able to integrate monetary theory and value theory by invoking the real balance effect, a concept introduced by the English economist A. C. Pigou. This concept, which takes into account changes in the value of money, allowed Patinkin to extend J. R. Hicks's theory of the consumer's behavior toward commodities to his behavior toward money.

> As its name implies this new effect measures the influence on demand of a change in real balances, other things being held constant. For example, if the individual is confronted with a change in the price of a single commodity, the corresponding change in the amount he demands of the various commodities is the resultant of all three effects: for there is a change in relative prices, and hence a substitution effect; there is a change in real income, and hence an income effect; and finally there is a change in the price level and therefore in the real value of his initial money holdings, and hence a real balance effect.[15]

Patinkin's synthesis also allowed him to integrate analyses of markets that neoclassical and monetary theorists generally treated separately: "Since monetary changes are assumed to affect all markets of the economy, their effects can be fully appreciated only by a simultaneous study of all these markets. Indeed, it will be seen that in most cases where we reach a conclusion at variance with the accepted ones, it is a direct result of taking into account the dynamic interactions between price-level variations in the commodity market and interest-rate variations in the bond market. This interdependence of markets is a fundamental and recurring element of the argument."[16]

In addition to integrating analyses of the real and financial sides of the economy, Patinkin's work helped explain how nations could pull themselves out of economic depressions, like the devastating depression of the 1930s. Irving Fisher introduced this principle in *Booms and Depressions* (1932), and Pigou formulated it again in "The Classical Stationary State" (1943). According to this theory, as unemployment rises and the prices of commodities fall, the value of a bank account in real money exceeds its nominal value. In theory at least, this "wealth effect" allows consumers who have money to help lift the nation out of depression by spending—although, in the absence of government programs designed to manage short-term demand, individuals' spending may take an unacceptably long time to stabilize the economy.

8.1b. The Econometrics of the Probability Approach

If the neoclassical synthesis provided Keynesian theory a more robust mathematics, another set of research programs elaborated an econometric dimension for the Keynes-Hicks models. Many of these research programs were associated with the Cowles Commission, which we introduced in chapter 7.[17] While not every theory or technique developed by the Cowles researchers applied directly to the Keynesian strand of American economics, Cowles was one sponsor of this version of econometrics. With the help of government sponsors, moreover, such as the Office of Naval Research, RAND, the Atomic Energy Commission, and NASA, the Cowles Commission helped make it possible for economists to transfer the classified work developed during the war to the larger community of economists.[18] This transfer occurred partly, although not exclusively, at a series of conferences that brought together members of the operations research community with researchers in several disciplines. From these conferences and the publications that followed, the theories and techniques associated with the neoclassical synthesis were elaborated, consolidated, and disseminated to the profession at large.

As we saw in chapter 7, the Norwegian economist Ragnar Frisch introduced a program for econometrics in his 1930 Yale lectures. This program could not be implemented, however, until Trygve Haavelmo, another Norwegian who studied with Frisch, anchored Frisch's "model worlds" in a new theory of probability. At the end of January 1945, the Cowles Commission, which had relocated to the University of Chicago in 1939, convened a conference to explore Haavelmo's probability approach to econometrics, which addressed the estimation of the statistical coefficients used in Keynesian macroeconometric models. Haavelmo championed an understanding of probability based on the paradigm for statistical inference developed by the Polish statistician and mathematician Jerzy Neyman, a Jewish émigré who escaped National Socialism by moving to LSE, then to Berkeley in 1938, and Egon Pearson, the LSE statistician who coined the term *biometrics*, which inspired the term *econometrics*. In adopting the Pearson-Neyman program for hypothesis testing to link the variables used in the equations of mathematical economics to statistical data, Haavelmo was targeting the least-squares method, which

Keynesian economists routinely used to estimate constants and parameters in equations for concepts like "the propensity to consume." Haavelmo insisted that statistics had to include techniques designed to accommodate stochasticity if theorists were to link their models to the actual world.

> The notion that one can operate with some vague idea about "small errors" without introducing the concepts of stochastic variables and probability distributions is, I think, based upon an illusion. Some such [stochastic] elements . . . must, in fact, be present in any equation which shall be applicable to actual observations. . . . In other words, if we consider a set of related economic variables, it is, in general, not possible to express any one of the variables as an exact function of the other variables only. There will be an "unexplained rest" and, for statistical purposes, certain stochastical properties must be ascribed to this rest, a priori. . . . We need a stochastical formulation to make simplified relations elastic enough for applications.[19]

Haavelmo's argument, which was published in *Econometrica* in 1944, challenged traditional statistics, which was not grounded in mathematical probability theory.[20] The majority of statisticians resisted the ideas that every observation belonged to a distribution, could pertain to random or unknowable populations, and had to be treated accordingly. Haavelmo argued that both statistical data and economic theories had to be constructed probabilistically and that some bridge had to connect the two. While this bridge had yet to be discovered, Haavelmo regarded Jerzy Neyman's statistical theory as a promising start.

Neyman had shown that any set of empirical observations upon which statistical inference could be based had to be understood as a sample of a distribution taken from a population with unknown characteristics. The only way to model this population was by repeated sampling against a hypothesis about the type of distribution the sample might represent. This method alone could generate two of the statistical contours (or "moments") of the observed data: the mean and the variance. Haavelmo's adaptation of Neyman's ideas required every term in the economist's equations to incorporate a coefficient to indicate stochasticity. Doing so would transform the interpretations offered by Tinbergen, Persons, and other inferential statisticians from single-value observations to observations of ranges of values within intervals, in populations characterized by fuzzy boundaries. If statisticians continued to take only the parts of probability that suited them, Haavelmo concluded, their work would be worthless because their tools were flawed. "No tool developed in the theory of statistics has any meaning—except, perhaps, for descriptive purposes—without being referred to some stochastic scheme."[21]

The "Statistical Inference in Dynamic Economic Models" conference registered the jolt Haavelmo's probability work gave to economics, econometrics, and statistics. At the Cowles Commission itself, Jacob Marschak, who became research director in 1943, adopted the challenge of incorporating probability into the Keynesian framework as the institution's primary focus. Cowles remained focused on the econometrics of the probability approach for the next five years—even though Haavelmo's preference for the Neyman objective approach to statistics was soon to be replaced by the more subjective Bayesian understanding of probability.

8.1c. Mathematical Probability Theory

In August 1945, a second influential conference aspired to integrate probability, this time into mathematical statistics. The inaugural Berkeley Symposium on Mathematical Statistics and Probability was held at the University of California, Berkeley, at the Statistical Laboratory, which Jerzy Neyman had founded when he arrived at the university in 1938. In addition to Neyman, speakers included Hans Reichenbach, the eminent philosopher who had figured prominently in the Berlin Circle, then joined the faculty of UCLA after fleeing Nazi Germany, and Harold Hotelling, the most prominent American statistician, who had championed R. A. Fisher's work in the early 1930s. While these papers did not contribute directly to the development of American Keynesianism, they did introduce mathematical and statistical techniques adopted by representatives of this school. Most directly, the papers amplified the impact the probabilistic revolution was having on statistics: Reichenbach announced the program that had transformed R. A. Fisher's probability method into functional notation using set theory and topology and that introduced axiomization into probability theory; Hotelling outlined how the teaching of statistics would have to change to accommodate probability; and Neyman provided new tests to evaluate hypotheses in experiments involving random samples.

The tone of the conference was set by the stirring conclusion of Reichenbach's paper, "Philosophical Foundations of Probability." Rejecting the "quest for certainty" pursued by economists like Irving Fisher, who viewed economics as an exact science tailored to a deterministic world, Reichenbach fully embraced the implications of stochasticity, yet refused to despair.

The use of the rule of induction . . . can be regarded as the fulfillment of a necessary condition of success in a situation in which a sufficient condition is unknown to us. To speak in such a case of a justified use of a rule appears in agreement with linguistic usage concerning the word "justification." Thus we call Magellan's enterprise justified because, if he wanted to find a thoroughfare through the Americas, he had to sail along the coast until he found one—that there was a thoroughfare was by no means guaranteed. He could act only on the basis of necessary conditions of success; that they would turn out sufficient was unknown to him.[22]

Reichenbach argued that the best guide for research in a world riven by randomness, where necessity must suffice, is a "formal system of axioms," which relates primitive terms so that logically consistent statements can be derived deductively. The axioms he cited point to the axiomization of probability theory introduced by the Russian probabilist A. N. Kolmogorov. Such a system offered the additional advantage of being amenable to geometrical and other kinds of mathematical representation. But the mathematics Reichenbach used was not the old mathematics of calculus or geometry but the new mathematics of set theory and topology. In a probabilistic world, this new mathematics was necessary because topology's "spaces" accommodated probability's "ranges" and "distributions" better than did the "points" of Euclidian geometry. In set theory, mapping replaces graphing as the way of representing functional relationships, and stochasticity and frequency can be factored into every concept. Using set theory, Reichenbach was able to integrate probability distributions into other mathematical, statistical, and—by extension—economic statements. In so doing, he announced a synthesis of two traditions that had previously been separate—philosophical logic and mathematics. This provided a rigorous basis for probability theory, which Keynes had merely invoked.

Reichenbach used as an example of the new tools that accommodated stochasticity the Markoff chain, a mathematical sequence of sequences, or what Reichenbach called a *"sequence lattice."*[23] The critical property of such sequences is that their iterative parts are independent: as the sequence undergoes transitions from one state to another, the new state does not depend upon what preceded it. This innovation provided a new way of doing time series that integrated randomness into the relatively straightforward method used by Persons and Tinbergen. It also offered an explanation for the origination of randomness particularly applicable to finance: the Markoff chain is a random process, and, as its sequences unfold, it introduces randomness into subsequent iterations. Many real-world situations where past events only partially determine future states—like asset prices and market volatility—were subsequently modeled with Markoff chains.

The contributions by Hotelling and Neyman illuminated what statistics had to become in a world reconceptualized as stochastic. Hotelling highlighted the discipline's "failure to make proper use of the theory of probability." "Without probability theory, statistical methods are of minor value," Hotelling declared. "Although they may put data into forms from which intuitive inferences are easy, such inferences are very likely to be incorrect."[24] Neyman attempted to show what a statistical practice imbued with probability theory would look like. Like R. A. Fisher, Neyman used a frequentist approach to address one of the central questions of statistical research: how can one extract knowledge from observations? Whereas Fisher worked with observations of natural phenomena, however, where regularities and normal distributions can be assumed, Neyman grappled with phenomena that might not conform to these conditions. He insisted that the repeated samples with which the statistician worked contained randomness, and his estimates of the relative frequency of particular events all incorporated random experiments. His technical paper was a contribution to Neyman's long-standing interest in "inductive behavior," or error tests (rules for rejecting or provisionally accepting a hypothesis). In his collaboration with Egon Pearson, which began before Neyman moved to Berkeley, the authors explained why their emphasis on behavior was superior to Fisher's emphasis on "inductive inference" or "inductive reasoning." "Without hoping to know whether each separate hypothesis is true or false, we may search for rules to govern our behavior with regard to them, in following which we insure that, in the long run of experience, we shall not too often be wrong."[25] Because every hypothesis was subject to error and every sample was both the origin and the effect of randomness, only rules—the axioms of mathematics and error tests—could serve as reliable guides.

8.1d. Game Theory and Bayesian Probability

The meeting of the Econometric Society held in Madison, Wisconsin, in the fall of 1948 was a harbinger of disciplinary things to come. Co-sponsored by the American Mathematical Society, the Mathematical Association of America, and the Institute of Mathematical Statistics, the conference explored the intersection of economic theory and developments within mathematics. The meeting featured a day-long symposium on game theory, and the two authors of the 1944 *Theory of Games and Economic Behavior*—John von Neumann and Oskar Morgenstern—delivered papers at the conference.[26] Jacob Marschak used the occasion to elaborate his view that game theory provided the Keynesian framework the microfoundations it so sorely needed: the postulate of a "rational" self-maximizing economic actor.[27] Also present at the Madison conference were other Cowles- or RAND-affiliated individuals who were developing a neo-Walrasian version of general equilibrium theory. These economists, statisticians, and mathematicians included George Dantzig, Tjalling Koopmans, Harold Hotelling, Kenneth Arrow, Leonard Jimmie Savage, and Abraham Wald. Marschak's contribution to the development of rationality postulates was formalized by Savage's *Foundations of Statistics* (1954). This Bayesian reformulation of statistical theory became central to American Keynesianism, largely displacing Neyman's more objective approach in much subsequent work in both economics and finance.[28]

Marschak praised the mathematical toolkit introduced by von Neumann and Morgenstern for the simplification and clarity their axiomatic approach introduced.[29] For Marschak, the mathematics used by von Neumann and Morgenstern had the additional advantage of weaning economics from its old reliance on physics and the mathematics associated with that discipline, specifically calculus and differential equations. Instead of calculus, game theory relied on set theory, topology, and the combinetrics of convex sets, which allowed von Neumann and Morgenstern to model some of the novel "relations relevant to games and markets (such as 'domination' and 'solution')."

Because Marschak was already interested in addressing the problem of choice in the presence of unknowns—the situation that confronted the investor—he made two important adjustments to the account of rationality von Neumann and Morgenstern provided in *Theory of Games*. The first concerned the statistical approach used in figuring probabilities. When dealing with games like poker, the analyst could use the objective, frequentist approach to statistics refined by R. A. Fisher and Neyman because the frequencies and probability distributions of such games are given by the rules of the game. The probability distributions of future economic variables and financial returns, by contrast, are not given in advance, and they require a statistical approach that can accommodate subjective factors such as belief and expectation.

Marschak's most important innovation was to add a fourth proposition to the axioms von Neumann and Morgenstern deemed essential to "rational" behavior in any "game."[30] The *Theory of Games and Economic Behavior* introduced three propositions: (1) the rational agent (player) had to make logical decisions, which expressed his preferences as choices among a range of ordered options; (2) the set of ordered choices available in the game must map to an arithmetic set of ordered options, so that mathematical rules could be applied; and (3) the player must express his preferences consistently. The postulate Marschak added accommodated the kind of intertemporal decisions an investor must make about an unknown future: the agent must be willing and able to choose consistently not only from a range of ordered (ranked) commodities, both real and monetary, but also from a range of statistical distributions or probabilities. In Marschak's example, the rational agent must choose among "prospects": "a car, a $1,000 bill, and the ticket to a lottery in which the chances of winning a car or a $1,000 bill are, respectively, .2 and .8, say" (120). The latter, the prospect of having *a chance* to win the car or the $1,000 bill under varying conditions of probability is equivalent to a financial claim, about which one can only estimate the future payout within a probability distribution. In Marschak's formulation, these probability distributions could be known because the lotteries had determinate likelihoods ("the chances . . . are, respectively, .2 and .8"). Even though Marschak was not yet fully embracing stochasticity, that is, he was insisting that the investor was not only the self-maximizing "economic man" but also "statistical man," willing and able to estimate varying probabilities of future returns.[31] What this formulation did *not* accommodate was the possibility that some of the patterns exhibited by the prices of financial assets could fall outside normal or recognized statistical distributions. This possibility, which Nassim Nicholas Taleb calls a "black swan," turns out to be a characteristic feature of financial markets.[32]

8.1e. Linear Programming of Activities

Even though the conferences held in Chicago and Berkeley as the war ended promised to bring the probability revolution to the social sciences and to economics in particular, many of the mathematical techniques invented during the war were still classified, and the novel approaches published in *Theory of Games and Economic Behavior* were not immediately assimilated by economists. The beginnings of a change can be found four years after the war when Cowles researchers, working under a research contract funded by RAND, formally and legally transferred the military technology characterized as "The Theory of Programming and Allocation" from the military to a university setting. At the conference held in June 1949, some of the mathematical techniques Marschak had celebrated were on display, now articulated as "the programming of interdependent activities," which came to be known as linear programming. So taken-for-granted were the mathematical values of rigor and axiomization epitomized by these methods that most of the conference's thirty-four papers were—and still are—incomprehensible to anyone not trained in these techniques. One of the very few exceptions was a terse, three-page paper by Morgenstern denouncing all attempts to estimate the errors in economic statistics and thus all but dismissing much of the conference's subject: "Linear programming, or any other similar utilization of great masses of economic data, cannot be expected to make decisive practical progress until there is satisfaction that the data warrant the implied extensive and costly numerical operations."[33] Had the conference participants heeded Morgenstern's admonition, they might have shifted their attention away from techniques like linear programming to the theoretical and practical adequacy of data—a return of the data problem that has always stalked economic theorizing, worried Keynes in his debate with Tinbergen, and resurfaces in every new version of econometric research.

Instead of engaging the data problem, the conference on activity analysis and linear programming marked the introduction of operations research into a nonmilitary setting.[34] The conference was sponsored by the Cowles Commission, whose research program was now directed by Tjalling Koopmans, a Dutch mathematician and economist who, before joining Cowles, had worked for the US government on wartime problems of transportation and optimal routing. In 1949, Koopmans signed a research contract with RAND for work on "resource allocation," and the conference, along with the research projects conducted by most of its participants, was sponsored by this contract. While still working within the Keynesian framework, these projects marked a departure from the work on probability Marschak had favored. As Till Düppe and E. Roy Weintraub have argued, the conference "defined . . . the emergence of a new kind of economic theory growing from game theory, operations research, and linear programming and the related mathematical techniques of convex sets, separating hyperplanes, and fixed-point theory." The conference, in the words of Düppe and Weintraub, "established the historical conditions for economics to become a modeling science"—partly by distancing the Cowles version of economics from the politicized debates earlier economists had waged and partly by affiliating its version of the discipline with the new mathematics, whose value, paradoxically, was based on the twin foundations of mathematicians' undeniable accomplishments during the war and the postwar "purity" claimed by mathematicians who scorned applied research.[35] While we agree with Düppe and Weintraub, we want to emphasize the conference's preference for models that dealt with allocation and optimality—or maximizing results under constraint. As we will see in chapter 9, *optimality* was central to the financial models spun off from the subdiscipline that was beginning to emerge within economics. As we will see in chapter 10, *allocation,* first in the form of distribution (the factors of production receive their marginal products) and then as stabilization (the intertemporally optimizing rational agent assures the full employment of all resources, subject only to random shocks), was to take over economic theory in the late twentieth century, in the guise of the rational expectation hypothesis and Real-Business Cycle Theory. That this emphasis on allocation to the exclusion of other topics made it impossible for theorists' models to include financial factors is one of the ironies we explore in chapter 10. For present purposes, it is primarily important to note the conference's airing of another mathematical contribution to economics—von Neumann's introduction of topology into economic theory.

The explicit purpose of the 1949 conference was to transfer the classified wartime techniques to business and management contexts. The essential task addressed by most of the papers was developing a method for identifying "the best allocation of limited means toward desired ends"—a formulation that simultaneously rendered optimization central yet remained capacious enough to accommodate numerous applications.[36] In rejecting *maximization,* which had traditionally been understood as the central goal of economic theory, for *optimization,* a value associated with operations research, participants acknowledged the real-world condition of constraint and provided a means of managing, or allocating, resources under certain kinds of constraint. At the conference, papers were delivered on several real-side issues—crop rotation, the aircraft industry, and transportation—but no one applied the theory to a financial situation. Within three years, however, this application was made, in the paper most historians present as the origin of modern finance: Harry Markowitz's 1952 application of optimality to the creation of an investor's portfolio. Thus, we can see a direct line from operations research, with its method of linear programming, to the emergent theory of finance, with economic applications as a sort of stepping stone.

Just as Reichenbach's opening address to the Berkeley conference set the tone for that gathering, so the paper by the economists Marshall K. Wood and George B. Dantzig identified the central problem for the 1949 conference. During the war, Wood had been the head of Project SCOOP, and Dantzig was its chief mathematician. Project SCOOP (Scientific Computation of Optimal Programs) was a US Air Force project that ran for eight years from 1947; its primary objective was to develop programming strategies for moving a complex organization, such as a complex of weapons or an economy, from one defined state to another. It was while working on SCOOP that Dantzig stated the first mathematical form of the general linear program, and, with Wood, identified the mathematical and economic components of planning. One part of their mathematical method was familiar—the simultaneous equation method that was the workhorse of the Cowles Commission—but, in an accompanying paper, Dantzig called for solving programming problems with the simplex algorithm. At the end of this technical paper, Dantzig mentioned some of the research programs to which linear programming might be applied. These included the studies of inter-industry relations addressed by Leontief and the Bureau of Labor Statistics; the transportation problem Koopmans had worked on during the war; the minimum-cost diet problem tacked by Jerome Cornfield and G. J. Stigler; and the warehouse problem proposed by A. Cahn.

As even this brief description makes clear, many of the watchwords of the activity analysis conference were operations research values: *optimization, efficiency, allocation,* and *programming,* although the socialist connotations of the last word led several participants to qualify or reject the term.[37] Dantzig explicitly added *model* to the conference's guiding terms, defining *model* as "a mathematical representation of a technology" (with *technology* defined as "the whole set of possible activities" being analyzed).[38] In "Analysis of Production as an Efficient Combination of Activities," Koopmans elaborated the idea of modeling, but, in doing so, he alluded to a distinction that was to prove consequential for economics, and for finance in particular.

> Managers choose between, or employ efficient combinations of, several processes to obtain in some sense the best results. . . . An efficient manager chooses that combination of productive activities which maximizes the amount produced for given available quantities of factors which have given qualitative characteristics. In this concept, the quality characteristics of the available factors and of the desired product specify the variables entering into the production function and the nature of the function. The available quantities of the factors specify the values of the variables, and the maximal output specifies the value assumed by that function.[39]

Koopmans's account of modeling might seem identical to the operations research version: efficiency was the desired outcome; resources were limited; qualities could be quantified because each "commodity" was "homogeneous qualitatively and continuously divisible quantitatively" (35); and each activity was "capable of continuous proportional expansion or reduction" because each activity returned to scale (36). In accounting terms, this version of modeling combined a flow concept (activities or programming) with a fund concept (allocation). In computational terms, its key was linear programming. But Koopmans was actually adding to the operations research version of modeling a new set of mathematical tools derived from a source that preceded operations research: John von Neumann's axiomatic approach to economic equilibrium. Von Neumann had demonstrated this axiomatic approach in a paper published in German in 1937, which was translated into English in 1945.[40] Koopmans had "learned of and benefited from" the literature related to von Neumann's approach before 1948, when he delivered a paper informed by it at the same Madison meeting of the Econometric Society where Marschak presented his work on rationality (33, n. 1).

Although Koopmans did not make this point explicitly, the mathematical shift he described—from calculus to topology and set theory—represented a radical alteration of the fundamental platform of economics—from a grounding metaphor of forces, which was taken from physics and implicitly referred to actual forces, to a grounding metaphor of mathematics, which referred to nothing beyond the logic of mathematics itself. As interpreted by Dantzig (and Marschak), von Neumann's work—both his early articles and the 1944 book on game theory—gave economists a new operating procedure: create an axiom system that can ground a mathematical structure; show the mathematical relations among the parts of the system; then add the economic content. Or one could work the opposite way: begin with the economic content, then generalize up to its inherent formal structure, which must be expressed in mathematical form. This is what Tjalling Koopmans did in his activity analysis conference papers: he began with the transportation problem that had engaged him during the war, then, using topology and the fixed-point theorem, generalized its formal structure to show that efficiency represented the limit point of a production system, of which transportation was one part. Harry Markowitz, one of Koopmans's students—who was also a student of Marschak—would soon use the toolkit comprised of the new mathematics, the new concept of rationality, and the method Koopmans applied to transportation to create a formal model showing how to construct the most "efficient" portfolio of securities. Few economic historians have acknowledged Markowitz's indebtedness to Marschak, Koopmans, or the platform created in the 1940s.[41] As we will see in chapter 9, the emergent discipline of finance embraced the mathematics of the linear programming conference immediately, but several years were to pass before dynamic programming became the workhorse of macroeconomics.

8.2. MEASUREMENT, MONETARISM, KEYNESIAN STABILIZATION POLICIES, AND GROWTH THEORY

Even though Keynes's *General Theory* did not rely on or cite empirical data, the categories Keynes introduced were ready for data, and, as we saw in chapter 6, national income estimates and accounts implicitly relied on the categories Keynes emphasized. During the 1950s and 1960s, economists and statisticians launched projects intended to provide data sets for areas not specified in the national accounts. In so doing, they also helped make finance and financial intermediation visible. Many of these researchers ignored the sophisticated mathematical and statistical toolkit we have just examined, preferring instead the basic tools of time series, index numbers, and sampling Simon Kuznets and Milton Gilbert used to construct national accounts. Most of these projects, which were sponsored either by the NBER or by Brookings and belong to the institutionalist tradition within economics, exhibit the characteristic NBER reluctance to be guided by theory or rush to theoretical conclusions. Nevertheless, when combined with the new mathematical framework, these empirical studies provided the basis for most of the century's subsequent applied and theoretical work within both economics and finance because they added an element that was conspicuously lacking in the GNP/GDP accounting framework developed in the 1930s—a fund view of the nation's balance sheet, which made the growing role of financial institutions visible and revealed the institutional structure of the intermediaries and markets that constitute the US financial system.[42] These empirical research projects played a key role in both American Keynesianism and monetarism, which not always successfully presented itself as an alternative to mainstream Keynesianism.

8.2a. Measuring Financial Flows

Neither Simon Kuznets's approach to national income estimates nor Milton Gilbert's revision of Kuznets's work proved satisfying to all economists. As early as 1932, Morris A. Copeland pointed out problems in the theory that informed Kuznets's estimates, and during the 1940s, Copeland developed an alternative to the national income accounts released annually by the US Department of Commerce.[43] Copeland offered his flow of funds accounts as another perspective on the US economy, one not aggregated at the same scale as the national income accounts, and able to combine sector statements of moneyflows and loanfunds to reveal how money of all kinds moved through the nation's economy. Influenced by his training in accounting as well as economics, Copeland conceptualized the empirical work sponsored by the NBER as part of an accounting process, which would finally provide detail for Keynes's theoretical declarations (e.g., savings equals investment) and enable Americans to see what had previously been invisible: the connections between the real side of the economy and the financial side.

Copeland received his PhD from the University of Chicago and spent much of his academic career at Cornell University. A disciple of Wesley Clair Mitchell, Copeland served as executive secretary of the Central Statistical Board from 1933 to 1939 before becoming director of the Bureau of the Budget. During World War II, he was chief of the munitions branch of the War Production Board. Copeland also taught at the Brookings Graduate School of Economics and was a member of the Federal Reserve Board's Division of Research and Statistics. At the NBER, he devoted himself to an empirical study of moneyflows between 1936 and 1942, which was published in 1952 as *A Study of Moneyflows in the United States*. While overlooked or misunderstood by many economists, Copeland's work had a powerful impact on the US government's official statistical representations of the economy. In 1955, the Board of Governors of the Federal Reserve issued its first exposition of the flow of funds accounts; in 1965, a statistical relationship between the flow of funds accounts and the national income accounts was established; and now the Federal Reserve compiles and issues flow of funds accounts quarterly.

Copeland's flow of funds accounts differ from the national income accounts in four primary ways.[44] First, unlike the national accounts, the flow of funds accounts record financial transactions, such as borrowing, lending, or hoarding. This allows one to see how finance underwrites production and consumption and, not incidentally, provides empirical evidence with which to test Keynes's theoretical claim that savings equals investment. Second, because the national accounts measure the current output of final products, they eliminate trading in already existing assets, something the flow of funds accounts include. This gives a more complete picture of the full range of the nation's economic transactions. Third, the national accounts treat all capital expenditures as business activities, not investments, whereas the flow of funds accounts treat consumers' purchases of durable goods as investments. This appreciably increases the amount of consumer saving shown in the accounts. And fourth, the flow of funds accounts use a much more detailed system of sectoring to reveal the channels through which finance flows. While the detailed sectoring in the flow of funds accounts makes integrating these accounts with the national income accounts challenging, the combination of the two provided for the first time "a complete and internally consistent body of data on financial flows, interlocked with national income data."[45]

While the title of Copeland's project highlighted "flows," his work was an explicit challenge to the hydraulic view of money championed by economists like Irving Fisher. Picturing the economy as a cistern, as Fisher had done at the beginning of the century, and money as water flowing through the cistern's reservoirs and pipes introduced several problems that Copeland's preferred metaphor was intended to solve. Instead of viewing money as water flowing through reservoirs and pipes, Copeland presented an electrical model of the economy, where batteries served the function performed by Fisher's reservoirs, and circuits took the place of Fisher's pipes. This metaphorical recasting eliminated the time lags that inevitably characterize flows of water and emphasized instead the simultaneity of the two sides represented by every transaction: at the very moment one transactor spends or borrows a sum of money, another transactor receives this money or contracts a debt for the same sum. "What one transactor spends is a receipt for someone else; what one transactor receives is an expenditure by someone else."[46]

Copeland's electrical analogy took issue with other economists' tendency to apply the neoclassical supply/demand model to money, and it also challenged two common misunderstandings about the money supply: that it consists of a finite sum and that, in difficult times, the Federal Reserve increases it simply by printing money.[47] Instead of presenting the money supply as fixed or as pooling in the lowest-lying reservoirs, Copeland's electrical metaphor cast money as a current that is everywhere at the same time, subject only to the operation of "circuit breakers," which can momentarily halt the flow of electricity. Instead of viewing the Federal Reserve as an all-powerful agent that prints money, Copeland emphasized the discretionary power of numerous economic actors, all of whom have the power to throw the breaker and interrupt the flow of currency. This is what happened during the Great Depression, he argued, when banks failed to make loans.

Copeland charged that the money supply view, which was integrally linked to Fisher's equation of exchange, revealed nothing about what the Federal Reserve's monetary policy actually was or did.[48] Nor could it show that the money supply was a continuum, to which all kinds of financial assets and activities also belonged. Indeed, as his data revealed, in the period between 1936 and 1942, financial assets such as mortgages, insurance, securities, and lines of credit had become as "real" as the products they enabled consumers and businesses to purchase, in the sense that they constituted a substantial part of the "wealth" of every transactor. Treating money and finance as a single continuum, composed of different kinds of elements and surging through the "channels" of banks and other financial institutions, provided the basis for what James Tobin theorized as a portfolio view of finance. This view has affinities with J. R. Hicks's and Jacob Marschak's presentation of an array of financial assets from which the investor chooses, but, unlike the model Marschak and Makower built up logically, on the theoretical framework of general equilibrium, Copeland offered statistical evidence to show how credit and money actually funded the purchases of individuals, companies, and governments, the relationship between money obtained through borrowing and the "equity structure of the economy," and the roles played by cash balances and credit in business expansion and contraction (5). Among the many questions for which Copeland's statistics provided new answers were those central to the business cycle projects underway since the 1920s: "How can we trace the cyclical impact of government fiscal policy on businesses and on households? The impact of business policy on households and on government? The impact of household finances on business and government? How can we determine which sectors of the economy are taking the initiative in the various changes in the level of economic activity?" (5–6).

The accounting framework Copeland used to illuminate the structural skeleton of the nation's economy consisted of three parts: a series of sectors, which added the financial sector to the three-sector approach of the national income accounts; a sources-and-uses-of-funds statement, a hybrid document that combined features of the corporate balance sheet and income statement; and a flow of funds matrix, which drew on Leontief's input-output accounts.[49] As a whole, the flow of funds accounts allowed the analyst to see a number of features that had previously been invisible: for any specified period, the new accounts showed the balanced sources and uses of funds for each sector, the interrelations among sectors, and the aggregate totals of saving, investment, hoarding, lending, and borrowing for the entire economy. The macroeconomic picture that emerged used accounting identities to make it possible to impute functions for which no data was available.

Any one sector may invest more or less than it saves, or borrow more or less than it lends. However, for the economy as a whole, saving must necessarily equal investment, and borrowing must equal lending plus hoarding. Thus deficit sectors, which invest more than they save, necessarily imply the existence of other surplus sectors. This is not only because the economy-wide total of saving must equal investment but also because a deficit sector *must* finance its deficit by borrowing, dishoarding, or selling off securities. This implies the existence of surplus sectors to do the lending, hoarding, or buying of the securities. Similarly, surplus sectors, which save more than they invest, necessarily imply the existence of other deficit sectors.[50]

8.2b. Financial Intermediaries

If Copeland's work made the channels of finance visible for the first time, Raymond W. Goldsmith revealed the actual institutions through which money, credit, and other forms of finance flowed. *Financial Intermediaries in the American Economy Since 1900* (1958) belonged to a series on major trends in capital formation, launched by the NBER in 1950. Of the series' seven works, five were devoted to the real side of the economy, and even Goldsmith's study of financial intermediation stressed repeatedly that the primary function of finance is to enhance *"real* capital formation" and, by extension, economic growth. Indeed, Goldsmith's title contained the word *intermediaries* instead of *institutions* to highlight the role financial institutions played "as channels between savers and users of funds."[51] For data, he drew on his own *A Study of Saving in the United States* (1955, 1956), as well as the aggregate sources-and-uses-of-funds statements for various corporations compiled by the Department of Commerce and the Board of Governors of the Federal Reserve (219).

Goldsmith was a German Jew working in the German statistical office in 1934 when he fled his home country for the United States. For the next seventeen years, he worked at the Securities and Exchange Commission and the War Production Board. While in Washington, Goldsmith teamed up with Gerhard Colm, the German émigré we have already encountered, to draft a plan for reform of the German currency, and in 1951, as a staff member of the NBER, he began work on his *Study of Saving.* Goldsmith's works provided data both for Keynesian theorists and for Milton Friedman's permanent income theory of consumption.

Goldsmith's work on financial intermediaries revealed several trends contemporaries must have already suspected: the federal government had played an outsized role in absorbing funds, especially during the two non-"normal" periods of the last half-century (the Great Depression and World War II); insurance companies of all kinds (including government-sponsored entities such as the Federal Deposit Insurance Corporation) had grown more rapidly than other financial institutions, especially commercial banks (11, 26, 30, 6);

and the share of financial intermediaries in "national assets" (real and financial assets) had dramatically increased during the period, rising from one-ninth of the total in 1900 to one-sixth in 1929 to one-fourth in 1955 (11, 16–26). Goldsmith also provided a typology of financial intermediaries, divided into five major categories (52), which affords a useful comparison to the survey Harold Moulton published in 1921. While the passage of time has overturned some of his more speculative predictions (he foresaw "a deceleration or retardation in the rate of increase of financial intermediaries' share in national assets," 49), Goldsmith's careful documentation of the sources and uses of funds for commercial banks, insurance companies, and savings and loan associations constituted a data goldmine for more theoretical treatments of finance, such as John Gurley and Edward Shaw's *Money in a Theory of Finance* (1960), to which we turn in a moment.

For our purposes, the most important point of Goldsmith's *Financial Intermediaries* is one he makes in passing, as part of his discussion of structural changes in the sources of bank funds. Goldsmith noted that "during the past fifty years the outstanding change in the sources of bank funds is the reduction in the proportion of equity funds [in relation to total assets and liabilities]. For the entire banking system the decline . . . is from approximately 20 per cent in the period from 1900 to 1929, to about 10 per cent in 1939, to as little as 8 per cent in 1952" (156). This reduction "reflects the relatively low level of retained earnings and the small volume of sales of new bank stock since the Great Depression," Goldsmith continued, but, he assured readers, it should not be reason for alarm.

> It should be emphasized that the decline of the ratio of equity funds to total assets or liabilities is not in itself an indication of a deterioration in the financial position of the banking system or of an increase in the risk taken by bank depositors. In interpreting the decline, account must be taken of the changes in the degree of risk involved in the assets held and of protective devices such as deposit insurance introduced since the thirties. Even without detailed investigation it is obvious that the risk of loss in the banking system has been considerably reduced by the increasing share of cash and short-term United States government securities among assets. (160)

In invoking deposit insurance, Goldsmith was alluding to the Federal Deposit Insurance Corporation (FDIC), which was mandated by the 1933 Glass-Steagall Act, the central piece of legislation FDR's administration used to reform and regulate the banking system. The FDIC helped quiet depositors' concerns about commercial bank failures by insuring deposits up to a specified amount. The government also created the Federal Savings and Loan Insurance Corporation (FSLIC) to insure deposits at savings and loan institutions. Both insurance corporations were designed to be self-financing through the fees they charged member banks, but, in emergencies, they were authorized to borrow up to $100 billion from the US Treasury. In addition to establishing insurance plans, the government also created regulatory agencies: beyond the Securities and Exchange Commission, which, as we saw in chapter 4, was charged with overseeing securities exchanges, legislators created the Federal Home Loan Bank Board to watch over the savings and loan industry (1933) and the Bureau of Federal Credit Unions to regulate credit unions. Regulating insurance companies remained an obligation of the individual states.

Glass-Steagall contained two further provisions that were to attract increasing attention after 1980. The first prohibited commercial banks from engaging in "non-banking activities," which included trading stocks or other securities. As we saw in chapter 4, this practice was widespread in the 1920s, when it led to a rapid increase in the volume and riskiness of securities. The second, a provision called Regulation Q (Reg Q), prohibited banks from paying interest on demand deposits and limited the interest rate banks could offer on other kinds of accounts, such as savings and time accounts. This was adopted to discourage competition among banking institutions for depositors' money, a practice policy makers charged with driving down the margin between lending rates and borrowing rates in the early 1930s.

Writing in the mid-1950s, Goldsmith could take these protections and regulations for granted and he could feel confident that commercial banks would continue to operate the relatively staid business they had practiced since the Great Depression. The kinds of intermediation that constitute the primary business of banks—"liquidity transformation," "maturity transformation," "asset substitution," and "asset transformation"—were intended to populate the channels Copeland had documented with machinery that worked efficiently, safely, and at a relatively low cost.[52] This system of insurance and regulation provided exactly the kind of protection Depression-era legislators had wanted. Between 1940 and 1970 the United States experienced no banking crises, and very few banks failed.

Such serenity exacted a toll on the banking industry itself, and the sources of bank funds documented by Goldsmith—depositors' savings, short-term borrowing in the money market, and long-term borrowing through bond issue, which was often sold to insurance companies or pension funds—came to seem insufficient for the kind of growth bankers and Wall Street investors demanded. In the 1970s, as the financial opportunities Goldsmith named were joined by innovations like NOW accounts and money market funds, Reg Q began to seem unbearably onerous, and with the insistent demands for economy-wide growth that accompanied the oil shocks of that decade, the entire edifice of Glass-Steagall began to seem oppressive. As we will soon see, between 1980 and 2008, the system of protection and regulation that underwrote Goldsmith's equanimity was laid waste by the fires of deregulation.

8.2c. The First Theoretical Account of Financial Intermediation

Money in a Theory of Finance, by John G. Gurley and Edward S. Shaw, was the first theoretical study to show the interrelations of all financial markets and financial institutions in the United States. The project, which was sponsored by the Brookings Institution, began as a study of trends in commercial banking and grew into a new approach to monetary theory designed to move beyond the monetarism of Friedman and Schwartz, to which we turn in the next section. Instead of limiting their analysis to the nation's stock of money, Gurley and Shaw addressed both the interplay among various financial markets (the markets for primary and indirect securities, bonds, etc.) and between financial markets and markets for real production and services. Using the data compiled by Copeland, Goldsmith, and Friedman and Schwartz, Gurley and Shaw demonstrated that a theoretical model of the entire economy anchored in empirical work could show how financial intermediation worked and how commercial banking was linked to the money supply.

After working in the Office of Price Administration during World War II, John Gurley joined the economics department at Stanford, where Edward Shaw was one of his students. Even though their work did not have the impact they wished, especially on Federal Reserve policy, it did introduce what Perry Mehrling has called a "new line" of monetary analysis.[53] Gurley and Shaw launched their "new line" with the assumptions of neoclassical economics: "full employment, price flexibility, absence of money illusion and distribution effects." They used these assumptions, however, not to endorse but to reverse the conclusions of neoclassical economists: "We have played the game according to the ground rules of neo-classical economics in order to show that even here money is not a veil, that it may have an important role to play in determining the level and composition of output."[54] According to their "gross money" doctrine (187), which considered nonmonetary financial institutions as well as the money-generating Federal Reserve, money enters the system not simply from the Fed, but also through the operations of commercial banks and other "nonmonetary financial intermediaries."[55] These nonmonetary financial intermediaries resemble the Federal Reserve in helping transfer the savings of some individuals to borrowers who need money, and both kinds of intermediaries also create indirect securities by purchasing primary securities. To omit the contributions of such intermediaries from an account of "money," as monetarists like Milton Friedman did, was thus to leave out of the story a major endogenous contribution to the nation's money supply.

Gurley and Shaw repeatedly emphasized the interrelation of all financial markets with the nation's real markets: "Financial development is incomprehensible apart from its context of real development. Markets of goods and markets for securities (including money) are simultaneously the media through which spending units seek optimal adjustment between income and spending, net worth and wealth. Excess demands, positive or negative, for current output are of necessity excess supplies of securities, and the sectoral location of excess demands partly determines the types of primary securities that will be issued. The real world and the financial world are one world" (122–23). To see this interrelation required the balance sheet approach made possible by Copeland's work on flow of funds, for only bank balance sheets reveal capital appreciation and loss. Balance sheets, moreover, reveal the portfolio decisions made by bank officers, and this could help show how monetary disequilibria occurred in the financial system. Indeed, as Mehrling has pointed out, Gurley and Shaw considered an imbalance between the supply and demand for money to be both the engine of economic growth and the "normal state of affairs" in a healthy economy. "For Shaw, economic growth was a matter of monetary *dis*equilibrium, an expansion of *ex ante* investment in advance of *ex ante* saving, and an expansion of the money supply in advance of money demand. At any given moment in time, money supply is not necessarily equal to money demand. 'If it is not, there is monetary disequilibrium . . . the normal state of affairs" (1958).' . . . 'The pressure of monetary disequilibrium on levels of output can raise or lower historic growth rates of real income.' (Gurley and Shaw 1961, 103). From this point of view, the secular tendency for money supply to lag behind money demand operates as a deflationary force on the growth of real output, a force that is countered by a secular expansion of financial intermediation."[56] According to this theory, the secular expansion of financial intermediation—increased activity by commercial banks and other nonmonetary intermediaries—can do what the Federal

Reserve alone cannot accomplish: increase real output by increasing the nation's financial resources.

Gurley and Shaw entertained some ideas that, with hindsight, seem dubious. They supported a merger movement within banking, for example, on the assumption that larger banks would reduce costs (298), and they briefly fantasized consolidating the Treasury and the Federal Reserve to link regulation of the nation's money supply to management of government debt (278–80). In many senses, however, Gurley and Shaw were ahead of their time. Their discussion of the process by which nonmonetary institutions create credit, for example, anticipated the acceleration of securitization that swept the United States after 1970, and their insights into the relationship between liquidity and spending were sufficiently prescient to prompt Doug Noland, who blogged for SafeHaven as PrudentBear, to resurrect their work in 2001. "One has to go back 40 years to find such insightful and prudent analysis as to the key importance of financial intermediaries," Noland wrote in 2001, just after the Federal Reserve unexpectedly cut interest rates. Noland cited Gurley's comments on financial intermediaries to support his own conviction that the U.S. had entered "an incredibly complex 'managed liquidity' monetary regime." "While spending is not directly affected by interest rates," Gurley wrote, "it is affected by liquidity, which is composed of the money supply and the money people can get hold of. The private sector's liquidity is increased by the lending of commercial banks and other financial intermediaries, because such lending increases the supply of loanable funds ('money people can get hold of'), and the growth of liquidity stimulates spending. The important thing about financial institutions is not the liquid liabilities (monetary or otherwise) they create but the lending they do—the assets they purchase."[57] During the long lead-up to the 2008 crisis, with the assistance of securitization, Gurley's observations proved prophetic, and PrudentBear's warnings finally found willing listeners.

8.2d. Monetarism

Milton Friedman had an outsized influence on the rise of finance in America, with his promotion of a floating dollar, repealing interest rate ceilings, and a new rule for monetary growth, later codified as the Taylor Rule and adopted by the Fed in the 1980s. Friedman also made important contributions to economics in the postwar period, in work devoted to the theory of consumption, stabilization policy, the theory of money demand, the natural rate of unemployment, and capitalism and freedom.[58] Friedman is also remembered for his methodological insistence on combining an empirical statistical approach with theoretical hypotheses. He defended his "positive economics" by insisting that an economic theory can only be measured by its success in prediction, not by the realism of its assumptions.[59] Friedman's empirical, statistical approach and his emphasis on the role played by expectations are reminiscent of Irving Fisher's *Appreciation and Interest* (1898), where Fisher recognized the role expectations play in investment markets and subjected his hypotheses to a series of quasi-empirical "thought experiments" using figures gathered from the US Comptroller of Currency and the British India Office.

Trained as a statistician, Friedman worked within the marginalist neoclassical tradition based on Alfred Marshall's *Principles of Economics* (1890). He was introduced to economics at Rutgers University by the NBER's future president, Arthur Burns, but he remained committed to statistics as well. Friedman's statistical sophistication was fine-tuned by two of America's most distinguished econometricians, Harold Hotelling, who taught Friedman at Columbia University, and Henry Schultz, who directed Friedman's research at the University of Chicago. Friedman's first journal article, "The Use of Ranks to Avoid the Assumption of Normality Implicit in the Analysis of Variance," was published in the *Journal of the American Statistical Association*, and his dissertation, "Income from Independent Professional Practice," used statistical analysis to study the stability of the income of professionals over time. On the basis of this study, Friedman introduced the Fisherian concept of permanent income, which Friedman used to challenge some of the assumptions of the Keynesian framework. Also well versed in utility theory, Friedman collaborated with Leonard Jimmie Savage on an article on expected utility theory, and, as a founding member of the Mont Pelerin Society, he wrote a critical book review of Oscar Lange's *Price Flexibility and Employment* (1944). Whereas Paul Samuelson built theoretical models at MIT as an engaged Keynesian, Friedman devoted his academic career at the University of Chicago to price theory, on the one hand, and money and banking, on the other. As a prominent public intellectual, he fiercely opposed Keynesian policies and advocated instead a free-market approach to economic challenges.

Even if Friedman viewed his work as a rebuke to American Keynesianism, many of his critiques of Keynesian concepts, such as "involuntary unemployment," strengthened the Keynesian ascendency in the short run, if only by making other economists answer his criticisms. Monetarism, which is arguably Friedman's most important contribution to economics, can be said to be related to Keynesian in the sense that it took a single component of aggregate demand—the demand for money—and elevated it to a position of theoretical and practical preeminence. Of course, Friedman reached conclu-

sions diametrically opposed to those of the American Keynesians who dominated Washington in the 1970s, for he resisted the central bank's use of the
money supply to stabilize prices and encourage employment. In "The Effects
of Full-Employment Policy on Economic Stability" (1953), which Edmund
Phelps characterized as "the magna carta" of monetarism, Friedman argued
that when the Federal Reserve uses an activist monetary policy, it risks destabilizing the economy because analysts cannot model the effects—or time
lags—of their actions.[60] In "The Quantity Theory of Money: A Restatement"
(1956), Friedman laid out the "'model' of a quantity theory in . . . the [Chi-
cago] oral tradition" that described a demand-for-money function in which
the real quantity of money demanded "was a function of the vector of returns
on alternatives to holding money—bonds, equities, physical goods, and human capital—of real income" and a "portmanteau variable." This variable
gave Friedman's model Marshallian microfoundations, for it reflected factors
that affect the tastes and preferences of individuals, as well as institutional
factors.[61] As the title of this article suggests, Friedman's monetarism harkened
back to Irving Fisher's quantity theory, but, unlike Fisher's hydraulic model,
Friedman's model explicitly rested "on maximization of a utility function [for
money] defined in terms of 'real magnitudes.'"[62] Friedman's monetary theory was not a theory of output, or of money income, or of the price level, for
"any statement about these variables requires combining the quantity theory
with some specifications about the conditions of supply of money and other
variables as well" (4). He concluded that the quantity theorist should hold a
number of "empirical hypotheses": "the demand for money is highly stable"
(16); it plays an important role in determining variables of great importance
for the analysis of the economy as a whole; and "there are important factors
affecting the supply of money that do not affect the demand for money" (16).
These empirical hypotheses were critical because a stable demand function
was useful to trace out the effects of changes in supply.

Friedman rested his conviction that money demand was relatively stable on
the data supplied by Goldsmith's study of US household savings. In *The Theory of Consumption Function* (1957), Friedman used Goldsmith's data again,
this time to reframe consumption theory based on the Fisherian concept of
"permanent income" (e.g., the annuity value of all expected lifetime income
streams and wealth) and to challenge the policies of American Keynesianism, which did not emphasize the forward-looking nature of financial decisions. In addition to criticizing the Keynesian emphasis on short-term decisions, Friedman also offered "the natural unemployment rate" as a rejoinder
to the Keynesian concept of involuntary unemployment, and he introduced

the concept of "adaptive expectations," which was a precursor to the rational expectations theory.

8.2e. The Fed on Trial

Working with Anna Jacobson Schwartz and under the auspices of the NBER, Milton Friedman made the empirical case for his theoretical monetarism in *A Monetary History of the United States, 1867–1960* (1963). This work represented a continuation of Friedman's earlier work in both empirical statistics and economic theory, but it constituted something of a departure for the NBER, which, as we have seen, prided itself on deferring the theoretical—not to mention political—implications of its research projects. In characterizing the actions—or inaction—of the Federal Reserve during the Great Depression as "inept," Friedman and Schwartz rejected the NBER's stance of impartiality and emphatically endorsed the free market economic liberalism to which Friedman devoted the rest of his career. This work is now generally considered the authoritative account of one hundred years of monetary history.[63]

A Monetary History belonged to a larger empirical project, launched in 1948, which was designed to analyze monetary factors in the business cycle.[64] While dense with tables and charts, the *Monetary History* did not contain the bulk of the statistical data generated by the larger project, nor did the authors' analysis feature correlation or regression analysis, as did some of the other volumes spun off from the monetary project.[65] Friedman and Schwartz presented the historical narrative of this work as "background for the statistical work," but they also acknowledged that the statistical work and the analytical narrative account shaped each other.[66] Beneath both the historical narrative and the statistical analysis lay a single "backbone," the money series the NBER began to compile in 1947 (xxi). The year 1947 was also the one in which Friedman, who had just been hired by the economics department of the University of Chicago, attended the first meeting of the Mont Pelerin Society, an organization devoted to preserving the free market values members feared endangered by the motley combination of Keynesianism, market socialism, and European politics.[67]

In the *Monetary History*, Friedman and Schwartz defined "money" rather loosely, as "all currency plus all deposits in commercial banks" (4). Friedman justified this definition in 1948 by calling attention to money's role as an asset: "There is no sharp dividing line between 'money' and 'near moneys' or between 'near moneys' and 'securities proper.' . . . Any study which is to take account of the role played by 'money' as an asset must clearly consider other assets as well; indeed from this point of view the arbitrary line between 'money' and other assets might well be drawn at a different point than it is when the emphasis is on the function of money as a circulating medium."[68] As this passage suggests—and as Friedman and Schwartz emphasized in the book's conclusion—money is "full of mystery and paradox" because money belongs to both the real and financial sides of the economy. As a medium of exchange, money facilitates real transactions; as an asset, money is one among many claims; and, to further complicate matters, money can be used in real transactions to buy and sell financial claims. If they allowed for some wiggle room in their definition of money, however, Friedman and Schwartz drew the line at treating endogenous institutions like banks as sources of the money supply. Indeed, when Walter Stewart, chair of the Rockefeller Foundation Board of Trustees, encouraged Friedman to begin with a study of banks' lending and investment activity, Friedman refused; Rockefeller, in turn, did not fund the project.[69] Friedman and Schwartz focused on changes in the stock of money, however loose their definition, because they considered money to be exogenous and an adequate money supply the most important factor in the nation's nominal income growth.[70] While they did mention other financial topics, such as credit supplies, and gave some attention to the factors many scholars considered central to the Great Depression (e.g., the collapse of the 1920s construction boom or poor lending decisions before the crash), they consistently returned to their central topic: "the monetary side" of the US economy (296).

In Friedman and Schwartz's account, three factors determine changes in the stock of a nation's money. The first, "high-powered money," combines "specie or . . . fiduciary money which is a direct or indirect liability of the government" and "vault cash," the bank reserves that, after the 1914 Federal Reserve Act, included not only the public's deposits but also the deposit liabilities of the Federal Reserve system to banks. "The total is called high-powered money because one dollar of such money held as bank reserves may give rise to the creation of several dollars of deposits" (50). The remaining two factors consist of the ratio of bank deposits to bank reserves and the ratio of bank deposits to currency. Of the three actors whose interactions affect the money supply—the government, banks, and the public—the most influential by far is the government. In the account given by Friedman and Schwartz, moreover, the government can, for all intents and purposes, be reduced to the Federal Reserve system, which Friedman and Schwartz often refer to simply as "the System." Note that Friedman's tendency to treat the Federal Reserve as if it were the only face of government—certainly the only part that could use financial policy to effect changes—played down the importance of both the Treasury, which was charged with managing debt, and fiscal policy more generally, even though taxation could raise revenue. This emphasis on the Fed is consistent with Friedman's career-long campaign to reduce the role played by any arm of the government in the economy. With Treasury and fiscal policy marginalized, he had only to impugn the Fed to discredit all government intervention.

According to Friedman and Schwartz, empirical data proved that the Federal Reserve was responsible for unpredictable changes in the money supply because the data showed a sharp contrast between an economy ruled by the gold standard and one subject to the Fed's "inept" decisions. "The blind, undesigned, and quasi-automatic working of the gold standard turned out to produce a greater measure of predictability and regularity—perhaps because its discipline was impersonal and inescapable—than did deliberate and conscious control exercised within institutional arrangements intended to promote monetary stability" (10). In their discussion of the Great Depression, they blamed the Fed explicitly: "The monetary collapse was not the inescapable consequence of other forces, but rather a largely independent factor which exerted a powerful influence on the course of events. The failure of the Federal Reserve System to prevent the collapse reflected not the impotence of monetary policy but rather the particular policies followed by the monetary authorities and, in smaller degree, the particular arrangements in existence" (300). Here is the central point of the history Friedman and Schwartz provided: monetary forces matter and, if the government refrains from meddling in the money supply, a stable money supply will lead to the growth of nominal income.

In this account of the New Deal, the measures intended to stabilize the country's economy both set a terrible precedent and strengthened the very agency that wrecked so much havoc in the 1930s.

> The broadening of the powers of the System was of greater significance than the change in its structure. The Board and the Banks naturally attributed the System's failure to stem the 1929–33 contraction and to prevent the banking panic to its inadequate powers rather than to the use of the powers it had. It both requested additional powers and was urged to accept them. The first measure along these lines preceded the panic: the Glass-Steagall Act, . . . which broadened acceptable collateral for Federal Reserve notes and permitted emergency advances to member banks on any asset. Other provisions of the Banking Act of 1935, all ex-

tending the System's powers are: (1) enlargement of the Board's power
to alter reserve requirements. . . . (2) broadening of the lending powers
of the [Federal Reserve] Banks. . . . (3) empowering the Board to set a
maximum limit to interest rates paid by member banks on time deposits. . . . (4) granting of power to the Board to regulate credit advanced
by bankers and brokers to their customers for purchasing and carrying
registered securities. (448)

Beyond inflicting pain on countless Americans, the Federal Reserve's supposed failure to moderate the 1930s decline in the stock of money had another
deleterious effect: it convinced economists and legislators that money played
only a minor role in the nation's productivity, unlike "governmental fiscal actions and direct interventions" (12). The additional powers the 1935 Banking
Act granted the Fed gave this institution even more power over the money
supply, but this added to the damage that Friedman and Schwartz thought the
Fed's meddling had caused. In the 1950s, with Keynesian theorists emphasizing the "credit effects" of monetary policy on interest rates instead of paying
attention to the stock of money, the nation drifted further from the free market
policies Friedman endorsed. The Fed attempted to guide the economy with
countercyclical policies, but unforeseen events—the Korean War and then the
cold war—revealed how difficult it was to devise and time appropriate interventions. In Friedman and Schwartz's history, it took the Fed's failure to make
good on the mandate of the 1946 Employment Act to return policy makers
to their senses. "The result was an increasing shift of emphasis to monetary
policy as a means of promoting 'full employment' and price stability" (596).

The conclusion Freidman and Schwartz drew from the end of the century
they surveyed was paradoxical but clear: "Confidence in the efficacy of monetary policy in the 1950s was inversely related to monetary stability. As that
confidence has grown, it has produced a growing instability in the stock of
money" (638). Only recognizing that the Fed's attempts to guide the economy were flawed, in other words, might lead policy makers to give markets—
including the money market—the freedom they need to thrive and grow.

Given his commitment to anchoring economic analysis in empirical work,
Friedman might have been surprised to discover that, in recent decades, the
Federal Reserve has become a more productive source of economic data than
the NBER, which played that role for much of the twentieth century. Given
his skepticism about the wisdom of the Fed's ability to intervene in markets,
he might have also expressed reservations about the aggressive policies implemented by the Fed in the 2008 crisis. But Friedman would almost certainly

not have been surprised by the increased power the Fed now exercises—not simply at the behest of policy makers alarmed by market volatility but also because of ties to the financial industry, which some economists charge with aiding and abetting a virtually autonomous and all-powerful Federal Reserve system.[71]

We can give a broader context for Friedman's monetarism by noting that it was fiercely debated in the 1960s and 1970s, then reconstructed in the 1980s by New Classical economists, such as Robert Lucas and Thomas Sargent, who departed from the Marshallian partial equilibrium model Friedman endorsed. Monetarism was not defined by an axiomatic set of propositions, however, but by a set of attitudes and technical assumptions shared by monetary economists allied with each other by their common objection to Keynesian stabilization policies. Among these shared assumptions, according to Thomas Mayer and Martin Bronfenbrenner, were "belief in the inherent stability of the private sector," "dislike of government intervention," "a relatively greater concern about inflation than about unemployment compared to other economists," "reliance on small rather than large econometric models," commitment to the quantity theory of money "in the sense of predominance of the impact of monetary factors on nominal income," and a "focus on the price level as a whole rather than on individual prices."[72] As we will see in chapter 10, monetarists also rejected the idea that there was a trade-off between unemployment and inflation, as the Phillips curve implied. Even though New Classical macroeconomists jettisoned Friedman's Marshallian partial equilibrium model in the 1980s, they retained many of the policy implications of Friedman's work.[73]

8.2f. The Celler-Kefauver Act

Friedman's reference to the Employment Act is a salutary reminder that these works were composed in the context of the social and institutional contexts we surveyed at the beginning of this chapter. In addition to the Bretton Woods Agreement, the 1946 Employment Act, and the Fed Accord, a fourth measure had a lasting impact on American finance, although it receives even less attention in most histories of economic thought than do the other three. This was the Celler-Kefauver Act, passed in 1950. This act prohibited companies from monopolizing their industries through the kind of horizontal mergers that had been used before the war.

In chapter 1, we saw that, even though the Sherman Act of 1890 made predatory trade practices, monopolies, and cartels illegal, new corporations were able to form by consolidating existing companies. During the Depression, when all business slowed, corporations tried to stay alive by cutting production and maintaining prices in hopes of earning short-term profits. After World War II, companies began to grow again. In 1950, in an effort to discourage mergers and the resulting centralization of economic activity, Congress passed the Celler-Kefauver Act. Instead of blocking all mergers, however, the act actually encouraged mergers between companies that grew through diversification rather than consolidation. In the wake of the act, the largest companies became more diversified, and this led to a new approach to company management. Instead of managers whose expertise derived from knowledge of specific product lines, the managers of these new companies used knowledge about finance to evaluate and manage parts of the company that had little in common except their ability to generate short-term profit. In this "finance conception of control," short-term gains and high rates of return were paramount, and product lines that did not generate surplus revenue were considered expendable.[74] The reference group for such corporations consisted of other corporations that operated across diverse industries, and the performance metrics were rates of return and stock prices.

Treating the corporation as a collection of assets, managers—who were often trained in finance or accounting—began to use innovative financial techniques such as the leveraged buyout to increase profits and market share.[75] In 1962, an article in *Fortune* signaled the magnitude of the changes that had transformed American corporations during the previous decade: "Top financial officers now have a hand in everything from mergers to budgets to personnel and marketing. They also woo bankers and stock analysts. Because they know more about the company than anyone else, they often move, finally, right into the driver's seat."[76] Financial officers not only moved into the driver's seat of major corporations. As they instituted performance metrics derived from finance, they also helped elevate financial principles like rate of return over the quantity metrics used to measure the output of real commodities. The resulting abstraction of commercial and industrial processes into financial measures was to become one of the hallmarks of the new industries that developed at the end of the twentieth century.

8.2g. From Institutionalism to Keynesianism in US Monetary and Fiscal Policy, 1950–1968

Now that we have surveyed some of the mathematical, empirical, and theoretical tools economists developed to advance their discipline, it is time to turn again to the setting in which economic theories and tools were applied—even though some did not prove as effective as their authors might have hoped and others were not intended for application. Indeed, a long-standing but always evolving split within the discipline of economics between those who favored "applied" work and economists who pursued more "theoretical" projects makes it impossible to link developments within the discipline directly to policies adopted by US legislators. What we can see is that in the 1950s, the federal government institutions staffed primarily by economists—the Council of Economic Advisors, which was established by the 1946 Employment Act, and the Board of the Federal Reserve—were dominated by individuals loosely associated with the institutionalist wing of the discipline, even though they did not use this term to describe themselves (and even when these men were not economists by training).[77] This was true even though, within some of the leading academic economics departments (e.g., the University of Chicago, Harvard, and MIT), the discipline's most prominent scholars worked within the monetarist, Walrasian general equilibrium, or Keynesian traditions. During the entire cold war period, the game theorists and Cowlesmen received abundant resources from government entities such as RAND, but, even though their theoretical insights and mathematical methods were valued by Robert McNamara and other architects of the national security state, these economists did not play prominent roles on the Council of Economic Advisors or the Federal Reserve Board.[78] After the brief reign of institutionalists in Washington, Keynesian economists, many of whom were trained by Alvin Hansen at Harvard and all of whom were versed in Paul Samuelson's 1948 Keynesian textbook, did contribute directly to monetary and fiscal policy. Many followed Gerhard Colm to Washington in the 1960s. Taking up positions in the Kennedy administration, they directly shaped some of the most important legislation of that short-lived administration, including the 1964 Tax Reduction Act. The model these economists used incorporated what proved to be a controversial—and consequential—understanding of the relationship between unemployment and inflation, the Phillips curve.

During the 1950s, most Washington spokesmen for economics belonged to the institutionalist wing of the discipline. We can get a sense of the official influence wielded by the institutionalists in the 1950s and beyond by invoking a few names, many of which no longer appear in undergraduate economics textbooks. Arthur F. Burns, Wesley Clair Mitchell's protégé at the NBER (then co-author of the final volume of Mitchell's work on business cycles), served as director of the NBER under President Truman (1945–53), chair of the Council of Economic Advisors (CEA) under President Eisenhower (1953–56), and

chair of the Federal Reserve under President Nixon (1970–78). Leon Keyserling, a lawyer who also worked on agricultural economics and helped draft
parts of the Social Security Act, served as chair of the CEA under Truman
(1950–53), then founded and headed the Conference on Economic Progress
(1954–87). Raymond J. Saulnier, a Columbia University economist, served as
chair of the CEA under Eisenhower (1956–61), as well as director of the Financial Research Program at the NBER (1946–61). And William McChesney
Martin, whose undergraduate degrees were in English and Latin and who
never earned an economics PhD, served as chair of the Import-Export Bank
(1946–49), before assuming his tenure as chair of the Federal Reserve in 1951.
Martin held this position for longer than any other Fed chairman, serving until 1970 under five US presidents.

We link these individuals to economic institutionalism because of their
commitment to applying empirical data to practical problems and because
they believed that the institutional conditions to which economic policies are
applied evolve over time. When data did not support particular economic
theories, these economists, like other institutionalists, were often willing to
suspend theoretical conclusions or even set theory aside. A good example
of the institutionalists' skepticism about theory-driven programs is their
complicated relationship to Keynesianism. While some endorsed parts of
Keynes's ideas, most were skeptical of Keynesians' simple models and expressed doubts about the models' empirical foundations and the wisdom of
theory-driven deficit spending over the long run.[79] In return, some of the most
prominent American Keynesians chided institutionalists for their apparent
indifference to theory. Paul Samuelson, for example, once quipped that "hostility to economic theory is the only sure badge identifying an Institutionalist,"
and Tjalling Koopmans's fierce attack on the business cycle book by Burns
and Mitchell sparked a rift between institutionalists and Keynesians known
as the "Measurement without Theory" debate.[80] But it is as unfair to say that
all institutionalists spurned theory as it would be to charge every member
of the Cowles Commission with being completely indifferent to data. Like
Thorstein Veblen and John C. Commons, two influential early institutionalists, the institutionalists of the 1950s did hold theoretical convictions; but
their theories emphasized that historical context was more important than
universal economic laws and that economic behavior was shaped by the institutions that cultivated habits and embodied conventions, rather than ema-
nating from an essential human nature. In short, game-theoretical methods
that assumed all economic actors to be rational agents, Keynesian models
that highlighted only a few aggregate variables, and monetarist theories that

emphasized rule-driven monetary policy over discretion made no sense to economists sympathetic to institutionalism. Many of the advanced mathematical techniques and dogmatic theories of the period seemed irrelevant to the economists who most closely advised the president and helped set monetary and fiscal policy at midcentury.

We can see this in William McChesney Martin's response to inflation. As chair of the Fed, Martin was one of the most influential economic advisers of the decade, and as one of the people responsible for realizing the 1946 Employment Act and steering a newly independent Fed, he established a precedent for managing the tension between maintaining "price stability" and promoting "full" employment. Martin called the policy he initiated "lean against the wind" to indicate how the Fed Open Market Committee used short-term interest rate adjustments to counteract unsustainable economic strengths or weaknesses. Martin's Fed engaged in open market purchases only in Treasury bills, thereby allowing long-term bond rates to be set by the market. A rise or fall in these long bond rates would tell the Fed whether markets believed the Fed would consistently implement Martin's stated goal of maintaining price stability. Because he repeatedly upheld his position, Martin was able by 1960 to create an environment in which markets produced the price stability his policy was intended to promote.

Martin's primary goal was to stabilize the price level—to protect "purchasing power," in the language of the 1946 Employment Act; he represented inflation as a "thief in the night" and used worries about inflation to gain support for his policy.[81] In a report to the House Banking and Currency Committee in May 1951, just weeks after taking office, Martin cast his monetary policy in the shadow of the "grave inflationary dangers" most people expected to accompany the conflict on the Korean peninsula. Urging legislators to renew the credit measures instituted by the 1950 Defense Production Act, Martin cited a host of positive developments—"tangible evidences that the availability of bank reserves has been reduced, that banks have become more restrictive in their lending policies, and that the over-all expansion of bank credit has definitely slackened despite acceleration of lending to finance defense production," and that restrictions on consumer credit (like minimum down payments on automobiles, durables, and real estate) had curtailed excessive borrowing. Despite these undeniable gains, Martin concluded that doubling defense spending, as President Truman wanted to do, meant that "the fundamental situation in this country and abroad is still strongly inflationary." Leaning against the inflationary wind he encouraged his audience to feel, Martin persuaded them to see things his way.[82] He successfully managed inflationary pressures throughout most of the decade, using a tight money policy in 1957 and again in 1960 to curtail the first signs of instability in prices, even at the cost of brief recessions.

Martin's monetary policy also expressed a point of view on unemployment—one shared by the decade's fiscal policy makers. Christina D. Romer and David H. Romer have argued that policy makers in the 1950s "believed that inflation began to rise at moderate rates of overall employment . . . [and] that attempting to push the economy above full employment would be self-defeating. . . . Thus, if anything, the 1950s model held that there was a *positive* long-run relationship between inflation and unemployment."[83] With an unemployment rate of 4% in August 1955, one member of the Federal Reserve Open Market Committee (FOMC) described the nation's economic situation as "ebullient" and worried that such frothiness "presses on the comfortable capacity of the economy . . . accordingly, an inflation is inevitable." Economic growth was deemed less important than the stability Martin championed: in 1958, the *Economic Report of the President* declared that "efforts to accelerate growth under these conditions may succeed only in generating inflationary pressures."[84] This affirmed the position expressed in the *Economic Report* of 1956: "As a Nation, we are committed to the principle that our economy of free and competitive enterprise must continue to grow. But we do not wish to realize this objective at the price of inflation, which not only creates inequities, but is likely, sooner or later, to be followed by depression."[85]

Worries about inflation during the mild recession of 1959 helped John F. Kennedy defeat the Republican candidate, Richard M. Nixon, and ushered in a new regime of fiscal policy. With unemployment at 7%, American industry beginning to lose its postwar head of steam, economic rivalry from Germany and Japan, and continued worries about the Communist threat from Russia and China, the "New Economists" of the Kennedy administration faced an array of challenges. William Martin was still chair of the Federal Reserve, and to his customary worries about inflation, he added new concerns about a drain of gold out of the United States and the impact this would have on the value of the US dollar. To discourage the outflow of gold and manage inflation, Martin wanted relatively high interest rates, but Kennedy's new Council of Economic Advisors (James Tobin, Kermet Gordon, and Walter Heller, as chair) had a different plan. Inspired by Keynesian theory and backed by new statistical models that estimated how an increase in employment could bolster the nation's GDP, these economists favored deficit spending and a flexible interest rate. Beginning in 1961, the CEA's economists began to formulate a tax-cut policy that, when implemented in 1964, represented the largest income tax reduction in US history.

The shift realized by the 1964 legislation represented a major turn in the philosophy behind the government's economic actions, as well as its mix of monetary and fiscal policies. Instead of promoting the government withdrawal advocated by Milton Friedman, or emphasizing price stability, monetary restraint, and fiscal prudence, as their predecessors had done, the New Economists promoted government deficit spending and policies that increased consumer demand to reduce unemployment in the short run, with the long-term aim of increasing overall growth. According to the model drawn up by Arthur M. Okun, a staff economist at the CEA, every 1% reduction in unemployment would yield (through direct impacts on the level of production and indirect reductions in the "underemployment" of contracted labor in slack times) a 3% increase in the GDP.[86] The nation's "reasonable and prudent" rate of unemployment, according to the first *Economic Report* published under the new Kennedy administration (in 1962) was 4%, and the tax cut represented the major stimulus for aggregate demand. To replace the fight against inflation with a campaign to control unemployment and enhance growth required economists to find alternative explanations for the bouts of inflation that continued to occur. The 1962 report thus attributed inflation not to excess demand but to the boom in the production of durables and to union and corporate power. The 1966 *Economic Report* blamed increases in food and commodity prices for the inflation of 1965 (when unemployment was 4.5%), and the report of the following year identified the persistent inflation as a sign that the economy was simply growing too fast, not as excessive economic demand. Even though fiscal policy makers insisted that inflation would abate, it continued to rise in the second half of 1967 (when unemployment was 3.9%).[87]

Along with the belief that reducing unemployment to incite growth was more important than price stability, the New Economists of the Kennedy administration believed in a trade-off between unemployment and inflation. The 1967 *Economic Report* stated this clearly: "The economy is now in the range of trade-off between falling unemployment and rising prices." "The choice of the ideal level of utilization is a social judgment that requires a balancing of national goals of high employment and reasonable price stability," the report continued. Even though Martin was still at the helm of the Fed, monetary policy makers were also optimistic about sustainable levels of output and employment, and, while more concerned about inflation than their counterparts at the CEA, as late as 1968, the FOMC agreed that inflation would soon begin to fall.[88]

The Revenue Act of 1964 accomplished what its architects desired: it stimulated consumer spending and reduced the rate of unemployment (to just over 4%). It also immeasurably enhanced the reputation of the discipline of economics, as even critics of Keynesian activism, such as Milton Friedman, had to admit. Through the informal meetings of the so-called Troika (members of the CEA, the Treasury Department, and the Bureau of the Budget), then the Quadriad (the previous three groups plus officials from the Fed), the success of the tax campaign also realigned the balance of economic power in Washington, giving the CEA more clout than it had previously enjoyed. Equally important, the Revenue Act helped convince legislators that the management made possible by macroeconomic modeling could promote the new goal of national growth.[89]

Many of the most important macroeconomic models that supported the Kennedy administration's New American Keynesian policies were created by James Tobin, who was both a member of the CEA and an economist at Yale. In the 1960s, Tobin positioned the tax-cut model in the context of his larger theoretical agenda: the specification of microfoundations for Keynes's theories. As president of the Cowles Foundation, which moved to Yale in 1955, Tobin continued both Alfred A. Cowles III's work on investment theory and Jacob Marschak's work on portfolio selection. We return to Tobin's contributions to investment theory in chapter 9. Here we examine Tobin's account of a model developed to estimate the relationship between monetary policy and financial intermediation, along with his 1981 Nobel Prize speech, for these papers reveal Tobin's theoretical contributions to elaborating the "channels" of finance laid bare by Copeland and Goldsmith.

In an article published in 1963 with William C. Brainard, a former graduate student who became a Yale colleague, Tobin offered a series of models that showed how financial intermediaries affect governmental monetary controls. All variants of the Hicks IS-LM model, the Tobin-Brainard models sought to clarify the "effects of financial intermediation by banks, the consequence of leaving their operation unregulated, and the effects of regulating them in various ways."[90] The models demonstrated that financial intermediation matters to the effectiveness of monetary controls: in some cases, the interrelation of banks and nonfinancial intermediaries and the relationships among regulations and interest rates diminish the impact of monetary controls, but, in all situations, "monetary controls can still be effective" (384). In keeping with the Kennedy tax plan, then, Tobin's models combined support for government management of the financial system (in this case, through monetary controls) with a refusal to use *only* the Fed's monetary controls, unmoored from other fiscal policies and without consideration for other factors. "Increasing the responsiveness of the system to instruments of control may also increase its sensitivity to random exogenous shocks. Furthermore, extension of controls over financial intermediaries and markets involves considerations beyond those of economic stabilization; it also raises questions of equity, allocative efficiency, and the scope of governmental authority" (384).

If Tobin's work in the 1960s anticipated later work on the "bank lending" or "credit channel" dimensions of monetary policy, the models he built in subsequent decades elaborated the interrelations of monetary, financial, *and* fiscal policies.[91] In his 1981 Nobel acceptance speech, Tobin prefaced his remarks with three observations: the macroeconomist's goal was to illuminate "economic interdependence"; his general equilibrium models were not closed but "depend on exogenous parameters including instruments controlled by policy-makers"; and his "alternative framework" built upon but was intended to repair some of the "defects" of the Keynes-Hicks IS-LM model.[92] Tobin acknowledged that the shared aspiration of monetary economists was to identify the "foundations" of people's willingness to choose among and hold financial assets "that make no intrinsic contribution to utility or technology," but he distinguished his work from Robert Lucas's rational expectations models, which emphasized the "optimizing behavior of individual agents," and Milton Friedman's tendency to treat monetary policy as the sole preserve of a central authority, "without clearly describing the operations that implement the policy" (14, 13). We return in a moment to rational expectations theory and the Real-Business Cycle economists, whom Tobin later characterized as "the enemy."[93] Tobin also distinguished his models from Kenneth Arrow's contingent state models, to which we return in chapter 9. Tobin agreed with Arrow that if futures markets and contingent states existed for all commodities, including financial assets, it would be possible to build a general equilibrium model for an entire economy. But the combination of the unique nature of saving and the absence of such markets meant that "financial and capital markets are at their best highly imperfect coordinators of saving and investment."[94] "This failure of coordination is a fundamental source of macro-economic instability," Tobin continued, "and of the opportunity for macro-economic policies of stabilization" (16).

To identify the best stabilization policies—which, in Tobin's account, consisted of monetary, fiscal, and financial policies—he designed models that integrated saving and portfolio decisions, combined the perspectives of stocks and flows, and put time stamps on the various components of financial intermediation and fiscal and monetary policies. His models also estimated the way that the demand for "inside money"—the credit and debt created in the private sector in the process of financial intermediation—affected demand for "outside money"—the high-powered or "base" fiat money created by the central monetary authority (35).[95] While his models were intended to inform government policies originating in the Federal Reserve and the Department of the Treasury, Tobin also noted that the overall "trend" of the financial system was toward a less predictable—and potentially less manageable—pattern of growth: "The trend of the financial system is to enlarge the range of assets that have variable market-determined rates, increasing the leverage of base money supplies and equivalent shocks on market interest rates. This trend makes the Hicksian 'LM' curve more nearly vertical, rendering fiscal policies and other 'IS' shocks less consequential" (36).

Tobin's 1981 lecture shows how components of the financial theories we examined in previous chapters were woven into the Keynesian macroeconomic models that dominated US policy in the 1960s. Tobin's models incorporated insights from Keynes's *General Theory* and John Hicks's 1935 article on money. They drew on the "money view" of the economy associated with Alvin Hansen, Macaulay's work on asset categories, Marschak's work on asset selection, Goldsmith's examination of the channels of finance, and the theoretical account given by Gurley and Shaw of the role inside money plays in the financial system. Tobin's models also relied on the balance-sheet approach made possible by Copeland's flow of funds accounts, and his emphasis on critical accounting balances—e.g., household demand for end-of-period holdings must equal household demand for end-of-period wealth—allowed him to move beyond the flow accounts common to most other macroeconometric models. His theorization of the "wealth effect," along with his development of "Q," as the ratio between a physical asset's market value and its replacement cost, constituted major contributions to economic theory and finance. Indeed, the latter—Q—as the "nexus between financial markets and markets for goods and services"—theorized the link between the real and financial sides of the economy.[96]

While the American Keynesians, with the help of institutionalist bureaucrats, ruled US monetary and fiscal policy in the 1960s, their reign was soon to be ended by a combination of external factors (the oil shocks of the 1970s) and administrative overreach (the attempt to fund both the Vietnam War and Johnson's War on Poverty). We return to these events in chapter 10. Here it is important to acknowledge that at least one American economist sounded warnings about Keynesian overreach even before the Gulf States created OPEC. In 1967, Milton Friedman presented an address to the American

Economic Association that insisted that monetary policies based on models like Tobin's Keynesian macroeconomic models would not be effective in the long run. Friedman made two critical points. First, he argued that the statistical trade-off between unemployment and inflation (the Phillips curve), which was a critical econometric assumption in Keynesian models, described only a short-term phenomenon because it did not factor in either the expectations people form as the government adjusts its monetary policy or the time lag between the implementation of a new policy and the dynamic of expectations. "Let the higher rate of monetary growth produce rising prices, and let the public come to expect that prices will continue to rise. Borrowers will then be willing to pay and lenders will then demand higher interest rates—as Irving Fisher pointed out decades ago. The price expectation effect is slow to develop and also slow to disappear. . . . These subsequent effects explain why every attempt to keep interest rates at a low level has forced the monetary authority to engage in successively larger and larger open market purchases."[97] Friedman's second argument was that the Phillips Curve fails to distinguish between nominal and real values—both nominal and real interest rates and nominal and real wages.

> The monetary authority controls nominal quantities—directly, the quantity of its own liabilities. In principle, it can use this control to peg a nominal quantity—an exchange rate, the price level, the nominal level of national income, the rate of growth of the quantity of money. It cannot use its control over nominal quantities to peg a real quantity—the real rate of interest, the rate of unemployment, the level of real income, or the rate of growth of the real quantity of money. (11).

When models using the Phillips curve failed in the 1970s, American Keynesianism was discredited. As the US economy swooned under the burden of stagflation—the dangerous combination of high inflation and stagnant growth—policy makers turned to a different set of macroeconomic models for guidance. The models they used, however—the dynamic stochastic general equilibrium models—had no place for the dramatic growth in the US financial sector, which had already begun to reshape the American economy.

8.2.h. Neoclassical Growth Theory

In his 1962 Economic Report to Congress, President John F. Kennedy praised the 1946 Employment Act for steering US policy in the 1950s, but he also identified a new goal intended to distinguish his administration from the Truman-Eisenhower years: "the acceleration of economic growth."[98] To achieve the growth rate Kennedy targeted—4.1% per year, or a 50% increase between 1960 and 1970—the United States had joined with the nineteen other members of the Organization for Economic Cooperation and Development (9). Going forward, the president told Congress, fiscal and monetary policy would support not only economic stabilization but also programs designed to accelerate growth. In addition to an investment tax cut and more liberal allowances for depreciation, these policies included increased spending in areas like education and the aerospace program, recently launched by NASA.

The accompanying report issued by the Council of Economic Advisors in 1962 delivered Kennedy's vision in more emphatic terms: "stabilization policy is not enough," the three-person Council declared; while the nation's previous focus on expanding demand was still important, it was now time for "a concerted effort, private and public, to speed the increase of potential output" (108). Lest Americans worry that shifting from policies that promoted demand to those encouraging supply would undermine the nation's well-being, the council assured its readers that "the objectives of stabilization policy and growth policy coalesce." The "capacity to produce is not an end in itself, but an instrument for the satisfaction of needs and the discharge of responsibilities," the council concluded (142).

The shift in emphasis from stabilization to supply signaled the Kennedy administration's openness to theoretical models economists had been developing since the 1930s; these models supported policies that encouraged growth, particularly (although not exclusively) the growth of technology. The accompanying economic theory also constituted an early version of what would resurface in the 1970s as supply-side economics. The variant of growth theory that influenced Kennedy and his economic advisers—Walter W. Heller, Kermit Gordon, and James Tobin—drew most immediately on models developed by Robert Solow in the 1950s. Solow, in turn, was trying to improve upon growth models introduced by Roy Harrod and Evsey Domar in 1939 and 1946, respectively; during the 1950s, Paul Samuelson, James Tobin, and other Keynesian theorists also devised growth models; and from the 1930s through the mid-1950s, as we saw in chapter 6, Wassily Leontief had worked on input-output models designed to depict the growth of various US industries.[99] In the early 1970s, decades of work on growth theory coalesced in what Dale W. Jorgenson hailed as a "rare professional consensus," epitomized by the publication, in 1970, of Solow's *Growth Theory* and, in 1971, of *Economic Growth of Nations* by Simon Kuznets, the architect of national income estimates.[100] Kuznets received the 1971 Nobel Prize for his work on growth theory, and Solow, who had served as Leontief's research assistant at Harvard, was awarded a Nobel Prize for his growth models in 1987.

According to Solow, growth theory "was invented to provide a systematic way to talk about and compare equilibrium paths for the economy" by investigating how technology change is labor-augmenting.[101] It is a method by which growth can be attributed to labor-augmenting technology or the rate of technology progress. While the growth theory of the 1950s was compatible with Keynesian theory—the devoted Keynesians Samuelson and Tobin both worked on growth models—the policy implications of these models departed from Keynesian policies designed to maintain (or restore) steady-state equilibrium. In fact, Solow's growth models constituted an implicit rejection of Keynes's *General Theory* in the sense that they presented the latter as a special theory that pertained only to the very short term. In Solow's view, to achieve growth, policies had to promote deferring current consumption in favor of enjoying a greater level of consumption in the future. As Solow phrased it, "growth theory provides a framework within which one can seriously discuss macroeconomic policies that not only achieve and maintain full employment but also make a deliberate choice between current consumption and future consumption" (Nobel speech). These models constituted a new direction for economic theory: they not only shifted emphasis from demand to supply but also supplemented economists' long-standing interest in short-term economic fluctuations (the business cycle) with a new focus on long-term trends.

The models Solow developed in the 1950s were neoclassical long-term growth models. They assumed full employment and a frictionless, competitive, causal system, and they treated technological change as an exogenous variable. Solow's models broke through the pessimistic implications of the Harrod-Domar models ("the economic system is at best balanced on a knife-edge of equilibrium growth")[102] by relaxing the earlier authors' fixed-proportion assumption. The conclusions Solow reached were that the most important variable in the model was the variation in capital intensity and that "the rate of technological progress in the broadest sense" determines "the permanent rate of growth of output per unit of labor input" (Nobel 3). "The basic conclusion of this analysis," Solow wrote in 1956, is that "the system can adjust to any rate of growth in the labor force, and eventually approach a state of steady proportional expansion" (Nobel Speech, 73).

Solow knew that his models did not solve all the problems involved in moving from short-term fluctuations to long-term trends. He acknowledged that the 1950s variant of growth theory could not figure out how to deal with deviations from the long-term equilibrium path caused by short-term fluctuations, and he knew that the theory of asset pricing implied by his growth model only worked in "tranquil conditions," not the "turbulent conditions" global stock markets experienced in 1987, when the Dow Jones Industrial Index fell 22.6%.[103] The optimism his models encouraged might have seemed justified in 1963, in other words, as John F. Kennedy announced the nation's pivot to growth, but as global equities markets began to grow in the 1970s in ways Solow's models did not predict, new ways of understanding growth—and pricing equities—became felt needs.

CHAPTER 9

Modern Finance

9.1. ORIGINS OF MODERN PORTFOLIO THEORY

The innovations in method, data, theory, modeling, and macroeconometrics we examined in the last chapter were developed within the discipline of economics, even when their creators were not academic economists. Although sometimes quite abstract or based on unrealistic assumptions, all these innovations were directly or indirectly designed to assist policy decisions. As tools for allocating limited resources, the innovations were thus the outward face of economics as theory and practice, even as the discipline experienced significant changes in its theoretical core.

In one sense, modern finance originated within the discipline of economics. In another sense, the roots of finance lay outside every university discipline: traces of finance can be found in business practices as old as exchange itself, in apprenticeships and guilds, in futures markets for agricultural crops, and in schools of commerce and accounting, where business skills were passed along to younger generations.[1] Once housed within universities, economics and finance have had a complicated relationship to each other. To a certain extent, the split between them acquired an institutional dimension from 1970 on: as the latter found a home in business schools, divisions between economists and finance theorists seemed to grow—even though two of the universities that have exercised the greatest influence on both disciplines—MIT and the University of Chicago—are homes to economics departments closely aligned with business schools. Just as economics generates theories that can be used to formulate policy, so finance typically generates products. Whether these products originated in business schools or departments of economics, they are typically used in securities markets, like the ones we surveyed in chapter 4, and, increasingly, in electronic exchanges, where billions of dollars now change hands daily through an enormous range of financial instruments. Taken together, these products, along with the material and theoretical platforms that support them, constitute the core of modern finance.

The idea that finance could be a distinct subfield within the discipline of economics was initially raised in 1940 when a group of interested economists launched the American Finance Association (AFA). Despite this flicker of recognition, however, finance remained at the margins of the interwar discipline: even though the American Economic Association's specification of fourteen subfields included both "public finance" and "private finance," membership in the new society remained "meager," with only twenty-three individuals listed on the organization's first rolls.[2]

In 1970, by contrast, membership in the AFA had grown to over five thousand, the subfield had identified a group of canonical primary texts, and finance and finance-related courses formed a staple of economics and business school curricula.[3] Soon after it was founded, the AFA began to publish its own journal, but publication was interrupted by the war, and the *Journal of Finance* began to appear regularly only in 1946. For the subfield, then, the war was a black box, which made it impossible for most people to see how tools and theories were being refined, applied, and profoundly altered as they were reshaped for wartime deployment. After the war, subscriptions to the journal began to increase and the field became visible to interested readers. The explosive growth of the academic field is only one face of the dramatic rise of finance in the last quarter of the twentieth century. The other is the transformation of investment centers such as Wall Street and London's City, whose firms began to hire freshly minted MBAs and students trained in finance. Long sites of frenetic but often seat-of-the-pants trading, these centers of modern finance gradually morphed into conglomerates of theory-driven, model-dependent, computerized businesses, with refined and carefully delineated investment styles, which both employed and helped train their staffs to market—and engineer—new products for an ever-growing population of institutional and private investors.

9.1a. Hedging

Even though a few scholars, most notably Franck Jovanovic, have noted the relationship between modern finance and agricultural economics—no one has explored the complex relationship between these fields in the first decades of the twentieth century.[4] The complexities of this relationship reflect the lag between the concerns of the two fields. On the one hand, because the futures market has always played an important role in the economics of crop production, agricultural economists repeatedly addressed financial topics such as speculative prices, which was to become central to modern portfolio theory. On the other hand, because there was no futures market in financial contracts before 1972—no formal exchange on which an investor could speculate on currency futures, for example—futures occupied only a marginal place in the syllabi of finance courses before the mid-1970s. As Richard Whitley has shown, these courses tended to focus on "institutional arrangements, legal structures, and long-term financing of companies and investment projects."[5] They tended to be practical, teach rule-of-thumb approaches to taxation, prices, insurance, and accounting, and limit discussion of "investments" to topics like liquidity and pension funding. In his survey of the articles published in the *Journal of Finance,* Peter L. Bernstein reports finding only five articles that "could be classified as theoretical rather than descriptive" and that contained any mathematics at all.[6]

In 1962, Holbrook Working, an agricultural economist recently retired from the Food Research Institute at Stanford, published an overview of agricultural economists' achievements during the previous forty years.[7] Working emphasized six of the breakthroughs agricultural economists had made, five of which were critical to the transformation of finance. First, in response to the robust data collection generated by the Grain Futures Administration, founded in 1922, economists like J. W. T. Duvel rethought the function of commodity futures markets. Instead of viewing such markets as sites where ownership is transferred, Duvel argued that futures markets "exist chiefly to facilitate the holding of contracts." Paradoxically, emphasizing that futures are contractual *claims held open* until they are settled by financial transfers made commodity futures a prototype for the *financial* dimension of all futures and for the *contractual* nature of all specifically financial claims. To explore how open contracts functioned in these markets, Duvel and his colleagues introduced new terminology—"long position," "short position," "long hedging," and "short hedging." Adopting the open-contract concept then led to new quantitative research on hedging, an activity that could not be measured as long as statisticians only tracked actual trades.[8]

Statistical and theoretical reconsiderations of hedging led to the second innovation introduced by agricultural economists: the hedging-market concept. Instead of viewing futures markets as speculative markets and hedging as a "fortunate by-product" of speculation, H. S. Irwin, a staff member at the

Grain Futures Administration, tracked the net amount of hedging in the butter and egg futures markets to show that the incentive to form futures markets came not from speculators but from hedgers. According to Working, this led Irwin to argue that "futures markets ought not to be regarded as primarily speculative, but as primarily hedging markets" and that long hedging "creates a need for short speculation." By reversing the priority of speculation and hedging, Irwin demonstrated the payoff of considering hedging on its own terms, as a discrete kind of investment strategy, and he also rehabilitated the concept of speculation, which had long suffered from proximity to gambling.[9]

Once agricultural economists began to investigate hedging, they could see it involved more than simply avoiding risk. Indeed, they argued, hedging performed numerous functions: it could be undertaken to assure profits, to anticipate profits in price relations (not simply in price changes), to simplify business decisions, to avoid loss (rather than simply avoid risk), to take advantage of current prices (in anticipation of future price changes), or to offset an expected loss. All these functions highlight two components of hedging: the expertise, or "special knowledge," the successful hedger needed to possess; and the comparative decisions, or "choice made between alternatives," such knowledge allowed him to make. The first was to prove critical to theories of modern finance because the combination of *information* and *expectations* was considered fundamental to market behavior. The second dovetails with not only game-theoretic paradigms, which always emphasized decisions and choice, but also the weighing of alternatives in terms of relative benefits, which was the bedrock of rationality postulates and asset allocation.

The fourth contribution of agricultural economists, in Working's account, elaborated the *relational* component of different economic factors—in this case, the relationship between spot and futures prices. Whereas economists had long argued that there was no necessary relationship between spot prices, which depend on the present abundance or scarcity of some commodity, and futures prices, which depend on a subsequent harvest, beginning in 1933 agricultural economists demonstrated that this relationship did exhibit regularity. "What happens in fact is that any change in price of a distant, new-crop, wheat-future tends to be accompanied by an equal change in prices paid for wheat from currently available supplies" (443). This relationship existed because of buyers' expectations about future prices, even when the commodities in question could be stored and even when the future was quite distant. This means, in turn, that even in the case of commodities, which are tangible and disappear once consumed, consumers' ideas about the future profoundly influence monetary value in the present. When viewed from the perspective of the futures market, commodities resemble financial claims more than economists had previously imagined.

The agricultural-economic breakthrough with the most obvious relationship to theories now associated with modern finance elaborated the roles played by information and expectations on the idea Louis Bachelier hit upon in 1900—the idea that securities prices change randomly, or follow a random walk. In Working's account, the random walk only acquired economic meaning once its relationship to the "perfect futures market" was understood. Working did not mention Paul A. Samuelson, one of the economists who discovered Bachelier's work; in his account, agricultural economists took the lead because they had experience with the futures market.

> When attention was drawn to that characteristic of certain prices, about a quarter of a century ago, the discovery aroused no comment and apparently no lasting interest on the part of either statisticians or economists. It was a factual observation that carried no economic meaning, even to people who understood the technical distinction between random variation and random walk. But presently the economic meaning of the discovery was found: Pure random walk in a futures price is the price behavior that would result from perfect functioning of a futures market, the perfect futures market being defined as one in which the market price would constitute at all times the best estimate that could be made from currently available information of what the price would be at the delivery date of the futures contract. (446)

According to Working, this insight led agricultural economists to devise "the economic concept that futures prices are *reliably* anticipatory; that is, they represent close approximations to the best possible current appraisals of prospects for the future" (447).

As Working elaborated the concept of "random walk" in the context of commodities futures, he highlighted features of this concept implied, but not always detailed, in accounts by other economists. For example, citing a paper by Alfred Cowles III and H. E. Jones, Working noted that "randomness of walk in a statistical series is not a specific characteristic detectable by any one specific test, but a term that designates absence of any systematic characteristic—absence of any sort of 'structure'" (447). Working pointed out that the most common kinds of "structure" found in futures and stock prices are trends and cycles, but in discussing both the absence of structure in the random walk and the "secondary sort of structure" revealed in phenomena like the dispersal of correlation (448), he also implied that, for some kinds of analysis—such as the analysis of speculative or anticipatory prices in conditions of uncertainty—it was necessary to *impose* structure on statistical series to make theoretical sense of them and rationally select securities with uncertain risks and returns. As he grappled with the inadequacy of the available concepts and data—"the concept that futures prices are reliably anticipatory, in the full sense of that term, evidently does not correspond wholly to the facts"—Working acknowledged the critical role modeling played in situations of this complexity. The concept of reliably anticipatory futures prices "avoids the gross misrepresentation involved in the concept that the variations in futures prices are in large part unwarranted, wave-like fluctuations; and its own misrepresentation is of a sort that is inevitable in a concept that, for the sake of simplicity, must fall short of representing the full facts" (449).

In presenting "speculative prices" as "anticipatory prices" and speculative risk as hedging, which could perform one of several functions, Working helped erase the pejorative connotations of risk taking and rendered the management of risk a central component of good business. These theoretical revisions anticipated the reevaluation of speculative prices that occurred in finance—a reevaluation used to justify trading in financial futures during the 1970s. As the concepts introduced by agricultural economists were adapted during the next two decades, they helped theorists make the transfer of risk central to transactions on the financial side of the economy and identify expectations and information as the critical components of such transfers.

9.1b. Correlation Analysis and Diversification

Most scholars identify the publication of Harry Markowitz's 1952 "Portfolio Selection" as the singular origin of modern financial theory.[10] In our account, Markowitz's article was not so much the beginning of something new as a logical extension of the mean/variance choice revolution launched by J. R. Hicks in 1935, extended by Helen Makower and Jacob Marschak in 1938, and augmented by the linear programming method described by Koopmans, Dantzig, and Wood in 1949. Nor was Markowitz's treatment of the portfolio problem the only mean/variance approach to portfolio selection published in 1952. That same year, A. D. Roy, who was studying Harald Cramér's *Mathematical Methods of Statistics* (1946), applied Cramér's approach to a theory of holding assets—not specifically portfolios of securities but assets in general, which could include financial assets. Roy showed how Cramér's actuarial technique of computing a mean and a standard deviation for the mathematical expectation of a loss could be generalized as a "safety-first" criterion for holding a portfolio of risky assets. Roy produced the safety-first criterion by combining computations of the mathematical expectation for the return of the asset and the return's expected variance with an analysis of the correlation among the assets the investor held.[11]

The critical idea in both Markowitz's theory of relative risk and Roy's safety-first criterion was the insight that correlation analysis held the key to portfolio diversification. In previous chapters, we have seen that Henry L. Moore, Alfred Cowles III, and Jan Tinbergen all used correlation analysis, and we have also seen that Irving Fisher, David Dodd, and Benjamin Graham advocated diversification. But it was only when correlation techniques were applied to the theory of holding assets, or portfolio selection, that a mathematical theory of diversification and a relative measure of risk became available. Applying the mathematics of correlation to the statistical facts of asset prices, Roy and Markowitz were both able to see that the expected returns from the assets held in a portfolio are additive—the overall return is attributable to each asset weighted proportionally to its representation in the portfolio—but the variance of the portfolio and its standard deviation, or risk, is *not* additive because noncorrelated assets go up and down in different patterns. If some securities prices are going up while others are going down, the combined volatility of the portfolio is less than the weighted average of the sum of volatilities of all securities. To the extent that individual security movements are independent of each other—potentially because they are influenced by different external factors—the fluctuations in price, and therefore the returns, form a protective shield of diversification. The benefits of this show up over time because of the magic of compounding: in the case of two portfolios characterized by the same expected return but different volatilities, the less volatile portfolio will generate wealth more rapidly than its more volatile counterpart.

The 1952 articles by Markowitz and Roy gave more specificity to the distinction Frank H. Knight introduced in 1921—between statistically measurable (thus insurable) risk and uncertainty, which was an effect of unknowable factors. These articles also moved beyond Benjamin Graham and David Dodd's characterization of risk in absolute terms, Irving Fisher's judgment that risk is "unadapted to mathematical formulation," and John Burr Williams's present-value treatment of returns.[12] We should note that, to reach his conclusion, Markowitz simply set aside what he defined as the first phase of portfolio selection, the process by which an investor forms "beliefs about the future performances of available securities," and highlighted instead the second phase, in which the investor moves from beliefs to rational choices.[13] Markowitz thus set aside the questions of how investors make decisions, form expectations, and develop their specific tolerances for risk, but he was able to show that diversification of "the right kind" could decrease variance (movement around the mean) and thus increase a portfolio's overall returns: if the selected stocks are not correlated with each other, the optimal relation of the expected risk/return ratios of all stocks in the portfolio, calculated in relation to each other, constitutes the most "efficient" portfolio.

Two additional applications of linear programming soon supplemented and simplified the labor-intensive method Markowitz described.[14] The first was formulated in 1958 by James Tobin, whose work with W. C. Brainard we discussed in chapter 8. While there are some continuities between Tobin's contributions to the analysis of financial intermediation and his portfolio analysis, the two bodies of work have different emphases. Tobin's financial theory largely dealt with the selection of a portfolio of assets. In "Liquidity Preference as Behavior toward Risk," Tobin introduced the "separation theorem," which generalized the available asset classes, presenting them simply as cash or not-cash. The former is riskless, and the latter carries risk. Tobin's riskless assets, which he presented as "marketable, fixed in monetary value, [and] free of default risk," can be represented by government-issued treasury bills but are generally simply referred to as "money." The advantage of Tobin's simplification was that it proved that the investor's risk tolerance and wealth did not affect the investment manager's choice of the liquidity ratio, which was independent of the basket of risky assets assembled into the portfolio. Tobin also extended Markowitz's model for establishing the relationship between risk and reward to portfolios that contain securities and money. Tobin's theory about the special relationship between riskless and risky assets also shed light on the behavioral foundations of Keynes's "liquidity preference"—that is, it helped Tobin explain why investors hold money, even though cash earns no interest.

Along with Markowitz's portfolio theory, Tobin's separation theorem was used to endorse money market funds, the first of which was introduced in 1971. Money market funds provided a way to skirt the restrictions of the Depression-era Regulation Q, which prohibited banks from paying interest on demand deposits. Regulated by the Securities and Exchange Commission, money market mutual funds limit the investor's risk of loss due to credit, market, or liquidity risk, and, typically, they have been safe ways for investors to hold money, for they seek to maintain a stable $1 per share payoff.

Two book-length treatments helped make portfolio theory part of the finance curriculum and, before long, easier for investors to use. Harry Markowitz's

1959 *Portfolio Selection* expanded his 1952 paper and provided accounts of the assumptions that underwrote his brief article. In a section entitled "Rational Choice under Uncertainty," Markowitz summarized many of the theories and techniques we have already encountered: the concepts of information and choice developed in game theory and statistical decision theory, the computing procedures associated with linear programming and activity analysis, the idea of the "rational man," the notion of the "expected utility maxim," and Bayesian (or "personal") probability distributions and preferences. Markowitz used set theory and provided three axioms of rational behavior, expressed in set-theoretic language. He used vector notation, stylized wheels, matrices, and schematic diagrams to represent the combinations available to the decision maker. But, while he mentioned Leonard Jimmie Savage by name once in his text and even though his bibliography included a few works by von Neumann and Morgenstern and Marschak, Markowitz did not discuss any of these works in detail. We make this point not to impugn Markowitz's forthrightness, but to underscore that, as portfolio theory was accepted, it came to seem less and less important to understand its origins or how ideas and methods emerged victorious from earlier disputes. By now, generations of students in the field of finance have read Markowitz's 1959 book, where the assumptions that inform portfolio theory were naturalized and purged of their military lineage. By this time, too, the investment strategies implied by portfolio theory have been used by countless investment advisers to help both individual and institutional investors construct "efficient" portfolios.

9.1c. Subjective Probability Theory

In the early 1950s, most economists interested in financial topics were beginning to reach consensus about at least one foundational assumption. After the publication of *Theory of Games and Economic Behavior,* they generally agreed that the idea that choice is based on utility should no longer be anchored in the nineteenth-century idea of marginal utility but in an epistemology of axiomized rationality. The rationality postulates introduced by von Neumann and Morgenstern, then extended by Marschak, were based on a frequentist framework and objective probability distributions, but, as we saw in chapter 8, by the 1950s, the frequentist approach to statistics was being supplemented by a subjective approach to probability formulated by statistical theorists such as Leonard Jimmie Savage, a statistician at the University of Chicago, and Howard Raiffa and Robert Schlaiffer, managerial economists at Harvard. These theorists formulated a subjective or Bayesian approach to expectations and the probability distributions understood to describe the future outcomes of the choices made on this basis. This approach to probability, which was to give a distinctive character to portfolio theory, distinguishes this phase of the probabilistic revolution in modern finance.

Because probability is so central to modern financial theory and practice—and such a complicated subject in its own right—a brief reprise of statistical approaches will help clarify the importance of the Bayesian view. The "classical" approach to probability is anchored in games like dice or choosing balls from an urn, where the probability distributions are assumed to be normal or Gaussian. The second, "frequentist" approach is based on repeated experiments, like those carried out by R. A. Fisher, and distributions, while not always Gaussian, are normally assumed to conform to the Bell curve. The Bayesian approach, by contrast, is founded on the assumption that the agent's choices are informed by subjective expectations about the future, which are, in turn, informed by experience. This means, among other things, that as an individual's experiences change, so do his expectations. The Bayesian approach to probability thus adds a performative component to the understanding of probability, for, as expectations are affected by experience, the agent begins to make decisions based on expectations about what will happen in the future—even though past, present, and future are not necessarily linked causally. In the Bayesian approach to probability, one cannot assume that distributions will be Gaussian in shape. Finding probability distributions that conformed to various expectation-informed decision processes was one of the most challenging aspects of implementing the Bayesian approach.

Influenced by the Italian probabilist Bruno de Finetti, Savage developed the theoretical rationale implicit in this approach in *The Foundations of Statistics* (1954). Savage carried over the von Neumann-Morgenstern idea that choice should be understood as the mathematical expectation about the outcome of a wager, but he based the value assigned to the wager—the amount the individual was willing to risk—on the individual's subjective degree of conviction about the likelihood of the best outcome; the agent reached this degree of conviction after weighing probabilities, either formally or informally. Both the von Neumann-Morgenstern frequentist notion of expected utility and Savage's Bayesian decision theory are used today, depending on the application.

Adding the Bayesian approach to probability and the decision theory that followed from it to the concepts and tools we surveyed in the last section meant that most of the platform of modern finance was in place by the mid-1950s. But it was still necessary to put some version of uncertainty and risk into financial theory and practice. In simplest terms, both uncertainty and risk were subsumed into stochasticity, or randomness. Efforts to conceptualize stochasticity appeared in several different research projects, which were only indirectly or intermittently concerned with finance. We have already examined the contribution made to modern finance by agricultural economists' treatment of hedging against price risk. We now return to game theory and linear programming, which, as we saw in chapter 8, were developed within the interdisciplinary wartime collaboration of operations research.

9.1d. Linear Programming and Finance

In chapter 8, section 8.1d, we showed how theories and methods developed in operations research were transferred, after the war, to nonmilitary logistical problems involving the allocation and optimization of resources. In the 1949 Activity Analysis conference, Tjalling Koopmans, George Dantzig, and Marshall Wood introduced linear programming and detailed a number of applications for which the method was suited—including transportation and resource allocation problems. Dantzig and Wood defined "programming, or program planning," as "the construction of a schedule of actions by means of which an economy, organization, or other complex entity may move from one defined state to another, or from a defined state toward some specifically defined objectives."[15] Harry Markowitz had studied with Koopmans at the University of Chicago and worked with Dantzig at the RAND Corporation, and his 1952 article applied linear programming to investment. In this context, the "complex of activities" linear programming addressed consisted of the selections an investor makes from all available securities, and the "specifically defined objective" involved the construction of an "efficient" portfolio that achieves the investor's desired ratio of return to risk. Markowitz's influential article thus provided both a theoretical statement of how risk could be incorporated into modern finance and a set of principles to guide financial advisers and institutional investors. Investment analysts now routinely use software programs that rely on Markowitz's portfolio selection principles to construct portfolios for clients, and more than one investment adviser has presented Markowitz's "efficient frontier" as graphical proof that the recommended portfolio offers the highest expected return for the client's tolerance for risk.

9.1e. Competitive Equilibrium Theory

Another research project critical to modern finance—the modern version of general equilibrium theory—was inaugurated in Vienna in the 1920s, in Karl

Menger's Mathematical Colloquium. There, the mathematicians Abraham Wald and John von Neumann introduced but failed to complete the challenge of modeling competitive equilibrium in uncertain conditions. Three decades were to pass before a conceptual device was introduced to solve this problem. Kenneth Arrow's contingent commodity—a contingent claim on a future state of the world—provided a theoretical solution to the general equilibrium problem by making it possible to include in the model not only goods that are priced in the present but also free goods and those whose future price is unknown. Arrow further theorized that the cost of betting on a future state—whether an event would occur or not—can be considered the price of risk. As we saw in chapter 8, it was the absence of actual markets for such contingent claims that led John Maynard Keynes and James Tobin to consider disequilibrium a natural state of the economy and to target the inefficiencies of financial intermediaries as a promising site for macroeconomic intervention.

The tools introduced in largely German-speaking prewar contexts such as the Vienna Mathematical Colloquium included von Neumann's higher algebra (the topological properties of convex cones), von Neumann's and Morgenstern's game theory, Wald's sequential decision theory, the significance tests developed by Jerzy Neyman and Egon Pearson, and (during World War II) Dantzig's linear programming techniques. These tools generalized the real numbers used in the price system as points in a choice space bounded by the geometrics of a cone in a hyperplane. In this very abstract space, the coordinates provided by J. Willard Gibbs's matrix and vector notation were dematerialized. In the interior of a topological space geometrically represented by a cone, convex and concave planes tracing utility and indifference curves converge at vanishing points known as the Nash or Brouwer "fixed points." According to their own account, economists like Koopmans and Arrow used set theory, combinatorics, and game theory instead of the traditional mathematics of calculus because the derivative applied in calculus cannot produce equilibrium solutions in welfare economics, which seeks to distribute resources optimally, or in general equilibrium theory, where countless unlike factors occur. The Newtonian derivative, which had been used to model equilibrium ever since the work of Antoine Cournot in the 1830s, can only value real commodities using positive numbers. Deterministic calculus cannot accommodate commodities that are not traded (zero quantities) or free goods (zero prices). But when offered a basket of commodities, a consumer needs to be able to express preference by choosing some quantity of some goods and none of others, and, sometimes, by substituting a free good for one that is priced. Because traditional calculus cannot differentiate zero or a negative number, the concept of marginal utility cannot adequately model general equilibrium.

Arrow's breakthrough led to contingent state pricing theory, an alternative to the mean/variance approach to risk we discussed in the work of J. R. Hicks and Jacob Marschak. Arrow's work, which he initially presented in Paris in 1952, drew on his discussions with Marschak and Leonard Jimmie Savage and used the tools we have just described (as well as what he had learned from the logician Alfred Tarsky, Arrow's undergraduate teacher) to propose what are known as "corner solutions." Ross M. Starr, an equilibrium theorist and student of Arrow at Stanford University, explains the problem Arrow addressed: "It is rare to find that all quantities of all possible goods and all possible inputs are used in strictly positive quantities. . . . There must be a welfare economics that includes corner solutions; it must be possible to present welfare economics without the calculus."[16] In the process of trying to model economic equilibrium without calculus—a project already underway in the paper Arrow delivered at the 1949 Activity Analysis conference—Arrow was led to formulate the concepts of the contingent claim and the Arrow Security.[17] The latter is a simple model of an instrument used to trade contingent claims on a future commodity, defined by a future state of the world. Arrow's theoretical breakthrough made general equilibrium theory more robust by specifying commodities not only by time, as J. R. Hicks had done, but also by "state."

In 1964, Arrow introduced the contingent commodity to the English-speaking world in "The Role of Securities in the Optimal Allocation of Risk-Bearing."[18] He hypothesized that equilibrium could be achieved in a competitive economy if every kind of commodity—including future commodities conceptualized on a contingent state preference basis—was included. Arrow used Savage's Bayesian approach to probability and the concept of trading contingent claims based on "states of nature" formulated by the Russian probabilist A. N. Kolmogorov.[19] To make such contingent claims imaginable, he developed the Arrow Security (or the Arrow-Debreu Security), as the simplest form a claim can take; it can be scaled up in various sized "bundles"; and, in its most "elementary" form, it characterizes risk at the most basic level: either an event will occur or it will not. Using this simple idea of an instrument by which investors can trade contingent risks, Arrow and the French economist Gérard Debreu went on to prove the existence of general equilibrium without recourse to calculus. Their representation of risk also provided the theoretical rationale for securitizing all kinds of claims and "events" that previously could not be traded on markets. In terms of financial products, the legacy of Arrow's contingent claims theory included the previously unimaginable range of new instruments made possible through securitization.[20] Arrow's state-preference theory was also to become essential to pricing all kinds of derivative claims.

9.2. THE YEARS OF HIGH THEORY

If the 1950s saw the platform of modern finance constructed from the disparate pieces we have just examined, the next two decades constituted a period of both theoretical consolidation and practical implantation, as products designed to put financial theory to work in securities markets proliferated. Against the backdrop of the Kennedy and Johnson administrations, as Keynesian New Economists' hopes that macroeconomic models could manage the nation's economy soared, then collapsed, theorists of finance constructed models and products designed to make money in the increasingly arcane world of securities trading. In the second half of the 1960s and 1970s, the real side of the American economy might have seemed headed for hell in a hand basket, but the financial side was finally coming into its own.

9.2a. The Capital Asset Pricing Model

In two articles, published in 1963 and 1964, the Stanford University economist William F. Sharpe introduced a technique that could compare the mean/variance ratio of a single security to the overall market. This technique, one of the most influential applications of portfolio theory, allowed the investment manager to focus on the risk a new asset would contribute to the investor's portfolio instead of needing to create a covariance matrix with the same number of factors as there were assets in the portfolio. The resulting model, the Capital Asset Pricing Model, or CAPM, uses a simple measure, later called beta, to show how much a security's return is explained by the level of the market.[21] Drawing a simple graph with axes for risk and return, Sharpe showed that, as prices adjust to changing demand, they yield a linear set of intersecting points—a straight line—which he called the "capital market line." Any portfolio with a risk/return ratio intersecting this line was considered an "efficient" (optimal) portfolio, and the linear line was held to be the "efficient frontier." Markowitz had also identified this line, but the more complicated method he used made finding it difficult for investment analysts. Sharpe's model shed light on the price of a security and the various components of its overall risk and on the return requirements of its risks, which could be eliminated by diversification. Sharpe assumed that the market portfolio contained all available securities, weighted by their relative capitalization and priced "efficiently"—or according to the risk of each security. He also assumed that all investors have the same information and that the market is "perfect"—that is, one in which trading involves no transaction costs or taxes, no trader can influence prices, assets can be traded in infinitely divisible amounts without penalty, and all traders are "rational" in wanting to maximize their utility. Given these assumptions, in considering whether to add a particular security to his portfolio, the investor was advised simply to consider the relationship between the risk/return ratio of the particular asset and that of the market portfolio. If the target asset rose and fell along with the market portfolio, they shared what Sharpe called "systematic risk." He initially called the fluctuations of the target asset that did not correspond to the movements of the market portfolio its "unsystematic risk"; later, this became known as the asset's "specific risk." While systematic risk cannot be diversified away, "diversification enables the investor to escape all but the risk resulting from swings in economic activity."[22] In later papers, Sharpe showed how to move from estimates of these different components of risk to the weights that optimize the portfolio's overall ratio of risk to return. The expected return of an optimal portfolio is based on the risk-free rate of return, typically represented in the United States by a Treasury bill, plus a risk premium based on the market variance.

9.2b. The Mathematics of Random Processes

As we have seen, probability theory played critical roles in various stages of the development of statistics, mathematics, game theory, and finance. As one way of engaging uncertainty, probability theory inevitably touches upon, even if it does not explicitly engage with, the problem of information, for as soon as one moves beyond the naïve notion that information is the sum total of data circulating in a given context, it becomes necessary to theorize how what counts as information is available and how it can be accessed. (The problem of information might well include the vast realm of what can*not* be known, but, in practice, theorists of information have rarely ventured into unknowable unknowns.)[23] Probability distributions provide one way of addressing this problem, but deciding the nature of the probability distribution within which data points and densities can be assumed to fall remained a challenge to economic and financial theorists alike. Coming to terms with this challenge was one of the most important contributions of modern finance's years of high theory.

Two early twentieth-century contributions to the mathematical theory of probability were particularly important for the reconceptualization of information. In 1903, in his PhD thesis, the Swedish actuary Filip Lundberg recognized that the standard Gaussian distribution did not obtain for some kinds of actuarial risk, especially reinsurance and collective risks.[24] While Lundberg's work was not immediately taken up, its implications were eventually developed by the Swedish mathematician and actuary Harald Cramér and by William Feller, a German émigré who taught mathematical statistics and probability theory in several US universities. Together, these theorists reconceptualized the Poisson distribution and introduced the concept of the central limit theorem, which provides approximate results for this distribution.

A second PhD thesis, also written early in the century but neglected for several decades, provided another critical component for the understanding of information central to modern finance. In a 1900 thesis to which we have already referred, Louis Bachelier, a student of the French mathematician Henri Poincaré, applied probability theory to the data available for options prices on the French bourse. Bachelier demonstrated that the prices of options closely resembled the distribution known as Brownian.[25] Brownian motion describes the "random walk" by which successive movements of an object or price "wander" away from its starting point. As the agricultural economist Holbrook Working noted in 1962, economists had long been aware that some phenomena exhibited such random steps, but until Bachelier's thesis was rediscovered in the 1960s, it was not obvious that these random movements could be mapped to a mathematically formalizable probability distribution. Indeed, the full significance of the random walk hypothesis could only be grasped when digital computers made it possible to empirically test Bachelier's mathematical formulations. Such testing began in the mid-1960s at the University of Chicago, when Merrill Lynch began to fund the computer analysis of stock prices at the Center for Research on Stock Prices (CRSP).

In 1964, Paul H. Cootner, a professor at the MIT Sloan School of Management, included a translation of Bachelier's thesis in *The Random Character of Stock Market Prices*. As Cootner's title suggests, the volume emphasized the importance of the random walk hypothesis for specifically financial applications, but the writers represented in the collection were not all specialists in financial theory or practice. In his introductory remarks, Cootner acknowledged that the topic might seem "rather narrow," but he defended focusing on the price formation of securities as a prime example of the theory of stochastic processes—in other words, as a study in the statistical analysis of randomness, which is how he understood uncertainty.[26] Cootner also explained the principles—or "rationality"—behind the random walk model. The basic proposition depends on a characteristic of competition in perfect markets: the idea that participants in such a market

> will eliminate any profits above the bare minimum required to induce them to continue in the market, except for any profits which might accrue to someone who can exercise some degree of market monopoly. . . . We should not expect, in such a market, that traders could continue to profit from the use of a formula depending only upon past price data and generally available rules of "technical analysis." If this is so, all changes in prices should be independent of any past history about a company which is generally available to the trading public. . . . It is from this concept of stock prices having independent increments that the idea of stock prices having a "random walk" arises. (3)

Cootner's explanation made the collection's affront to the profession of stock forecasters clear: no "chartists" or "technical" analysts can hope to outperform the market if stock prices fluctuate randomly. It also alluded to, without elaborating, two critical attributes of well-functioning securities (and commodities) markets: equity or fairness to both buyer and seller, which is a function of the 50/50 chance that each price change will go up (down) in the next interval; and the absence of persistent arbitrage opportunities, which follows from the eagerness of traders to take advantage of any such opportunity that arises. The former—fairness—can also be mathematically formulated as or attributed to the presence of the martingale property; the latter—no arbitrage—can be formulated as the presence of a convergence property in a security's prices over time, as those prices approach the mathematical expectation of its intrinsic value. A stochastic model of a speculative security has to take into account both the trading interval and the investment horizon; equity is measured over small intervals, like the trading day, the trading hour, or the trading tick; while the market's rationality is measured by the presence or absence of arbitrage opportunities over longer intervals.

Even though the information (statistical description) provided by the probability distribution of Brownian motion can provide objective probabilities for price movements over short intervals, it was not self-evident that returns over a longer period of time, such as the holding period required for the expiration of a warrant or option, conformed to this distribution. In 1963, the Polish-born mathematician Benoit Mandelbrot tested both the long-standing assumption that the distribution for such returns was Gaussian and the newer idea that it was Brownian. Using an IBM computer to track the US Department of Agriculture's records of changes in spot prices for cotton between 1815 and 1940, Mandelbrot demonstrated that neither Gaussian nor Brownian patterns described these changes, which were too "peaked" to conform to either distribution. Mandelbrot proposed analyzing speculative prices with another family of probability laws, which he referred to as a "stable Paretian" distribution.[27] This distribution contains "jumps," in which a stock's price suddenly changes dramatically, either up or down.

At almost the same time that Cootner's volume introduced the random walk hypothesis, but too late for inclusion in the volume, Harvard economist Paul A. Samuelson also invoked the random walk. He did so deductively, using an a priori model of stochastic speculative prices. In "Proof that Properly Anticipated Prices Fluctuate Randomly," Samuelson posited a "rather general stochastic model of price change" to deduce "a fairly sweeping theorem in which next-period's price differences are shown to be uncorrelated with (if not completely independent of) previous period's price differences."[28] Samuelson's article is noteworthy for at least two reasons. First, like mathematical probabilists influenced by A. N. Kolmogorov, Samuelson used an axiomatic approach: his fundamental axioms were that the expected price for a security is subject to a probability distribution and that a "fair game" could be assumed to exist if the mathematical property of a martingale were present. Second, Samuelson's approach required him to leave unspecified or simply posit a number of characteristics of speculative stock behavior. These include whether the price change series is stationary, whether it forms a Markov process, whether the relevant probability distribution is Gaussian or some other distribution, and whether a recognizable pattern will emerge in the time path of the security's price.[29] Each of these issues set an agenda for future work on security prices, but the major implication of Samuelson's paper, as of Cootner's collection, was that "there is no way of making an expected profit by extrapolating past changes in the futures price."

Two further formulations of the random walk model were published in 1965, this time by University of Chicago's Eugene Fama. Fama's "Random Walks in Stock Market Prices" and "The Behavior of Stock Prices" introduced a phrase his contemporaries had begun to take for granted: the "efficient market." Not every financial theorist agreed that the so-called efficient-market hypothesis was identical to the random walk model, but Fama's phrase captured for many what was beginning to seem like a truism about the securities market when it was viewed probabilistically—that is, as operating in conditions of uncertainty.[30] Fama defined the assumptions inherent in this truism in the less technical "Random Walks": "an 'efficient' market is defined as a market where there are a large number of rational, profit-maximizers actively competing, with each trying to predict future market values of individual securities, and where important current information is almost freely available to all participants."[31] While many of these assumptions would be qualified or relaxed in subsequent decades, Fama's formulation neatly captures what was gradually being accepted as the essence of the transformed discipline of finance: efficient-market participants are "rational profit-maximizers"; the market is competitive and sets prices by an equilibrium process; uncertainty, almost always conceptualized as "risk,"[32] mandates making decisions on the basis of expectations; information is "almost freely available" to everyone; and, by implication, the combination of equity and the market's tendency to eliminate arbitrage opportunities means that "the actions of many competing participants should cause the actual price of a security to wander randomly about its intrinsic value" (56).

Unlike Samuelson, who deduced the random walk theorem, Fama wanted to test it empirically, and he devoted much of his career to developing adequate tests. In these two papers, the primary targets of his tests were the claims of Wall Street analysts that they could outperform the market, by either chartist techniques or some other form of analysis. Like Alfred Cowles III and Paul Cootner, Fama demonstrated the emptiness of such claims. Indeed, more explicitly than Cowles or Cootner, Fama emphasized the performative effects of what Benjamin Graham and David Dodd celebrated as fundamental analysis. "The existence of many sophisticated analysts helps make the market more efficient which in turn implies a market which conforms more closely to the random walk model. Although the returns to these sophisticated analysts might be quite high, they establish a market in which fundamental analysis is a fairly useless procedure both for the average analyst and the average investor" (58).[33]

Financial theorists remain divided about the efficient-market hypothesis, with some granting its validity only in the long term and others preferring, as Fama did in 1970, to discriminate among weak, semi-strong, and strong versions of the claim.[34] Paul Samuelson also admitted ambivalence about the basic theorem of the random walk model: "I must confess to having oscillated over the years in my own mind regarding it as trivially obvious (and almost trivially vacuous) and regarding it as remarkably sweeping." He concluded with a warning "not to read too much into the . . . theorem": "It does not prove that actual competitive markets work well. It does not say that speculation is a good thing or that randomness of price changes would be a good thing. It does not prove that anyone who makes money in speculation is *ipso facto* deserving of the gain or even that he has accomplished something good for society or for anyone but himself."[35] Whatever reservations theorists have expressed about the efficient-market hypothesis and the random walk model, these concepts have played critical roles in the expansion of the infrastructure of modern finance: they are now routinely used to provide a benchmark by which investors can evaluate investment managers and as proof that statistical analysis trumps the fundamental analysis promoted by Graham and Dodd. Most importantly, the efficient-market hypothesis and the random walk model were used to create index funds—mutual funds containing a portfolio that matches the components of a specific market index, such as the S&P 500. With their low operating costs and broad market exposure, index funds have soared in popularity and market share from their humble 1970 origin in the Qualidex Fund, which tracked the Dow Jones Industrial Average.

9.2c. The Canonization of Modern Finance

The textbook that helped make modern finance a staple of business school and economics courses was *The Theory of Finance,* published by Eugene Fama and Merton H. Miller in 1972. Providing what its authors called a "rigorous grounding in the basic theory of finance," this text pruned away both "institutional and descriptive material" and empirical tests of the efficient-market hypothesis; it treated uncertainty as risk, within the mean/variance framework, assumed that securities are traded in perfect markets, and emphasized the "microdecision problems of the investor and the corporate manager" rather than the "macroeconomic problems of social policy."[36] This textbook, which Michael Jensen called the "white bible," shepherds the student through a series of successively more complex models, which deal, first, with the allocation of resources in conditions of certainty, and second, with resource allocation in a world of uncertainty. In this second part, Markowitz's portfolio selection model features prominently, but Fama and Miller also work through the simplifications and extensions of the mean/variance framework formulated by Sharpe and Tobin. As in Markowitz's 1959 book, *The Theory of Finance* cited these authors in bibliographies, but Fama and Miller presented their material not as a narrative of the historical development of ideas and models but as a series of models whose increasing complexity simply reflects the student's increased technical skill. In defense of employing the assumption that markets are "perfect" and "efficient" throughout the book, Fama and Miller affirmed the truism of the efficient-market hypothesis: "The most striking single impression that emerges from the mass of empirical work that has been done in the last ten years is how robust the perfect and efficient market models are in confrontation with the data, despite what seem to be the outrageous simplifications that have gone into their construction" (ix).

9.3. OPTIONS PRICING THEORY, FINANCIAL ENGINEERING, AND FINANCIAL ECONOMETRICS

9.3a. The Theoretical and Mathematical Pillars of Modern Finance

In the 1960s, models based on CAPM dominated financial theory. By the middle of the following decade, many Wall Street investment firms had adopted these models and routinely used them to make investment decisions. During the 1970s, however, even as investment managers embraced CAPM, some financial theorists returned to the objections Benoit Mandelbrot had raised in 1963.[37] While CAPM models were never discarded, the theoretical assumptions on which they were based were soon joined—and, to a certain extent, supplanted—by a new approach to financial theory and practice. This new approach was not based primarily on pricing securities, matching risk/return ratios to an investor's risk preference, or evaluating investment managers. Nor did the new approach need the assumptions that anchored CAPM: assumptions about symmetrical information, investor rationality, and profit-maximizing investors. Instead of trying to model the behavior of individuals making choices under uncertainty, financial engineers began to model the structure of the financial market itself. Instead of simply pricing securities, they began to create new financial assets, which were derived from the primary securities and could be traded independently. These derivatives could be priced using a model devised by Fischer Black, Myron Scholes, and Robert C. Merton in 1973. As increasing kinds of assets were converted into underlying securities for such derivatives, trading in derivatives helped realize Arrow's dream of a "complete" market that accommodates hedging on every possible kind of asset and for every conceivable future state. Before the derivatives revolution, common stocks and insurance contracts were examples of this kind of contingent contract, and at the outset of the revolution, it appeared to observers that the new derivative-based trading instruments would usher in the ideal of the Pareto-efficiency state. As the financial crisis of 2008 taught us, however, there is no reason to assume in advance that the actual contracts commercially available to hedge risks will be appropriate to the moment at hand. (Witness the difficulty speculators faced when they tried to short residential real estate before the crisis.) In addition, as Kenneth Arrow insisted, in conditions of uncertainty, "we have the possibility of information and, of course, also the possibility of its absence. No contingent contract can be made, at the time of execution, if either of the parties does not know whether the specified contingency has occurred or not."[38]

Quantitative finance and financial engineering, based on the mathematics of derivatives pricing, emerged in the 1970s, the tumultuous decade to which we return in chapter 10. This decade inherited the 1960s' combination of increased inflation and unsustainable US expenditures on the Vietnam War and the War on Poverty, and the 1973 oil shock made price volatility even more extreme. The new volatility was also a response to additional factors: the breakdown of the Bretton Woods agreement; the globalization of markets and the rise of new economic powers like Japan; the rapid industrialization of many underdeveloped countries where cheap labor was newly available to multinational corporations; and the increased speed and decreased cost of acquiring, processing, and implementing information (the digital revolution).[39]

The price volatility of the 1970s roiled global capital markets. In hindsight, the 1960s, when CAPM was the darling of financial theorists, look more like the roaring twenties than any decade before or since. Both decades recorded outstanding returns in the capital markets, and both ended with devastating financial losses and widespread questioning of academic theories and the tools professionals used to manage money. The CAPM was not ridiculed quite as much as Edgar Lawrence Smith's buy-and-hold approach to common stocks, and Paul Samuelson's quip that the business cycle had been tamed did not damage his reputation as much as Irving Fisher's notorious assertion that the stock market high of 1929 was simply a new plateau. Nevertheless, the exogenous shocks of the 1970s in the currency and real commodity markets and the devastation of the US stock and bond markets between 1971 and 1975 left many wondering whether financial theorists and economists had any understanding of what was beginning to seem like the new normal. Particularly perplexing was the increase in inflation during a recessionary slowdown. Slack production during a recession is supposed to moderate the demand for money and thus contain inflation. But in what came to be called "stagflation," this did not happen, and, when the Bretton Woods agreement was abandoned in 1971, a worldwide flight from the dollar began. Without a global fixed exchange rate system, the value of all currencies was free to fluctuate—and traders were given license to speculate in currency futures and exchange rates.

The phase of finance that followed CAPM and the efficient-market hypothesis—the triumvirate of quantitative finance, financial engineering, and financial econometrics—was developed partly as a response to the shocks that price volatility, inflation, and stagflation inflicted on global capital markets and investor confidence. As we will see in chapter 10, the tax asymmetries and investment opportunities introduced by changing conditions and technological innovations also aroused the interest of financial entrepreneurs, who exploited the crisis to make money in new ways. Either explanation might account for the swift-footed, back-door negotiations that led to the founding of a new exchange for trading currency futures, the Chicago Mercantile Exchange's International Money Market (IMM). As soon as the fixed exchange rate system enforced by Bretton Woods collapsed, Leon Melamed, founder of the IMM, commissioned free-market advocate Milton Friedman to write a paper promoting a futures market in currencies. Armed with Friedman's theoretical justification, George Schultz, incoming secretary of the Treasury, blessed the exchange "because he philosophically agreed."[40] The IMM opened in 1972; the first interest rate swap was traded in 1981; and in 1983, the Merc introduced its first option contract on an index, the S&P 500 Stock Index. The number, kind, and value of such derivatives—traded either on formal exchanges like the Chicago Mercantile Exchange (CME), the Chicago Board of Trade (CBOT), the New York Mercantile Exchange (NYMEX), and the London International Financial Futures and Options Exchange (LIFFE) or in over-the-counter transactions—have increased dramatically since then. By December 2011, the worldwide market of outstanding contracts in interest rate derivatives alone had a notional value of $500 trillion.[41]

Such trades were facilitated not only by the financial theories and mathematics we discuss below but also by innovations in information technology. Computer hardware innovations like high-speed processing, desktop computers, networked systems, and high-speed data entry completely overcame the computing difficulties that impeded Alfred Cowles III and his team in the 1930s. With the arrival of real-time international conferencing and instantaneous data transmission, through both hard-wiring and satellite transmission, international securities trading became possible on a previously unimaginable scale. Software programs designed to facilitate spreadsheet construction made it possible to model complex financial deals previously beyond the capacity of Wall Street traders. After their introduction, the volume of currency and interest-rate swaps increased exponentially. By the mid-1980s, the New

York Stock Exchange was using an order-matching computer system known as the Designated Order Turnaround System (DOT), and financial engineers began to work out the mathematical relationships capable of not only pricing options but also exploiting temporary discrepancies between the market price of a derivative and its fair value. Often modeled first as a solution to a specific problem or need, the resulting financial products were then written into software programs that other professional traders could apply to more generic problems. By late 1985, the trading strategy known as *program trading* or *futures-cash arbitrage* was helping enrich major investment banks (and financial engineers) at the same time it increased short-term equity price volatility. These developments also helped accelerate the information technology (IT) industry, whose advances were so critical to the transformation of finance. The symbiotic relationship between the two industries is clear from the disproportionate investment the US finance industry made in IT. In the decades after the IMM opened, the financial sector became the leading purchaser of information technology, accounting for 32.5% of investment in computers in 1979, 38.7% in 1989, and 37.8% in 1992. At the same time, the cost of computing relative to other capital purchases dropped substantially, and microchip performance showed uninterrupted exponential growth.[42] Analysts cite the finance industry's expenditures for risk management as a primary source of this disproportionate allocation of the nation's IT resources. In 1984, Robert C. Merton, to whom we return below, convinced Goldman Sachs to hire its first "quant"—or quantitative financial theorist. The new hire, Fischer Black, had already helped devise the options pricing model that helped launch quantitative finance.

Given the technical nature of modeling financial derivatives, it might be helpful to summarize the components of the revolution that transformed financial theory and practice after 1973 before turning to the models themselves. The probabilistic revolution in finance, which culminated in the derivatives revolution, followed its counterparts in the physical and natural sciences, where the mathematics of stochastic processes and measure-theoretic probability theory were used to develop new applications in quantum physics, engineering, and the biological sciences. After the 1970s, experts in the emergent field of quantitative finance—many trained in theoretical physics or mathematics—began to apply the same stochastic process techniques to financial problems. This generation of "quants" used modified versions of stochastic methods like the Weiner process, named after the mathematician and used in physics to describe the drift of a particle bombarded by neutrons, to give more specificity to the "random walk" of stock prices, which Louis

Bachelier had described in 1900. This random walk, as we have seen, can also be described as a geometric Brownian motion with a drift (the mean expected return). Bachelier had also provided early descriptions of the concept of risk-neutral probability, the premise of market rationality, and the idea that the mathematical feature of a martingale property in a time series reflects a "fair game" in a market transaction. (The martingale is a mathematical property of a time series in which the future price of a security is identical to the present price.) In the 1960s, Paul Samuelson redefined the characteristics of the financial asset's "geometric" motion, using as an example the asymmetry of returns for securities under bankruptcy laws.

The probabilistic revolution in finance was also premised on Kenneth Arrow's idea that risk bearing involves bets and payoffs linked to future objective states of the world. The concept of "state prices"—the pricing of contingent outcomes—is based on the idea that one can price the risks of contingent claims as payoffs. In a world conceptualized as stochastic (but not unknowable), the future is treated as a "state space," in which various outcomes generate various payoffs. Working only with this primitive concept, the modeler can create different combinations of investments and payoffs to construct various kinds of market models—models that enforce the law of one price (the no-arbitrage condition), models of complete markets (where every asset and derivative can be hedged), and models of risk-neutral price measures in a two-period world (where risk has been backed out of the model and the expiration date of the option constitutes the second period).

Derivatives theory also drew on the work of Franco Modigliani and Merton Miller, Fischer Black and Myron Scholes, and Robert C. Merton. In different ways, all these theorists explored the implications of the no-arbitrage condition assumed to operate in a working market. This assumption enforces a rational pricing strategy for options and, by extension, other securities. Later theorists extended some of the critical elements of the Black-Scholes-Merton model to probabilistic models and multiperiod security markets. In these multiperiod models, as we will see in a moment, theorists developed the critical attribute of the martingale taken under a risk-neutral probability measure.

Finally, as we will see, Robert C. Merton introduced continuous-time models, which use stochastic calculus and Kiyoshi Itô's formula to create both hedged portfolios (in which a security is hedged by creating a call option) and replicating portfolios (in which the underlying security and a bank or money market account can be dynamically balanced to replicate the value of the call).[43] Both anchor long-term trading strategies and each constitutes a financial application of the linear programming techniques set out in the Activity Analysis conference of 1949. Merton's insight about the importance of continuous-time modeling, which was a natural extension of the Black-Scholes-Merton formula, provided a critical component of financial engineering.

9.3b. Arbitrage Theory

One of the most important concepts that distinguishes contingent-claims pricing from CAPM is the theory of arbitrage—or, more precisely, no-arbitrage. As Stephen Blyth explained in 2014, "The *assumption of no-arbitrage*—that is, there exist no arbitrage portfolios—underpins quantitative finance."[44] One of the first papers to formulate this idea, "The Cost of Capital, Corporation Finance, and the Theory of Investment," was published in 1958 by Franco Modigliani and Merton H. Miller, members of the Graduate School of Industrial Administration at the Carnegie Institute of Technology (now Carnegie Mellon). The explicit subject of the paper was the old question of company valuation, which had been raised by investors since the first US corporations were formed. Instead of trying to assess the likelihood that corporations were "watering" their shares or continuing the fundamental analysis of a firm's capital structure advocated by Benjamin Graham and David Dodd, Modigliani and Miller argued that corporate financial structure—the mixture of debt and equity—was irrelevant to the value of a company. While this claim was startling enough, even more consequential was the arbitrage argument by which they demonstrated it.

> The market value of any firm is independent of its capital structure because otherwise an investor could buy and sell stocks and bonds in such a way as to exchange one income stream for another stream, identical in all relevant respects but selling at a lower price. The exchange would be advantageous to the investor quite independently of his attitude toward risk. As investors exploit these arbitrage opportunities, the value of the overpriced shares will fall and that of the underpriced shares will rise, thereby tending to eliminate the discrepancy between the market value of the firms.[45]

With these words, Modigliani and Miller dispensed with two pieces of received wisdom: every firm has an optimal capital structure, and an investor's attitude toward risk is fundamental to investment decisions. Assuming only that investors behave rationally (i.e., they prefer more income to less),

Modigliani and Miller emphasized one of the cornerstones of any competitive market: if two securities with identical costs and payoffs trade for different prices, an arbitrage opportunity will exist, someone will exploit the price differential and, in doing so, the arbitrageur will help return the overpriced share to its fair price.

Assuming that competitive markets are governed by the no-arbitrage principle allows the financial engineer to order the securities available in a market in relation to each other, according to their payoffs. After 1973, the available securities could include not only stocks and bonds but also various kinds of derivatives, which trade in a determinate relation to the value of the underlying security from which they derive their value. Once it became possible to create and price derivatives, and operating in an environment where the risk preferences of individual investors are deemed irrelevant (a risk-neutral environment), investment managers and financial engineers could develop expectations about the stochasticity of each security's returns, up to the point of the option's expiration date, and construct a portfolio or a new security in which the riskiness of one contract is offset or hedged by another security whose risk moves in the opposite direction. Modigliani and Miller did not pursue the arbitrage argument into the problem of pricing derivatives, but they made it clear that the no-arbitrage assumption was critical to doing so.

9.3c. The Options Pricing Model

In the early 1970s, in the aftermath of the debate between Keynesians and monetarists, Fischer Black and Myron Scholes solved the problem of how to price derivatives. At the time, Black was working in his own financial consulting practice, and Scholes was an economist in the MIT Sloan School of Management. In his many moves back and forth between private financial institutions and the academic world, Black embodied the synergy that animated financial theory and securities trading in the 1970s, and in bringing his Chicago PhD to Cambridge, Scholes closed the gap between the fresh-water and salt-water schools, which so often divided the ranks of economists in this decade.[46] Central to the solution Black and Scholes proposed was the no-arbitrage assumption: "If options are correctly priced in the market, it should not be possible to make sure profits by creating portfolios of long and short positions in options and their underlying stocks. [This is the no-arbitrage principle.] Using this principle, a theoretical valuation formula for options is derived. Since almost all corporate liabilities can be viewed as combinations of options, the formula and the analysis that led to it are also applicable to corporate liabilities such as common stock, corporate bonds, and warrants. In particular, the formula can be used to derive the discount that should be applied to a corporate bond because of the possibility of default."[47] For a stock, equity can be viewed as a call option on a residual claim during the liquidation of the firm in bankruptcy; due to the principle of limited liability, this protects the equity investor from a loss larger than his original investment.[48]

A derivative is a contract or trade between two parties whose value derives from the underlying asset (the "underlying"). Derivatives trading allows investment banks and sovereign states to do what farmers and commodity producers have long been able to do in commodity futures markets: hedge their risks. Instead of using futures contracts to hedge against future increases (decreases) in prices for crops, as farmers have long done, investment banks and financial engineers use financial derivatives to hedge the risks associated with the ownership of financial assets: foreign currencies, changes in interest rates, or any other underlying asset specified by the contract. With the construction of increasingly "exotic" derivatives, it has become possible to use ever-more complicated products to hedge against countless kinds of risk.[49]

Of course, financial assets are not exactly like their counterparts in the real side of the economy. In particular, the former have a more complex relationship to liquidity than do real assets. On the one hand, financial assets are more liquid than a house or car in the sense that financial assets can be and are marked to market—their "fair" price is generated every instant and made public (to traders) by the Autoquote system, which continuously generates prices for all options. This enhanced liquidity means that their holder is more willing to lend money against collateral than a homeowner or car owner might be. The greater liquidity of financial assets allows for leverage, in other words, and this can encourage more aggressive trading. The greater liquidity of these assets also means—and this is the other hand—that the risk surrounding derivatives exceeds risk in the real side of the economy. In particular, derivatives risk causing—and then suffering the effects of—a liquidity crisis, and, when this occurs, they cannot be traded at all. In a liquidity crisis, such as those that triggered the collapse of Long Term Capital Management in 1998 and the global financial crisis in 2008, liquidity suppliers (e.g., broker-dealers, hedge funds) recognize that the demand for liquidity is rising and pull back from the market. If the ensuing fall in securities' prices is sufficiently large, the very need for aggressive liquidation can spiral out of control. In severe cases, such as the two we have just named, financial markets can freeze altogether, and this is when repercussions begin to be felt in the real side of the economy as well.[50]

Needless to say, the creators of options pricing theory did not have such liquidity crises in mind when they devised a formula for pricing derivatives. They were simply trying to "perfect" financial markets in the sense of making them more responsive to investors' desires—for quicker trades with a more complete array of options and other derivatives instruments. With the introduction of options pricing theory, investment analysts were able to optimize the return process dynamically by hedging the underlying against the option in re-optimized proportion as each security traded in a stochastic manner. Of course, modeling randomness is tricky—as much art as science—and no model can take account of moral hazard, fraud, liquidity crises, or the kind of arbitrage "violations" that occurred in 2008–9.[51] Because models are simulations, based on limit-setting assumptions, the most they can do is try out the properties of potential solutions, not predict what will happen.

The Black-Scholes (or Black-Scholes-Merton) options pricing model was based on three variables the modeler could observe and thus know in advance: the price of the underlying (e.g., common stock), the time to expiration of the options contract, and the risk-free rate of the benchmark security; in addition, one variable, the volatility or standard deviation of the security, could be observed *ex post* but not *ex ante* or in advance. Using the variables that could be observed, the Black-Scholes equation allowed the modeler to calculate the theoretical value of the call. By extension, the modeler could also derive a near-perfect hedged position using a trading strategy that combined a long position in the stock and a short position in the option.[52] The result was a hedged position that grew at the risk-free rate. Because of the implications of the hedge process, the investment professional could calculate the value of the call by discounting its future value back to the present based on the risk-free rate. The boundaries of the price of the call could also be determined: they are set by the volatility of the stock and the time to expiration of the call. These boundary conditions established the parameters for the relationship between the underlying and the call.

The options pricing model laid the foundation for pricing all securities issued by a corporation, relative to each other: its common stock, bonds, options, and warrants. Equally important, the model made it possible for an investment professional to replicate the value of the option with a trading strategy that included the common stock and a bank account.[53] By deconstructing securities into packages of embedded options, this model changed finance forever because it brought the rational cohesiveness of the no-arbitrage principle to all financial markets. Because it was based almost completely on observable variables, moreover, the Black-Scholes options pricing model did not have to rest on the "homogeneous beliefs" necessary to CAPM, nor did it assume a Gaussian probability distribution. Because of the widespread practical application of options pricing theory for derivatives pricing, hedging, and arbitrage, contingent-claim pricing, using the mathematics of quantitative finance, became one of the foundations of contemporary portfolio management.

As powerful and influential as the Black-Scholes model has been, the role played by unobservable variables should not be discounted. In particular, it is impossible to observe the future volatility of the price of a given financial asset; typically, modelers use past volatility as a proxy for this variable. To use past volatility as a proxy for its future counterpart assumes that the processes generating the relevant data are stationary—that is, that the future will be a repetition of the past. This is not only a version of the kind of theoretical unknown that so worried Keynes in his critique of Tinbergen. As we will see in chapter 10, it also became an observable fact after the stock market crash of 1987, when the relationship between the implied volatility of an equity and the strike price of the option with the same expiration date began to diverge from the log normal straight-line distribution assumed by the Black-Scholes model. The resulting "volatility skew" or "volatility smile" might indicate changes in investor behavior as a result of fear of unpredictable future events. Or it might indicate the presence of structural issues that contradict the predicates of the Black-Scholes model. In any case, one legacy of the 1987 crash was a version of "crashophobia" that challenged the model that seemed to promise so much.

9.3d. Options Pricing in Continuous Time

In 1973, shortly after the publication of the groundbreaking article by Black and Scholes, Robert C. Merton, another MIT Sloan School economist, elaborated the role stochastic calculus plays in options pricing. In "Theory of Rational Option Pricing," Merton also laid out the relationship between arbitrage theory, options pricing, and the contingent-claim (or contingent-state) theory introduced by Kenneth Arrow and Gérard Debreu. In 1973, of course, options represented a tiny proportion of the universe of financial securities, a situation Merton acknowledged by calling them "relatively unimportant."

Because options are specialized and relatively unimportant financial securities, the amount of time and space devoted to the development of a pricing theory might be questioned. One justification is that, since the option is a particularly simple type of contingent-claim asset, a theory of options pricing may lead to a general theory of contingent-claims pricing. Some have argued that all such securities can be expressed as combinations of basic option contracts, and, as such, a theory of options pricing constitutes a theory of contingent-claims pricing. Hence, the development of an options pricing theory is, at least, an intermediate step toward a unified theory to answer questions about the pricing of a firm's liabilities, the term and risk structure of interest rates, and the theory of speculative markets.[54]

What Merton's article added to the Black-Scholes options pricing model was a "rigorous derivation"—that is, a mathematical derivation—of the model. Using stochastic calculus, Merton showed other financial engineers how to combine a small amount of stock plus a bank account to create a replicating portfolio that matched the value of the call. So closely does Merton's work follow on Black and Scholes's model that the result is now known as the Black-Scholes-Merton options pricing model.

As Donald MacKenzie has argued, this model had a profound—and performative—effect on financial markets for the fifteen-year period following the publication of these articles. Because the model was readily available, easy to use, and relatively inexpensive, traders quickly adopted it, and, as they put it to use, market prices of options began to resemble the model's predictions. "From 1973 on, market prices fell toward Black-Scholes-Merton levels."[55] The model not only helped eliminate the speculative connotations previously associated with the trading of financial options; it also provided traders a theoretical rationale to support the prices they assigned to options. Largely as a result of reliance on this model, the options market soon reached $668 trillion. This figure represents $100,000 for every human being alive at that time.[56]

Merton was able to elaborate the mathematical hints Black and Scholes dropped in their article because he had been using stochastic calculus since 1969. That year, in collaboration with his teacher Paul Samuelson, Merton applied stochastic calculus to warrant pricing to model the optimal exercise date of a given warrant.[57] In his dissertation, Merton used stochastic calculus again to develop what he called "continuous-time finance." This allowed him to produce a model of lifetime consumption and investment in which an investor revises his or her decisions continuously in time.[58] As he explained in a volume published in 1990, "time and uncertainty are the central elements that influence financial behavior. It is the complexity of their interaction that provides intellectual challenge and excitement to the study of finance."[59]

Stochastic calculus was able to capture the Brownian movements of a security's price because it uses stochastic differential equations instead of the simple differential equations used in traditional calculus. The challenge security prices pose to the latter is that even though the sample path of the price is continuous, it is so jagged that it is impossible to compute its rate of change over even a small interval. (The price is nowhere differentiable.) Continuous-time models, combined with stochastic calculus's ability to derive the laws of motion for the nonlinear Browning movement, allowed the financial engineer to replicate the payoffs of options and other derivatives by dynamically adjusting portfolios of simpler securities like stocks and bonds. In Merton's model, the price of the call was linked to the random pattern of the underlying stock's price and a model for the risk-free bond. Modeling the underlying stock's prices required a formula developed by the Japanese mathematician Kiyoshi Itô in 1944; modeling the risk-free bond was simple, for it earns a return simply as a function of time. This array of mathematical techniques for pricing options—collectively called quantitative finance—is now used to replicate the risk/return characteristics of securities, portfolios, and risk exposures.

9.3e. Three Approaches to Pricing Derivatives

The countless models now used to price securities (including derivatives), hedge portfolios using financial claims, and develop strategies for continuous-time or discrete-time trading exemplify one or some combination of three approaches to pricing. These include stochastic calculus, which Black, Scholes, and Merton introduced; the binomial tree, which was developed by Mark Rubenstein, John C. Cox, and Stephen A. Ross; and the measure-theoretic probability approach, which was elaborated by David M. Kreps, J. Michael Harrison, and Stanley R. Pliska.[60] Chronologically, the Black-Scholes-Merton calculus approach came first; the results of the other two research platforms were published in 1979. Conceptually, the binomial tree is the simplest of the three and the most computationally efficient; the measure-theoretic probability approach is the most abstract. In terms of application, the binomial tree has simplified computing the price of options and has become the go-to model for options traders; the stochastic calculus approach has generated options pricing models that accommodate factors like volatility, interest rates, and other pricing parameters ("the Greeks"); and the probability approach has led to models that both theorize and model risk (as the time path of stochastic variables) and model the information structure of the financial market (as information is filtered through probability matrices). Taken together, the models derived from these approaches are the basis for the complex valuation technologies that now link financial institutions all over the world into a single, complexly interrelated global financial market. While they are specifically designed to manage and distribute risk, these models have also generated risk that is now systemic, in the sense that the interconnectedness of the world's financial institutions can and does lead to worldwide failure when the risk models fail.

We have already described the stochastic differential equation method central to Merton's approach. We offer here a brief description of the other two approaches to pricing options. Each approach was developed by a team of economists, for, as the models have become increasingly complex in mathematical and theoretical terms, the team approach to modeling has replaced the single-researcher and the pair approach. The binomial tree options pricing formula described by Rubenstein, Cox, and Ross in "Option Pricing: A Simplified Approach" (1979) seeks to simplify the daunting task of factoring time and uncertainty into options pricing.[61] It is based on a binomial tree that provides a picture of the process of filtration, a term that refers to the structure of a diffusion process. The diffusion process occurs in the transfer of heat; it also appears in electrical circuits and in the movement of particles in quantum space. When used in finance, filtration refers to the movement securities' prices take as new information hits the market. As new information arrives, investors' probability expectations change (are filtered), and the price of a security moves up or down in the random walk Bachelier described.

The binomial tree allows the modeler to represent this process as a series of binomial movements taken over discrete periods. Time is assumed to be finite, with a definite end point, and discrete—that is, composed of distinct episodes or segments. The passage of time is represented by moving from left (the starting point) to right (the end). The discrete segments are represented as branches, and the points at which new information hits the market as nodes, which sponsor the splitting off of new branches. At each node, the modeler assigns probabilities to the two possible future directions the new branch can take—say, a 70% likelihood that the price will move higher (the branch forks up) and a 30% likelihood that it will move lower (the branch forks down). The model does not demand restrictive assumptions about the risk preference of the investor or the investor's assumptions about the kind of distribution governing the return-generating process. Instead, it uses the critical application of a "risk-neutral measure," which simply assumes that the investor prefers more gain to less, by equally weighting the probability of an upturn and a downturn at each node. By equally weighting every expectation, the modeler effectively renders irrelevant an individual investor's expectations about the pattern up versus down at each node. Modelers can adapt the tree diagram by changing the probabilities of the up-and-down spread at any given node, and they can extend it sequentially by increasing the number of probability nodes and stopping points. Because information enters the market both randomly and continuously, its impact is filtered by changes in expected probabilities; the binomial tree standardizes representation of this filtration process and makes it simpler to calculate the random walk of a call's price. Although it is obviously a simplification, this model nevertheless provides a richer treatment of information than we encountered in the work of Berle and Means or Marschak in the 1930s.

Measure-theoretic probability theory provides a more abstract way to model the movements of a security's price. This approach conjures a measurable sample space, which is said to be equipped with a probability measure and a filtration. To price a derivative, the modeler characterizes the sample space by the random process that models the convergence between the price of the derivative and its underlying security at the former's day of expiration. To model the securities market in general in order to develop a long-term trading strategy, the modeler reconceives the sample space as Kenneth Arrow's "all future states of the world"; the probability measure on this space is defined by the investor's expectation about contingent outcomes of the processes by which securities are priced in the "real world," and the filter describes the probabilistic path the security's price will take through the existential wilderness of randomness.

Measure-theoretic mathematical probability theory supplies quantitative finance with the concept of the martingale, which is an important object in probability space. The martingale is a mathematical attribute of a variable's path in a stochastic diffusion process, which is represented in a time series. If the price process is equipped with the martingale property, then the mathematical expectation is that the next price of the security will be no greater (or less) than its value at the present. This concept defines a "fair game" (neither the buyer nor the seller has an advantage) and constitutes the condition for a no-arbitrage market (the market contains no opportunities for a "free lunch").

The martingale was first described by J. L. Doob, who was a student of the statistician Harold Hotelling, the statistician we encountered in earlier chapters. In *Stochastic Processes* (1953), Doob described a stochastic process as "the mathematical abstraction of an empirical process whose development is governed by probabilistic laws"; this stochastic process is a martingale if the expected return of a variable at each successive stopping point is the same as the prior stopping point.[62] In 1979, the Stanford economists David M. Kreps and J. Michael Harrison gave this concept economic content, thus expanding Bachelier's assertion that the presence of a martingale was the sign of a fair game in an investment market. In "Martingales and Arbitrage in Multiperiod Securities Markets," Kreps and Harrison modeled security markets as a price system. In their multiperiod model, Kreps and Harrison placed investment theory in a macroeconomic context and gave it a microeconomic foundation: the financial market as a whole allows individuals to secure resources for future consumption; individuals make investment decisions based on their subjective expectations about future states of the world; contingent claims (derivatives and options) are priced according to the expectations of investors as a group; and prices are modeled as stochastic vectors. One of the important insights of this paper is the concept of the "equivalent martingale measure," which helps define the concept of a no-arbitrage price in a stochastic universe, where risk bearing is defined by pricing a contingent claim. It also provided theoretical justification for the important technique of risk-neutral pricing. Finally, it supplied the first formal link between no-arbitrage theory and martingale theory, which lies at the heart of what has been called the "fundamental theorem of finance."[63] All these pricing strategies constitute critical components of the derivatives revolution, which transformed modern finance in the 1970s and 1980s.

9.3f. The Arbitrage Theory of Capital Asset Pricing Model

At the same time the Black-Scholes-Merton model was simplified with tools like the binomial tree and extended into measure-theoretic models using martingale theory, financial theorists began to relax some of the more limiting assumptions of the 1960s version of CAPM. This reconsideration began with Stephen A. Ross's elaboration of CAPM into what he called the arbitrage theory of the Capital Asset Pricing Model. In 1973, Ross, then a professor of finance at Penn's Wharton School, proposed a simple factor model that extended CAPM's linear pricing relation between an asset's return and risk by placing these variables in a stochastic investment/payoff set-up, which was based on bets about the future states of the world and the condition of no-arbitrage.[64] Ross wanted to expand the model's factors beyond risk and return by relaxing CAPM's crucial assumptions about the risk preference of the investor and the *ex ante* treatment of the security's volatility. Unlike Black and Scholes, moreover, who had developed their model using the general equilibrium argument, Ross's model priced securities on the condition of no-arbitrage—the condition that, in an economy where equilibrium obtains, identical securities cannot trade at different prices. Ross's model, which is called the APT (arbitrage pricing theory), does not specify the risk tolerance of the investor, only that he prefer a greater return to a lesser one. Instead of restricting information about the future distribution of returns to a Gaussian probability distribution, as CAPM does, APT allows for different classes of probability distributions, including the Levy process with its characteristic jump functions. Instead of restricting the model to the linear relationship of return to variance (risk), the hallmark of CAPM pricing, APT theorizes that many kinds of factors, from macroeconomic to local, can account for an expected price change. Thus the factors that can be modeled, based on a Bayesian approach to the modeler's expectations, include everything from expectations about overall inflation to industry- or company-specific developments, to purely financial factors. Along with CAPM, which is still used (especially to evaluate the performance of fund managers), the Black-Scholes-Merton options pricing model and its offshoots, and models based on risk-neutral pricing (RNP), APT models form one of the core groups of financial models in widespread use today.

9.3g. A Manual for Financial Engineers

In 1982, J. Michael Harrison teamed with Stanley R. Pliska of the University of Illinois-Chicago Circle to investigate the conditions necessary for a "complete market"—a market in which every asset can be hedged with an engineered derivative. This work was a first step toward Pliska's graduate-level textbook, *Introduction to Mathematical Finance: Discrete Time Models* (1997). In 1995, Pliska, who was also the editor and founder of *Mathematical Finance*, showcased this work at a conference held at Cambridge University's Isaac Newton Institute for Mathematical Sciences. Sponsored by the Bank of England, the conference was entitled "Mathematical Theories of Finance: Models, Theories, and Computations." Both the conference's sponsor and its setting suggest the mathematical and business orientation quantitative finance had taken by the mid-1990s, and the term associated with Pliska's work— financial engineering—highlights what work in advanced finance had become by the last decade of the twentieth century.

Financial engineering first appeared in the 1970s, in the period of economic instability associated with stagflation. In that decade, the Black-Scholes-Merton model made it possible to price a host of new derivatives products and to manage portfolio, business, and government risk exposures. The defining characteristic of financial engineering—the feature that distinguishes it from the interwar theory of investments and postwar portfolio theory—is that financial engineering is anchored in the theory of no-arbitrage instead of the concept of equilibrium, which lies at the heart of modern economics. The graduate textbook Pliska workshopped at the 1995 conference provides the theoretical foundations, economic theory, and mathematics of financial engineering. He begins with the idea that building a portfolio of investments (or a lifetime consumption/investment plan) is a linear programming exercise, which involves setting objective functions for risk and reward. The financial engineer develops models of trading strategies by specifying submodels for the value, gain, and discounting processes, recognizes certain specifications and restrictions based on "arbitrage and other economic considerations," and prices claims based on contingent future states of the world. The latter "will be logically consistent if there is a *linear pricing measure*"—if the securities market permits no-arbitrage opportunities. The price of each claim (each financial asset) can be modeled in matrix terms as a "price vector."[65] This leads to the critical synthesis that combines investor behavior, pure mathematics, and economic theory: the initial price of each security is assumed to represent a positive expectation under the given probability measure. "In order to rule out arbitrage opportunities . . . there must exist a linear pricing measure which gives a positive mass" to every state of the world (11). Pliska satisfies this condition by using the martingale depiction of the fair game in a risk-neutral world: under the indicated probability measure (the risk-neutral probability measure), "the discounted price of each risky security is equal to its initial price. Hence a risk-neutral probability measure is just a linear pricing measure giving strictly positive mass" to every state of the world (11). With these assumptions in place—trading strategies conceptualized as linear processes, return processes providing the bookkeeping to convert price dividends and interest into capital gains, the no-arbitrage restriction, a positive probability measure based on expectations, and the risk-neutral pricing process—the financial engineer can build models that price securities relative to each other and that depict financial markets in either discrete-time, two-period variants or continuous-time variants. In 2009, Stephen A. Ross referred to these foundations as "the fundamental theorem of finance." From this fundamental theorem, financial engineers could build not only models to price options but also yield-curve models, models of coupon bonds, bond options, interest rate derivatives, swaps and swaptions, credit default swaps, and collateralized debt obligations—in short, an entire universe of models designed to posit purely theoretical prices for securities that trade, in ever-greater volume, in the global financial market. As we will see in chapter 10, however, the theoretical purity of this fundamental theorem can be—and regularly is—violated by the actual behavior of financial markets: in the real world, asset prices can vary in nonlinear ways, the structure of some kinds of instruments creates complexity that models do not capture, the financial system as a whole can operate as a tightly coupled system, and the payoffs of options and other derivatives may not be related in a linear way to the prices of their underlying securities. The stock market crash of 1987 and the collapse of Long Term Capital Management eleven years later provided ample warnings that financial engineers' most compelling theories and powerful models could fall short of the results they promised.[66]

9.3h. Financial Econometrics

According to Andrew Lo, professor of finance at MIT's Sloan School, financial econometrics emerged from a "confluence of three parallel developments": the increasing complexity of the global financial system; breakthroughs in the quantitative modeling of financial markets (based on modern portfolio theory and financial engineering); and developments in digital technology, including innovations in hardware, software, data collection and organization, and the creation of international systems of digital communication such as Swift (the Society for Worldwide Interbank Telecommunications, created in 1973).[67] By the mid-1970s, finance had become an important major in MBA programs offered by American business schools, and courses in finance could also be found in undergraduate and graduate departments of economics. By the end of the next decade, the subdiscipline of finance had begun to spin off its own subspecialties, the most important of which was financial econometrics.[68] Within the academy, financial econometrics pioneered a new array of statistical tools and econometric concepts, which directly bore fruit in Wall Street applications. In addition, relatively inexpensive financial econometrics software packages became available, and this made courses in econometrics among the most popular in undergraduate as well as graduate economics departments. With this software, even students could perform sophisticated time series and regression analyses on data sets at every possible time scale and level of aggregation. It became possible to download data from an enormous range of multidecade indexes into statistical regression packages for portfolio simulations and regression analysis. Combined with ever-more powerful desktop and laptop computers, this software also made it possible for Wall Street traders to create and trade securities in any number of forms—

closed-end funds, open-end funds, or electronically traded securities and funds (ETS and ETFs). By the end of the twentieth century, financial econometrics had become the common language of financial engineers, investment managers, arbitrageurs, and traders of all stripes—from professionals working in global trading centers in New York or Singapore to day traders sitting at home in Racine, Wisconsin. Beginning in 1982, when E-Trade was founded, individual investors were able to trade, invest, hedge, and arbitrage on the world's global capital markets.

Some of the most important tools of financial econometrics were developed in the early 1980s, but the new specialty did not launch its signature organization—the Society for Financial Econometrics (SoFiE)—until 2007. Financial econometrics, like the Econometric Society, its 1930s antecedent, fuses theory—in this case, financial theory—with mathematics and statistics. Like the econometrics of the interwar period once more, financial econometrics aspires to confront theory with data and to use empirical data to refine or develop theories. The theories financial econometrics has challenged are the underlying assumptions of CAPM: the average returns of all assets and portfolios can be explained by their market betas, returns are unpredictable, simple indexes always outperform managed funds, and securities markets are efficient.[69]

9.3i. Efficient Capital Markets II

In 1991, Eugene Fama, one of the architects of the efficient-market hypothesis, published a sequel to his influential 1970 survey of that hypothesis. In "Efficient Capital Markets II," Fama organized the mushrooming field of capital market research and testing into three areas, which reflected some of the major theoretical breakthroughs associated with financial econometrics. "Tests for return predictability" had been revolutionized by a new understanding that the volatility of financial time series was itself time-variant; "event studies" had been updated by cross-sectional studies of time series; and "tests for private information" had begun to incorporate analyses of asymmetrical information flows—between market makers and securities firm customers and among insiders, professional managers, and the investing public.[70] The result was a reconsideration of widely used models: CAPM, the Black-Scholes-Merton options pricing model, and APT multifactor models have all been reappraised with financial econometric techniques.

Developments in financial econometrics in the 1970s and 1980s paralleled the macroeconomic and macroeconometric research programs of those decades. Both, moreover, were in part at least responses to stagflation, which persisted for almost a decade. Just as the failure of Keynesian New Economists to deal with stagflation led to Robert Lucas's New Classics and the rational expectations revolution, which we examine in chapter 10, so the failure of the Cowles simultaneous equation approach to the same problem led other financial theorists to offer improvements on this method. One was the vector autoregressive technique (VAR) introduced by Clive Granger, Christopher Sims, and Lars Peter Hansen, faculty at the University of California-San Diego, Princeton University, and the University of Chicago, respectively. This approach placed fewer a priori restrictions on the identification and estimation of model equations than did the Cowles simultaneous equation method.

In addition to VAR, three additional econometric techniques, all developed in the 1980s, had important applications in finance: the general method of moments (GMM), the ARCH/GARCH time series techniques, and cointegration. The general method of moments, which was introduced by Lars Peter Hansen, led to an estimation approach that by-passed some of the technical impasses that had impeded researchers' attempts to select, estimate, and test statistical models for financial variables. It also allowed financial theorists to model stochastic return-generating processes in the capital market with a generalized model that could accommodate many kinds of stochastic return-generating processes—that is, different kinds of financial instruments. The autoregressive conditional stochastic model (ARCH), created by the University of California-San Diego's Robert Engle, allowed econometricians to relax one of the assumptions used in CAPM and the original Black-Scholes options pricing model: the assumption that volatility does not vary with time. Within a few years, the Danish-born economist Tim Bollersev was able to model the persistence and stationarity of time series, measures that are necessary to forecast future variance in prices. The ability to measure changes in volatility in financial markets is extremely important, and work continues on this project at various sites, including New York University's Volatility Institute's V-Lab.[71] Time-variant volatility measurement allows financial econometricians to quantify changes in investors' "animal spirits," the irrational force to which Keynes attributed individuals' eagerness to trade. Cointegration was developed by Clive Granger, Robert Engle, Charles R. Nelson (University of Washington), and Charles Plosser (University of Rochester) to mitigate the problem of "spurious correlation" between time series with deterministic and stochastic properties. Robert J. Shiller of Yale University, who won a Nobel

Prize in 2013, conducted research in stock price volatility in the 1980s, using all these techniques. With his student John Y. Campbell (later at Harvard), Shiller conducted econometric analyses that showed that the variability of prices broke rational "variance bounds" and thus should be understood as "irrational exuberance." Autoregressive and cointegrative techniques helped econometricians answer two questions: "First, what components of stock returns can be *predicted* given the information in the VAR system? Second, what component of stock returns can be *accounted for* ex-post by news about future dividends?"[72] The work of Shiller and Campbell exemplifies the way financial econometrics can both test existing theory (the theory of rational markets) and introduce new research areas.

9.3j. Behavioral Finance

In 2003, Robert Shiller took up the evaluation of efficient-market theory that Eugene Fama had initiated in 1970 and updated in 1991. Shiller's conclusions dramatically departed from Fama's, however, for, instead of finding ways to reconcile the volatility of aggregate stock prices, which financial econometricians had observed for at least a decade, to the efficient-market hypothesis, Shiller announced that the data had inspired a new approach. "In the 1990s, a lot of the focus of academic discussion shifted away from these economic analyses of time series on prices, dividends and earnings toward developing models of human psychology as it relates to financial markets." Citing his own NBER conference seminar on behavioral finance, codirected with the University of Chicago's Richard Thaler, which had been running since 1991, and the 1996 publication of *The Econometrics of Financial Markets,* edited by John Y. Campbell, Andrew Lo, and A. Craig MacKinlay, Shiller announced that "the foundation for a revolution in finance" was already in place.[73] By the turn of the century, this revolution was well underway, and it remains one of the liveliest areas in financial theory.

Jeremy Bentham's attempt to anchor economic analysis in an assessment of "hedonics," or the ratio of pleasurable to painful sensations, and later nineteenth-century efforts to measure "utility" had famously led the discipline into alleys that, if not always blind, did require some contortions to negotiate. Irving Fisher's suggestion that the "util" could be used to measure the psychological payoff of rewards and Paul A. Samuelson's notion of "revealed preference" both represented attempts to reconcile a discipline whose analytic framework was moving ever-closer to mathematics with the notoriously elusive matter of human psychology.[74] After over half a century of trying to reduce psychological motivations—including behaviors that violated the strictures of rationality—to patterns that could be formulated in mathematical terms, economists and financial theorists understandably found it difficult to allow psychology back into the discipline, and analyses that emphasized agents' lack of information or "imperfect information" can be seen as efforts to position psychology within the mathematical rubric economists had chosen so as to rein in the havoc psychology might play if "animal spirits" were taken seriously.

One basis for changing the discipline's tortured relation to psychology appeared in 1979 when two psychologists, Daniel Kahneman and Amos Tversky, both fellows at the Stanford Center for Advanced Study in the Behavioral Sciences, published "Prospect Theory: An Analysis of Decisions under Risk."[75] Along with Richard Thaler's "Toward a Positive Theory of Consumer Choice" (1980), this paper helped launch behavioral economics. While mainstream economists did not immediately embrace prospect theory, many Wall Street firms did, for it seemed to explain behaviors analysts had observed in investors and it promised to identify investment trends that violated the efficient-market hypothesis, at least in the short run.

Among the claims of prospect theory was the argument that individuals systematically deviate from making the decisions game theorists and theorists of rational choice would predict. Sometimes people "draw insufficient distinctions among small probabilities"; sometimes they are overconfident about their own judgment ("biased self-attribution"); sometimes, in hindsight, they claim to have made better predictions than they actually did; and almost always, individuals are irrationally more upset by losses than pleased by equivalent gains.[76]

While incorporating these conclusions into financial theory is a work-in-progress, behavioral finance has undeniably loosened the efficient-market hypothesis's stranglehold on theory and practice. In 2003, Shiller was cautiously optimistic about the impact behavioral theory could have on the discipline: "We should not expect market efficiency to be so egregiously wrong that immediate profits should be continually available. But market efficiency can be egregiously wrong in other senses. For example, efficient markets theory may lead to drastically incorrect interpretations of events such as major stock market bubbles. . . . While theoretical models of efficient markets have their place as illustrations or characterizations of an ideal world, we cannot maintain them in their pure form as accurate descriptors of actual markets."[77]

Whether to build and rely on models of an ideal world or create models that somehow move closer to "actual markets" remains an unresolved issue for practitioners of both economics and finance.

The 2008 failure of Lehman Brothers induced a new urgency in this project. With a repetition of the Great Depression suddenly a very real possibility, Shiller returned to the idea of animal spirits, this time with the help of the behavioral macroeconomist George Akerlof. Akerlof had identified five additional factors, beyond the excessive volatility of the stock market, that were not explained by neoclassical assumptions about the rational optimizing economic agent. These factors, according to Akerlof, required behavioral foundations. They included the existence of involuntary unemployment; the impact of monetary policy on output and employment; the prevalence of undersaving for retirement; and the stubborn persistence of an underclass.[78] After the global financial crisis, Shiller and Akerlof collaborated on two books that sought to synthesize behavioral finance and behavioral macroeconomics. In *Animal Spirits: How Human Psychology Drives the Economy and Why It Matters for the Global Economy* (2009) and *Phishing for Phools: The Economics of Manipulation and Deception* (2015), Shiller and Akerlof explored the limitations and inherent contradictions of the dynamic stochastic general equilibrium model view of markets. In doing so, they also advanced a radically new way to think about markets, market participants, and behavior both rational and irrational.

CHAPTER 10

The Transformation of American Finance

10.1. THE INTER-CRISIS PERIOD: THE VOLCKER DEFLATION TO THE LEHMAN BANKRUPTCY, 1982-2008

While economic historians have yet to assign it a name, the period between 1982 and 2008 is sufficiently distinctive to deserve recognition. We call this the inter-crisis period because even though its middle years were characterized by subdued volatility and increased national prosperity, its beginning was marked by one crisis—the Volcker deflation of 1982—and its climax (though not conclusion) by a second—the bankruptcy of the fourth largest investment bank in the United States, Lehman Brothers, on September 15, 2008. The period is also bookended by two recessions: the 1981–82 recession and the onset of the Great Recession, which began in the fourth quarter of 2007. The Volcker deflation was the result of a Federal Reserve monetary policy designed to crush inflation after more than a decade of attempts to bring it under control.[1] This policy had two phases: a brief monetarist experiment, which began in 1979 and attempted to peg monetary aggregates, and a second phase, which pegged not aggregates but the Federal funds rate. The policy was part of a two-part strategy that paired a major tax cut with a strict monetary policy, assuming that the stimulus of the first could produce a high-growth economy without inflation if it was accompanied by the second. Volcker kept interest rates high through the summer of 1982, even though, by that point, the US economy had been in a deep recession for a year. As unemployment exceeded 10%, manufacturing and industries like construction suffered, and the public began to lobby the Fed to loosen its grip on the nation's money. Volcker's punishing policy, which was relaxed late in the summer of 1982, did reduce inflation—from 13% when he joined the Fed in 1979 to 4% in 1982. Even though the policy was heavy-handed, it created the impression that the market, not the state, was governing the economy, for all the Federal Reserve seemed to have done was identify and maintain a non-inflationary growth rate for the money supply.[2]

After the Volcker deflation, the US economy entered a period that economists have named. This period, which was characterized by a reduction in the volatility of the US business cycle and overlapped Alan Greenspan's chairmanship of the Fed, was designated "the great moderation" by another Fed chair, Ben S. Bernanke.[3] This widely celebrated reduction in macroeconomic volatility was attributed to the enlightened macro and monetary policies of the supply-side revolution introduced by Ronald Reagan in 1981 and continued under presidents George H. W. Bush and William J. Clinton. The "great moderation" that began in 1984 saw a decline in aggregate output volatility in the United States (although not a decline in aggregate stock price volatility).[4] Incomes rose for nearly all workers, and an increase in stock prices created even more wealth for investors. The two Clinton administrations (1993–2000) used policies collectively known as "progressive fiscal conservatism" to modestly redistribute national income while exercising budget discipline. Financial deregulation, to which we return in a moment, had given consumers a new array of financial innovations, ranging from credit cards and home equity loans to derivatives, which theoretically allowed them to allocate spending and investment over longer periods of time.[5] From 1984 through 2007, the United States experienced only two, relatively brief recessions—in 1990–91 and 2001—and periods of expansion were correspondingly long. During Clinton's second term, real economic growth averaged 4.5% per year, and unemployment reached the goal of 4% specified in the Humphrey-Hawkins legislation of 1978.[6] Inflation remained low and stable, and the budget deficits of the early 1980s were replaced by budget surpluses. Because the boom of the 1990s was led by private-sector spending and private-sector employment, moreover, instead of expansionist fiscal or monetary policies, the great moderation offered what seemed like incontrovertible proof that market forces offered more stability and prosperity than the Keynesian policies of the 1950s.

We subsume the years known as the great moderation into a longer period because "the inter-crisis period" captures a reality masked by Bernanke's more upbeat periodization. Not only did the great moderation emerge from and collapse back into severe recessions, but the very years marked by tamed economic volatility and aggregate real-side prosperity also contained worrisome signs of deeper forces at work. During the so-called great moderation, the number of personal bankruptcies increased; the personal savings rate, as measured in the national income statistics, decreased; the trade deficit expanded dramatically; and in 1987, a stock market crash that saw the Dow Jones industrial average fall 22.6% and the S&P 500 lose 20% in a single day suggested that there were problems in the financial markets. That the stock market crash was almost certainly related to the widespread use of portfolio insurance, one of the financial innovations introduced by financial engineers, should have raised questions about financial markets.[7] Less obvious, but more dangerous in terms of the real economy, was what has been called the "great risk shift"—the transfer of risks that had been borne by governments and corporations to individuals and households.[8] New Deal legislation, such as the Glass-Steagall Act, the Social Security Act, and the Federal Deposit Insurance Act, had been designed to shield individuals from a variety of risks, from the imprudence of banks to the risk of underinsurance for health care or old age. With aggregate employment more stable in the 1990s, policy makers assumed that out-of-work Americans would soon move to other jobs; with private health insurance offering more options (and after the failure, in 1994, of the Health Security Act), they assumed that individuals would supplement Social Security with personal policies; and with almost all securities prices going up, many assumed that it would be more cost-effective for companies to replace pensions and defined benefit plans with defined contribution retirement plans, such as 401(k)s. The investment of these funds, as well as the IRAs individuals were allowed to open, would theoretically be overseen by fund managers. The Employee Retirement Income Security Act (ERISA), which was signed into law by President Gerald Ford in 1974, dramatically increased the funds under management invested in the stock market, as we will see in a moment.

The great risk shift did not cause widespread hardship in the United States as long as incomes were rising, inflation remained low, and most people were employed. The international scene also supported US prosperity: world prices for oil remained low, and US import prices were generally low, partly because the value of the dollar appreciated and partly because other nations, particularly in East Asia, experienced deflation.[9] Even though volatility in the real side of the US economy seemed to have been tamed, however, economies in other countries began to show serious strains in the 1990s. Partly because of capital flows into developing economies, foreign debt-to-GDP ratios soared in the four major Asian nations represented by the Association of Southeast Asian Nations (ASEAN), moving from 100% in 1993 to 167% in 1996. In July 1997, the currency of Thailand collapsed, and economic downturns rapidly followed in Indonesia, South Korea, Hong Kong, Laos, Malaysia, and the Philippines. In an attempt to contain the damage, the International Monetary

Fund offered South Korea, Thailand, and Indonesia $40 billion. The Asian financial crisis was not confined to the region, however. In 1998, the crisis spread to Russia, forcing the government to devalue the ruble and default on its debt.

While these crises had many causes, including swings in oil prices, one contributing factor was the deregulation of international capital flows. This allowed money to flow into projects many of which were speculative in nature, and it encouraged governments of developing nations to borrow more than they could repay—in the dollars that were the world's only reserve currency. While the damage initially seemed safely offshore, the United States did not completely escape blow-back from the deregulated global capital market. In 1998, Long-Term Capital Management (LTCM) collapsed, and shock waves rippled through the US financial sector. Long-Term Capital Management was a hedge fund founded in 1994. Two of the architects of modern finance, Myron Scholes and Robert C. Merton, sat on the board of LTCM, and the firm relied heavily on the absolute return and high leverage trading strategies the two Nobel laureates modeled. This hedge fund lost $4.6 billion in just four months in 1998. Under supervision of Greenspan's Federal Reserve Board, sixteen financial institutions agreed to recapitalize the company, but it was liquidated and dissolved in 2000.[10]

In macro and monetary theory, economists had forged a new synthesis by 2000, the new neoclassical synthesis. This theory combined elements of the Keynesian and monetarist theories we discussed in chapter 8 and enhanced them with new theories—endogenous growth theory, New Classical macro and monetary economics, and Real-Business Cycle Theory—as well as sophisticated econometric modeling closely aligned with the stochastic framework of modern finance—dynamic stochastic general equilibrium modeling. This new synthesis was the outcome of a paradigm shift that had occurred in macroeconomics after 1980. For many macroeconomists, neoclassical (endogenous) growth theory (an offshoot of the exogenous model Robert Solow had proposed in 1957) displaced the paradigm inherent in the Keynesian IS-LM framework to become the dominant paradigm of the discipline. Endogenous growth theory focused on the welfare effects of long-term growth, based on the augmentation of productivity led by technology and the enhancement of workforce skills instead of addressing the destabilizing effects of short-term fluctuations in output or employment. Based on New Classical macroeconomic assumptions, Real-Business Cycle theorists modeled stochastic technology shocks—not Keynesian dislocations in the process of investment and savings—as the source of fluctuations in the business cycle, or, as they construed it, fluctuations in the rate of growth of the economy. Economic growth, fueled by technological innovation, and supply-side incentives such as tax policies and investment in human capital were modeled as a linear, stochastic, vector growth process. From the perspective of this model, fluctuations of economic output and unemployment around the vector's growth trajectory were not a Keynesian problem to be solved by macroeconometric short-term stabilization policies. Instead, fluctuations in the time path of economic growth, much like fluctuations in the stock market, needed to be put in a long-term perspective, because such fluctuations are considered unavoidable.

The New Classical models were built on a set of highly restrictive theoretical assumptions: markets that clear at Arrow-Debreu equilibrium; the neutrality of money; models of aggregate household behavior that assume rational agents; atomistic self-interested behavior; and rational expectations. The aggregation technique that undergirded these assumptions abstracted such issues as household income inequality. The New Classical models assumed that firms exhibit competitive profit-maximizing behavior unconstrained by finance or the money illusion; they also assumed that government-level policy interventions would be ineffective because rational households and firms can anticipate and neutralize these interventions. Although the highly abstract assumptions of the New Classical set-up simply ignored many facts of everyday life, their policy implications fit well with the politics of the emergent free market ideology. By implication, New Classical models made institutional arrangements and federal actions irrelevant, even dangerous. Casting the federal government as an illegitimate economic agent was consistent with the principles set out by the Mont Pelerin Society from its inception; this idea was tirelessly promoted by Milton Friedman; and it was given new life by the supply-side economic theories and policies launched under President Reagan. Later, the same dynamic stochastic equilibrium framework was used to incorporate traditional Keynesian themes, which emphasized labor and market inefficiencies. These New Keynesian model assumptions reintroduced a rationale for government policy interventions. The so-called New Neoclassical Synthesis brought the New Classical, New Keynesian, and monetarist perspectives together in dynamic stochastic general equilibrium models.

Under the paradigm assumed by the New Neoclassical Synthesis, macroeconomists focus on policies that encourage economic growth in the real economy, and monetary economists at the Fed concentrate on maintaining a credible inflation targeting program using the tools of the open market committee. While both groups of economists did their jobs during the great moderation, before the 2008 financial crisis neither macro nor monetary economists considered financial regulation to be an instrument of monetary policy. Instead, under the doctrine of supply-side economics, regulation of almost any kind was considered an impediment to economic growth. As a result, regulation of the burgeoning financial sector was not considered the province of either macro or monetary economists, even though regulatory oversight was theoretically the responsibility of the Federal Reserve, the SEC, and the Treasury. What went unnoticed during the giddy years of the great moderation was that the US financial system was changing—in size, structure, and influence. What went unnoticed—what prevailing macroeconometric and monetary models did not make visible—was that the US financial system was becoming even more of a market-based system than it had always been, whose oversight demanded policy tools not currently in use by regulatory agencies.

The financial system described by Harold Moulton in 1921, quantified by Raymond Goldsmith in the 1950s, and theorized by Gurley and Shaw in 1960 was organized by central-bank oversight and consisted of various channels of financial intermediation, which linked financial institutions to each other and, ultimately, moved money from depositors to borrowers. In the market-based system that began to develop in the 1980s, by contrast, the process of securitization made banking and capital markets inseparable. Whereas previously, banks reacted to changes in the external environment by expanding or decreasing lending, under the new conditions, banks and other financial intermediaries—including security broker-dealers—tend to respond to credit losses by reducing their exposure to risk, curtailing lending, and charging higher risk premiums. As we will see when we describe the market-based financial system in sections 10.4 and 10.5, this can have—and has had—a serious impact on the real economy.

Of course, the new conditions signaled by a more fully elaborated market-based economy have also meant a dramatic increase in the scale and importance of the US financial system. Measured as a percentage of the nation's GDP, the financial sector rose from 2.8% in 1950 to 4.9% in 1980. By 2006, it had reached 8.3% of GDP.[11] During the great moderation, the influence of senior Wall Street executives over agencies of the federal government also increased: Donald Regan, former president of Merrill Lynch, helped shape the Reagan Economic Recovery Act, which led to a sweeping tax cut in 1986; Robert Rubin, formerly co-chairman of Goldman Sachs, served as secretary of the Treasury under President Clinton; later, as vice chairman of Citigroup under Sanford Weill, Rubin lobbied for passage of the Gramm-Leach-Bliley Act, which drove the last nail in the coffin of the Glass-Steagall Act in 1999. Henry Paulson, chairman and CEO of Goldman Sachs, was secretary of the

Treasury under President George W. Bush. Perhaps most important was Alan Greenspan, who was appointed chair of the Fed by Ronald Reagan in 1987 and, after William McChesney Martin, was the longest-serving Fed chair to date. Greenspan, the son of a stock broker, began his career as a Wall Street analyst at Brown Brothers Harriman, and went on to found the consulting firm, Townsend-Greenspan Associates.

To understand the factors that have transformed the American financial system since the 1980s, and to see why the "great moderation" is best understood as part of "the inter-crisis period," we need to understand four inter-related processes: disintermediation and the creation of a shadow banking system, deregulation, financial engineering, and securitization. Together, these processes helped create the market-based global economy we occupy today.

10.2. EARLY SIGNS OF THE TRANSFORMATION

While few contemporaries recognized its significance at the time, the most visible indication that changes were occurring in the structure of the American economy was a dramatic increase in financial disintermediation.[12] In the 1960s and 1970s, financial institutions subject to restrictions such as Regulation Q lost investment assets to products that returned higher rates because they were not subject to the Reg Q ceilings; often, these assets were invested directly in capital markets instead of being mediated by other financial institutions. Because US regulations covered all national banks and savings institutions, early competitors for American investment dollars were located in other countries. An important early player was the market in Eurodollars, launched by Citibank in London in the 1960s. Eurodollars are US dollar-denominated funds, which are largely unregulated and fall outside the jurisdiction of the Federal Reserve. Citibank-London offered its first Eurodollar issues in 1966 for large deposits (in the millions of dollars), and many of its early clients were US mutual funds. Because the issuing bank could operate on a narrower margin than US banks, and because deposits were less liquid, these funds offered investors higher yields than Reg Q–restricted financial institutions in America. As we will see in a moment, the US government soon responded to the threat such international competition posed by dramatically scaling back its system of financial regulation—as part of a program of deregulation designed to help the real and financial sides of the US economy compete in global markets.

For economic theorists, an early sign that money and finance were beginning to affect the US economy was the failure of the macroeconomic relationship known as the Phillips curve. The Phillips curve depicts the relationship between unemployment in the real economy and inflation, which is a financial phenomenon. The Phillips curve was based on a century-long data set introduced by Alban W. Phillips in 1958, which showed an inverse relation between unemployment and the rate of change of money wages. During the early 1960s, American Keynesians embraced Phillips's findings because they seemed to provide empirical evidence that supported Keynes's theories. If the Phillips curve was a fixed relation, policy makers could choose a point on the curve and devise policies to promote or "buy" more employment by accepting higher rates of inflation. In the early 1970s, economists' confidence in the Phillips curve was shattered when stagflation—the combination of stagnant wages and high inflation—revealed the shortcomings of macroeconometric models based on estimations of this changing theoretical relation. These shortcomings signaled that the Keynesian view of business cycles was in trouble—not, according to many economists, because new empirical evidence challenged it, but because Keynesian theory lacked adequate microfoundations.[13] Even as they pointed out this shortcoming of the Keynesian framework, however, most economists failed to see the underlying cause of the woes besetting the US economy in the 1970s: the global financial economy from which the United States had previously been insulated had begun to affect the very conditions in which theories were spun and policies drawn up. With the nation having abrogated the Bretton Woods agreements between 1968 and 1973, the value of currencies had become flexible, currency had begun to flow to the most advantageous markets, and the United States faced global competitors it had not previously had to consider. When dramatic changes occurred in the real side of the international economy—in agriculture and oil—effects rippled through the global economic system and the United States had no buffer.

After the giant corporation and the US government, the market-based US financial system, which was elaborated during the 1980s, constitutes the third institution that has profoundly shaped the history of finance in America. Of course, the structural transformation that manifested itself in this market-based system was more difficult to see than the new corporations that altered American life at the beginning of the twentieth century or the federal government, whose growth was obvious in inescapable waves of taxation, regulation, and public finance. As early as the 1970s, some signs of this emergent transformation began to be felt, yet these effects were staggered, and they remained inchoate rather than defined. Undeniably part of the larger process known as globalization, the structural transformation that elaborated the market-based financial system in the United States rapidly affected the financial side of the economy, gradually transformed international trade in real goods, and belatedly altered the way Americans imagined their place in the world. Before it was given a name or theoretical explanation, this transformation made its effects known—not least in the way assets were bought and sold and risk was managed.

Like blind men naming parts of the elephant closest to hand, economists and financial theorists reacted to the parts of this structural transformation that most immediately affected them.[14] In the 1970s the primary objective of economic policy makers at the Council of Economic Advisors and the Federal Reserve's twelve research departments was to design monetary, fiscal, regulatory, and supervisory policies to meet the dual mandates of the Employment Act of 1946; in the shadow of stagflation, they fell short on both goals. These economists were charged with maintaining America's global preeminence in the face of rising interest rates, declining domestic output, persistent increases in the level of inflation, rising unemployment, increased capital market volatility, and investor anxiety—all signs of the still-unrecognized transformation remaking the global and national financial systems.[15] The objective of financial theorists, model builders, and Wall Street consultants, by contrast, was to find innovative ways to minimize taxes, avoid regulation, and devise strategies that allowed portfolios to benefit from high inflation, high interest rates, and the investment psychology of markets.[16] The market volatility to which financial theorists responded constituted another face of the structural transformation already underway, and, although they were quick to capitalize on them, few realized why new arbitrage opportunities were opening around them.

Paradoxically, their shared inability to recognize the nature of the transformation both groups were experiencing was masked by the differences that seemed to separate them. Even though, by 1970, both disciplines—macroeconomics and finance—relied heavily on the sophisticated econometrics of time-series analysis and the stochastic mathematics of probability theory, the level of aggregation, timeliness, and quality of data used in macroeconomics posed problems different in kind from those presented by financial data, which was generated instantaneously and in large volume by trading on auction markets. This led to the second revolution in econometric practice, which we introduced as financial econometrics in chapter 9.[17]

The transformation in the structure of global finance struck the United States not simply in disturbing phenomena like financial disintermediation, the appearance of competitors for American investment dollars, and the failure of the macroeconometrics of the Phillips curve, but also in a series of shocks that emanated from all quarters of the real and financial sides of the economy. On the financial side, America's abrogation of the Bretton Woods monetary agreements allowed the value of the dollar, now trading as a global fiat currency, to fluctuate widely. Volatility affected not only the foreign exchanges but also domestic bond and stock markets. The precipitous stock market decline of 1973–74 was second only to the 1929 crash, and the bear market in fixed income that began in the early 1950s after the Fed Accord continued until 1982—raising domestic inflation rates, just as instability in the external value of the dollar raised interest rates. As a result, investors began to expect—and factor into their decisions—rising interest rates and growing inflation. These expectations, along with the inflation that fueled them, were targets of the Volcker deflation. On the real side of the economy, shortages in agricultural commodities and the unprecedented rise in oil prices caused by an oil embargo, then the formation of the OPEC cartel, coincided with an increase in the number of US bankruptcies, falling economic output, a loss of productivity for American labor, and rising unemployment.[18] The 1970s also witnessed major disruptions in the American political landscape, as the Watergate scandal erupted in 1972 and the ensuing impeachment proceedings against Richard M. Nixon led to the president's resignation in 1974. In December 1969, Nixon had declared an end to the prolonged, unsuccessful war in Southeast Asia, but the nation's entanglement in distant conflicts continued. After the American-backed Shah of Iran was deposed in February 1979, protestors stormed the Tehran Embassy in November, and the rescue operation finally authorized by President Jimmy Carter ended in failure in April 1980.

In the decade after the United States abandoned Bretton Woods, the nation's economy suffered three recessions, each apparently induced by an administration's policies. The last, and most severe was finally ended by the Volcker deflation, which also broke the back of the bear market in fixed income that began after the Fed Accord in 1951.[19] But the very turbulence that accompanied the recessions opened new opportunities for financiers eager to take advantage of the innovative models we described in chapter 9. As we have seen, the Chicago Mercantile Exchange launched the first financial futures contracts in 1972, offering contracts on seven major currencies, and it marketed the first interest rate future, a contract on the Government National Mortgage Association, in 1981. All the while, the Eurodollar market flourished in London as the still-unrecognized harbinger of changes to come. After the enactment of ERISA in 1974, which regulated the funding of defined benefit and contractual retirement plans, asset managers created new institutional offerings that competed for the pools of retirement funds in search of positive investment returns. In subsequent decades, retirement funds became the bread and butter of traditional asset managers and of the lucrative hedge fund industry.[20]

10.3. MACROECONOMIC THEORIES DURING THE INTER-CRISIS PERIOD

10.3a. New Classical Macroeconomic Theory, Dynamic Stochastic General Equilibrium Models, and Real-Business Cycle Theory

The same shocks that opened opportunities for financial theorists and investors posed a decade-long challenge for macroeconomic theorists. To many, the challenge seemed to emanate from the inability of Keynesian theory to explain the pattern of unemployment and inflation that appeared in the 1970s. Some argued that this inability stemmed from the lack of microfoundations in Keynesian theory—its failure to anchor changes in economic phenomena in an account of agents' optimizing behavior. The roots of the solution one influential group of macroeconomists devised to redress this failure lay in the period we have already examined: the end of World War II, when the classified techniques associated with operations research were transferred to nonmilitary applications.

In chapter 8, we saw that George Dantzig and Marshall Wood applied operations research techniques to the problem of transportation in the late 1940s. Within a few years, industrial economists, who wanted to address problems associated with business administration, were also adopting the dynamic programming technique, as well as the underlying mathematical structure of probability flows. In fact, funding for at least one of these early industrial applications came from the same source that supported much OR research: the US Air Force Scientific Computation of Optimal Programs (Project SCOOP). In 1949, Project SCOOP awarded the newly formed Graduate School of Industrial Administration at Carnegie Mellon University a three-year grant for research on "Intra Firm Planning and Control." Under the auspices of this grant, economists, econometricians, and computer scientists applied dynamic programing, stochastic processes, and NASA-engineered control theory to problems emerging from interfirm business activity. In 1960, Charles Holt, Franco Modigliani, John Muth, and Herbert Simon published *Planning, Production, Inventory & Employment,* a volume one economic historian calls a canonical operations research text.[21] The next year, Muth took the research project in a slightly different direction in "Rational Expectations and the Theory of Price Movements." In this article, Muth, who was a mathematical economist, developed a rationale for a stronger set of assumptions about how agents form expectations in anticipatory forecasting. Instead of using bounded rationality, the idea developed by his teacher and colleague Herb Simon, Muth insisted that agents make decisions not only by looking backward but also by looking forward. Indeed, Muth argued, agents' decisions are informed not simply by their own personal or anticipated experience but also by the economic theories used to model such decisions. As a consequence, according to Muth, far from overemphasizing the rationality of economic agents, "dynamic economic models do not assume enough rationality." As Muth explained, "expectations, since they are informed predictions of future events, are essentially the same as the predictions of the relevant economic theory."[22] Muth's formulation was soon applied to every branch of macroeconomics—business cycle theory, monetary theory, international trade, and growth theory. As it was developed and elaborated by Robert E. Lucas, Thomas Sargent, Edward Prescott, and Finn Kydland, Muth's rational expectations hypothesis launched a revolution that successfully challenged Keynesian macroeconomics.[23] By the 1980s, the models associated with rational expectations had attained general acceptance, especially in the United States.

The class of macroeconomic models associated with rational expectations is called dynamic stochastic general equilibrium models (DSGE). These models are *dynamic* in showing economic relations in time, especially the forward-looking behavior of economic agents, and they are *stochastic* in including shocks, which allow the models to accommodate a non-Knightian version of uncertainty. They are also *general* (Walrasian) because they include the entire economy, and they are *equilibrium* models because they impose explicit constraints and objectives for households and firms. In their most basic form, these models provide a mathematical mechanism for viewing processes. They do not have a specified content but can be used to model everything from inter-industry flows of goods to securities prices to business fluctuations. In fact, the options pricing model introduced by Fischer Black, Myron Scholes, and Robert C. Merton was closely allied to this class of models. Despite their proximity to financial models like the Black-Scholes-Merton model, in their macroeconomic form DSGE models assume that in the long-term, the influence of money is neutral. Economists call this a "neutrality" assumption.

The DSGE models were originally most closely associated with a theoretical school of macroeconomists known as the New Classical School, which was led in the 1970s by Lucas at the University of Chicago, Thomas Sargent at the University of Minnesota, and the team of Prescott and Kydland at Carnegie Mellon. Initially, Lucas used the models to explain fluctuations in the business cycle by placing aggregate fluctuations on a choice-theoretical framework: he demonstrated that agents' reactions to stochastic shocks adequately account for the positive relationship between the rate of inflation and the rate of employment. The implication of this theoretical reconsideration was that it was not possible for the government to exploit or adjust this relationship, as the Phillips curve-based policy assumed.[24] Lucas elaborated this idea in the Lucas critique—the argument that because economic agents can anticipate the actions of governments and central banks, they will factor these expectations into their behavior and thus neutralize the government's attempts to influence the economy. The New Classical approach to macroeconomic issues involved two technical innovations as well as new theoretical assumptions: to the modeling approach introduced by Keynesians such as Hicks, Lucas and Sargent added new mathematical tools, which they borrowed from the engineering sciences, and the advanced computational capacity made possible by breakthroughs in computer science.[25]

Beginning in the 1980s, Prescott and Kydland elaborated the rational expectations paradigm and New Classical assumptions in a modeling approach called Real-Business Cycle Theory (RBC). RBC added to New Classical macroeconomics a new empirical strategy, known as calibration, and it substituted for the monetary shocks Lucas had emphasized stochastic autocorrelated technology shocks.[26] These amendments were made in an attempt to synthesize Lucasian business cycle assumptions with optimal control theory as a way of integrating business cycle economics into a theory of growth. In their modeling approach, Prescott and Kydland followed Lucas in combining elements of two traditions: the NBER reference cycle approach and Ragnar Frisch's impulse propagation model. From the first, they adopted Wesley Mitchell's observation that each business cycle is unique; from the latter, they took the convention of decomposing growth trends and viewing fluctuations as driven by an impulse and propagation mechanism. Prescott and Kydland's "Time to Build and Aggregate Fluctuations" (1982) identified the propagation mechanism as technology shocks, and it substituted the controversial but widely imitated technique of calibration for the estimation technique used in the Cowles Commission simultaneous equation approach. This allowed them to "quantitatively derive the implications of theory and measurement for business cycle fluctuations using the full discipline of dynamic stochastic general equilibrium theory and national accounts statistics."[27]

Calibration required the enhanced computational power that was becoming available in the 1980s. As Prescott and Kydland used it, calibration relied on a software program that incorporated an algorithm known as the Kalman filter, introduced by the electrical engineer and mathematician Rudolf Kalman. In computer and aerospace applications, the Kalman filter was used to extract a signal from long sequences of technical measurements; in Prescott and Kydland's macroeconomic models, it handled the assumption of rational expectations. As Michel De Vroey explains, the advantage of using calibration was "negative: it avoided, first, the refutation conclusion that would have followed with econometric testing and, second, it side-stepped the difficult enterprise of constructing 'deeply structural' econometric models."[28] De Vroey argues that Kydland and Prescott performed the same service for Lucas that J. R. Hicks had performed for Keynes: both sets of "followers" consolidated the revolutionary implications of the pioneer by extending an original insight into a usable framework, which could be widely adopted and applied.[29]

New Classical and RBC macroeconomic models flourished during the 1970s and 1980s. New econometric techniques, the ever-increasing computational power of mainframe, then personal, computers, and funding from the National Science Foundation and the Federal Reserve Board allowed researchers to conduct important research programs using these models. Early on, Lucas and Prescott modeled investment as a stochastic dynamic programming problem.[30] Later, they applied extensions of this model, under rational expectations, to monetary, business cycle, and growth economics, using a common framework of Walrasian general equilibrium theory and New Classical assumptions. Christopher Sims at Princeton developed an "atheoretical" variant of this model based on the Vector AutoRegressive approach to time series analysis. Large, mainframe-dependent Keynesian macroeconometric models, such as the Federal Reserve-MIT-Penn Model, based on the original Klein-Goldberger and Brookings models, continued to be used to generate forecasts for central bankers and government agencies, but, by the end of the 1980s, dynamic stochastic general equilibrium models, using VAR techniques written into econometric software programs and running on personal computers, became the workhorses of the economics profession.[31]

As influential as the rational expectations revolution and the DSGE models have been, it is important to note that, even in the heyday of this macroeconomic approach, serious objections were raised to its assumptions, omissions, and empirical applicability. One early sign of dissent from the position that was rapidly becoming macroeconomic orthodoxy appeared at a conference intended to celebrate the demise of the Keynesian paradigm. Held in 1978 and sponsored by the Boston Federal Reserve, "After the Phillips Curve: Persistence of High Inflation and High Unemployment" culminated in a two-volume collection of essays edited by Lucas and Sargent. The title of this collection—*Rational Expectations and Econometric Practice*—announced the triumphant arrival of the new guard.[32] The paper Lucas and Sargent delivered at the conference, provocatively entitled "After Keynesian Macroeconomics," was intended to be both a manifesto for the new macroeconomics and last rites for its displaced and discredited predecessor. In Boston, ground-zero for Keynesian orthodoxy, the rational expectations revolutionaries announced that Keynesian models were "widely incorrect," "fundamentally flawed," "of no value," represented "failure on a large scale," and offered "no hope."[33] Lucas and Sargent concluded their paper with a nod to the policy implications of their work: "While such a theory predicts positive correlations between the inflation rate and the money supply, on the one hand, and the level of output, on the other, it also asserts that those correlations do not depict trade-offs that can be exploited by a policy authority"[34]. In essence, they were saying that the Phillips curve-based policy was wrong and the government should leave the economy alone.

Even as Lucas and Sargent danced on the grave of the Keynesians, however, the limitations of the New Classical approach were being exposed. In the presentation that immediately followed the Lucas-Sargent paper, Lawrence Klein identified one factor left out of the DSGE model: the impact of globalization. Klein was the primary architect of the Keynesian, structural, large-scale Wharton macroeconometric model that Sargent and Lucas had just denominated "wreckage." In "Disturbances in the International Economy," Klein reported on the construction of an international trading model, as part of a program titled Project LINK, which was designed to augment the closed model of a domestic economy by adding a much richer specification of a national economy's relationship to the global economy. This massive international project, which linked macroeconometric models of developed and developing nations together in a single model, coincided with Richard M. Nixon's New Economic Policy, which included abandoning the Bretton Wood agreement. As Klein reported to conference participants, this was simply one of many shocks the model had to accommodate.

In the second full year of operation of the international trading model built under the auspices of Project LINK, we encountered the first of a series of world-scale shocks, NEP (President Nixon's New Economic Policy) with the closing of the gold window, surcharging of automobile imports, and a host of domestic economic restrictions. This phase, known in Japan as Nixon shocks, led to the Smithsonian agreement on exchange rates and a later dollar devaluation in 1973. This was only the beginning of a tumultuous period with many other shocks of a comparable magnitude to the Nixon shocks and the Smithsonian agreement: (i) Soviet grain purchases, rising food prices, rising raw material prices; (ii) oil embargo and quadrupling of OPEC prices; (iii) protectionism; (iv) capital transfers; (v) wage offensives.[35]

Klein cautioned his audience that to focus exclusively on a nation's domestic economy, as did closed-economy macroeconomic models such as the DSGE, risked obscuring the possibility that additional global shocks might be on the horizon. In his account, these shocks included "debt default, speculative waves in currencies and commodities, [and] famine as a result of large-scale crop failure."[36]

A second sign that objections were being raised to the innovations of New Classical and RBC macroeconomics can be found in another conference, this one held at the interdisciplinary Santa Fe Institute in September 1987, one month before the US stock market plummeted. The "Evolutionary Paths of the Global Economy Workshop" brought together leading economic theorists and natural scientists to explore how best to understand nonlinear dynamical systems, such as the global economy and biological symbiotic systems. Chaired by Kenneth J. Arrow and Philip W. Anderson, the workshop was designed to foster mutual appreciation of the contributions made by disciplines that rarely spoke to each other. Instead, if the questions raised at the final plenary session are a fair indication, the workshop provoked incredulity in the natural scientists, who were struck by the methodological and theoretical limitations in macroeconomists' approach to systems that might not be stationary but evolving. In his summary comments, the physicist Richard Palmer posed three questions, which summed up his frustration at the economists' theory and method: "Why do economists downplay or ignore the role of psychological, sociological, and political forces in economic systems? . . . Rational Expectations (RE) theory with infinite foresight appears obviously wrong. Why is it so well accepted? . . . Can a system with a fixed number of variables adequately model innovation?"[37]

What the physicists considered theoretical and methodological limitations were not unknown to the New Classical and RBC macroeconomists, of course. The economists attending the Santa Fe workshop were willing to accept these limitations, however, as constraints imposed by modeling itself. Indeed, as many economists were ready to acknowledge, neither the rational expectations hypothesis nor the Kalman filter technique was intended to refer to the real world. Instead, these were properties of the model world, the use of which had become central to macroeconomic theorizing since the days of Frisch and Marschak. "One can ask . . . whether expectations are rational in the Klein-Goldberger model of the United States economy," Robert Lucas explained; "one cannot ask whether people in the United States have rational expectations." Rudolf Kalman was even more emphatic. "To put it more bluntly, control theory does not deal with the real world, but only with mathematical models of certain aspects of the real world."[38]

It is important to underscore this characteristic of the DSGE models, for it is precisely the relationship between the world of the models and the real-world economy that captures both the strengths and weaknesses of these models. Like all mathematical models, models built on this framework simplify the complexities of the real-world economy in order to isolate variables and test hypotheses. As developed by Lucas, however—and, to an even greater extent, by Prescott and Kydland—DSGE models shifted the balance between what Frisch called the model world and the world outside the model: instead of simply capturing a simplified aspect of the real-world economy, the DSGE model creates a fictitious economy and makes propositions about it. These propositions might be consistent with the model world, just as they had been used to construct it, but the fit between the model world and the propositions has little say about the relevance of these propositions for the world outside the model.[39] This is true even though Prescott and Kydland claimed that their advance over Lucas consisted both in making Lucas's models quantitative and in relating them to data about the real economy. Of the five steps required to make their models answer the question with which Prescott and Kydland began ("To what extent [can] observed output fluctuations in the United States . . . be attributed to technology shocks?"), only the last—comparing the time series generated by the model to the time series provided by US national income statistics—attempted to map the model to the real world.[40] In elevating the criteria of consistency and mathematical precision over accuracy or relevance, and in using the homogenizing construct of the representative agent to simplify human behavior, DSGE models may have completed the move toward formalization economics had been making since the days of Irving Fisher, but they left much to be desired as guides to policy.

At first, and in keeping with the tenuous relationship Lucas and Sargent acknowledged between the model and the world, the small dynamic models developed on the DSGE rational expectation framework were not used for policy or forecasting purposes. After 2000, however, estimated DSGE models were used for forecasting and policy, where they complemented large structural models, simpler trend-extrapolating models, and the ad hoc judgment that policy makers continued to use around the world.[41]

10.3b. Developments in Information Technology, New Keynesian Macroeconomics, the New Neoclassical Synthesis, and Hyman Minsky

We have already seen that breakthroughs in digital computing were essential to the development of DSGE and RBC models. Indeed, even though "Time to Build and Aggregate Fluctuations" was a paradigmatic example of a parsimonious model, which explained fluctuations in real output and labor hours based on the measured standard deviation and correlation of only eight variables against the ninth—output—it took advantage of the information technology revolution underway in the late 1960s, as new software was developed and reliance on centralized mainframe computers was decreased by the proliferation of personal, desktop computers. By the 1980s, the econometric techniques developed in the post–World War II period by the Cowles Commission researchers had been consolidated in textbooks and had begun to be made commercially available in software programs, such as TPS (developed by Robert Hall at MIT), MODLR (developed at Brookings), and PcGive (originally AUTOREG, developed at LSE).[42] The commercial company Mathworks, founded in 1984, sold and distributed a software program called Matlab, which enabled modelers to take advantage of powerful new algorithms for dynamic analysis and econometrics. PcGive provided diagnostics for sophisticated tests of whether "good" models had been estimated.

Although the coincidence of the advent of the personal computer and the formulation of Lucasian New Classical theory on a framework of rational expectations partially explains the influence of DSGE models, it can be argued that the paradigm shift from Keynesian IS-LM models to the New Classical and RBS/DSGE models was not complete until a group of theorists called New Keynesians brought to the technology of DSGE a new set of assumptions. These assumptions replaced the New Classical emphasis on perfect competition and a flexible price framework with a framework that emphasized monopolistic competition and rigid prices. The New Keynesians also returned the monetary side of the economy to center stage, whereas the New Classical and RBC theorists had abstracted money.[43] Despite these differences, the New Keynesian models continued the tradition of Lucas, Prescott, and Kydland's DSGE models, and were, in fact, an outgrowth of RBC modeling. The most important intervention of the New Keynesian models was the idea that the behavior of the macroeconomic system cannot be derived simply from microfoundations—bottom-up, as it were, from the behavior of individuals. Instead, they argued, emergent properties that emanate from group behaviors, such as herding and contagion, required a top-down analysis as well. Furthermore, they objected, the parable of the atomistic, self-interested, rational agent was misleading; the labor market should not be assumed to be in equilibrium; and flexible prices for goods, labor, and services meant that contractual obligations and customer obligation maintenance practices, explicit or tacit, were at play. Finally, they assumed that involuntary employment is the result of market imperfections, and that information cannot be assumed to be perfect. With these assumptions, the New Keynesians built variants of DSGE models such as imperfect competition models, sticky wages models, contract models, information asymmetry models, and consumer uncertainty models.[44]

In 2003, Columbia University professor Michael Woodford published *Interest and Prices: Foundations of A Theory of Monetary Policy*, in which he called the recent convergence of these macroeconomic programs the "New" Neoclassical Synthesis. According to Woodford, the New Neoclassical Synthesis includes the DSGE econometric framework (with or without rational expectations), John Taylor's monetarist rule-based inflation-targeting approach, and New Keynesian macro-analysis.[45] Under the Taylor rule, the Fed's Fund rates operating target is set as a linear function of a measure of the current inflation rate and the current gap between real and potential output, with an implicit inflation target of 2% per annum.[46] Marvin Goodfriend and Robert King have explained the most important policy implications of the new synthesis:

> The New Neoclassical Synthesis inherits the spirit of the old [synthesis] in that it combines Keynesian and classical elements. Methodologically, it involves the systematic application of intertemporal optimization and rational expectations as stressed by Robert Lucas. In the synthesis these ideas are applied to the pricing and output decisions at the heart of Keynesian models, new and old. . . . Moreover the new synthesis also embodies the insights of monetarists, such as Milton Friedman and Karl Brunner regarding the theory and practice of monetary policy. . . . The NNS models suggest that monetary actions have an important effect on

real economic activity persisting over several years. . . . The models suggest little long run-trade off between inflation and real activity. . . . The models suggest significant gains from eliminating inflation . . . and the models imply that credibility plays an important role in understanding the effect of monetary policy.[47]

Before we leave the economic and financial theories spun out during the inter-crisis period, we need to mention one of the few economists who did recognize the tremors of these years as signs of structural transformation. This was Hyman P. Minsky, who warned as early as 1957 that the modern financial system was inherently unstable, but whose writings of the next four decades were ignored by nearly all mainstream macroeconomists and financial theorists. During his formative years, Minsky came into contact with many of the figures we have met in this book: he studied with Frank Knight and Oscar Lange at the University of Chicago, and was Alvin Hansen's research assistant at Harvard; also at Harvard, he began his dissertation under Joseph Schumpeter, then completed the thesis (after Schumpeter's death) with Wassily Leontief; he spent a year at Cambridge University, where he engaged with Joan Robinson and Frank Hahn; his mature work drew on the financial writing of John Gurley and Edward Shaw; and, in 1996, he was awarded the Veblen-Commons Award by the Association of Evolutionary Economics. As this award suggests, Minsky is best understood as an institutionalist in the tradition of Veblen; but he also considered himself a "financial Keynesian," by which he meant that he wanted to resurrect in Keynes's work the financial themes that American Keynesianism had all but erased.[48] Minsky was both behind the times and ahead of his day, however. Primarily rediscovered in the wake of the financial crisis of 2008, Minsky largely toiled at the margins of the discipline during his lifetime—primarily because he wanted to show how institutional constraints affected an economy understood as evolutionary, while the rest of this discipline embraced mathematics and modeling and viewed the economy as naturally tending toward equilibrium states.

Viewing the economy in evolutionary terms, Minsky identified four stages in the history of capitalism. Each was characterized by a unique financial structure. The commercial capitalism of the nineteenth century was dominated by commercial banks and short-term loans. At the beginning of the twentieth century, this system was replaced by finance capitalism, governed by investment banks and long-term loans. At the end of World War II, the New Deal initiatives we examined in chapter 4 constrained financial activity, and the result was the emergence of managerial welfare-state capitalism. This persisted through the next several decades, until the large pool of accumulated savings began to encourage ever-greater risk taking, and the consolidation of the shadow banking system encouraged growth of private debt relative to income and led investors to rely on short-term finance. Minsky called this last stage money-manager capitalism. This stage corresponds closely to what we are calling the market-based financial system.

In addition to recognizing both the structural transformation that was altering the face of American finance and the interpenetration of the financial and real sides of the economy, Minsky is noteworthy for what has been called the "financial instability hypothesis." According to this elaboration of Keynes's argument that fluctuations of investment spending drive the business cycle, Minsky argued that financing—which is necessary to investment but which is also, by nature, expensive—generates structural instability. L. Randall Wray summarizes Minsky's position as follows:

> During an upswing, profit-seeking firms and banks become more optimistic, taking on riskier financial structures. Firms commit larger portions of expected revenues to debt service. Lenders accept smaller down payments and lower quality collateral. In the boom, financial institutions innovate new products and finesse rules and regulations imposed by supervisory authorities. Borrowers use more external finance (borrowing rather than using savings or retained earnings) and increasingly issue short-term debt that is potentially volatile (it must be "rolled over" or renewed, so there is risk that lenders might refuse to do so). As the economy heats up, the central bank hikes its interest rate to cool things down—but with greater use of short-term finance, borrowers face higher debt service costs (with short-term finance they cannot "lock in" rates). . . . Over the business cycle, fragility rises, exposing the system to the possibility of a crisis coming from a variety of directions: income flows turn out to be lower than expected, interest rates rise, lenders curtail lending, or a prominent firm or bank defaults on payment commitments. Just as finance accelerates the boom, it fuels the collapse as debtors need to cut back spending and sell assets to make contractual payments. As spending falls, income and employment fall; as assets are sold, their prices fall. In the extreme, debt-deflation dynamics that Irving Fisher saw in the Great Depression can be generated—asset values plummet, wealth is wiped out, and widespread bankruptcies occur. This causes people and firms to cut back spending, so output and employment collapse.[49]

In the context of DSGE models and rational expectations macroeconomic theory—whether of the New Classical, New Keynesian, or New Neoclassical Synthesis variety—Minsky's argument seems both out of synch and eerily prescient. While other blind men were stroking the elephant, Minsky was describing the damage the beast could inflict. For the most part, unfortunately, his argument fell on deaf ears.

10.3c. New Research Initiatives

During the inter-crisis period, the DSGE framework was not only augmented and elaborated. It was also challenged from perspectives embodied in a dizzying number of research projects—not all of which were as marginalized as Minsky's. Many drew on empirical work; they sometimes used experimental approaches; and some took advantage of work in disciplines as disparate as psychology, sociology, politics, mathematics, philosophy, and the science of institutions. When taken as a whole, these initiatives reveal that, even though the New Classical-RBC-New Keynesian-New Neoclassical Synthesis DSGE models did "downplay [and] ignore the role of psychological, sociological, and political forces in economic systems," as the Santa Fe scientists complained, the discipline as a whole should be cleared of this charge. Although the jury is still out, it may well be that what Robert Shiller described in 2003 as an "elegant theory," which would heal the rift between macroeconomics and finance, may emerge from one of these research projects.[50] While a comprehensive survey of these initiatives lies beyond the scope of this book, we can summarize a representative sampling of approaches to modeling economic agents, information, corporate finance, economic growth, and dynamics. These projects have taken on new relevance in the wake of the global financial crisis.

Modeling the behavior of economic agents, *experimental studies* in prospect theory and behavioral economics have demonstrated the regularity of cognitive bias in the formulation of judgments under conditions of uncertainty, and *experimental game theorists* have demonstrated the limitations of Nash equilibrium in experiments that simulate market behavior.[51] *Behavioral economics and behavioral finance* model the influence of beliefs, social norms, and values in economic behaviors.[52] *Information economics* deconstructs the assumption of perfect information with models of asymmetric information and signaling.[53] *Empirical studies* of prices and returns in the foreign exchange and securities markets investigate the limits of rationality assumptions in such market phenomena as excess volatility, the equity risk premium puzzle, and movements of nominal exchange rates.[54] The *economic and finance theory concerned with "unknowable unknowns" and "unique un-knowable unknowns"* explores the implications of Frank Knight's version of uncertainty, as theorists apply philosophical and experiential insights to push beyond all rationality postulates.[55] *New institutional economics* examines the formal and informal constraints that underlie economic activity, social and legal norms, and rules with respect to such factors as organizational structure, transaction costs, property rights, governance structure and contracts; and the *modern theory of corporate finance* models the fault lines caused by agency problems, information asymmetry, moral hazard, and incentives and motivations within corporations and financial intermediaries.[56] The *theory of endogenous economic growth* extends Joseph Schumpeter's theory of development, which introduced the role of entrepreneurial "creative destructive" as a source of technological innovation, to explore synergies between the evolution of technology and finance.[57] Regarding system dynamics, *complex-system theory* demonstrates the limitations of the representative agent in the New Classical models, and the mathematics of multiple equilibria in complex systems allows these theorists to model the formation of asset bubbles as nonlinear explosions or implosions.[58] From a social accounting perspective, *consistent stock/flow models* have pointed out the blind spots in the flow-based DSGE models.[59] And *new geographical economics* examines spatial aspects of the economy using modeling techniques developed to analyze industrial organization, international trade, and economic growth.[60]

10.4. THE TRANSITION TO A MARKET-BASED FINANCIAL SYSTEM

10.4a. Deregulation and the Growth of Finance in America after 1980

While we leave a full account of the future of economic and financial theory to others, we cannot quit the inter-crisis period without exploring in more depth the largely unrecognized forces that caused the disturbances inaugurated by the 1970s crisis to erupt into view after 1980. Together, these forces—deregulation, securitization and the shadow banking system (disintermediation), and financial innovation—transformed the US financial system by amplifying what had been an emergent orientation toward the market into a full-fledged market-based system, with all the instabilities that implies.

Deregulation, which was a central plank of the supply-side policies promoted by Ronald Reagan, was intended to help the economy grow its way out of economic trouble by releasing market forces. Financial deregulation was an important part of deregulation in general. Begun under the Carter administration, financial deregulation continued under the next four US presidents.[61] Its early phase was epitomized by the 1980 passage of the Depository Institutions Deregulation and Monetary Control Act, which lifted Regulation Q, the restriction imposed on the rate of interest banks could pay on demand deposits.[62] Other significant milestones in financial deregulation include the Supreme Court's 1978 ruling that banks could export the usury laws of their home state to other states; the 1982 Garn-St. Germain Depository Institutions Act, which deregulated the thrift industry; the 1989 Financial Institutions Reform and Recovery Act, which abolished the Federal Home Loan Bank Board and created the Resolution Trust Corporation to resolve the problem of failed thrifts; the 1994 Riegel-Neal Interstate Banking and Breaching Efficiency Act, which removed restrictions on interstate bank branches; the 1996 reinterpretation, by the Federal Reserve Board, of the Glass-Steagall Act; the 1998 merger of Citicorp and Travelers, which married a commercial bank to an insurance company to create the world's largest financial services company; the 1999 Gramm-Leach Bliley Act, which repealed the Glass-Steagall Act entirely; and the 2000 Commodities Futures Modernization Act, which prevented the Commodity Futures Trading Commission from regulating most over-the-counter derivative contracts, including credit default swaps.[63] Not only were these acts adopted by four different administrations—the Carter, Reagan, George H. W. Bush, and Clinton administrations—but many were enacted with strong bipartisan congressional support. Financial deregulation continued under the George W. Bush administration (2001–9).

Deregulation led to, and was also accelerated by, dramatic growth in the US financial sector. This growth began in 1980 and, in addition to deregulation, was fed by both the innovative products created by financial theorists and engineers in the 1960s and 1970s and technological breakthroughs in digital communications. In the context of deregulation, financial services and fees soared in the decades between 1980 and 2007. As a percentage of the nation's GDP, the size of the financial sector increased at a faster rate than in the previous thirty years, increasing at a rate of thirty basis points of GDP a year in 2007, up from the rate of a seven-basis-point increase per annum during the prior thirty years.[64] At the same time, connections between the US financial system and counterparts all over the world were strengthened, as digital innovations like the Global telex network (from 1966), the Clearing House Interbank Payments System (from 1970), Swift (the Society for Worldwide Interbank Telecommunications, from 1973), online securities trading (from 1982), and Citibank's Financial Services Technology Consortium (from 1993) helped create a global financial system in which the United States was simply one—albeit generally the most important—player.

In 2013, Robin Greenwood and David Scharfstein, research associates at the NBER and faculty members of the Harvard Business School, published an analysis of the magnitude and drivers of financial growth in the United States. The data Greenwood and Scharfstein used came from many of the sources whose history we have traced, including the Federal Reserve's flow of funds accounts. Among their findings, two are particularly telling: first, in 1980, "the value of total financial assets was approximately five times U.S. GDP; by 2007, this ratio had doubled"; and second, "over the same period, the ratio of financial assets to tangible assets (like plant and equipment, land, and residential structures) increased as well" (446). These observations succinctly convey how the relationship between the real and the financial sides of the US economy has been transformed since 1980.

Equally important is Greenwood and Scharfstein's analysis of the factors that have caused the financial sector to grow. In their account, the two principal drivers of the growth of finance are asset management (fees) and the expansion of household credit (debt). Output from asset management, mostly in the form of fees, has soared as the value of financial assets under professional management has increased. This increase began after the Volcker deflation in 1982 initiated the gradual decline in interest rates, a decline that continued for two decades. The increase in output from asset management reflects a growth in the percentage of households that own stock—from 32% in 1989 to 51% in 2007 (13–14). It also reflects an increase in the share of household equity holdings under professional management—up from 25% in 1980 to 53% in 2007 (12). But the increased output also speaks to the soaring value of the managed assets: between 1980 and 2007, the value of traded equity and fixed income securities increased from 107% of GDP to 323% of GDP (11). For mutual funds alone (including money market funds), assets under management grew from $134 billion in 1980 to over $12 trillion in 2007 (9), and the fees for all managed assets, fluctuating between 1.1% and 1.6% of managed assets, have swelled the financial sector as a whole. "All told, during the period 1980–2007, total asset management fees grew by 2.2 percentage points of GDP, which is over one-third of the growth in financial sector output" (11). Asset values rose so dramatically in part because the two-decade-long regime of low interest rates proved the duration rule Fredrick Macaulay laid out in the 1930s: the value of fixed income assets goes up when interest rates go down.

The growth in household credit since 1980 is equally telling. In chapter 4 we saw how the frothiness of 1920s "new era" finance was whipped by innovative credit arrangements like installment buying plans. We also saw that one aspect of the New Deal response to the collapse of credit in 1929 was to extend Hoover's promotion of home ownership and increase government involvement in the housing market, both through underwriting mortgage loans and by extending tax advantages to mortgage holders. While Americans took out mortgages and other forms of debt in the decades between the 1930s and 1980, the percentage of GDP represented by household credit, mostly mortgage debt, only began to increase dramatically in 1980. Between that year and 2007, household credit grew from 48% of GDP to 99%. In the same period, corporate credit grew from 31% to 50% of GDP (21).

10.4b. Securitization and the Shadow Banking System

The growth in household credit was facilitated by—and also accelerated—two further changes in the financial system: the rise in securitization and the extension of the shadow banking system. Greenwood and Scharfstein point out that the percentage of household credit as a share of GDP held by banks did not change between 1980 and 2007, remaining at about 40% (21). What did change were the volume and value of asset-backed securities held by banks and other financial intermediaries. Generally, banks created securitized assets (loans) to remove the mortgage loans they had financed from their balance sheets. "As early as 1995," Greenwood and Scharfstein point out, "more than half of all outstanding single-family mortgages and a sizeable share of commercial mortgages and consumer credit were securitized" (21).

Commercial banks did not want to keep mortgage loans on their balance sheets partly because worries over the levels of the reserve capital banks held had provoked the government to impose tougher bank rules in the late 1980s. When the rules took effect in the mid-1990s, banks began bundling the loans into asset-backed securities, in the form of collateralized loan obligations (CLOs) and collateralized debt obligations (CDOs), which they broke up into risk-specific tranches and sold to outside investors, such as security broker-dealers, pension funds, and insurance companies. Securitization was driven by several factors: an increase in consumer demand; an increase in supply, made possible by technological breakthroughs in administering large pools of securities; and inadequate legislative oversight. Whatever its causes, the growth of credit associated with securitization (and the increase in fees that accompanied it) fed the extension of shadow banking.

Shadow banking is a term used to refer to the institutions that perform the core bank-intermediation functions (maturity transformation, liquidity transformation, leverage, and credit risk transformation) outside the regulated system of official banking. For this reason, the shadow banking system is an example of the disintermediation of finance. The shadow banking system originated in the 1930s, when the US government created agencies such as Fannie Mae to backstop mortgage loans. In addition to government-sponsored entities like Fannie Mae and Freddie Mac, the shadow banking system now includes hedge funds, money market funds, finance companies, security broker-dealers who fund their assets with repurchase agreements (repos), and structured investment vehicles (SIVs). The entities that compose the shadow banking system have historically faced the same risks banks face, but before 2008, they were not regulated or insured by federal deposit insurance, and they did not have access to the Federal Reserve's lender-of-last resort credit facilities.[65] The institutions of the shadow banking system developed new ways of supplying credit to household consumers, but their immunity to oversight by the Fed, the SEC, and other institutions of central oversight left them vulnerable to exogenous shocks such as the collapse in housing prices and the ensuing defaults on mortgages that began in 2006. The vulnerability of the shadow banking system, in turn, exposed millions of borrowers to risks they did not know they were assuming.

The shadow banking system generated two apparently antithetical effects. On the one hand, it removed a significant percentage of the bank-intermediation process, which Goldsmith and Copeland made visible in the 1950s, from the official banking system. As a result, much of the business of finance, which the Federal Reserve flow of funds accounts were designed to track, disappeared from official view. Then, too, many financial activities previously conducted through institutions became functions of relationships that formed outside the regulated financial system. Because institutions have traditionally been targets of regulation, these activities slipped out of the regulatory network. On the other hand, the shadow banking system installed layers of mediation between financial products and the assets that backed them. Simply because the shadow banking system removed intermediation from the regulated banking system does not mean that intermediation no longer occurred. On the contrary. Within the shadow banking system, credit is intermediated through a variety of instruments, ranging from securitized products like asset-backed securities to repurchase agreements (repos) and money market funds. Intermediation within the shadow banking system tends to use short-term liabilities to fund illiquid long-term assets, and, while this may have reduced the cost of credit for some consumers, it also helped make the market-based system vulnerable to shocks.

Greenwood and Scharfstein have created a credit intermediation index to measure the number of steps involved in credit creation. Their index reveals that most of the increase in the layering of credit intermediation occurred in the 1990s, when nonbank financial intermediaries began to purchase large amounts of asset-backed securities. Because these financial intermediaries funded their purchases with debt, they exponentially increased the number of layers within the process of credit intermediation (22–25).

10.4c. Structured Investment Vehicles

Structured investment vehicles provide a good example of the layering of credit mediation within the shadow banking system and help demonstrate how this layering increased risk in the lead-up to 2008. A structured investment vehicle (SIV) is an entity created to profit from the credit spread between the portfolio of long-term assets it holds and the short-term liabilities it issues. Such nonbank institutions are permanently capitalized and have an active management team, and they are often registered as offshore companies to avoid taxation. Before 2008, their activities were typically not recorded on the balance sheet of the bank or sponsor that set them up. Essentially, the activity of the SIV is identical to traditional credit-spread banking: the SIV raises capital, generally by borrowing from the money market at low rates; leverages the capital by issuing short-term securities, such as commercial paper or public bonds; then uses that money to purchase longer-term securities, in the form of securitized pools of residential mortgage-backed securities or student loans or credit card debt, which earn rates higher than the cost of funding. The profits of the SIV come from the spread between its income on the assets it holds and the cost of funding its liabilities. An SIV performs two kinds of intermediation and accepts the attendant risks: a credit transformation (lending to less qualified borrowers while issuing high-rated liabilities) and a maturity transformation (borrowing short while lending long). In number, SIVs never represented a large component of the shadow banking system, but the assets they managed were substantial: in 2004 there were only eighteen SIVs, managing assets valued at $147 billion; by 2007, the number had increased to thirty-six, and their assets under management exceeded $400 billion.[66]

The first SIVs were created in the late 1980s by Citibank as a response to volatility in the capital markets. Because the AAA rating assigned them by credit rating agencies seemed to guarantee high quality, these SIVs were considered safe ways for investors to earn stable returns on their capital. The SIVs faced several risks, however, which partly derived from the densely mediated nature of the assets they bought and sold. Because all securitized products are composed of assets that are different in kind, it was difficult to assess the composite risk of the assets that secured the derivatives bought and sold by the SIVs. When some SIVs invested in subprime US mortgage-backed securities, they exposed themselves to risk no one was monitoring. The rating agencies' mathematical models, which were supposed to replace the first-hand monitoring performed by traditional banks, turned out to rely on assumptions that were, in some cases, disastrously wrong, such as the assumption that house prices would continue to rise at an annual rate of 6% forever or that mortgage default would not trigger defaults in other loans, such as automobile loans. Coupled with the injudicious—in some cases, criminal—marketing of mortgages to individuals unable to meet the re-set interest rates of variable-rate mortgages, the failure of the models meant that the bundled loans held by the SIVs began to underperform against statistical expectations, and SIVs found it difficult to sell commercial paper. This caused a run on the entire shadow banking system, and because many banks relied on the SIVs and other parts of the shadow banking system for short-term funds, the run created pressure on the official banking system. We return to the 2008–9 financial crisis below, but here we merely note that by the time the US Congress passed the Troubled Asset Relief Program (TARP) in October 2008, the last remaining SIV, Sigma Finance, had entered liquidation.

10.4d. Credit Derivatives

The Commodities Futures Modernization Act of 2000 made it possible for financial engineers to create a bewildering variety of new financial products, most of which were derivatives. These included synthetic credit derivatives such as credit-linked notes, credit default swaps, collateralized debt obligations (CDOs), and collateralized debt obligations squared. These products resemble the derivatives we examined in chapter 9 (forwards, swaps, options, and futures), in that their value derives from an underlying asset, but credit derivatives are designed to allow investors to manage their exposure to risk by separating risk from the product or event with which it is associated and transferring it to a buyer. The first credit derivative was created in 1993 by J. P. Morgan; by 1996, the value of outstanding credit derivatives had reached $40 billion; and as of September 15, 2008, the day Lehman Brothers filed for bankruptcy, the worldwide credit derivatives market was valued at $62 trillion, according to the *Times* of London.[67]

Funded credit derivatives, which are usually created by a financial institution, involve an initial payment by the party that assumes the credit risk; this payment is used to settle the contract if the credit event (a default or credit downgrade) occurs. A common form of funded credit derivative is the CDO. Unfunded credit derivatives are bilateral contracts in which neither party puts up money unless the credit event occurs. The most common unfunded credit derivative is a credit default swap. Unfunded credit derivatives can be combined with funded credit derivatives, in another example of the layering that creates a daisy chain of securitized financial products. This is the process that led to the near-collapse and government bailout of the insurance giant AIG in September 2008. Financial engineers in the London branch of AIG called AIG Financial Products created credit default swaps designed to insure CDOs against default. AIG sold this insurance to investors who held the various kinds of debt pooled into the CDOs, and the business proved extremely profitable for the division; in five years, its revenues rose from $735 million to $3 billion. Because insured CDOs contained bundled mortgage debt, however, they were subject to risk if homeowners defaulted on their loans. When this began to happen, AIG incurred enormous losses, its stock price fell, and a reduction in the credit rating of AIG forced it to post collateral for its own outstanding loans. When the US government stepped in with $85 billion to save the company from insolvency, the London division alone had lost $25 billion.[68]

The US government saved AIG because the company was deemed "too big to fail." In the judgment of US officials like Ben Bernanke (chair of the Federal Reserve) and Timothy Geithner (secretary of the Treasury), the insurance giant was so connected, through both insurance contracts and debt obligations, to so many other financial institutions around the world that its failure could have ricocheted throughout the global financial system, destroying pension funds, hedge funds, investment banks, and even sovereign funds.[69] The layering typical of derivative products such as credit default swaps is one source of the systemic risk that can threaten the global financial system, not just national economies like that of the United States.[70]

10.5. THE MARKET-BASED FINANCIAL SYSTEM IN TROUBLE

All the features we have just described—the acceleration of securitization in the context of deregulation, the expansion of the shadow banking system, the growth of assets invested in SIVs, and the proliferation of engineered financial products like credit derivatives—are symptoms of the structural transformation of the US financial system to which we have repeatedly referred. While a comprehensive picture of this emergent system would require placing the US financial system in a global context, here we offer only a snapshot of the domestic situation. We draw our account of the market-based financial system from "The Changing Nature of Financial Intermediation and the Crisis of 2007–2009," prepared by Tobias Adrian and Hyun Song Shin, staff members of the Federal Reserve Bank of New York.

Adrian and Shin contrast the market-based financial system that has been developing since 1980 with the traditional bank-based financial system. In the latter, banks serve as intermediaries between depositors and borrowers, and the central bank oversees and backstops banks and other commercial lenders. In the market-based financial system, by contrast, the banking sector is inextricably linked to the capital market, and the credit market provides the best barometer for the stability of the system as a whole. Behind the emergence of the market-based system lie two interconnected developments: the growth of asset-backed securities as an asset class and the growth of the broker-dealer sector of the economy.[71] Commercial banks still represent an important part of the market-based financial system, but, as the distinction between financial institutions' banking and investment functions was erased by the Gramm-Leach-Bliley and Commodities Futures Modernization acts, even they became increasingly enmeshed in the dynamics of the credit market.

According to Adrian and Shin, the growth in securitization gave broker-dealers and SIVs a greater role in supplying credit, especially to the home mortgage market. Like other financial institutions, these financial intermediaries use short-term liabilities, generally repos, to finance long-term illiquid liabilities, such as securitized pools of mortgages. Indeed, the balance sheets of broker-dealers consist almost entirely of short-term market borrowing (606). The balance sheets of these financial intermediaries are more volatile than those of commercial bank both because they rely so heavily on short-term market borrowing and because they mark the value of their balance sheets to current market prices. Adrian and Shin identify the most distinctive feature of these financial intermediaries as their mark-to-market balance-sheet valuation. This form of valuation synchronizes broker-dealers' responses to market conditions and to each other, and, in the case of a system-wide move to deleverage, can lead to a general reduction in lending.

The interconnection of financial intermediaries forged by the combination of securitization, reliance on leverage, and short-term borrowing meant that, increasingly in the years since 1980, the *financial system as a whole* began to hold long-term illiquid assets financed by short-term liabilities (604). In other words, the system as a whole had a maturity mismatch, and if market conditions began to change, some part of the system would begin to give. By September 2008, signs of this structural problem had begun to appear—not only in the failure of Bear Stearns in March 2008 but in the bankruptcy of Lehman Brothers in the middle of September. Institutions that were highly leveraged and held long-term illiquid assets financed with short-term debt served as "pinch points" when their lenders reduced exposure in response to the deteriorating market conditions. Market conditions were deteriorating, in turn, because the securitized assets that backed many of the investment products consisted of home mortgages, too many of which had been made to unqualified borrowers. When borrowers began to default on mortgage payments as the value of their homes fell, the securities backed by these mortgages lost value. In the crisis that began in 2008, the liquidity crisis initially suffered by individual investment banks and broker-dealers rapidly spread to the system as a whole, and a general pull-back in lending occurred. Because so many financial institutions, not just in the United States but across the globe, had significant positions in asset-backed securities—or held insurance products, such as credit default swaps, created to backstop these investments—the combination of a frozen market in US short-term lending, an unsustainable strain on the primary insurer (AIG), and the failure of an important broker-dealer (Lehman Brothers) pushed the global financial system to the brink of failure.

The events of 2008-9 were not the first signs of trouble in the US financial system, of course, and the way previous crises were managed helped make the underlying structural transformation both difficult to recognize and, when the crisis finally exploded, expensive to address. During Alan Greenspan's leadership of the Fed—between 1987 and 2006—trouble in the financial system was typically addressed by a sharp reduction in the Federal funds target rate and by flooding the markets with liquidity. Indeed, despite economists' embrace of the New Neoclassical Synthesis and DSGE models, Greenspan did not consistently follow the dictates of any econometric or monetary model. As Alan Blinder and Ricardo Reis explained in a 2005 celebration of "the maestro's" management of the Fed, "Greenspan . . . never accepted the idea that *any* model with unchanging coefficients, or even with an unchanging structure, can describe the U.S. economy adequately."[72] Blinder and Reis described a "Greenspan standard" rather than a theory-, rule-, or model-driven policy, and they characterize the "Greenspan non-model" (9) as "risk management rather than optimization" (9), "putting out fires" (13) rather than following a single rule, and "the resurrection of fine tuning" instead of adherence to a pre-set policy. Calling Greenspan "the greatest central banker who ever lived" (3), Blinder and Reis credit him with successfully managing a series of potentially destructive financial crises. These include the stock market crash of October 1987, the collapse of the savings and loan industry between 1986 and 1995, the currency crises that roiled emerging markets between 1994 and 2002, the 1997–98 crisis that followed the collapse of Long Term Capital Management and Russia's debt default, the collapse of the technology stock bubble in 2000, and the stock market reaction to the terrorist attack on September 11, 2001.

Greenspan managed these potentially devastating events by manipulating short-term interest rates and by telegraphing to the markets the Fed's willingness to supply liquidity. According to Blinder and Reis, "the Fed more or less announced that it stood ready to supply as much liquidity as necessary to keep markets functioning after the stock market crash of 1987, during the international financial crisis of 1998, and after the 9/11 attacks" (70). After the dot.com crash obliterated $8 trillion in wealth in 2000, Greenspan's approach was not to intervene but simply to wait it out, then "mop up" the damage; by doing so, he prevented all but a tiny recession, which Blinder and Reis described as a successful "soft landing" for the economy (70–71).

We want to make two points about Greenspan's management of the Fed—and, through Fed monetary policy, the US economy and, especially, the emergent market-based financial system. First, the macroeconometric and monetary models we described in section 10.3 can inform central bank policy—or these models may simply be set aside by a Fed chair willing to depend on his (or her) judgment, discretion, and flexibility. Second, the precedent set by Greenspan—flooding the market with liquidity in times of crisis—can, in the short run, impose extremely high costs on American taxpayers. The first point is echoed by Adrian and Shin, who recommended in 2008 that monetary authorities not use the New Neoclassical Synthesis models then in vogue.[73] The problem with such models, according to Adrian and Shin, is that they treat financial intermediaries as passive, largely irrelevant players, which the central bank uses simply to implement its policies. Adrian and Shin recommended moving away from all models that seek to manage investors' expectations and that assume that the price stickiness of goods constitutes the primary friction in the economy. Instead of these models, Adrian and Shin advised using models that highlight the "agency relationships embedded in the organization of market-based financial intermediaries," treat the supply of credit as a major source of friction, and recognize that financial intermediaries do more than passively transmit Fed policy. Adrian and Shin also advised economists to adopt new measures to gauge the nation's economy: instead of the money stock, which was Milton Friedman's go-to metric, they recommended monitoring collateralized borrowings. The money stock is a measure of the liabilities of deposit-taking banks, and, as the credit provision of banks is increasingly rivaled by broker-dealers, the size of the money stock falls short of the probative value it once held.[74] The second point—that a Federal Reserve willing and able to flood a system in crisis with liquidity can be costly—was driven home in the financial crisis of 2008: in three rounds of purchases known as "quantitative easing," the Fed bought billions of dollars of mortgage-backed securities, agency-backed securities, and Treasury securities in order to stabilize the US financial system.[75]

10.6. FINAL THOUGHTS

In describing the transformation of the US financial system into a market-based system, we have already summarized many of the details of the crisis that erupted into visibility in 2008–9. So many articles and books have narrated the unfolding of this crisis that we relegate our skeletal summary of these events to a footnote.[76] The point we want to add to the thousands of pages of analysis already in print and online is simply that the growth of modern finance—its emergence outside of, but also within and then in parallel to, a discipline that embraced theories and methods that relied heavily on mathematics, logic, and probability—occurred within a context and in a way that negated the oversight macroeconomic and monetary models might have provided. The models most macroeconomists and central bankers used—or set aside—did not make the developments that were transforming the US and global financial systems visible.[77] And there was so much money to be made from lightly regulated financial innovations—including securitized home mortgages and derivatives of these securities—that there was little incentive for anyone profiting from them to raise concerns.

In *Finance in America: An Unfinished Story*, we have traced a number of stories, all of which lead to—but do not end with—the financial crisis of 2008. One is the story of the corporations, which were created at the beginning of the twentieth century to increase the productivity of the real side of the US economy. Rendered "persons" by law and made more efficient and calculable by new accounting practices, the corporations were the antecedents of the giant, (in some cases) multinational financial institutions that began to proliferate after the merger of Travelers Insurance and Citicorp in 1998. We need to keep in mind that some of the largest, most powerful financial institutions only incorporated in the context of deregulation, in the decades since the market-based financial system began to take shape. Goldman Sachs, for example, became a corporation in 1998, and JPMorgan Chase assumed its modern corporate form in 2000, when Chase Manhattan Corporation merged with J. P. Morgan & Co. Like their early twentieth-century counterparts, these institutions are also protected by legal provisions—but the legal environment in which they have prospered is shaped by deregulation as much as by restrictive laws. Partly because of the new merger movements whose first signs were visible in the 1970s, the United States is now populated by many corporations—especially financial corporations—considered "too big to fail" because the well-being of the nation (and the world) depends upon their stability.

Side by side with corporate growth, we have chronicled the growth of the federal government, including the Federal Reserve system. At the beginning of the twentieth century, the federal government was relatively weak, and the Supreme Court had recently denied it the ability to tax its citizens' income. The nation's banking system was also weak, and the money supply was insufficiently elastic to provision farmers in times of planting or to reward depositors for saving. Two world wars dramatically accelerated the growth of the federal government, and two measures—the 1946 Employment Act and the Fed Accord of 1951—significantly expanded the power of the Federal Reserve. By the end of our period, the federal government has become enormously powerful (although it still wrestles with the states over jurisdiction of some issues, such as the criminalization of marijuana), and the Federal Reserve has been given both the power and the budget to manage the nation's economy, not simply serve as lender of last resort. Of course, at the same time that the Fed has been charged with managing the national economy, other measures that might assist the Fed's efforts have been curtailed. Most significantly, fiscal policy, which was used to great effect in the 1930s and 1940s, has been handcuffed by political descendants of the Mont Pelerin initiative, such as the Tea Party, who have successfully fomented skepticism about both the efficacy of all government initiatives and the wisdom of raising taxes in particular. Partly because of objections launched by the Tea Party and other conservative groups, Americans still vigorously debate whether—or to what extent—the growth of the federal government and the extension of the central bank's power have proved beneficial to the nation's stability and security. After the Great Recession, which followed the 2008 crisis, the issue of income inequality in the United States has come to the fore and the benefits (or threats) that modern financial practices and liberal capital rules pose to long-term growth are being debated anew. This is the context in which the Fed's virtual hegemony in managing the US economy through monetary policy, the neutralization of fiscal policy, and existing measures for regulating the financial system must now be evaluated.

In the disciplines of economics and finance, we have seen parallel developments in the reliance on mathematical, statistical, and probability techniques, many of which were refined during World War II. At the core of the policies and products developed by the two professional groups lie assumptions about how best to manage uncertainty and, most striking, a widespread tendency to reduce the form of uncertainty Frank Knight declared to be beyond measures of probability to statistically manageable risk. The reduction of uncertainty to risk has been repeatedly criticized—not only by Knight but by John Maynard Keynes and contemporary economists such as Tony Lawson and Nassim Taleb—but this reduction is written into nearly every model created since World War II.[78] In order to use the tools borrowed from mathematicians, logicians, physicists, and aerospace engineers, moreover, modern economists have also assumed that the general equilibrium paradigm of competitive markets (where finance is assumed to complete markets by developing opportunities to hedge future risks) applies to economies driven by modern financial practices. In these economies, however, only a limited and arbitrary number of factors can be hedged, and the techniques to do so are subject to model-risk, human error, market psychology, and, sometimes, prohibitive costs. Modern financial theorists and engineers have assumed the principle of no arbitrage and nearly efficient markets, but both these assumptions implicitly rest on institutional guarantees—at the very least, a legal system of contracts and enforcement that allows individuals to believe that present agreements will be honored in the future. Yet the models that drive economists' policies and financial theorists' products typically omit any consideration of institutions or historical context, and any model assuming the concept of the representative agent is silent on income distribution effects—a critical consideration given the rise of inequality in the United States since 1970. Then, too, the belief in concepts such as bounded rationality and efficient markets has made it possible to create economic policies divorced from institutions and financial products with only a tangential relationship to the assets that theoretically back them.

Modern economic and financial models also assume a kind of rationality that permits the application of linear programming to identify optimal results. This platform, which is used in both modern economics and finance, requires the user to bet on unknown and unknowable probability distributions and to assume that markets real and financial are not fraught with moral hazard, information asymmetries, and imperfections. New Classical economics effaces nominal values in favor of "real" values; in so doing, these models effectively mask an entire range of financial relationships—including changes in the very structure of the financial system itself. Overconfidence in particular models (and in financial engineering in general) has also been a recurrent problem in the story we have told, as has the Fed's overconfidence in the monetary view—as opposed to the credit view, which would have helped illuminate the role financial intermediaries have always played in the financial system. Even though Fed chairman Ben Bernanke's commitment to the credit view, based on his work on the Great Depression, informed the Fed's response to the 2008 crash, macroeconomic policy makers did not consider financial regulation to be a viable tool before the subprime crisis.[79] Going back to the debates between these two points of view, the decade when the nature of index numbers was still a matter of dispute, or the years when early models still betrayed their limitations might encourage more humility and more caution on the part of economists, financial engineers, and policy makers who make and use models as part of their daily work.

In *Finance in America,* we have also told the story of the collection, management, and dissemination of data—whether to raise taxes to support a war or to enhance transparency in corporate productivity and national accounts. In the financial crisis of 2008, the earlier efforts at transparency whose history these pages tell were undermined by the combination of economists' reliance on the arcane language of advanced mathematics, the opacity of the financial products engineered by Wall Street quants, and off-balance-sheet vehicles such as structured investment vehicles. The latter have made excessive leverage and risk invisible even to the most diligent Wall Street analysts who follow the principles of Graham and Dodd. Today, even though data is bigger and more readily available than ever, fewer Americans can understand financial economics; hedge funds, to which the nation's largest pools of financial assets have committed large sums, are nontransparent by design; hedge-fund fee arrangements for profit sharing are hidden by nondisclosure agreements; and the system of offshore arrangements by which fund managers benefit from advantageous carried interest provisions are located in jurisdictions not open to public scrutiny. Today even the most prestigious public funds do not know how much they are paying Wall Street for investment management services. Efforts at postcrash legislation, such as the Dodd–Frank Wall Street Reform and Consumer Protection Act and the Basel III Regulatory Framework, are beyond the scope of this work. We do note, however, that as of this writing the financial system is more exposed to a handful of large, complex financial institutions than before the 2008 financial crisis.

Finance in America: An Unfinished Story has focused primarily on the construction of assumptions, techniques, and models, and the financial crisis of 2008 has exposed the shortcomings in many of these components of modern finance. The belief that properly estimated models, which factor probability into their very form, allow us to anticipate future prices and events has been challenged by the black swan of falling real estate prices and the bankruptcies of venerable investment houses. The assumption that actors are rational and consistently serve their own interests has been challenged by the exposure of agency costs and credit frictions within the system of financial intermediation. The role accounting conventions played in helping companies (and nations) manage their affairs is now shadowed by accountancy's darker role in moving debt off company balance sheets and into the nontransparent world of offshore accounts and SIVs. The role financial engineering played in managing risk through diversification and securitization is now exposed for its deleterious effects: investment products so complicated and interconnected that they helped make risk systemic have subjected ordinary investors to the cruelties of true Knightian uncertainty.

What we have learned in the years we have researched *Finance in America* is that finance in all its guises is difficult to see, efforts to render it transparent have always been stalked by demands for more privacy and claims about the opacity of technical language, and the very models that have made financial engineering so profitable can fall short as the conditions in which they are applied change. What we have learned from writing *Finance in America* is that the story truly is unfinished and that making finance visible will require the work of many hands.

NOTES

INTRODUCTION

1. Robin Greenwood and David Scharfstein, "The Growth of Finance," *Journal of Economic Perspectives* 27, no. 2 (Spring 2013): 4.

2. Dani Rodrik, *Economics Rules: The Rights and Wrongs of the Dismal Science* (New York: Norton, 2015); Ben S. Bernanke, *The Courage to Act: A Memoir of a Crisis and Its Aftermath* (New York: Norton, 2015).

3. Schumpeter, *Ten Great Economists from Marx to Keynes* (New York: Oxford University Press, 1951), 223; Tobin, "Fisher, Irvin (1867–1947)," in Steven N. Durlauf and Lawrence E. Blume, eds., *The New Palgrave Dictionary of Economics*, 2nd ed. (1987), 369–76; Milton Friedman, *Money Mischief: Episodes in Monetary History* (New York: Harcourt Brace, 1994), 37.

4. Paul Davidson, *Financial Markets, Money, and the Real World* (Cheltenham: Edward Elgar, 2002).

5. For statistical measures of "financialization," see Greta R. Krippner, *Capitalizing on Crisis: The Political Origins of the Rise of Finance* (Cambridge, MA: Harvard University Press, 2011), chap. 2.

6. Robert M. Solow, "How Did Economics Get That Way and What Way Did It Get?" *Deadalus* 126, no. 1 (Winter 1997): 39–58.

7. See Alvin H. Hansen, Seymour E. Harris, and John M. Keynes, *A Guide to Keynes*, chap. 7 (New York: McGraw-Hill, 1979), 140–53.

8. On modeling in economics, see Mary S. Morgan, *The World in the Model: How Economists Work and Think* (Cambridge: Cambridge University Press, 2012), Marcel Boumans, *How Economists Model the World into Numbers* (Abington: Routledge, 2007), and Rodrik, *Economics Rules*.

9. The performative nature of economics and finance, and of models in particular, has been explored by Michel Callon and Donald MacKenzie. See Callon, "Introduction: The Embed-

dedness of Economic Markets in Economies," in Callon, ed., *The Laws of the Markets* (Oxford: Blackwell, 1998); and MacKenzie, *An Engine, Not a Camera: How Financial Models Shape Markets* (Cambridge, MA: MIT Press, 2006).

10. MacKenzie argues that the Black-Scholes option pricing model was performative in this strong sense: "the use of the model shifted practice towards the results of the model" (*Engine*, 19).

11. See Charalambos D. Aliprantis and Kim C. Border, "A Foreword to the Practical: Why We Use Infinite Dimensional Analysis: A Hitchhiker's Guide," in *Infinite Dimensional Analysis*, 3rd ed. (Berlin: Springer, 2007), xix–xxiv.

12. See, e.g., John G. Gurley and Edward S. Shaw, *Money in a Theory of Finance* (Washington, DC: Brookings Institution: 1960).

13. Veblen, "The Preoccupations of Economic Science, III," *Quarterly Journal of Economics* 14, no. 2 (February 1900): 254–55. Veblen coins the term "neo-classical" on p. 261. This is the third in a series of articles about the nature of economics. See also "The Preoccupations of Economic Science, I," *Quarterly Journal of Economics* 13, no. 2 (1899): 121–50; and "The Preoccupations of Economic Science, II," *Quarterly Journal of Economics* 13, no. 4 (1899): 396–426.

14. Colander, "The Death of Neoclassical Economics," *Journal of the History of Economic Thought* 22, no. 2 (2000): 131–32.

15. "Death," 132, 130.

16. Philip Mirowski, *Never Let a Serious Crisis Go to Waste: How Neoliberalism Survived the Financial Meltdown* (London: Verso, 2013), 22. Implicitly and without pausing over the implications of this, Colander agrees with Mirowski that heterodox economists have been banished from "major graduate schools." In fact, he defines "heterodox" as "an approach to problems that is not accepted as legitimate. Thus, my litmus test of heterodox economists is their ability to get jobs at major graduate schools" ("Death," 137).

17. Lawson, "What Is This 'School' Called Neoclassical Economics?" *Cambridge Journal of Economics* 37 (2013): 950, 953, 957, 954. See also Lawson, *Reorienting Economics* (New York: Routledge, 2003), and "The Current Economic Crisis: Its Nature and the Course of Academic Economics," *Cambridge Journal of Economics* 33, no. 4 (2009): 759–88. Thanks to Ylva Hasselberg for calling our attention to Lawson's work.

18. The attributes Colander lists are: a focus on the allocation of resources at a given moment in time; the acceptance of some variation of utilitarianism; a focus on marginal tradeoffs; the assumption of far-sighted rationality; and the acceptance of methodological individualism ("Death," 134).

19. Monboit, "Neoliberalism—The Ideology at the Root of All Our Problems," http://www.theguardian.com/books/2016/apr/15/neoliberalism-ideology-problem-george-monbiot?CMP=share_btn_link

20. According to Mirowski, the core principles of neoliberalism include the idea that modern society must be constructed, rather than being a natural phenomenon; the belief that the heart of this society is the market, whose ability to process information will always exceed that of the state; the conviction that the market is "natural" (even if the society it centers is not); the idea that the state must be redefined, not destroyed; the claim that the neoliberal market state needs popular support, which must continuously be reinforced; a conviction that the

"self" in a neoliberal state must continuously monitor and regulate the "self" in which identity is invested; the belief that "freedom" in such a state consists of "autonomous self-governing entities, all coming naturally equipped with some version of 'rationality' and motives of ineffable self-interest, striving to improve their lot in life by engaging in market exchange" (61); the conviction that capital has the natural right to flow freely, even across national borders; the assumption that inequality is a natural characteristic of the market system and the motor for progress; the belief that corporations are constructive players in the neoliberal market society; the conviction that the market can provide solutions to all problems, even those apparently caused by the market; and the assumption that an expanded system of incarceration prevents wayward individuals from sidestepping the efficient market (*Never*, 53-67).

21. *Never*, 190.

22. Brett Christophers, "The Limits to Financialization," *Dialogues in Human Geography* 5, no. 2 (2015): 183-85.

23. Martin J. Sklar, *The Corporate Reconstruction of American Capitalism, 1890-1916: The Market, The Law, and Politics* (Cambridge: Cambridge University Press, 1988); Alfred D. Chandler Jr., *The Visible Hand: The Managerial Revolution in American Business* (Cambridge, MA.: Harvard University Press, 1977); Philip Mirowski, *Machine Dreams: Economics Becomes a Cyborg Science* (Cambridge: Cambridge University Press, 2002); Peter L. Bernstein, *Capital Ideas: The Improbable Origins of Modern Wall Street* (New York: Free Press, 1992); Perry Mehrling, *The Money Interest and the Public Interest: American Monetary Thought, 1920-1970* (Cambridge, MA.: Harvard University Press, 1997) and *Fischer Black and The Revolutionary Idea of Modern Finance* (New York: John Wiley & Sons, 2005); Colin Read, *The Rise of the Quants: Marschak, Sharpe, Black, Scholes, and Merton* (Basingstoke: Palgrave Macmillan, 2012) and *The Portfolio Theorists: Von Neumann, Savage, Arrow, and Markowitz* (Basingstoke: Palgrave Macmillan, 2012); Geoffrey Poitras, ed., *Pioneers of Financial Economics: Volume Two, Twentieth-Century Contributions* (Cheltenham, UK: Edward Elgar, 2007); Franck Jovanovic, "The Construction of the Canonical History of Financial Economics," *History of Political Economy* 40, no. 2 (2008): 213-42.

24. Merton, *Continuous-Time Finance*, rev. ed. (Oxford: Blackwell, 1992); Bingham and Kiesel, *Risk-Neutral Valuation* (London: Springer-Verlag, 2004); Cochrane, *Asset Pricing*, rev. ed. (Princeton, NJ: Princeton University Press, 2005); Joshi, *Concepts and Practice*, 2nd ed. (Cambridge: Cambridge University Press, 2008); Blyth, *Introduction to Quantitative Finance* (Oxford: Oxford University Press, 2014); Kreps, *Microeconomic Foundations* (Princeton, NJ: Princeton University Press, 2013); Pliska, *Introduction to Mathematical Finance: Discrete-Time Models* (Oxford: Blackwell, 1997).

25. Hendry and Morgan, *The Foundations of Econometric Knowledge* (Cambridge: Cambridge University Press, 1995), and Morgan, *The History of Econometric Ideas* (Cambridge: Cambridge University Press, 1992); Morgan, *The World in the Model*; Boumans, *How Economists Model the World*; Weintraub, *General Equilibrium Analysis: Studies in Appraisal* (Cambridge: Cambridge University Press, 1985), *Stabilizing Dynamics: Constructing Economic Knowledge* (Cambridge: Cambridge University Press, 1991), and *How Economics Became a Mathematical Science* (Durham, NC: Duke University Press, 2002); Donald MacKenzie, *Engine*; Krippner, *Capitalizing*; and Rubenstein, *A History of the Theory of Investments: My Annotated Bibliography* (Hoboken, N. J.: John Wiley and Sons, 2006).

26. Goetzmann, *Money Changes Everything* (Princeton, NJ: Princeton University Press, 2016), 19.

27. Piketty, *Capital in the Twenty-First Century*, trans. Arthur Goldhammer (Cambridge, MA: Harvard University Press, 2014), 16.

28. As James K. Galbraith has argued, in an analysis that extends the famous Cambridge controversy of the 1950s and 1960s, "it is not possible to add up the values of capital objects to get a common quantity without a prior rate of interest, which (since it is prior) must come from the financial and not the physical world. . . . If the actual interest rate is a financial variable, varying for financial reasons, the physical interpretation of a dollar-valued capital stock is meaningless" ("James K. Galbraith Takes on Thomas Piketty's *Capital in the Twenty-First Century*," *Dissent Magazine* [April 21, 2014], http://www.alternet.org/economy/james-k-galbraith-takes-thomas-pikettys-capital-twenty-first-century). The main participants in the Cambridge Controversy, sometimes called the "Cambridge-Cambridge Controversy" because one group spoke from the UK Cambridge and the other from the US Cambridge, included Joan Robinson, Piero Sraffa, and Luigi Pasinetti, on the UK side, and Robert Solow and Paul Samuelson, on the US side. In 1966, Samuelson conceded that the UK argument was correct. The classic account of this controversy is G. C. Harcourt, *Some Cambridge Controversies in the Theory of Capital* (Cambridge: Cambridge University Press, 1972). A more recent treatment of the controversy is Roger Backhouse, "MIT and the Other Cambridge," *History of Political Economy* 46 (2014): 252–71.

29. Solow and Tobin, "Introduction," in *Two Economic Revolutions in Economic Policy: The First Economic Reports of Presidents Kennedy and Reagan*, ed. James Tobin and Murray Weidenbaum (Cambridge, MA: MIT Press, 1988), 5.

CHAPTER ONE

1. Thomas Philippon, "The Evolution of the U.S. Financial Industry from 1860 to 2007: Theory and Evidence" (November 2008, http://pages.stern.nyu.edu/-tphilipp/papers/finsize_old.pdf), appendix: table 1 and figure 1.

2. On the cultural implications of corporatization, see Alan Trachtenberg, *The Incorporation of America: Culture and Society in the Gilded Age* (New York: Hill & Wang, 1982; rpt. 2007), esp. chaps. 2–5. Among the many historical treatments of these developments, the most pertinent are Alfred D. Chandler Jr., *The Visible Hand: The Managerial Revolution in American Business* (Cambridge, MA: Harvard University Press, 1977); Martin J. Sklar, *The Corporate Reconstruction of American Capitalism, 1890–1916: The Market, The Law, and Politics* (Cambridge: Cambridge University Press, 1988), esp. Part I; and James Livingston, *Origins of the Federal Reserve System: Money, Class, and Corporate Capitalism, 1890–1913* (Ithaca, NY: Cornell University Press, 1986), esp. Part I.

3. Edward S. Meade, *Trust Finance: A Study of the Genesis, Organization, and Management of Industrial Corporations* (New York: D. Appleton, 1903), chap. 1. While contemporaries sometimes used the terms "trusts," "industrials," and "corporations" interchangeably, legal differences distinguished these company forms. See William Z. Ripley, *Trusts, Pools, and Corporations* (New York: Ginn & Co., 1905), introduction. Except when a contemporary uses "trust," we prefer "corporation" for the publicly traded but not public service companies cre-

ated in this era. The modern historian who has estimated the number of consolidated companies is Naomi Lamoreaux, *The Great Merger Movement in American Business, 1895–1904* (Cambridge: Cambridge University Press, 1985), 2. Both contemporaries and modern historians debate the precise boundaries of the first merger movement. Meade defined the "Real Trust Movement" as 1898–1903 (*Trust Finance*, 149). On modern historians' discussion of how to date the movement, see Sklar, *Corporate Reconstruction*, 46; and Lawrence C. Mitchell, *The Speculation Economy: How Finance Triumphed over Industry* (San Francisco: Berrett-Koehler, 2007), 283–84, n. 12. Mitchell also discusses the controversy about the number of corporations and the amount of capitalization added to the US economy (*Speculation Economy*, 12 and 284, n. 12). Also essential to this subject is *A History of Corporate Finance*, by Jonathan Barron Baskin and Paul J. Miranti Jr. (Cambridge: Cambridge University Press, 1997), esp. chaps. 4 and 5. For contemporaries' estimates about numbers of corporations and the amount of wealth they added to the economy, see John Moody, *The Truth about the Trusts* (New York: Moody, 1904), 485–89.

    4. Meade, *Trust Finance*, 78.

    5. Some historians attribute the success of the merger movement to the adoption of marginalist theories. See Sklar, *Corporate Reconstruction*, chap. 2; and Mary Susan Murname, *The Mellon Tax Plan: The Income Tax and the Penetration of Marginalist Economic Thought into American Life and Law in the 1920s* (unpublished PhD thesis, Case Western Reserve, UMI ProQuest, 2007), 52, 80–88.

    6. Jeremiah Whipple Jenks and Walter F. Clark, *The Trust Problem* (1900; rev. ed. New York: Doubleday, 1925), 50.

    7. Sklar, *Corporate Reconstruction*, 49–50. As Sklar explains, the Santa Clara decision was crucial to the emergence of the corporations. "The corporate reorganization required proprietors to surrender ownership of their physical units or assets in exchange for securities that, as equities, were claims upon a share of earnings. Upon that claim, in turn, rested the exchange value of the securities. That value found itself enhanced in the market in proportion as the consolidated prestige, goodwill, and reinforced market power, of previously separated enterprises, raised the putative earning power of the new corporation. The legal protection of the value of intangibles as essential to property rights, along with the Court's strengthening of limited stockholder liability in its 'natural entity' doctrine, reduced the risk and enhanced the value of corporate stock, and thereby facilitated the exchange of tangibles for securities and hence the separation of operational control from legal ownership characteristic of the corporate form of property" (*Corporate Reconstruction*, 50). Despite this pro-corporate decision, as Sklar explains, between 1897 and 1911 the Supreme Court also inhibited corporate-administered markets through its interpretation of the Sherman Anti-Trust Act (see *Corporate Reconstruction*, chap. 3). We should also note that corporations were (and are) governed by state, not federal, law. This meant that, until a corporation's business activity crossed state lines, jurisdiction remained with the state where the corporation was registered. Different states could and did pass legislation that either restricted the growth of corporations, as Massachusetts did, or encouraged it, as did Delaware and New Jersey. Predictably, the legal status of corporations was a matter of ongoing debate during this period. Despite the 1886 Santa Clara decision, corporations were still sometimes treated as aggregates of partners as well as legal persons. For a discussion of these debates and legal nuances, see Marjorie E. Kornhauser, "Corporate

Regulation and the Origins of the Corporate Income Tax," *Indiana Law Journal* 66, no. 53 (1990–91): 62–68.

8. One measure of the interest provoked by the new corporations is the number of official reports and economic articles published on the subject. In 1901, Charles J. Bullock of Wellesley College reported that in 1899–1900 alone, twenty-eight books, reports, and pamphlets had appeared, "together with a flood of periodical articles that will reach probably one hundred and fifty titles when the returns for 1900 have all been received" ("Trust Literature: A Survey and a Criticism," *Quarterly Journal of Economics* 15 [1901]: 168).

9. In the meantime, states could and did pass legislation that either promoted corporate formation, as was the case with New Jersey, Delaware, and New York, or inhibited it, as was the case with Massachusetts in particular.

10. Quoted in Eric R. Hake, "The Stock Watering Debate: More Light, Less Heat," *Journal of Economic Issues* 35, no. 2 (June 2001): 424.

11. See Ripley, "Stock Watering," *Political Science Quarterly* 26, no. 1 (March 1911): 117. While Jenks seems to have favored this method of valuation, his comments are so guarded and equivocal that it is often difficult to determine exactly what policies he supported. On the question of overcapitalization, see Jenks and Clark, *Trust Problem*, chap. 7.

12. See Meade, *Trust Finance*; and Francis Cooper, *Financing an Enterprise: A Manual of Information and Suggestion for Promoters, Investors and Business Men Generally,* 3rd ed. (New York: Ronald, 1909), I, chaps. 21 and 22. Meade taught at the Wharton School, where he developed courses entitled "Investments," "Corporation Finance," and "Railway, Finance, and Accounting." See Paula A. McLean and D. G. Brian Jones, "Edward Sherwood Mead (1874–1956)," *European Business Review* 19, no. 2 (2007): 118–28. (Meade changed the spelling of his last name sometime between 1912 and 1915.)

13. Frenyear, "The Ethics of Stock Watering," *Annals of the American Academy of Political and Social Science* 8 (1896): 78.

14. In 1906, Arthur W. Spencer described how the "value-of assets" theory, which he supported, could "become a cloak for excessive capitalization." This could occur when a corporation accumulated property whose value had appreciated or equipment that it did not need for immediate production and held onto to this property in order to stave off possible competition. Such "excess assets" could also appear when two companies merged and were left with duplicate plants or equipment. Instead of liquidating such holdings to pay for improvements and ongoing costs, the corporation would then pay for improvements out of earnings, so as to count the unused property as assets against which capital stocks could be issued. To permit such excessive assets "to be capitalized has precisely the same effect on the public as the issue of an equal amount of capital where there are no visible assets on which to base it," Spencer complained ("The Prevention of Stock-Watering by Public-Service Corporations," *Journal of Political Economy* 14, no. 9 [November 1906]: 547).

15. Ripley, "Stock Watering," 98. Stephen A. Zeff explains stock watering as follows: "valuing non-cash assets received in exchange for capital stock at the par value of the stock, when the worth of the assets is significantly less than that amount" (*Henry Rand Hatfield: Humanist, Scholar, and Accounting Educator* [Bingley: Emerald, 2000], 98).

16. For this, Ripley cites the example of the way the Union Pacific Railway Company used the Oregon Short Line Railway Company: "the net result was certainly to increase the funded

debt of the Union Pacific system, without any commensurate addition to its actual assets at that time" ("Stock Watering," 100).

17. Ripley, "Stock Watering," 103–4.

18. Cooper, *Financing an Enterprise*, 241.

19. Ibid., 174, 174–75, 178.

20. Ibid., chapters 19–22.

21. Meade, *Trust Finance*, 46.

22. Ibid., 89.

23. Ibid., 62.

24. Ibid., 129.

25. For Meade's suggestions, see *Trust Finance*, chaps. 16, 19, and 20.

26. *Trust Finance*, 368. These two phrases hint at the remedy Meade proposed to what he saw as the basic problem of the day—that corporations were being capitalized on a basis designed to appeal to speculators. In addition to recommending that the federal government oversee corporations and require them to disclose more information, Meade also suggested enforcing a "conservative disposition of profits" by requiring publicly traded companies to put profits into a reserve fund up to a certain percentage of estimated earning power before paying dividends. See *Trust Finance*, 368–75.

27. In 1907, Frederick Douglas, another New York attorney, suggested that laws requiring companies to assign a par value to their stock be repealed. See "The Par Value of Stock," *The Yale Law Review* 16, no. 4 (February 1907): 247–52. In 1900, Jeremiah Jenks had also raised the possibility of eliminating par valuation, citing a permissive, though not compulsory plan of stock issue adopted in New York. Jenks did not pursue this idea, however, and he commented that "there is no general interest" in such a change. See *The Trust Problem*, 101–3. Cooper also suggested this, in passing; see *Financing a Company*, 175–76. No-par stock rules were passed beginning in 1912. At least one modern scholar believes that eliminating the par requirement really did resolve the problem of stock watering, even though complaints about this practice persisted into the 1920s. See Hake, "The Stock Watering Debate," 423–30.

28. In 1908, Arthur Lowes Dickinson reminded the American Association of Professional Accountants that accounting was an art as much as a science: "It is very seldom that you find two cases exactly alike. You have to take every case on its own merits and deal with it as you see it. If you should put down all the rules in the world you would have cases to which the rules would not apply. You have to use your experience . . . and that is the reason we are here as professional accountants—because we have to gain experience, judgement and tact in dealing with accounts and taking the best of the many different ways of determining matters" (quoted in Gary John Previts and Barbara Dubis Merino, *A History of Accounting in America: An Historical Interpretation of the Cultural Significance of Accounting* [New York: John Wiley & Sons, 1979], 105). On the professionalization of accounting, see Paul J. Miranti, "Birth of a Profession," *CPA Journal* 1996; http://www.nysscpa.org/cpajournal/1996/0496/features/f14 .htm. The "postulates" eventually formulated and taught in accountancy courses consisted of principles general enough to establish a methodological baseline for the profession (such as that the accountant's method should be consistent and that a corporation should be treated as a "going concern") yet specific enough to address some, but not all, of the practical questions an accountant might encounter (like the suggestion that accountants use historical cost, not

replacement cost, to value a purchase). See William Andrew Paton, *Accounting Theory with Special Reference to the Corporate Enterprise* (New York: Ronald Press, 1922), chap. 20. That it is always necessary to temper rules with the use of more flexible principles in the case of accountancy is also visible in the most recent treatment of this practice. The Generally Accepted Accounting Practices (GAAP), codified in 2009, provides a set of principles that function as a standard, not a set of rules that can be enforced by the federal government. The GAAP, in turn, was derived from similar sets of principles, all issued by committees of professional accounting organizations: the fifty-one accounting research bulletins issued by the American Institute of Accountants' Committee on Accounting (formed in 1929), the thirty-one accounting principles issued by the Accounting Principles Board, and the 169 Statements of Financial Accounting Standards published by the Financial Accounting Standards Board (formed in 1973). Thus even after the federal government imposed requirements for disclosure (through the Interstate Commerce Law of 1887 and the adoption of a federal income tax in 1913, for example), accountancy retained the ability—indeed, the necessity—to police itself by principles, not to obey strict laws. For this reason, accountancy is best understood as a practice that operates within boundaries, rather than one strictly governed by law. An extremely interesting acknowledgment of this property of accounting, as well as an attempt to derive and describe accountancy principles schematically is George H. Sorter, *Boundaries of the Accounting Universe: The Accounting Rules of Selection* (Manchester, NH: Ayer Publishing Company, 1978). A capsule history of the codification of accounting principles can be found at http://accountinginfo.com/financial-accounting-standards/asc-100/105-gaap-history.htm.

29. See Previts and Merino, *History of Accounting*, 93–148; Paul J. Miranti, "Associationism, Statism, Professional Regulation: Public Accountants and the Reform of Financial Markets, 1896–1940," *Business History Review* 60:3 (Autumn 1986): 438–45, and "Birth of a Profession," *CPA Journal* 1996; http://www.nysscpa.org/cpajournal/1996/0496/features/f14.htm.

30. Previts and Merino, *History of Accounting*, 105, 107.

31. Hatfield complained about the lack of a common terminology in 1909 (*Modern Accounting*, vi) and again in the 1915 revised version of this text. Committees devoted to terminology continued to be appointed within the American Association of Public Accountants until 1915. See John Gary Previts, *A Critical Evaluation of Comparative Financial Accounting Thought in America 1900 to 1920* (New York: Arno Press, 1980), 3.

32. See Previts and Merino, *History of Accounting*, 165–76, 222–29. Previts and Merino discuss entity theory, which was introduced by William Paton as a rival to proprietary theory, on 176–80.

33. Charles Ezra Sprague, *The Philosophy of Accounts* (New York: Ronald Press, 1908), 61–62.

34. Hatfield, *Modern Accounting*, 196. See Previts and Merino, *History of Accounting*, 169.

35. Sprague, *Philosophy of Accounts*, 61.

36. Thorstein Veblen, *The Theory of Business Enterprise* (1904; reprint Mansfield Centre, CT: Martino, 2013), 78.

37. The double-entry bookkeeping system could represent profits, but the temporality of those profits was not visible in the balance sheet. See B. S. Yamey, "Scientific Bookkeeping and the Rise of Capitalism," *Economic History Review*, 2nd series, 1, nos. 2–3 (1949): 99–113.

38. Hatfield, "Some Neglected Phases of Accounting," *Electric Railway Journal* 46, no. 16 (October 15, 1915), 800; quoted Previts, *Critical Evaluation*, 171. A related issue, as Thomas A. King explains, concerns the future profitability of particular resources: "Perhaps the most important accounting decision a bookkeeper can make is determining whether resources consumed today will generate revenue in future accounting periods. If the answer is yes, then the charge should be *capitalized* and classified on the balance sheet as an asset. If not, then the balance should be *expensed,* flow through the income statement, and accumulate as a reduction in retained earnings" (*More Than a Numbers Game: A Brief History of Accounting* [Hoboken, NJ: Wiley, 2006], 9).

39. Stephen A. Zeff has long insisted that the differences between the two theories were not as important as some historians have maintained. See *A Critical Examination of the Orientation Postulate in Accounting, with Particular Attention to Its Historical Development in New York* (New York: Arno Press, 1978). See also Steven A. Bank, "Entity Theory as Myth in the Origin of the Corporate Income Tax," *William and Mary Law Review* 43, no. 2 (2001), 447.

40. Richard K. Fleischman and Thomas N. Tyson, "Cost Accounting during the Industrial Revolution: The Present State of Historical Knowledge," *Economic History Review* 46, no. 3 (1993): 503–17; and Previts and Merino, *History of Accounting*, 62–64, 113–19. Early courses were taught at Columbia by two CPAs, Jerome Lee Nicholson and John Francis Deems Rohrbach. In 1913, Nicholson published a textbook, *Cost Accounting, Theory and Practice*, in which he referred to the dramatic increase in literature on this subject. Ninety percent of this material had been published since 1903, he claimed, and 75% since 1908 (*Cost Accounting, Theory and Practice* [New York: Ronald Press, 1913], 19). Nicholson and Rohrbach updated the text in 1919, in response to the Federal Trade Commission's advocacy of cost accounting and the need exposed by World War I to collect information about US corporations' profits (*Cost Accounting* [New York: Ronald Press, 1919]), iii.

41. Previts, *Critical Evaluation*, 179–81. On the development of the income statement, see also Clifford D. Brown, *The Emergence of Income Reporting: An Historical Study* (East Lansing, MI.: Michigan State University Business Studies Division of Research, 1971). Brown's summary corroborates our findings: "There was a gradual emergence, not a sudden or dramatic appearance, of the presentation of income statement data as they are reported today" (40–41).

42. "Profits of a Corporation," *Cyclopedia of Commerce, Accountancy, Business Administration* (Chicago: American Technical Society, 1909), 285, 275. Dickinson recognized that "partial realizations" (261) and the need to price them properly made the balance sheet no longer sufficient for the modern corporation, but, for a document that has had so much impact on the profession, he devoted remarkably little attention to the income statement itself. It is clear from the way he presents it that he still considered what he called "the Profit and Loss Account" (272, 275) from the perspective of proprietary theory. Dickinson explicitly stated that the balance sheet—for the consolidated corporation—was the primarily financial document of a company (293–94).

43. See Richard J. Joseph, *The Origins of the American Income Tax: The Revenue Act of 1894 and Its Aftermath* (Syracuse, NY: Syracuse University Press, 2004), 169.

44. Brief, "Corporate Financial Reporting at the Turn of the Century," *Journal of Accountancy* (May 1987): 149.

45. John L. Carey, "The Origins of Modern Financial Reporting," in *The Evolution of Corporate Financial Reporting*, ed. T. A. Lee and R. H. Parker (Sunbury-on-Thames: Thomas Nelson, 1979), 242.

46. *Accountants' Handbook*, ed. Earl A. Saliers, 14th ed. (New York: Ronald Press, 1923), 338. Both the balance sheet and the income statement are included in a section entitled "Financial Statements" (319-43). Saliers notes that the balance sheet and the income statement need to be considered together (321). Thanks to Stephen A. Zeff for directing us to this source.

47. Paton discusses the income statement in *Principles of Accounting* (1916), the text he wrote with Stevenson. See pp. 176-86. "Such a statement consists of all the accounts showing the expenses and revenues for the period, together with the appropriations made from net income" (176). In his 1922 *Accounting Theory with Special Reference to the Corporation*, by contrast, Paton only glances at the "income sheet" or "revenue statement" (269-70).

48. By 1965, the income statement was not considered a "supporting schedule," as it was at the beginning of the twentieth century. Instead, the figures that appeared on the balance sheet were held to be "residual figures," the results of decisions made "from the point of view of the income statement" (Willard J. Graham, "Some Observations on the Nature of Income, Generally Accepted Accounting Principles, and Financial Reporting," *Law and Contemporary Problems* 30, no. 4 [Autumn 1965]: 661).

49. N. Loyall McLaren, *Annual Reports to Stockholders, Their Preparation and Interpretation* (New York: Ronald Press, 1947), 253.

50. McLaren explains that companies did use the income form in audit reports but they were slow to adopt the form for routine reporting to shareholders. See *Annual Reports*, 154. The Federal Reserve model form was revised in 1929 and 1936.

51. In his 1922 book on accounting theory, Paton noted the impact of the Interstate Commerce Commission's dictates about where to enter interest. The ICC treats "interest charges as deductions from 'income' rather than 'revenue.' . . . The Commission seems to be emphasizing primarily the distinction between 'operating' and 'non-operating' charges in a technical sense," he explains, "rather than the line dividing true expenses and distributions of income to equities" (*Accounting Theory*, 269). The issue about where to enter interest charges remained controversial through this period. In this text, Paton does not discuss income statements apart from this discussion of where to enter interest charges on what he alternately calls an "income sheet" and a "revenue statement" (269-70).

52. In 1965, Graham stated this principle in no uncertain terms. "The primary objective of the measurement of business income is to furnish data for decision making. Decision making is concerned with the future, and what has happened in the past is largely irrelevant unless it provides a basis for sound estimates of the future. . . . Most business decision are (or should be) based on future expectations about the earning power of a business. . . . It is incumbent upon management and the accounting profession to provide a measurement of past business income that gives the most useful basis for estimating future earning power" ("Some Observations," 672, 673).

53. Charles Arthur Conant, *A History of Modern Banks of Issue, with an Account of the Economic Crises of the Nineteenth Century and the Crisis of 1907* (4th ed., 1909), 424.

54. Eugene N. White, "Were Banks Special Intermediaries in Late Nineteenth-Century America?" *Review of the Federal Reserve Bank of St. Louis* (May/June 1998), 13.

55. Ellis W. Tallman and Jon R. Moen, "Lessons from the Panic of 1907," *Economic Review of the Federal Bank of Atlanta* 75 (May/June 1990): 9.

56. Conant, *History of Modern Banks of Issue*, 714–15.

57. Tallman and Moen, "Lessons," 11.

58. Allan H. Meltzer, *A History of the Federal Reserve* (Chicago: University of Chicago Press, 2003), 1:71.

59. Charles W. Calomiris, "Volatile Times and Persistent Conceptual Errors: U.S. Monetary Policy 1914–1951," in Michael D. Bordo and William Roberds, eds., *The Origins, History, and Future of the Federal Reserve: A Return to Jeckyl Island* (Cambridge: Cambridge University Press, 2010), 172. See also William L. Silber, *When Washington Shut Down Wall Street: The Great Financial Crisis of 1914 and the Origins of America's Monetary Supremacy* (Princeton, NJ: Princeton University Press, 2007).

60. The metaphor comes from Perry Mehrling. "The web of interlocking debt commitments, each one a more or less rash promise about an uncertain future, is like a bridge that we collectively spin out into the unknown future toward shores not yet visible. As a banker's bank, the Fed watches over the construction of that bridge at the point where it is most vulnerable, right at the leading edge between present and future" (*The New Lombard Street: How the Fed Became the Dealer of Last Resort* [Princeton, NJ: Princeton University Press, 2011], 3–4). Mehrling discusses the early years of the Fed on pp. 32–36.

61. Mehrling uses the term "commercial loan theory" (*New Lombard Street*, 33). Our analysis is indebted to Merhling's discussion in *New Lombard Street*, pp. 33–34. The phrase "commercial-bill theory of banking" comes from Joseph A. Schumpeter, *History of Economic Analysis*, ed. Elizabeth Boody Schumpeter (1954; New York: Oxford University Press, 1994), 729.

62. Mehrling, *New Lombard Street*, 34.

63. See Perry Mehrling "The Money Muddle: The Transformation of American Monetary Thought, 1920–1979," *History of Political Economy* (1998), 293–306, and *The Money Interest and the Public Interest: American Monetary Thought, 1920–1970* (Cambridge, MA: Harvard University Press, 1997), esp. chaps. 2–3 and 6.

CHAPTER TWO

1. For treatments of the early years of the AEA, see Mary O. Furner, *Advocacy and Objectivity: A Crisis in the Professionalization of American Social Science, 1865–1905* (Lexington: University Press of Kentucky, 1975), esp. chap. 3; Dorothy Ross, *The Origins of American Social Science* (New York: Cambridge University Press, 1991), 63, 110, 159; and A. W. Coats, "The First Two Decades of the American Economic Association," *American Economic Review* 50 (1960): 555–74. For discussions of economists' efforts to gain social authority, see Robert L. Church, "Economists as Experts: The Rise of an Academic Profession in the United States, 1870–1920," in *The University in Society*, vol. 2: *Europe, Scotland, and the United States from the 16th to the 20th Century*, ed. Lawrence Stone (Princeton, NJ: Princeton University Press, 1974), 571–609; and Michael A. Bernstein, *A Perilous Progress: Economists and Public Purpose in Twentieth-Century America* (Princeton, NJ: Princeton University Press, 2001), esp. chap. 1.

2. See, e.g., Wesley Clair Mitchell, *Types of Economic Theory: From Mercantilism to Institutionalism,* ed. Joseph Dorfman (New York: Augustus M. Kelley, 1969), 2 volumes; Joseph A. Schumpeter, *History of Economic Analysis,* ed. Elizabeth Boody Schumpeter (1954; New York: Oxford University Press, 1994); and Malcolm Rutherford and Mary S. Morgan, "American Economics: The Character of the Transformation," *History of Political Economy* 30, no. 1 (1998): 1–26. In *A Perilous Progress,* Michael Bernstein provides a helpful summary of what was at stake in the split between these two positions: "The belief (and the determination) of orthodox theorists that economics could be a truly objective science of society rested on a commitment to the legitimacy of understanding the whole by studying its parts; a focus on individual transactions and behavior thus served as an appropriate (and defensible) starting point for the science. If, however, this methodological posture were destabilized, if the parts were understood to be dependent on the whole, the need to address a diverse array of historical, sociological, and descriptive issues would leave economics bereft of a strong case for its disciplinary birthright. To be sure, the struggle between the institutionalists and the neoclassical theorists was a contest over the nature of economics itself; more than this, it was a confrontation over the professionalizing project that had virtually defined the field since the 1880s" (45).

3. Wesley Clair Mitchell, Veblen's student, admirer, and editor, presents Veblen's work as so at odds with the discipline that many orthodox economists would say "there is no economic theory in Veblen." Veblen, Mitchell added, "has so little of the academic about him that he is *persona non gratis* to a great many of his professional colleagues" (*Types of Economic Thought,* 2: 609, 651).

4. On institutionalism in the period, see Malcólm Rutherford, *The Institutional Movement in American Economics, 1918–1947: Science and Social Control* (Cambridge: Cambridge University Press, 2011). On the continuing tradition of institutionalism, see Rutherford, "Institutional Economics: Then and Now," *Journal of Economic Perspectives* 15, no. 3 (Summer 2001): 173–94. Rutherford says that the term "institutional economics" was introduced in 1919 by Walter Hamilton ("Institutional Economics," 173). In a footnote to Mitchell's *Types of Economic Theory,* however, Joseph Dorfman says that Mitchell began referring to Veblen's work as "institutional theory" in 1917–18, after having previously called it "evolutionary theory" (*Types of Economic Thought,* 2: 610, n. 3).

5. Veblen, *The Theory of Business Enterprise* (1904; reprint Manfield Centre, CT: Martino Publishing, 2013), 160. Future citations refer to this edition.

6. Mitchell, *Types of Economic Theory,* 2: 667.

7. Veblen, "Preoccupations of Economic Science, III," *Quarterly Journal of Economics* 14, no. 2 (1900): 267. "Neo-classical" appears on p. 261. Veblen was drawing a distinction between some economists, such as Marshall, who pursued "taxonomic" projects but were moving toward the evolutionary approach Veblen preferred, and others who could not escape ahistorical taxonomy. Veblen was strongly critical of the taxonomic project because it made the "science" of economics inapplicable to the actual world. "The laws of the science, that which makes up the economist's theoretical knowledge, are laws of the normal case. The normal case does not occur in concrete fact. These laws are . . . 'hypothetical' truths; and the science is a 'hypothetical' science. They apply to concrete facts only as the facts are interpreted and abstracted from, in the light of the underlying postulates. The science is, therefore, a theory of the normal case, a discussion of the concrete facts of life in respect of their degree of approximation to the normal

case" (254–55). For a probing discussion of Veblen's article, see Tony Lawson, "What Is the 'School' Called Neoclassical Economics?" *Cambridge Journal of Economics* 37, no. 5 (2013): 947–83.

8. Henry Schultz, one of the founders of American mathematical economics, explained why mathematics was necessary to depict the complex interrelations of multiple factors: "Even when a quantity of a commodity demanded is a function of all prices, an increase of its price will decrease, and increase of income will increase the amount taken as long as the commodity in question does not compete in consumption with any other commodity. When the consumption of a commodity is related to that of another an increase in its price may increase and an increase in income may decrease the amount taken" (*The Theory and Measurement of Demand* [Chicago: University of Chicago Press, 1938], p. 1950).

9. John B. Clark, "Distribution as Determined by a Law of Rent," *Quarterly Journal of Economics* 5, no. 3 (1891): 293.

10. Major works include William Stanley Jevons, *Principles of Political Economy* (1871), Carl Menger, *Principles of Economics* (1871), and Léon Walras, *Éléments d'économie politique* (1874).

11. Richard S. Howey, "The Origins of Marginalism," in R. D. Collison Black, A. W. Coats, and Crauford D. W. Goodwin, *The Marginal Revolution in Economics: Interpretation and Evaluation* (Durham, NC: Duke University Press, 1973), 24. John A. Hobson used the word *marginalism* in 1914 in *Work and Wealth* to refer to both marginal utility and marginal productivity.

12. "Literary" is a term used by George J. Stigler, for example, in *Production and Distribution Theories: The Formative Period* (New York: Agathon Press, 1968), 1; and by Schumpeter, *History of Economic Analysis,* 960.

13. Quoted Mitchell, *Types of Economic Theory,* 2:240–41.

14. Joseph Dorfman implies that Clark was responding to the May Haymarket strike and bombing in Chicago, and he argues that this explains why Clark shifted away from the Christian socialist position he had taken in *The Philosophy of Wealth,* which was published in book form in 1886 but contained essays written during the previous decade. See *Economic Mind in American Civilization* (New York: Viking, 1946–49), 3:195. See also Joseph Persky, "The Neoclassical Advent: American Economics at the Dawn of the 20th Century," *Journal of Economic Perspectives* 14, no. 1 (Winter 2000): 98, n. 4.

15. Clark, "Distribution as Determined by a Law of Rent," *Quarterly Journal of Economics* 5, no. 3 (April 1891): 312. All future references cited in the text.

16. Clark repeatedly referred to the "scientific" nature of economics, calling it an "economic science" and an example of "scientific thought" ("Capital and Its Earnings," *Publications of the American Economics Association* 3, no. 2 [1888]: 32, 17).

17. Clark, "The Law of Wages and Interest," *Annals of the American Academy of Political and Social Science* 1 (July 1890): 52. All future references cited in the text.

18. Clark, *The Distribution of Wealth: A Theory of Wages, Interest, and Profits* (1889: New York, 1902), 327, 328, 329, 330.

19. Economic historians have debated Clark's claims to be impartial. Wesley Clair Mitchell, for example, refers to Clark's "set purpose" and "definite end," which guided his supposedly objective theoretical formulations (*Types of Economic Theory,* 2:237). See also Morris A. Copeland, "Institutional Economics and Model Analysis," *American Economic Review* 41, no. 2

(1951), 58; Thomas C. Leonard, "'A Certain Rude Honesty': John Bates Clark as a Pioneering Neo-Classical Economist," *History of Political Economy* 35, no. 3 (2003): 548–49; and Dorfman, *The Economic Mind,* 3:191–204.

20. Mary S. Morgan points out that Americans in this period faced "monopoly, monopsony, or a variety of sharp practices" instead of the level playing field or customary pricing practices that might support fair trade and fair prices. See "Marketplace Morals and the American Economists: The Case of J. B. Clark," in *Transactors and Their Markets, History of Political Economy* 26 (1994), Annual Supplement, 230.

21. See Persky, "Neoclassical Advent," 97, 100. Persky argues that Clark believed that unless *labor* was treated fairly in the matter of wages in particular, America would face serious violence, possibly even revolution (98). For this reason, Clark's economic theory functioned as an admonition, not just a rhetorical plea for justice in the abstract.

22. For a discussion of static analysis, its relation to abstraction, and its distance from data, see Schumpeter, *History of Economic Analysis,* 963. Schumpeter discusses partial analysis, which he describes as another way of generating simplification, on pp. 990–91.

23. Samuelson, "On the Problem of Integrability in Utility Theory," *Economica* 17 (1950): 355. At the end of his life Fisher enumerated the chief points of his dissertation. He credited his approach with contributing (1) A concept of utility and marginal utility based on desire, not, as Jevons and others had attempted, on pleasure (the gratification of desire)—and which was thus amenable to statistical measurement; (2) hydrostatic and other mechanical analogies; (3) distinctive price determining equations; (4) applications to economics of Gibb's vector concepts; (5) indifference curves; and (6) reversal of cause and effect ("Fisher's Unpublished Annotations" in *The Works of Irving Fisher,* ed. William J. Barber, volume I [London: Pickering & Chatto, 1997], 173).

24. George J. Stigler "The Development of Utility Theory II," *Journal of Political Economy* 58, no. 5 (October 1950), 377–79. When Fisher asked one of his favorite teachers, William Graham Sumner, for advice about a dissertation topic in the spring of 1890, the young student admitted being torn between economics and mathematics, the two disciplines he had thus far studied. Sumner, who taught political economy and sociology at Yale, suggested that Fisher look into mathematical economics, a subject then unknown to Fisher. Beginning with two books—Jevons's 1971 *Theory of Political Economy,* and Rudolf Auspitz and Richard Lieben's *Untersuchungen euber die Theorie des Prises (Researches in Price Theory,* 1887, 1889) —Fisher worked his way through the few works available on mathematical economics, and he added to them Gibbs's vector analysis. See Robert Loring Allen, *Irving Fisher: A Biography* (Cambridge, MA: Blackwell, 1993), 53.

25. Fisher's formulation of general equilibrium theory also differed in other ways from the Walrasian formulation, as it differed from the subsequent elaboration of the theory of demand, using indexes of utilities and indifference curves, developed by the Italian theorist Vilfredo Pareto and extended by the Russian economist Eugen Slutsky in 1915. Fisher was aware of some of the differences between his approach and that of Walras, whose work he had not read before writing his dissertation. In his preface, he noted that the equations he used "are essentially those of Walras in *Éléments d'économie politique pure.* The only fundamental differences are that I use marginal utility throughout and treat it as a function of the quantities of commodity, whereas Professor Walras makes the quantity of each commodity a function of the prices"

(*MI* 4). As E. Roy Weintraub has demonstrated, modern proofs in general equilibrium theory are based on a later tradition begun by the Swedish economist Gustav Cassel and do not rely on either Fisher's or Walras's formulations. See *General Equilibrium Analysis: Studies in Appraisal* (Ann Arbor: University of Michigan Press, 1985), 59.

26. Gibbs's most important works include "Graphic Methods in the Thermodynamics of Fluids" (*Scientific Papers of J. Willard Gibbs,* ed. H. A. Bumstead and R. G. Van Name [London: Longmans Green, 1906], 1:1–32); "A Method of Geometrical Representation of the Thermodynamic Properties of Substances by Means of Surfaces" (*Scientific Papers* 1:33–54); and *On the Equilibrium of Heterogeneous Substances* (*Scientific Papers,* 1:55–353).

27. Thus, for example, the elaborate plan for a bath that would float differently shaped and sized cisterns in water could display the coordinates of a commodity spatially and present the utility of this commodity as a force (*Mathematical Investigations in the Theory of Value and Prices* [1902; reprint Old Chelsea Station, NY: Cosimo, 2007], 85; hereafter *MI*). While the machine could show some of the interrelations that connected the cisterns in the bath, however, "there also exist other connections between the shapes of the cisterns which could not be mechanically exhibited" (*MI* 66). Fisher viewed the inadequacy of each successive mode of representation as unavoidable, and he considered even the analysis that might result from adding them all together incomplete: "Neither economics nor any other science can expect an exhaustive analysis" (*MI* 67).

28. "Mathematics is the lantern by which what before was dimly visible now looms up in firm, bold outlines," Fisher explained (*MI* 119). Fisher was not the first writer to use mathematical equations and symbols in a printed text, but previous examples tended to be mathematical textbooks or treatises intended to illustrate mathematical principles. The latter is true of the text Fisher rediscovered and had translated: Cournot's 1838 *Récherches sur les principes mathematic de la theorie des richesses.* To modern scholars, this feature of Fisher's work makes it seem methodologically rigorous, in a way and to a degree that the work of Fisher's contemporaries does not. This is an example of the extent to which mathematical notation and argumentation have been naturalized within the practice of economics and it also shows how what was simply one— albeit the favored—representational mode in Fisher's own work subsequently came to seem like the *optimum* way to set out an economic theory. See, for example, William J. Baumol, who writes that "it is only in mathematical economics—notably in the work of Irving Fisher—that I have found work that stands up in terms of its use of method, to more recent writings" ("On Method in U.S. Economics a Century Earlier," *American Economic Review* 75, no. 6 [December 1985], 1).

29. He placed the mathematical demonstrations in the body of *The Theory of Interest* (1930).

30. The 1926 edition of Fisher's PhD thesis includes not only Fisher's original diagrams but also photographs of both physical constructions of Fisher's model. The 1893 model is the smaller of the two; its container is a box set on what appear to be sawhorse supports. The model built in 1925, by which time the first model had worn out from repeated classroom use, seems to fill an entire room. Fisher never discussed the complexities introduced when he converted his two-dimensional diagrams into a three-dimensional machine. Nor did he belabor the precision (or lack thereof) of the fit between the diagram and the economic principles it helped him visualize. The former is the subject of Mary S. Morgan's and Marcel Boumans's treatment of another hydraulic machine, built by yet another economist (Bill Phillips): "Secrets Hidden by Two-Dimensionality: The Economy as a Hydraulic Machine," in *Models: The Third Dimen-*

sion of Science, ed. Soraya de Chadarevian and Nick Hopwood (Stanford, CA: Stanford University Press, 2004), 369–401. The latter is the subject of Mary S. Morgan's "The Technology of Analogical Models: Irving Fisher's Monetary Worlds," *Philosophy of Science* 64, Supplement Proceedings of the 1996 Biennial Meetings of the Philosophy of Science Association, Part II: Symposium Papers (December 1997): S 304–14.

31. These relationships included (but were not limited to) *"the quantities of each commodity consumed by each individual during the year"* (*MI* 42); *"the given total quantities of each commodity consumed by the whole market"* (*MI* 42); *"the marginal utility of each commodity to each individual"* (*MI* 43); *"the prices of commodities in terms of each other"* (*MI* 43); and *"the marginal utility of money to each individual"* (*MI* 43).

32. Anne Mayhew, "Copeland on Money as Electricity," *Real World Economics Review* 53 (2010).

33. This is the argument pursued with great vigor by Philip Mirowski. Mirowski argues that "the neoclassical theory of exchange was an offshoot of the metaphor of energy, buttressed by the mathematics of rudimentary rational mechanics" (*More Heat Than Light: Economics as Social Physics, Physics as Nature's Economics* [Cambridge: Cambridge University Press, 1989], 196).

34. This is part of the title of Fisher's text in its initial publication form, which appeared in *Publications of the American Economic Association* 11 (August 1996): 331–442. The edition of *AI* we cite is bound with *Mathematical Investigations* (Reprint, Old Chelsea Station, NY: Cosimo, 2007). Future references cited in text.

35. The Fisher effect states that the real interest rate (the amount by which the purchasing power grows over time) is not affected by monetary measures such as the nominal interest rate and the expected inflation rate. The real interest rate equals the nominal interest rate minus the expected inflation rate.

36. Under recessionary conditions with interest rates at zero, as they were after the 2008 financial crisis, deflationary expectations stimulate negative feedback effects and exacerbate the downturn. In such periods, the Fed does not have access to the typical strategy of lowering interest rates to stimulate the economy. See Kenneth S. Rogoff, *The Curse of Cash* (Princeton, NJ: Princeton University Press, 2016), chaps. 8–10; and Michael D. Bordo and Andrew J. Filardo, *Deflation and Monetary Policy in a Historical Perspective: Remembering the Past or Being Condemned to Repeat It?* (Cambridge, MA: National Bureau of Economic Research, 2004). We discuss Milton Friedman's criticism of the actions of the Federal Reserve during the Great Depression in chapter 8.

37. Fisher did not bother to prove the "general theorems" that present-value calculations assume because, as he explained, "their proof is accessible in most treatises on interest, annuities, insurance, etc." (*AI* 20, n. 1). So numerous were the texts containing these "elaborate tables" that Fisher merely gestures, here and elsewhere, to the sources he clearly assumed his reader would know: "See, *e.g.,* the 'Encyclopedia Britannica,' 'Annuities'" (*AI* 20, n. 1). Fisher also refers to "Horner's Method" (*AI* 27), which was a technique of synthetic division used to evaluate polynomials. Horner's Table (or Tableau) provided a shortcut so that one would not have to make laborious calculations. Fisher was intimately familiar with such tables and their usefulness; in 1894 he and a Yale colleague, Andrew W. Phillips, published a five-figure table of logarithms to accompany the geometry textbook that Fisher and Phillips published in 1896.

38. We see Fisher's frustration with the data (as well as the labor necessary to make it usable) in a note explaining how he generated a table that compares India bonds whose interest was paid in gold and in silver between 1875 and 1895 to the estimated and actual percentages of appreciation of gold in terms of silver: "The methods by which the first column [showing rates of interest in silver] is computed are the same as those explained in the preceding chapter, account being taken of the fact that the price quotations for rupee paper are not 'flat,' so that no corrections for accrued interest need be applied. For computing the second column [interest rates in gold] a more laborious method was necessary, due to the fact that the quotations are not continuous of the same bond. The earlier ones are for a 4% bond and the later for a 3% bond. The buyer of a 4% bond is regarded as converting it into the 3% at the current price in 1888, the date of maturity of the earlier bond. As no bond tables apply to such conversions, tables of present values were used and that rate was found by trial (and interpolation) which would make the present value of all benefits equal to the purchase price" (*AI* 50 n. 6).

39. To make expectations conducive to modeling, Milton Friedman introduced the idea of "adaptive expectations" and John Muth advanced the notion of "rational expectations." To make behavior amenable to modeling, Daniel Kahneman and Amos Tversky developed prospect theory.

40. *The Theory of Interest as Determined by Impatience to Spend Money and Opportunity to Invest It* (1930; reprint Mansfield Centre, CT: Martino, 2012), ix.

41. *The Nature of Capital and Income* (New York: Macmillan Co., 1906), vii.

42. In response to Fisher's attempt to introduce new definitions for economics' central terms, Charles A. Tuttle voiced an objection shared by many of his peers: "Such a revolution in economic terminology, instead of 'removing certain verbal obstacles which now block the way to important ideas,' would render mutual understanding well-nigh impossible" ("The Fundamental Notion of Capital, Once More," *Quarterly Journal of Economics* 19, no. 1 (November 1904): 8. Fisher reviewed some of these terminological debates in "Precedents for Defining Capital," *Quarterly Journal of Economics* 18, no. 3 (May 1904): 386–408.

43. That the bond and its interest is the foundational model for Fisher's work is even more explicit in *The Theory of Interest:* "There is no more definite and universally accepted formula in the whole realm of economics and business than [the formula written into the bond table]. It is used *every day* in brokers' offices. . . . It is the type, par excellence, of the capitalization principle both in theory and practice" (465). See also pp. 17 and 26.

44. Maurice Allais, "Fisher, Irving," in David L. Sills, ed., *International Encyclopedia of the Social Sciences,* vol. 5 (New York: Macmillan and Free Press, 1968), 477.

45. Jérôme de Boyer des Roches and Rebeca Gomez Betancourt, "American Quantity Theorists Prior to Irving Fisher's *Purchasing Power of Money,*" *Journal of Economic Perspectives* 26, no. 4 (2012), 1. The period of decreasing prices extended from 1873 to 1897 and is sometimes called the Great Deflation. The authoritative discussion of secular trends in the money supply is Milton Friedman and Anna Jacobson Schwartz, *A Monetary History of the United States, 1867–1960* (Princeton, NJ: Princeton University Press, 1963); especially chaps. 3 and 4.

46. Schumpeter, *History of Economic Analysis,* 1088.

47. Des Roches and Betancourt, "American Quantity Theorists," 13–15.

48. *The Works of Irving Fisher,* ed. William J. Barber (London: Pickering & Chatto, 1997), 4:563.

49. Schumpeter, *History of Economic Analysis*, 1102, 1103. Lance Girton and Don Roper also identify tensions in Fisher's quantity theory. See "J. Laurence Laughlin and the Quantity Theory of Money," International Finance Discussion Paper 103 (March 1977): 17–19.

50. Quinn and Roberds, "Evolution," 14. By 1915, there were 229 bank clearinghouses.

51. Allen Meltzer, the foremost historian of the Federal Reserve, characterized Fisher's contribution to business-cycle theory as follows: "According to Fisher (1920, chap. 4) bank loans and bank deposits increased much more than currency during the early stages of expansion. In his notation, M$'$ (deposits) rose relative to M (currency) following an inflow of gold or other source of base money. Later in the expansion, consumer expenditures increased and the ratio of currency to deposits rose. This rise forced fractional reserve banks, operating under gold standard rules, to surrender reserves. Faced with a loss of reserves, the banks raised loan rates, called loans, and reduced deposits. The reduction in money brought the expansion to an end and started the contraction. . . . The key element in his explanation of cycles is that businesses, banks and households failed to anticipate the inflation caused by monetary expansion. A central bank operating on the currency principle (or gold standard rules) would always react too slowly to prevent inflation" (*A History of the Federal Reserve*, 2 vols. [Chicago: University of Chicago Press, 2003], 1:61).

52. Banks also created credit in the period by discounting short-term commercial paper, working capital, and fixed capital. For an analysis of banks' use of "shiftability" of their investment portfolios to remain liquid, see Perry Mehrling, *The New Lombard Street: How the Fed Became the Dealer of Last Resort* (Princeton, NJ: Princeton University Press, 2011), 34.

53. Mehrling, "The Money Muddle: The Transformation of American Monetary Thought, 1920–1970," *History of Political Economy* (1998): 293–306.

54. Irving Fisher, "Recent Changes in Price Levels and Their Causes," *American Economic Review* 1, no. 2 (April 1911): 37, 38.

55. Laughlin, "Causes of the Changes in Prices since 1896," *American Economic Review* 1, no. 2 (April 1911): 35.

56. D. E. F. Houston, W. Kemmerer, Joseph French Johnson, Murray S. Wildman, T. N. Carver, W. F. Taussig, Ralph H. Hess, J. Laurence Laughlin, and Irving Fisher, "Money and Prices: Discussion," *American Economic Review* 1, no. 2 (April 2011): 65. Of the seven economists who responded to Fisher and Laughlin, four supported Fisher and three endorsed Laughlin's position.

57. Houston et al., "Money and Prices: Discussion," 67.

58. Knight, *Risk, Uncertainty, and Profit* (1921; reprint Chicago: University of Chicago Press, 1971), 237. Future references cited in the text.

59. Keynes, *A Treatise on Probability* (London: Macmillan & Co., 1921), chap. 1.

60. A useful discussion of forms of unknowns that lie beyond uncertainty can be found in Richard Zeckhauser, "Investing in the Unknown and Unknowable," *Capitalism and Society* 1, no. 2 (2006): 1–39. Richard Bookstaber refers to these unknown unknowables as "primal risk." See *A Demon of Our Own Design: Markets, Hedge Funds, and the Perils of Financial Innovation* (Hoboken, NJ: John Wiley & Sons, 2007), 232.

61. Robert Riegel and Henry James Loman, *Insurance, Principles and Practices*, 2nd ed. (New York: Prentice-Hall, 1922), 5, 8.

62. Knight, "The Limitations of Scientific Method in Economics," in *The Trend of Econom-*

ics, ed. Rexford Tugwell (New York: Knopf, 1924), 137, 135. See Malcolm Rutherford, "Chicago Economics and Institutionalism," in *The Elgar Companion to the Chicago School of Economics*, ed. Ross B. Emmett (Cheltenham, UK: Edward Elgar, 2010).

63. Mary Murname provides a compelling case for the centrality of marginalism in these debates, especially in the 1920s. J. B. Clark was one of the economists most involved in these campaigns. See Murname, *The Mellon Tax Plan: The Income Tax and the Penetration of Marginalist Economic Thought into American Life and Law in the 1920s* (PhD diss., Case Western Reserve, 2007), 80, 182–84. Here is the marginalist position on progressive taxation in a nutshell: "If the last dollar earned by a rich person delivered less utility than a dollar earned by a poor person, progressive income taxation increased total social well-being" (Murname, 88; she is citing Edwin R. A. Seligman).

64. See Murname, *The Mellon Tax Plan*, and W. Elliot Brownlee, "Economists and the Formation of the Modern Tax System in the United States: The World War I Crisis," in Mary O. Furner and Barry Supple, eds., *The State and Economic Knowledge: The American and British Experiences* (Cambridge: Cambridge University Press, 1990), 401–35. In his more extended discussion of taxation, Brownlee barely mentions the 1909 Corporate Tax Act. See *Federal Taxation in America* (Cambridge: Cambridge University Press, 1996), chap. 1.

65. Reuven S. Avi-Yonah, "9," http://www.enotes.com/major-acts-congress/corporate-income-tax-act.

66. See Brownlee, *Federal Taxation*, 45.

67. Some states had attempted to tax corporations, but only Pennsylvania and New York had succeeded in passing corporate tax laws.

68. As Marjorie E. Kornhauser explains, "net income was to be computed by subtracting from gross income dividends received from other corporations that paid the tax and all 'ordinary and necessary expenses,' depreciation, losses, and 'interest actually paid within the year on its bonded or other indebtedness to an amount of such bonded and other indebtedness not exceeding the paid-up capital stock of such corporation . . . outstanding at the close of the year'" ("Corporate Regulation and the Origins of the Corporate Income Tax" [1990] http://heinonline; citation 66 Ind. L. J. 53 1990–91, 101). While this definition seems quite specific, the debates that followed, as well as the fact that accountants had to make decisions about when to realize "ordinary and necessary expenses," indicate that it was always subject to interpretation.

69. Willard J. Graham, "Some Observations on the Nature of Income, Generally Accepted Accounting Principles, and Financial Reporting," *Law and Contemporary Problems* 30, no. 4 (Autumn 1965): 655. In the *Eisner v. Macomber* decision, Justice Pitney wrote: "'Income may be defined as the gain derived from capital, from labor, or from both combined,' provided it be understood to include profit gained through a sale or conversion of capital assets. . . . Here we have the essential matter: *not* a gain *accruing* to capital, not a *growth* or *increment* of value *in* the investment; but a gain, a profit, something of exchangeable value *proceeding from* the property, *severed* from the capital however invested or employed, and *coming in,* being '*derived*'; that is, *received* or *drawn by* the recipient . . . for his *separate* use, benefit and disposal:—*that* is income derived from property" (quoted in Graham, 655). Graham notes that the essential elements of this definition turn on realization ("to be income it must be severed from the capital"), gain (it must be above costs), production (the gain must be realized from labor or capital or both), appreciation of the capital assets that is realized (taken by the owner), and a monetary concept

("Some Observations," 654–55). In subsequent decisions, Graham states, courts have insisted that net incomes are not all the same and should not be treated as such.

70. Brownlee chronicles the impact these events had on the profession of economics. See "Economists and the Formation of the Modern Tax System," 406–26.

71. Paton, *Accounting Theory, with Special Reference to the Corporate Enterprise* (New York: Ronald Press, 1922), 470.

72. Murname, *Mellon Tax Plan*, 386.

73. Seligman, "Federal Taxes Upon Income and Excess Profits—A Discussion," *American Economic Review* 8, no. 1, Supplement (March 1918), 41, 44. Seligman was responding to a paper presented by Thomas Sewell Adams, the Yale political economist who was generally considered the leading expert on federal taxation.

CHAPTER THREE

1. Stephen M. Stigler, *The History of Statistics: The Measurement of Uncertainty before 1900* (Cambridge, MA: Harvard University Press, 1986).

2. North, "The Relation of Statistics to Economics and Sociology," *Publications of the American Statistical Association* 11, no. 85 (March 1909): 432.

3. Ibid., 441. Walker was president of the ASA from 1882 until his death in 1897. He was also the first president of the American Economic Association (1886), served as chief of the Bureau of Statistics (1869–70), and directed the US censuses in 1870 and 1880. In 1884, Walker became the president of the Massachusetts Institute of Technology.

4. Charles Camic and Yu Xie cite Johns Hopkins, where Henry Ludwell Moore studied with J. B. Clark; Yale; the University of Pennsylvania; Cornell; the University of Michigan; Harvard; the University of Chicago; and the University of Wisconsin as the only universities other than MIT and Columbia to offer training in statistics. See "The Statistical Turn in American Social Science," *American Sociological Review* 59, no. 5 (October 1994): 778.

5. Moore explicitly justified his reference to the "normal" wage by invoking the marginal product of labor. See Henry L. Moore, *Laws of Wages: An Essay in Statistical Economics* (New York: Macmillan, 1911), 46–47. David Card and Craig A. Olsen note that Moore's evaluation of strikes as either "successful" or "unsuccessful," never partially so, was typical of early twentieth-century analysts, including the authors of the US Bureau of Labor reports. See "Bargaining Power, Strike Durations, and Wage Outcomes: An Analysis of Strikes in the 1880s," *Journal of Labor Economics*, 13, no. 1 (January 1995): 32.

6. Henry Schultz, *The Theory and Measurement of Demand* (Chicago: University of Chicago Press, 1938), 48. Here is Schultz's summary of Moore's accomplishments: "Professor Moore's contributions to the solution of the problem are three: (1) he restated the hypothetical statistical law of demand in a form admitting of concrete inductive treatment; (2) he devised ingenious statistical techniques, such as the method of link relatives and the method of trend ratios, for handling the time variable, and was among the first to apply the method of multiple correlation to the study of demand; and (3) he succeeded in deducing for the first time the statistical demand curves for several important commodities, and in measuring their elasticities of demand" (65).

7. Henry L. Moore, *Forecasting the Yield and the Price of Cotton* (New York: Macmillan, 1917), 65–92.

8. Fisher also alludes to mathematical models: "Formulae, diagrams, and models are instruments of higher study. The trained mathematician uses them to clarify and extend his previous unsymbolic knowledge" (*Mathematical Investigations in the Theory of Value and Prices* [1902; reprinted Old Chelsea Station, N. Y.: Cosimo, 2007], 108).

9. To forecast the probable price of cotton, Moore explained, one had to know the "law of demand for cotton"—that is, "the probable variation in the price that will accompany a computed variation in the supply" (*Forecasting*, 8). This formulation reveals both Moore's emphasis on the demand side of the marginalist paradigm and his endorsement of one of the most basic marginalist claims: price represents the intersection between the supply and demand curves.

10. Inverse probability calculations can use the following: the normal, or Gaussian, curve which depicts the distribution of errors; the method of least squares, which figures regression in terms of the root-means-square of the differences between the line and the data points; standard deviation from an arithmetic mean; or the law of large numbers, which involves performing the same calculation a large number of times.

11. George J. Stigler, "Henry L. Moore and Statistical Economics," *Econometrica* 30, no. 1 (1962): 1.

12. Dorothy Ross's important book on the origins of the social sciences in America stresses their shared ambition to be "scientific." Since "science" was held to be a more abstract enterprise than the data-dependent discipline of historical analysis, linking social sciences like economics to science rather than history inevitably raised the status of the discipline; it also introduced the data problem. See *The Origins of American Social Science* (Cambridge: Cambridge University Press, 1991), chap. 3.

13. Guy Alchon, *The Invisible Hand of Planning: Capitalism, Social Science, and the State in the 1920s* (Princeton, NJ: Princeton University Press, 1985), 53. Greene asked for suggestions for the economic institute in 1913 and soon formed an exploratory committee, with Gay as chair. In June 1914, the committee issued a memorandum that called for an impartial investigation of "the basic facts" about wages, prices, and rents. See also Herbert Heaton, *A Scholar in Action: Edwin F. Gay* (Cambridge, MA: Harvard University Press, 1952), 91–93. Another version of the prehistory of the NBER stresses the role played by Malcolm C. Rorty, an electrical engineer and statistical expert who worked at the American Telephone and Telegraph Corporation, and Nahum I. Stone, an economist and expert on tariffs. According to this version, Rorty and Stone first discussed the idea of an institute in 1916 and Rorty soon approached Gay, Mitchell, and John Commons. Rorty's particular interest was in being able to anticipate the "industrial readjustment that [would] necessarily arise" in America as a response to the European war. Rorty's plan, like Greene's, was interrupted by the US entry into World War I. See Alchon, *Invisible Hand*, 53–56; and Solomon Fabricant, "Toward a Firmer Basis of Economic Policy: The Founding of the National Bureau of Economic Policy" (New York: NBER, 1984), 3–4.

14. Quoted in Alchon, *Invisible Hand*, 76. Rakesh Khurana discusses the founding of HBS in *From Higher Aims to Hired Hands: The Social Transformation of American Business Schools and the Unfulfilled Promise of Management as a Profession* (Princeton, NJ: Princeton University Press, 2007), 111–21.

15. Heaton, *Scholar*, 77–78.

16. Ibid., 81.

17. Letter to Lucy Sprague Mitchell, June 19, 1910, in Lucy Sprague Mitchell, "A Personal Sketch," in *Wesley Clair Mitchell: The Economic Scientist* (New York: NBER, 1952), 91.

18. *Survey of Current Business* (Washington, DC: US Government Printing Office, 1921). R. G. D. Allen points out that index numbers do not have to represent changes over time; they can also represent two situations in a spatial sense (e.g., two regions of a country) or two groups of individuals (*Index Numbers in Theory and Practice* [Houndsmills: Macmillan Press, 1975]).

19. One mid-twentieth-century attempt to identify the origin of index numbers is M. G. Kendall, "Studies in the History of Probability and Statistics, XXI: The Early History of Index Numbers," *Review of the International Statistical Institute* 37, no 1 (1969): 1–12. Kendall associates these index numbers with Bishop Fleetwood, who tried to capture the decrease in the purchasing power of money on a basket of goods in 1707. The theory of index numbers was formulated, according to Kendall, in the mid-eighteenth century, when the fall in the value of money decade by decade was severe enough to cause fixed-price contracts to become a hardship. See also Joseph Persky, "Retrospectives: Price Indexes and General Exchange Values," *Journal of Economic Perspectives* 12, no. 1 (Winter 1998): 197–205. By 1900, the elementary theory of index numbers was fairly well established. For a snapshot of this consensus, see F. Y. Edgeworth, "Index Numbers," *Dictionary of Political Economy*, ed. R. H. Inglis Palgrave (London: Macmillan, 1900), 384–87. In 1905, Mitchell identified Ronald P. Falkner, the statistician who helped compose the 1893 Aldrich Report, as the first person to use index numbers in preparing price tables, but by 1821, he had pushed the origin further back—to the mid-eighteenth century, when the Italian G. I. Carli calculated the changes in the prices of oil, grain, and wine between 1500 and 1750. See Mitchell, "Methods of Presenting Statistics of Wages," *Publications of the American Statistical Association* 9, no. 72 (December 1905): 325. The best study of the history of time series is Judy L. Klein, *Statistical Visions in Time: A History of Time Series Analysis, 1662–1938* (Cambridge: Cambridge University Press, 1997).

20. Frisch, "Annual Survey of General Economic Theory: The Problem of Index Numbers," *Econometrica* 4, no. 1 (January 1936): 1.

21. Warren Persons, "Indices of Business Conditions," *The Review of Economic Statistics* 1 (January 1919): 7.

22. The survey contains three kinds of data sets. Most of the data sets (nineteen of the twenty sets of tables) depict the real view of the economy, using "commodities" to include both goods and services. One data set ("Banking and Finance") depicts both the money view of the economy, in its survey of current money (e.g., "new capital issues"), and the financial view, in its tables showing capital assets (e.g., stocks, bonds, and dividends and interest), 3.

23. See Evan B. Metcalf, "Secretary Hoover and the Emergence of Macroeconomic Management," *Business History Review* 49, no. 1 (Spring 1975): 60–80. Metcalf briefly discusses the *Survey of Current Business* on 66–68, explaining that "a Goodyear executive called the *Survey* 'the most important step in our industrial life since the inauguration of the Federal Reserve System.'"

24. R. D. G. Allen notes that it is not unusual to find the kind of misnomer represented by the *Survey*'s use of "index numbers" to refer to this kind of figure. "It is quite common . . . to

see the term 'index number' applied to a variation of a magnitude which is directly measurable. It is often convenient to express the changes in such a magnitude, given (for example) as an annual series, in the form of one year as a percentage of another, of one year as showing a percentage increase or decrease over another. The reference base, written as 100, can be any one year of the series found convenient. The result looks very much like an index number, and by extension, it is often described as such" (*Index Numbers*, 3). We should note that some of the figures included in the *Survey*'s tables are, technically speaking, index numbers. But the authors do not distinguish between the figures that record measurable quantities, as do the figures for the bank clearings, and those that are proper index numbers because they are aggregates constructed out of unmeasurable or incommensurate entities.

25. See William J. Barber, *From New Era to New Deal: Herbert Hoover, the Economists, and American Economic Policy, 1921–1933* (Cambridge: Cambridge University Press, 1985), 13.

26. Mitchell, *History of Prices during the War* (Washington, DC: Government Printing Office, 1919), 3.

27. Tjalling C. Koopmans, "Measurement without Theory," *Review of Economics and Statistics* 29, no. 3 (August 1947): 161–72.

28. Calling the data presented in the Aldrich Report "an invaluable source of information to students of economics and statistics," Edith Abbott reported that "the unanimous verdict of statisticians [about this report] has been that these data are unimpeachable" ("The Wages of Unskilled Labor in the United States, 1850–1900," *Journal of Political Economy* 13, no. 3 [1905], 339).

29. Mitchell faulted the report for not weighting its index numbers: "No computations," Mitchell complained, whether arithmetic or geometric, that produce "a single average of relative wages" can reveal "the complex facts of wage-changes between two periods." Despite his criticism of the Aldrich Report, Mitchell agreed with most of his peers in calling it the "best collection" of wage data then available ("Statistics of Wages," 331–32).

30. Mitchell et al. *Income in the United States, Its Amount and Distribution, 1909–1919*, vol. I (New York: Harcourt Brace, 1921), ix.

31. Hoover approached the NBER in 1927 with a request to undertake this study, which was intended to focus on the prosperity of the previous four years. Published in 1929 as the Committee on Recent Economic Changes's *Recent Economic Changes*, the book failed to record ominous signs of the impending 1929 crash. The NBER's next project was even more controversial, for work on the President's Research Committee's *Recent Social Trends in the United States* (1933) became entangled with the presidential campaign as well as the financial frenzy that preceded the stock market crash. The budget for the NBER was slashed during the Depression, in part because of anger about its apparent collusion with the Hoover administration. A director of the Carnegie Corporation said that the NBER had "disgraced itself" because, "presumably under political pressure," it "disregarded the prospect of disaster" (quoted Jeff Biddle, "Social Science and the Making of Social Policy: Wesley Mitchell's Vision," *Economic Mind in America: Essays in the History of American Economics* [London: Routledge, 1998], 64).

32. Mitchell had grappled with the complexities of this tool since his earliest work on the greenback, and Fisher's 1911 study of inflation, *The Purchasing Power of Money*, devotes an

entire section (the appendix to chapter 10) to a deductive evaluation of the relative merits of various modes of constructing index numbers. In December 1920, Fisher read a paper on index numbers at the annual meeting of the American Statistical Association, and, the following April, he presented another version of it to the American Academy of Arts and Sciences. While Fisher's paper was never published, an abstract was printed in the Association's journal in March 1921. In response to other economists' objections, Fisher devoted a full-length book to the subject. The four-hundred-plus-page *The Making of Index Numbers: A Study of their Varieties, Tests, and Reliability* appeared in 1922. Meanwhile, in the reports of the WIB we have already examined, as well as in commentaries on these price series, Mitchell also returned repeatedly to the subject of index numbers; in a footnote to a 1921 article on price indexes, Mitchell credits Fisher with having read this essay in draft form. In the first volume of the NBER project on business cycles, which extended and elaborated Mitchell's earlier work on this topic, index-number construction is a recurrent topic, and Mitchell devotes many pages to explaining the complexities involved in using this measurement tool. We should also note that, in 1923, Fisher founded the Index Number Institute, the purpose of which was to prepare and sell index numbers to newspapers like the *New York Times*. The Institute became the first organization to provide the public systematic economic data in index-number form. By 1929, Fisher's wholesale price index was regularly reaching 5 million newspaper readers. On the last topic, see Robert Loring Allen, *Irving Fisher: A Biography* (New York: John Wiley & Sons, 1993), 173. In the mid-1930s, Fisher sold the Index-Number Institute to the Institute of Applied Econometrics.

33. In what might have been a slighting nod to the cistern Fisher built to illustrate equilibrium, Mitchell criticized this method of analysis. "Perhaps an ingenious person who thought the game worthwhile might design a mechanical contrivance which would work somewhat after the fashion of cyclical business fluctuations. If he did so, however, most economists would find his machine so difficult to understand and the real similarity of its operations to business processes so uncertain, that they would leave its intricacies to the pleased contemplation of the inventor" (*Business Cycles: The Problem and Its Setting* [New York: National Bureau of Economic Research, 1927], 186–87).

34. Mitchell, "Index Numbers of Wholesale Prices," 11. "While index numbers are a most convenient concentrated extract of price variations, they are far from being a competent representation of all the facts which they summarize. Most 'consumers of statistics' lack the time to go back of the finished products to the data from which they are made. But the increase of knowledge concerning the causes and consequences of price variations depends much more upon intensive study of the ultimate data than upon the manipulation of averages or aggregates" (114).

35. From a modern standpoint, Mitchell's position may look naïve, as the title of a recent collection reminds us: see Lisa Gitelman, ed., *"Raw Data" Is an Oxymoron* (Cambridge, MA: MIT Press, 2013). From the perspective of 1927, Mitchell's position looks less naïve, for he was focused on the havoc that premature theorizing—or political preconceptions—seemed to inflict on the way data were collected and used.

36. Weintraub, *How Economics Became a Mathematical Science* (Durham, NC: Duke University Press, 2002), esp. chaps. 1 and 2. See also the earlier versions of these chapters: "From

Rigor to Axiomatics: The Marginalization of Griffith C. Evans," in *From Interwar Pluralism to Postwar Neoclassicism* (Durham, NC: Duke University Press, 1998), 227–59; and "Measurement and Changing Images of Mathematical Knowledge," in *The Age of Economic Measurement* (Durham, NC: Duke University Press, 2001), 303–21. The latter contains the phrase we quote: "changing images of mathematics" (311).

37. "When a formula is especially erratic it is called 'freakish'" (1922, 356).

38. One of Person's new technologies was the "Illuminated Box with Glazed Top to Facilitate Comparison of Cycle Charts." He describes this in "An Index of General Business Conditions," *Review of Economic Statistics* 2 (April 1919).

39. Persons credits Moore and Fisher in "Statistics and Economic Theory," *Review of Economic Statistics* 7, no. 3 (July 1925): 194. He acknowledges Mitchell in the same article (194).

40. Persons, "An Index of General Business Conditions," 78.

41. A. W. Magret, "Morgenstern on the Methodology of Economic Forecasting," *Journal of Political Economy* 37 (1929); quoted David F. Hendry and Mary S. Morgan, eds., *The Foundations of Econometric Analysis* (Cambridge: Cambridge University Press, 1995), 181.

42. The chart is reproduced in Paul Crosthwaite, Peter Knight, and Nicky Marsh, *Show Me the Money: The Image of Finance, 1700 to the Present* (Manchester: Manchester University Press, 2014), 46–47.

43. Quoted in Harold Glenn Moulton, *The Financial Organization of Society* (Chicago: University of Chicago Press, 1921), 765, 767. Future page references are to this book.

44. Moulton, "Commercial Banking and Capital Formation I," *Journal of Political Economy* 26 (May 1918), 487.

45. See Clark Warburton, "Monetary Control under the Federal Reserve Act," *Political Science Quarterly* (1946): 505–34.

CHAPTER FOUR

1. Thomas Philippon, "The Evolution of the U.S. Financial Industry from 1860 to 2007: Theory and Evidence" (November 2008), 6; http://pages.stern.nyu.edu/~tphilipp/papers/finsize_old.pdf.

2. Allan H. Meltzer, *A History of the Federal Reserve, Volume I: 1913–1951* (Chicago: University of Chicago Press, 2003), 109.

3. Peter Temin, "The Great Depression" (Historical Working Paper Series no. 62, NBER, New York, 1994), 1. For the second reversal, see the Federal Reserve figures at https://fred .stlouisfed.org/series/M0892AUSM156SNBR, and R. Gordon and R. Krenn, *The End of the Great Depression 1939–41: Fiscal Multipliers, Capacity Constraints, and Policy Contributions*, available at http://economics.weinberg.northwestern.edu/robert-gordon/researchPapers.php. Thanks to Bill Janeway for these citations.

4. See H. T. Warshow, "The Distribution of Corporate Ownership in the United States," *Quarterly Journal of Economics* 39, no. 1 (November 1924): 15–38; and Gardiner Means, "The Diffusion of Stock Ownership in the United States," *Quarterly Journal of Economics* 44, no. 4 (August 1930). See also Mary O'Sullivan, "The Expansion of the U.S. Stock Market, 1885–1930: Historical Facts and Theoretical Fashions," *Enterprise & Society* 8, no. 3 (2007): 533.

5. Frederick Lewis Allen, *Only Yesterday: An Informal History of the Nineteen-Twenties* (New York: John Wiley & Sons, 1931), 72. The bomb was presumably set off by the American Anarchists or the Bolsheviks.

6. Michael E. Parrish, *Anxious Decades: America in Prosperity and Depression, 1920–1941* (New York: W. W. Norton & Co., 1992), 228. Cedric Cowing estimates that the number of Americans who held securities rose to 17 million because of Liberty Bonds. See *Populists, Plungers, and Progressives: A Social History of Stock and Commodity Speculation, 1890–1936* (Princeton, NJ: Princeton University Press, 1965), 95. While he agrees that the number of people investing in stocks increased after 1915, David Hochfelder attributes this rise as much to the effective campaign against illegal bucket shops as to the Liberty Bond campaign. See "'Where the Common People Could Speculate': The Ticker, Bucket Shops, and the Origins of Popular Participation in Financial Markets, 1880–1920," *Journal of American History* 93, no. 2 (September 2006): 335–58. For a discussion of the relationships among companies, stock issuance, and the financing of innovation in the automobile, aviation, and radio industries, see Mary A. O'Sullivan, "Funding New Industries: A Historical Perspective on the Financing Role of the U.S. Stock Market in the Twentieth Century," in *Financing Innovation in the United States, 1870 to the Present*, ed. Naomi R. Lamoreaux and Kenneth L. Sokoloff (Cambridge, MA: MIT Press, 2007), 163–216.

7. David M. Tucker, *The Decline of Thrift in America: Our Cultural Shift from Saving to Spending* (New York: Praeger, 1991), 84. It is not clear whether these certificates were ever sold.

8. James Grant, *Money of the Mind: Borrowing and Lending in America from the Civil War to Michael Milken* (New York: Farrar, Straus & Giroux, 1994), 150.

9. On the absence of these data, and their importance, see O'Sullivan, "The Expansion of the U.S. Stock Market," 537. One reason we do not have data about what percentage of the nation's GDP was contributed by finance is that the first aggregate figures for the nation's income did not consistently break this sector out.

10. O'Sullivan has found that, while the percentage of securities in the holdings of national banks remained steady between 1900 and 1916 (at about 16%), this percentage began to increase after 1920. It reached 25% by 1928. O'Sullivan, "The Expansion of the U.S. Stock Market," 532. See also Julia Ott, *When Wall Street Met Main Street* (Cambridge, MA: Harvard University Press, 2011).

11. Barry Eichengreen considers "the causes of the Wall Street boom of the 1920s . . . one of the great unsolved mysteries in the literature on financial history" (*Golden Fetters: The Gold Standard and the Great Depression, 1919–1939* [New York: Oxford University Press, 1992], 14, n. 18). Among the most prominent attempts to solve this mystery, see John Kenneth Galbraith, *The Great Crash 1929* (Boston: Houghton Mifflin, 1954); Charles P. Kindleberger, *Manias, Panics, and Crashes: A History of Financial Crises* (New York: Basic Books, 1978); Milton M. Friedman and Anna J. Schwartz, *A Monetary History of the United States, 1867–1960* (Princeton, NJ: Princeton University Press, 1963), 305–8, 334–42; and Eugene N. White, "When the Ticker Ran Late: The Stock Market Boom and Crash of 1929," in *Crashes and Panics: The Lessons from History*, ed. Eugene N. White (Homewood, IL: Dow Jones-Irwin, 1990), 143–87.

12. Lawrence Chamberlain and William Wren Hay, *Investment and Speculation: Studies of Modern Movements and Basic Principles* (New York: Henry Holt, 1931), 109. Chamberlain and

Hay, experienced bond salesmen of the period, explained that the previously modest demand for securities had been dramatically increased by the government's sale of Liberty bonds. "The Liberty loans had engendered quantity consumption, and dealers with the aid of commercial banks perforce had created the machinery for quantity manufacture and distribution" (108–9). Twenty-two million patriotic Americans had purchased Liberty and Victory bonds between 1917 and 1919, at a cost of $27 billion.

13. Quoted in Joel Seligman, *The Transformation of Wall Street: A History of the Securities and Exchange Commission and Modern Corporate Finance* (Boston: Houghton Mifflin, 1982), 24.

14. Quoted in Seligman, *The Transformation of Wall Street,* 24.

15. The 1932–33 Pecora Hearings revealed how much Mitchell's ambition had cost shareholders: in 1927, his compensation from the two companies was $1,056,230; in 1929, he took home $1,108,000 (Seligman, *The Transformation of Wall Street,* 26).

16. William Nelson Peach, *The Security Affiliates of National Banks* (Baltimore, MD.: Johns Hopkins University Press, 1941), 28.

17. Ibid., 37.

18. Ibid., 83.

19. Ibid., 107. Investment banks financed most of the rest of the security purchases.

20. Allen, *Only Yesterday,* 313.

21. Winfield W. Riefler, David Friday, Walter Lichtenstein, and J. H. Riddle, *A Program of Financial Research, Vol. 1: Report of the Exploratory Committee on Financial Research* (New York: NBER, 1937), 4.

22. See White, "When the Ticker Ran Late," 162–63. White observes that "after moving together with the other two rates [the discount and the commercial paper rates] for 1926 and 1927, the call rate increased sharply. Although the differential was not constant for the whole boom, it remained very large, suggesting that it was the rising tide of speculation that attracted funds, not any independent credit creation."

23. Alexander Noyes, *The Market Place: Reminiscences of a Financial Editor* (Boston: Little, Brown, 1938), 332.

24. Ibid., 333.

25. Chamberlain and Hay, *Investment and Speculation,* 65.

26. Ibid., 66.

27. Ibid., 107. White provides the following numbers: Only forty investment trusts existed in the US before 1921, and in the next five years, 139 additional trusts were added. In 1927, an additional 140 trusts were founded; and 1928 and 1929 saw 186 and 265 additional trusts, respectively ("When the Ticker Ran Late," 147).

28. Chamberlain and Hay, *Investment and Speculation,* 189–90, xi. Chamberlain and Hay pointed out that almost every corporation had made outsize profits after the war, and that most investors, including the supposedly expert investors who made decisions for investment trusts, only looked at short-term earnings histories. "Only the earnings made in the recovery from the collapse of 1920 were considered. As a whole the inference was that these earnings would go on increasing, whereas they represented the recovery after a depression. In this way a false idea of the trend of future earnings was insinuated into the minds of investors and speculators alike,

and this in turn led to another and more serious mistake. Early in 1928 speculators commenced to mistake cyclical expansion for long-term growth" (190).

29. Irving Fisher, *The Stock Market Crash—and After* (New York: Macmillan, 1930), x. Fisher's primary argument in the book is that the rise in stock prices that occurred in the 1920s was justified by business fundamentals, rather than being simply an effect of a speculative mania. Even though Fisher's contemporaries, as well as many economic historians, have mocked his analysis, some, like White, see more wisdom in Fisher's assessment. See White, "When the Ticker Ran Late," 151–52. Fisher did acknowledge that one practice of investment trusts contributed to the crash. These trusts frequently merged with each other, and, when they did, they issued new securities to replace the securities in the previous trusts; before these new issues were listed on the exchange, they were not liquid. "By some fatality," Fisher explained, "the crash seemed to be exactly so timed that many people with plenty of collateral could not use it because it consisted temporarily of investment trust certificates unlisted and non-liquid. That this factor played a part [in the crash] was evidenced by the fact that in the panic many investment trust securities which, a few weeks before, were selling above their liquidation value, thus capitalizing the investment trust management, came to sell below their liquidation value; that is, the constituent stocks held by these investment trusts were worth more than the titles to them in the form of the trust's certificates" (Fisher, *The Stock Market Crash—and After*, 49).

30. Edgar Lawrence Smith, *Common Stocks As Long Term Investments* (New York: Macmillan, 1928), 81.

31. Fisher, *The Stock Market Crash—and After*, 202.

32. Ibid., 203.

33. Ibid., 206.

34. Ibid., 207–8.

35. Ben Bernanke revived Fisher's thesis in his work on the Depression. See Ben Bernanke, *Essays on the Great Depression* (Princeton, NJ: Princeton University Press, 2000), 23–35.

36. See Gauti B. Eggertsson and Paul Krugman, "Debt, Deleveraging, and the Liquidity Trap: A Fisher-Minsky-Koos Approach," *Quarterly Journal of Economics* 127, no. 3 (2012): 1469–1513.

37. William W. Bartlett, *Mortgage-Backed Securities: Products, Analysis, Trading* (New York: New York Institute of Finance, 1989), 5.

38. Gries and Taylor, *How to Own Your Own Home: A Handbook for Prospective Homeowners* (Washington, DC: US Government Printing Office, 1923). See Alyssa Katz, *Our Lot: How Real Estate Came to Own Us* (New York: Bloomsbury, 2009), 3–5.

39. "We are promoting thrift by promoting home ownership," the speaker declared. President Harding, along with his commerce secretary, Herbert Hoover, repeatedly sounded this line: "No greater contribution can be made towards perpetuating the democracy of our country than to make our Nation a nation of home owners" (*Thrift Education: Being the Report of the National Conference on Thrift Education; Held in Washington, D. C., June 27 and 28, 1924, Under the Auspices of the Committee on Thrift Education of the National Education Association and the National Council of Education*, 9 [http://lcweb2.10c.gov:808/ammem/amrlhtm/inthrift.html]). The first Thrift Week was held in 1916, as an offshoot of the activities of the Committee on Thrift Education, which was founded in 1915. Thrift Week began on January 17,

the birthday of Benjamin Franklin, America's great apostle of thrift, and it was celebrated annually until 1966, when a lack of sponsors led to its demise.

40. Simon William Strauss, *A History of the Thrift Movement in America* (New York: Lippincott, 1920), 23, 111.

41. Quoted in Grant, *Money of the Mind,* 163.

42. Edwin R. A. Seligman, the first economist to theorize installment purchasing, explicitly cited the purchase of Liberty Bonds as an instance of installment buying. See *The Economics of Instalment Selling: A Study in Consumers' Credit* (New York: Harper & Bros., 1927), 1:7.

43. Grant, *Money of the Mind,* 48–49.

44. Ibid., 51.

45. Ibid., 165–69. Strauss escaped with only a reprimand from the New York state attorney general, but his bonds did eventually suffer a catastrophic fall in value during the panic of 1831–32 (Grant 200).

46. Quoted in Katz, *Our Lot,* 3.

47. Quoted in Seligman, *The Transformation of Wall Street,* 41.

48. Important scholarly treatments of this book include William W. Bratton and Joseph A. McCahery, "The Content of Corporate Federalism" (paper presented at the Law and Economics Workshop, University of California at Berkeley, 2004); William W. Bratton and Michael L. Wachter, "Shareholder Primacy's Corporatist Origins: Adolf Berle and the Modern Corporation," *Journal of Corporation Law* 34, no. 1 (September 2008): 99–152; John C. C. Macintosh, "The Issues, Effects and Consequences of the Berle–Dodd Debate, 1931–1932," *Accounting, Organizations and Society* 24: 2 (1999): 139–53; Fenner L. Stewart Jr., "Berle's Conception of Shareholder Primacy: A Forgotten Perspective for Reconsideration during the Rise of Finance," *Seattle University Law Review* 34 (Summer 2011): 1457–99; and Elizabeth Pollman, "Reconceiving Corporate Personhood," *Utah Law Review* 2011, no. 4 (November 2011): 1629–75. On the modern concept of agency costs see Eugene F. Fama and Michael C. Jensen, "Separation of Ownership and Control," *Journal of Law and Economics* 26, no. 2 (June 1983): 301–25; Michael Jensen, "Agency Cost of Free Cash Flow, Corporate Finance, and Takeovers," *American Economic Review* 76, no. 2 (May 1986): 223–29.

49. Adolf Berle and Gardiner Means, *The Modern Corporation and Private Property* (1932; revised, New Brunswick, NJ: Transaction Publishers, 2011), 255. Future references cited in the text.

50. "It is thus plain that the concept of a share of stock must now be vigorously changed. No longer can it be regarded, from the point of view of the investor as primarily a *pro rata* share in an asset fund, or as a continuing, *pro rata* participation in earnings. . . . The factual concept must be not what these legal participations and rights are, but what expectation the shareholder has of their being fulfilled in the form of distributions and what appraisal an open market will make of these expectations" (Berle and Means, *The Modern Corporation and Private Property,* 251–52).

51. "Out of this mechanism primarily designed to secure liquidity and resulting in an apparatus permitting an open market appraisal through the operation of buyers and sellers and a free market, the security markets have evolved a totally different function. They serve as a yardstick by which security values are measured not only in respect of the floating supply but

also in respect of tremendous immobile holdings throughout the country. This measurement of value, coupled with liquidity, makes securities available as a basis of credit or exchange; and at the same time it measures their monetary worth for these purposes" (Berle and Means, *The Modern Corporation and Private Property,* 262).

52. Seligman, *The Transformation of Wall Street,* 40, 38, 20. Seligman discusses FDR's preference for the disclosure philosophy over more punitive regulation; see 41–42, 50.

53. For their discussion of "deceit," which is one of the transgressions the plaintiff might argue against a corporation's promoter or banker, and "rescission," a remedy that allowed the plaintiff to recover his losses by returning shares to the company, see bk. 3, chap. 2, of Berle and Means, *The Modern Corporation and Private Property,* esp. 264–77.

54. Quoted in Seligman, *The Transformation of Wall Street,* 71. One contemporary, Brunson MacChesney, evaluated the 1933 act three years after its implementation and judged its publicity requirements relatively effective—especially in curbing fraud by promoters. See Brunson MacChesney, "The Securities Act and the Promoter," *California Law Review* 25, no. 1 (September 1936): 66–79.

55. Quoted in Seligman, *The Transformation of Wall Street,* 100.

56. Geoffrey Poitras, *Security Analysis and Investment Strategy* (Malden, MA: Wiley-Blackwell, 2005), 91. Graham and Dodd's *Security Analysis* has been in print continuously since it was published in 1933. Each new edition contains revisions that incorporate new developments in financial theory and practice. The most recent edition, the sixth, was published in 2009. It contains an introduction by Warren Buffett, who is one of Graham's most well-known students. Additional discussions of Graham and Dodd's work include: Peter L. Bernstein, *Capital Ideas: The Improbable Origins of Modern Wall Street* (New York: Free Press, 1992), chap. 8; and Justin Fox, *The Myth of the Rational Market: A History of Risk, Reward, and Delusion on Wall Street* (New York: HarperCollins, 2009), chap. 3.

57. Irving Kahn and Robert D. Milne, "Benjamin Graham: The Father of Financial Analysis" (Occasional Paper Series 5 [Charlottesville: Financial Analysts Research Foundation, 1977], 18). The biographical information about Graham comes largely from this paper.

58. When a corporation offered warrant options, for example, this tended to dilute the value of the common stocks it had already issued. See Benjamin Graham and David L. Dodd, *Security Analysis* (New York: McGraw-Hill, 1934), chaps. 23–26. Future references cited in the text by page number. The corporation's decisions about how to raise capital, which is now called capital budgeting, constituted one of the most important applications of financial modeling. The formal calculation of the weighted-average cost of capital for the corporation's cost of equity, based on its mix of debt and equity, was not popularized until 1951 in Joel Dean, *Capital Budgeting: Top-Management Policy on Plant, Equipment, and Product Development* (New York: Columbia University Press, 1951). See also Mark Rubenstein, "Great Moments in Financial Economics: I. Present Value," *Journal of Investment Management* 1, no. 1 (2003): 48.

59. "An investment operation is one which, upon thorough analysis, promises safety of principal and a satisfactory return. Operations not meeting these requirements are speculative" (Graham and Dodd, *Security Analysis,* 54).

60. M. J. Gordon, who introduced the formal dividend discount model, complained that "Graham and Dodd go so far as to state that stock prices should bear a specified relation to

earnings and dividends, but they neither present nor cite data to support the generalization" ("Dividends, Earnings, and Stock Prices," *Review of Economics and Statistics* 41, no. 2 [May 1959]: 99). Marshall Blume and Jeremy J. Siegel also note that American finance during the interwar period had "no formal theory explaining why the market price and intrinsic price may differ" ("The Theory of Security Pricing and Market Structure," *Journal of Financial Markets, Institutions, and Instruments* 1, no. 3 [August 1992]: 10).

61. What Graham and Dodd presented as historically specific responses to a changing investment environment many analysts now call investment "styles." One style emphasizes growth and the other emphasizes value. Some modern analysts do offer versions of the historical account Graham and Dodd favored. See, e.g., Janette Rutterford, "From Dividend Yield to Discounted Cash Flow: A History of U. K. and U.S. Equity Valuation Techniques," *Accounting, Business, and Financial History* 14, no. 2 (2004): 115–49; and Geoffrey Poitras, *Valuation of Equity Securities: History, Theory, and Application* (Singapore: World Scientific Publishing, 2011), 97–149.

62. John Burr Williams, *The Theory of Investment Value* (1938; facsimile, Burlington, VT: Fraser Publishing, 1997), vii, ix.

63. A few historians have recognized Williams's importance, but they do not credit his work with introducing a significant epistemological innovation, as we do here. See Mark Rubenstein, *A History of the Theory of Investments: My Annotated Bibliography* (New York: John Wiley & Sons, 2006), 75. Other engagements with Williams include Bernstein, *Capital Ideas,* 151–54, 182–83; Donald R. Stabile, *Forerunners of Modern Financial Economics: A Random Walk in the History of Economic Thought* (Northampton, MA: Edward Elgar, 2005), 122–28; and Fox, *The Myth of the Rational Market,* 53–54, 214–16.

64. Harold T. Davis, *The Theory of Econometrics* (Bloomington, IN: Principia Press, 1941), 210–211.

65. See Mary S. Morgan, "Business Cycles: Representation and Measurement," in *Monographs of Official Statistics: Papers and Proceedings of the Colloquium on the History of Business-Cycle Analysis,* ed. Dominique Ladiray (Luxembourg: Office for Official Publications of the European Communities, 2001), 184.

66. Stabile explains the way Williams factored in probability. See *Forerunners of Modern Financial Economics,* 125, 127–28. "Williams, even if he did not use statistical measures of risk, had a solid understanding of probability theory" (128).

67. In 1951, Morris A. Copeland identified economists' widespread use of mathematics as beginning in the mid-1930s: "prior to the mid-thirties economists in the English-speaking world used mathematical symbols somewhat sparingly." But in the fifteen years that followed, "a much more liberal use of algebraic and calculus notation" began to appear in academic publications" ("Institutional Economics and Model Analysis," in *Fact and Theory in Economics: The Testament of an Institutionalist; Collected Papers of Morris A. Copeland,* ed. Chandler Morse [Ithaca, NY: Cornell University Press, 1958], 55). By 1998, when Laurence A. Boland contributed an essay on method to the new Palgrave dictionary, the discipline had been completely transformed. "While the [economic] journals in the early 1950s contained very little formal mathematics, by the late 1970s almost all leading journals were devoting most of their space to articles that were either completely concerned with the mathematical analysis of invented

mathematical models or with methods of presenting economic ideas using mathematical formalism" ("Methodology," in *The New Palgrave: A Dictionary of Economics,* ed. John Eatwell, Murray Milgate, and Peter Newman, 3rd ed. [London: Macmillan, 1998], 456).

68. William N. Goetzmann and Roger G. Ibbotson credit Williams with formalizing the equity-risk premium; see "History and the Equity Risk Premium" (working paper, International Center for Finance, Yale School of Management, New Haven, April 2005), 5.

69. See, e.g., Lawrence Klein and Arthur Goldberger, *An Econometric Model of the United States, 1929–1952* (Amsterdam: North-Holland, 1955).

CHAPTER FIVE

1. Quoted George J. Stigler, "Henry L. Moore and Statistical Economics," *Econometrica* 30, no. 1 (January 1962): 17.

2. Wallace's 1920 book is *Agricultural Prices*; his co-authored work with Snedecor, "Correlation and Machine Calculation," initially appeared in the *Iowa State College Bulletin* 23, no. 35 (1925). Wallace served as secretary of agriculture from 1933 to 1940, and as vice president, in Franklin Delano Roosevelt's third term, from 1941 to 1945.

3. See David Alan Grier, *When Computers Were Human* (Princeton, NJ: Princeton University Press, 2005), 162–66.

4. The theoretical statement of this idea can be traced to two Frenchmen: Jules Regnault, who set out the idea in 1863, and Louis Bachelier, whose 1900 *The Theory of Speculation* elaborated it. MIT professor Paul Cootner picked up the idea in *The Random Character of Stock Market Prices* (1964) and Burton Malkiel of Princeton University helped popularize it in *A Random Walk down Wall Street* (1973). In 1965, Eugene Fama published "Random Walks in Stock Market Prices" in the *Financial Analysts Journal* 21, no. 5 (1965): 55–59.

5. For details about Cowles and the foundation of the Cowles Commission, see Carl F. Christ, "History of the Cowles Commission, 1932–52," *Economic Theory and Measurement: A Twenty Year Research Report, 1932–1952* (Chicago: Cowles Commission for Research in Economics, 1952): 3–65; Peter L. Bernstein, *Capital Ideas: The Improbable Origins of Modern Wall Street* (New York: Free Press, 1992), 12; Grier, *When Computers Were Human*, 2; Justin Fox, *The Myth of the Rational Market: A History of Risk, Reward, and Delusion on Wall Street* (New York: HarperCollins, 2009).

6. Harold Hotelling, "Statistical Methods for Research Workers," *Journal of the American Statistical Association* 22, no. 159 (September 1927): 411–12.

7. In 1922, R. A. Fisher published "On the Mathematical Foundations of Theoretical Statistics," *Philosophical Transactions of the Royal Society of London* 222 (1922): 309–68; and in 1925, the first edition of *Statistical Methods for Research Workers* appeared.

8. Snedecor wrote to Fisher that the former's *Statistical Methods* was "designed to lead the beginner to an appreciation of your books" (quoted Erich L. Lehmann, *Fisher, Neyman, and the Creation of Classical Statistics* [New York: Spring Science and Business, 2011], 27). Snedecor's book, *Statistical Methods Applied to Experiments in Agriculture and Biology*, was published in 1937. It went through numerous editions and eventually sold more than 200,000 copies. Fisher's *Statistical Methods for Research Workers* sold well for a relatively technical

statistics text—going through fourteen editions between 1925 and 1970—but its sales never approached those of Snedecor's more accessible text (Lehmann, 28, 25). Joan Fisher Box, R. A. Fisher's daughter and biographer, revealed that it was through Snedecor that Fisher became popular in the United States: "It was George W. Snedecor, working with agricultural applications, who was to act as midwife in delivering the new statistics in the United States" (*R. A. Fisher: The Life of a Scientist* [New York: John Wiley & Sons, 1978], 313).

9. Box, *R. A. Fisher*, 313–24. Box summarized the influence Fisher's work was to have during the 1930s and 1940s by listing the statistical textbooks used during World War II. "All of these books were, in effect, introductions to Fisher's statistical ideas and commentaries, explications and elaborations of what he had written. Several of them he saw in manuscript form and discussed with their authors; only [E. F.] Lindquist, from Iowa City, and [G.] Freedman, from Harvard, were not immediately associated with Fisher" (320).

10. One of the conceptual foundations of inferential statistics and theories about sampling was probability theory. In probability theory, the whole to which the sample is assumed to belong is generally called the "universe"; when probability theory was imported into biometrics, the whole was called the "population."

11. The father/daughter height correlation table is reproduced in R. A. Fisher, *Statistical Methods for Research Workers* (Edinburgh: Oliver & Boyd, 1925), 180–81. Fisher took this data from Karl Pearson. Sometimes, the research worker was told to make the table *after* constructing the scatter-diagram graph because the table "serves as a compact record of extensive data" (33).

12. This method of introducing the student to the concept of frequency distribution was followed by H. T. Davis and W. F. C. Nelson in the textbook they published in 1935. See *Elementary Statistics with Applications to Economic Data* (Bloomington, IN: Principia Press, 1935).

13. Fisher, *Statistical Methods for Research Workers*, 367.

14. Ibid., 314.

15. These tests include tests of goodness of fit (ibid., 78), as well as more technical tests, such as the t test ("Student's test") and the z test (later named the f test, for Fisher).

16. Declaring that a hypothesis is *adequate* or *satisfactory* from the point of view of the statistical tests performed upon it is not equivalent to saying that it is an accurate representation of the "real" world. Aris Spanos explains that every hypothesis "is a conceptual construct which purports to provide an idealised description of the phenomena within its intended scope. . . . Economic 'reality' is much too complicated for such an exact copy to be comprehensible and thus useful in explaining the phenomena in question" (*Statistical Foundations of Econometric Modeling* [Cambridge: Cambridge University Press, 1986], 662).

17. None of the secondary descriptions of Cowles's article mention his having read Fisher, but Cowles cites Fisher's method several times in "Can Stock Market Forecasters Forecast?" For discussions of this article, see Fox, *Myth of the Rational Market*, 36–38; Bernstein, *Capital Ideas*, 31–36; Robert W. Dimand, "The Cowles Commission and Foundation on the Functioning of Financial Markets from Irving Fisher and Alfred Cowles to Harry Markowitz and James Tobin," *Révue d'histoire des sciences humaines* 1, no. 20 (2009): 79–100; and Robert W. Dimand and William Veloce, "Alfred Cowles and Robert Rhea on the Predictability of Stock Prices," *Journal of Business Inquiry* 9, no. 1 (2010): 56–64. Dimand and Veloce call

this article "one of the landmarks in the development of the efficient market hypothesis," and Dimand says in the 2009 article that Cowles's essay contributes "a technical innovation of lasting value" (84).

18. Cowles, "Can Stock Market Forecasters Forecast?" *Econometrica* 1, no. 3 (July 1933), 310. Future references cited in the text.

19. At one point, Cowles mentions the Standard Statistics Company index of ninety representative stocks ("Can Stock Market Forecasters Forecast?" 316). We assume he used this index to construct "the stock market."

20. The sixteen financial services security recommendations and the actual securities choices made by the fire insurance companies allowed him to test securities selection, and the *Wall Street Journal* columns and the twenty-four newsletters' suggestions allowed him to test stock market timing.

21. Cowles demonstrated that he was operating within the epistemology of inferential statistics and probabilism when he cast his data in a probabilistic equation: "A.D.(t) = 5.42 + 1.5t (A. D. = average deviation, t, in units of four weeks ≥), representing the deviation for all periods from one month up to one year, of the average individual stock from the average of all stocks" ("Can Stock Market Forecasters Forecast?" 311).

22. The program for the ninety-fourth meeting of the American Statistical Association, which was held December 28–31, 1932, can be found in *Journal of the American Statistical Association* 28, no. 181 (March 1933): 1–9. These organizations met together because the US State Department had asked Americans to keep holiday travel at a minimum to conserve the nation's resources. The panel at which Cowles presented his paper was the last panel of the conference. The importance of this panel was signaled by the fact that it was chaired by Irving Fisher (who also gave one of the conference's plenary addresses). Discussants for the panel were Harold T. Davis, Ragnar Naess of Goldman Sachs, Ray Westerfield of Yale, and Harry C. Carver of the University of Michigan. Members of some fire insurance companies spoke at earlier sessions and one of the other sessions addressed the "Record of Insurance in the Depression." One can only imagine how some of the experts involved in making or using stock forecasts responded to Cowles's remarks, although when he was interviewed in 1970, he provided a hint of the response: "Of course, I got a lot of complaints. Who had appointed me to keep track? Also, I had belittled the profession of investment adviser. I used to tell them that it isn't a profession, and of course that got them even madder" (quoted Murray Teigh Bloom, *Rogues to Riches* [New York: G. P. Putnam's Sons, 1971], 28).

23. In 1937, Cowles and Herbert E. Jones published "Some A Posteriori Probabilities in Stock Market Action," *Econometrica* 5, no. 3 (1937): 280–94. The findings of this exercise were inconclusive. On the one hand, Cowles and Jones found "conclusive evidence of structure in stock prices"; on the other hand, they offered no assurance that speculators could exploit this structure to earn "consistent or large profits" (294).

24. Harold T. Davis's book on time series helps clarify parts of Cowles's paper, for in chapter 11 Davis works through the examples Cowles gives step by step, and Davis provides some of the tables and formulae to which Cowles only alludes. See *The Analysis of Economic Time Series* (Bloomington, IN: Principia Press, 1941), chap. 11. So close are the two accounts of the procedure and calculations Cowles describes—with Davis sometimes repeating Cowles word for word—that we assume the two men collaborated on the 1933 article.

25. Stephen M. Stigler has identified 1933 as the origin of modern mathematical statistics. Although Stigler does not cite Cowles's article or the issue of *Econometrica* in which it appeared, Harold Hotelling, who reviewed R. A. Fisher's work in 1927 and who was a member of the Cowles Commission, does feature prominently in Stigler's account. See Stigler, "The History of Statistics in 1933," *Statistical Science* 11, no. 3 (1996): 244–52. For an account of a meeting attended by both Cowles and Hotelling, see H. T. Davis, "Report of the Meeting of the Econometric Society, Colorado Springs, June 22–24, 1935," *Econometrica* 3, no. 4 (October 1935): 473–76.

26. Macaulay, a Canadian by birth, earned a BA and an MA (in Commerce) from the University of Colorado, then joined the faculties at, successively, the University of Washington and the University of California, Berkeley. In 1924, he earned a PhD from Columbia University under Mitchell and joined the NBER, where he worked until 1938. In 1934, Macaulay had joined the father of Peter L. Bernstein (the founder of the *Journal of Portfolio Management*) to launch an investment counsel firm, Bernstein Macaulay, Inc. His final research project was a study of short selling sponsored by the New York Stock Exchange. See Geoffrey Poitras, "Frederick R. Macaulay, Frank M. Redington and the Emergence of Modern Fixed Income Analysis," in *Pioneers of Financial Economics*, vol. 2, eds. Geoffrey Poitras and Franck Jovanovic (Cheltenham, U. K.: Edward Elgar, 2007), 5–9.

27. Robert W. Dimand, "The Cowles Commission," 86.

28. "Macaulay duration," set out in chapter 2 of the 1938 text, and its extension, "Macaulay adjusted duration," are statistics derived from present-value methodology. The statistics can be used to measure the sensitivity of a bond or portfolio to movements in interest rates—a critical measure of security risk. Macaulay's technical insight concerned how to weight the future cash flows accruing to the owner of a fixed-income security on a present-value basis in order to establish a relationship between future cash flows and the current price. As he explains, "the 'duration' of a bond is an average of the durations of the separate single payment loans into which the bond may be broken up. To calculate this average the duration of each individual single payment loan must be weighted in proportion to the size of the individual loan; in other words, by the ratio of the present value of the individual future payments to the sum of all the present values, which is, of course, the price paid for the bond" (Frederick R. Macaulay, *Some Theoretical Problems Suggested by the Movements of Interest Rates, Bond Yields and Stock Prices in the United States Since 1856* [New York: NBER, 1938], 48). Future references cited in the text. The application of Macaulay duration and its extension to the management of fixed income portfolios was popularized in 1972 by *Inside the Yield Book*, which Martin Leibowitz and Sidney Homer originally wrote for Solomon Brothers bond traders. See Leibowitz and Homer, *Inside the Yield Book: The Classic that Created the Science of Bond Analysis* (Princeton, NJ: Bloomberg, 2004). For the history of the theory and application of Macaulay duration, see Poitras, "Frederick R. Macaulay," 9–16. We note that Macaulay did not present duration in 1938 as a measure of interest rate *risk*. Macaulay's treatment of duration was an empirical problem, which later theorists elaborated as risk. This provides another example of the NBER's insistence that measurement must provide the groundwork for financial theories, which were to be developed later. The risk concept was articulated in 1971 by Lawrence Fisher and Roman Weil, "Coping with Risk of Interest-Rate Fluctuations: Returns to Bondholders from Naïve and Optimal Strategies," *Journal of Business* 44:4 (October 1971): 408–31.

29. "Stylized facts" is a term coined by Nicholas Kaldor in 1961. It captures the simplified presentation or broad generalization that summarizes complex statistical calculations. See Nicholas Kaldor, "Capital Accumulation and Economic Growth," in *The Theory of Capital*, eds. Friedrich A. Lutz and D. C. Hague (London: Macmillan, 1961), 177–222.

30. Eugene F. Fama, *Foundations of Finance: Portfolio Decisions and Securities Prices* (New York: Basic Books, 1976).

31. Cowles refers to the "average investment experience" (37), but he also carefully distinguishes between his sense of "average" and the more common usage of this term. "Our hypothetical investor was assumed merely to distribute his holdings in *proportion* to the value of stock outstanding, and as long as we do not suppose him to be 'average' in the sense that all investors might have behaved just as he did, with the same results, the correction for cash dividends seems appropriate" (Alfred Cowles, *Common-Stock Indexes: 1871–1937* [Bloomington, IN: Principia Press, 1938], 14, n. 15). Future references cited in the text.

32. Macaulay, *Theoretical Problems*, 3.

33. The statistical method of chain linking joins together two indexes that overlap in one period. To place the two indexes in a single time series, the statistician rescales one index to make its value equal to that of the other in the same period. See *Concepts and Methods of the United States National Income and Products Accounts* (July 2009), by US Chamber of Commerce, 11–23. This publication is the "NIPA Handbook."

34. One of the most important projects to adopt this design was Clark Warburton's work on the quantity of money. This enabled Warburton to discover the money-income relationship that Keynes theorized—that is, the influence that changes in the stock of money have on the flow of national money income and expenditure. Warburton's articles on monetary economics appeared in the *American Economic Review* and the *Journal of Political Economy* between 1943 and 1945. On Warburton's work, see Paul B. Trescott, "Discovery of the Money-Income Relationship in the United States, 1921–1944," *History of Political Economy* 14, no. 1 (1982): 85–87.

35. The first note reads: "Director's Note: 'This, while true, does not imply the contrary contention that economic stability would be more certain under rigid forms of social regimentation. The recurring unbalances under complete "laissez-faire" may be less serious than the economic unwisdom of a dictatorship. The path to stability should lie between the two extremes.' M. C. Rorty" (Macaulay, *Some Theoretical Problems* 14, n. 4).

CHAPTER SIX

1. It may be best to understand the Keynesian revolution as an amalgamation of British, Swedish, Austrian, German, and American ideas erected on a Keynesian framework. See David Laidler, *Fabricating the Keynesian Revolution: Studies of the Inter-War Literature on Money, the Cycle, and Unemployment* (Cambridge: Cambridge University Press, 1999).

2. "Keynesian theory needed the national income and product accounts to make contact with reality, and the availability of national income and product accounts made Keynesian macroeconomics fruitful (and helped to shape it)" (Robert M. Solow, "How Did Economics Get That Way and What Way Did It Get?" *Daedalus* 126, no. 1 [Winter 1997]: 47–48).

3. In England, national income estimates were calculated as early as the seventeenth century by John Graunt, William Petty, and Geoffrey King. In the interwar period, the Netherlands,

Norway, and Germany joined the United States and the United Kingdom in compiling national aggregates. This task intensified during the interwar period because of a series of counter-vailing forces, which also gave these efforts their distinctive character. On the one hand, the recently concluded conflict made it obvious that the warring nations were connected to each other in complex political, economic, and monetary ways. On the other hand, because these countries had only been recently freed from an international system of relatively unimpeded capital flows based on the shared standard of gold, they were newly isolated from each other monetarily. The abandonment of the gold standard in the early 1930s made it possible for na-tions to draw up accounts that respected national (currency) boundaries—in other words, that represented national economies as "closed." See Brett Christophers, *Banking across Bound-aries: Placing Finance in Capitalism* (Malden, MA: Wiley-Blackwell, 2013).

4. In a very real sense, "the economy" did not exist as a discrete object that could be mea-sured until national income and product estimates made it visible. See Daniel Breslau, "Eco-nomics Invents the Economy: Mathematics, Statistics, and Models in the Work of Irving Fisher and Wesley Mitchell," *Theory and Society* 32, no. 3 (June 2003): 379–411; and Adrienne van den Bogaard, "Past Measurement and Future Prediction," in *Models as Mediators*, ed. Mary S. Morgan and Margaret Morrison (Cambridge: Cambridge University Press, 1999), 296.

5. A sixth issue, now important in national aggregates, is the *boundary* issue. This addresses where production occurred and helps accountants distinguish between GDP (gross domestic product) and GNP (gross national product). Kuznets and Gilbert did not directly engage this issue.

6. Simon Kuznets's first article on national income estimates, published in the *Encyclopedia of the Social Sciences,* volume 9, caught the attention of an assistant to Wisconsin senator Mar-ion La Follette. This led to a resolution that directed the Department of Commerce to provide income estimates for the years leading up to the Depression. Unable to think of anyone quali-fied to undertake this project, the Commerce secretary, Daniel Roper, asked Wesley Mitch-ell's advice, and Mitchell suggested Kuznets. With the help of two students—Milton Gilbert and Robert Nathan—Kuznets completed the research, then continued working on national estimates throughout the 1930s. For an examination of Kuznets's work, see Vibha Kapuria-Foreman and Mark Perlman, "An Economic Historian's Economist: Remembering Simon Kuznets," *Economic Journal* 105, no. 433 (November 1995): 1524–47.

7. The other members of Gilbert's team were George Jaszi, Edward F. Denison, and Charles Schwartz.

8. Simon Kuznets, "National Income," in *Readings in the Theory of Income Distribution* (1933; reprint, Homewood, IL: Richard D. Irwin, 1946), 8.

9. Richard E. Kane, "Measures & Motivations: National Income and Product Estimates During the Great Depression and World War II," Munich Personal RePEc Archive (Febru-ary 2013), 6. This reference (available at http://mpra.ub.uni-muenchen.de/44336/) is the best scholarly treatment of the interwar debates about national aggregates.

10. Ibid., 9.

11. Milton Gilbert and George Jaszi, "National Product and Income Statistics as an Aid in Economic Problems," in *Readings in the Theory of Income Distribution*, 44–45. Future refer-ences cited in the text. Originally published in *Dun's Review* for February 1944 (on pages 9–11 and 28–32).

12. Kane, "Measures & Motivations," 13.

13. Here is Gilbert's definition of gross national product: "It may be defined as the aggregate value of the current production of goods and services flowing to the Government, to consumers, and—for the purposes of gross capital formation—to business" (Gilbert and Jaszi, "National Product and Income Statistics," 46–47). See Carol S. Carson, "The History of the United States National Income and Product Accounts: The Development of an Analytical Tool," *Review of Income and Wealth* 21, no. 2 (June 1975): 169–70.

14. "The result on wartime policy analysis from using GNP instead of national income was that the anticipated effect from WWII mobilization would not be quite as dire as many were then predicting, which alternatively implied that more aggressive war program goals for production were attainable. This was true not only because GNP was, by definition, larger in value than national income produced, but also because the final expenditure composition revealed by GNP showed how the income generated from national product was being spent. Using final expenditure measures, GNP estimates showed that despite the large reduction in non-war output needed to achieve the goals of the war effort, much of the decrease would be absorbed through a reduction in private investment and consumer durables, rather than a curtailment in the consumption of food, clothing, and shelter" (Kane, "Measures & Motivations," 13).

15. A 1947 report of the United Nations describes the recommended way of treating imputed items. "The items in the tables may be divided, from one point of view, into cash terms and imputed items, the former being those elements which reflect market transactions, and the latter being those for which a calculation has to be made in the absence of market transactions. In view of the difficulty of finding a commonly accepted basis for the second type of estimate it is desirable that, as far as possible, items of this kind should be shown separately" (Sub-Committee on National Income Statistics of the League of Nations Committee of Statistical Experts, "Measurement of National Income and the Construction of Social Accounts," Richard Stone, chairman, *Studies and Reports on Statistical Methods*, report no. 7 [Geneva: United Nations, 1947], 18).

16. Simon Kuznets, "National Income: A New Version," *Review of Economics and Statistics* 30, no. 3 (August 1948): 151–79; and Milton Gilbert, George Jaszi, Edward F. Denison, and Charles Schwartz, "Objectives of National Income Measurement: A Reply to Professor Kuznets," *Review of Economics and Statistics* 30, no. 3 (August 1948): 179–95. Future references to these works cited in the text. A more extensive set of readings that capture the differences between the two teams' positions would include Kuznets's 1934 report for the Senate Finance Committee (*National Income, 1929–1932* [Washington, DC: US Government Printing Office, 1934]); Kuznets's 1944 work on war accounting (*National Product, War and Prewar* [Occasional Paper 17; New York: NBER, 1944]); Gilbert, et al.'s response to Kuznets's paper ("National Product, War and Prewar: Some Comments on Professor Kuznets' Study and a Reply by Professor Kuznets," *Review of Economics and Statistics* 26, no. 3 [August 1944]: 109–35); and Kuznets's 1946 presentation of his findings (*National Income: A Summary of Findings* [New York: NBER, 1946]).

17. George Jaszi, "The Conceptual Basis of the Accounts: A Reexamination," in *A Critique of the United States Income and Product Accounts* (*Studies in Income and Wealth*, vol. 22; Princeton, NJ: Princeton University Press, 1958), 31.

18. The most helpful scholarly works on the development of the expenditure approach

are Carson, "The History of the United States National Income and Product Accounts"; and Gérard Duménil and Dominique Lévy, "Pre-Keynesian Themes at Brookings," in *The Impact of Keynes on Economics in the Twentieth Century*, ed. L. Pasinetti and B. Schefold (Aldershot, UK: Edward Elgar, 1999), 182–201.

19. By 1939, some institutionalist American economists had embraced Keynes's work. These included Leon Keyserling, J. M. Clark, and Clarence Ayres. Others, including two of the most important Brookings economists—Edwin Nourse and Harold Moulton—did not. See Malcolm Rutherford and C. Tyler Desroches, "The Institutionalist Reaction to Keynesian Economics," *Journal of the History of Economic Thought* 30, no. 1 (March 2008): 29–48. We return to this topic in chap. 8.

20. Brookings Institution, "Brookings Institution History," Annual Report (2008), 20.

21. Clark Warburton, "Three Estimates of the Value of the Nation's Output of Commodities and Services: A Comparison," in *Studies in Income and Wealth*, vol. 3 (New York: NBER, 1939), 317–98.

22. Harold Glenn Moulton, *Income and Economic Progress* (Washington, DC: Brookings Institution, 1935), 46. For a discussion of Moulton's work, see Duménil and Lévy, "Pre-Keynesian Themes at Brookings," 2–5.

23. Samuelson's books are *Foundations of Economic Analysis* (1947) and *Economics: An Introductory Analysis* (1948). On the influence of the latter, see Kenneth G. Elzinga, "The Eleven Principles of Economics," *Southern Economic Journal* 58, no. 4 (April 1992): 861–79.

24. Martin Kohli, "Leontief and the U.S. Bureau of Labor Statistics, 1941–54: Developing a Framework for Measurement," supplement, *History of Political Economy* 33 (2001): 199–212. On Leontief's early work, see J. Adam Tooze, *Statistics and the German State, 1900–1945: The Making of Modern Economic Knowledge* (Cambridge: Cambridge University Press, 2001), 201. For a discussion of government funding of the IOA project, see Milton P. Reid III and Stacey L. Schreft, "Credit Aggregates from the Flow of Funds Accounts," *Federal Reserve Bank of Richmond Economic Quarterly* 79, no. 3 (Summer 1993), 51.

25. Wassily Leontief, *The Structure of American Economy, 1919–1939: An Empirical Application of Equilibrium Analysis* (New York: Oxford University Press, 1951). This edition contains both the 1941 text, in Parts I-III, and the additions published in 1951, as Part IV. The four chapters that comprise Part IV are based on more extensive statistical data, compiled by the Bureau of Labor Statistics, and add to the material presented in the first three parts the concept of an "open" system. Part IV also benefited from the availability of "large-scale computational procedures to numerical solutions of a system containing ninety and more linear equations"—i.e., the availability of computers. See "Preface to the Second Edition," ix. Future references cited in the text.

26. Leontief may have invented this particular inferential technique, but he was not the first to depict economic relations in a *tableau*. Francois Quesnay had drawn up a *tableau économique* in the eighteenth century, and Léon Walras also experimented with this format in the nineteenth century. In addition, Alexander Bogdanov presented an input-output analysis in 1921 to the All Russia Conference on the Scientific Organization of Labor and Production. See A. A. Belykh, "A Note on the Origins of Input-Output Analysis and the Contribution of the Early Soviet Economists: Chayanov, Bogdanov and Kritsman," *Soviet Studies* 41, no. 3 (1989): 426–29.

27. Leontief made the role played by the Walrasian general equilibrium model in his matrix

method clear: "The picture of the economic system underlying every general equilibrium theory is that of a large set of data which determine in their totality the magnitudes of all the dependent variables of the system. Variables are the 'unknowns' we try to explain; data are those elements which are used as a basis of explanation. . . . If the data are constant, the variables remain unchanged. As soon as the determining conditions are modified, some or all of the variables react with corresponding changes. The character of such reactions depends upon the initial structural properties of the empirically given system. This particular aspect of the general equilibrium problem constitutes the central issue of this investigation" (Leontief, *The Structure of American Economy*, 34–35).

28. Our treatment of taxation in this section relies heavily on Joseph J. Thorndike, *Their Fair Share: Taxing the Rich in the Age of FDR* (Washington, DC: Urban Institute Press, 2012). Thorndike explains his thesis that the "class tax" was replaced by a "mass tax," but his emphasis falls on the rise in income tax at the very end of the interwar period, not on the entire period between 1932 and 1943. "Between 1939 and 1943, Congress transformed [the individual income tax] from a 'class tax' to a 'mass tax.' Exemptions fell dramatically and the number of taxpayers increased more than sixfold. Almost overnight, it was later said, the income tax 'changed its morning coat for overalls.' Meanwhile, lawmakers pushed rates upward, with the top bracket eventually peaking at 94%. Together, these changes made the income tax a fiscal workhorse, boosting revenue from $1.0 billion in fiscal year 1939 to $18.4 billion in 1945. By war's end, the tax was raising more than 40 percent of total revenue, displacing excise taxes—which dominated the tax system through the mid-1930s—as the principal source of federal funds" (6). Thorndike calls the 1932 Revenue Act the largest tax hike in American history (*Their Fair Share*, [159]). For taxation in the first decade of this period. see also Mark H. Leff, *The Limits of Symbolic Reform: The New Deal and Taxation, 1933–1939* (Cambridge: Cambridge University Press, 1984).

29. Mellon, who had left the Treasury in 1932, was charged with criminal tax evasion in 1934. The case dragged on until after Mellon's death. He was eventually absolved of criminal liability, but his estate was assessed $480,000 in back taxes (Thorndike, *Their Fair Share*, 143–45). As Thorndike points out, the Morgan case was even more complicated, for many of the strategies he used to avoid taxes were perfectly legal, but, when made public, seemed grossly unfair. Thorndike concludes that "the Morgan disclosures contributed to a sense of crisis surrounding the income tax. Tax avoidance struck many critics as profoundly undemocratic. And by discrediting the income tax's claim to fairness, it raised doubts about the very foundation of national fiscal policy" (91).

30. Ibid., chap. 4.

31. Ibid., chap. 7 and 314, n. 73.

32. Ibid., 201.

33. See https://www.ssa.gov/history/reports/trust/tf1941.html.

34. The campaign to discover and punish tax evaders was most virulent in the first two years of Roosevelt's first term, and it is often associated with Ferdinand Pecora, chief counsel for the Senate Banking Committee. Newspaper headlines were especially splashy in May 1933, when the Committee hearings revealed that, in 1931 and 1932, J. P. Morgan, the banking magnate, had paid no income taxes (Thorndike, *Their Fair Share*, 83–94). The "soak the rich" approach to taxation reflected the influence of Herman Oliphant, general counsel to the Department of the

Treasury; but it also appealed to Roosevelt's strong commitment to tax justice. This campaign helped earn passage for the Revenue Act of 1935, often called "the wealth tax" (131–75). The idea of "social taxation" was also promoted by Oliphant and was picked up by the popular press, especially liberal periodicals like the *Nation* (Thorndike, *Their Fair Share*, 132–37).

35. The first year of the Harvard Fiscal Policy seminar coincided with the beginning of a sharp recession in the United States. At the beginning of the fall term, Walter Salant remembers, the economy's real GNP had risen by more than 44%, thus reaching the point last seen in October 1929; but within four months, industrial production had declined an alarming 30%. "The recession of 1937–38 was an intellectually traumatic episode," Salant recalls, and the seminar focused on how to restart the recovery. Among the topics to which it repeatedly returned was taxation, and experts in tax law were among the guests invited to the seminar that year. See Salant, "Alvin Hansen and the Fiscal Policy Seminar," *Quarterly Journal of Economics* 90, no. 1 (February 1976): 16, 18.

36. David C. Colander and Harry H. Landreth, "Introduction," in *The Coming of Keynesianism to America*, ed. David C. Colander and Harry H. Landreth (Cheltenham, UK: Edward Elgar, 1996), 3–9. The two students were Robert Bryce and Lorie Tarshis. Their notes, along with those taken by other students, were reconstructed and published as Thomas K. Rymes, ed., *Keynes's Lectures 1932–35: Notes of a Representative Student* (Ann Arbor, MI: Michigan University Press, 1989).

37. Byrd L. Jones, "The Role of Keynesians in Wartime Policy and Postwar Planning, 1940–1946," *American Economic Review* 62: 1/2 (March 1972):125–33.

38. Quoted in Colander and Landreth, *The Coming of Keynesianism to America*, 219–20.

39. Quoted in ibid., 84.

40. Johnson used the term "University in Exile" as a fund-raising device. He sought support from two hundred leading philanthropists and social scientists, all but four of whom responded positively. Within a month, Johnson had raised $17,000, but the rescue effort would nevertheless have failed had not a wealthy US industrialist, Hiram J. Halle, promised Johnson $120,000. Johnson also received funding from other foundations, including the Doris Duke Charitable Foundation, the Rockefeller Foundation ($54,000 from 1933 through 1940); and the Rosenwald Family Association ($110,000). By 1941, the faculty of the institution, renamed the Graduate Faculty of the New School for Social Research, included twenty-six members, and the student body had risen from 153 to 520 students (Lewis A. Coser, *Refugee Scholars in America: Their Impact and their Experiences* [New Haven, CT: Yale University Press, 1984], 104). Not all Americans supported the rescue effort, nor was the State Department eager to issue the visas necessary to allow the émigrés to stay. This attitude partly stemmed from worries that the Europeans would take academic positions held by young Americans, over two thousand of whom (10% of the professoriate) were to lose their jobs during the Depression. The attitude sometimes also stemmed from anti-Semitic or anti-German sentiments. See Claus-Dieter Krohn, *Intellectuals in Exile* (Amherst, MA: University of Massachusetts Press, 1993), 22, 76–77.

41. The full name of the original Kiel Institute was the Royal Institute for Maritime Transport and World Economics. Founded in 1914, it was the only institute in the world dedicated to studying the world economy, as opposed to national economies. The founding director was Bernhard Harms, and the institute housed the world's largest research library in economics.

In 1926, the institute created a new department for statistical economics and business cycle research, headed by Adolph Lowe. Along with Hans Neisser, Jacob Marschak, and Wassily Leontief, Gerhardt Colm was a staff member in this department. Leontief left Kiel for the NBER in 1931, and then joined the Harvard Economics Department; Marschak fled to Paris in 1933 when the provost at Kiel demanded proof of "Arian descent," and he soon went to Oxford; Neisser left Kiel with Colm in 1933, as another of the original twelve tapped by Johnson to staff the University in Exile in 1933. The Kiel Institute, now the Kiel Institute for the World Economy, is still a vibrant center of international economic research.

42. Tooze, *Statistics and the German State*, 103.

43. Colm's team arrived at a prewar figure for national income that was much greater than Helffrich's estimate. See Tooze, *Statistics and the German State*, 124.

44. Ibid., 104. As Tooze points out, part of the appeal of Wagemann's vision of the power of statistical data rested on his claim to have "the power of prediction, providing policy-makers with a definite outlook on which to make long-term decisions."

45. Ibid., 126 and the figure on 127.

46. For a description of the scandals and infighting that descended on the IfK in 1930, see ibid., 161–76.

47. Krohn, *Intellectuals in Exile*, 52–58. These economists were sometimes called the "new classicals" because they focused on the relationships among accumulation, technical progress, and unemployment—as Ricardo, J. S. Mill, and Marx had done—rather than focusing on the equilibrium of supply and demand studied in isolation, as the neoclassical school did.

48. Ibid., 120.

49. Quoted in ibid., 41.

50. See Gerhard Colm, "The Ideal Tax System," in *Essays in Public Finance and Fiscal Policy*, ed. Helen Nicol (New York: Oxford University Press, 1955), 62, 63, 65. This article was initially published as "The Ideal Tax System," *Social Research* 1, no. 3 (Fall 1934): 319–42, but we refer here to the page numbers given in the collected volume.

51. Ibid., 67. Colm qualifies this pessimism in a footnote added in 1954. By that date, with the number of people subject to income tax so much higher and the proportion of tax revenue so much greater relative to the entire national income, he considered tax policy a more important instrument of cyclical policy (67, n. 20).

52. Colm, "Technical Requirements for an Effective Fiscal Policy," in *Essays in Public Finance*, 176.

53. Ibid., 172–87. The Employment Act advocated, but stopped short of mandating, the kind of budget projections that Colm repeatedly recommended. It also set up an interdepartmental finance committee that could help the president develop economic strategies; this was another of Colm's suggestions. The act also created the Council of Economic Advisors, the small advisory committee of which Colm became a member. This group was charged with working out long-term economic goals and issuing reports designed to educate the public, as well as to inspire investment. In these reports, "financial and political perspectives were presented that appeared in none of the textbooks of the time. . . . From now on, budgetary decisions would no longer be based on past developments but would be made with a view to the future and be oriented toward politically defined macrogoals that budgetary policies would

help achieve. . . . These reports were intended to have 'an announcement effect,' that private businesses could use" (Krohn, *Intellectuals in Exile*, 128). The Employment Act disappointed Colm in some respects, but it did implement many of the policies he had long supported.

54. "Public Finance in the National Income," in *Essays in Public Finance and Fiscal Policy*, 229. Colm's argument about the place that government revenue and expenditures should have in the national income accounts was derived from his argument that the government constitutes a "third pillar" of the economy: along with, but operating independently of, individuals and companies, the government has unique economic and social responsibilities. Central to these responsibilities were the two functions of stabilizing the economy and protecting the population. See the 1948 essay by Colm, "Why Public Finance?" in *Essays in Public Finance and Fiscal Policy*, 3–23.

55. On American attitudes toward planning, see Marcia L. Balisciano, "Hope for America: American Notions of Economic Planning between Pluralism and Neoclassicism, 1930–1959," in *From Interwar Pluralism to Postwar Neoclassicism*, ed. Mary S. Morgan and Malcolm Rutherford (Durham, NC: Duke University Press), 153–78.

56. "National Economic Budgets," in *Essays in Public Finance and Fiscal Policy*, 253.

57. In "National Economic Budgets," Colm defines models as "tools for demonstrating and appraising in quantitative terms the results of theoretical analysis" (ibid., 244).

58. "Public Spending," in *Essays in Public Finance and Fiscal Policy*, 113, n. 1.

59. Ibid., 127. The charts appear on pages 125 and 126.

60. Ibid., 133.

61. For further discussion of Colm, see Krohn, *Intellectuals in Exile*, 112–29. Salant and Keyserling's respect for Colm is recorded in Colander and Landreth, *The Coming of Keynesianism to America*, 127 and 233.

62. Claus-Dieter Krohn, "An Overlooked Chapter of Economic Thought: The 'New School's' Effort to Salvage Weimar's Economy," *Social Research* 50, no. 2 (Summer 1983): 452–68; Krohn, *Intellectuals in Exile*, 112–29; and Coser, *Refugee Scholars in America*, 104, 108.

63. Hebert Stein, *The Fiscal Revolution in America: Policy in Pursuit of Reality* (Chicago: University of Chicago Press, 1969), 168. For a discussion of the relationship between the German reform economists and Keynes's ideas, see Krohn, *Intellectuals in Exile*, 110–19.

64. See Laidler, *Fabricating the Keynesian Revolution*, 323–24.

65. Thorndike, *Their Fair Share*, 249. This act "created the modern U.S. tax regime." On the withholding provision, see pages 253, 257, and 259.

CHAPTER SEVEN

1. See Robert M. Solow, "How Did Economics Get That Way and What Way Did It Get?" *Daedalus* 126, no. 1 (Winter 1997): 39–58. Marcel Boumans identifies Tinbergen's 1935 paper, delivered to the Fifth European Conference of the Econometric Society, as the "first time an economist used the term 'model' to denote a specific mathematical product of one's empirical research" (*How Economists Model the World into Numbers* [London and New York: Routledge, 2005], 21). On economic modeling in general, see Mary S. Morgan, *The World in the Model: How Economists Work and Think* (Cambridge: Cambridge University Press, 2012), chap. 1; and

Dani Rodrik, *Economics Rules: The Rights and Wrongs of the Dismal Science* (New York and London: W. W. Norton, 2015), chapters 1, 2, and 4.

2. Ragnar Frisch, *A Dynamic Approach to Economic Theory: The Yale Lectures of Ragnar Frisch*, ed. Olav Bjerkhold and Duo Qin (London: Routledge, 2013), 29, 30, 31 32. Future references cited in the text. Frisch made significant contributions to both mathematical modeling and statistical modeling. The 1933 article "Propagation Problems and Impulse Problems in Dynamic Economics" laid the foundation for future generations of dynamic growth models. In addition, as Hendry and Morgan have shown, the statistical technique developed in his *Statistical Confluence Analysis by Means of Complete Regression Systems* (1934) was "the first all purpose statistical method developed specially for the problems of economic data" (David F. Hendry and Mary S. Morgan, eds., *The Foundations of Econometric Analysis* [Cambridge: Cambridge University Press, 1995], 41).

3. Histories of the Econometric Society include Carl F. Christ, "History of the Cowles Commission, 1932–52," in *Economic Theory and Measurement: A Twenty Year Research Report* (Chicago: Cowles Commission for Research in Economics, 1952); Roy Epstein, *A History of Econometrics* (Amsterdam: North Holland, 1987); Mary S. Morgan, *The History of Econometric Ideas* (Cambridge: Cambridge University Press, 1990); Olav Bjerkholt, "Ragnar Frisch and the Foundation of the Econometric Society and *Econometrica*," in *Econometrics and Economic Theory in the Twentieth Century: The Ragnar Frisch Centennial Symposium*, ed., S. Strom (Cambridge: Cambridge University Press, 1998), 26–57; and Francisco Louçã, *The Years of High Econometrics: A Short History of the Generation That Reinvented Economics* (New York: Routledge, 2007), esp. chap. 2. The founding group elected ten individuals to form the first governing council. Its American members included Irving Fisher, Charles Roos, and Edwin Wilson. The European members were Frisch (Norway), Schumpeter (Germany), Luigi Amoroso (Italy), Ladislaus von Bortkiewicz (Germany), Arthur Bowley (England), François Divisia (France), and Wladislaw Zawadzki (Poland). See Louçã, *The Years of High Econometrics*, 29, 16.

4. Frisch, *A Dynamic Approach to Economic Theory*, 17.

5. Joseph A. Schumpeter, *Business Cycles: A Theoretical, Historical and Statistical Analysis of the Capitalist Process* (1939; abridged edition, New York: McGraw-Hill, 1964), 23. At the time this work was published, Schumpeter was teaching at Harvard, where he supervised John Burr Williams's dissertation. We do not know how much of the project, which he had been writing since 1933, Schumpeter shared with his Harvard graduate students, so we cannot know how much, if at all, Williams's method was influenced by his dissertation director's work, but Schumpeter's approach to modeling is consistent with Williams's algebraic budgeting.

6. Ronald Bodkin, Lawrence Klein, and K. Marwah, *A History of Macroeconomic Model-Building* (Cheltenham, UK: Edward Elgar, 1991), 5. Marcel Boumans offers an amusing analogy for the model-building process: "Model building is like baking a cake without a recipe. The ingredients are theoretical ideas, policy views, mathematisations of the cycle, metaphors, and empirical facts." To build the model, "you start a trial and error process till the result is what you would like to call a cake: the colour and taste are satisfactory. Characteristic for the result is that you can not distinguish the ingredients in the cake any more" ("Built-In Justification," in *Models as Mediators: Perspectives on Natural and Social Science*, ed. Mary S. Morgan and Margaret Morrison [Cambridge: Cambridge University Press, 1999], 67).

7. Trygve Haavelmo, "The Probability Approach in Econometrics," supplement, *Econometrica* 12 (July 1944): iii-vi, 1–115. "The method of econometric research aims, essentially, at a conjunction of economic theory and actual measurement, using the theory and technique of statistical inference as a bridge-pier. But the bridge itself was never completely built." Quoted in Olav Bjerkholt, "Writing 'The Probability Approach' With Nowhere to Go: Haavelmo in the United States," *Econometric Theory* 23, no. 5 (October 2007): 775, 1.

8. Stephen Stigler, *The History of Statistics: The Measurement of Uncertainty before 1900* (Cambridge, MA: Harvard University Press, 1986); Anders Hald, *A History of Mathematical Statistics from 1750 to 1930* (New York: Wiley, 1998); and Aris Spanos, "Curve-Fitting, the Reliability of Inductive Inference and the Error-Statistical Approach," *Philosophy of Science* 74, no. 5 (2007): 357–81.

9. John Maynard Keynes, *General Theory of Employment, Interest and Money* (New York: Harcourt Brace, 1936), 298.

10. Keynes did address modeling, which he understood to be central to economic analysis, in a letter to Roy Harrod. "It seems to me that economics is a branch of logic, a way of thinking. . . . But one cannot get very far except by devising new and improved models. This requires, as you say, 'a vigilant observation of the actual working of our system.' . . . Economics is a science of thinking in terms of models joined to the art of choosing models which are relevant to the contemporary world. It is compelled to be this, because, unlike the typical natural science, the material to which it is applied is, in too many respects, not homogeneous through time. The object of a model is to segregate the semi-permanent or relatively constant factors from those which are transitory or fluctuating so as to develop a logical way of thinking about the latter, and of understanding the time sequences to which they give rise in particular cases . . . Progress in economics consists almost entirely in a progressive improvement in the choice of models" (John Maynard Keynes to Roy Harrod, July 4, 1938, in *The Collected Interwar Papers and Correspondence of Roy Harrod*, ed. Daniele Besomi, http://economia.unipv.it/harrod/edition/editionstuff/rfh.346.htm). Thanks to Bill Janeway for calling our attention to this passage, which also gestures toward the form of unknowns Keynes recognized: "material . . . not homogeneous through time."

11. In 1940, Irving Fisher commented on the "trend" of mathematical reasoning newly visible in the social sciences. See Irving Fisher, "Mathematical Method in the Social Sciences," *Econometrica* 9, nos. 3–4 (July-October 1941), 188. On mathematical economics, see Alpha C. Chiang, *Fundamental Methods of Mathematical Economics*, 3rd ed. (New York: McGraw-Hill, 1967), 4.

12. Fisher, "Mathematical Method in the Social Sciences," 189.

13. Keynes, *General Theory*, 161.

14. These quotations are all taken from Don Patinkin, "Anticipations of the *General Theory*? The Significance of the Central Message," in Patinkin, *Anticipations of the General Theory? And Other Essays on Keynes* (Chicago: University of Chicago Press, 1982), 79–80.

15. David C. Colander and Harry H. Landreth, eds., *The Coming of Keynesianism to America* (Cheltenham, UK: Edward Elgar, 1996), 15. In distinguishing between a research program's "complex core" and its "surface structure," Colander and Landreth are referring to the work of the Hungarian philosopher of science and mathematics Imre Lakatos.

16. Here is a brief example of Keynes's distinctive style: "To say that net output to-day is greater, but the price-level lower, than ten years ago or one year ago, is a proposition of a similar character to the statement that Queen Victoria was a better queen but not a happier woman than Queen Elizabeth—a proposition not without meaning and not without interest, but unsuitable as material for the differential calculus" (Keynes, *General Theory*, 40).

17. J. R. Hicks, "A Suggestion for Simplifying the Theory of Money," *Economica*, n.s., 2, no. 5 (February 1935): 3. Future references cited in the text.

18. Keynes, *General Theory*, 208.

19. Keynes's involvement with national data was linked to Colin Clark's work on national statistics; by 1940, when Keynes published *How to Pay for the War*, he was not only using Clark's statistics but also basing policy recommendations on them, as well as offering his own ideas about sectoring. The first official UK accounting estimates were published in 1941 in the White Paper prepared by James Meade and Richard Stone; Keynes wrote the text that accompanied these estimates, which were published as *An Analysis of the Sources of War Finance and an Estimate of the National Income and Expenditure in 1938 and 1940*. On Keynes and national aggregates, see Geoff Tily, "John Maynard Keynes and the Development of National Income Accounts in Britain, 1895–1941," *Review of Income and Wealth* 55, no. 2 (June 2009): 347–51. On Keynes and macroeconomics, see Victoria Chick, *Macroeconomics after Keynes* (Cambridge, MA: MIT Press, 1983).

20. On Reddaway's model, see David Laidler, *Fabricating the Keynesian Revolution: Studies of the Inter-war Literature on Money, the Cycle, and Unemployment* (Cambridge: Cambridge University Press, 1999), 305.

21. Michel De Vroey and Kevin D. Hoover explain that Hicks's model became canonical in two stages: in 1944, Franco Modigliani "sharpened the contrast between the classical and the Keynesian submodels"; and in 1949, Hansen "reinterpreted Keynes and rewrote elementary macroeconomics using Hicks's model." Hansen also substituted for Hicks's LL curve the name "LM." See "Introduction: Seven Decades of the IS-LM Model," in *The IS-LM Model: Its Rise, Fall, and Strange Persistence*, ed. Michel De Vroey and Kevin Hoover (Durham, NC: Duke University Press, 2004), 5. Samuelson's presentations of the IS-LM model, as part of what became known as the "neoclassical synthesis," appeared in *Foundations of Economic Analysis* (1947) and *Economics: An Introductory Analysis* (1948). For a discussion of the role played by Samuelson's work and the IS-LM model in the neoclassical synthesis, see Martin Goodfriend and Robert G. King, "The New Neoclassical Synthesis and the Role of Monetary Policy," in *NBER Macroeconomics Annual*, vol. 12, ed. Ben S. Bernanke and Julio Rosenberg (Cambridge: MIT Press, 1997), 233–34. David Laidler argues that "the IS-LM diagram and the model it portrayed were, from the early 1950s until the mid 1970, the *sine qua non* of macroeconomics" (*Fabricating the Keynesian Revolution*, 303). He also points out that the model is sometimes called the Hicks-Hansen model (303–4).

22. Luigi L. Pasinetti and Gian Paolo Mariutti argue that converting Keynes's literary prose into a system of simultaneous equations generated precisely the opposite of what Keynes had intended. See Pasinetti and Mariutti, "Hicks's 'Conversion'—from J. R. to John," in *Markets, Money and Capital*, ed. Roberto Scazzieri (Cambridge: Cambridge University Press, 2009), 61.

23. J. R. Hicks, "Mr. Keynes and the 'Classics'; A Suggested Interpretation," *Econometrica* 5, no. 2 (April 1937): 153.

24. "This brings us to what, from many points of view, is the most important thing in Mr. Keynes' book. It is not only possible to show that a given supply of money determines a certain relation between Income and interest (which we have expressed by the curve *LL); it* is also possible to say something about the shape of the curve. . . . It will probably tend to be nearly horizontal on the left, and nearly vertical on the right. This is because there is (1) some minimum below which the rate of interest is unlikely to go, and (though Mr. Keynes does not stress this) there is (2) a maximum to the level of income which can possibly be financed with a given amount of money. If we like we can think of the curve as approaching these limits asymptotically. . . . Therefore, if the curve *IS* lies well to the right (either because of a strong inducement to invest or a strong propensity to consume), *P (static equilibrium point)* will lie upon that part of the curve which is decidedly upward sloping, and the classical theory will be a good approximation, needing no more than the qualification which it has in fact received at the hands of the later Marshallians. An increase in the inducement to invest will raise the rate of interest, as in the classical theory, but it will also have some subsidiary effect in raising income, and therefore employment as well. . . . But if the point *P* lies to the left of the *LL* curve, then the *special* form of Mr. Keynes' theory becomes valid. A rise in the schedule of the marginal efficiency of capital only increases employment, and does not raise the rate of interest at all. We are completely out of touch with the classical world" (Ibid., 154).

25. Ibid., 158.

26. The comparative static IS-LM model became the lens through which American Keynesian economists approached macroeconomics until the 1960s, but it did receive criticism. After the publication of Axel Leijonhufvud's *On Keynesian Economics and the Economics of Keynes: A Study in Monetary Theory* (New York: Oxford University Press, 1968), parsing the difference between Keynes and his American followers became a cottage industry. One line of questioning targeted the model's neglect of time; another argued that Hicks's emphasis on the neoclassical rational agent suppressed some of Keynes's most important insights ("animal spirits"); a third was pursued by members of the British "Keynes circus," led by Richard Kahn and Joan Robinson, and argued that American "Bastard Keynesianism" was really the offspring of Hicks, Hansen, and Samuelson, not Keynes. For discussions of these lines of criticism, see Roger Backhouse and David Laidler, "What Was Lost with IS-LM?" *History of Political Economy* 36 (2004): 25–56; Marc Lavoie, *Post-Keynesian Economics: New Foundations* (Cheltenham: Edward Elgar, 2015); and Roger Backhouse and Bradley W. Bateman, eds. *The Cambridge Companion to Keynes* (Cambridge: Cambridge University Press, 2006).

27. Don Patinkin, *Money, Interest, and Prices: An Integration of Monetary and Value Theory* 2nd. ed. (New York: Harper & Row, 1965), Part 2.

28. Scholarship on the European émigrés includes Earlene Craver, "Patronage and the Directors of Research in Economics: The Rockefeller Foundation in Europe, 1924–38," *Minerva* 24, no. 2 (1986): 205–22; Claus-Dieter Krohn, "Dismissal and Emigration of German-Speaking Economists after 1933," in *Forced Migration and Scientific Change: Émigré German-Speaking Scientists and Scholars after 1933*, ed. Mitchell G. Ash and Alfons Söllner (Cambridge: Cambridge University Press, 1996), 175–97; Harald Hagemann and Claus-Dieter Krohn, eds., *Biographisches Handbuch Der Deutschsprachigen Wirtschaftswissenschaftlichen Emigration Nach 1933* (Munich: K. G. Saur, 1999); F. M. Scherer, "The Emigration of German-Speaking Economists after 1933," *Journal of Economic Literature* 38, no. 3 (September 2000): 614–26; and

Keith Tribe, "German Émigré Economists and the Internationalization of Economics," *Economic Journal* 111, no. 475 (November 2001): F740–F746. On émigré mathematicians, see Reinhard Siegmund-Schultze, *Mathematicians Fleeing from Nazi Germany: Individual Fates and Global Impact* (Princeton, NJ: Princeton University Press, 2009); and Steve Batterson, "The Vision, Insight, and Influence of Oswald Veblen," *Notices of the AMS* 54, no. 5 (2007): 606–18.

29. Quoted in Harald Hagemann, "European Émigrés and the 'Americanization' of Economics," *European Journal of the History of Economic Thought* 18, no. 5 (2011): 660. For Marschak's biographical details, see 657–63; Kenneth J. Arrow, "Portrait: Jacob Marschak," *Challenge* 21, no. 1 (March/April 1978): 69–71; and Colin Read, *The Rise of the Quants: Marschak, Sharpe, Black, Scholes, and Merton* (Basingstoke: Palgrave Macmillan, 2012), 7–38.

30. Faculty associated with the Cambridge School included A. C. Pigou, Dennis Robertson, Frederick Lavington, and the younger Keynes.

31. A. W. Coats, "The Distinctive LSE Ethos in the Inter-War Years," *Atlantic Economic Journal* 10, no. 1 (1982): 26; and Lionel Robbins, *The Nature and Significance of Economics* (London: Macmillan, 1935), chap. 6.

32. On the Robbins Circle, see Coats, "The Distinctive LSE Ethos," 18–30; and Yuichi Kimura, "The 'Robbins Circle' of the London School of Economics and Political Science: The Liberalism Group's Counterattack of Laissez-Faire against Cambridge," *Journal of Saitama University Faculty of Education* 59: 2 (September 2010): 119–34.

33. Hans Staehle, "Report of the Fifth European Meeting of the Econometric Society," *Econometrica* 5, no. 1 (January 1937): 91. Jan Tinbergen presented a paper at the conference in which he set out a mathematical model of business-cycle policy (which he called a "mechanism," not a "model"). Ragnar Frisch was also present, and he and Marschak were among the most active participants in all the summarized discussions.

34. Ibid., 91.

35. Ibid.

36. Ibid., 92–93.

37. In 1939, Makower was tapped by Churchill to join a small team of statisticians, called S Branch, which worked on allocating the nation's resources in the lead-up to war. Makower's specializations after joining the LSE faculty included rationing, activity analysis, linear programming, customs unions, and international trade. She was the teacher of noted economists Richard G. Lipsey, L. M. Lachmann, and Harry G. Johnson, and she later co-authored papers with W. G. Baumol, Joseph Schumpeter, Irving Fisher, and H. W. Robinson. She was fondly remembered by George G. S. Shackle, "George G. Shackle (1903–1992)," in *A Biographical Dictionary of Dissenting Economists*, 2nd edition, ed. Philip Arestis and Malcolm Sawyer (Cheltenham, UK: Edward Elgar, 2000), 587.

38. The first footnote reads, in part: "This article reconsiders certain ideas which were treated by one of the present authors [Marschak] in a memorandum on Investment circulated privately in 1935 and in a paper read at the 1935 Meeting of the Econometric Society. A mathematical version of the article is to appear shortly in *Econometrica*. . . . The subject was also treated by the writers [Makower] in an unpublished thesis called *The Theory of Value on the Capital Market*" (H. Makower and J. Marschak, "Assets, Prices and Monetary Theory," new series, *Economica* 5, no. 19 [August 1938]: 261).

39. The unpublished thesis is typed, and Makower had to handwrite the equations in the body of the text and to add pages containing the hand-drawn curves at the end of the thesis. Many thanks to Martin Giraudeau for finding and photocopying Makower's thesis.

40. Helen Makower, "The Theory of Value in the Capital Market" (unpublished PhD thesis, London School of Economics, 1937). This quotation appears in the abstract, but the pagination begins anew with each of the three parts of the thesis, so citation by page number is not helpful.

41. See Matthias Klaes, "The History of the Concept of Transaction Costs: Neglected Aspects," *Journal of the History of Economic Thought* 22, no. 2 (2000): 191–216.

42. Jacob Marschak, "Money and the Theory of Assets," *Econometrica* 6, no. 4 (October 1938): 312. Future references cited in the text.

43. Mary S. Morgan makes this point about Tinbergen's project. See Morgan, *The History of Econometric Ideas,* chap. 4.

44. Bodkin, Klein, and Marwah identify antecedents to Tinbergen's models in François Quesnay's stylized *tableau économique* and Walras's abstract general equilibrium models as pre-twentieth-century candidates for this honor. They also mention two mathematical models of the business cycle created in the early 1930s by Ragnar Frisch and Michal Kalecki as more proximate anticipations. See *A History of Macroeconomic Model-Building,* xiii. The prize awarded to economists is not officially called a "Nobel Prize" but the Sveriges Riksbank Prize in Economic Sciences in Memory of Alfred Nobel (Swedish: *Sveriges riksbanks pris i ekonomisk vetenskap till Alfred Nobels minne*).

45. Bodkin, Klein, and Marwah discuss Tinbergen's model in Bodkin, Klein, and Marwah, *A History of Macroeconomic Model-Building,* 31–41.

46. On the relationship between the business-cycle project and Tinbergen's model project, see Adrienne van den Bogaard, "Past Measurement and Future Prediction," in *Models as Mediators: Perspectives on Natural and Social Science,* ed. Mary S. Morgan and Margaret Morrison (Cambridge: Cambridge University Press, 1999), 297–305. Tinbergen had begun working at the Dutch Central Board of Statistics in 1928 and rose to a position of leadership in Department II. He had written his thesis on physics and economics, and, in 1935, he presented his first model ("Past Measurement," 300–305).

47. Victor Zarnowitz, *Business Cycles: Theory, History, Indicators, and Forecasting* (Chicago: University of Chicago Press, 1992), 171.

48. See Morgan, *The History of Econometric Ideas,* 114. Frisch defines a dynamic theory as one that "explains how one situation grows out of the foregoing" ("Propagation Problems and Impulse Problems in Dynamic Economics" in *The Foundations of Econometric Analysis,* ed. David F. Hendry and Mary S. Morgan [1933; reprint, Cambridge: Cambridge University Press, 1995], 333).

49. Jan Tinbergen, *Statistical Testing of Business-Cycle Theories: Business Cycles in the United States of America 1919–1932,* vol. II (Geneva: League of Nations, 1939), 15–18.

50. Ibid., 15–20.

51. Ibid., 21.

52. John Maynard Keynes, "Professor Tinbergen's Method," in *The Foundations of Econometric Analysis,* 382. Keynes's review initially appeared in *Economic Journal* 49 (1939): 558–

68. Hendry and Morgan interpret Keynes's use of rhetoric as an expression of skepticism about econometrics in general: "In part, Keynes was using rhetoric to try and dampen enthusiasm in a field which he believed had a smaller role to play than that envisaged by the econometricians themselves," but they also point out that Robert Stone insisted that Keynes was not "anti-econometrics" ("Introduction," in *The Foundations of Econometric Analysis*, 55).

53. "Am I right in *thinking* that the method of multiple correlation analysis essentially depends on the economist having furnished, not merely a list of the significant causes, which is correct so far as it goes, but a *complete* list? . . . The method is one neither of discovery nor of criticism. It is a means of giving quantitative precision to what, in qualitative terms, *we know already as a result of a complete theoretical analysis*" (Keynes, "Professor Tinbergen's Method," 383; emphasis added).

54. Ibid., 387.

55. This combines Keynes's fifth and sixth objections, as is best captured by his comment in the latter: "How far are these curves and equations meant to be no more than a piece of historical curve-fitting and description and how far do they make inductive claims with reference to the future as well as the past?" (Ibid., 387-88).

56. Ibid., 388.

57. Keynes was all too aware of the practical and theoretical problems presented by the statistical data available in 1939 and by economic measurement in general. He refers to "the frightful inadequacy of most of the statistics employed" in Tinbergen's model, and he notes that Tinbergen used different kinds of measures; many were "indirect," in that they consisted of index numbers rather than "direct measures of the factor itself," and others seemed to have been chosen arbitrarily. "He insists that his factors must be measurable, but about the units in which he measures them he remains singularly care-free, in spite of the fact that in the end he is going to add them all up." This complaint provoked one of Keynes's most memorable thrusts at Tinbergen's entire project: "It becomes like those puzzles for children where you write down your age, multiply, add this and that, subtract something else, and eventually end up with the number of the Beast in Revelation" (Ibid., 388, 386, 385).

58. One econometrician who departed from what came to be the official position of the Econometric Society was Ragnar Frisch. In a paper written for, but delivered too late to be read at, the society's 1938 Cambridge conference, Frisch argued, in Louçã's paraphrase, that "if the true causal relation, the autonomous structural equation, cannot be estimated, policy makers cannot base their projections on the use of traditional but defective tools, since they may just suggest fictions. Only highly autonomous equations could shed a light on reality, but that required other information than that of the equation system itself . . ." As Louçã went on to suggest, "For Frisch, this required information from outside the system, obtained from interviews and experimentation—which of course the other econometricians were not available to concede" (Louçã, *The Years of High Econometrics*, 205).

59. Paul B. Trescott, "Discovery of the Money-Income Relationship in the United States, 1921-1944," *History of Political Economy* 14, no. 1 (1982): 65-88.

60. Tinbergen, *Statistical Testing of Business-Cycle Theories*, vol. II, 72, n. 3. Hereafter cited in the text.

CHAPTER EIGHT

1. Till Düppe and E. Roy Weintraub, "Siting the New Economic Science: The Cowles Commission's Activity Analysis Conference of June 1949," EHES Working Paper 40 (June 2013), 9, n. 10 (http://ehes.org/EHES.n040.pdf).

2. C. D. C. Goodwin, "The Patrons of Economics in a Time of Transformation," in Mary S. Morgan and Malcolm Rutherford, eds., *From Interwar Pluralism to Postwar Neoclassicism* (Durham, NC: Duke University Press, 1998): 62–63.

3. See Roger E. Backhouse and Mauro Boianovsky, *Transforming Modern Macroeconomics: Exploring Disequilibrium Microfoundations, 1956–2003* (Cambridge: Cambridge University Press, 2013), 32.

4. See Anita Wells, "Legislative History of Excess Profits Taxation in the United States in World Wars I and II," *National Tax Journal* 4, no. 3 (September 1951): 232–54.

5. Marc Labonte and Mindy Levit, "CRS Report for Congress: Financing Issues and Economic Effects of American Wars," Congressional Research Service, RL31176, 6–7 (https://www.fas.org/sgp/crs/natsec/RL31176.pdf).

6. Robert Leeson, "The Eclipse of the Goal of Zero Inflation," *History of Political Economy* 29, no. 3 (1997): 448, 459–60.

7. Allan H. Meltzer, *A History of the Federal Reserve* (Chicago: University of Chicago Press, 2003–9), vol. I, 579–724; vol. II, 2–41.

8. Samuelson, *Economics*, 3rd edition (New York: McGraw-Hill, 1955), vi.

9. Samuelson, quoted in Michel De Vroey, "The History of Macroeconomics Viewed against the Background of the Marshall-Walras Divide," in *The IS-LM Model: Its Rise, Fall, and Strange Persistence*, ed. Michel De Vroey and Kevin D. Hoover (Durham, NC: Duke University Press, 2004), 75.

10. Franco Modigliani, "The Monetarist Controversy or, Should We Forsake Stabilization Policies?" *American Economic Review* 67, no. 2 (March 1977): 2.

11. See David Laidler, *Fabricating the Keynesian Revolution: Studies in the Inter-War Literature on Money, the Cycle, and Unemployment* (Cambridge: Cambridge University Press, 1999), chap. 11.

12. "It so happens that in a wide number of economic problems it is admissible and even mandatory to regard our equilibrium equations as maximizing (minimizing) conditions. A large part of entrepreneurial behavior is directed towards maximization of profits with certain implications for minimization of expenditure, etc." (Samuelson, *Foundations of Economic Analysis*, enlarged edition [Cambridge, MA: Harvard University Press, 1983], 21). Future references cited in the text.

13. See Olivier Jean Blanchard and Stanley Fischer, *Lectures in Macroeconomics* (Cambridge, MA: MIT Press, 1989), 26–27.

14. Backhouse and Boianovsky, *Transforming*, 37.

15. Patinkin, *Money, Interest and Prices: An Integration of Monetary and Value Theory* (Evanston, IL: Row, Peterson, 1956), 21. Ironically, Patinkin's resurrection of Pigou's real balance effect restored the economics that Keynes had tried to overthrow with his *General Theory*.

16. Ibid., xxiv.

17. Düppe and Weintraub, "Siting," and Mirowski, *Machine Dreams: Economics Becomes a Cyborg Science* (Cambridge: Cambridge University Press, 2002), chaps. 5 and 6.

18. RAND sponsored an eclectic range of projects, from abstract mathematics to weapons system engineering. According to Düppe and Weintraub, the only "shared vision" was a commitment "to apply the principles of rational agency to politics and warfare" ("Siting," 12). Unlike Mirowski, who strongly implies that RAND, with its military agenda, profoundly shaped post-war economics, Düppe and Weintraub insist that RAND had "no disciplinary commitments" and was not interested in remaking economics ("Siting," 12).

19. Haavelmo, "The Statistical Implications of a System of Simultaneous Equations," *Econometrica* 11, no. 1 (January 1943): 5, 1–2.

20. Haavelmo, "The Probability Approach in Econometrics," *Econometrica*, Supplement (1944): iii–115. On Haavelmo's development of the probability thesis and his consultations with other economists, see Olav Bjerkholt, "Frisch's Econometric Laboratory and the Rise of Trygve Haavelmo's Probability Approach," *Econometric Theory* 21, no. 3 (June 2005): 491–533, and "Writing 'The Probability Approach' with Nowhere to Go: Haavelmo in the United States, 1939–1944," *Econometric Theory* 23, no. 5 (October 2007): 775–837.

21. Haavelmo, "Probability Approach," lii.

22. Reichenbach, "Philosophical Foundations of Probability," in Jerzy Neyman, ed., *Proceedings of the Berkeley Symposium on Mathematical Statistics and Probability* (Berkeley: University of California Press, 1949), 20.

23. Ibid., 5.

24. Hotelling, "The Place of Statistics in the University," in *Berkeley Symposium*, 25.

25. Quoted E. L. Lehmann, "The Fisher, Neyman-Pearson Theories of Testing Hypotheses: One Theory or Two?" *Journal of the American Statistical Association* 88, no. 424 (December 1993): 1243.

26. Philip Mirowski provides an account of von Neumann's rejection of John Nash's version of game theory in *Machine Dreams*, 334–49.

27. Marschak's paper belonged to a series of papers and reviews he devoted to game theory: "Neumann's and Morgenstern's New Approach to Static Economics," *Journal of Political Economy* 54, no. 2 (April 1946): 97–115; "Measurable Utility and the Theory of Assets" (conference paper); and "Rational Behavior, Uncertain Prospects, and Measurable Utility," *Econometrica* 18, no. 2 (April 1950): 111–41.

28. For interpretations of game theory, see E. Roy Weintraub, *Toward a History of Game Theory* (Durham, NC: Duke University Press, 1992); and *John von Neumann and Modern Economics*, eds. Mohammed Dore, Sukhamoy Chakravarty, and Richard Goodwin (Oxford: Clarendon Press, 1989), esp. part 4. A compelling account of the discipline's tardiness in incorporating the central tenets of game theory can be found in Nicola Giocoli, *Modeling Rational Agents: From Interwar Economics to Early Modern Game Theory* (Cheltenham, UK: Edward Elgar, 2003). We want to note, contra Giocoli, that James Tobin was using these mathematical techniques by the mid-1950s.

29. "The main achievement of the book lies, more than in its concrete results, in its having introduced into economics the tools of modern logic and in using them with an astounding power of generalization. Every empirical situation—be it poker or bilateral monopoly—is divested of inessential features and expressed in unambiguous symbols. . . . 'Intuitive' or

'heuristic' considerations generated in the authors' minds by experience are formalized into concepts and propositions which, once stated, are detached from experience until the final conclusions are reached. Such detached reasoning safeguards against any subconscious smuggling-in of undefined terms and operations or of assertions that have not been proved, yet had not been stated explicitly as axioms" (Marschak, "Neumann's and Morgenstern's New Approach," 114–15).

30. In defining rationality or "rational behavior," Marschak was not describing the behavior of real human beings. Instead, as he acknowledged in the first paragraph of the 1950 article, "the theory of rational behavior is a set of propositions that can be regarded either as idealized approximations to the actual behavior of men or as recommendations to be followed" ("Rational Behavior," 111).

31. Marschak, "Neumann and Morgenstern's New Approach," 109.

32. Nassim Nicholas Taleb, *The Black Swan: The Impact of the Highly Improbable* (New York: Random House, 2007).

33. "The Accuracy of Economic Observations," *Activity Analysis of Production and Allocation: Proceedings of a Conference*, ed. Tjalling C. Koopmans (New York: John Wiley & Sons, 1951), 283.

34. The first paper to introduce linear programming to a civilian audience was an earlier draft of the paper Marshall K. Wood and George B. Dantzig delivered at the Cowles Conference. They presented this early draft to the Cleveland meeting of the Econometric Society on December 27, 1948. An expanded version of the paper was published as "Programming of Interdependent Activities: I. General Discussion," in *Econometrica* 17, nos. 3–4 (July-October 1949): 193–99.

35. Düppe and Weintraub, "Siting," 1–2. The postwar "purity" of mathematics was epitomized by the Bourbaki group. In 1946, Marshall Stone hired one of the group's leaders, André Weil, as part of his campaign to rebuild the mathematics department at the University of Chicago. Düppe and Weintraub describe the mutually influential relationship between the Cowles Commission and the mathematics department in "Siting," 18–21. The Bourbaki group focused on set theory, typology, algebra, functions of one real variable, and integration.

36. Tjalling C. Koopmans, "Introduction" to Koopmans, ed., *Activity Analysis of Production and Allocation*, 1.

37. Koopmans, for example, was careful to distance programming from war work. "There is, of course, no exclusive connection between defense or war and the systematic study of allocation and programming problems. It is believed that the studies assembled in this volume are of equal relevance to problems of industrial management and efficiency" ("Introduction," 4). Marshall K. Wood and George B. Dantzig, the latter the creator of the simplex method, also defined *programming* in a way that extended it beyond work on ballistics. "Programming, or program planning, may be defined as the construction of a schedule of actions by means of which an economy, organization, or other complex of activities may move from one defined state to another" ("The Programming of Interdependent Activities: I. General Discussion," in *Activity Analysis*, 15).

38. Dantzig, "The Programming of Interdependent Activities: Mathematical Models," in *Activity Analysis*, 21, 20.

39. Koopmans, "Analysis of Production," in *Activity Analysis*, 34. Future references cited in the text.

40. Von Neumann, "A Model of General Economic Equilibrium," *Review of Economic Studies* 13, no. 1 (1945):1–9.

41. Peter L. Bernstein mentions that Markowitz studied with both Marschak and Koopmans, but he follows Markowitz's own account of the origin of "Portfolio Selection" in emphasizing the influence of John Burr Williams's *Theory of Investment* over the work of either of his mentors. See *Capital Ideas: The Improbable Origins of Modern Wall Street* (New York: Free Press, 1992), chap. 2.

42. See, e.g., the stock-flow consistent models introduced by Wynne Godley and Marc Lavoie (*Monetary Economics: An Integrated Approach to Credit, Money, Income, Production and Wealth* [Houndsmills, Basingstoke: Palgrave Macmillan, 2006], chaps. 3, 12, and 13).

43. Morris A. Copeland, "Some Problems in the Theory of National Income," *Journal of Political Economy* 40, no. 1 (1932): 1–55; "National Wealth and Income—An Interpretation," *Journal of the American Statistical Association* 30, no. 190 (June 1935): 377–86; and "Social Accounting for Money Flows," *The Accounting Review* 24, no. 3 (1949): 254–64. See also Morris A. Copeland and Edwin M. Martin, "National Income and Capital Formation," *Journal of Political Economy* 47, no. 3 (June 1939): 398–407.

44. See Lawrence S. Ritter, "An Exposition of the Structure of the Flow-of-Funds Accounts," *Journal of Finance* 18, no. 2 (May 1963): 229–30.

45. Ritter, "Exposition," 230.

46. Copeland, *A Study of Moneyflows in the United States* (New York: National Bureau of Economic Research, 1952), 30. Future references cited in text.

47. See Anne Mayhew, "Copeland on Money as Electricity," *Real-World Economics Review* 53 (2010): 53–54.

48. Copeland, *Study of Moneyflows*, 271. This is part of "A Note on the Quantity Theory of Money" (267–79), where Copeland directly addresses the challenge posed by his electrical model to the quantity theory of money (277–79).

49. See Ritter, "Exposition," 220, 227–28.

50. Ritter, "Exposition," 228–29.

51. Goldsmith, *Financial Intermediaries in the American Economy since 1900* (Princeton, NJ: Princeton University Press, 1958), xiv, xv, 180. Future references cited in the text.

52. See Frederic R. Mishkin, *The Economics of Money, Banking, and Financial Institutions*, 8th ed. (Upper Saddle River, N.J.: Pearson Addison Wesley, 2007), 223; and Anat Admati and Martin Hellwig, *The Bankers' New Clothes: What's Wrong with Banking and What to Do about It* (Princeton, NJ: Princeton University Press, 2013), chap. 4.

53. Mehrling, *The Money Interest and the Public Interest: American Monetary Thought, 1920–1970* (Cambridge, MA: Harvard University Press, 1997), 164.

54. John G. Gurley and Edward S. Shaw, *Money in a Theory of Finance* (Washington, DC: Brookings Institution, 1960), 10. Future references cited in the text. While they avoid "mathematical pyrotechnics" in the body of the text (ix), the book contains a mathematical appendix by Alain C. Enthoven, of the RAND Corporation.

55. "There is an approach to monetary theory . . . that would say that development of nonmonetary finance is irrelevant to real aggregative behavior and in particular to analysis of

the money market. This is net-money doctrine. . . . Net-money doctrine consolidates private domestic accounts so that private domestic debt cancels out against an equivalent amount of private domestic financial assets in both monetary and nonmonetary form. The only financial assets remaining in aggregative analysis are those held by the private sectors as net claims against the outside world—against, that is, government and the foreign sector. Thus, money, as part of these outside financial assets, is entirely of the outside variety. According to net-money doctrine, the quantity and quality of private domestic debt and its counterparts—inside debt and financial assets—are irrelevant to aggregative analysis and in particular to the demand for money and to the stock of money. . . . This overlooks the desire for diversified financial positions by both firms and consumers" (Gurley and Shaw, *Money in a Theory of Finance*, 187–88).

56. Mehrling, *The Money Interest*, 190.

57. Doug Noland, "John G. Gurley and Edward S. Shaw on Financial Intermediaries," (April 20, 2001) www.safehaven.com/browse/articles/by_month/2001/04. Noland is quoting from Gurley's response to a 1957 British Chancellor of the Exchequer report on the findings of the Radcliffe Committee. The report was issued in 1959.

58. Thomas I. Palley, "Milton Friedman's Economics and Political Economy: An Old Keynesian Critique," IMK working paper 134 (July 2014), 4. Reprinted in *Milton Friedman: Contributions to Economics and Public Policy*, ed. Robert Cord (Oxford: Oxford University Press, 2015).

59. Friedman, "Methodology of Positive Economics," in *Essays in Positive Economics* (Chicago: University of Chicago Press, 1953), 3–34.

60. According to Phelps, Friedman "showed that a continuously activist [monetary] policy, one that changes the money supply, say, in response to every wriggle in the data on employment etc., may be *destabilizing* in the sense that it actually increases the variance of unemployment because in comparing the variance and correlation between the two variables (money growth and unemployment) policy intervention may inadvertently make unemployment more volatile and unstable because, among other things: (1) the data is often highly inaccurate, especially before data revisions, and (2) by the time the policy action takes effect it might be no longer desirable. Therefore the 'passive' policy . . . may be better than any of the activist policies that are apt to be chosen" (*Seven Schools of Macroeconomic Thought: The Arne Memorial Lectures* [Oxford: Clarendon Press, 1990], 30).

61. James R. Lothian, "Milton Friedman's Monetary Economics and the Quantity-Theory Tradition," *Journal of International Money and Finance* 28, no. 7 (209): 1087; and Friedman, "The Quantity Theory of Money: A Restatement," in *Studies in the Quantity Theory of Money*, ed. Milton Friedman (Chicago: University of Chicago Press, 1956). Mark Blaug contrasted Friedman's work to that of Hicks and Keynes: "He set out a precise specification of the relevant constants and opportunity cost variables entering a household's demand function. His independent variables included wealth or 'permanent income'—the present value of expected future receipts from all sources. . . . Like Hicks, Friedman specified wealth as an appropriate budget constraint, but his concept of wealth was much broader than that adopted by Hicks. Whereas Keynes had viewed bonds as the only asset competing with cash, Friedman regarded all types of wealth as potential substitutes for cash holding in an individual's balance sheet; thus instead of a single interest variable in the Keynesian liquidity preference equation, we get a whole list of relative yields in Friedman. An additional novel feature, entirely new with

Friedman, is the inclusion of the expected rate of change of P as a measure of the anticipated rate of depreciation in the purchasing power of cash balances" (Blaug, *Economic Theory in Retrospect* [Cambridge: Cambridge University Press, 1996], 627–28).

62. Friedman, "The Quantity Theory of Money: A Restatement," *Studies in the Quantity Theory of Money*, 10. Friedman continued: "A more fundamental point is that all demand analysis resting on maximization of a utility function, this demand equation must be considered independent in any essential way of the nominal units to measure monetary variables." Future references cited in the text.

63. Many economic historians and macroeconomists have disputed Friedman and Schwartz's contention that the Federal Reserve was solely responsible for prolonging the Depression. While Stephen G. Cecchetti agrees that "the Federal Reserve played a key role in nearly every policy failure during this period," for example, he states that "there is now a broad consensus supporting three conclusions. First, the collapse of the finance system could have been stopped if the central bank had properly understood its function as lender of last resort. Second, deflation played an extremely important role deepening the Depression. And third, the gold standard, as a method for supporting a fixed exchange rate system, was disastrous" ("Understanding the Great Depression: Lessons for Current Policy," NBER Working Paper no. 6015 [1997], 1). See also Ben S. Bernanke, "The Macroeconomics of the Great Depression: A Comparative Approach," *Journal of Money, Credit and Banking* 27, no. 1 (1995): 1–28; Barry Eichengreen and Jeffrey Sachs, "Exchange Rates and Economic Recovery in the 1930s," *Journal of Economic History* 45, no. 4 (December 1985): 925–46; Ehsan U. Choudhri and Levis A. Kochin, "The Exchange Rate and the International Transmission of Business Cycle Disturbances: Some Evidence from the Great Depression," *Journal of Money, Credit and Banking* (November 1980): 565–74; and Peter Temin, "Transmission of the Great Depression," *Journal of Economic Perspectives* 7, no. 2 (Spring 1993): 87–102.

64. Friedman considered this project a "co-operative endeavor" between the NBER and Friedman's University of Chicago Money and Banking workshop (J. Daniel Hammond, *Theory and Measurement: Causality Issues in Milton Friedman's Monetary Economics* [Cambridge: Cambridge University Press, 1996], 47). Another part of the project, *Monetary Trends*, was published in 1982, but the third part remained unfinished.

65. See, e.g., Phillip Cagan, *Determinants and Effects of Changes in the Stock of Money, 1875–1960* (New York: National Bureau of Economic Research, 1965). Cagan participated in Friedman's Money and Banking workshop and also worked at the NBER. Cagan explained that his work was a "supplement" to Friedman and Schwartz's *Monetary History* (*Determinants*, xx).

66. Milton Friedman and Anna Jacobson Schwartz, *A Monetary History of the United States, 1867–1960* (Princeton, NJ: Princeton University Press, 1963), xvi. Because they were recounting the history of changes in the money supply, Friedman and Schwartz referred to the Great Depression as the "Great Contraction." Future references appear in the text.

67. For a sustained critique of the neoliberalism associated with the Mont Pelerin Society, see Philip Mirowski, *Never Let a Serious Crisis Go to Waste: How Neoliberals Survived the Financial Meltdown* (London: Verso, 2013), especially chap. 1. At the first meeting, and critical to formulating the society's free market ideology, were Friedrich Hayek, Ludwig von Mises, and Lionel Robbins.

68. Quoted Hammond, *Theory and Measurement*, 60.

69. Hammond, *Theory and Measurement*, 63. The foundation did help finance Friedman's Banking and Money workshop (65, n. 1 2, 78–9, n. 6).

70. Thomas Mayer explains that Friedman considered it desirable but unnecessary to trace the channels by which money affects income or consumption. Friedman believed that "one can document numerous cases in which changes in nominal income have followed exogenous changes in money, and combine this fact with the general explanation from price theory, that when there is an exogenous increase in the supply of one asset (money) the demand for the other asset (goods) increases" ("The Influence of Friedman's Methodological Essay," in *The Methodology of Positive Economics: Reflections on the Milton Friedman Legacy*, ed. Uskali Mäki [Cambridge: Cambridge University Press, 2009], 136–37).

71. "The entire governance structure of the Federal Reserve has evolved to guarantee responsiveness to its main constituency, the pinnacle of finance. . . . The member private banks 'own' stock in the regional Feds, and indeed, are paid dividends on their stock. The twelve regional Feds are governed by nine-member boards, six elected by member banks, and the remaining three by the Board of Governors. Each of the twelve regional Federal Reserve banks is a separately incorporated not-for-profit that is privately owned by the member banks in its district. Further, the entire Fed system is self-funded from its operations, freeing it from the rigors of an external budgetary control or any serious accountability. The Federal Reserve Board of Governors, to be sure, has seven members appointed by the president and confirmed by the Senate for nonrenewable fourteen-year terms, but almost inevitably they are chosen from those with previous experience in the regional Feds, or representatives of the banks or Treasury, although they may have concurrently served as academics. The Fed is technically run by the twelve regional Fed presidents plus the seven-member Board of Governors. Substantial power is vested in the chairman of the board, also appointed by the president for renewable four-year terms. This neither fish-nor-fowl organization chart dating from 1935 has admirably served to camouflage many of the activities of the Fed in the past. Indeed, the Fed is a bulwark of industry 'self-regulation,' decked out as a government entity dedicated to the public welfare; a sheep in wolf's clothing.

"Fed directors typically hold down a full-time job elsewhere, so in practice, most directors are officers of banks, or academics who are somehow connected to them. This level of private control of a central government regulatory agency . . . accomplishes an enhanced degree of 'self-regulation' of the industry, covered over with a patina of plausible deniability. This is combined with a critical dynamic wherein the Fed has engineered greater concentration in the financial sector over time (through shotgun mergers of failing banks, plus other blandishments), such that there are fewer banks to provide and elect qualified directors, and therefore, the entire system is increasingly being 'regulated' by the few oversized firms that conveniently dictate the staffing of the Fed. . . . This leads to those very same banks being bailed out in times of crisis" (Mirowski, *Never*, 190). Dean Baker is equally blunt: "The Fed has been deliberately designed to insulate it from democratic control and leave it instead a tool of the financial industry" (*The End of Loser Liberalism* [Washington: Center for Economic and Policy Research, 2011], 59).

72. Mayer, *The Structure of Monetarism* (New York: W. W. Norton, 1978), 2.

73. Kevin D. Hoover, *The New Classical Macroeconomics: A Sceptical Inquiry* (Oxford: Basil Blackwell, 1988), 213–32.

74. Neil Fligstein, *The Transformation of Corporate Control* (Cambridge, MA: Harvard University Press, 1990), 191–92.

75. According to Fligstein, before 1959, only two of the presidents or CEOs of the 100 largest firms in the United States held MBAs. "By 1979, 20 of the largest 100 corporations had presidents with MBAs. Of these, thirteen were from the Harvard Business School" (*Transformation,* 282).

76. Quoted in Fligstein, *Transformation,* 252.

77. Malcolm Rutherford argues that institutionalism all but disappeared after World War II, but we find it useful to link these individuals to institutionalism because many had connections to the Brookings Institution or NBER, which were homes to many interwar institutionalists, and because, by contrast with the neoclassical general equilibrium theory economists and the Keynesians, these individuals held positions consistent with many of the ideas of Veblen and Commons. See Rutherford, "Institutional Economics: Then and Now," *Journal of Economic Perspectives* 15, no. 3 (Summer 2001): 173–94.

78. Michael A. Bernstein, *A Perilous Progress: Economists and Public Purpose in Twentieth-Century America* (Princeton, NJ: Princeton University Press, 2001), 94–103.

79. Malcolm Rutherford and C. Tyler DesRoches, "The Institutionalist Reaction to Keynesian Economics" (May 30, 2006), esp. 12–24. Available at SSRN: https://ssrn.com/abstract=905613.

80. Samuelson, "In Search of the Elusive Elite," *New York Times* (26 June 1975), 845. On the "Measurement without Theory" debate, see David F. Hendry and Mary S. Morgan, eds., *The Foundations of Econometric Analysis* (Cambridge: Cambridge University Press, 1995), 491–524.

81. Robert L. Hertzel, "The Treasury-Federal Reserve Accord to the Mid-1960s," www.federalreservehistory.org/Events, 1. The specified aims of the 1946 Employment Act commanded the Council of Economic Advisors to "promote employment, production, and purchasing power under free competitive enterprise" (http://fraser.stlouisfed.org; Public Law 304 [S. 380], section 4).

82. "Statement by William McChesney Martin, Jr., Chairman of the Board of Governors of the Federal Reserve System before the House Banking and Currency Committee" (May 10, 1951), http://fraser.stlouisfed.org, 1, 3, 13.

83. Romer and Romer, "The Evolution of Economic Understanding and Postwar Stabilization Policy," NBER Working Paper 9274 (2002), http://nber.org/papers/w9274, 6.

84. Cited in ibid., 7.

85. Cited in ibid., 8.

86. Bernstein, *Perilous Progress,* 134. Our discussion is indebted to chapter 5 of Bernstein's work.

87. Romer and Romer, "Evolution," 9–10.

88. Ibid., 10–12.

89. Bernstein, *Perilous Progress,* 137–40.

90. Tobin and Brainard, "Financial Intermediaries and the Effectiveness of Monetary Controls," *American Economic Review* 53, no. 2 (May 1963): 384. Future references cited in the text.

91. Willem H. Buiter, "James Tobin: An Appreciation of his Contribution to Economics," *Economic Journal* 113 (November 2003): 585–631.

92. Tobin, "Money and Finance in the Macro-Economic Process," Nobel Memorial Lecture, December 8, 1981. Available at http://www.nobelprize.org/nobel_prizes/economic -sciences/laureates/1981/tobin. Future references cited in the text.

93. David Colander, "Conversations with James Tobin and Robert J. Shiller," in *Inside the Economist's Mind: Conversations with Eminent Economists*, ed. Paul A. Samuelson and William A. Barnett (Malden, MA: Blackwell, 2007), 400.

94. To explain the unique nature of saving, Tobin quoted Keynes: "Because the act of saving implies, not a substitution for present consumption of some specific additional consumption which requires for its preparation just as much immediate economic activity as would have been required by present consumption equal in value to the sum saved, but a desire for 'wealth' as such, that is for a potentiality of consuming an unspecified article at an unspecified time" (q. 15–16).

95. See Richard Lagos, "Inside and Outside Money," *New Palgrave Dictionary of Economics*, 2 edition, eds. Steven N. Durlauf and Lawrence E. Blum (London: Palgrave Macmillan, 2016). "Inside" money consists of any asset that represents or is backed by any form of private credit. The term "outside," which is used to describe fiat (unbacked) money issued by a central monetary authority, means that the money originates outside the private sector.

96. James Tobin and William C. Brainard, "Asset Markets and the Cost of Capital," in *Economic Progress, Private Values, and Public Policy* (Amsterdam: North Holland, 1977), 235.

97. Friedman, "The Role of Monetary Policy," *American Economic Review* 58:1 (March 1968), 6. Future references cited in the text.

98. *Economic Report of the President Together with the Annual Report of the Council of Economic Advisors* (Washington, DC: Government Printing Office, 1962), 7. Future references cited in the text.

99. The best overview of these early variants of growth models is F. H. Hahn and R. C. O. Matthews, "The Theory of Economic Growth: A Survey," *Economic Journal* 74, no. 296 (December 1964): 779–902.

100. Jorgenson, "Technology in Growth Theory," 45, in *Technology and Growth: Conference Proceedings* ed. Jeffrey C. Fuhrer and Jane Sneddon Little (Boston: Federal Reserve Bank of Boston, 1996); 45–77.

101. Solow's Nobel Prize speech can be found at http://www.nobelprize.org/nobel_prizes/ economic-sciences/laureates/1987/solow-facts.html.

102. Solow, "A Contribution to the Theory of Economic Growth," *Quarterly Journal of Economics* 70, no. 1 (February 1956): 65.

103. Solow, Nobel 6, 5. The October 1987 crash, whose US onset is known as Black Monday, began in Hong Kong and rapidly engulfed securities markets around the world. We return to this event in chapter 10.

CHAPTER NINE

1. The best long history of finance is William N. Goetzmann, *Money Changes Everything: How Finance Made Civilization Possible* (Princeton, NJ: Princeton University Press, 2016). Goetzmann finds evidence of finance in the ancient Near East.

2. On the origins of the AFA, see Robert Kavesh, J. Fred Weston, and Harry Suvain, "The American Finance Association: 1939–1969," *Journal of Finance* 25, no. 1 (1970): 1–17. For the AEA list of subfields, see Michael A. Bernstein, *A Perilous Progress: Economists and Public Purpose in Twentieth-Century America* (Princeton, NJ: Princeton University Press, 2001), 83.

3. While the master's degree in business requires subjects in addition to various courses in finance, the growth in the number of business master's degrees awarded in the United States is one measure of the increased popularity of finance. In the mid-1950s, US universities awarded slightly more than 3,000 business master's degrees each year. By 1997–98, this number had reached over 100,000. In 1980, MBA degrees surpassed the combined advanced degrees awarded in medicine and law, and in 2000, more than twice as many MBAs were awarded as bachelor's degrees in engineering. See Esteban Perez Caldentey and Matias Vernengo, "Modern Finance, Methodology, and the Global Crisis," *Real-World Economics Review* 52 (2010): 74. Franck Jovanovic points out that *two* canons for financial economics were established during the 1960s. One, centered at MIT, represented financial markets as imperfect; the other, centered at the University of Chicago, represented financial markets as perfect. See "The Construction of the Canonical History of Financial Economics," *History of Political Economy* 40, no. 2 (2008): 230–36. Perry Mehrling dates the full acceptance of finance by economists to the mid-1970s. In 1970, Stephen Ross, a graduate student at Wharton, was warned that "finance is to economics as osteopathy is to medicine." Mehrling says that finance in 1970 was still "substantially a descriptive field, involved mainly with recording the range of real-world practice and summarizing it in rules of thumb rather than analytical principles and models" (*Fischer Black and the Revolutionary Idea of Finance* [New York: John Wiley & Sons, 2005], 136).

4. Jovanovic, "Construction of the Canonical History," 213–42.

5. Whitley, "The Rise of Modern Finance Theory: Its Characteristics as a Scientific Field and Connections to the Changing Structure of Capital Markets," *Research in the History of Economic Thought and Methodology* 4 (1986): 154–55. See also Donald MacKenzie, *An Engine, Not a Camera: How Financial Models Shape Markets* (Cambridge, MA: MIT Press, 2006), chap. 2.

6. Peter A. Bernstein, *Capital Ideas: The Improbable Origins of Modern Wall Street* (New York: Free Press, 1992), 42. Robert C. Merton reiterates this point: "Finance was first treated as a separate field of study early in this century, and for the next forty years it was almost entirely a descriptive discipline with a focus on institutional and legal matters. As recently as a generation ago, finance theory was still little more than a collection of anecdotes, rules of thumb, and manipulations of accounting data. The most sophisticated tool of analysis was discounted value and the central intellectual controversy centered on whether to use present value or internal rate of return to rank corporate investments" (Merton, "Preface," *Continuous Time Finance* [New York: Wiley-Blackwell, 1992], xii).

7. Working held a PhD in economics from Cornell University; he taught agricultural economics at the University of Minnesota from 1920 to 1925, and held non-tenure-track appointments at the University of Chicago (summer 1928) and the University of Michigan (1934–35) before moving to the Food Research Institute at Stanford. He was associate director of the Institute from 1952 through 1960.

8. Holbrook Working, "New Concepts Concerning Futures Markets and Prices," *American Economic Review* 52, no. 3 (June 1962): 433–34. Future references cited in the text.

9. Ibid., 435–36.

10. See Mark Rubenstein, "Markowitz's 'Portfolio Selection': A Fifty Year Retrospective," *Journal of Finance* 57, no. 3 (2002): 1041–45; and Bernstein, *Capital Ideas*, 41–55.

11. Harald Cramér, *Mathematical Methods of Statistics* (Princeton, NJ: Princeton University Press, 1946); and A. D. Roy, "Safety First and the Holding of Assets," *Econometrica* 20, no. 3 (July 1952): 431–49.

12. Fisher, *The Theory of Interest: As Determined by Impatience to Spend Income and Opportunity to Invest It* (1930; Mansfield Centre, CT: Maritime Publishing, 2012), 316.

13. Markowitz, "Portfolio Selection," *Journal of Finance* 7, no. 1 (1952): 77.

14. Markowitz's method required the security analyst to calculate a covariance matrix of a rank equal to the number of assets in the portfolio—and, for shares issued by a publicly traded company, the rank could be as large as 100,000 (Colin Read, *The Rise of the Quants: Marschak, Sharpe, Black, Scholes, and Merton* [Basingstoke: Palgrave Macmillan, 2012], 74).

15. Wood and Dantzig, "The Programming of Interdependent Activities: I General Discussion," in Tjalling C. Koopmans, ed., *Activity Analysis of Production and Allocation: Proceedings of a Conference* (New York: John Wiley & Sons, 1951), 15.

16. "Arrow, Kenneth Joseph (Born 1921)," http://www.nobelprize.org/nobel_prizes/economic-sciences/laureates/1972/arrow-bio.html. The class of general equilibrium models developed by Arrow with Gérard Debreu and Lionel McKenzie used the fixed point theorem as an equilibrium solution, akin to the equilibrium in a game, as developed by the mathematician John Nash. This is often referred to as the Arrow-Debreu model. See Arrow and Debreu, "Existence of Equilibrium for a Competitive Economy," *Econometrica* 22, no. 3 (July 1954): 265–90; and Ross M. Starr, *General Equilibrium Theory: An Introduction* (Cambridge: Cambridge University Press, 2011).

17. Arrow's Activity Analysis paper was entitled "Alternative Proof of the Substitution Theorem for Leontief Models in the General Case" (in Koopmans, ed., *Activity Analysis*, 155–64).

18. The paper was published in English in the *Journal of Economic Studies* 31, no. 2 (1964): 91–96.

19. The idea of "states of nature" was introduced by Kolmogorov. J. Hirshleifer and J. Riley describe Arrow's contribution as part of an "intellectual revolution," which also included von Neumann's expected utility function. "Just as intertemporal analysis requires subscripting commodity claims by *date,* uncertainty analysis requires subscripting commodity claims by *state*" ("The Analytics of Uncertainty and Information: An Expository Survey," *Journal of Economic Literature* 17, no. 4 [1979]: 1376).

20. Securitization refers to the process by which a group of assets—e.g., home mortgages, student debts, outstanding automobile loans—are bundled into a single security, which can then be subdivided into "tranches," the prices of which depend upon each tranche's exposure to risk (and the tranches' relations to each other). With the advent of financial engineering, pricing such securities and tranches has become a critical stage in creating and trading financial derivatives.

21. Sharpe's model considered pricing from the investor's point of view; similar results were obtained for the point of view of the security-issuing corporation by Jack Traynor and John Lintner. Only Sharpe was awarded the Nobel for this work, even though the results of the three

economists were similar. On Traynor, see Mehrling, *Fischer Black and The Revolutionary Idea of Modern Finance* (New York: John Wiley & Sons, 2005), chap. 2; on Lintner, see Mehrling, *Fischer Black*, chap. 3.

22. Sharpe, "Capital Asset Prices: A Theory of Market Equilibrium under Conditions of Risk," *Journal of Finance*, rpt. in Howard R. Vane and Chris Mulhearn, eds., *Pioneering Papers of the Nobel Memorial Laureates in Economics: Harry M. Markowitz, Merton H. Miller, William F. Sharpe, Robert C. Merton and Myron S. Scholes*, vol. 2 (Cheltenham, UK: Edward Elgar, 2009), 260.

23. For an exception to this generalization, see Richard Zeckhauser, "Investing in the Unknown and Unknowable," *Capitalism and Society* 1, no. 2 (2006): 1–39.

24. Lundberg's thesis was entitled *Approximations of the Probability Function/Reinsurance of Collective Risks.*

25. The movement of prices Bachelier described is often called "Brownian" because the pattern resembles the physical movements of a particle suspended in gas or fluid and subject to random shocks. This was first observed by Robert Brown, a British physicist, in the 1820s. See Paul H. Cootner, "Introduction" to Part I in Cootner, ed., *The Random Character of Stock Market Prices* (Cambridge, MA: MIT Press, 1964), 4.

26. Cootner, "Preface," *Random Character*, xxiii.

27. Mandelbrot, "The Variation of Certain Speculative Prices," in Cootner, ed., *Random Character*, 369–412. See also Paul H. Cootner, "Comments on the Variation of Certain Speculative Prices," in Cootner, ed., *Random Character*, 413–18. In addition to methodological issues, some economists expressed reservations about Mandelbrot's "messianic tone" (413).

28. Samuelson, "Proof," *Industrial Management Review* 6, no. 2 (Spring 1965): 42.

29. Such a pattern was theorized as an "ergodic state."

30. Among the financial theorists who did not equate the random walk model with the efficient-market hypothesis was Andrew W. Lo. "The reason for this distinction [between the two concepts] comes from one of the central ideas of modern financial economics . . . : the necessity of some trade-off between risk and expected return. If a security's expected price change is positive, it may be just the reward needed to attract investors to hold the asset and bear the corresponding risks. Indeed, if an investor is sufficiently risk averse, he or she might gladly pay to avoid holding a security which has unforecastable returns. In such a world, prices do not need to be perfectly random, even if markets are operating efficiently and rationally" ("Introduction" to Cootner, ed., *Random Character*, ix).

31. Fama, "Random Walks in Stock Market Prices," *Financial Analysts Journal* 21, no. 5 (Sept.-Oct. 1965): 56. Future references cited in the text.

32. Stephen Nelson and Peter J. Katzenstein argue that the financial theorists of the 1960s and 1970s almost all ignored Knight's distinction between risk and uncertainty. See "Risk, Uncertainty, and the Financial Crisis of 2008," *International Organization* 68, no. 2 (2014): 361–92.

33. Lo argues that, in order to test the efficient-market hypothesis, "one must specify additional structure, e.g., investors' preferences, information structure, etc. But then a test of market efficiency becomes a test of several auxiliary hypotheses as well, and a rejection of such a joint hypothesis tells us little about which aspect of the joint hypothesis is inconsistent with the data" ("Introduction" to Cootner, ed., *Random Character*, x).

34. Lo, "Efficient Market Hypothesis," *New Palgrave*, 2:124. Burton G. Malkiel describes the three versions of the hypothesis in "Efficient Market Hypothesis," in John Eatwell, Murray Milgate, and Peter Newman, eds., *The New Palgrave: A Dictionary of Economics* (London: Macmillan, 1998), 2:120–23.

35. Samuelson, "Proof," 45, 48.

36. Eugene F. Fama and Merton H. Miller, *The Theory of Finance* (Hinsdale, IL: Dryden Press, 1972), vii, viii, ix. Future references cited in the text.

37. Mandelbrot's initial objection was to CAPM's assumption that price changes followed the Gaussian distribution. He argued that the "peaked" distribution evident in empirical studies of price changes suggested a class of stochastic distributions called Levy processes. See "The Variation of Certain Speculative Prices," in Cootner, ed, *Random Character*. Further empirical studies also reappraised CAPM: see Michael C. Jensen, Fischer Black, and Myron S. Scholes, "The Capital Asset Pricing Model: Some Empirical Tests," https://ssrn.com/abstract=908569); Richard Roll, "A Critique of the Asset Pricing Theory's Tests: Part I: On Past and Potential Testability of the Theory," *Journal of Financial Economics* 4, no. 2 (1977): 129–76; Marshall E. Blume and Irwin Friend, "A New Look at the Capital Asset Pricing Model," *Journal of Finance* 28, no. 1 (1973): 19–34. By 1991, even Eugene Fama, one of the architects of CAPM, declared that "beta is dead" ("Efficient Capital Markets II," *Journal of Finance* 46, no. 5 [1991] 1575–1617). The quotation comes from Eric Berg's interview with Fama, published in "Market Place: A Study Shakes Confidence in the Volatile-Stock Theory," *New York Times* (February 18, 1992). The assumptions implicit in neoclassical finance, including CAPM, were also questioned by new work on organizations, investor behavior, and transaction costs. See Michael Jensen and William H. Meckling, *Theory of the Firm: Managerial Behavior, Agency Costs, and Ownership Structure* (Netherlands: Springer, 1979); and Daniel Kahneman and Amos Tversky, "Prospect Theory: An Analysis of Decision under Risk," *Econometrica* 47, no. 2 (March 1979): 263–91.

38. Arrow, "The Organization of Economic Activity," in *General Equilibrium: Collected Papers of Kenneth J. Arrow* (Cambridge, MA: Belknap Press, 1983), 142. Taking two examples from the insurance industry, Arrow showed that "adverse selection" and "moral hazard" demonstrated that "it is not a priori obvious" that free market arrangements are Pareto-efficient. Under adverse selection, insurance buyers with different risks, unknown to the insurers, could respond disproportionately to insurance offerings, causing the insurer to underprice the risk. Under moral hazard, "any system which, in effect, insures against adverse final outcomes automatically reduces the incentives to good decision making" (145).

39. See John F. Marshall and Vipul K. Bansal, *Financial Engineering: A Complete Guide to Financial Innovation* (New York: New York Institute of Finance, 1992), chap. two.

40. Leon Melamed, "The International Money Market," in *The Merits of Flexible Exchange Rates: An Anthology,* ed. Leon Melamed (Fairfax, VA: George Mason University Press, 1988), 41. See also Mehrling, *Fischer Black*, 188–89.

41. Stephen Blyth, *An Introduction to Quantitative Finance* (Oxford: Oxford University Press, 2014), 21.

42. Eirk Brynjolfsson, "The Productivity Paradox of Information Technology," *Communications of the ACM* 36, no. 12 (1993): 66–77. See table 4 and figs. 3a and 3b.

43. See Steven E. Shreve, *Stochastic Calculus for Finance I: The Binomial Asset Pricing Model* (Springer Science and Business, 2012), I:3, 4; 156–59.

44. Blyth, *An Introduction to Quantitative Finance*, 147.

45. Modigliani and Miller, "The Cost of Capital, Corporation Finance and the Theory of Investment," *American Economic Review* 48, no. 3 (June 1958): 269.

46. The best treatment of Fischer Black is Mehrling, *Fischer Black*.

47. Black and Scholes, "The Pricing of Options and Corporate Liabilities," *Journal of Political Economy* 81, no. 3 (May-June 1973): 637.

48. See Aswath Damodaran, *Damodaran on Valuation: Security Analysis for Investment and Corporate Finance* (Hoboken, NJ: John Wiley & Sons, 2006), 16.

49. The four basic kinds of derivatives are futures, forwards, swaps, and options, and the two fundamental contractual relationships to these derivatives are puts and calls. A futures contract is an agreement to trade an underlying asset at a specified price and a specific time in the future; it involves cash flows up to the stated expiration date; and futures are almost always traded on an exchange. A forward is also an agreement to trade an underlying asset at a specified price and future date; but, unlike a futures contract, a forward contract does not involve constant cash flows, and many forwards trade between two parties, as over-the-counter contracts. A swap is a contract binding two parties to exchange a series of cash flows at a given time; these can derive from interest rates or currency exchange rates or any other cash-generating financial underlying. Finally, an option is a contract that gives the buyer the option—but not the obligation—to exchange the underlying asset at a specified price and time. Various kinds of options include the European option, in which the agreement can only be exercised at the point of the asset's expiration date; the American option, which allows exercise of the option at any point up to and including the expiration date; and the Bermudan option, which allows exercise of the option at specified points in time. A put is a contractual agreement to sell; and a call is a contractual agreement to buy.

50. For a discussion of the relationship between financial assets and liquidity, see Richard Bookstaber, *A Demon of Our Own Design: Markets, Hedge Funds, and the Perils of Financial Innovation* (Hoboken, NJ: John Wiley & Sons, 2007), esp. chaps. 1, 2, and 6.

51. Blyth describes the situations that violated the no-arbitrage principle in 2008–9 in *Introduction*, 18–19, 49, 131.

52. Black and Scholes, "Pricing," 641.

53. The model allows a financial engineer to replicate a portfolio by constructing it in such a way that the cash flows the portfolio generates over time reproduce the cost of the underlying assets. This simplifies the work of traders because they do not need to set a discount rate on the assets or calculate the term structure of interest rates. See Bruce Kogut and Hugh Patrick, "Executive Summary," in "The Quantitative Revolution and the Crisis: How Have Quantitative Financial Models Been Used and Misused?" (Columbia Business School, December 4, 2009), 8 (http://markleehunter.free.fr/documents/quant_crisis.pdf. See also https://www8.gsb.columbia.edu/leadership/research/dec2009).

54. The article initially appeared in a RAND Corporation periodical, *Bell Journal of Economics and Management Science* 4 (Spring 1973): 141–83. It was reprinted in Merton, *Continuous-Time Finance*, rev. ed. (Malden, MA: Blackwell, 1992), 255–308. This quotation appears on p. 256.

55. Quoted Kogut and Patrick, "Executive Summary," 7. See also Mackenzie, *Engine, Not a Camera*, "Introduction."

56. MacKenzie, *Engine, Not a Camera*, 6.

57. Paul A. Samuelson and Robert C. Merton, "A Complete Model of Warrant Pricing That Maximizes Utility," *Industrial Management Review* 10, no. 2 (1969): 17–46. Stochastic calculus was developed after World War II for applications in engineering, theoretical physics, and biology, where researchers paid particular attention to stochastic diffusion processes such as the process of heat transfer. By analogy, heat transfer equations could be applied to security prices modeled as a stochastic process (as Bachelier had shown them to be). This analogy had been made clear in 1966 when Paul Samuelson's "Rational Theory of Warrant Pricing" was published with an appendix by Henry P. McKean called "A Free Boundary Problem for the Heat Equation Arising from a Problem of Mathematical Economics."

58. The name is somewhat misleading because investors cannot trade continuously: even in a digital environment, every exchange closes. "Continuous-time finance" nevertheless stands in opposition to "discrete-time finance." The former requires stochastic calculus.

59. Merton, "Preface," *Continuous-Time Finance*, xiii.

60. Merton, *Continuous-Time Finance*; Cox, Ross, and Rubenstein, "Option Pricing: A Simplified Approach," *Journal of Financial Economics* 7, no. 3 (1979): 229–63; and Harrison and Kreps, "Martingales and Arbitrage in Multiperiod Securities Markets," *Journal of Economic Theory* 20, no. 3 (1979): 381–408. John C. Cox and Stephen A. Ross teach in MIT's Sloan School of Business, and Mark Rubenstein teaches in the Hass School of Business at the University of California-Berkeley. J. Michael Harrison and David M. Kreps are members of the business school faculty at Stanford University, and Stanley R. Pliska teaches at the University of Illinois, Chicago.

61. Cox, Ross, and Rubenstein, "Option Pricing," 229–63.

62. Doob, *Stochastic Processes* (New York: Wiley, 1953), 91.

63. Stephen A. Ross, *Neoclassical Finance* (Princeton, NJ: Princeton University Press, 2005), chap. 1; and Philip H. Dybvig and Ross, "Arbitrage" in *New Palgrave: A Dictionary of Economics*, ed. J. Eatwell, M. Milgate, and P. Newman (London: Macmillan, 1987) I:100–106.

64. Stephen A. Ross, "The Arbitrage Theory of Capital Asset Pricing," Working Paper no. 2 (Wharton School Rodney L. White Center for Financial Research) (https://rodneywhitecenter .wharton.upenn.edu/working-papers/papers-1973/).

65. Pliska, *Introduction to Mathematical Finance: Discrete Time Models* (Oxford: Blackwell, 1997), 6. Future references cited in the text.

66. Bookstaber, *Demon*, chap. 8.

67. Lo, "Introduction," Financial Econometrics (unpublished PDF [2006]), 1–2.

68. In a draft completed in 2006, Andrew Lo pointed out that the term *financial econometrics* had not been coined in 1986, but that this specialty was rapidly becoming "one of the fastest growing branches of economics today, both in academia and in industry" ("Introduction," Financial Econometrics), 1, 14.

69. John H. Cochrane, *Asset Pricing*, revised ed. (Princeton, NJ: Princeton University Press, 2005), 390–91.

70. Fama, "Efficient Capital Markets II," 1575–1617.

71. http://vlab.stern.nyu.edu/en/. Further reading on ARCH and GARCH can be found in Robert F. Engle and C. W. J. Granger, *Long-run Economic Relationships: Readings in Cointegration* (Oxford: Oxford University Press, 1991); and Robert F. Engle, ed., *ARCH: Selected Readings* (Oxford: Oxford University Press, 1995).

72. Robert J. Shiller, *Market Volatility* (Cambridge, MA: MIT Press, 1989), 154. See also Shiller, *Irrational Exuberance* (Princeton, NJ: Princeton University Press, 2000).

73. Shiller, "From Efficient Markets Theory to Behavioral Finance," *Journal of Economic Perspectives* 17, no. 1 (Winter 2003): 90, 91. In addition to Shiller's *Irrational Exuberance*, examples of behavioral finance include Hersh Shefrin, *Beyond Greed and Fear: Understanding Behavioral Finance and the Psychology of Investing* (Boston: Harvard Business School Press, 2000); Andrei Shleifer, *Inefficient Markets* (Oxford: Oxford University Press, 2000); George A. Akerlof and Robert J. Shiller, *Animal Spirits: How Human Psychology Drives the Economy and Why It Matters for Global Capitalism* (Princeton, NJ: Princeton University Press, 2009); José A. Scheinkman, *Speculation, Trading, and Bubbles* (New York: Columbia University Press, 2014).

74. See Nicola Giocoli, *Modeling Rational Agents: From Interwar Economics to Early Modern Game Theory* (Cheltenham: Edward Elgar, 2003), chap. 2.

75. *Econometrica* 47, no. 2 (1979): 263–91.

76. Zeckhauser, "Investing in the Unknown and Unknowable."

77. Shiller, "From Efficient Markets Theory," 101–2.

78. Akerlof, "Behavioral Macroeconomics and Macroeconomic Behavior," *American Economic Review* 92, no. 3 (June 2002): 411–33.

CHAPTER TEN

1. Olivier J. Blanchard, "The Lucas Critique and the Volcker Deflation," *American Economic Review* 74, no. 2 (May 1984): 211–15.

2. Greta R. Krippner, *Capitalizing on Crisis: The Political Origins of the Rise of Finance* (Cambridge, MA: Harvard University Press, 2011), 120.

3. "The Great Moderation: Remarks by Governor Ben S. Bernanke" (February 20, 2004), Federal Reserve Board (http://www.federalreserve.gov/boarddocs/speeches/2004/20040220/).

4. Olivier Blanchard, "The State of Macro," NBER Working Papers Series, n. 14259 (2008), 17, n. 7 (http://www.nber.org/papers/w14259).

5. Diners Club introduced the first credit card in the 1950s, but this was really a charge card, which had to be repaid every billing cycle. That same decade, Bank of America issued the BankAmericard, which was the first all-purpose credit card. In the mid-1970s, this became the VISA card.

6. Jeffrey Frankel and Peter Orszag, "Introduction," to Frankel and Orszag, eds., *American Economic Policy in the 1990s* (Cambridge, MA: MIT Press, 2002), 1.

7. Portfolio insurance was an investment strategy that applied the Black-Scholes-Merton option pricing theory. It was intended to protect a stock portfolio from falling below a specified

floor value. As Donald MacKenzie explains, "a floor below which the value of an asset cannot fall is, in effect, a put option on the asset: an option to sell the asset at the guaranteed price level. In principle, therefore, the value of a portfolio can be insured by buying a put on the portfolio with a strike price equal to the desired floor" (*An Engine, Not a Camera: How Financial Models Shape Markets* [Cambridge, MA: MIT Press, 2006], 179). Two professors of finance, Hayne E. Leland and Mark Rubenstein, both of the University of California-Berkeley, developed portfolio insurance (which was a trading strategy, not insurance) in the late 1970s and, in 1981, they joined John O'Brien in founding Leland O'Brien Rubenstein Associates, Inc. (LOR). They realized it was unrealistic to assume that asset prices would display log-normal volatility, as the Black-Scholes model assumed, so the strategy they modeled and sold did not "insure" a portfolio for a given period of time but merely produced a replicating portfolio—and then only for a given number of stock-price moves. So popular did portfolio insurance become in the mid-1980s that, by the fall of 1987, $50 billion worth of stock was covered by LOR and its licensees; another $50 billion was covered by LOR's imitators, including Morgan Stanley. The problem with the strategy was that, if stock prices began to plunge discontinuously, it would be impossible to produce a replicating portfolio quickly enough. This is what happened when so many investors used the portfolio insurance technique: when computer programs governing trades according to the LOR formula demanded that all investors sell simultaneously, the price fall began to snowball in a feedback loop. The sell-off in stocks represented on the Dow Jones industrial average on Monday, October 19, 1987 was the largest one-day fall in the history of the US market. After the crash, which was followed by an almost equal rise in prices in the next two days, the so-called "volatility skew" or "volatility smile" began to appear in the ratio between the implied volatility and the strike price of an option with the same expiration date. This phenomenon revealed shortcomings in the Black-Scholes option pricing model. See MacKenzie, *Engine*, chap. 7; and Richard Bookstaber, *A Demon of Our Own Design: Markets, Hedge Funds, and the Perils of Financial Innovation* (Hoboken, NJ: John Wiley & Sons, 2007), chap. 2.

8. Jacob Hacker, *The Great Risk Shift: The Assault on American Jobs, Families, Health Care, and Retirement, and How You Can Fight Back* (New York: Oxford University Press, 2006).

9. Frankel and Orszag, "Introduction," 8.

10. On the collapse of LTCM, see MacKenzie, *Engine*, chap. 8.

11. Robin Greenwood and David Sharfstein, "The Growth of Finance," *Journal of Economic Perspectives* 27, no. 2 (Spring 2013): 1. Future references cited in the text.

12. The transformation of the US economy was inextricably linked to changes in other economies—and to the global economy as well. Unregulated capital flows, the outsourcing of risk through sales of securitized assets, and fluctuations in the value of various currencies all affected changes in the US economy and the financial structure. While these factors are critical, they do not form part of our story. Important studies of globalization include Assaf Razin, *Understanding Global Crises: An Emerging Paradigm* (Cambridge, MA: MIT Press, 2014); Paul Langley, *The Everyday Life of Global Finance: Saving and Borrowing in Anglo-America* (Oxford: Oxford University Press, 2008); Rawi Abdelal, *Capital Rules: The Construction of Global Finance* (Cambridge, MA: Harvard University Press, 2007); Xavier Freixas, Luc Laeven, and José-Luis Peydró, *Systemic Risk, Crises, and Macroprudential Regulation* (Cambridge, MA:

MIT Press, 2015); and Edward LiPuma and Benjamin Lee, *Financial Derivatives and the Globalization of Risk* (Durham, NC: Duke University Press, 2004).

13. N. Gregory Mankiw and David Romer, eds., *New Keynesian Economics, Volume I: Imperfect Competition and Sticky Prices* (Cambridge, MA: MIT Press, 1991), 1–2. The Phillips curve debates can be found in Edmund Phelps, ed., *The Microeconomic Foundations of Employment and Inflation Theory* (New York: W. W. Norton, 1970).

14. The different faces economists and financial theorists saw of this structural transformation help explain the schism between the two disciplines described by Lawrence H. Summers in 1985. See "On Economics and Finance," *Journal of Finance*, 40, no. 3 (July 1985): 633–35.

15. Ezra Solomon, *The Anxious Economy* (San Francisco: W. H. Freeman, 1975). Solomon was a staff member of the Council of Economic Advisors.

16. Merton H. Miller, "Financial Innovation: The Last Twenty Years and the Next," *Revue De La Banque* (1986): 35–42.

17. Christopher A. Sims, "Macroeconomics and Reality," *Econometrica* 48, no. 1 (1980): 1–48.

18. For a summary of these shocks, see Alan S. Blinder, *Economic Policy and the Great Stagflation* (New York: Academic Press, 1979), 42. Steven K. McNees identifies six shocks: "(1) The imposition and relaxation of several different phases of wage and price controls; (2) the switch from fixed to flexible exchange rates and the subsequent experience of learning to live with exchange rate-induced variations in prices of traded commodities; (3) the sudden quadrupling of the price of imported oil; (4) the changes in demographics, public policy, and social attitudes and their alleged impact on the 'natural' rate of unemployment; (5) the growing importance of governmentally mandated supply-restricting or cost-raising measures; (6) the introduction of a new framework for conducting monetary policy" ("An Empirical Assessment of New Theories of Inflation and Unemployment," in *After the Phillips Curve: Persistence of High Inflation and High Unemployment: Proceedings of a Conference Held at Edgartown, Massachusetts, June, 1978* [Boston: Federal Reserve Bank of Boston, Public Information Centre, 1978], 45).

19. James Tobin, "Stabilization Policy Ten Years After," *Brookings Papers on Economic Activity*, 11, no. 1 (1980): 20–89.

20. Fees for managing the retirement savings of millions of Americans, along with advantageous tax carve-outs such as the carried-interest provision for investment managers, helped the financial sector grow exponentially in the 1980s and underwrote a new gilded age for multibillionaire hedge fund managers, private equity advisers, and venture capital titans. For the compensation of hedge fund managers in 2015, see Institutional Investors Alpha's 2015 Hedge Fund Ranking at http://www.institutionalinvestorsalpha.com/HedgeFundCompensationReport/html.

21. July L. Klein, "The Cold War Hot House for Modeling Strategies at the Carnegie Institute of Technology," Working Paper No. 19, Institute for New Economic Thinking.

22. John F. Muth, "Rational Expectations and the Theory of Price Movements," *Econometrica* 29, no. 3 (1961): 316.

23. Roger E. A. Farmer calls Muth's rational expectations a "revolution" in *How the Economy Works: Confidence, Crashes and Self-Fulfilling Prophecies* (Oxford: Oxford University Press, 2010), 65. Michel De Vroey agrees, although he gives Muth less credit than does Farmer:

"The notion of scientific revolution has often been overused. But if there is one episode in the history of microeconomics that deserves the label, it is the transformation initiated by Lucas and brought to completion by Kydland and Prescott—the movement from the Keynesian to the Lucasian program" (*A History of Macroeconomics from Keynes to Lucas and Beyond* [Cambridge: Cambridge University Press, 2016], 280).

24. Lucas, "Expectations and the Neutrality of Money," in *Studies in Business Cycle Theory* (Cambridge, MA.: MIT Press, 1981), 65–89. Other important articles by Lucas include "An Equilibrium Model of the Business Cycle" (1975) in *Studies*, 179–214; and "Understanding Business Cycles" (1977) in *Studies*, 215–39.

25. De Vroey, *History*, chap. 9.

26. See Kevin D. Hoover, *The New Classical Macroeconomics* (Oxford: Basil Blackwell, 1988); and De Vroey, *History*, chaps. 15–17.

27. Prescott, "Nobel Lecture: The Transformation of Macroeconomic Policy and Research," *Journal of Political Economy* 114 (2006): 231–32.

28. De Vroey, *History*, 264–65. On the conceptualization of "structural parameters" and the limitations of this concept, see Duo Qin, *A History of Econometrics: The Reformation from the 1970s* (Oxford: Oxford University Press, 2013), 115–17.

29. De Vroey, *History*, 281. While Qin concurs that the RBC models were innovative, she argues that "the DSGE approach has carried forward and formalized the NBER tradition of emphasizing the role of sector-specific shocks in business cycle research, but at the expense of replacing econometric estimation by calibration and consequently nullifying the relevant econometric criteria for model testing" (*History of Econometrics*, 102).

30. Robert E. Lucas and Edward C. Prescott, "Investment under Uncertainty," *Econometrica* 39, no. 5 (1971): 659–81.

31. Charles G. Renfro, *The Practice of Econometric Theory: An Examination of the Characteristics of Econometric Computation* (Berlin: Springer, 2009).

32. Authors published in the collection include John Muth, Clive Granger, Christopher Sims, Bennett T. Macallum, John Taylor, Robert J. Barrow, Edwin Kydland, Edward C. Prescott, and Guillermo A. Calvo.

33. These were some of the phrases Robert Solow culled from the Lucas-Sargent presentation, which Solow characterized as containing a "polemic vocabulary reminiscent of Spiro Agnew" ("Summary and Evaluation," in *After the Phillips Curve*, 203–4). For Paul Romer's comment on this exchange, see "Solow's Choice" (August 14, 2015), http://paulromer.net/solows-choice/.

34. Robert E. Lucas and Thomas J. Sargent, "After Keynesian Macroeconomics," in *Rational Expectations and Econometric Practice*, ed. Robert E. Lucas Jr. and Thomas J. Sargent (Minneapolis: University of Minnesota Press, 1981), 307.

35. Lawrence Klein, "Disturbances in the International Economy," in *After the Phillips Curve*, 84–85.

36. Klein, "Disturbances," 85.

37. Richard Palmer, "Final Plenary Discussion," in Philip W. Anderson, Kenneth J. Arrow, and David Piner, eds., *The Economy as an Evolving Complex System* (Westview, CT: Westview Press, 1988), 258, 259, 261.

38. Quoted Klein, "Cold War Hot House" 45–46.

39. "It is mistaken to write, as Prescott's phrasing suggests, that the Kydland-Prescott model explains that, for the period studied, US business fluctuations up to a certain percentage result from agents' optimizing reactions to exogenous shocks. The correct phrasing should rather be: 'Kydland and Prescott have constructed a model economy in which agents are by definition in equilibrium; simulating it, they found that several of its moments replicate the moments calculated from U.S. statistics over the period considered.' Methodologically, this difference is far from negligible: neglecting it makes one think that rational expectations, the equilibrium discipline, and so on are features of reality, while in fact they are just devices to construct models" (De Vroey, *History*, 305).

40. De Vroey, *History*, 264. The demotion of econometrics by RBC helps explains the criticism the historian of econometrics Duo Qin levels at all rational expectations models, although she explicitly targets the gap between the models and the worlds they claim to illuminate. "The significance of the formalization becomes more difficult to identify when it is assessed from the applied perspective, especially when the success rate in ex-ante forecasts of recessions is used as a key criterion. The fact that the onset of the 2008 financial-crisis-triggered recession was predicted by only a few 'Wise Owls' while missed by regular forecasters armed with various models serves us as the latest warning that the efficiency of the formalization might be far from optimal" (Qin, *History of Econometrics*, 111).

41. Lawrence J. Christiano, Martin S. Eichenbaum, and Charles Evans, *Nominal Rigidities and the Dynamic Effects of a Shock to Monetary Policy* (Cambridge, MA: National Bureau of Economic Research, 2001).

42. Renfro, *Practice of Econometric Theory*, chap. 7. TSP was developed between 1965 and 1966; MODLR and PcGive were created in 1968. The first was designed to avoid, not take advantage of, desktop computing machines (234).

43. De Vroey calls this group of models "second-generation New Keynesian" models (*History*, chap. 18). Economists associated with New Keynesianism include Jordi Gali, Michael Gertler, and Miles Kimball.

44. In addition to De Vroey, *History*, chap. 11, see David Colander, "Introduction" to Colander, ed., *Post-Walrasian Microeconomics: Beyond the Dynamic Stochastic General Equilibrium Model* (Cambridge: Cambridge University Press, 2006), 1–23.

45. Michael Woodford, *Interest and Prices: Foundations of a Theory of Monetary Policy* (Princeton, NJ: Princeton University Press, 2003).

46. Woodford, *Interest and Prices*, 39.

47. "New Neoclassical Synthesis and the Role of Monetary Policy," in Ben S. Bernanke and Julio Rotemberg, eds., *NBER Macroeconomics Annual* (1997), 232–33.

48. L. Randall Wray, *Why Minsky Matters: An Introduction to the Work of a Maverick Economist* (Princeton, NJ: Princeton University Press, 2016), 24. Our discussion of Minsky is indebted to Wray's timely study of Minsky's work.

49. Wray, *Why Minsky Matters*, 31–33.

50. Shiller, "From Efficient Markets Theory to Behavioral Finance," *Journal of Economic Perspectives* 17, no. 1 (Winter 2003): 83–104.

51. Daniel Kahneman and Amos Tversky, *Choices, Values, and Frames* (New York: Russell Sage Foundation, 2000); Richard H. Thaler, *Misbehaving: The Making of Behavioral Econom-*

ics (New York: W. W. Norton & Co., 2015); and Herbert Gintis, *The Bounds of Reason: Game Theory and the Unification of the Behavioral Sciences* (Princeton, NJ: Princeton University Press, 2009). For comprehensive reviews of game theory, see Robert J. Aumann and Sergiu Hart, *Handbook of Game Theory with Economic Applications* (Amsterdam: North-Holland, 1992); Aumann and Hart, *Handbook of Game Theory with Economic Applications*, vol. 2. (Amsterdam: North-Holland, 1995); Aumann and Hart, *Handbook of Game Theory with Economic Applications*, vol. 3 (Amsterdam: Elsevier, 2002) and H. P. Young, Shmuel Zamir, and Ken Binmore, *Handbook of Game Theory*, vol. 4 (Amsterdam: Elsevier, 2015).

52. Colin Camerer, George Lowenstein, and Matthew Rabin, *Advances in Behavioral Economics* (New York: Russell Sage Foundation, 2004); and Peter A. Diamond and Hannu Vartiainen, *Behavioral Economics and Its Applications* (Princeton, NJ: Princeton University Press, 2007).

53. Carl Shapiro and Hal R. Varian, *Information Rules: A Strategic Guide to the Network Economy* (Boston, MA: Harvard Business School Press, 1999). In 2001, George Akerlof, Michael Spence, and Joseph E. Stiglitz shared the Nobel Prize in Economics for their analysis of markets with asymmetric information.

54. William N. Goetzmann and Roger G. Ibbotson, *The Equity Risk Premium: Essays and Explorations* (New York: Oxford University Press, 2004).

55. Roman Frydman and Michael D. Goldberg, *Imperfect Knowledge Economics: Exchange Rates and Risk* (Princeton, NJ: Princeton University Press, 2007).

56. Claude Ménard and Mary M. Shirley, *Handbook of New Institutional Economics* (Berlin: Springer, 2008); and Jean Tirole, *The Theory of Corporate Finance* (Princeton, NJ: Princeton University Press, 2006).

57. Philippe Aghion and Peter Howitt, with Maxine Brant-Collett and Cecilia Garcia-Penalosa, *Endogenous Growth Theory* (Cambridge, MA: MIT Press, 1998) and Stelios Michalopoulos, Luc Laeven, and Ross Levine, *Financial Innovation and Endogenous Growth* (Cambridge, MA: National Bureau of Economic Research, 2009).

58. Sunny Y. Auyang, *Foundations of Complex-Systems Theories in Economics, Evolutionary Biology, and Statistical Physics* (Cambridge: Cambridge University Press, 1998).

59. Wynne Godley, Marc Lavoie, and Gennaro Zezza, *The Stock-Flow Consistent Approach: Selected Writings of Wynne Godley* (New York: Palgrave Macmillan, 2006).

60. Masahisa Fujita, Paul R. Krugman, and Anthony Venables, *The Spatial Economy: Cities, Regions, and International Trade* (Cambridge, MA: MIT Press, 1999).

61. Under Carter, deregulation initially affected trucking, airlines, natural gas, and banking. Under Reagan, deregulation was extended to telecommunications, electricity, and some parts of environmental protection.

62. Krippner, *Capitalizing*, chap. 3.

63. Matthew Sherman, "A Short History of Financial Deregulation in the United States," Center for Economic and Policy Research (July 2009), 1–2 (http://cepr.net/documents/publications/dereg-timeline-2009-07.pdf).

64. Greenwood and Scharfstein, "The Growth of Finance," 3.

65. Zoltan Pozsar, Tobias Adrian, Adam Ashcroft, and Haley Boesky, "Shadow Banking," Federal Reserve Bank of New York Staff Report (2010).

66. *The Financial Crisis Inquiry Report* (Washington, DC: US Government National Commission on the Causes of the Financial and Economic Crisis in the United States, 2011), 252.

67. Patrick Hosking et al., "Dow Dives as Federal Reserve Lines Up $75b loan for AIG," *Times* (London), September 16, 2008.

68. Gregory Gethard, "Falling Giant: A Case Study of AIG," www.investopedia.com/articles/economics/09/american-investment-group-aig-bailout.asp.

69. Ben S. Bernanke, *The Courage to Act: A Memoir of a Crisis and its Aftermath* (New York: W. W. Norton & Co., 2015), chap. 13.

70. See Freixas, Laeven, and Peydro, *Systemic Risk*, chaps. 2, 3, 6.

71. Tobias Adrian and Hyun Song Shin, "The Changing Nature of Financial Intermediation and the Financial Crisis of 2007–2009," *Annual Review of Economics* 2 (2010): 603–8, C1–C14, 609–18. Future references cited in the text. See also Tobias Adrian and Hyun Song Shin, "Liquidity and Leverage," http://hdl.handle.net/10419/60918. This paper, delivered at an International Fund conference on April 18, 2008, was written as the crisis was unfolding.

72. Alan S. Blinder and Ricardo Reis, "Understanding the Greenspan Standard," Paper presented at the Fed Reserve Bank of Kansas Symposium, "The Greenspan Era" (September 12, 2005), 48, 8 (https://www.kansascityfed.org/publicat/sympos/2005/pdf/Blinder-Reis2005.pdf). Future references cited in the text.

73. Adrian and Shin, "Liquidity and Leverage," 12.

74. Ibid., 26, 28.

75. Quantitative Easing 1 (QE1) began in November 2008, when the Fed bought $600 billion in mortgage-backed securities; QE1 reached a peak of $2.1 trillion in June 2010. QE2 began in November 2010, when the Fed bought $600 billion of Treasury securities. QE3 began in September 2012. Initially, this consisted of a series of $40 billion-per-month purchases of agency-backed securities, but the open-ended monthly purchase amount was raised to $85 billion in December 2012. The Fed began tapering off its purchases in February 2014 and halted them in October 2014.

76. Partial Timeline of the 2007–9 Financial Crisis:

March 2007	Mortgage delinquencies and home foreclosures reach new highs
	New Century Financial halts new loans
April 2007	New Century Financial files for Chapter 11 bankruptcy
May 2007	USB closes its US subprime lending arm
July 2007	S&P and Moody's downgrade bonds backed by subprime mortgages
August 2007	American Home Mortgage files for bankruptcy
	BNP Paribus freezes three funds affected by subprime
	Bank of America acquires $2 billion equity stake in Countrywide Mortgages
	Lehman Brothers closes subprime mortgage origination unit
December 2007	Recession begins (quarter 1)
	UBS announces writedown of $10 billion
	Citigroup bails out seven affiliated SIVs
March 2008	JPMorgan Chase announces it will buy Bear Stearns
May 2008	Moody's initiates ratings error probe

June 2008	S&P reveals error in its ratings model
July 2008	IndyMac fails
August 2008	Consumer credit contracts
September 2008	Fannie Mae and Freddie Mac put into receivership
	A large money market fund "breaks the buck"
	US government seizes control of AIG
	Lehman Brothers fails
	Barclays agrees to buy Lehman Brothers
	Bank of America buys Merrill Lynch
	Washington Mutual fails
October 2008	Consumer spending falls for the first time in seventeen years
November 2008	Fed begins QE1
December 2008	US government bails out automobile industry
	Goldman Sachs posts first loss since 1999
March 2009	AIG posts Q4 loss of $61.7b
November 2010	Fed begins QE2
September 2012	Fed begins QE3
December 2012	Fed increases QE3 purchases
February 2014	Fed begins tapering QE3 purchases

The primary source for this timeline is www.centerforfinancialstability.org/timeline.php.

77. For the implications of the global financial crisis for American policy, see Martin N. Baily and John B. Taylor, *Across the Great Divide: New Perspectives on the Financial Crisis* (Stanford: Hoover Institution Press, 2014); Alan S. Blinder, Andrew W. Lo, and Robert M. Solow, *Rethinking the Financial Crisis* (New York: Sage, 2013); George O. Akerlof, Olivier Blanchard, David Romer, and Joseph E. Stiglitz, *What Have We Learned?: Macroeconomic Policy after the Crisis* (Washington, DC: International Monetary Fund, 2014); Carmen M. Reinhart and Kenneth S. Rogoff, *This Time Is Different: Eight Centuries of Financial Folly* (Princeton, NJ: Princeton University Press, 2009). For a historical perspective on the microfoundations debates of the 1970s see Roman Frydman and Edmund S. Phelps, *Rethinking Expectations: The Way Forward for Macroeconomics* (Princeton, NJ: Princeton University Press, 2013). For a modern interpretation of the implications of the Phillips Curve in historical perspective, see Jeffrey C. Fuhrer et al., *Understanding Inflation and the Implications for Monetary Policy: A Phillips Curve Retrospective* (Cambridge, MA: MIT Press, 2009).

78. See Nassim N. Taleb, *The Black Swan: The Impact of the Highly Improbable* (New York: Random House, 2007).

79. Ben Bernanke, *Essays on the Great Depression* (Princeton, NJ: Princeton University Press, 2000). See Olivier Blanchard, Giovanni Dell'Aricca, and Paolo Mauro, "Rethinking Macroeconomic Policy," *Journal of Money, Credit and Banking* 42 (2010): 199–215.

BIBLIOGRAPHY

Abbott, Edith. "The Wages of Unskilled Labor in the United States, 1850–1900." *Journal of Political Economy* 13, no. 3 (1905): 321–67.

Abdelal, Rawi. *Capital Rules: The Construction of Global Finance.* Cambridge, MA: Harvard University Press, 2007.

Accountants' Handbook. Edited by Earl A. Saliers. 14th ed. New York: Ronald, 1923.

Adams, T. S. "Federal Taxes upon Income and Excess Profits." *American Economic Review* 8, no. 1, suppl. (March 1918): 18–35.

Admati, Anat, and Martin Hellwig. *The Bankers' New Clothes: What's Wrong with Banking and What to Do about It.* Princeton, NJ: Princeton University Press, 2013.

Adrian, Tobias, and Hyun Song Shin. "Liquidity and Leverage." Staff Report no. 328. New York: Federal Reserve Bank of New York, 2008. https://www.econstor.eu/handle/10419/60918.

———. "The Changing Nature of Financial Intermediation and the Financial Crisis of 2007–2009." *Annual Review of Economics* 2 (2010): 603–18.

Aghion, Philippe, and Peter Howitt with Maxine Brant-Collett and Cecilia García-Peñalosa. *Endogenous Growth Theory.* Cambridge, MA: MIT Press, 1998.

Akerlof, George A. "Behavioral Macroeconomics and Macroeconomic Behavior." *American Economic Review* 92, no. 3 (June 2002): 411–33.

Akerlof, George, Olivier Blanchard, David Romer, and Joseph Stiglitz, eds. *What Have We Learned? Macroeconomic Policy after the Crisis.* Washington, DC: International Monetary Fund, 2014.

Akerlof, George A., and Robert J. Shiller. *Animal Spirits: How Human Psychology Drives the Economy, and Why It Matters for Global Capitalism.* Princeton, NJ: Princeton University Press, 2009.

Alchon, Guy. *The Invisible Hand of Planning: Capitalism, Social Science, and the State in the 1920s.* Princeton, NJ: Princeton University Press, 1985.

Aliprantis, Charalambos D., and Kim C. Border. "A Foreword to the Practical." In *Infinite Dimensional Analysis: A Hitchhiker's Guide*, 3d ed., xix–xxiv. Berlin: Springer, 2007.

Allais, Maurice. "Irving Fisher." In *International Encyclopedia of the Social Sciences* (17 vols.), ed. David L. Sills, 5:475–85. New York: Macmillan/Free Press, 1968.

Allen, Frederick Lewis. *Only Yesterday: An Informal History of the 1920s*. New York: John Wiley & Sons, 1931.

Allen, R. G. D. *Index Numbers in Theory and Practice*. Houndsmills: Macmillan, 1975.

Allen, Robert Loring. *Irving Fisher: A Biography*. New York: John Wiley & Sons, 1993.

An Analysis of the Sources of War Finance and an Estimate of the National Income and Expenditure in 1938 and 1940. Command Paper 6261. London: HM Stationery Office, 1941.

Arrow, Kenneth J. "Alternative Proof of the Substitution Theorem for Leontief Models in the General Case." In *Activity Analysis of Production and Allocation: Proceedings of a Conference*, ed. Tjalling C. Koopmans, 155–64. New York: Wiley, 1951.

———. "The Role of Securities in the Optimal Allocation of Risk-Bearing." *Journal of Economic Studies* 31, no. 2 (April 1964): 91–96.

———. "The Organization of Economic Activity: Issues Pertinent to the Choice of Market versus Nonmarket Allocation." 1969. In *Collected Papers of Kenneth J. Arrow*, vol. 2, *General Equilibrium*, 133–55. Cambridge, MA: Belknap Press of Harvard University Press, 1983.

———. "Portrait: Jacob Marschak." *Challenge* 21, no. 1 (March/April 1978): 69–71.

Arrow, Kenneth J., and Gérard Debreu. "Existence of an Equilibrium for a Competitive Economy." *Econometrica* 22, no. 3 (July 1954): 265–90.

Aumann, Robert J., and Sergiu Hart. *Handbook of Game Theory with Economic Applications*. 3 vols. Amsterdam: North-Holland, 1992–2002.

Auspitz, Rudolf, and Richard Lieben. *Untersuchungen über die Theorie des Preises* (Researches in price theory). Leipzig: Duncker & Humblot, 1889.

Auyang, Sunny Y. *Foundations of Complex-Systems Theories in Economics, Evolutionary Biology, and Statistical Physics*. Cambridge: Cambridge University Press, 1998.

Avi-Yonah, Reuven S. "Corporate Income Tax of 1909." Major Acts of Congress, 2004. http://www.encyclopedia.com/doc/1G2-3407400068.html.

Bachelier, Louis. "Theory of Speculation." 1900. Translated by A. James Boness. In *The Random Character of Stock Prices* (rev. ed.), ed. Paul H. Cootner, 17–78. Cambridge, MA: MIT Press, 1964.

Backhouse, Roger E. "MIT and the Other Cambridge." *History of Political Economy* 46, suppl. 1 (2014): 252–71.

Backhouse, Roger E., and Bradley W. Bateman, eds. *The Cambridge Companion to Keynes*. Cambridge: Cambridge University Press, 2006.

Backhouse, Roger E., and Mauro Boianovsky. *Transforming Modern Macroeconomics: Exploring Disequilibrium Microfoundations, 1956–2003*. Cambridge: Cambridge University Press, 2013.

Backhouse, Roger E., and David Laidler. "What Was Lost with IS-LM?" *History of Political Economy* 36, suppl. (2004): 25–56.

Baily, Martin Neil, and John B. Taylor, eds. *Across the Great Divide: New Perspectives on the Financial Crisis*. Stanford, CA: Hoover Institution Press, 2014.

Baker, Dean. *The End of Loser Liberalism: Making Markets Progressive.* Washington, DC: Center for Economic and Policy Research, 2011.

Balisciano, Marcia L. "Hope for America: American Notions of Economic Planning between Pluralism and Neoclassicism, 1930–1959." In "From Interwar Pluralism to Postwar Neoclassicism," ed. Mary S. Morgan and Malcolm Rutherford, *History of Political Economy* 30, suppl. (1998): 153–78.

Bank, Steven A. "Entity Theory as Myth in the Origins of the Corporate Income Tax." *William and Mary Law Review* 43, no. 2 (2001): 447–537.

Barber, William J. *From New Era to New Deal: Herbert Hoover, the Economists, and American Economic Policy, 1921–1933.* Cambridge: Cambridge University Press, 1985.

Bartlett, William W. *Mortgage-Backed Securities: Products, Analysis, Trading.* New York: New York Institute of Finance, 1989.

Baskin, Jonathan Barron, and Paul J. Miranti, Jr. *A History of Corporate Finance.* Cambridge: Cambridge University Press, 1997.

Batterson, Steve. "The Vision, Insight, and Influence of Oswald Veblen." *Notices of the American Mathematical Society* 54, no. 5 (May 2007): 606–18.

Baumol, William J. "On Method in U.S. Economics a Century Earlier." *American Economic Review* 75, no. 6 (December 1985): 1–12.

Belykh, A. A. "A Note on the Origins of Input-Output Analysis and the Contribution of the Early Soviet Economists: Chayanov, Bogdanov and Kritsman." *Soviet Studies* 41, no. 3 (July 1989): 426–29.

Berg, Eric N. "Market Place: A Study Shakes Confidence in the Volatile-Stock Theory." *New York Times,* February 18, 1992.

Berle, Adolf A., and Gardiner C. Means. *The Modern Corporation and Private Property.* 1932. With a new introduction by Murray L. Weidenbaum and Mark Jensen. 1991. New Brunswick, NJ: Transaction, 2011.

Bernanke, Ben S. "The Macroeconomics of the Great Depression: A Comparative Approach." *Journal of Money, Credit, and Banking* 27, no. 1 (February 1995): 1–28.

———. *Essays on the Great Depression.* Princeton, NJ: Princeton University Press, 2000.

———. "The Great Moderation." Remarks by Governor Ben S. Bernanke at the meetings of the Eastern Economic Association, Washington, DC, February 20, 2004. Federal Reserve Board. http://www.federalreserve.gov/boarddocs/speeches/2004/20040220.

———. *The Courage to Act: A Memoir of a Crisis and Its Aftermath.* New York: Norton, 2015.

Bernstein, Michael A. *A Perilous Progress: Economists and Public Purpose in Twentieth-Century America.* Princeton, NJ: Princeton University Press, 2001.

Bernstein, Peter L. *Capital Ideas: The Improbable Origins of Modern Wall Street.* New York: Free Press, 1992.

Besomi, Daniele, ed. *The Collected Interwar Papers and Correspondence of Roy Harrod.* 3 vols. Cheltenham: Edward Elgar, 2003.

Biddle, Jeff. "Social Science and the Making of Social Policy: Wesley Mitchell's Vision." In *Economic Mind in America: Essays in the History of American Economics,* ed. Malcolm Rutherford, 43–79. London: Routledge, 1998.

Bingham, N. H., and Rüdiger Kiesel. *Risk-Neutral Valuation: Pricing and Hedging of Financial Derivatives.* 1998. 2nd ed. London: Springer, 2004.

Bjerkholt, Olav. "Ragnar Frisch and the Foundation of the Econometric Society and *Econometrica.*" In *Econometrics and Economic Theory in the Twentieth Century: The Ragnar Frisch Centennial Symposium,* ed. Steinar Strøm, 26–57. Cambridge: Cambridge University Press, 1998.

———. "Frisch's Econometric Laboratory and the Rise of Trygve Haavelmo's Probability Approach." *Econometric Theory* 21, no. 3 (June 2005): 491–533.

———. "Writing 'The Probability Approach' with Nowhere to Go: Haavelmo in the United States, 1939–1944." *Econometric Theory* 23, no. 5 (October 2007): 775–837.

Black, Fischer, Michael C. Jensen, and Myron S. Scholes. "The Capital Asset Pricing Model: Some Empirical Tests." In *Studies in the Theory of Capital Markets,* ed. Michael C. Jensen, 79–124. New York: Praeger, 1972.

Black, Fischer, and Myron Scholes. "The Pricing of Options and Corporate Liabilities." *Journal of Political Economy* 81, no. 3 (May–June 1973): 637–54.

Blanchard, Olivier J. "The Lucas Critique and the Volcker Deflation." *American Economic Review* 74, no. 2 (May 1984): 211–15.

———. "The State of Macro." Working Paper no. 14259. Cambridge, MA: National Bureau of Economic Research, 2008. http://www.nber.org/papers/w14259.

Blanchard, Olivier, Giovanni Dell'Ariccia, and Paolo Mauro. "Rethinking Macroeconomic Policy." *Journal of Money, Credit, and Banking* 42, suppl. (2010): 199–215.

Blanchard, Olivier Jean, and Stanley Fischer. *Lectures on Macroeconomics.* Cambridge, MA: MIT Press, 1989.

Blaug, Mark. *Economic Theory in Retrospect.* 1962. 5th ed. Cambridge: Cambridge University Press, 1996.

Blinder, Alan S. *Economic Policy and the Great Stagflation.* New York: Academic, 1979.

Blinder, Alan S., Andrew W. Lo, Robert M. Solow, eds. *Rethinking the Financial Crisis.* New York: Russell Sage Foundation, 2013.

Blinder, Alan S., and Ricardo Reis. "Understanding the Greenspan Standard." Paper presented at the Federal Reserve Bank of Kansas City symposium "The Greenspan Era," Kansas City, MO, September 12, 2005. https://www.kansascityfed.org/publicat/sympos/2005/pdf/Blinder-Reis2005.pdf.

Bloom, Murray Teigh. *Rogues to Riches: The Trouble with Wall Street.* New York: Putnam's, 1971.

Blume, Marshall E., and Irwin Friend. "A New Look at the Capital Asset Pricing Model." *Journal of Finance* 28, no. 1 (March 1973): 19–34.

Blume, Marshall E., and Jeremy J. Siegel. "The Theory of Security Pricing and Market Structure." *Journal of Financial Markets, Institutions, and Instruments* 1, no. 3 (August 1992): 1–58.

Blyth, Stephen. *An Introduction to Quantitative Finance.* Oxford: Oxford University Press, 2014.

Bodkin, Ronald G., Lawrence R. Klein, and Kanta Marwah. *A History of Macroeconomic Model-Building.* Cheltenham: Edward Elgar, 1991.

Boland, Laurence A. "Methodology." In *The New Palgrave: A Dictionary of Economics* (4 vols.), ed. John Eatwell, Murray Milgate, and Peter Newman, 3:455–58. London: Macmillan, 1998.

Bookstaber, Richard. *A Demon of Our Own Design: Markets, Hedge Funds, and the Perils of Financial Innovation.* Hoboken, NJ: Wiley, 2007.

Bordo, Michael D., and Andrew Filardo. "Deflation and Monetary Policy in a Historical Perspective: Remembering the Past or Being Condemned to Repeat It?" Working Paper no. 10833. Cambridge, MA: National Bureau of Economic Research, October 2004.

Boumans, Marcel. "Built-in Justification." In *Models as Mediators: Perspectives on Natural and Social Science,* ed. Mary S. Morgan and Margaret Morrison, 66–96. Cambridge: Cambridge University Press, 1999.

———. *How Economists Model the World into Numbers.* London: Routledge, 2005.

Box, Joan Fisher. *R. A. Fisher: The Life of a Scientist.* New York: John Wiley & Sons, 1978.

Bratton, William W., and Joseph A. McCahery. "The Equilibrium Content of Corporate Federalism." *Wake Forest Law Review* 41, no. 3 (2006): 619–96.

Bratton, William W., and Michael L. Wachter. "Shareholder Primacy's Corporatist Origins: Adolf Berle and the Modern Corporation." *Journal of Corporation Law* 34, no. 1 (September 2008): 99–152.

Breslau, Daniel. "Economics Invents the Economy: Mathematics, Statistics, and Models in the Work of Irving Fisher and Wesley Mitchell." *Theory and Society* 32, no. 3 (June 2003): 379–411.

Brief, Richard A. "Corporate Financial Reporting at the Turn of the Century." *Journal of Accountancy* 163, no. 5 (May 1987): 142–57.

Brown, Clifford D. *The Emergence of Income Reporting: An Historical Study.* East Lansing: Michigan State University, Graduate School of Business Administration, Division of Research, 1971.

Brownlee, W. Elliot. "Economists and the Formation of the Modern Tax System in the United States: The World War I Crisis." In *The State and Economic Knowledge: The American and British Experiences,* ed. Mary O. Furner and Barry Supple, 401–35. Cambridge: Cambridge University Press, 1990.

———. *Federal Taxation in America: A Short History.* Cambridge: Cambridge University Press, 1996.

Brynjolfsson, Erik. "The Productivity Paradox of Information Technology: Review and Assessment." *Communications of the Association for Computing Machinery* 36, no. 12 (December 1993): 66–77.

Buiter, Willem H. "James Tobin: An Appreciation of His Contribution to Economics." *Economic Journal* 113, no. 491 (November 2003): F585–F631.

Bullock, Charles J. "Trust Literature: A Survey and a Criticism." *Quarterly Journal of Economics* 15 (1901): 167–217.

Burns, Arthur F., and Wesley C. Mitchell. *Measuring Business Cycles.* New York: National Bureau of Economic Research, 1946.

Cagan, Phillip. *Determinants and Effects of Changes in the Stock of Money, 1875–1960.* New York: National Bureau of Economic Research, 1965.

Caldentey, Esteban Pérez, and Matías Vernengo. "Modern Finance, Methodology and the Global Crisis." *Real-World Economics Review,* no. 52 (March 2010): 69–81.

Callon, Michel. "Introduction: The Embeddedness of Economic Markets in Economics." In *The Laws of the Markets,* ed. Michel Callon, 1–57. Oxford: Blackwell, 1998.

Calomiris, Charles W. "Volatile Times and Persistent Conceptual Errors: U.S. Monetary Policy, 1914–1951." In *The Origins, History, and Future of the Federal Reserve: A Return to Jeckyll Island,* ed. Michael D. Bordo and William Roberds, 166–218. Cambridge: Cambridge University Press, 2010.

Camerer, Colin F., George Loewenstein, and Matthew Rabin, eds. *Advances in Behavioral Economics.* New York: Russell Sage Foundation, 2004.

Camic, Charles, and Yu Xie. "The Statistical Turn in American Social Science: Columbia University, 1890 to 1915." *American Sociological Review* 59, no. 5 (October 1994): 773–805.

Card, David, and Craig A. Olson. "Bargaining Power, Strike Durations, and Wage Outcomes: An Analysis of Strikes in the 1880s." *Journal of Labor Economics* 13, no. 1 (January 1995): 32–61.

Carey, John L. "The Origins of Modern Financial Reporting." In *The Evolution of Corporate Financial Reporting,* ed. T. A. Lee and R. H. Parker, 142–57. Sunbury-on-Thames: Thomas Nelson, 1979.

Carson, Carol S. "The History of the United States National Income and Product Accounts: The Development of an Analytical Tool." *Review of Income and Wealth* 21, no. 2 (June 1975): 153–81.

Cecchetti, Stephen G. "Understanding the Great Depression: Lessons for Current Policy." Working Paper no. 6015. Cambridge, MA: National Bureau of Economic Research, April 1997.

Chamberlain, Lawrence, and William Wren Hay. *Investment and Speculation: Studies of Modern Movements and Basic Principles.* New York: Henry Holt, 1931.

Chandler, Alfred D., Jr. *The Visible Hand: The Managerial Revolution in American Business.* Cambridge, MA: Harvard University Press, 1977.

Chiang, Alpha C. *Fundamental Methods of Mathematical Economics,* 3rd ed. New York: McGraw-Hill, 1967.

Chick, Victoria. *Macroeconomics after Keynes: A Reconsideration of the General Theory.* Cambridge, MA: MIT Press, 1983.

Choudhri, Ehsan U., and Levis A. Kochin. "The Exchange Rate and the International Transmission of Business Cycle Disturbances: Some Evidence from the Great Depression." *Journal of Money, Credit, and Banking* 12, no. 4, pt. 1 (November 1980): 565–74.

Christ, Carl F. "History of the Cowles Commission, 1932–52." In *Economic Theory and Measurement: A Twenty Year Research Report, 1932–1952,* 3–65. Chicago: Cowles Commission for Research in Economics, 1952.

Christiano, Lawrence J., Martin Eichenbaum, and Charles Evans. "Nominal Rigidities and the Dynamic Effects of a Shock to Monetary Policy." Working Paper no. 8403. Cambridge, MA: National Bureau of Economic Research, July 2001.

Christophers, Brett. *Banking across Boundaries: Placing Finance in Capitalism.* Malden, MA: Wiley-Blackwell, 2013.

———. "The Limits to Financialization." *Dialogues in Human Geography* 5, no. 2 (2015): 183–200.

Church, Robert L. "Economists as Experts: The Rise of an Academic Profession in the United States, 1870–1920." In *The University in Society,* vol. 2, *Europe, Scotland, and the*

United States from the 16th to the 20th Century, ed. Lawrence Stone, 571–609. Princeton, NJ: Princeton University Press, 1974.

Clark, John B. *The Philosophy of Wealth: Economic Principles Newly Formulated.* Boston: Ginn, 1886.

———. "Capital and Its Earnings." *Publications of the American Economic Association,* vol. 3, no. 2 (May 1888).

———. "The Law of Wages and Interest." *Annals of the American Academy of Political and Social Science* 1 (July 1890): 43–65.

———. "Distribution as Determined by a Law of Rent." *Quarterly Journal of Economics* 5, no. 3 (April 1891): 289–318.

———. *The Distribution of Wealth: A Theory of Wages, Interest, and Profits.* 1889. Reprint, New York: Macmillan, 1914.

Coats, A. W. "The First Two Decades of the American Economic Association." *American Economic Review* 50, no. 4 (September 1960): 555–74.

———. "The Distinctive LSE Ethos in the Inter-War Years." *Atlantic Economic Journal* 10, no. 1 (March 1982): 18–30.

Cochrane, John H. *Asset Pricing.* 2001. rev. ed. Princeton, NJ: Princeton University Press, 2005.

Colander, David. "The Death of Neoclassical Economics." *Journal of the History of Economic Thought* 22, no. 2 (2000): 127–43.

———. Introduction to *Post Walrasian Macroeconomics: Beyond the Dynamic Stochastic General Equilibrium Model,* ed. David Colander, 1–23. Cambridge: Cambridge University Press, 2006.

———. "Conversations with James Tobin and Robert J. Shiller on the 'Yale Tradition' in Macroeconomics." In *Inside the Economist's Mind: Conversations with Eminent Economists,* ed. Paul A. Samuelson and William A. Barnett, 392–419. Malden, MA: Blackwell, 2007.

Colander, David C., and Harry Landreth. Introduction to *The Coming of Keynesianism to America: Conversations with the Founders of Keynesian Economics,* ed. David C. Colander and Harry H. Landreth, 1–38. Cheltenham: Edward Elgar, 1996.

Colm, Gerhard. "The Ideal Tax System." *Social Research* 1, no. 3 (August 1934): 319–42. Reprinted in Gerhard Colm, *Essays in Public Finance and Fiscal Policy,* ed. Helen Nicol, 44–67. New York: Oxford University Press, 1955.

———. "Technical Requirements for an Effective Fiscal Policy." Original title: "Maintaining High-Level Production and Employment." *American Political Science Review* xxxix (December 1945): 1126–37. Reprinted in Gerhard Colm, *Essays in Public Finance and Fiscal Policy,* ed. Helen Nicol, 172–87. New York: Oxford University Press, 1955.

———. "Why Public Finance?" *National Tax Journal* 1, no. 3 (September 1948): 193–206. Reprinted in Gerhard Colm, *Essays in Public Finance and Fiscal Policy,* ed. Helen Nicol, 3–23. New York: Oxford University Press, 1955.

———. "Public Finance in the National Income" (in Spanish). *Bulletin of the Central Bank of Venezuela* (June–February 1950): 17–26. Reprinted in Gerhard Colm, *Essays in Public Finance and Fiscal Policy,* ed. Helen Nicol, 223–40. New York: Oxford University Press, 1955.

———. "National Economic Budgets" (in Spanish). *Bulletin of the Central Bank of Venezuela* (May–June 1951): 13–21. Reprinted in Gerhard Colm, *Essays in Public Finance and Fiscal Policy*, ed. Helen Nicol, 241–57. New York: Oxford University Press, 1955.

Colm, Gerhard, and Fritz Lehman. "Public Spending and Recovery in the United States." *Social Research* 3, no. 2 (May 1936): 129–66. Reprinted in Gerhard Colm, *Essays in Public Finance and Fiscal Policy*, ed. Helen Nicol, 113–35. New York: Oxford University Press, 1955.

Committee on Recent Economic Changes. *The Recent Economic Changes in the United States.* 2 vols. New York: National Bureau of Economic Research, 1929.

Conant, Charles A. *A History of Modern Banks of Issue: With an Account of the Economic Crises of the Nineteenth Century and the Crisis of 1907.* 1896. 4th ed. New York: Putnam's, 1909.

Concepts and Methods of the U.S. National Income and Products Accounts (Chapters 1–5). US Chamber of Commerce/Bureau of Economic Analysis, July 2009. http://www.bea.gov/national/pdf/NIPAhandbookch1–4.pdf.

Cooper, Francis [Hugh Ronald Conyngton]. *Financing an Enterprise: A Manual of Information and Suggestion for Promoters, Investors and Business Men Generally.* 3rd ed. New York: Ronald, 1909.

Cootner, Paul H. "Comments on the Variation of Certain Speculative Prices." In *The Random Character of Stock Market Prices,* ed. Paul H. Cootner, 413–18. Cambridge, MA: MIT Press, 1964.

———. Introduction to *The Random Character of Stock Market Prices,* ed. Paul H. Cootner, 1–6. Cambridge, MA: MIT Press, 1964.

———. Preface to *The Random Character of Stock Market Prices,* ed. Paul H. Cootner, [unpaginated]. Cambridge, MA: MIT Press, 1964.

———, ed. *The Random Character of Stock Market Prices.* Cambridge, MA: MIT Press, 1964.

Copeland, Morris A. "Some Problems in the Theory of National Income." *Journal of Political Economy* 40, no. 1 (February 1932): 1–51.

———. "National Wealth and Income—an Interpretation." *Journal of the American Statistical Association* 30, no. 190 (June 1935): 377–86.

———. "Social Accounting for Money Flows." *Accounting Review* 24, no. 3 (1949): 254–64.

———. *A Study of Moneyflows in the United States.* New York: National Bureau of Economic Research, 1952.

———. "Institutional Economics and Model Analysis." *American Economic Review* 41, no. 2 (1951): 56–65. Reprinted in *Fact and Theory in Economics: The Testament of an Institutionalist; Collected Papers of Morris A. Copeland,* ed. Chandler Morse (Ithaca, NY: Cornell University Press, 1958), 54–66.

Copeland, Morris A., and Edwin M. Martin. "National Income and Capital Formation." *Journal of Political Economy* 47, no. 3 (June 1939): 398–407.

Coser, Lewis A. *Refugee Scholars in America: Their Impact and Their Experiences.* New Haven, CT: Yale University Press, 1984.

Cournot, Augustin. *Récherches sur les principes mathématic de la théorie des richesses.* Paris: Hachette, 1838. Translated by Nathaniel T. Bacon as *Researches into the Mathematical*

Principles of the Theory of Wealth, with a bibliography of mathematical economics by Irving Fisher (New York: Macmillan, 1897).

Cowing, Cedric B. *Populists, Plungers, and Progressives: A Social History of Stock and Commodity Speculation, 1890–1936.* Princeton, NJ: Princeton University Press, 1965.

Cowles, Alfred, III. "Can Stock Market Forecasters Forecast?" *Econometrica* 1, no. 3 (July 1933): 309–24.

———. *Common-Stock Indexes: 1871–1937.* Bloomington, IN: Principia, 1938.

Cowles, Alfred, III, and Herbert E. Jones. "Some A Posteriori Probabilities in Stock Market Action." *Econometrica* 5, no. 3 (July 1937): 280–94.

Cox, John C., Stephen A. Ross, and Mark Rubenstein. "Option Pricing: A Simplified Approach." *Journal of Financial Economics* 7, no. 3 (September 1979): 229–63.

Cramér, Harald. *Mathematical Methods of Statistics.* Princeton, NJ: Princeton University Press, 1946.

Craver, Earlene. "Patronage and the Directions of Research in Economics: The Rockefeller Foundation in Europe, 1924–1938." *Minerva* 24, nos. 2–3 (Summer–Autumn 1986): 205–22.

Crosthwaite, Paul, Peter Knight, and Nicky Marsh. *Show Me the Money: The Image of Finance, 1700 to the Present.* Manchester: Manchester University Press, 2014.

Damodaran, Aswath. *Damodaran on Valuation: Security Analysis for Investment and Corporate Finance.* 1994. 2nd ed. Hoboken, NJ: Wiley, 2006.

Dantzig, George B. "The Programming of Interdependent Activities: Mathematical Model." In *Activity Analysis of Production and Allocation: Proceedings of a Conference,* ed. Tjalling C. Koopmans, 19–32. New York: Wiley, 1951.

Davidson, Paul. *Financial Markets, Money, and the Real World.* Cheltenham: Edward Elgar, 2002.

Davis, Harold T. "Report of the Meeting of the Econometric Society, Colorado Springs, June 22–24, 1935." *Econometrica* 3, no. 4 (October 1935): 473–76.

———. *The Analysis of Economic Time Series.* Bloomington, IN: Principia, 1941.

———. *The Theory of Econometrics.* Bloomington, IN: Principia, 1941.

Davis, H. T., and W. F. C. Nelson. *Elementary Statistics with Applications to Economic Data.* Bloomington, IN: Principia, 1935.

Dean, Joel. *Capital Budgeting: Top-Management Policy on Plant, Equipment, and Product Development.* New York: Columbia University Press, 1951.

des Roches, Jérôme de Boyer, and Rebeca Gomez Betancourt. "American Quantity Theorists Prior to Irving Fisher's *Purchasing Power of Money.*" *Journal of the History of Economic Thought* 35, no. 2 (June 2013): 135–52.

De Vroey, Michel. "The History of Macroeconomics Viewed against the Background of the Marshall-Walras Divide." In "The IS-LM Model: Its Rise, Fall, and Strange Persistence," ed. Michel De Vroey and Kevin Hoover, *History of Political Economy* 36, suppl. (2004): 57–91.

———. *A History of Macroeconomics from Keynes to Lucas and Beyond.* Cambridge: Cambridge University Press, 2016.

De Vroey, Michel, and Kevin D. Hoover. "Introduction: Seven Decades of the IS-LM Model."

In *The IS-LM Model: Its Rise, Fall, and Strange Persistence,*" ed. Michel De Vroey and Kevin Hoover, 1–11. Durham, NC: Duke University Press, 2004.

Diamond, Peter, and Hannu Vartiainen, eds. *Behavioral Economics and Its Applications.* Princeton, NJ: Princeton University Press, 2007.

Dickinson, Arthur Lowes. "Profits of a Corporation: A Paper Read Before the Congress of Accountants at St. Louis, on September 27, 1904." N.p.: privately printed by Jones, Caesar, Dickinson, Wilmot & Co. and Price, Waterhouse & Co, 1904.

Dickinson, Arthur Lowes. "Profits of a Corporation." Cyclopedia of Commerce, Accountancy, Business Administration. Chicago: American Technical Society, 1909: 272–94.

Dimand, Robert W. "The Cowles Commission and Foundation on the Functioning of Financial Markets from Irving Fisher and Alfred Cowles to Harry Markowitz and James Tobin." *Révue d'histoire des sciences humaines* 1, no. 20 (2009): 79–100.

Dimand, Robert W., and William Veloce. "Alfred Cowles and Robert Rhea on the Predictability of Stock Prices." *Journal of Business Inquiry* 9, no. 1 (May 2010): 56–64.

Doob, J. L. *Stochastic Processes.* New York: Wiley, 1953.

Dore, Mohammed, Sukhamoy Chakravarty, and Richard Goodwin, eds. *John von Neumann and Modern Economics.* Oxford: Clarendon, 1989.

Dorfman, Joseph. *The Economic Mind in American Civilization.* 5 vols. New York: Viking, 1946–59.

Douglas, Frederick. "The Par Value of Stock." *Yale Law Review* 16, no. 4 (February 1907): 247–52.

Duménil, Gérard, and Dominique Lévy. "Pre-Keynesian Themes at Brookings." In *The Impact of Keynes on Economics in the Twentieth Century*, ed. Luigi L. Pasinetti and Berträm Schefold, 182–201. Aldershot: Edward Elgar, 1999.

Düppe, Till, and E. Roy Weintraub. "Siting the New Economic Science: The Cowles Commission's Activity Analysis Conference of June 1949." European Economics Historical Society Working Paper no. 40. June 2013. http://ehes.org/EHES_N040.pdf.

Dybvig, Philip H., and Stephen A. Ross. "Arbitrage." In *New Palgrave: A Dictionary of Economics* (4 vols.), ed. John Eatwell, Murray Milgate, and Peter Newman, 1:100–106. London: Macmillan, 1998.

Economic Report of the President: Together with the Annual Report of the Council of Economic Advisors. Washington, D.C: US Government Printing Office, 1962.

Edgeworth, F. Y. "Index Numbers." In *Dictionary of Political Economy,* ed. R. H. Inglis Palgrave, 384–87. London: Macmillan, 1900.

Eggertsson, Gauti B., and Paul Krugman. "Debt, Deleveraging, and the Liquidity Trap: A Fisher-Minsky-Koos Approach." *Quarterly Journal of Economics* 127, no. 3 (August 2012): 1469–1513.

Eichengreen, Barry. *Golden Fetters: The Gold Standard and the Great Depression, 1919–1939.* New York: Oxford University Press, 1992.

Eichengreen, Barry, and Jeffrey Sachs. "Exchange Rates and Economic Recovery in the 1930s." *Journal of Economic History* 45, no. 4 (December 1985): 925–46.

Elzinga, Kenneth G. "The Eleven Principles of Economics." *Southern Economic Journal* 58, no. 4 (April 1992): 861–79.

Engle, R. F., and C. W. J. Granger. *Long-Run Economic Relationships: Readings in Cointegration.* Oxford: Oxford University Press, 1991.

Engle, Robert F., ed. *ARCH: Selected Readings: Advanced Texts in Econometrics.* Oxford: Oxford University Press, 1995.

Epstein, R. J. *A History of Econometrics.* Amsterdam: North Holland, 1987.

Fabricant, Solomon. "Toward a Firmer Basis of Economic Policy: The Founding of the National Bureau of Economic Research." Working Paper. New York: National Bureau of Economic Research, 1984.

Fama, Eugene F. "Random Walks in Stock Market Prices." *Financial Analysts Journal* 21, no. 5 (September/October 1965): 55–59.

———. *Foundations of Finance: Portfolio Decisions and Securities Prices.* New York: Basic, 1976.

———. "Efficient Capital Markets II." *Journal of Finance* 46, no. 5 (December 1991): 1575–1617.

Fama, Eugene F., and Michael C. Jensen. "Separation of Ownership and Control." *Journal of Law and Economics* 26, no. 2 (June 1983): 301–25.

Fama, Eugene F., and Merton H. Miller. *The Theory of Finance.* Hinsdale, IL: Dryden, 1972.

Farmer, Roger E. A. *How the Economy Works: Confidence, Crashes and Self-Fulfilling Prophecies.* Oxford: Oxford University Press, 2010.

"Final Plenary Discussion." In *The Economy as an Evolving Complex System,* ed. Philip W. Anderson, Kenneth J. Arrow, and David Pines, 257–61. Boulder, CO: Westview, 1988.

The Financial Crisis Inquiry Report: Final Report of the National Commission on the Causes of the Financial and Economic Crisis in the United States. Official Government ed. Washington, DC: Financial Crisis Inquiry Commission, January 2011.

Fisher, Irving. "Mathematical Investigations in the Theory of Value and Prices." PhD diss., Yale University, 1891. A revised version was issued as "Mathematical Investigations in the Theory of Value and Prices," *Transactions of the Connecticut Academy of Arts and Sciences* 9 (1892): 1–124. The latter was reprinted as *Mathematical Investigations in the Theory of Value and Prices* (New Haven, CT: Yale University Press, 1902).

———. "Appreciation and Interest: A Study of the Influence of Monetary Appreciation and Depreciation on the Rate of Interest, with Applications to the Bimetallic Controversy and the Theory of Interest." *Publications of the American Economic Association* 11, no. 4 (July 1896): 1–100.

———. *Appreciation and Interest* (bound with *Mathematical Investigations*). Reprint, Old Chelsea Station, NY: Cosimo, 2007.

———. *Mathematical Investigations in the Theory of Value and Prices.* New Haven, CT: Yale University Press, 1902. Reprint, Old Chelsea Station, NY: Cosimo, 2007.

———. "Precedents for Defining Capital." *Quarterly Journal of Economics* 18, no. 3 (May 1904): 386–408.

———. *The Nature of Capital and Income.* New York: Macmillan, 1906.

———. *The Rate of Interest: Its Nature, Determination, and Relation to Economic Phenomena.* New York: Macmillan, 1907.

———. *The Purchasing Power of Money: Its Determination and Relation to Credit Interest and Crises.* New York: Macmillan, 1911.

———. "Recent Changes in Price Levels and Their Causes." *American Economic Review* 1, no. 2 (April 1911): 37–45.

———. "The Best Form of Index Number." *Quarterly Publication of the American Statistical Association*, n.s., 17, no. 133 (March 1921): 533–37.

———. *The Making of Index Numbers: A Study of Their Varieties, Tests, and Reliability.* Boston: Houghton Mifflin, 1922.

———. *The Stock Market Crash—and After.* New York: Macmillan, 1930.

———. *The Theory of Interest: As Determined by Impatience to Spend Income and Opportunity to Invest It.* New York: Macmillan, 1930. Reprint, Mansfield Centre, CT: Maritime, 2012.

———. "Mathematical Method in the Social Sciences." *Econometrica* 9, nos. 3–4 (July–October 1941): 185–97.

Fisher, Lawrence, and Roman Weil. "Coping with Risk of Interest-Rate Fluctuations: Returns to Bondholders from Naïve and Optimal Strategies." *Journal of Business* 44, no. 4 (October 1971): 408–31.

"Fisher's Unpublished Annotations." In *The Works of Irving Fisher* (14 vols.), ed. William J. Barber, 1:171–75. London: Pickering & Chatto, 1997.

Fisher, R. A. "On the Mathematical Foundations of Theoretical Statistics." *Philosophical Transactions of the Royal Society of London* 222 (1922): 309–68.

———. *Statistical Methods for Research Workers.* Edinburgh: Oliver & Boyd, 1925.

Fleischman, Richard K., and Thomas N. Tyson. "Cost Accounting during the Industrial Revolution: The Present State of Historical Knowledge." *Economic History Review* 46, no. 3 (1993): 503–17.

Fligstein, Neil. *The Transformation of Corporate Control.* Cambridge, MA: Harvard University Press, 1990.

Fox, Justin. *The Myth of the Rational Market: A History of Risk, Reward, and Delusion on Wall Street.* New York: HarperCollins, 2009.

Frankel, Jeffrey A., and Peter R. Orszag. Introduction to *American Economic Policy in the 1990s*, ed. Jeffrey A. Frankel and Peter R. Orszag, 1–16. Cambridge, MA: MIT Press, 2002.

Freeman, Harold A. *Industrial Statistics: Statistical Technique Applied to Problems in Industrial Research and Quality Control.* New York: Wiley, 1942.

Freixas, Xavier, Luc Laeven, and José-Luis Peydró. *Systemic Risk, Crises, and Macroprudential Regulation.* Cambridge, MA: MIT Press, 2015.

Frenyear, T. C. "The Ethics of Stock Watering." *Annals of the American Academy of Political and Social Science* 8 (November 1896): 77–82.

Friedman, Milton. "The Methodology of Positive Economics." In *Essays in Positive Economics*, 3–34. Chicago: University of Chicago Press, 1953.

———. "The Quantity Theory of Money: A Restatement." In *Studies in the Quantity Theory of Money*, ed. Milton Friedman, 3–21. Chicago: University of Chicago Press, 1956.

———. "The Role of Monetary Policy." *American Economic Review* 58, no. 1 (March 1968): 1–17.

———. *Money Mischief: Episodes in Monetary History.* New York: Harcourt Brace, 1994.

Friedman, Milton, and Anna Jacobson Schwartz. *A Monetary History of the United States, 1867–1960.* Princeton, NJ: Princeton University Press, 1963.

———. *Monetary Trends in the United States and the United Kingdom: Their Relation to Income, Prices, and Interest Rates, 1867–1975.* Chicago: University of Chicago Press, 1982.

Frisch, Ragnar. "Propagation Problems and Impulse Problems in Dynamic Economics." In *The Foundations of Econometric Analysis,* ed. David F. Hendry and Mary S. Morgan, 333–46. Cambridge: Cambridge University Press, 1995. Reprinted (abridged) from *Economic Essays in Honour of Gustav Cassel,* 171–205 (London: Allen & Unwin, 1933).

———. *Statistical Confluence Analysis by Means of Complete Regression Systems.* Publication no. 5. Oslo: Universitetets Økonomiske Instituut, 1934.

———. "Annual Survey of General Economic Theory: The Problem of Index Numbers." *Econometrica* 4, no. 1 (January 1936): 1–38.

———. *A Dynamic Approach to Economic Theory: The Yale Lectures of Ragnar Frisch.* Edited by Olav Bjerkhold and Duo Qin. London: Routledge, 2013.

Frydman, Roman, and Michael D. Goldberg. *Imperfect Knowledge Economics: Exchange Rates and Risk.* Princeton, NJ: Princeton University Press, 2007.

Frydman, Roman, and Edmund S. Phelps. Introduction to *Individual Forecasting and Aggregate Outcomes: "Rational Expectations" Examined,* ed. Roman Frydman and Edmund S. Phelps, 1–30. Cambridge: Cambridge University Press, 1983.

———, eds. *Rethinking Expectations: The Way Forward for Macroeconomics.* Princeton, NJ: Princeton University Press, 2013.

Fuhrer, Jeff, Yolanda K. Kodrzycki, Jane Sneddon Little, and Giovanni P. Olivei, eds. *Understanding Inflation and the Implications for Monetary Policy: A Phillips Curve Retrospective.* Cambridge, MA: MIT Press, 2009.

Fujita, Masahisa, Paul Krugman, and Anthony J. Venables. *The Spatial Economy: Cities, Regions, and International Trade.* Cambridge, MA: MIT Press, 1999.

Furner, Mary O. *Advocacy and Objectivity: A Crisis in the Professionalization of American Social Science, 1865–1905.* Lexington: University Press of Kentucky, 1975.

Galbraith, James K. "James K. Galbraith Takes on Thomas Piketty's *Capital in the Twenty-First Century.*" *Dissent,* April 21, 2014. http://www.alternet.org/economy/james-k-galbraith-takes-thomas-pikettys-capital-twenty-first-century.

Galbraith, John K. *The Great Crash, 1929.* Boston: Houghton Mifflin, 1954.

Gethard, Gregory. "Falling Giant: A Case Study of AIG." Investopedia. Updated August 31, 2016. http://www.investopedia.com/articles/economics/09/american-investment-group-aig-bailout.asp.

Gibbs, J. Willard. "Graphic Methods in the Thermodynamics of Fluids." In *Scientific Papers of J. Willard Gibbs* (2 vols.), ed. H. A. Bumstead and R. G. Van Name, 1:1–32. London: Longmans Green, 1906.

———. "A Method of Geometrical Representation of the Thermodynamic Properties of Substances by Means of Surfaces." In *Scientific Papers of J. Willard Gibbs* (2 vols.), ed. H. A. Bumstead and R. G. Van Name, 1:33–54. London: Longmans Green, 1906.

———. *On the Equilibrium of Heterogeneous Substances.* In *Scientific Papers of J. Willard Gibbs* (2 vols.), ed. H. A. Bumstead and R. G. Van Name, 1:55–353. London: Longmans Green, 1906.

Gilbert, Milton, and George Jaszi. "National Product and Income Statistics as an Aid in Economic Problems." *Dun's Review* 52, no. 2190 (February 1944): 9–11, 30–38. Reprinted in

Readings in the Theory of Income Distribution, ed. William Fellner and Bernard F. Haley (1944; reprint, Homewood, IL: Richard D. Irwin, 1951), 3–43.

Gilbert, Milton, George Jaszi, Edward F. Denison, and Charles Schwartz. "Objectives of National Income Measurement: A Reply to Professor Kuznets." *Review of Economics and Statistics* 30, no. 3 (August 1948): 179–95.

Gilbert, Milton, Hans Staehle, W. S. Woytinsky, and Simon Kuznets. "National Product, War and Prewar: Some Comments on Professor Kuznets' Study and a Reply by Professor Kuznets." *Review of Economics and Statistics* 26, no. 3 (August 1944): 109–35.

Gintis, Herbert. *The Bounds of Reason: Game Theory and the Unification of the Behavioral Sciences.* Princeton, NJ: Princeton University Press, 2009.

Giocoli, Nicola. *Modeling Rational Agents: From Interwar Economics to Early Modern Game Theory.* Cheltenham: Edward Elgar, 2003.

Girton, Lance, and Don Roper. "J. Laurence Laughlin and the Quantity Theory of Money." International Finance Discussion Paper 103. Washington, DC: Board of Governors of the Federal Reserve System, March 1977. Reprinted as "J. Laurence Laughlin and the Quantity Theory of Money," *Journal of Political Economy* 86, no. 4 (August 1978): 599–625. Also available at http://www.federalreserve.gov/pubs/ifdp/1977/103/ifdp103.pdf.

Gitelman, Lisa, ed. *"Raw Data" Is an Oxymoron.* Cambridge, MA: MIT Press, 2013.

Godley, Wynne, and Marc Lavoie. *Monetary Economics: An Integrated Approach to Credit, Money, Income, Production and Wealth.* Basingstoke: Palgrave Macmillan, 2006.

Goetzmann, William N. *Money Changes Everything: How Finance Made Civilization Possible.* Princeton, NJ: Princeton University Press, 2016.

Goetzmann, William N., and Roger G. Ibbotson. *The Equity Risk Premium: Essays and Explorations.* New York: Oxford University Press, 2004.

———. "History and the Equity Risk Premium." Working Paper no. 05–04. New Haven, CT: International Center for Finance, Yale School of Management, April 2005.

Goldsmith, Raymond W. *Financial Intermediaries in the American Economy since 1900.* Princeton, NJ: Princeton University Press, 1958.

Goodfriend, Martin, and Robert G. King. "The New Neoclassical Synthesis and the Role of Monetary Policy." In *NBER Macroeconomics Annual* (vol. 12), ed. Ben S. Bernanke and Julio Rosenberg, 231–96. Cambridge, MA: MIT Press, 1997.

Goodwin, Craufurd D. "The Patrons of Economics in a Time of Transformation." In "From Interwar Pluralism to Postwar Neoclassicism," ed. Mary S. Morgan and Malcolm Rutherford, *History of Political Economy* 30, suppl. (1998): 53–81.

Gordon, M. J. "Dividends, Earnings, and Stock Prices." *Review of Economics and Statistics* 41, no. 2 (May 1959): 99–105.

Gordon, Robert J., and Robert Krenn. *The End of the Great Depression, 1939–41: Fiscal Multipliers, Capacity Constraints, and Policy Contributions.* February 14, 2014; http://economics.weinberg.northwestern.edu/robert-gordon/files/RescPapers/EndGreatDepression.pdf.

Graham, Benjamin, and David L. Dodd. *Security Analysis.* New York: McGraw-Hill, 1934. 6th ed. Updated with a new preface and new commentary. New York: McGraw-Hill, 2009.

Graham, Willard J. "Some Observations on the Nature of Income, Generally Accepted Accounting Principles, and Financial Reporting." *Law and Contemporary Problems* 30, no. 4 (Autumn 1965): 652–73.

Grant, James. *Money of the Mind: Borrowing and Lending in America from the Civil War to Michael Milken.* New York: Farrar, Straus, Giroux, 1994.

Greenwood, Robin, and David Scharfstein. "The Growth of Finance." *Journal of Economic Perspectives* 27, no. 2 (Spring 2013): 3–28.

Grier, David Alan. *When Computers Were Human.* Princeton, NJ: Princeton University Press, 2005.

Gries, John M., and James S. Taylor. *How to Own Your Own Home: A Handbook for Prospective Homeowners.* Washington, DC: US Government Printing Office, 1923.

Gurley, John G., and Edward S. Shaw. "Reply" [to Culbertson]. *American Economic Review* 48, no. 1 (March 1958): 132–38.

———. *Money in a Theory of Finance.* Washington, DC: Brookings Institution, 1960.

———. "Money." In *American Economic History*, ed. Seymour E. Harris, 101–29. New York: McGraw-Hill (1961).

Haavelmo, Trygve. "The Statistical Implications of a System of Simultaneous Equations." *Econometrica* 11, no. 1 (January 1943): 1–12.

———. "The Probability Approach in Econometrics." *Econometrica* 12, suppl. (July 1944): iii–vi, 1–115.

Hacker, Jacob S. *The Great Risk Shift: The Assault on American Jobs, Families, Health Care, and Retirement and How You Can Fight Back.* New York: Oxford University Press, 2006.

Hagemann, Harald. "European Émigrés and the 'Americanization' of Economics." *European Journal of the History of Economic Thought* 18, no. 5 (December 2011): 643–71.

Hagemann, Harald, and Claus-Dieter Krohn, eds. *Biographisches Handbuch der deutschsprachigen wirtschaftswissenschaftlichen Emigration nach 1933.* 2 vols. Munich: K. G. Saur, 1999.

Hahn, F. H., and R. C. O. Matthews. "The Theory of Economic Growth: A Survey." *Economic Journal* 74, no. 296 (December 1964): 779–902.

Hake, Eric R. "The Stock Watering Debate: More Light, Less Heat." *Journal of Economic Issues* 35, no. 2 (June 2001): 423–30.

Hald, Anders. *A History of Mathematical Statistics from 1750 to 1930.* New York: Wiley, 1998.

Hammond, J. Daniel. *Theory and Measurement: Causality Issues in Milton Friedman's Monetary Economics.* Cambridge: Cambridge University Press, 1996.

Hansen, Alvin H., Seymour E. Harris, and John M. Keynes. *A Guide to Keynes.* New York: McGraw-Hill, 1979.

Harcourt, G. C. *Some Cambridge Controversies in the Theory of Capital.* Cambridge: Cambridge University Press, 1972.

Harrison, J. Michael, and David M. Kreps. "Martingales and Arbitrage in Multiperiod Securities Markets." *Journal of Economic Theory* 20, no. 3 (1979): 381–408.

Hatfield, Henry Rand. *Modern Accounting: Its Principles and Some of Its Problems.* New York: Appleton, 1909. Reprint, New York: Appleton, 1915.

———. "Some Neglected Phases of Accounting." *Electric Railway Journal* 46, no. 16 (October 15, 1915): 799–802.

Heaton, Herbert. *A Scholar in Action: Edwin F. Gay.* Cambridge, MA: Harvard University Press, 1952.

Hendry, David F., and Mary S. Morgan, eds. *The Foundations of Econometric Analysis.* Cambridge: Cambridge University Press, 1995.

———. Introduction to *The Foundations of Econometric Analysis,* ed. David F. Hendry and Mary S. Morgan, 1–82. Cambridge: Cambridge University Press, 1995.

Hetzel, Robert L. "The Treasury–Federal Reserve Accord to the Mid-1960s." Federal Reserve History, November 2013. http://www.federalreservehistory.org/Period/Essay/12.

Hicks, J. R. "A Suggestion for Simplifying the Theory of Money." *Economica,* n.s., 2, no. 5 (February 1935): 1–19.

———. "Mr. Keynes and the 'Classics': A Suggested Interpretation." *Econometrica* 5, no. 2 (April 1937): 147–59.

Hirshleifer, J., and John G. Riley. "The Analytics of Uncertainty and Information—an Expository Survey." *Journal of Economic Literature* 17, no. 4 (December 1979): 1375–1421.

Hobson, J. A. *Work and Wealth: A Human Valuation.* New York: Macmillan, 1914.

Hochfelder, David. "'Where the Common People Could Speculate': The Ticker, Bucket Shops, and the Origins of Popular Participation in Financial Markets, 1880–1920." *Journal of American History* 93, no. 2 (September 2006): 335–58.

Hoover, Kevin D. *The New Classical Macroeconomics: A Sceptical Inquiry.* Oxford: Blackwell, 1988.

Hosking, Patrick, Miles Costello, and Marcus Leroux. "Dow Dives as Federal Reserve Lines Up $75bn loan for AIG." *The Times* (London), September 16, 2008.

Hotelling, Harold. Review of *Statistical Methods for Research Workers,* by Irving Fisher. *Journal of the American Statistical Association* 22, no. 159 (September 1927): 411–12.

———. "The Place of Statistics in the University." In *Proceedings of the Berkeley Symposium on Mathematical Statistics and Probability,* ed. Jerzy Neyman, 21–40. Berkeley: University of California Press, 1949.

Houston, D. F., E. W. Kemmerer, Joseph French Johnson, Murray S. Wildman, T. N. Carver, F. W. Taussig, Ralph H. Hess, J. Laurence Laughlin, and Irving Fisher. "Money and Prices: Discussion." *American Economic Review* 1, no. 2 (April 2011): 46–70.

Howey, Richard S. "The Origins of Marginalism." In *The Marginal Revolution in Economics: Interpretation and Evaluation,* ed. R. D. Collison Black, A. W. Coats, and Craufurd D. W. Goodwin, 15–36. Durham, NC: Duke University Press, 1973.

Jaszi, George. "The Conceptual Basis of the Accounts: A Reexamination." In *A Critique of the United States Income and Product Accounts* (*Studies in Income and Wealth,* vol. 22), 13–127. Princeton, NJ: Princeton University Press, 1958.

Jenks, Jeremiah Whipple, and Walter F. Clark. *The Trust Problem.* 1900. 4th ed. New York: Doubleday, 1925.

Jensen, Michael C. "Agency Cost of Free Cash Flow, Corporate Finance, and Takeovers." *American Economic Review* 76, no. 2 (May 1986): 223–29.

Jensen, Michael C., Fischer Black, and Myron S. Scholes. "The Capital Asset Pricing Model: Some Empirical Tests." Available at SSRN: https://ssrn.com/abstract=908569.

Jensen, Michael C., and William H. Meckling. "Theory of the Firm: Managerial Behavior,

Agency Costs and Ownership Structure." *Journal of Financial Economics* 3, no. 4 (October 1976): 305–60.

Jevons, W. Stanley. *The Theory of Political Economy.* London: Macmillan, 1871.

Jones, Byrd L. "The Role of Keynesians in Wartime Policy and Postwar Planning, 1940–1946." *American Economic Review* 62, nos. 1–2 (March 1972): 125–33.

Jorgenson, Dale. "Technology in Growth Theory." In *Technology and Growth: Conference Proceedings,* ed. Jeffrey C. Fuhrer and Jane Sneddon Little, 45–77. Boston: Federal Reserve Bank of Boston, 1996.

Joseph, Richard J. *The Origins of the American Income Tax: The Revenue Act of 1894 and Its Aftermath.* Syracuse, NY: Syracuse University Press, 2004.

Joshi, Mark S. *The Concepts and Practice of Mathematical Science.* 2003. 2nd ed. Cambridge: Cambridge University Press, 2008.

Jovanovic, Franck. "The Construction of the Canonical History of Financial Economics." *History of Political Economy* 40, no. 2 (2008): 213–42.

Jovanovic, Franck, and Philippe Le Gall. "Does God Practice a Random Walk? The 'Financial Physics' of a Nineteenth-Century Forerunner, Jules Regnault." *European Journal of the History of Economic Thought* 8, no. 3 (Autumn 2001): 332–62.

Kahn, Irving, and Robert D. Milne. "Benjamin Graham: The Father of Financial Analysis." Occasional Paper no. 5. Charlottesville, VA: Financial Analysts Research Foundation, 1977.

Kahneman, Daniel, and Amos Tversky. "Prospect Theory: An Analysis of Decision under Risk." *Econometrica* 47, no. 2 (March 1979): 263–91.

———, eds. *Choices, Values, and Frames.* New York: Russell Sage Foundation, 2000.

Kahneman, Daniel, Paul Slovic, and Amos Tversky, eds. *Judgment under Uncertainty: Heuristics and Biases.* Cambridge: Cambridge University Press, 1982.

Kaldor, Nicholas. "Capital Accumulation and Economic Growth." In *The Theory of Capital,* ed. Friedrich A. Lutz and D. C. Hague, 177–222. London: Macmillan, 1961.

Kane, Richard. "Measures and Motivations: U.S. National Income and Product Estimates during the Great Depression and World War II." February 2012. Munich Personal RePEc Archive, http://mpra.ub.uni-muenchen.de/44336.

Kapuria-Foreman, Vibha, and Mark Perlman. "An Economic Historian's Economist: Remembering Simon Kuznets." *Economic Journal* 105, no. 433 (November 1995): 1524–47.

Katz, Alyssa. *Our Lot: How Real Estate Came to Own Us.* New York: Bloomsbury, 2009.

Kavesh, Robert. "The American Finance Association: 1939–1969." *Journal of Finance* 25, no. 1 (March 1970): 1–17.

Kemmerer, Edwin Walter. *Money and Credit Instruments in Their Relation to General Prices.* New York: H. Holt, 1907.

Kendall, M. G. "Studies in the History of Probability and Statistics, XXI: The Early History of Index Numbers." *Review of the International Statistical Institute* 37, no. 1 (1969): 1–12.

Keynes, John Maynard. *A Treatise on Probability.* London: Macmillan, 1921.

———. *The General Theory of Employment, Interest and Money.* New York: Harcourt Brace, 1936.

———. "Professor Tinbergen's Method." In *The Foundations of Econometric Analysis*, ed. David F. Hendry and Mary S. Morgan. Cambridge: Cambridge University Press, 1995. Reprinted (abridged) from *Economic Journal* 49, no. 195 (September 1939): 558–77.

———. *How to Pay for the War: A Radical Plan for the Chancellor of the Exchequer*. New York: Harcourt Brace, 1940.

Khurana, Rakesh. *From Higher Aims to Hired Hands: The Social Transformation of American Business Schools and the Unfulfilled Promise of Management as a Profession*. Princeton, NJ: Princeton University Press, 2007.

Kimura, Yuichi. "The 'Robbins Circle' of the London School of Economics and Political Science: The Liberalism Group's Counterattack of Laissez-Faire against Cambridge." *Journal of Saitama University Faculty of Education* 59, no. 2 (September 2010): 119–34.

Kindleberger, Charles P. *Manias, Panics, and Crashes: A History of Financial Crises*. New York: Basic, 1978.

King, Thomas A. *More Than a Numbers Game: A Brief History of Accounting*. Hoboken, NJ: Wiley, 2006.

Klaes, Matthias. "The History of the Concept of Transaction Costs: Neglected Aspects." *Journal of the History of Economic Thought* 22, no. 2 (2000): 191–216.

Klein, Judy L. *Statistical Visions in Time: A History of Time Series Analysis, 1662–1938*. Cambridge: Cambridge University Press, 1997.

———. "The Cold War Hot House for Modeling Strategies at the Carnegie Institute of Technology." Working Paper no. 19. New York: Institute for New Economic Thinking, October 2015.

Klein, Lawrence R. "Disturbances to the International Economy." Paper presented at the Federal Reserve of Boston conference "After the Phillips Curve: Persistence of High Inflation and High Unemployment," Edgartown, MA, June 1978.

Klein, L. R., and A. S. Goldberger. *An Econometric Model of the United States, 1929–1952*. Amsterdam: North-Holland, 1955.

Knight, Frank H. *Risk, Uncertainty and Profit*. 1921. Reprint, Chicago: University of Chicago Press, 1971.

———. "The Limitations of Scientific Method in Economics." In *The Trend of Economics*, ed. Rexford Guy Tugwell, 229–67. New York: Knopf, 1924.

Kogut, Bruce, and Hugh Patrick. "Executive Summary." In "The Quantitative Revolution and the Crisis: How Have Quantitative Financial Models Been Used and Misused?" Columbia Business School, December 4, 2009. http://markleehunter.free.fr/documents/quant_crisis.pdf.

Kohli, Martin. "Leontief and the U.S. Bureau of Labor Statistics, 1941–54: Developing a Framework for Measurement." *History of Political Economy* 33, suppl. (2001): 199–212.

Koopmans, Tjalling C. "Measurement without Theory." *Review of Economics and Statistics* 29, no. 3 (August 1947): 161–72.

———. "Analysis of Production as an Efficient Combination of Activities." In *Activity Analysis of Production and Allocation: Proceedings of a Conference*, ed. Tjalling C. Koopmans, 33–97. New York: Wiley, 1951.

———. Introduction to *Activity Analysis of Production and Allocation: Proceedings of a Conference*, ed. Tjalling C. Koopmans, 1–12. New York: Wiley, 1951.

Kornhauser, Marjorie E. "Corporate Regulation and the Origins of the Corporate Income Tax." *Indiana Law Journal* 66, no. 53 (1990–91): 62–68.

Kreps, David M. *Microeconomic Foundations I: Choices and Competitive Markets.* Princeton, NJ: Princeton University Press, 2013.

Krippner, Greta R. *Capitalizing on Crisis: The Political Origins of the Rise of Finance.* Cambridge, MA: Harvard University Press, 2011.

Krohn, Claus-Dieter. "An Overlooked Chapter of Economic Thought: The 'New School's' Effort to Salvage Weimar's Economy." *Social Research* 50, no. 2 (Summer 1983): 452–68.

———. *Intellectuals in Exile: Refugee Scholars and the New School for Social Research.* Amherst: University of Massachusetts Press, 1993.

———. "Dismissal and Emigration of German-Speaking Economists after 1933." In *Forced Migration and Scientific Change: Émigré German-Speaking Scientists and Scholars after 1933,* ed. Mitchell G. Ash and Alfons Söllner, 175–97. Cambridge: Cambridge University Press, 1996.

Kuznets, Simon. *National Income, 1929–1932.* Report prepared for the Senate Finance Committee. Washington, DC: US Government Printing Office, 1934.

———. *National Product, War and Prewar.* Occasional Paper 17. New York: National Bureau of Economic Research, 1944.

———. "National Income." In *Encyclopedia of the Social Sciences* (15 vols.), 11:205–24. New York: Macmillan, 1933). Reprinted in *Readings in the Theory of Income Distribution: Selected by a Committee of the American Economic Association* (Philadelphia: Blakiston, 1946), 3–43.

———. *National Income: A Summary of Findings.* New York: National Bureau of Economic Research, 1946.

———. "National Income: A New Version." *Review of Economics and Statistics* 30, no. 3 (August 1948): 151–79.

Labonte, Marc, and Mindy Levit. "CRS Report for Congress: Financing Issues and Economic Effects of American Wars." Congressional Research Service Report RL31176. Updated July 28, 2008. https://www.fas.org/sgp/crs/natsec/RL31176.pdf.

Lagos, Richard. "Inside and Outside Money." Staff Report 374. Minneapolis: Federal Reserve Bank of Minneapolis, May 2006. https://www.minneapolisfed.org/research/sr/sr374 .pdf. This report was prepared for the *New Palgrave Dictionary of Economics* (2nd ed.), ed. Steven N. Durlauf and Lawrence E. Blum. Manchester: Palgrave Macmillan, 2008.

Laidler, David. *Fabricating the Keynesian Revolution: Studies of the Inter-War Literature on Money, the Cycle, and Unemployment.* Cambridge: Cambridge University Press, 1999.

Lamoreaux, Naomi. *The Great Merger Movement in American Business, 1895–1904.* Cambridge: Cambridge University Press, 1985.

Langley, Paul. *The Everyday Life of Global Finance: Saving and Borrowing in Anglo-America.* Oxford: Oxford University Press, 2008.

Laughlin, J. Laurence. "Causes of the Changes in Prices since 1896." *American Economic Review* 1, no. 2 (April 1911): 26–36.

Lavoie, Marc. *Post-Keynesian Economics: New Foundations.* Cheltenham: Edward Elgar, 2015.

Lavoie, Marc, and Gennaro Zezza, eds. *The Stock-Flow Consistent Approach: Selected Writings of Wynne Godley.* New York: Palgrave Macmillan, 2011.

Lawson, Tony. *Reorienting Economics.* New York: Routledge, 2003.

———. "The Current Economic Crisis: Its Nature and the Course of Academic Economics." *Cambridge Journal of Economics* 33, no. 4 (2009): 759–88.

———. "What Is This 'School' Called Neoclassical Economics?" *Cambridge Journal of Economics* 37, no. 5 (2013): 947–83.

Leeson, Robert. "The Eclipse of the Goal of Zero Inflation." *History of Political Economy* 29, no. 3 (Fall 1997): 445–96.

Leff, Mark H. *The Limits of Symbolic Reform: The New Deal and Taxation, 1933–1939.* Cambridge: Cambridge University Press, 1984.

Lehmann, E. L. "The Fisher, Neyman-Pearson Theories of Testing Hypotheses: One Theory or Two?" *Journal of the American Statistical Association* 88, no. 424 (December 1993): 1242–49.

———. *Fisher, Neyman, and the Creation of Classical Statistics.* New York: Springer Science & Business, 2011.

Leibowitz, Martin L., and Sidney Homer. *Inside the Yield Book: The Classic That Created the Science of Bond Analysis.* Princeton, NJ: Bloomberg, 2004.

Leijonhufvud, Axel. *On Keynesian Economics and the Economics of Keynes: A Study in Monetary Theory.* New York: Oxford University Press, 1968.

Leonard, Thomas C. "'A Certain Rude Honesty': John Bates Clark as a Pioneering Neoclassical Economist." *History of Political Economy* 35, no. 3 (Fall 2003): 521–58.

Leontief, Wassily. *The Structure of the American Economy, 1919–1939: An Empirical Application of Equilibrium Analysis.* New York: Oxford University Press, 1951.

Lindquist, E. F. *Statistical Analysis in Educational Research.* Boston: Houghton Mifflin, 1940.

LiPuma, Edward, and Benjamin Lee. *Financial Derivatives and the Globalization of Risk.* Durham, NC: Duke University Press, 2004.

Livingston, James. *Origins of the Federal Reserve System: Money, Class, and Corporate Capitalism, 1890–1913.* Ithaca, NY: Cornell University Press, 1986.

Lo, Andrew W. "Financial Econometrics." October 2006. http://papers.ssrn.com/s013/papers.cfm?abstract_id=991805. This is the introduction to the first volume of the forthcoming Edward Elgar series The International Library of Financial Economics.

———. "Efficient Markets Hypothesis." n.d. http://papers.ssrn.com/s013/papers.cfm?abstract_id=991509. This report was prepared for the *New Palgrave Dictionary of Economics* (2nd ed.), ed. Steven N. Durlauf and Lawrence E. Blum. Manchester: Palgrave Macmillan, 2008.

Lothian, James R. "Milton Friedman's Monetary Economics and the Quantity-Theory Tradition." *Journal of International Money and Finance* 28, no. 7 (November 2009): 1086–96.

Louçã, Francisco. *The Years of High Econometrics: A Short History of the Generation That Reinvented Economics.* New York: Routledge, 2007.

Lucas, Robert E., Jr. "Expectations and the Neutrality of Money." 1972. In *Studies in Business Cycle Theory,* 66–89. Cambridge, MA: MIT Press, 1981.

———. "An Equilibrium Model of the Business Cycle." 1975. In *Studies in Business Cycle Theory,* 179–214. Cambridge, MA: MIT Press, 1981.

———. "Understanding Business Cycles." 1977. In *Studies in Business Cycle Theory,* 215–39. Cambridge, MA: MIT Press, 1981.

Lucas, Robert E., Jr., and Edward C. Prescott. "Investment under Uncertainty." *Econometrica* 39, no. 5 (September 1971): 659–81.

Lucas, Robert E., Jr., and Thomas J. Sargent. "After Keynesian Macroeconomics." In *Rational Expectations and Econometric Practice,* ed. Robert E. Lucas Jr. and Thomas J. Sargent, 295–320. Minneapolis: University of Minnesota Press, 1981.

———, eds. *Rational Expectations and Econometric Practice.* 2 vols. Minneapolis: University of Minnesota Press, 1981.

Lundberg, Filip. "Approximations of the Probability Function/Reinsurance of Collective Risks" (in Swedish). PhD diss., University of Uppsala, 1903.

Macaulay, Frederick R. *Some Theoretical Problems Suggested by the Movements of Interest Rates, Bond Yields and Stock Prices in the United States since 1856.* New York: National Bureau of Economic Research, 1938.

MacChesney, Brunson. "The Securities Act and the Promoter." *California Law Review* 25, no. 1 (September 1936): 66–79.

Macintosh, John C. C. "The Issues, Effects and Consequences of the Berle-Dodd Debate, 1931–1932." *Accounting, Organizations and Society* 24, no. 2 (February 1999): 139–53.

MacKenzie, Donald. *An Engine, Not a Camera: How Financial Models Shape Markets.* Cambridge, MA: MIT Press, 2006.

Magret, Arthur W. "Morgenstern on the Methodology of Economic Forecasting." In *The Foundations of Economic Analysis,* ed. David F. Hendry and Mary S. Morgan, 180–90. Cambridge: Cambridge University Press, 1995. Reprinted (abridged) from *Journal of Political Economy* 37, no. 3 (June 1929): 312–39.

Makower, Helen. "The Theory of Value in the Capital Market." PhD diss., London School of Economics, 1937.

Makower, H., and J. Marschak. "Assets, Prices and Monetary Theory." *Economica,* n.s., 5, no. 19 (August 1938): 261–88.

Malkiel, Burton. *A Random Walk Down Wall Street.* New York: Norton, 1973.

———. "Efficient Market Hypothesis." In *The New Palgrave: A Dictionary of Economics* (4 vols.), ed. John Eatwell, Murray Milgate, and Peter Newman, 2:120–23. London: Palgrave Macmillan, 1998.

Mandelbrot, Benoit. "The Variation of Certain Speculative Prices." 1963. In *The Random Character of Stock Market Prices,* ed. Paul H. Cootner, 369–412. Cambridge, MA: MIT Press, 1964.

Mankiw, N. Gregory, and David Romer. Introduction to *New Keynesian Economics,* vol. 1, *Imperfect Competition and Sticky Prices,* ed. N. Gregory Mankiw and David Romer, 1–26. Cambridge, MA: MIT Press, 1991.

Markowitz, Harry. "Portfolio Selection." *Journal of Finance* 7, no. 1 (March 1952): 77–91.

Marschak, J. "Money and the Theory of Assets." *Econometrica* 6, no. 4 (October 1938): 311–25.

———. "Neumann's and Morgenstern's New Approach to Static Economics." *Journal of Political Economy* 54, no. 2 (April 1946): 97–115.

———. "Measurable Utility and the Theory of Assets." Paper presented at the meeting of the Econometric Society, University of Wisconsin, Madison, September 7–10, 1948. Subsequently published as "Rational Behavior, Uncertain Prospects, and Measurable Utility" (see below).

———. "Rational Behavior, Uncertain Prospects, and Measurable Utility." *Econometrica* 18, no. 2 (April 1950): 111–41.

Marshall, John F., and Vipul K. Bansal. *Financial Engineering: A Complete Guide to Financial Innovation.* New York: New York Institute of Finance, 1992.

Mayer, Thomas. *The Structure of Monetarism.* New York: Norton, 1978.

———. "The Influence of Friedman's Methodological Essay." In *The Methodology of Positive Economics: Reflections on the Milton Friedman Legacy,* ed. Uskali Mäki, 119–42. Cambridge: Cambridge University Press, 2009.

Mayhew, Anne. "Copeland on Money as Electricity." *Real-World Economics Review,* no. 53 (July 2010): 213–22.

McKean, Henry P., Jr. "Appendix: A Free Boundary Problem for the Heat Equation Arising from a Problem of Mathematical Economics." *Industrial Management Review* 6, no. 2 (Spring 1965): 32–39.

McLaren, N. Loyall. *Annual Reports to Stockholders: Their Preparation and Interpretation.* New York: Ronald, 1947.

McLean, Paula A., and D. G. Brian Jones. "Edward Sherwood Mead (1874–1956)." *European Business Review* 19, no. 2 (2007): 118–28.

McNees, Steven K. "An Empirical Assessment of 'New Theories' of Inflation and Unemployment." Paper presented at the Federal Reserve Bank of Boston conference "After the Phillips Curve: Persistence of High Inflation and High Unemployment," Edgartown, MA, June 1978. Subsequently published in *After the Phillips Curve: Persistence of High Inflation and High Unemployment: Proceedings of a Conference Held at Edgartown, Massachusetts, June, 1978,* 29–49. Boston: Federal Reserve Bank of Boston, Public Information Centre, 1978.

Meade, Edward S. *Trust Finance: A Study of the Genesis, Organization, and Management of Industrial Corporations.* New York: D. Appleton, 1903.

"'Measurement without Theory' Debate." In *The Foundations of Economic Analysis,* ed. David F. Hendry and Mary S. Morgan, 491–524. Cambridge: Cambridge University Press, 1995.

Means, Gardiner C. "The Diffusion of Stock Ownership in the United States." *Quarterly Journal of Economics* 44, no. 4 (August 1930): 561–600.

Melamed, Leo. "The International Money Market." In *The Merits of Flexible Exchange Rates: An Anthology,* ed. Leo Melamed, 417–27. Fairfax, VA: George Mason University Press, 1988.

Mehrling, Perry. *The Money Interest and the Public Interest: American Monetary Thought, 1920–1970.* Cambridge, MA: Harvard University Press, 1997.

———. "The Money Muddle: The Transformation of American Monetary Thought, 1920–1979." *History of Political Economy* 30, suppl. (1998): 293–306

———. *Fischer Black and the Revolutionary Idea of Modern Finance.* New York: Wiley, 2005.

———. *The New Lombard Street: How the Fed Became the Dealer of Last Resort.* Princeton, NJ: Princeton University Press, 2011.

Meltzer, Allan H. *A History of the Federal Reserve.* 2 vols. Chicago: University of Chicago Press, 2003–9.

Ménard, Claude, and Mary M. Shirley, eds. *Handbook of New Institutional Economics.* Berlin: Springer, 2008.

Menger, Carl. *Grundsätze der Volkswirthschaftslehre* (Principles of Economics). Vienna: Wilhelm Braumuller, 1871.

Merton, Robert C. "Theory of Rational Option Pricing." *Bell Journal of Economics and Management Science* 4, no. 1 (Spring 1973): 141–83. Reprinted in Robert C. Merton, *Continuous-Time Finance* (1990), rev. ed. (Oxford: Blackwell, 1992), 255–308.

———. *Continuous-Time Finance.* 1990. rev. paperback ed., 1992. Reprint, Oxford: Blackwell, 2004.

Metcalf, Evan B. "Secretary Hoover and the Emergence of Macroeconomic Management." *Business History Review* 49, no. 1 (Spring 1975): 60–80.

Michalopoulos, Stelios, Luc Laeven, and Ross Levine. "Financial Innovation and Endogenous Growth." Working Paper no. 15356. Cambridge, MA: National Bureau of Economic Research, September 2009.

Miller, Merton H. "Financial Innovation: The Last Twenty Years and the Next." *Revue de la Banque* (Brussels) (September 1986): 35–42. An expanded version appears in *Journal of Financial and Quantitative Analysis* 21, no. 4 (December 1986): 459–71.

Miranti, Paul. J. "Associationism, Statism, Professional Regulation: Public Accountants and the Reform of Financial Markets, 1896–1940." *Business History Review* 60, no. 3 (Autumn 1986): 438–45.

———. "Birth of a Profession." *CPA Journal* 66, no. 4 (April 1996): 14–20, 72. http://archives.cpajournal.com/1996/0496/features/f14.htm.

Mirowski, Philip. *More Heat Than Light: Economics as Social Physics, Physics as Nature's Economics.* Cambridge: Cambridge University Press, 1989.

———. *Machine Dreams: Economics Becomes a Cyborg Science.* Cambridge: Cambridge University Press, 2002.

———. *Never Let a Serious Crisis Go to Waste: How Neoliberalism Survived the Financial Meltdown.* London: Verso, 2013.

Mishkin, Frederic S. *The Economics of Money, Banking, and Financial Institutions.* 8th ed. Upper Saddle River, NJ: Pearson Addison Wesley, 2007.

Mitchell, Lawrence C. *The Speculation Economy: How Finance Triumphed over Industry.* San Francisco: Berrett-Koehler, 2007.

Mitchell, Lucy Sprague. "A Personal Sketch." In *Wesley Clair Mitchell: The Economic Scientist* (Publications of the National Bureau of Economic Research, no. 53), ed. Arthur F. Burns, 55–106. New York: National Bureau of Economic Research, 1952.

Mitchell, W. C. "Methods of Presenting Statistics of Wages." *Publications of the American Statistical Association* 9, no. 72 (December 1905): 325–43.

———. *History of Prices during the War.* Washington, DC: US Government Printing Office, 1919.

———. "Index Numbers of Wholesale Prices in the United States and Foreign Countries." *Bulletin of the U.S. Department of Labor Statistics,* no. 284 (October 1921).

———. *Business Cycles: The Problem and Its Setting.* New York: National Bureau of Economic Research, 1927.

———. *Types of Economic Theory: From Mercantilism to Institutionalism.* Edited by Joseph Dorfman. 2 vols. New York: Augustus M. Kelley, 1969.

Mitchell, Wesley C., Willford I. King, Frederick R. Macaulay, and Oswald W. Knauth. *Income in the United States: Its Amount and Distribution, 1909–1919.* Vol. 1, *Summary.* New York: Harcourt Brace, 1921.

Modigliani, Franco. "Liquidity Preference and the Theory of Interest and Money." *Econometrica* 12, no. 1 (1944): 45–88.

———. "The Monetarist Controversy; or, Should We Forsake Stabilization Policies?" *American Economic Review* 67, no. 2 (March 1977): 1–19.

Modigliani, Franco, and Merton H. Miller. "The Cost of Capital, Corporation Finance and the Theory of Investment." *American Economic Review* 48, no. 3 (June 1958): 261–97.

Monbiot, George. "Neoliberalism—the Ideology at the Root of All Our Problems." *The Guardian,* April 15, 2016. https://www.theguardian.com/books/2016/apr/15/neoliberalism-ideology-problem-george-monbiot?CMP=share_btn_link.

Moody, John. *The Truth about the Trusts.* New York: Moody, 1904.

Moore, Henry L. *Laws of Wages: An Essay in Statistical Economics.* New York: Macmillan, 1911.

———. *Forecasting the Yield and the Price of Cotton.* New York: Macmillan, 1917.

Morgan, Mary S. *The History of Econometric Ideas.* Cambridge: Cambridge University Press, 1992.

———. "Marketplace Morals and the American Economists: The Case of John Bates Clark." In *Higgling: Transactors and Their Markets* (*History of Political Economy,* annual suppl., vol. 26), ed. Neil De Marchi and Mary S. Morgan, 229–52. Durham, NC: Duke University Press, 1994.

———. "The Technology of Analogical Models: Irving Fisher's Monetary Worlds." In "Proceedings of the 1996 Biennial Meetings of the Philosophy of Science Association: Pt. 2, Symposia Papers." *Philosophy of Science* 64, suppl. (December 1997): S304–S314.

———. "Business Cycles: Representation and Measurement." In *Monographs of Official Statistics: Papers and Proceedings of the Colloquium on the History of Business-Cycle Analysis,* ed. Dominique Ladiray, 175–90. Luxembourg: Office for Official Publications of the European Communities, 2001.

———. *The World in the Model: How Economists Work and Think.* Cambridge: Cambridge University Press, 2012.

Morgan, Mary S., and Marcel Boumans. "Secrets Hidden by Two-Dimensionality: The Economy as a Hydraulic Machine." In *Models: The Third Dimension of Science,* ed. Soraya de Chadarevian and Nick Hopwood, 369–401. Stanford, CA: Stanford University Press, 2004.

Morgan, Mary S., and Malcolm Rutherford. "American Economics: The Character of the Transformation." *History of Political Economy* 30, suppl. (1998): 1–26.

Morgenstern, Oskar. "The Accuracy of Economic Observations." In *Activity Analysis of Production and Allocation: Proceedings of a Conference,* ed. Tjalling C. Koopmans, 282–84. New York: Wiley, 1951.

Moulton, Harold Glenn. "Commercial Banking and Capital Formation I." *Journal of Political Economy* 26, no. 5 (May 1918): 484–508.

———. *The Financial Organization of Society.* Chicago: University of Chicago Press, 1921.

———. *Income and Economic Progress.* Washington, DC: Brookings Institution, 1935.

Murname, Mary Susan. "The Mellon Tax Plan: The Income Tax and the Penetration of Marginalist Economic Thought into American Life and Law in the 1920s." PhD diss., Case Western Reserve University, 2007.

Muth, John F. "Rational Expectations and the Theory of Price Movements." *Econometrica* 29, no. 3 (July 1961): 315–35.

Nelson, Stephen, and Peter J. Katzenstein. "Risk, Uncertainty, and the Financial Crisis of 2008." *International Organization* 68, no. 2 (March 2014): 361–92.

Nicholson, J. Lee. *Cost Accounting: Theory and Practice.* New York: Ronald, 1913.

Nicholson, J. Lee, and John F. D. Rohrbach. *Cost Accounting.* New York: Ronald, 1919.

"Ninety-Fourth Annual Meeting." *Journal of the American Statistical Association* 28, no. 181, suppl. (March 1933): 1–9.

Noland, Doug. "John G. Gurley and Edward S. Shaw on Financial Intermediaries." Safe Haven, April 20, 2001. http://www.safehaven.com/article/185/john-g-gurley-and-edward -s-shaw-on-financial-intermediaries.

North, S. N. D. "The Relation of Statistics to Economics and Sociology." *Publications of the American Statistical Association* 11, no. 85 (March 1909): 431–43.

Noyes, Alexander. *The Market Place: Reminiscences of a Financial Editor.* Boston: Little, Brown, 1938.

O'Sullivan, Mary. "The Expansion of the U.S. Stock Market, 1885–1930: Historical Facts and Theoretical Fashions." *Enterprise and Society* 8, no. 3 (September 2007): 489–542.

———. "Funding New Industries: A Historical Perspective on the Financing Role of the U.S. Stock Market in the Twentieth Century." In *Financing Innovation in the United States, 1870 to the Present,* ed. Naomi R. Lamoreaux and Kenneth L. Sokoloff, 163–216. Cambridge, MA: MIT Press, 2007.

Ott, Julia C. *When Wall Street Met Main Street: The Quest for an Investors' Democracy.* Cambridge, MA: Harvard University Press, 2011.

Palley, Thomas I. "Milton Friedman's Economics and Political Economy: An Old Keynesian Critique." Working Paper no. 134. Dusseldorf: Institut für Makroökonomie und Konjunkturforschung, July 2014. Reprinted as "The Economics and Political Economy of Milton Friedman: An Old Keynesian Critique." In *Milton Friedman: Contributions to Economics and Public Policy,* ed. Robert Cord and J. Daniel Hammond, 631–56. Oxford: Oxford University Press, 2015.

Palmer, Richard. "Final Plenary Discussion." In *The Economy as an Evolving Complex System,* ed. Philip W. Anderson, Kenneth J. Arrow, and David Piner, 257–61. Westview, CT: Westview Press, 1988.

Pareto, Vilfredo. *Manual of Political Economy: A Critical and Variorum Edition.* Edited by Aldo Montesano, Alberto Zanni, Luigino Bruni, John S. Chipman, and Michael McLure. Oxford: Oxford University Press, 2014.

Parrish, Michael E. *Anxious Decades: America in Prosperity and Depression, 1920–1941.* New York: Norton, 1992.

Pasinetti, Luigi L., and Gianpaolo Mariutti. "Hicks's 'Conversion'—from J. R. to John." In *Markets, Money and Capital: Hicksian Economics for the Twenty-First Century,* ed. Roberto Scazzieri, Amartya Sen, and Stefano Zamagni, 52–71. Cambridge: Cambridge University Press, 2009.

Patinkin, Don. *Money, Interest, and Prices: An Integration of Monetary and Value Theory.* Evanston, IL: Row, Peterson, 1956.

———. "Anticipations of the *General Theory?* Conclusion: The Significance of the Central Message." In *Anticipations of the General Theory? And Other Essays on Keynes,* 79–92. Chicago: University of Chicago Press, 1982.

———. "Keynesian Monetary Theory and the Cambridge School." In *Anticipations of the General Theory? And Other Essays on Keynes,* 165–80. Chicago: University of Chicago Press, 1982.

Paton, William Andrew. *Accounting Theory: With Special Reference to the Corporate Enterprise.* New York: Ronald, 1922.

Paton, William A., and Russell A. Stevenson. *Principles of Accounting.* Ann Arbor, MI: Ann Arbor, 1916.

Peach, William Nelson. *The Security Affiliates of National Banks.* Baltimore: Johns Hopkins University Press, 1941.

Persky, Joseph. "Retrospectives: Price Indexes and General Exchange Values." *Journal of Economic Perspectives* 12, no. 1 (Winter 1998): 197–205.

———. "The Neoclassical Advent: American Economics at the Dawn of the 20th Century." *Journal of Economic Perspectives* 14, no. 1 (Winter 2000): 95–108.

Persons, Warren M. "Indices of Business Conditions." *Review of Economic Statistics* 1, no. 1 (January 1919): 1–107.

———. "An Index of General Business Conditions." *Review of Economic Statistics* 1, no. 2 (April 1919): 111–205.

———. "Statistics and Economic Theory." *Review of Economic Statistics* 7, no. 3 (July 1925): 179–197.

Phelps, Edmund S., et al., eds. *The Microeconomic Foundations of Employment and Inflation Theory.* New York: Norton, 1970.

———. *Seven Schools of Macroeconomic Thought: The Arne Ryde Memorial Lectures.* Oxford: Clarendon Press, 1990.

Philippon, Thomas. "The Evolution of the US Financial Industry from 1860 to 2007: Theory and Evidence." November 2008. http://pages.stern.nyu.edu/~tphilipp/papers/finsize_old.pdf.

Piketty, Thomas. *Capital in the Twenty-First Century.* Translated by Arthur Goldhammer. Cambridge, MA: Harvard University Press, 2014.

Pliska, Stanley R. *Introduction to Mathematical Finance: Discrete Time Models.* Oxford: Blackwell, 1997.

Poitras, Geoffrey. *Security Analysis and Investment Strategy.* Malden, MA: Wiley-Blackwell, 2005.

———. "Frederick R. Macaulay, Frank M. Redington and the Emergence of Modern Fixed Income Analysis." In *Pioneers of Financial Economics,* vol. 2, *Twentieth-Century Contributions,* ed. Geoffrey Poitras and Franck Jovanovic, 5–16. Cheltenham: Edward Elgar, 2007.

———, ed. *Pioneers of Financial Economics.* Vol. 2, *Twentieth-Century Contributions.* Cheltenham: Edward Elgar, 2007.

———. *Valuation of Equity Securities: History, Theory and Application.* Singapore: World Scientific, 2011.

Pollman, Elizabeth. "Reconceiving Corporate Personhood." *Utah Law Review* 2011, no. 4 (November): 1629–75.

Pozsar, Zoltan, Tobias Adrian, Adam Ashcroft, and Haley Boesky. "Shadow Banking." Staff Report no. 458. New York: Federal Reserve Bank of New York, July 2010/rev. February 2012.

Prescott, Edward C. "Nobel Lecture: The Transformation of Macroeconomic Policy and Research." *Journal of Political Economy* 114, no. 2 (April 2006): 203–35.

President's Research Committee on Social Trends. *Recent Social Trends in the United States.* New York: McGraw-Hill, 1933.

Previts, Gary John. *A Critical Evaluation of Comparative Financial Accounting Thought in America, 1900 to 1920.* New York: Arno Press, 1980.

Previts, Gary John, and Barbara Dubis Merino. *A History of Accounting in America: An Historical Interpretation of the Cultural Significance of Accounting.* New York: Wiley, 1979. Revised as *A History of Accountancy in the United States: The Cultural Significance of Accounting* (Columbus: Ohio State University Press, 1998).

"Public Law 79–304, 79th Congress, S. 380." https://fraser.stlouisfed.org/scribd/?title_id= 1099&filepath=/docs/historical/congressional/employment-act-1946.pdf.

Qin, Duo. *A History of Econometrics: The Reformation from the 1970s.* Oxford: Oxford University Press, 2013.

Quinn, Stephen, and William Roberds. "The Evolution of the Check as a Means of Payment: A Historical Survey." *Economic Review of the Federal Reserve* 93, no. 4 (December 2008): 10–14.

Razin, Assaf. *Understanding Global Crises: An Emerging Paradigm.* Cambridge, MA: MIT Press, 2014.

Read, Colin. *The Portfolio Theorists: Von Neumann, Savage, Arrow and Markowitz.* Basingstoke: Palgrave Macmillan, 2012.

———. *The Rise of the Quants: Marschak, Sharpe, Black, Scholes, and Merton.* Basingstoke: Palgrave Macmillan, 2012.

Regnault, Jules. *Calcul des chances, et philosophie de la bourse.* Paris: Mallet-Bachelier, 1863. https://archive.org/details/calculdeschances00regn.

Reichenbach, Hans. "Philosophical Foundations of Probability." *Proceedings of the Berkeley Symposium on Mathematical Statistics and Probability,* ed. Jerzy Neyman, 1–20. Berkeley: University of California Press, 1949.

Reid, Milton P., III, and Stacey L. Schreft. "Credit Aggregates from the Flow of Funds Accounts." *Federal Reserve Bank of Richmond Economic Quarterly* 79, no. 3 (Summer 1993): 49–63.

Reinhart, Carmen M., and Kenneth S. Rogoff. *This Time Is Different: Eight Centuries of Financial Folly.* Princeton, NJ: Princeton University Press, 2009.

Renfro, Charles G. *The Practice of Econometric Theory: An Examination of the Characteristics of Econometric Computation.* Berlin: Springer, 2009.

Riefler, Winfield W., David Friday, Walter Lichtenstein, and J. H. Riddle. *A Program of Financial Research.* Vol. 1, *Report of the Exploratory Committee on Financial Research.* New York: National Bureau of Economic Research, 1937.

Riegel, Robert, and Henry James Loman. *Insurance: Principles and Practices.* 1921. 2nd ed. New York: Prentice-Hall, 1922.

Ripley, William Z. *Trusts, Pools, and Corporations.* New York: Ginn & Co., 1905.

———. "Stock Watering." *Political Science Quarterly* 26, no. 1 (March 1911): 98–121.

Ritter, Lawrence S. "An Exposition of the Structure of the Flow-of-Funds Accounts." *Journal of Finance* 18, no. 2 (May 1963): 219–30.

Robbins, Lionel. *An Essay on the Nature and Significance of Economic Science.* 1932. London: Macmillan, 1935.

Rodrik, Dani. *Economics Rules: The Rights and Wrongs of the Dismal Science.* New York: Norton, 2015.

Rogoff, Kenneth S. *The Curse of Cash.* Princeton, NJ: Princeton University Press, 2016.

Roll, Richard. "A Critique of the Asset Pricing Theory's Tests: Part 1, On Past and Potential Testability of the Theory." *Journal of Financial Economics* 4, no. 2 (March 1977): 129–76.

Romer, Christina D., and David H. Romer. "The Evolution of Economic Understanding and Postwar Stabilization Policy." Working Paper no. 9274. Cambridge, MA: National Bureau of Economic Research, October 2002.

Romer, Paul. "Solow's Choice." August 14, 2015. https://paulromer.net/solows-choice.

Ross, Dorothy. *The Origins of American Social Science.* Cambridge: Cambridge University Press, 1991.

Ross, Stephen A. "The Arbitrage Theory of Capital Asset Pricing." Working Paper no. 2–73. Philadelphia: University of Pennsylvania, Wharton School, Rodney L. White Center for Financial Research, 1973. https://rodneywhitecenter.wharton.upenn.edu/wp-content/uploads/2014/03/73-02.pdf.

———. *Neoclassical Finance.* Princeton, NJ: Princeton University Press, 2005.

Roy, A. D. "Safety First and the Holding of Assets." *Econometrica* 20, no. 3 (July 1952): 431–49.

Rubenstein, Mark. "Markowitz's 'Portfolio Selection': A Fifty-Year Retrospective." *Journal of Finance* 57, no. 3 (June 2002): 1041–45.

———. "Great Moments in Financial Economics: I, Present Value." *Journal of Investment Management* 1, no. 1 (2003): 45–54.

———. *A History of the Theory of Investments: My Annotated Bibliography.* New York: Wiley & Sons, 2006.

Rutherford, Malcolm. "Institutional Economics: Then and Now." *Journal of Economic Perspectives* 15, no. 3 (Summer 2001): 173–94.

———. "Chicago Economics and Institutionalism." In *The Elgar Companion to the Chicago School of Economics,* ed. Ross B. Emmett, 25–40. Cheltenham: Edward Elgar, 2010.

———. *The Institutional Movement in American Economics, 1918–1947: Science and Social Control.* Cambridge: Cambridge University Press, 2011.

Rutherford, Malcolm, and C. Tyler DesRoches. "The Institutionalist Reaction to Keynesian Economics." May 2006. http://papers.ssrn.com/s013/papers.cfm?abstract_id=905613.

———. "The Institutionalist Reaction to Keynesian Economics." *Journal of the History of Economic Thought* 30, no. 1 (March 2008): 29–48.

Rutherford, Malcolm, and Mary S. Morgan. "American Economics: The Character of the Transformation." *History of Political Economy* 30, no. 1 (1998): 1–26.

Rutterford, Janette. "From Dividend Yield to Discounted Cash Flow: A History of UK and US Equity Valuation Techniques." *Accounting, Business and Financial History* 14, no. 2 (2004): 115–49.

Rymes, Thomas K., ed. *Keynes's Lectures, 1932–35: Notes of a Representative Student.* Ann Arbor: University of Michigan Press, 1989.

Salant, Walter. "Alvin Hansen and the Fiscal Policy Seminar." *Quarterly Journal of Economics* 90, no. 1 (February 1976): 14–23.

Samuelson, Paul A. *The Foundations of Economic Analysis.* Cambridge, MA: Harvard University Press, 1947. Enlarged ed. Cambridge, MA: Harvard University Press, 1983.

———. *Economics: An Introductory Analysis.* New York: McGraw-Hill, 1948. 3rd ed. New York: McGraw-Hill, 1955.

———. "The Problem of Integrability in Utility Theory." *Economica* 17, no. 68 (November 1950): 355–85.

———. "Proof That Properly Anticipated Prices Fluctuate Randomly." *Industrial Management Review* 6, no. 2 (Spring 1965): 41–49.

———. "Rational Theory of Warrant Pricing." *Industrial Management Review* 6, no. 2 (Spring 1965): 13–32.

———. "In Search of the Elusive Elite." *New York Times,* June 26, 1975, 845.

Samuelson, Paul A., and Robert C. Merton. "A Complete Model of Warrant Pricing That Maximizes Utility." *Industrial Management Review* 10, no. 2 (1969): 17–46.

Scheinkman, José A. *Speculation, Trading, and Bubbles.* New York: Columbia University Press, 2014.

Scherer, F. M. "The Emigration of German-Speaking Economists after 1933." *Journal of Economic Literature* 38, no. 3 (September 2000): 614–26.

Schultz, Henry. *The Theory and Measurement of Demand.* Chicago: University of Chicago Press, 1938.

Schumpeter, Joseph A. *Business Cycles: A Theoretical, Historical and Statistical Analysis of the Capitalist Process.* 1939. Abridged ed. New York: McGraw-Hill, 1964.

———. *Ten Great Economists: From Marx to Keynes.* New York: Oxford University Press, 1951.

———. *History of Economic Analysis.* Edited by Elizabeth Boody Schumpeter. 1954. With a new introduction by Mark Perlman. New York: Oxford University Press, 1994.

Seligman, Edwin R. A. "Federal Taxes upon Income and Excess Profits—Discussion." *American Economic Review* 8, no. 1, suppl. (March 1918): 36–54.

———. *The Economics of Instalment Selling: A Study in Consumers' Credit.* 2 vols. New York: Harper & Bros., 1927.

Seligman, Joel. *The Transformation of Wall Street: A History of the Securities and Exchange Commission and Modern Corporate Finance.* Boston: Houghton Mifflin, 1982.

"Shackle, George L. S. (1903–1992)." In *A Biographical Dictionary of Dissenting Economists* (2nd ed.), ed. Philip Arestis and Malcolm Sawyer, 585–89. Cheltenham: Edward Elgar, 2000.

Shapiro, Carl, and Hal R. Varian. *Information Rules: A Strategic Guide to the Network Economy.* Boston: Harvard Business School Press, 1999.

Sharpe, William F. "Capital Asset Prices: A Theory of Market Equilibrium under Conditions of Risk." *Journal of Finance* 19, no. 3 (September 1964): 425–42. Reprinted in *Harry M. Markowitz, Merton H. Miller, William F. Sharpe, Robert C. Merton and Myron S. Scholes* (Pioneering Papers of the Nobel Memorial Laureates in Economics, vol. 2), ed. Howard R. Vane and Chris Mulhearn, 244–61. Cheltenham: Edward Elgar, 2009.

Shefrin, Hersh. *Beyond Greed and Fear: Understanding Behavioral Finance and the Psychology of Investing.* Boston: Harvard Business School Press, 2000.

Sherman, Matthew. "A Short History of Financial Deregulation in the United States." Washington, DC: Center for Economic and Policy Research, July 2009. http://cepr.net/documents/publications/dereg-timeline-2009-07.pdf.

Shiller, Robert J. *Market Volatility.* Cambridge, MA: MIT Press, 1989.

———. *Irrational Exuberance.* Princeton, NJ: Princeton University Press, 2000.

———. "From Efficient Markets Theory to Behavioral Finance." *Journal of Economic Perspectives* 17, no. 1 (Winter 2003): 83–104.

Shleifer, Andrei. *Inefficient Markets: An Introduction to Behavioral Finance.* Oxford: Oxford University Press, 2000.

Shreve, Steven E. *Stochastic Calculus for Finance I: The Binomial Asset Pricing Model.* 2004. New York: Springer, 2012.

Siegmund-Schultze, Reinhard. *Mathematicians Fleeing from Nazi Germany: Individual Fates and Global Impact.* Princeton, NJ: Princeton University Press, 2009.

Silber, William L. *When Washington Shut Down Wall Street: The Great Financial Crisis of 1914 and the Origins of America's Monetary Supremacy.* Princeton, NJ: Princeton University Press, 2007.

Sims, Christopher A. "Macroeconomics and Reality." *Econometrica* 48, no. 1 (January 1980): 1–48.

Sklar, Martin J. *The Corporate Reconstruction of American Capitalism, 1890–1916: The Market, the Law, and Politics.* Cambridge: Cambridge University Press, 1988.

Slutsky, Eugene. "Sulla teoria del bilancio del consumatore." Roma: Athenaeum, 1916. Reprinted from *Giornale degli economisti e rivista statistica* 51 (July 1915): 1–26.

Smith, Edgar Lawrence. *Common Stocks as Long Term Investments.* 1924. Reprint. New York: Macmillan, 1928.

Snedecor, George W. *Statistical Methods Applied to Experiments in Agriculture and Biology.* Ames, IA: Collegiate, 1937.

Solomon, Ezra. *The Anxious Economy.* San Francisco: Freeman, 1975.

Solow, Robert M. "A Contribution to the Theory of Economic Growth." *Quarterly Journal of Economics* 70, no. 1 (February 1956): 65–94.

———. "Summary and Evaluation." *After the Phillips Curve: Persistence of High Inflation and High Unemployment: Proceedings of a Conference Held at Edgartown, Massachusetts, June, 1978, 203–9.* Boston: Federal Reserve Bank of Boston, Public Information Centre, 1978.

———. "Growth Theory and After." Nobel Prize lecture, December 8, 1987. http://www.nobelprize.org/nobel_prizes/economic-sciences/laureates/1987/solow-lecture.html.

———. "How Did Economics Get That Way and What Way Did It Get?" *Daedalus* 126, no. 1 (Winter 1997): 39–58.

Solow, Robert M., and James Tobin. Introduction to *Two Revolutions in Economic Policy: The First Economic Reports of Presidents Kennedy and Reagan*, ed. James Tobin and Murray Weidenbaum, 3–16. Cambridge, MA: MIT Press, 1988.

Sorter, George H. *Boundaries of the Accounting Universe: The Accounting Rules of Selection*. Manchester, NH: Ayer, 1978.

Spanos, Aris. *Statistical Foundations of Econometric Modeling*. Cambridge: Cambridge University Press, 1986.

———. "Curve-Fitting, the Reliability of Inductive Inference, and the Error-Statistical Approach." In "Proceedings of the 2006 Biennial Meeting of the Philosophy of Science Association," pt. 1, "Contributed Papers," ed. Cristina Bicchieri and Jason Alexander, *Philosophy of Science* 74, no. 5 (2007): 1046–66.

Spencer, Arthur W. "The Prevention of Stock-Watering by Public-Service Corporations." *Journal of Political Economy* 14, no 9 (November 1906): 542–52.

Sprague, Charles Ezra. *The Philosophy of Accounts*. New York: Ronald, 1908.

Stabile, Donald R. *Forerunners of Modern Financial Economics: A Random Walk in the History of Economic Thought, 1900–1950*. Northampton, MA: Edward Elgar, 2005.

Staehle, Hans. "Report of the Fifth European Meeting of the Econometric Society." *Econometrica* 5, no. 1 (January 1937): 87–102.

Starr, Ross M. *General Equilibrium Theory: An Introduction*. Cambridge: Cambridge University Press, 2011.

Stein, Hebert. *The Fiscal Revolution in America: Policy in Pursuit of Reality*. Chicago: University of Chicago Press, 1969.

Stewart, Fenner L., Jr. "Berle's Conception of Shareholder Primacy: A Forgotten Perspective for Reconsideration during the Rise of Finance." *Seattle University Law Review* 34 (Summer 2011): 1457–99.

Stigler, George J. "The Development of Utility Theory II." *Journal of Political Economy* 58, no. 5 (October 1950): 373–96.

———. "Henry L. Moore and Statistical Economics." *Econometrica* 30, no. 1 (January 1962): 1–21.

———. *Production and Distribution Theories: The Formative Period*. 1941. Reprint, New York: Agathon, 1968.

Stigler, Stephen M. *The History of Statistics: The Measurement of Uncertainty before 1900*. Cambridge, MA: Harvard University Press, 1986.

———. "The History of Statistics in 1933." *Statistical Science* 11, no. 3 (August 1996): 244–52.

Strauss, Simon. *History of the Thrift Movement in America*. New York: Lippincott, 1920.

Sub-Committee on National Income Statistics of the League of Nations Committee of Statistical Experts. "Measurement of National Income and the Construction of Social Accounts." In Richard Stone, chairman, *Studies and Reports on Statistical Methods* (Report 7). Geneva: United Nations, 1947.

Summers, Lawrence H. "On Economics and Finance." *Journal of Finance* 40, no. 3 (July 1985): 633–35.

Survey of Current Business. Washington, DC: US Government Printing Office, 1921.

Taleb, Nassim Nicholas. *The Black Swan: The Impact of the Highly Improbable*. New York: Random House, 2007.

Tallman, Ellis W., and Jon R. Moen. "Lessons from the Panic of 1907." *Economic Review of the Federal Reserve Bank of Atlanta* 75 (May–June 1990): 2–13.

Temin, Peter. "Transmission of the Great Depression." *Journal of Economic Perspectives* 7, no. 2 (Spring 1993): 87–102.

———. "The Great Depression." Historical Working Paper Series no. 62. New York: National Bureau of Economic Research, November 1994.

Thaler, Richard H. *Misbehaving: The Making of Behavioral Economics.* New York: Norton, 2015.

Thorndike, Joseph J. *Their Fair Share: Taxing the Rich in the Age of FDR.* Washington, DC: Urban Institute Press, 2012.

Thrift Education: Being the Report of the National Conference on Thrift Education; Held in Washington, D.C., June 27 and 28, 1924, under the Auspices of the Committee on Thrift Education of the National Education Association and the National Council of Education. Washington, DC: National Education Association, 1924. http://lcweb2.10c.gov/gc/amrlg/lg26/lg26.html.

Tily, Geoff. "John Maynard Keynes and the Development of National Income Accounts in Britain, 1895–1941." *Review of Income and Wealth* 55, no. 2 (June 2009): 331–59.

Tinbergen, Jan. *Statistical Testing of Business-Cycle Theories.* Vol. 2, *Business Cycles in the United States of America, 1919–1932.* Geneva: League of Nations, 1939.

Tirole, Jean. *The Theory of Corporate Finance.* Princeton, NJ: Princeton University Press, 2006.

Tobin, James. "Stabilization Policy Ten Years After." *Brookings Papers on Economic Activity* 11, no. 1 (1980): 19–90.

———. "Money and Finance in the Macro-Economic Process." Nobel Memorial Lecture, December 8, 1981. http://www.nobelprize.org/nobel_prizes/economic-sciences/laureates/1981/tobin-lecture.pdf.

———. "Fisher, Irving (1867–1947)." In *The New Palgrave: A Dictionary of Economics* (4 vols.), ed. John Eatwell, Murray Milgate, and Peter Newman, 2:369–76. London: Palgrave Macmillan, 1998. Reprinted in "Celebrating Irving Fisher: The Legacy of a Great Economist," ed. Robert W. Dimand and John Geanakoplos, special issue, *American Journal of Economics and Sociology* 64, no. 1 (January 2005): 19–42.

Tobin, James, and William C. Brainard. "Financial Intermediaries and the Effectiveness of Monetary Controls." *American Economic Review* 53, no. 2 (May 1963): 383–400.

———. "Asset Markets and the Cost of Capital." In *Economic Progress, Private Values, and Public Policy: Essays in Honor of William Fellner,* ed. Béla A. Balassa and Richard R. Nelson, 235–62. Amsterdam: North-Holland, 1977.

Tooze, J. Adam. *Statistics and the German State, 1900–1945: The Making of Modern Economic Knowledge.* Cambridge: Cambridge University Press, 2001.

Trachtenberg, Alan. *The Incorporation of America: Culture and Society in the Gilded Age.* 1982. 25th anniversary ed. New York: Hill & Wang, 2007.

Trescott, Paul B. "Discovery of the Money-Income Relationship in the United States, 1921–1944." *History of Political Economy* 14, no. 1 (Spring 1982): 65–88.

Tribe, Keith. "German Émigré Economists and the Internationalisation of Economics." *Economic Journal* 111, no. 475 (November 2001): F740–F746.

Tucker, David M. *The Decline of Thrift in America: Our Cultural Shift from Saving to Spending.* New York: Praeger, 1991.

Tuttle, Charles A. "The Fundamental Notion of Capital, Once More." *Quarterly Journal of Economics* 19, no. 1 (November 1904): 1–110.

"Unemployment Rate for United States." Updated August 17, 2012. Economic Research, Federal Reserve Bank of St. Louis. https://fred.stlouisfed.org/series/M0892AUSM156SNBR.

"U.S. GAAP Codification of Accounting Standards." n.d. http://accountinginfo.com/financial-accounting-standards/asc-100/105-gaap-history.htm.

van den Bogaard, Adrienne. "Past Measurement and Future Prediction." In *Models as Mediators: Perspectives on Natural and Social Science,* ed. Mary. S. Morgan and Margaret Morrison, 282–325. Cambridge: Cambridge University Press, 1999.

Veblen, Thorstein. "The Preoccupations of Economic Science, I." *Quarterly Journal of Economics* 13, no. 2 (January 1899): 121–50.

———. "The Preoccupations of Economic Science, II." *Quarterly Journal of Economics* 13, no. 4 (July 1899): 396–426.

———. "The Preoccupations of Economic Science, III." *Quarterly Journal of Economics* 14, no. 2 (February 1900): 240–69.

———. *The Theory of Business Enterprise.* 1904. Reprint, Mansfield Centre, CT: Martino, 2013.

v[on] Neumann, J[ohn]. "A Model of General Economic Equilibrium." *Review of Economic Studies* 13, no. 1 (1945–46): 1–9.

Wallace, Henry A. *Agricultural Prices.* Des Moines, IA: Wallace Publishing, 1920.

Wallace, Henry A., and George W. Snedecor. "Correlation and Machine Calculation." *Iowa State College of Agriculture and Mechanic Arts Bulletin* 23, no. 35 (January 1925): 1–47.

Walras, Léon. *Éléments d'économie politique pure; ou, Théorie de la richesse sociale* (Elements of pure economics; or, The theory of social wealth). Lausanne: L. Corbaz, 1874.

Warburton, Clark. "Three Estimates of the Value of the Nation's Output of Commodities and Services: A Comparison." In *Studies in Income and Wealth* (vol. 3), 317–98. New York: National Bureau of Economic Research, 1939.

———. "Monetary Control under the Federal Reserve Act." *Political Science Quarterly* 61, no. 4 (December 1946): 505–34.

———. *Depression, Inflation, and Monetary Policy: Selected Papers, 1945–1953.* Baltimore: Johns Hopkins University Press, 1966.

Warshow, H. T. "The Distribution of Corporate Ownership in the United States." *Quarterly Journal of Economics* 39, no. 1 (November 1924): 15–38.

Weintraub, E. Roy. *General Equilibrium Analysis: Studies in Appraisal.* 1985. With a new preface. Ann Arbor: University of Michigan Press, 1993.

———. *Stabilizing Dynamics: Constructing Economic Knowledge.* Cambridge: Cambridge University Press, 1991.

———. *Toward a History of Game Theory.* Durham, NC: Duke University Press, 1992.

———. "From Rigor to Axiomatics: The Marginalization of Griffith C. Evans." In "From Interwar Pluralism to Postwar Neoclassicism," ed. Mary S. Morgan and Malcolm Rutherford, *History of Political Economy* 30, suppl. (1998): 227–59.

———. "Measurement and Changing Images of Mathematical Knowledge." In "The Age of Economic Measurement," ed. Judy L. Klein and Mary S. Morgan, *History of Political Economy* 33, suppl. (2001): 303–12.

———. *How Economics Became a Mathematical Science.* Durham, NC: Duke University Press, 2002.

Wells, Anita. "Legislative History of Excess Profits Taxation in the United States in World Wars I and II." *National Tax Journal* 4, no. 3 (September 1951): 237–54.

White, Eugene N. "When the Ticker Ran Late: The Stock Market Boom and Crash of 1929." In *Crashes and Panics: The Lessons from History,* ed. Eugene N. White, 143–87. Homewood, IL: Dow Jones–Irwin, 1990.

———. "Were Banks Special Intermediaries in Late Nineteenth-Century America?" *Review of the Federal Reserve Bank of St. Louis* 80, no. 3 (May–June 1998): 13–32.

Whitley, Richard. "The Rise of Modern Finance Theory: Its Characteristics as a Scientific Field and Connections to the Changing Structure of Capital Markets." *Research in the History of Economic Thought and Methodology* 4 (1986): 147–78.

Williams, John Burr. *The Theory of Investment Value.* 1938. Reprint, Burlington, VT: Fraser, 1997.

Wood, Marshall K., and George B. Dantzig. "Programming of Independent Activities." Paper presented to the meeting of the Econometric Society, Cleveland, December 27, 1948.

———. "Programming of Interdependent Activities: I. General Discussion." *Econometrica* 17, nos. 3–4 (July–October 1949): 193–99.

———. "Programming of Independent Activities." In *Activity Analysis of Production and Allocation: Proceedings of a Conference,* ed. Tjalling C. Koopmans, 15–18. New York: Wiley, 1951.

Woodford, Michael. *Interest and Prices: Foundations of a Theory of Monetary Policy.* Princeton, NJ: Princeton University Press, 2003.

Working, Holbrook. "New Concepts concerning Futures Markets and Prices." *American Economic Review* 52, no. 3 (June 1962): 431–59.

Wray, L. Randall. *Why Minsky Matters: An Introduction to the Work of a Maverick Economist.* Princeton, NJ: Princeton University Press, 2016.

Yamey, B. S. "Scientific Bookkeeping and the Rise of Capitalism." *Economic History Review,* 2nd ser., 1, nos. 2–3 (1949): 99–113.

Young, H. Peyton, and Shmuel Zamir. *Handbook of Game Theory.* Vol. 4. Amsterdam: Elsevier, 2015.

Yule, G. Udny. *Introduction to the Theory of Statistics.* London: Charles Griffin; Philadelphia: Lippincott, 1911.

Zarnowitz, Victor. *Business Cycles: Theory, History, Indicators, and Forecasting.* Chicago: University of Chicago Press, 1992.

Zeckhauser, Richard. "Investing in the Unknown and Unknowable." *Capitalism and Society* 1, no. 2 (2006): 1–39.

Zeff, Stephen A. *A Critical Examination of the Orientation Postulate in Accounting, with Particular Attention to Its Historical Development in New York.* New York: Arno, 1978.

———. *Henry Rand Hatfield: Humanist, Scholar, and Accounting Educator.* Bingley: Emerald, 2000.

INDEX

AAA. *See* Agricultural Adjustment Act
(AAA)
AAPA. *See* American Association of Public
Accountants (AAPA)
Accountant's Handbook (Dickinson), 44
accounting, 38, 381n28, 383n38; algebraic
budgeting, 154–58; balance sheet (*see*
balance-sheet systems); classifications of,
38; corporations and, 35, 36, 38, 47 (*see
also* corporations); cost accounting, 41–42,
79, 201, 383n40; decision making and,
384n52; double-entry (*see* double-entry
system); GDP and, 38, 198 (*see also* gross
domestic product); GNP and, 38, 198 (*see
also* gross national product); national,
38, 198 (*see also* gross domestic product;
gross national product); principles of,
38, 198 (*see also specific topics*); public,
36–49 (*see also specific topics*); as a science,
381n28; transformation of, 29. *See also
specific topics, texts, persons*
Adams, T. S., 94
Adrian, Tobias, 367, 369
AEA. *See* American Economic Association
(AEA)
AFA. *See* American Finance Association
(AFA)

Agricultural Adjustment Act (AAA), 204
agriculture, 80, 98, 129, 160–66, 295–99. *See
also specific persons, topics*
AIG, 366, 368
Akerlof, George, 336
Aldrich, Nelson W., 91
Aldrich Report, 112, 113, 396n19, 397n28
Aldrich-Vreeland Act, 53
algebraic budgeting method, 154–58
Allais, Maurice, 77
Allen, Frederick, 132
American Association of Public Accountants
(AAPA), 37, 47
American Economic Association (AEA),
57, 295
American Finance Association (AFA), 295
American Statistical Association (ASA), 97
Appreciation and Interest (Fisher), 72, 75, 274
Approach to Business Problems (Shaw), 102
arbitrage theory, 310, 312, 318–22, 328, 329,
345, 372
Arrow-Debreu models, 66, 288, 305, 306,
307, 435n16
ASA. *See* American Statistical Association
(ASA)
Asian financial crisis, 339–40
Autoquote system, 321

Bachelier, Louis, 298, 309, 318, 406n4

balance-sheet systems, 78, 289; arrangement of, 44; banking and, 272 (*see also* banking); capitalization, 49 (*see also* capitalization); commercial banks and, 50; corporations and, 40, 41, 383n42 (*see also* corporations); equilibrium and, 115 (*see also* equilibrium theory); Federal Reserve and, 44 (*see also* Federal Reserve); income statement and, 42, 44, 47 (*see also* income statement); limitations, 40; partial realizations and, 383n42; profits and, 40. *See also* accounting

banking, 80; balance sheets and, 272 (*see also* balance-sheet systems); bank failures, 49; British, 54; capital markets and, 342; CDOs and, 362; central banking, 49, 52, 73, 159 (*see also* Federal Reserve); checking deposits, 83–84, 270; commercial loan theory, 54, 385n61; credit and, 363, 364, 392n52 (*see also* credit); equity funds and, 269; Federal Reserve (*see* Federal Reserve); fractional reserve system and, 84; Great Depression and, 132; insuring deposits, 270; merger movement in, 273; monetary theory and, 53, 81–86, 223 (*see also* monetary theory); mortgage loans and, 140–41, 362, 364, 365; regulation of, 269–72; securitization and, 130, 132, 342, 362–64, 367; shadow banking system, 362–64

barter model, 81

Bayesian theory, 257–58, 302–3

behavioral economics, 335

bell curve, 169–70, 237, 303, 395n10, 437n37

Berle, Adolf, 141, 142, 143, 145, 146, 149

Bernanke, Ben S., 338, 373

Bernstein, Michael, 386n2

big data, 96

bimetallism, 81

binomial tree model, 326

Black, Fischer, 314, 318, 320

Black-Scholes-Merton model, 318, 319, 322, 325, 348, 440n7

Black-Scholes option pricing, 323, 375n9, 376n10, 441n7

black swan metaphor, 374

Blaug, Mark, 429n61

BLS. *See* Bureau of Labor Statistics (BLS)

blue-sky laws, 141, 146

Boissevain, Charles H., 164

bonds, 150, 177, 400n6; government, 131, 157; interest rates and, 136, 158, 391n43; risk premium and, 156, 157; stocks and, 131, 135–37, 152, 181; war and, 131, 156. *See also* specific types, topics

Booms and Depressions (Fisher), 137, 252

Boulding, Kenneth, 163

Bourbaki group, 427n35

Brainard, William C., 287, 301

Bretton Woods, 247, 248, 315, 344, 346

Brief, Richard A., 44

Brookings Institution, 185, 194–95

Brownian motion, 309, 310, 318, 436n25

Bryan, William Jennings, 55, 72, 81

Bureau of Labor Statistics (BLS), 197

Burns, Arthur F., 282

business cycles, 58, 73, 101, 115, 120, 206, 207, 208, 349; barometers of, 96, 154, 155; equilibrium and, 115 (*see also* equilibrium theory); exogenous model and, 340; fiscal policy and, 267; indexes for, 154; Keynes and (*see* Keynes, John Maynard); mathematical models and, 159, 423n44 (*see also* mathematical models); monetary factors and, 244 (*see also* monetary theory); NBER project and, 398n32; rocking horse model, 238; taxation and, 209–10 (*see also* taxation); Tinbergen on, 422n33; volatility and, 178 (*see also* volatility)

Business Cycles (Mitchell), 115

calculus, 62, 305, 306, 325, 405n67. *See also* mathematical models

Cambridge controversy, 378n28

capital: capitalism, 356–57; claims and, 32, 306; concepts of, 59–60, 63; corporations and, 32–36, 78, 149, 180, 379n3, 381n26 (*see also* corporations); financial theory and, 32; marginalist law, 64–65 (*see also* marginalist theory); redefinition of, 32; supply side and, 64, 338, 342; theory of, 60; valuation and, 36, 63, 78; workers and, 64. *See also specific topics*

Capital Asset Pricing Model (CAPM), 100, 307, 314, 315, 328–29, 437n37

capitalization, 49, 78; balance sheet and, 49 (*see also* balance-sheet systems); corporations and, 32–36, 149, 180, 379n3, 381n26; defined, 32; expectation and, 77 (*see also* expectation); future and, 32, 78; index funds, 175, 176, 179 (*see also* index funds); market and, 34, 175–76 (*see also* stock markets); overcapitalization, 34, 36, 380n12, 380n14; promoters and, 33; stocks and, 34, 49, 78, 172, 342 (*see also* stock markets); uncertainty and, 90 (*see also* uncertainty)

CAPM. *See* Capital Asset Pricing Model (CAPM)

case study method, 96, 100–103, 155

Cassel, Gustav, 389n25

cause/effect paradox, 67

CDOs. *See* collateralized debt obligations (CDOs)

CEA. *See* Council of Economic Advisors (CEA)

Celler-Kefauver Act, 280–81

central banking system, 49, 52, 73, 159. *See also* Federal Reserve

ceteris paribus convention, 85, 199

Chamberlain, Lawrence, 134, 135

cistern model, 68–70

Citibank, 364

Clark, Colin, 189

Clark, J. M., 211

Clark, John Bates, 62, 63, 65, 66, 75, 77, 94, 97, 100, 114

Clayton Act, 123

Clinton administration, 338

collateralized debt obligations (CDOs), 362, 365, 366

Colm, Gerhard, 206–13

commercial banks, 49–55

Commercial Economy Board, 103

commodities: agricultural, 80, 98, 129, 160–66, 295–99; capital goods, 63; cistern model, 68–70; contingent, 305, 306; futures markets (*see* futures markets); gold, 50–53, 72, 83, 278, 391n38, 430n63; money and (*see* monetary theory); random walk and, 298 (*see also* randomness); spot prices, 297. *See also specific topics*

Commodities Futures Modernization Act, 360, 365, 367

Commons, John R., 58, 283

Common-Stock Indexes (Cowles), 175–82

Common Stocks as Long-Term Investments (Smith), 134, 152, 153

communism, 182

computers, 316, 331, 354, 360. *See also* mathematical models; *and specific topics*

consumption, 78, 140, 185, 191, 196–97

Conyngton, Thomas, 32, 34, 35

Coolidge, Calvin, 129

Cooper, Francis, 32, 34, 35

Cootner, Paul H., 309

Copeland, Morris A., 68, 190, 264, 266, 267

Corporation Income Tax Act (1909), 92

corporations, 32, 54, 141, 370; accounting and, 35, 36, 38, 39, 47, 201 (*see also* accounting); affiliated companies, 132; aggregation and, 186; articles on, 380n8; balance sheet and, 40, 41, 383n42 (*see also* balance-sheet systems); banking and, 133 (*see also* banking); bonds, 77 (*see also* bonds); capitalization, 32–36, 149, 180, 379n3, 381n26 (*see also* capitalization); cost accounting and, 41–42, 79, 201, 383n40; credit insurance and, 87; disclosure and, 141–47, 150, 158; dynamics of, 47, 49; earning power, 32; emergence of, 379n7; excess assets, 94, 380n14; expectation and, 36 (*see also* expectation); federal government and, 381n26; finance models, 359; financial activities, 40, 42, 77;

corporations (*continued*)
  financial institutions, 133; growth of, 142,
    157, 371; income statement and, 44 (*see
    also* income statement); information and,
    143–44, 145; insurance industry and, 89,
    437n38; investment and, 31, 47, 49, 130–33,
    142, 148, 152 (*see also* investment; stock
    markets); legal status of, 30, 31, 379n7;
    liquidity, 142; logistic curve and, 157; man-
    agement theory, 88, 101 (*see also specific
    persons, topics*); merger movements, 30,
    59, 142, 154, 371, 379n3, 379n5; monopo-
    listic combinations, 85; neoliberalism
    and, 377n20; number of, 379n3; overcapi-
    talization and, 36, 380n14; part-shares
    owned, 41; pricing and (*see* price theory);
    production in, 40, 42; promoters and, 33,
    35, 36; property and, 32, 77, 379n7; rights
    of, 30; rise of, 28–56; risk and, 88 (*see also*
    risk); Santa Clara decision, 30, 379n7; sec-
    tors and, 186; securities and, 143, 379n7
    (*see also* securities markets); shareholders
    and, 31, 47, 49, 142, 148, 152, 177 (*see also*
    investment); specialization and, 88; state
    and, 146, 379n7; static representation, 47;
    stock market (*see* stock markets); taxation
    and, 91, 94, 203, 379n3, 393n67 (*see also*
    taxation); trusts and, 29, 30, 51, 85, 134–37,
    379n3, 401n27, 402n29; uncertainty and,
    88; undistributed profits, 203; valuation
    and, 31, 34–36; warrant options, 404n58;
    wealth and, 379n3. *See also specific per-
    sons, topics*
correlation analysis, 98–99, 198, 299–302
Correlation and Machine Calculation
    (Wallace/Snedecor), 162, 164
cost accounting, 41–42, 79, 201, 383n40
cotton prices, 98–99
Council of Economic Advisors (CEA), 205,
    247, 282, 285, 345, 416n53
Cowles, Alfred A., III, 105, 135, 164, 165, 171,
    172, 173, 174, 177, 178, 180
Cowles Commission, 164, 218, 242, 253

Cramér, Harald, 299
crash of 1929, 47, 120, 129–38, 140, 148, 159,
    165, 181, 397n31, 400n11
crash of 1987, 323, 331, 339, 369
credit, 124, 130; banks and, 363, 364, 392n52
    (*see also* banking); corporations and,
    87; credit cards, 440n5; debt and, 137;
    deflation and, 137; discount rate, 133, 156;
    Federal Reserve and (*see* Federal Reserve);
    Great Depression and, 137; insurance and,
    87; interest rate (*see* interest rates); inter-
    mediation index, 364; money and, 60, 61,
    124, 130, 373 (*see also* monetary theory);
    speculative/productive, 54; Veblen and,
    60. *See also specific topics*
crisis of 1907, 50
crisis of 2008, 314, 355, 370, 371, 446n76
currency markets, 127, 137, 316, 369
Currie, Lauchlin, 195
cyclical movement. *See* business cycles

Dantzig, George B., 261, 299, 304
data: accounting and (*see* accounting); analy-
    sis of (*see* statistical methods; *and specific
    topics*); collection of, 103–4; computers
    and, 316, 331, 354, 360 (*see also* mathemati-
    cal models); dissemination of, 105–10;
    index number and, 105–7; information
    and, 96; national, 103–4, 105 (*see also
    specific topics*); statistics and (*see* statistical
    methods); time and, 99, 105–10, 154, 177,
    240, 408n24. *See also specific types, topics*
Davis, Harold T., 154, 164, 167
Dawes Committee, 207
Debreu, Gérard, 66, 306
deficit, national, 192
deflation, 272, 337, 391n45; credit and, 137;
    dollar and, 127; Fisher and, 137–38; inter-
    est rates and, 390n36 (*see also* interest
    rates); money and (*see* monetary theory);
    Volcker deflation and, 346
demand, 67, 97–100, 210. *See also* markets
depreciation, 48

deregulation, 343, 359–62, 445n61
derivatives, 307, 314–18, 321, 325–28, 360, 365–66, 438n49
deterministic models, 255
De Vroey, Michel, 350
Dickinson, Arthur Lowes, 42, 79
digital technology, 316, 331, 332, 354, 360. *See also* mathematical models; *and specific topics*
diminishing returns, 62, 67
disclosure, corporations and, 143–45, 150, 158
discount rate, 133, 156
Distribution of Wealth, The (Clark), 64
diversification, 152, 299–302
dividend discount model, 153–60
Dodd, David, 147–53
Dodd-Frank Act, 373
dollar, U.S., 127, 129, 135, 352. *See also* monetary theory; *and specific topics*
Doob, J. L., 326
Doolittle, Myrrick, 163
Dos Passos, John, 32
double-entry system, 382n37; Fisher and, 79; income and, 115; inflation and, 192; input-output model, 196–99, 201; national aggregates and, 191; proprietary theory and, 38, 39
Dow Jones Industrial Index, 106, 171
DSGE models, 348, 351–55, 358, 443n29
Dunbar, Charles, 82
Duvel, J. W. T., 296
dynamic models, 115, 120, 348–58, 423n48, 443n29. *See also* mathematical models; *and specific types, topics*

Eccles, Marriner, 140
Econometrica, 164
econometrics, 164, 239, 314–19, 331–32, 345, 439n68. *See also* mathematical models; *and specific persons, topics, texts*
Econometric Society, 98, 105, 164, 215–19, 332

Economic Cycles (Moore), 98, 162
Economic Growth of Nations (Kuznets), 291
Economics (Samuelson), 250
efficient markets, 164, 302, 304, 307, 312, 316, 335, 372, 377n20
Eisner v. Macomber, 93
electronic trading, 332. *See also* digital technology
empiricism, 72, 76, 100, 107, 117
employment, 108, 127, 183, 275, 282, 285, 290, 344
Employment Act, 249, 345, 371, 416n53
endogenous growth model, 359
energy, metaphor of, 390n33
equilibrium theory, 66–68, 115, 198, 223, 227, 230–34, 251, 304–7, 372, 388n25
equities. *See* stock markets
ethics, 77, 97, 202, 208, 224, 322, 359, 395n12, 437n38
Eurodollars, 343
expectation: Bayesian approach and, 257–58, 302–3; choice and, 303; corporations and, 36; early models, 72–75; Fisher and, 74, 77, 79; futures and (*see* futures markets); income and, 77; information and, 145, 297; investors and, 301; likelihood principle, 237; mathematical theory and (*see* mathematical models; *and specific topics*); probability and, 302–3 (*see also* probability theory); risk and, 436n30 (*see also* risk); valuation and, 35, 36, 145, 297 (*see also* price theory)
expenditure approach, 184, 194–95

Falkner, Ronald P., 396n19
Fama, Eugene, 176, 311, 313–14
Fannie Mae, 140, 363
Federal Deposit Insurance Corporation (FDIC), 138, 269
Federal Housing Authority (FHA), 140
Federal National Mortgage Association, 140
Federal Reserve, 249, 265, 266, 278; balance sheet and, 44, 46; banking and, 46, 49–54,

Federal Reserve (*continued*)
157 (*see also* banking); Board of Governors, 44, 46, 52, 126, 247, 431n71; call rate
and, 52, 133; commercial loans and, 54, 55;
credit and, 124 (*see also* interest rates); discount rate and, 133; Fed Accord, 249, 371;
Federal Reserve Act, 52, 53, 54, 123; gold
and, 50–55, 72, 83, 278, 391n38, 430n63;
governance structure, 431n71; Great
Depression and, 430n63; growth of, 371;
history of, 392n51; income statement and,
47; interest rates and, 157 (*see also* interest
rates); monetary policy, 55, 266, 370 (*see
also* monetary theory); quantitative easing
and, 370; research departments, 345;
World War I and, 53
Federal Savings and Loan Insurance Corporation (FSLIC), 270
Federal Trade Commission (FTC), 126, 146
FHA. *See* Federal Housing Authority (FHA)
fiduciary/trust paradigm, 141
financial crisis of 1907, 50
financial crisis of 2008, 314, 355, 370, 371,
446n76
financial instability hypothesis, 357
Financial Intermediaries (Goldsmith), 269
Financial Organization of Society, The
(Moulton), 123
Financial Reserve, 28–56
Finetti, Bruno de, 303
Fisher, Irving, 32–35, 55, 93, 100, 114, 137,
142, 171, 176, 180, 196, 223, 252, 266;
agricultural economics, 166; bond tables
and, 391n38, 391n43; boom of 1920s, 129;
ceteris paribus convention, 66; cistern
model, 68, 82, 389n30; Clark and, 66, 75;
contributions of, 388n23; deflation and,
137–38; deterministic models, 255; diversification and, 152; double-entry system
and, 79; equation of exchange, 82, 83;
expectations and, 74–79; financial view,
79; Fisher effect, 72–75, 390n35; Friedman and, 275; general equilibrium theory

and, 388n25; Hicks and, 224; hydraulic
model, 68, 82, 389n30; ideal formula,
179; income concept and, 77, 78; index
numbers, 75, 116, 119, 178; inflation and,
397n32; interest and, 79; investment trusts
and, 135–37, 401n27, 402n29; Kemmerer
and, 82; Laughlin and, 85, 86; mathematics and, 60–61, 66, 67, 76, 80, 96, 119, 220,
389n28 (*see also* mathematical models);
measurability problem, 66; Mitchell and,
115, 116, 117, 118; monetary theory and, 66,
68, 73, 82, 160 (*see also* monetary theory);
present-value approach, 91; quantity
theorem, 83; Schumpeter and, 83; sources
for, 390n37; utility and, 68, 70; Walras
and, 67. *See also specific persons, texts,
topics*
Fisher, Ronald A., 166, 167, 169–74, 237, 257
fixed income, 161–82
Fleetwood, Bishop, 396n19
flow, of funds, 263, 265, 267, 289
Forecasting the Yield and Price of Cotton
(Moore), 98, 99
Foundations of Economic Analysis (Samuelson), 251
Foundations of Statistics (Savage), 258, 303
fractional reserve system, 84
Frankfurter, Felix, 146
free market, 65, 274, 276, 278, 280, 437n38
Frenyear, T. C., 33
frequentist approach, 302, 303
Friedman, Milton, 55, 62, 73, 76, 86, 247,
273–75, 278, 279, 289
Frisch, Ragnar, 106, 215, 216, 238, 253,
424n58
Frobenius, Georg, 199
FSLIC. *See* Federal Savings and Loan Insurance Corporation (FSLIC)
FTC. *See* Federal Trade Commission (FTC)
fundamental theorem of finance, 330
futures markets, 296; accounting and,
383n38; agricultural, 80, 98, 160–66,
295–99; capitalization and, 78; commodi-

ties and, 298; currency markets, 127, 137, 316, 367; decision making and, 384n52; hedging and, 297; interest rates and, 78; random walk and, 298

GAAP. *See* Generally Accepted Accounting Practices (GAAP)
Galbraith, James K., 378n28
Galton, Francis, 100, 167
game theory, 66, 257–58, 426n28
Gaussian distribution, 169–70, 237, 303, 395n10, 437n37
Gay, Edwin F., 101, 103, 104, 112
GDP. *See* gross domestic product (GDP)
general equilibrium theory (GET), 66, 68, 115, 198, 223, 227, 230–34, 251, 304–7, 372, 388n25
Generally Accepted Accounting Practices (GAAP), 382n28
General Motors Acceptance Corporation (GMAC), 140
General Theory of Employment, Interest, and Money (Keynes), 137, 159, 183, 195, 205, 218, 224, 226, 250. *See also* Keynes, John Maynard; *and specific topics*
GET. *See* general equilibrium theory (GET)
Gibbs, Willard J., 67, 70, 71
Gilbert, Milton, 186, 189, 191, 193, 194, 196, 198, 248
Glass-Stegall Act, 269, 270, 271, 278, 360
globalization, 351, 352, 441n12
GMAC. *See* General Motors Acceptance Corporation (GMAC)
GNP. *See* gross national product (GNP)
gold, 50–53, 72, 83, 84, 278, 391n38, 430n63
Goldsmith, Raymond W., 268
Gordon growth model, 153–60
government spending, 157, 186, 188, 191–92, 211–12. *See also specific administrations, topics*
Graham, Benjamin, 147–53
Graham, Willard J., 93
Gramm-Leach-Bliley acts, 367

Grant, James, 129
gravity, law of, 68
Great Depression, 127, 137, 155, 159, 163, 183, 188, 201, 211, 252, 266, 270, 277, 278, 415n40, 430n63
Great Recession, 337, 371
Greene, Jeremy, 101, 112
Greenspan, Alan, 368, 369
Greenwood, Robin, 361
Gries, John M., 138
Gross Capital Formation (Kuznets), 211
gross domestic product (GDP), 29, 38, 184, 196, 198, 248, 264, 342, 360, 411n5
gross money doctrine, 271–72
gross national product (GNP), 189, 190, 193, 196, 264, 411n5, 412n13, 412n14
growth theory, 153–60, 291, 292, 340, 359
Growth Theory (Solow), 291
Gurley, John G., 11, 55, 269–73, 356

Haavelmo, Trygve, 219, 253
Hamilton, William Peter, 171, 172
Hansen, Alvin, 154, 159, 195, 204, 213
Harrison, J. Michael, 329
Harrod-Domar models, 292
Harvard Business School, 100–103, 120–21, 155
Hatfield, Henry Rand, 37, 38, 41
Hawtrey, Ralph, 86
Hay, William Wren, 134, 135
Haymarket strike, 64, 387n14
hedging, 295–99, 321
Heinze, F. Augustus, 51
Helffrich, Karl, 207, 208
Hess, Ralph H., 86
Hicks, John R., 218–25, 250–52, 299
History of the Thrift Movement (Strauss), 139
Holt, Charles, 347
home ownership, 138, 139, 140, 402n39
Home Owners' Loan Corporation, 140
Hoover, Herbert, 108, 109, 110, 139
Hotelling, Harold, 166, 255, 409n25
household sector, 186, 191, 197, 200, 361–62

How to Pay for the War (Keynes), 247, 248, 420n19

Hull, Cordell, 91

Hume, David, 61

hypothesis testing, 257, 407n16

IBM. *See* International Business Machines (IBM)

IBRD. *See* International Bank for Reconstruction and Development (IBRD)

ICC. *See* Interstate Commerce Commission (ICC)

identification problem, 67

IfK. *See* Institute for Business-Cycle Research (IfK)

IMF. *See* International Monetary Fund (IMF)

income, 184, 187; consumption and, 194–96; defined, 94; double-entry format and, 115; expectation and, 77 (*see also* expectation); income statement (*see* income statement); interest and, 77, 78 (*see also* interest rates); investment and, 196 (*see also* investment); marginalist theory, 64 (*see also* marginalist theory); National Income, 113–14; NBER method and, 113; NIPA and, 184; production theory and, 64; savings and, 196 (*see also* savings); tax and, 90–94, 414n28; wages, 62–65, 97, 112, 388n21, 394n5

Income in the United States (Mitchell et al.), 114, 185

income statement, 44, 78, 384n46, 384n48; AAPA and, 47; arrangement of, 44; balance sheet and, 42, 44, 46, 47; cost accounting and, 41–42; defined, 93; depreciation and, 48; Dickinson form, 79; Federal Reserve and, 47; financial aspects, 42, 46; introduction of, 47; manufacturing operations, 46; production and, 41–42; sections of, 46, 47; surplus and, 47; time of purchase in, 48; timing of, 48

income tax, 90–94, 414n28. *See also* taxation

index funds, 313; capitalization and, 179; data and, 105; dispute over, 114–16, 118; Fisher and, 75, 116; ideal, 115; Index Number Institute, 398n32; index-number problem, 96, 99, 105–6, 178, 179–80; limitations of, 398n34; mathematical models, 118 (*see also* mathematical models); Mitchell and, 117; origin of, 396n19; personal, 90–95; prices and, 105–10; time series and, 106, 107; use of term, 396n24

indifference, utility and, 71

inflation, 115, 157, 192, 282, 284, 285, 290, 315, 344, 397n32

information, 308, 335, 358; computers and (*see* digital technology); corporations and, 143–44, 145; data and, 96 (*see also* data); disclosure rules and, 143–45; expectations and, 145, 297; IT systems, 316, 317, 354, 358; market and, 376n20; price and, 143, 144; stocks and, 158

input-output models, 196–99, 201

instability hypothesis, 357

Institute for Business-Cycle Research (IfK), 206, 207

institutionalism, 57–61, 90, 123, 156, 160, 281–90, 386n4, 413n19, 432n77

insurance industry, 89, 437n38. *See also* risk

inter-crisis period, 337

Interest and Prices (Woodford), 355

interest rates, 74, 77, 180, 182, 337, 346, 384n51; bonds and, 136, 157, 158; calculation of, 73–74; central banks and, 73; consumption and, 78; deflation and, 390n36 (*see also* deflation); discount rates and, 156; Federal Reserve (*see* Federal Reserve); future and, 78; household credit and, 361; income and, 77; Keynes on (*see* Keynes, John Maynard); money and, 72–73 (*see also* monetary theory); portfolio theory and, 182 (*see also* portfolio theory); public finance and, 159; pure, 157, 182; real, 78; recession and, 390n36; stocks and, 136 (*see also* stock markets); valuation and, 76

International Bank for Reconstruction and Development (IBRD), 248
International Business Machines (IBM), 163, 165
International Monetary Fund (IMF), 247
Interstate Commerce Commission (ICC), 384n51
interwar period, 126–60, 183
Introduction to the Theory of Statistics (Yule), 162
investment, 36, 259; as an art, 153; banking and, 130 (*see also* banking); corporations and, 129, 130, 148, 152, 259, 403n50 (*see also* corporations); diversification and, 152, 299–302; expectations and, 301 (*see also* expectation); expenditure approach, 185; fixed income, 161–82; hedging, 295–99, 321; incomes and, 196; interest and, 182 (*see also* interest rates); investment trusts, 29–30, 51, 59, 85, 130–38, 379n3, 401n27, 402n29, 442n20; Leontief and, 200; managers, 152, 299–302, 304, 442n20; mathematical models, 153, 179, 233 (*see also* mathematical models); P/E ratios, 152, 153; portfolios, 152, 299–302, 304 (*see also* portfolio theory); pricing and (*see* price theory); rational agent and, 259; risk and, 154, 180, 301 (*see also* risk); savings and, 265 (*see also* savings); speculation and, 36, 149, 297, 404n59; state control, 181; statistics and (*see* statistical methods); styles of, 405n61; technical analysis, 310; weighted indices, 176, 179
invisible hand, 181
Irwin, H. S., 296
IS-LM model, 218, 225, 250

Jackson, Robert H., 203
Jaszi, George, 194
Jenks, Jeremiah, 30, 32
Jevons, William Stanley, 61
Johnson, Alvin, 206
Jovanovic, Frank, 295

Kahler, Alfred, 206, 208
Kahn, R. F., 211
Kalman filter, 350, 353
Kane, Richard, 190
Kemmerer, Edwin Walter, 82
Keynes, John Maynard, 88, 127, 176, 247, 305, 323, 443n23; Colm and, 211, 213; Dawes Committee and, 207; demise of, 4, 6, 351; equilibrium models and, 227; Fiscal Policy seminar, 205; *General Theory* (see *General Theory of Employment, Interest, and Money*); Hicks and, 219–25, 226, 250, 251; institutionalism and, 283, 413n19; interest and (see *General Theory of Employment, Interest, and Money*); IS-LM model and, 250; liquidity preference and, 236, 301; marginalist theory and, 222; Marschak and, 236; mathematical modeling and, 218, 219, 220, 221, 224, 419n10; monetarism and, 264, 410n34 (*see also* monetary theory); national income and, 410n2; New Deal and, 213, 215; New Keynesians, 4, 250–53, 354, 444n43; rational expectations and, 348; savings and, 433n94; taxation and, 202; temporality and, 240; Tinbergen and, 218, 238–39, 355, 424n57; uncertainty and, 242. *See also specific persons, texts, topics*
Klein, Lawrence, 221, 351, 353
Knight, Frank H., 56, 87, 90, 152, 223, 234, 242
Kolmogorov, A. N., 256, 311
Koopmans, Tjalling, 260, 263
Koos, Richard, 138
Kuznets, Simon, 185, 186, 187, 188, 193, 194, 198, 211, 264, 292
Kydland, Finn, 348, 349, 353, 444n39

labor: employment and, 108, 127, 275, 285, 290, 344; income distribution and, 64; marginalist law and, 64–65; strikes and, 6, 387n14, 394n5; supply side and, 64; uprisings, 108; wages, 62–65, 97, 112, 388n21, 394n5

laissez-faire, 181
Lakatos, Imre, 419n15
Laughlin, J. Laurence, 55, 58, 84–86
Laws of Wages (Moore), 97
leakage, 211–12
Leontief, Wassily, 154, 196–201, 209
Lewis, Frederick Allen, 128
Liberty Bonds, 128, 138, 248, 400n6
linear programming, 259–64, 299–301, 304, 347, 372, 427n37
LINK Project, 351
liquidity crisis, 301, 321
Lo, Andrew W., 436n30
loan certificates, 50
logistic curve, 154, 157
Loman, Henry James, 89
London School of Economics (LSE), 229, 230
Long-Term Capital Management (LTCM), 321, 331, 340, 369
Lough, W. H., 196
Lowe, Adolf, 206, 208
Lucas, Robert E., 288, 348, 349, 350, 353, 443n23
Lundberg, Filip, 309

Macaulay, Frederick R., 176, 177, 180, 181, 182, 409n28
macroeconomics, 160, 183, 208, 219, 233, 242–45, 247. *See also specific persons, topics*
Making of Index Numbers, The (Fisher), 115
Makower, Helen, 232, 234, 250
Mandelbrot, Benoit, 311, 437n37
marginalist theory, 32, 56, 393n63; Keynes and, 222; labor and, 64–65; marginal utility, 62, 67, 76; mathematics and, 63, 66, 95, 97, 99; mergers and, 379n5; price theory and, 61–62; statistical tools, 97; tax and, 94; value and, 67, 68
Margret, A. W., 121
markets: banking and, 367–70 (*see also* banking); commodities (*see* commodities); competitive, 304–7, 320; complete, 329; corporations and (*see* corporations);

efficient, 164, 302–7, 312, 332–34, 377n20, 436n30, 436n33; financial system and, 342, 344, 359–70; fixed income, 161–82; futures (*see* futures markets); information and, 376n20 (*see also* information); marginalist theory (*see* marginalist theory); mechanism, 142, 149; neoliberalism and, 376n20, 377n20; prices and (*see* price theory); stock markets (*see* stock markets); voting and, 149. *See also specific types, topics*
Markoff chains, 256
Markowitz, Harry, 263, 299, 300, 302, 304
Marschak, Jacob, 206, 218, 227–38, 250, 258, 259
Marshall, Alfred, 61
Martin, William McChesney, 284
martingale theory, 311, 318, 326, 328, 330
Mathematical Investigations in the Theory of Value and Price (Fisher), 66, 67, 70
Mathematical Methods of Statistics (Cramér), 299
mathematical models, 70, 183, 256, 395n8, 418n6, 427n35; algebraic budgeting, 154; business cycle and, 159; calculus and, 405n67; Clark and, 63; Colm and, 211, 212; digital systems and, 316, 331, 332, 354, 360; econometrics, 164, 239, 314–19, 331, 332, 345, 439n68 (*see also specific topics*); economics and, 62, 96, 127, 196, 215, 219–25, 387n8 (*see also specific topics*); empiricism and, 117; environment and, 241; equilibrium theory, 66–68, 115, 198, 223, 227, 230–34, 251, 304–7, 372, 388n25; Fisher and, 67, 76, 77, 119, 389n28 (*see also* Fisher, Irving); Hicks and, 219–25; index numbers, 118 (*see also* index funds); institutionalism and, 160 (*see also* institutionalism); investment and, 153 (*see* portfolio theory); Keynes and, 219, 419n10 (*see also* Keynes, John Maynard); linear programming, 259–64, 299–301, 304, 372, 427n37; marginalism and, 63–64, 66; martingale theory, 311, 326, 328, 330; Matlab program, 354; matrix methods, 67,

71, 98, 198, 199, 218, 262; need for, 387n8; neoclassicism and, 156–57; notation and, 119; operations research, 263; pricing and (*see* price theory); probability theory (*see* probability theory); quantitative analysts, 317; random process and, 308–13 (*see also* randomness); risk and (*see* risk); set theory, 263; statistics and, 99, 107, 117, 169, 215, 409n25 (*see also* statistical methods); temporality and, 240; terminology, 417 (*see also specific topics*); uncertainty and, 89; utility and, 66 (*see also* utility). *See also specific persons, texts, topics*

matrix methods, 67, 71, 98, 198, 199, 218, 262

Mayer, Thomas, 431n70

McAdoo, William G., 53, 94

McFadden Act, 131

Meade, Edward Sherwood, 30, 32, 35, 36

Means, Gardiner, 128, 141–45, 149, 180

mean/variance choice revolution, 299, 300

Mehrling, Perry, 54, 385n60, 385n61

Mellon, Andrew W., 94, 95, 201, 209

Meltzer, Allen, 392n51

Menger, Carl, 61

merger movements, 30, 59, 154, 371, 379n3, 379n5. *See also* corporations

Merton, Robert C., 314, 318, 323, 324, 340, 434n6

Mill, John Stuart, 61

Miller, Merton H., 313–14, 318, 319–20

Mills, Ogden, 201

Minsky, Hyman P., 138, 355, 357

Mirowski, Philip, 390n33

Mitchell, Charles E., 131

Mitchell, Wesley Clair, 59, 100, 104, 112–17, 176–80, 185, 206

Modern Corporation and Private Property, The (Berle/Means), 141, 142, 143, 145, 176

Modigliani, Franco, 250, 318, 319–20, 347

moments, method of, 333

Monetary History of the United States, A (Friedman), 276–80

monetary theory, 55, 234, 273–80; banking and, 53, 81–86, 223 (*see also* banking);

business cycles, 244 (*see also* business cycles); checking deposits, 83–84; cistern model, 68–70, 266; commercial paper, 49–50; commodity prices, 72; creation of, 192; credit and, 49–50, 60, 61, 124, 373; currency markets, 127, 137, 316, 369; dollar and, 127, 129, 135, 352; electrical model, 68, 266; equilibrium models and, 66–68, 115, 227, 230–34, 251, 304–7, 372, 388n25; Federal Reserve (*see* Federal Reserve); Fisher and, 66, 68, 73, 82, 160 (*see also* Fisher, Irving); gold reserves and, 50–53, 72, 83, 278, 391n38, 430n63; gravity and, 68; hydraulic view of, 68–70, 266; inflation (*see* inflation); inside/outside, 433n95; interest rates and, 72–74 (*see also* interest rates); Keynes and, 264, 410n34 (*see also* Keynes, John Maynard); liquidity and, 301, 321; mathematical models (*see* mathematical models); monetarism, 55, 81, 82, 272, 276–80 (*see also specific persons, topics*); net-money doctrine, 429n55; price theory and, 62, 81–82, 431n70 (*see also* price theory); purchasing power, 191; quantity theory, 55, 81–86, 410n34, 421n24, 428n48, 429n60, 429n61, 430n66; Tinbergen and, 243; value theory and, 62, 72, 234, 252; velocity, of money, 82. *See also specific persons, texts, topics*

Money, Interest, and Prices (Patinkin), 252

Money and Credit Instruments in Their Relation to General Prices (Kemmerer), 82

"Money and the Theory of Assets" (Marschak), 237–38

Money in a Theory of Finance (Gurley/ Shaw), 11, 55, 269–73, 356

Money Trust, 3, 121–25

Mont Pelerin Society, 87

Moody's, 177

Moore, Henry Ludwell, 97, 121, 161, 162, 394n6

Morgan, J. P., 51, 122, 414n29

Morgenstern, Oskar, 121, 258

mortgage bonds, 138–41, 364, 365

Moulton, Harold, 53, 342
Moulton, Henry Glenn, 123, 124, 126, 130, 195, 196
Murname, Mary, 94
Muth, John, 347, 348
mutual funds, 301, 313, 343, 361

Nash, John, 305, 358, 426n26, 435n16
national aggregates, 28, 60, 114, 184–89, 191, 194, 195, 197, 210, 410n2. *See* gross domestic product (GDP); gross national product (GNP); *and specific topics*
National Banking Act, 83
national banks, 49, 52, 73, 131, 159. *See also* Federal Reserve
National Bureau of Economic Research (NBER), 101, 105, 111, 113, 114, 176, 182, 397n31, 398n32
National Income (Kuznets), 185
National Income and Product Accounts (NIPA), 184–86, 193–97
naturalization, 109
natural law, 100
Nature of Capital and Income, The (Fisher), 32, 34, 60, 77, 79, 80, 91
Nazi movement, 206
NBER. *See* National Bureau of Economic Research (NBER)
Neisser, Hans, 206, 208
neoclassical theory, 162, 220, 271; assumptions of, 80; growth and, 290–93; marginalists and, 97; mathematics and, 156–57; New Synthesis, 341, 355; price theory, 61–72; supply side and, 64
neoliberalism, 376n20, 377n20
New Classical theory, 208, 280, 341, 349–55, 359, 373, 416n47
Newcomb, Simon, 82
New Deal, 138, 144, 146, 213, 278
New School for Social Research, 205, 209
New York Curb Exchange, 177
Neyman, Jerzy, 253, 254
NIPA. *See* National Income and Product Accounts (NIPA)

Nixon, Richard M., 346
no-arbitrage principle, 318, 320, 322, 328, 372
Noland, Doug, 273
normal distribution, 169–70, 237, 303, 395n10, 437n37
Norse, Edwin G., 195
North, S. N. D., 97
Noyes, Alexander, 133

OECD. *See* Organization for Economic Cooperation and Development (OECD)
oil prices, 346
Okun, Arthur M., 286
OPEC cartel, 346
operations research, 260, 261, 262, 263, 307
options pricing models, 314–22, 323, 325, 348, 440n7. *See also specific types, topics*
Organization for Economic Cooperation and Development (OECD), 291
overcapitalization, 34, 36, 380n12, 380n14
Oxford Institute, 229

panic of 1907, 51, 52, 123
Pareto, Vilfredo, 66, 388n25
Pareto-efficient market, 311, 314, 437n38
Parrish, Michael E., 128
Patinkin, Don, 221, 227, 251, 252
Paton, William, 38, 44
Pearson, Egon, 253
Pearson, Karl, 97, 100, 167
Pecora, Ferdinand, 34, 130, 401n15, 414n34
P/E ratios, 152, 153
Persons, Warren S., 107, 119, 120, 154
Phillips curve, 280, 282, 290, 344, 346, 351
physics, 71, 115–18, 258, 263, 317, 423n45, 439n57
Pigou, A. C., 252
Pliska, Stanley R., 329, 330
Poisson distribution, 309
portfolio theory, 174, 294–307; diversification and, 152, 299–302; efficiency and, 301, 304, 307; hedging, 295–99, 321; index funds and, 313; insurance and, 440n7; interest rates, 182; investment and, 302

(*see also* investment); models for, 267, 302
(*see also* mathematical models); pricing in
(*see* price theory); probability and, 303;
replication of, 438n53, 441n7; risk and (*see*
risk). *See also specific topics*
Prescott, Edward, 348, 349, 350, 353
present-value theory, 79, 91, 145, 155–56, 300,
  390n37
price theory, 62, 68, 80, 83, 150, 232, 300,
  307–9, 312; Autoquote system, 321;
  Brownian motion and, 310; commodities,
  111 (*see also* commodities; *and specific
  topics*); data and, 104, 105; derivatives and,
  325–28; index numbers and, 103, 105, 110;
  information and, 143, 144; marginal utility
  and, 61–62 (*see also* marginalist theory);
  market factors and, 99 (*see also* markets);
  mathematical models (*see* mathematical
  models; *and specific types, topics*); money
  and, 81, 82, 431n70 (*see also* monetary
  theory); options pricing, 314–22, 325, 348,
  440n7 (*see also specific types, topics*); portfolio theory (*see* portfolio theory); profits
  and, 310; risk and (*see* risk); security
  analysis and, 149–50, 403n51; state prices
  and, 318; time series and, 110; volatility
  and, 315, 323 (*see also* volatility). *See also
  specific topics*
Principles of Money (Laughlin), 85
probability theory, 87, 99, 237, 255, 256, 308,
  374, 407n10; Bayesian theory, 257–58, 303–
  4; central limit theorem, 309; expectations
  and, 302–3 (*see also* expectation); Fisher
  and, 80 (*see also* Fisher, Irving); likelihood
  principle, 237; mathematical models (*see*
  mathematical models); measure-theoretic
  models, 326; normal distribution, 169–70,
  237, 303, 395n10, 437n37; Paretian theory,
  66, 311, 314, 388n25, 437n38; portfolio
  theory and, 303 (*see also* portfolio theory);
  randomness (*see* randomness); statistics
  (*see* statistical methods); subjective approach and, 302–4
production theory, 40, 64, 184, 194–95

property rights, 31–32, 77–78, 379n7
proprietary theory, 38, 39
prospect theory, 391n39
psychology, 335
public disclosure, 141–47
Pujo investigation, 121–25
purchasing power, 82–85, 210
Purchasing Power of Money, The (Fisher),
  82, 83, 85

Q ratio, 289
Q Regulation, 343
quantitative easing, 370, 446n75
quantitative theorists (quants), 317
quantity theory of money (QTM), 54–55,
  81–86
Quesnay, Francois, 413n26

Raiffa, Howard, 302
RAND, 426n18
randomness, 256, 257; asset pricing and, 309;
  commodities and, 298; efficient-market
  hypothesis and, 436n30; experiment
  design and, 170; Fisher and, 174; frequentist approach, 105, 167, 302, 303; futures
  markets and, 298; mathematical models,
  308–13 (*see also* mathematical models);
  probability and (*see* probability theory);
  random walk, 164, 298–99, 309–12, 318;
  statistics and, 169–70 (*see also* statistical
  methods); stochastic models, 245, 251,
  254, 304, 310, 325, 333, 439n57; uncertainty and (*see* uncertainty)
Rate of Interest, The (Fisher), 77
rationality, 60, 358, 376n18, 442n23; assumption of, 302, 358, 372; expectation
  and, 261, 348, 352, 444n40 (*see also*
  expectation); investment and, 259 (*see also*
  investment); Keynes and, 348; mathematical models (*see* mathematical models); risk
  and (*see* risk); theory of, 427n30; uncertainty and, 359 (*see also* uncertainty)
RBC. *See* real-business cycle theory (RBC)
Reagan, Ronald, 359

real-bills doctrine, 54
real-business cycle theory (RBC), 261, 288, 340, 349, 350, 355, 443n29, 444n40
real estate bonds, 139
recession, 14, 51, 113, 204, 285, 315, 337–38, 371, 390n36, 415n35
recession of 1921, 127
recession of 1981–82, 337
recession of 1990–91, 338
Regnault, Jules, 406n4
Regulation Q, 343
Reichenbach, Hans, 255
Revenue Acts, 203, 209, 287
Riegel, Robert, 89
Ripley, William Z., 32, 33
risk, 152, 237; Arrow-Debreu models, 66, 288, 306, 435n16; bonds and, 157; characterization of, 300; conviction and, 303; corporations and, 88 (*see also* corporations); derivatives and, 307, 314–18, 321, 325–28, 365, 438n49; equity risk premium and, 180; expected return and, 436n30 (*see also* expectation); financial institutions and, 135; frequentist theory, 105, 167, 302, 303; great risk shift, 339; hedging and, 295–99, 321; holding period and, 135; insurance and, 89; investment and, 136, 154, 301 (*see also* investment); limited liability, 321; liquidity ratio and, 301; Makower and, 234; Markowitz and, 300, 304; Marschak and, 234; mean/standard deviation and, 180, 300; models and, 326 (*see also* mathematical models; *and specific types, topics*); portfolio selection and, 300 (*see also* portfolio theory); premiums, 157; primal, 392n60; profit and, 88; quantitative finance and, 325; risk-neutral models, 308, 318, 322, 328, 330; risk/return ratio, 301; savings and, 223; separation theorem and, 301; specific, 308; speculation and, 36, 149, 297, 404n59; standard deviation and, 180, 300; stocks and, 135, 157 (*see also* stock markets); subjective approach, 303; systematic, 308; uncertainty and, 87, 223,

300, 372, 436n32 (*see also* uncertainty); volatility and, 174, 180 (*see also* volatility)
Risk, Uncertainty, and Profit (Knight), 87, 88, 90
Robbins, Lionel, 229
Robinson, Joan, 221
Rogoff, Kenneth, 73
Roosevelt administration, 127, 138, 141, 188, 195, 202–5, 211, 213
Rorty, Malcolm C., 182, 395n13
Ross, Stephen A., 328–29, 330
Rule, Taylor, 273

safety-first criterion, 300
sampling theory, 105, 165–75, 217, 254. *See also* statistical methods
Samuelson, Paul A., 66, 67, 76, 196, 250, 251, 274, 298, 311, 312
Santa Clara decision, 30, 379n7
Savage, Leonard Jimmie, 302, 303
savings, 442n20; consumption and, 78, 191; government deficit and, 192; hoarding and, 223; household sector and, 191; imputation and, 191; incomes and, 196; investment and, 196, 265, 268 (*see also* investment); Keynes and, 433n94 (*see also* Keynes, John Maynard); Leontief and, 200; liquidity preference, 301; risk and, 223
savings and loan industry crisis, 369
Scharfstein, David, 361
Schlaiffer, Robert, 302
Scholes, Myron, 314, 318, 320, 340
Schultz, Henry, 98, 163, 387n8
Schumpeter, Joseph A., 81, 83, 154, 215, 217, 359
SCOOP Project, 261, 347
SEC. *See* Securities and Exchange Commission (SEC)
Securities and Exchange Acts, 141, 144, 146, 148, 151
Securities and Exchange Commission (SEC), 146
securities markets, 131–32, 143, 149, 150,

379n7, 400n6, 403n51. *See also* stock markets; *and specific topics*

securitization, 13, 141, 273, 307, 342, 362–67, 435n20

Security Analysis (Graham/Dodd), 147–53, 155, 176

Seligman, E. R., 95

shadow banking, 13, 141, 343, 357, 359, 362–66

shareholders. *See* investment

Sharpe, William F., 307, 308

Shaw, Arch W., 102

Shaw, Edward Stone, 55, 86, 269–73, 356

Sherman Anti-Trust Act, 103, 110, 379n7

Shiller, Robert, 334, 335, 336

Shin, Hyun Song, 367, 369

shocks, 442n18

silver, 72, 81, 391n38

Simon, Herbert, 347, 348

simultaneous equation method, 67, 71, 98, 198, 199, 218, 262

SIV. *See* structured investment vehicles (SIV)

Sixteenth Amendment, 93

Smith, Adam, 61

Smith, Edgar Lawrence, 134, 135

SNA. *See* System of National Accounts (SNA)

Snedecor, George, 162, 166, 407n8

social sciences, 77, 97, 202, 208, 224, 322, 359, 395n12, 437n38

Social Security Administration, 23, 138, 156, 204, 283, 339

Solow, Robert, 292, 340, 443n33

speculative mania, 127–33, 402n29

Spencer, Arthur W., 380n14

stagflation, 3, 5, 290, 315, 329, 333, 344–45

Standard and Poor 500, 176

Standard Statistics, 144, 177, 408n19

state-preference theory, 307

statistical methods: agronomics and, 162–63; ASA and, 97; Bayesian models, 257–58, 302–33; correlation coefficients, 98, 168; data in, 103–7 (*see also specific types, top-*
ics); demand and, 97–100; Econometric Society and, 217; experiment design, 169–70; Fisher and, 166, 170 (*see also* Fisher, Ronald A.); frequency distributions, 105, 167, 180 (*see also specific types, topics*); frequentist approach, 302, 303; Harvard Barometer, 100–103, 120–21, 155; inference from, 107, 169–70, 217; input-output models, 196–99, 201; logistic curve, 154, 157; models and (*see* mathematical models); normal distribution, 169–70, 237, 303, 395n10, 437n37; portfolios and, 173 (*see also* portfolio theory); probability and (*see* probability theory); quantitative analysts, 317; randomness and (*see* randomness); regression analysis, 169–70, 211, 333, 350; sampling theory and, 105, 165–75, 217, 254; standard deviation, 168; static analysis, 98, 115; stochastic models, 245, 251, 254, 304, 310, 325, 326, 333, 439n57; time series, 99, 105–10, 154, 177–78, 408n24; VAR models, 333, 350. *See also specific methods, persons, topics*

Stevenson, Russell Alger, 38

Stigler, George J., 62, 66, 100, 163

stochastic models, 245, 251, 254, 304, 310, 325, 326, 333, 439n57. *See also* mathematical models

Stochastic Processes (Doob), 327–28

Stock Market Crash—and After, The (Fisher), 137

stock markets, 49, 127, 128, 133; arbitrage and, 318, 320, 322, 328, 372; bonds and, 135–36, 137, 152, 181; capitalization and, 34, 175–76 (*see also* capitalization); commodities and (*see* commodities); complete market, 329; concept of, 403n50; corporations and, 34, 36, 142 (*see also* corporations); Cowles and, 164; currency markets and, 127, 137, 316, 369; cycles in (*see* business cycles); derivatives in, 307, 314–18, 321, 325–28, 360, 365–66, 438n49; disclosure and, 143, 150, 158; dividends, 156; Dow-Jones index, 106, 171; forecasting, 164, 171,

stock markets (*continued*)
175; futures (*see* futures markets); holding period and, 135; information and, 158 (*see also* information); interest rates and, 136 (*see also* interest rates); investment (*see* investment); market timing, 175; par requirement, 381n27; P/E ratios, 152, 153; portfolios (*see* portfolio theory); present-value theory, 155–56; prices (*see* price theory); risk and (*see* risk); sample theory and, 165–75, 217, 254; savings and, 196 (*see also* savings); securities markets, 131–32, 143, 149, 150, 379n7, 400n6, 403n51; statistical methods and, 173 (*see also* statistical methods); stock selection, 174; technical analysis, 310; valuation and, 36; volatility and, 174, 181 (*see also* volatility); watering in, 34–36, 147, 381n27. *See also specific topics*　·
Stone, Nahum I., 395n13
Strauss, Simon William, 139
Strong, Benjamin, 127
structured investment vehicles (SIV), 364–65
Structure of American Economy, The (Leontief), 197
Study of Saving (Goldsmith), 268
subjective approach, 62–67, 302–4
Sumner, William Graham, 388n24
supply, demand and, 62, 65–67
supply-side economics, 64, 338, 342
Supreme Court, 30, 31, 44, 93. *See also specific decisions*
Survey of Current Business (GPO), 105, 107, 108
System of National Accounts (SNA), 196

Taft, William H., 91, 109
Taleb, Nassim Nicholas, 259
Taussig, F. W., 85
taxation, 95, 188, 214; business cycle and, 209–10 (*see also* business cycles); Colm and, 209; corporations and, 91, 94, 203, 393n67; income tax and, 90–94, 414n28; Keynesian theory and, 202 (*see also*

Keynes, John Maynard); rise in, 202; Roosevelt administration and, 202, 203; World War II and, 188–89
Taylor, Frederick Wilson, 101
Taylor, James S., 138
Taylor, John, 355
Tea Party, 371
technology, 83–84, 209, 291, 353. *See also* digital technology; *and specific topics*
temporality, 105, 240. *See also* time series
terrorist attacks, 369
"Theory of Assets" (Marschak), 227–38
Theory of Business Enterprise, The (Veblen), 58
Theory of Consumption Function, The (Friedman), 275
Theory of Finance, The (Fama/Miller), 313–14
Theory of Games and Economic Behavior (von Neumann/Morgenstern), 258, 302
Theory of Interest, The (Fisher), 77, 78, 391n43
Theory of Investment Value, The (Williams), 154, 155
thermodynamic systems, 67, 70
Thorndike, Joseph J., 414n28
Thrift Campaign, 139
time series, 99, 105–10, 154, 177–78, 408n24
Tinbergen, Jan, 88, 215; business-cycle policy and, 422n33; Keynes and, 218, 238–39, 355, 424n57; Marschak and, 244; trial-and-error method, 238, 239, 240; US economy, 243
Tintner, Gerhard, 163
Tobin, James, 267, 287, 288, 289, 301, 305
topology, 261, 263
total-return analysis, 177, 179, 180
trusts, 29, 30, 51, 59, 85, 134–37, 379n3, 401n27, 402n29
Tuttle, Charles A., 391n42

uncertainty, 87, 392n60; capitalization and, 90; insurance and, 88–89; Keynes and, 242; Marschak and, 234–38; probability and (*see* mathematical models; probability theory); rationality and, 359; risk and, 87, 223, 300, 372, 436n32 (*see also* risk); statistical models (*see* statistical methods)

unemployment, 127, 275, 282, 285, 290, 344

Uniform Accounting (Federal Reserve Board), 44

unions, labor, 64, 97, 387n14

universities, 37, 163, 294, 394n4, 415n40, 434n3. *See also specific topics, programs, persons*

utilitarianism, 61, 376n18

utility, 62, 68, 70, 71. *See also* marginalist theory

value theory: expectation and, 35, 36, 145 (*see also* expectation); financial view, 76; interest rates and, 76 (*see also* interest rates); marginal utility and, 67 (*see also* marginalist theory); monetary theory and, 234, 252 (*see also* monetary theory); present-value theory, 145, 380n14; pricing (*see* price theory); promoters and, 36; value ratio, 178; watering and, 36

variable proportions, law of, 62

VAR models, 333, 350

Veblen, Thorstein, 56–63, 84, 90, 117, 130, 283, 386n3, 386n7

vector analysis, 67, 70, 196, 333, 350

Victory bonds, 128, 248

Vietnam War, 289

volatility, 345, 346, 441n7; cycles and, 178 (*see also* business cycles); human nature, 180; price and, 315 (*see also* price theory); risk and, 174, 180 (*see also* risk); skew, 441n7; stock market and, 174, 181 (*see also* stock markets); time series and, 178 (*see also* time series)

Volcker deflation, 337, 346

von Neumann, John, 258, 263, 305, 426n26, 435n19

wages, 62–65, 97, 112, 388n21, 394n5

Wald, Abraham, 305

Walker, Francis A., 97

Wallace, Henry A., 162, 163

Walrus, Léon, 61, 66, 67, 162, 199, 222, 388n25, 413n26

war: bonds, 128, 139; interwar period, 126–60, 183; production and, 192; taxation and, 188–89; World War I and (*see* World War I); World War II and (*see* World War II)

Warburton, Clark, 195, 410n34

Warshow, H. T., 128

wealth, defined, 77, 94, 379n3

Weimar Germany, 206–7

Weintraub, E. Roy, 117, 389n25

Wharton School, 37

Whitley, Richard, 296

Williams, John Burr, 153, 154, 159, 180, 206, 216, 225

Williams, John H., 205

Wilson, Woodrow, 53, 94

Wood, Marshall K., 261

Working, Holbrook, 296, 297, 298, 309

World War I, 94, 105; Federal Reserve system and, 53; interwar period and, 126–60, 183; war bonds and, 128, 139; WIB and, 103–4

World War II: GNP and, 412n14; interwar period and, 126–60, 183; postwar economics, 246–94; production and, 188, 192; taxation and, 188–89

Young, Allyn, 55, 86

Yule, G. Udny, 162